EXCURSIONS IN
WORLD MUSIC

SIXTH EDITION

Timothy Rommen–Editor
UNIVERSITY OF PENNSYLVANIA

Bruno Nettl
UNIVERSITY OF ILLINOIS URBANA-CHAMPAIGN

Charles Capwell
UNIVERSITY OF ILLINOIS URBANA-CHAMPAIGN

Isabel K.F. Wong
UNIVERSITY OF ILLINOIS URBANA-CHAMPAIGN

Thomas Turino
UNIVERSITY OF ILLINOIS URBANA-CHAMPAIGN

Philip V. Bohlman
UNIVERSITY OF CHICAGO

Byron Dueck
ROYAL NORTHERN COLLEGE OF MUSIC

PEARSON

Boston   Columbus   Indianapolis   New York   San Francisco   Upper Saddle River
Amsterdam   Cape Town   Dubai   London   Madrid   Milan   Munich   Paris   Montréal   Toronto
Delhi   Mexico City   São Paulo   Sydney   Hong Kong   Seoul   Singapore   Taipei   Tokyo

Editorial Director: Craig Campanella
Editor in Chief: Sarah Touborg
Executive Editor: Richard Carlin
Editorial Assistant: Lily Norton
Vice President Director of Marketing: Brandy Dawson
Executive Marketing Manager: Kate Stewart Mitchell
Marketing Assistant: Lisa Kirlick
Managing Editor: Melissa Feimer
Project Manager: Marlene Gassler
Senior Manufacturing Manager: Mary Fischer

Senior Operations Specialist: Brian Mackey
Senior Art Director: Pat Smythe
Cover Designer: Dutton & Sherman Design
Senior Media Editor: David Alick
Media Project Manager: Rich Barnes
Full-Service Project Management: Jenna Gray, PreMediaGlobal
Composition: PreMediaGlobal
Printer/Binder: R.R. Donnelley/ Willard
Cover Printer: Lehigh-Phoenix Color/Hagerstown

Cover Photo: Malian musician Habib Koite. Photograph © Jack Vartoogian/FrontRowPhotos
Table of Contents and Chapter Opening Photo Credits: Chapter 1: Megapress/Alamy. **Chapter 2:** Robert Harding Picture Library Ltd/Alamy. **Chapter 3:** Lebrecht Music and Arts Photo Library/Alamy. **Chapter 4:** Bobbie Lerryn/Alamy. **Chapter 5:** Peter Arnold, Inc./Alamy. **Chapter 6:** Hans Kemp/Alamy. **Chapter 7:** Hisham Ibrahim/PhotoV/Alamy. **Chapter 8:** MERVYN REES/Alamy. **Chapter 9:** World Pictures/Alamy. **Chapter 10:** Blaine Harrington III/Alamy. **Chapter 11:** H. Mark Weidman Photography/Alamy. **Chapter 12:** Aurora Photos/Alamy.

Library of Congress Cataloging-in-Publication Data

Excursions in world music / Bruno Nettl ... [et al.]. — 6th ed.
    p. cm.
  ISBN 978-0-205-01285-5
  1. World music—Analysis, appreciation. I. Nettl, Bruno
MT90.E95 2011
780.9—dc22

2011015144

10 9 8 7 6 5 4 3 2 1

ISBN-10:	0-205-01285-X
ISBN-13:	978-0-205-01285-5
Exam Copy ISBN 10:	0-205-01286-8
Exam Copy ISBN 13:	978-0-205-01286-2
à la Carte ISBN 10:	0-205-21488-6
à la Carte ISBN 13:	978-0-205-21488-4

PEARSON

To the Memory of John Blacking (1928-1990)
"In a world such as ours...
It is necessary to understand why
a madrigal by Gesualdo or a Bach Passion, a sitar melody from
India or a song from Africa, Berg's 'Wozzeck' or Britten's
'War Requiem,'
a Balinese gamelan or a Cantonese opera, or a symphony by
Mozart, Beethoven, or Mahler, may be profoundly necessary for
human survival..."
"How Musical Is Man?" (1973)

CONTENTS

NOTES ON THE SIXTH EDITION

The sixth edition of *Excursions in World Music* responds to many of the significant changes that the world of music has experienced, but it also provides timely additions that increase its value to educators and students. It continues its aim of interpreting the rapidly changing conditions, repertories, and styles of world music since the beginning of the twenty-first century. In addition to presenting the world of music as a group of societies in which each has its own unique musical system, the authors explore the world as a place in which globalization, the explosion of new technologies, and the often dramatically shifting landscapes of a postcolonial and neonationalist world dominate the musical scene.

Each chapter has been revised to incorporate new musical developments and new approaches to scholarship and teaching. The most significant new component of this sixth edition is the inclusion of a new chapter, written by Byron Dueck, which re-explores the Music of Ethnic North America, and that replaces Philip V. Bohlman's chapter on this topic from previous editions. Integrated sidebar definitions of key terms, additional photos, and a wide range of new content available at MyMusicLab (www.mymusiclab.com) make this edition more user friendly. The reader will also discover that the listening guides have been revised throughout in order to create a more explicit connection between the musical examples and the text and with a view toward making them more central to the pedagogical aims of each chapter.

To those who have used the fifth edition of *Excursions in World Music*, this sixth edition will seem in many respects like a familiar but more user friendly and integrated book. The authors of *Excursions in World Music* continue in this edition their commitment to the approach, structure, and content with which they have always conceived this work. It remains a set of chapters—essays—by scholars writing, with conviction and a sense of devotion, about cultures in which they have had substantial field experience and done personal research, providing information and in-depth syntheses of the musical cultures of the world. We remain committed to a belief that knowledge of world music not only opens many doors to a better understanding of today's most pressing social, political, and cultural problems, but also engenders respect for those who make and experience music everywhere.

Listening Options

As in the past, we are offering an optional CD set containing the listening examples found in the text. However, we are also offering full streaming audio on *MyMusicLab* for those students who prefer to listen on line.

MyMusicLab

The online website, MyMusicLab, is an integral part of this new edition. Its features include the following:

- Chapter-based assessment, including pre-tests to test basic comprehension of the chapter; post-tests to measure understanding and application of these concepts; and chapter exams that help students and professors better measure their progress in the course.

- A musical instruments gallery which affords students the chance to explore the many instruments discussed in the text by means of photo, video, and audio content.

- Needle-drop activities in which students have to apply their knowledge of world music to specific listening examples and answer a series of questions.

- The Interactive Globe, a new and exciting feature that allows students to focus on each area studied in the book and access a wealth of additional information including online video.

- A fully integrated etext with hyperlinks to all of the MyMusicLab Lab assets.

- Full streaming audio for all music examples.

Acknowledgments

Many thanks to Damon Sink (University of Dayton) for preparing a new study guide for the sixth edition, Joseph Kaminski for revising the Instructor's Manual, and Sandy Karp for composing the index for this edition. Many thanks also to Jessica Swanston and Myles Karp for their assistance in preparing the manuscript for production and to Laura Donnelly, Jessamyn Doan, and Monique Ingalls, who compiled the online content. We also wish to express our gratitude for the numerous helpful suggestions provided by our students, anonymous readers, and all loyal users of the book alike.

We also thank our reviewers of this edition, *Edward Orgill* (Westfield State College), *Scott Warfield* (Univeristy of Central Florida), *Terry O'Mahoney* (St. Francis Xavier University), *Benjamin Koen* (Florida State University), *Lydia Hamessley* (Hamilton College), *Jay Kesiter* (University of Colorado, Boulder), *Paula Conlon* (University of Oklahoma), *Michael Varner* (The University of Texas at Arlington), *Stephen Blum* (CUNY Graduate Center), *Lindsay Weightman* (Temple University), *R Anderson Sutton* (University of Wisconsin-Madison), *David Harnish* (Bowling Green State University), *John Robison* (University of South Florida), *Arlene Caney* (Community College of Philadelphia), *Peter Marsh* (California State University, East Bay), *Sonya Lawson* (Westfield State College).

Timothy Rommen, Bruno Nettl, Charles Capwell, Isabel K.F. Wong, Thomas Turino, Philip V. Bohlman, Byron Dueck

ABOUT THE AUTHORS

Timothy Rommen studied at the University of Chicago and is an associate professor of ethnomusicology at the University of Pennsylvania. Working primarily in the Caribbean, his research interests include folk and popular sacred music, popular music, ethics, diaspora, critical theory, and the intellectual history of ethnomusicology. He is the author of *"Funky Nassau:" Roots, Routes, and Representation in Bahamian Popular Music*, and *"Mek Some Noise": Gospel Music and the Ethics of Style in Trinidad*.

Bruno Nettl studied at Indiana University; has taught at the University of Illinois since 1964; has done fieldwork in Iran (where he studied the Persian setar), among the Blackfoot people of Montana, and in South India; and is the author of *The Study of Ethnomusicology, Blackfoot Musical Thought: Comparative Perspectives, Heartland Excursions: Ethnomusicological Reflections on Schools of Music*, and *Nettl's Elephant: On the History of Ethnomusicology*.

Charles Capwell, a Harvard Ph.D., did field research among the Bauls of Bengal, India, and in Calcutta (where he also studied sarod), and he has studied Muslim popular music in Indonesia. He is the author of *Music of the Bauls of Bengal* and of numerous articles on aspects of South Asian musical culture and has been on the faculty of the University of Illinois since 1976, where he also supervises the gamelan program.

Isabel K.F. Wong studied at Brown University and teaches Chinese and other East Asian musics at the University of Illinois. She has done research on a large variety of music of her native China, including music drama, urban popular music, politics and music, and the history of musical scholarship in Chinese culture. More recently she has devoted herself also to the study of Chinese American musical culture.

Thomas Turino studied at the University of Texas and has taught at the University of Illinois since 1987. He is the author of *Moving Away from Silence* and *Nationalists, Cosmopolitans, and Popular Music in Zimbabwe* and *Music as Social Life: The Politics of Participation*. In 1992 and 1993 he lived in Zimbabwe, where he did research on village music and musical nationalism. He is an expert performer on the African mbira and founder of the Peruvian panpipe ensemble at Illinois.

Philip V. Bohlman studied at the University of Illinois and has been, since 1987, at the University of Chicago. He has done fieldwork in ethnic communities in Wisconsin, Chicago, and Pittsburgh, as well as Israel, Germany, and Austria, He is the author of *The Land Where Two Streams Flow, The Study of Folk Music in the Modern World, World Music: A Very Short Introduction, Jewish Music and Modernity*, and *Music, Nationalism, and the Making of the New Europe*.

He is the artistic director of The New Budapest Orpheum Society, a Jewish cabaret ensemble at the University of Chicago.

Byron Dueck is Lecturer in Music at the Royal Northern College of Music in Manchester, UK. He studied ethnomusicology at the University of Chicago. His research interests include aboriginal music and dance in Canada, popular music in Cameroon, and jazz performance in the United Kingdom. He is the author of *Musical Intimacies and Indigenous Imaginaries* (forthcoming with Oxford University Press) and coeditor with Jason Toynbee of *Migrating Music* (Routledge).

PREFACE

It's about 7:00 P.M. on July 25, 2009 and my daughter, Natalia, and I have just managed to find our seats at the Mann Center for the Performing Arts in Philadelphia, PA. The Center is presenting a double billing that has brought people out *en masse*. It's still an hour before show time, and already the amphitheater is full. The lawn behind the covered seating area, moreover, is almost completely covered in blankets and lawn chairs as patrons mill about, making preparations for the evening's entertainment. Natalia and I have been looking forward to this evening, because we're going to hear the South African vocal group, Ladysmith Black Mambazo, open a show that also features the famous gospel group, the Blind Boys of Alabama. Both of these Grammy Award winning ensembles are iconic in their own way, the former for showcasing a South African style of singing called *isicathamiya* and the latter for sustaining upwards of seven decades of innovation within the African-American gospel tradition in the United States (the group was founded in 1939).

Both of these groups have achieved fame within their respective national contexts, but they have also garnered tremendous international standing. Ladysmith Black Mambazo tours extensively and visits the United States regularly. They've already played shows all across the United States, Singapore, South Korea, China, and Australia this year, and they'll play a series of dates in the United Kingdom in the fall. The Blind Boys of Alabama are also veterans of heavy international touring schedules and have already performed in the Caribbean, Australia, New Zealand, Denmark, Italy, Spain, Switzerland, Sweden, and Slovakia this year. They are also slated to perform in Austria, Norway, Slovenia, France, Scotland, Hungary, and the United Kingdom later this year.

Five Blind Boys of Alabama, in concert, 1992. *Source:* Jack Vartoogian/ Front Row Photos © 1992

Lady Smith Black Mambazo in concert, 2005. *Source:* Jack Vartoogian/ Front Row Photos © 1992

Ladysmith Black Mambazo take the stage around 8:10 P.M. and perform their trademark show, complete with stories from Joseph Shabalala, the group's leader and principal arranger, humorous and playful interactions between members of the ensemble, choreographed dancing, heavy on Zulu aesthetics, and, of course, complete control over their subtle and virtuosic vocal production. Most of the songs are sung in Zulu, and only a few are performed in English. The Blind Boys of Alabama, for their part, take everyone to "church." Dressed in matching, bright blue suits and gathering emotional momentum as the set wears on, they call boisterously to the audience for participation (and receive it), tell jokes, and generally put on a great show, singing in their trademark, close harmony while treating us to a series of gospel standards. The concert, as it turns out, is amazing, and both groups live up to their considerable reputations, leaving the audience buzzing about the night's musical experiences.

As Natalia and I walk to the parking lot, I am struck by how well this concert highlights many of the issues with which ethnomusicologists (and this book) are concerned. For instance, the concert offers a glimpse at the ambiguity of the terminology we use to discuss the music of groups like Ladysmith Black Mambazo. The music industry, based largely in the North Atlantic, tends to market groups like Ladysmith Black Mambazo as "World Music," whereas the Blind Boys of Alabama are categorized as "gospel" musicians. Ironically, the expansive-sounding label—World Music—achieves a rather delimiting effect. It inscribes difference, otherness, and, at times, exoticism onto musical practices that do not squarely fit into North Atlantic modes of traditional, popular, or art music. The many musics of the world are, thus, homogenized into a category that serves as a catchall for the performances of artists who, unlike, say, the Blind Boys of Alabama, do not sing primarily in English and do not, generally, hail from a North Atlantic nation-state.

And yet, both of these groups are clearly "world musicians" in the broadest and best sense of the word—in the sense that opens the world to new sounds, new encounters, and new possibilities. The authors of this book explore the world's music in this broad, open-ended way. They consider each of the many musics of the world as offering meaningful and vital experiences both on the local and translocal levels. In this book, the authors explore how music functions in communities throughout the world; how musical practice intersects with politics and economics; how it is bound up in questions of ethnicity, class, race, and identity; how religion, aesthetics, and ideology affect the production and consumption of music; and how dance and art are intertwined with it, to name but a few of the book's major themes.

Setting the music industry's flaws and ambiguities aside for a moment, however, the industry markets "World Music" with recourse to difference precisely because it is a quantifiable (if often over-determined and essentialized) performative and sonic reality. Indeed, the musics of the world are endlessly diverse. This evening's musical performances offer a good case in point, for the styles of these two groups are quite different. Ladysmith Black Mambazo sing relatively softly, though there are many members in the group, while the Blind Boys of Alabama are few in number but their vocal production is loud. Ladysmith's music is called i*sicathamiya*, a Zulu-derived word that means something like "walk softly," which conveys in the name of the genre itself the necessity for low volume required of the early performers and innovators of this style. These performers, active in the early decades of the twentieth century, were employed as migrant laborers at South African mines and thus lived in the mine barracks. Their after-hours singing and dancing had to be quiet enough so that security would not notice and shut them down. The gospel music sung by the Blind Boys, by contrast, is rooted in the notion of proclamation and is, thus, intended to be heard both far and wide.

Ladysmith works with small units of musical material that they gradually transform over the course of performances often lasting more than ten minutes, a compositional technique sometimes referred to as *cellular construction* and a hallmark of many sub-Saharan African musical traditions (see Chapter 7). The Blind Boys work mainly within a shorter, verse-chorus structure that easily opens up to an improvisatory vamp toward the end of the song—a vamp that can extend these three or four minute compositions to well over ten minutes as well. Ladysmith is an *a capella* group, which means that they sing unaccompanied by instruments, once again because the genre developed within a context where playing instruments would have, in many cases, been impractical. The Blind Boys, though, travel with a small gospel band (organ and piano, guitar, bass, and drums). One group sings primarily in African languages; the other sings exclusively in English.

These divergent approaches to musical structure, aesthetics, language, dance, and style suggest an important way of thinking about musical difference. Difference, like sameness, is best understood as a matter of perspective. Sameness is constructed out of identifying difference and, as such, is bound up in who you are, the experiences you've accumulated, and the traditions from which you are selecting in the process of assembling your own sense of the world. As we all know, throughout history, difference has been mobilized to tragically destructive purpose—genocide, slavery, the holocaust, exile, religious fundamentalisms, and exoticisms of one stripe or another have all been justified through such mobilizations of difference. And yet, difference can also become truly productive if it is mobilized in service of mutual exchange and open encounter. It is in this sense that ethnomusicology is engaged with the musics of the world.

Importantly, acknowledging the ways that the musics of the world differ from each other can (and often does) lead to new insights and to rich and meaningful musical encounters that illustrate sameness, solidarity, and shared horizons. Difference can, in other words, enable us to see (and hear) ourselves in the other and the other in ourselves. This is especially the case if we approach these musical encounters open to the possibility that our own perspective is subject to reinterpretation and to change in the face of new experiences. Returning to this evening's concert, these two ensembles share several significant themes. First, both groups have overcome devastating social inequality tied to race and class. Ladysmith Black Mambazo was formed during the height of apartheid in South Africa, while the Blind Boys of Alabama have lived and performed through Jim Crow laws and the Civil Rights Movement in the United States. In this sense, they have both been affected by the prior movements of money, goods, and people that characterized the colonial period. Ladysmith's ancestors witnessed the colonial subjugation of the Zulu and the successive injustices that culminated in apartheid. The ancestral heritage of the Blind Boys is rooted in West Africa, the slave trade, and the southern plantation economy. Both groups have chosen to perform music of deep spiritual significance, raising their voices in defense of social justice and contributing in significant ways to the ongoing process of articulating a way forward after apartheid and in building on the as yet unfulfilled promise of the Civil Rights Movement, respectively.

Both groups have also benefitted from the long-term exchange of musical practices. This exchange has seen African practices inform musical lives throughout the African diaspora, including the musical practices of African Americans and Afro-Caribbean communities. As such, a host of musical ideas—often called African retentions, and including instruments, drumming styles, ensemble structures, dance styles, and rhythmic cells—have been incorporated into and adapted to the musical contexts of traditional, sacred, and popular musics throughout the African diaspora. This exchange has also witnessed the return of new genres and practices from the diaspora to Africa. For instance, *isicathamiya* itself is informed by the sounds of vaudeville and ragtime groups such as the Virginia Jubilee Singers and Orpheus McAdoo who toured South Africa during the 1890s.

A closer exploration of these two groups, then, reveals a deep solidarity, born of shared social and political histories (though experienced in different contexts) and worked out in shared musical horizons through the multiple crossings and recrossings of what has been called the Black Atlantic. Both groups, moreover, have remained committed to the musical traditions they grew into locally while collaborating with a wide range of other musical artists (including Peter Gabriel, the English Chamber Orchestra, Lucky Dube, Paul Simon, Bonnie Raitt, and Ben Harper to name but a few), thereby modeling the possibility of pursuing shared musical horizons and solidarity—of seeing the other in one's self and one's self in the other.

The historical, economic, political, and social horizons of Ladysmith Black Mambazo and the Blind Boys of Alabama are thus different in detail and local context, but similar in terms of the way that music is being mobilized to address these local issues and struggles. When viewed from this perspective, the concrete musical differences so obvious in their back-to-back performances are no longer central to an analysis of the musical power of these two groups. What emerges instead is an appreciation for the shared human concerns and histories that these two ensembles have consistently confronted throughout their careers, an appreciation that is deepened by the powerful illustration these two ensembles offer of the multiple musical paths that artists forge in addressing these concerns.

The title of this book, *Excursions in World Music*, then, is chosen in order to question the overarching category "World Music." The book engages the many musics of the world, offering excursions that highlight the concrete differences and sheer diversity to be experienced in the world of music. At the same time, however, the text illustrates the often profound ways through which a deeper exploration of these diverse communities of practice can reveal overlaps, shared horizons, and common concerns in spite of and, at times, because of this very diversity.

Welcome to the study of World Music!

Timothy Rommen
Philadelphia, April 2011

Introduction: Studying Musics of the World's Cultures

BRUNO NETTL

PRESENTING THE WORLD OF MUSIC

The purpose of this book is to introduce the reader to the world of music, the music of the world's cultures, emphasizing the diversity and the uniqueness of each. Directing ourselves to students—particularly those without a technical background—and to general readers, we want to give a sense of the character of music and musical life of all the world's peoples. Given that there are thousands of peoples, each with their own music, we can accomplish this only by careful sampling and judicious synthesis—through crafting excursions in world music. These excursions take the form of eleven chapters, each of which is devoted to presenting a representative set of case studies within a major culture area. Even so, we have had to leave large areas untouched.

In order to provide a degree of depth as well as breadth, we have had to be selective. We therefore work with case studies that, taken together, will provide the reader a picture of the way the world's peoples make music, think about it,

use it in their lives, and also what all this music sounds like and how it is structured. The world's musical diversity is reflected to some degree in the diversity of the organization of our chapters, but all chapters have commonalities. In each chapter, we first focus on a detailed description of a musical event that may be considered broadly representative of its culture area. Ordinarily, this is followed by an introduction to the cultures and societies of the area; an exploration of musical life and ideas about music, of musical style (described in terms comprehensible by nonspecialists), music history, and musical instruments; a brief description of a few additional musical genres or contexts; and finally, a consideration of recent developments and popular music. We describe musical cultures as they exist today, but wherever possible we provide some information about their history. We do this in some measure to dispel the notion that western academic or art music lives in a sense through its history, whereas the musics of other societies have no history at all, or at best a very different sort of history. We should make one thing clear from the start: every musical system—that is, the music and

✳ Explore
*Learning Objectives
for this chapter on*
mymusiclab.com

musical life of each society, from the multifarious society of New York City to a native Amazonian tribe of two hundred persons—is a complex phenomenon that may be analyzed and comprehended from many perspectives. We certainly would not be able to provide the amount of detail necessary to illustrate this point for all the cultures and musics with which we deal. We therefore introduce the world's musical complexity selectively, each chapter featuring one or a few concepts. Thus, in addition to providing a set of general and essentially parallel introductions to the musics of eleven world areas, this book may also be read as an introduction to the topics within world music study:

- Chapter 2, on India, devotes special attention to the relationship of music and dance.
- Chapter 3, on the Middle East, concentrates on different conceptions of music in the world's cultures and on ways musicians learn to improvise.
- Chapter 4, on China, presents a detailed examination of the role of music in the political development of a modernizing nation.
- Chapter 5, on Japan, shows the survival, in a modernized society, of its older traditions.
- Chapter 6, on Indonesia, examines the place of Indonesian music in musical contexts around the globe and explores the role of artists and tourists from abroad in Indonesian musical culture.
- Chapter 7, on sub-Saharan Africa, provides special insight into the world of popular music in the area's urban societies.
- Chapter 8, on Europe, concentrates on the interrelationships among folk, art, and popular musics in the contemporary world of Europe and looks at its attempts, since World War II, to become an integrated musical unit.
- Chapter 9, on Latin America, analyzes the relationships of social values and musical style through case studies drawn from the area.
- Chapter 10, on the Caribbean, gives a sampling of the diverse musical styles and genres from the multitude of island cultures, showing how in many ways, music serves to unify the contrastive cultures often living in close proximity, while at the same time giving each society an emblem of its identity.
- Chapter 11, on Native Americans, provides information on the study of history and prehistory of musical cultures without written records.
- Chapter 12 provides insight into the interaction between unity, diversity, and difference within both traditional, rural folk music, and modern, urbanized music in multiethnic North America.

✳ Explore
*regional maps on the
Interactive Globe on*
mymusiclab.com

For each area of the world covered by a chapter, we have tried to provide an overview; thus, Chapter 2 speaks at least briefly to many of the kinds of music found in India; Chapter 7 tells of the differences between East, Central, and West Africa, and between rural and urban musics; Chapter 11 gives an overview of the musics of the hundreds of Native North American tribes.

Mariachi Band Moyahua from the state of Zacatecas, performing on the streets in Mexico. *Source:* Peter M. Wilson/Alamy

Although we believe that our accounts achieve this kind of breadth, we also wish to show the reader the depth of musical culture, the many things that go into the composing, performance, and understanding of even a basic song or ritual, its history and the effects it has, and how it is perceived and judged by the people who render it and who hear it. We have tried to accomplish this by concentrating, in each chapter, on a limited number of representative cultures, communities, events, and even instruments within the broad geographical area that it covers. Thus, Chapter 3 concentrates on Iran, where one of the authors has done original research, to impart a sense of the many things to be noted, even though space limitations prevent giving the same attention to the Arab peninsula or Turkey. Chapter 8 presents the scope of European music, with all its variety, through the prism of the city of Vienna.

One of our purposes is to explain music as a cultural phenomenon. We do hope to persuade readers to listen to music of at least some of the world's many societies and to find it enjoyable. But much of the music we will be discussing has purposes far beyond enjoyment. The significance of much of the world's music is in the realm of religion and society, in the way humans interact with the supernatural and with each other. In some societies, music identifies clans and social classes, confirms political status, expresses communication from the supernatural, and cures the sick. Thus, although readers will want to know how the musical pieces of the world's cultures are put together and what general principles of composition may dominate in a given society, it is perhaps even more important for them to understand each culture's ideas of what music is, what its powers are, how it relates to other aspects of life, and how it reflects

RECITATIVE
A style of barely sung recitation in which the action or plot is carried forward. Often used in operas, oratorios, and cantatas, it imitates the rhythm and cadence of speech and is generally sparsely accompanied.

ARIA
A self-contained, often highly virtuosic piece for solo voice, most commonly used in opera, that affords the character a moment of reflection on a particular sentiment, issue, or dilemma taking place within the plot.

important things about its people and their view of the world. For this reason, although we wish to explain the nature of musical sound, we also have tried to present a holistic picture of musical life and musical culture.

LOOKING AT MUSIC IN SEVERAL WAYS

Our purpose is to present the varieties of the world's musics and to present several ways of looking at music, all of them necessary for understanding a particular work of music as it interacts with its culture in many ways. The world's music includes the music of Europe, and we illustrate our approach first by commenting on a work that is likely familiar to some readers, Mozart's opera, *The Marriage of Figaro* (originally named *Le Nozze di Figaro*). Its structure is an alternation of **recitatives**, in which the action is carried forward through quick dialogue barely sung, with **arias** and vocal ensembles such as trios and quartets, in which characters make lyrical and contemplative statements or react to what has just happened. Knowing this tells us something about the aesthetics and, if you will, the attention span of the patrons. But it also tells us about the relationship of opera to spoken drama, about the way Mozart and other composers of his time, and their audience, perceived the relationship of music and language.

The fact that this is an opera with Italian words about events in Spain perhaps a century earlier, composed by a German-speaking Austrian for a German-speaking audience in Vienna, speaks to this relationship as well. The well-educated audience of patrons for whom *Figaro* was composed presumably understood Italian and felt that this knowledge set them off from the general population, which would have wished for operas in German, and so we see this work as directed toward an elite segment of society. But this elite also comes in for criticism in the content of the opera, because the plot actually depicts a kind of social revolution. Figaro, the lowly but clever barber, wants to protect his fiancée from having to spend the night before their honeymoon with his boss, the count; this was, at the time the opera took place, part of the contract between landowners and their employees. Figaro succeeds, of course, without violence and through his wit, and everyone lives happily ever after, but when this opera was first presented, it definitely raised the eyebrows of the Austrian aristocracy.

Mozart was not widely regarded as a great genius in his own day, but now he holds that status among classical music historians. In his lifetime (1756–1791), the concept of "great master" of music had not really been developed, and when they were writing music, composers did not expect it to become great art for all times. Today, *Figaro* is considered one of the great musical works of all time, but in its day it was seen, at best, to be fine entertainment. In Mozart's time, the difference in musical style between academic music and music for popular entertainment wasn't all that great; the two sounded rather alike. Around 1800 this began to change, and today we expect academic music, what we call "classical" or "art" music, to sound quite different from popular music.

By now Mozart has become legendary among composers, and much is said and written about the greatness of *Figaro*. In today's American society, the concepts of genius and talent, innate abilities that set an artist apart, are important to musical culture. Underlying these beliefs are the oft-repeated stories that Mozart had composed acceptable music by the age of seven and that he composed masterworks with enormous speed, as if they sprang ready-made from his brain. We have developed, it seems, a kind of athletic view of music: We are impressed when something takes many hours to accomplish, or when someone can carry out significant work quickly, or when a composer or performer can accomplish an extremely difficult task of memory or dexterity. A quick look at *The Marriage of Figaro* tells us certain essential things about the culture of Mozart's time, but more significantly, because this opera is an important component of musical life within some sections of society today, it also conveys the musical values and attitudes of the musical culture of at least some North Americans.

But these observations raise several questions. For one thing, the members of one society such as those of the United States don't necessarily share musical identities and values. Those of us for whom classical music is the "home" music have different criteria for judging music than those whose normal musical experience is rock music, or salsa, or country music, or hip-hop, or norteño, or zydeco, to name but a few possibilities. And of course, the attitudes that make some of us extol Mozart and *Figaro* may not be the attitudes of other societies. For example, possessing great technical skill may not have been a criterion for judging a song in most Native American societies, and the concept of the musical work as something that may not be altered and must always be performed as the composer intended it is not relevant to understanding the music of India.

But it also would be a mistake to see the musical world as bifurcated, the classical tradition with its masterworks such as *Figaro* on one side and the rest of the world's music on the other. *Figaro* actually fits well into the world's musical picture. Many societies have drama rather like opera, in which the characters sing; many have forms of communication that, like Italian recitative, fall between ordinary speech and song; in many societies, music is used to express criticism of society. Social elites everywhere have musical ways of symbolizing their superiority: artistic resources such as the orchestra, linguistic techniques such as having opera in a foreign language. And we will need to remember that just as the European view of Mozart has changed since his death, all societies change in their views of music as well as in their musical styles. And, further, although so-called Western academic musical culture requires constant innovation and rapid change as a hallmark of its series of masterworks, other societies may restrict and inhibit change as detrimental to the function of music. The ideas about music that a society has, and contexts of creation and performance, help us to understand the music itself, which in turn provides insight into the values that led to it and the culture of which it is a part.

BASIC ASSUMPTIONS

In presenting the world's musical cultures, these chapters employ certain basic assumptions.

BASIC ASSUMPTIONS

- A relativistic view (no musical style is "better" than another)
- World music embraces a group of musics
- The three-part model of music: sound, behavior, and conception or ideas

---

A Relativistic View

If *The Marriage of Figaro* is a great work of music, this must be because for its consumers—those of us who listen to operas, that is—it satisfies certain criteria: It is a work of great complexity; its structure has internal logic; it has harmony and counterpoint, whereby several simultaneous melodies are both independent and united; the composer shows an ability to write music particularly suited to voices, instruments, and orchestra, and is facile in relating words and music; the work carries a particular social and spiritual message; and so on. Using these criteria to judge the musics of other cultures would quickly lead us to conclude that Western art music is the best and greatest. But from the viewpoint of an Indian musician, whose task is improvising within a framework of melodic and rhythmic rules, the performers of *Figaro* might not come off so well, because they must reproduce an existing work precisely and rely on notation to keep them from deviating, thus finding little opportunity to be creative. A Native American who considers a song to be a way for spirits to communicate with humans might marvel at the counterpoint of Bach, but he might also feel that this whole notion of what is "good" or "better" (or "lousy") music makes no sense. Performers in a West African percussion ensemble might find the melodic and harmonic structure of *Figaro* interesting, but its rhythms downright pedestrian.

As students of all the world's music, we cannot reconcile these divergent viewpoints. We are better off taking a relativistic attitude. We—the authors—believe that each society has a musical system that suits its culture, and although we may compare these systems in terms of their structure and function, we avoid making these comparisons the basis of qualitative judgments. Instead, we recognize that each society evaluates its own works of music by its own criteria and that there are also multiple—and often opposing—points of view on these works of music within each society. In the United States, we generally take it for granted that music should be an enjoyable auditory experience; elsewhere, the musical ideal may be quite different. We want to understand each music as an aspect of its own culture, and we recognize that each human community creates the kind of music it needs for its particular rituals and cultural events, to support its social system, and thus, to reflect its principal values.

World Music Is a Group of Musics

We see the world of music as consisting of a group of *musics*. It makes sense to think of *a* music as something like a language. Each society—a people or nation, but more typically an ethnic group—has its own principal music, and the members of a society know and respond to their music with a kind of common understanding, in the way they communicate through their language. But whereas few people know more than a couple of languages, many people learn to appreciate and respond to musics other than their "own." Still, most individuals feel most at home in one music.

But just as languages borrow words from each other, musics also influence each other. Indeed, as mass media and the Internet facilitate worldwide communication, most people of the world have access to the same body of popular music. And just as a society sometimes replaces one language with another (the Anglo-Saxons learned Middle English after the Norman invasion in 1066, and native peoples of South America took up Spanish after 1500), a community of people may cease using their tradition of music and replace it with another. Some individuals and some entire communities are bilingual; this is true of many North American Native American peoples today. Similarly, many Native American communities are "bimusical," using traditional Native American music and Western music equally but for different purposes, considering both to now be their cultural property.

If the world of music can be seen as a large group of *musics*, each music can be interpreted as a system, in the sense that change in one component causes changes in the others as well. A couple of imaginary examples: If a society begins using the piano to perform its traditional musical repertory, its melodies might be affected by the ubiquity and multiplicity of chords, easy and normal on the piano, but unusual on the older instruments. Bringing in the piano might also cause performance contexts to change. Consider, for example, a kind of music performed by traveling street musicians. If this music were taken up by the piano, it would no longer be possible to perform it while traveling, and if the piano were located in a concert hall, the idea of what this music should be and do would also change radically. Or, imagine a culture in which most music is improvised and transmitted orally. Bringing in the piano with its notated exercises for learning virtuosic technique might make musicians increase their respect for the performance of complex composed pieces that are best transmitted through notation and decrease their interest in improvising.

The Three-Part Model

This leads us to the third basic assumption. Using a model suggested by Alan P. Merriam, we look at music as a phenomenon that has three sides: sound, behavior, and conception or ideas. These three are closely interrelated, as each plays a role in determining the nature of the others.

✳ **Explore**
*the life and work of
Alan P. Merriam on*
mymusiclab.com

Let me illustrate. At a concert, we sit to hear musicians make sounds, and that to us is music. But if it's a classical piano recital, the performer usually plays as if she were alone and acknowledges the audience only when bowing before and after the numbers. If it's a folk concert, the singer always addresses the audience, makes jokes about himself, and sings "at" the audience. If it's an orchestra concert, the audience sits quietly; if a rock concert, members of the audience may make all sorts of sounds, sing along, or get up and dance. These different kinds of behavior are just as important to the music as a social and aesthetic event as are the sounds.

Now imagine a church service. The congregation sings a hymn, but the minister doesn't think, "My, they sang that hymn badly today; last week it was much better." The idea behind this music is that the congregation communicates with God, and musical virtuosity isn't an issue. But at the same service, the organist improvises on a theme by Bach during the offertory and does this so well that each of the members of the music committee, listening in the congregation, determines to renew the organist's contract and give her a raise.

Imagine now a Native American medicine man. He has experienced a vision in which he was visited by his guardian spirit, Muskrat, who sang a song for him. The man does not say to himself, "This was a particularly beautiful song I learned," but rather perhaps, "This song is powerful," and he would be

Close view of peyote cacti (*Lophophorus williamsii*) being held by a Native American medicine man. *Source:* IRA BLOCK/National Geographic Stock

sure to remember it precisely and not forget a note of it. But Mozart, suddenly inspired with one of his grand themes, may have said to himself, "This tune that came to me is fine, but I had better change it, fix it, work it out so it will be just right." To be properly understood, music should be studied as a group of sounds, as behavior that leads to these sounds, and as a group of ideas or concepts that govern the sound and the behavior.

So, in considering the music of the world's societies, the chapters in this book will concentrate on music as sound, or "the music itself" and also on the kinds of activities music accompanies that go into music-making and the consumption of music by audiences and communities, and also on societies' ideas about music. It is actually this third area that seems to be paramount, because it is the basic ideas about music—what it does for human society and how it relates to other components of culture such as religion, economic life, class structure, relationship of genders—that determine in the end the quality of a society's musical life. The ideas about music determine what the contexts for music will be and how the music will sound. If, for example, innovation is an important component of the system of ideas about music, the music will change frequently. If the notion of masterworks is present in the culture, great technical complexity and stylistic uniqueness may characterize its pieces. If the idea of conformity is important, well-disciplined orchestral performances may result. If individualism is important, then solo performances or improvised jam sessions may be the musical counterpart. If a society has complex music, then the notion of virtuosity in the realm of ideas may be reinforced, and social contexts for performances by virtuosi may be established.

UNIVERSALS OF MUSIC

Throughout the chapters that follow, the reader will be struck by the great differences among musics. Each society has a unique musical system related to the character of its culture. The most important thing that the reader should take away from this book is the enormous diversity in the world's music in sound, behavior, and ideas. But are there not some things about music that all, or virtually all, societies share? There surely are, and we use, for them, the term *universals* to mean the following:

UNIVERSALS

- All societies have music.
- All people sing.
- Music is used in religious rituals to experience the supernatural.
- Musical genres occur in all societies (such as songs associated with the seasons; children's songs; works songs).
- "Songs" or "pieces" are identified and distinguished from each other as common musical "units."

The most obvious universal is music itself: all societies, to our knowledge, at least have something like music. Not many societies, however, have a concept of music for which they have one word—"music." In the Persian language (spoken in Iran), there is one word for instrumental music and another for vocal. The Blackfoot language has a word for "song," but it includes dancing and ritual as well as music-making. Certain African languages have no term for music but a separate term for each of many genres of song. But all societies do have music in the sense that all have some kind of vocal production (it may sound like song, or chant, or ceremonial speech), which they themselves distinguish from ordinary speech. So, we are justified in identifying music, and especially vocal music, as a cultural universal. But the matter is complicated. For Americans, music is a broad concept—it may be vocal or instrumental, sacred or secular, solo or ensemble—and it has its metaphoric extensions, such as the notion that a "pleasant" sound is said to be "musical," that birds sing and elephants trumpet. But actually not all societies share our idea that all of these sounds—singing and instruments, ritual and entertainment, human and animal—can be brought together under one conceptual umbrella.

The first musical universal, then, is singing. All peoples sing. Virtually all peoples also have instruments, though in some instances they are rudimentary. And in the realm of instruments, virtually all peoples have percussion instruments. The most widespread are rattles and notched sticks that are rubbed, with drums actually not quite so universal. Virtually all peoples, even the most isolated tribal societies, have some kind of flutes. And everywhere one finds singing that is accompanied by percussion.

There are universals in the way music functions in societies—the "behavior" and "ideas" part of our three-part model. In all societies, music is used in religious rituals—almost everywhere it is a mainstay of sacred ceremonies—leading some scholars to suggest that perhaps music was actually "invented" for humans to have a special way of communicating with the supernatural. And, too, it seems that in all cultures music is used in some sense for transforming ordinary experience, producing anything from trance in a ritual to ecstasy or edification in a concert. Everywhere, dance is accompanied by musical sound. And everywhere, too, an important function of music is helping society to reinforce boundaries between social groups, who almost universally view their music as an emblem of identity. Music is used to integrate society and to provide a way of showing its distinctiveness.

Most societies, urban and rural, traditional and modernized, share some important genres of music. These include ritual and religious music; ritual calendric music (music appropriate to certain times in the year's cycle, such as winter solstice, spring, harvest songs); and music appropriate to rituals in the course of life, such as songs for adolescent ceremonies, wedding music, and funeral music; children's game songs; songs involving love and romance; narrative music (everything from folk ballads to music for dramas and operas); music for entertainment (evening family sings or concerts); and music to accompany labor (work songs or factory background music).

Bermudian Gombey dancer with a mask covering his face. *Source:* Doug Traverso/Robert Harding

Returning to universals in musical sound, music everywhere is presented in units that can be identified as "songs" or "pieces," with some kind of identity, a name, opus number, ritual designation, or owner. Nowhere do people "just" sing; they always sing *something*, and in this respect, music contrasts with some other art forms, such as dance. And everywhere, people can recognize and identify a tune or a rhythmic pattern, tell whether it is performed high or low or sung by a man or a woman.

There is then the question of the innate musicality of humans. We know that all normal humans inherit the ability to learn language—it is somehow "hardwired" in the human brain—but whether the same is true of music, whether all humans are basically musical is not clear, in part because cultures differ so much in their conception of "singing." Yet it seems likely that (with the occasional exception of individual disabilities) all humans can learn to sing minimally, to beat rhythms accurately, and to recognize simple pieces. Not all can attain professional proficiency; but then, although all humans can learn to speak, not all can become great orators. The world's societies differ in the degree to which they encourage individuals to participate in music. In some rural societies, most people are considered about equally good at singing, and everyone participates in music-making at public events. In many urban societies, musical participation is largely limited to listening to live music and even more to recordings, whereas performance is left to professionals with training and with the ascription of special talent.

The world's societies also differ greatly in the participation of men and women in music. In earlier times in Europe and North America and in certain devout Muslim nations of the Middle East, public performance by women was discouraged, and in some Native American societies, women were traditionally thought to lack musical ability. By contrast, in some traditional rural European cultures, women were the main transmitters of music and the prime participants in folkloric activities. In virtually all the world's societies, the late twentieth century saw a significant trend toward equalization of participation by gender, and musical roles that were once reserved for men (e.g., playing trumpet or singing in a Native American powwow group) are now filled by women as well.

If music is a cultural universal, it is not a universal language. Language is a human attribute, but humans speak many mutually unintelligible languages. Music is found in all cultures, but the world of music consists of musics that are not mutually compatible.

MUSICAL TRANSMISSION, HISTORY, AND CHANGE

All musics have a history, and all music changes, has always been changing, though at various rates and not always in the same direction. It would be foolish to assume that the music of India, because it is largely melodic and without harmony, somehow represents an "earlier stage" through which Western music has already passed, or that Europeans, in the days when they

MUSIC TRANSMISSION, HISTORY, AND CHANGE

- Different cultures' musics are affected differently when they come into contact with other musical cultures.
- In many societies, music is often transmitted aurally (by being heard).
- In some societies, notation is favored for preserving certain kinds of musical compositions.
- In the twentieth century, music from the North Atlantic has spread throughout the world with profound results.
- Today, all kinds of music seem to be available to everyone everywhere, leading to new musical styles.

lived in tribes, had music similar to that of Native Americans. Musics do not uniformly change from simple to complex. Each music has its own unique history, related to the history of its culture, to the way people adapt to their natural and social environment. The patterns we may discern in the world's music history usually have to do with the relationships of cultures to one another. Thus, in the twentieth century, as Western-derived culture has affected most others, most non-Western musics now show some influences of Western music. However, the results of this influence vary from culture to culture.

For example, when (shortly after 1800) the violin was introduced into the music of South India, it was incorporated into the Indian soundscape and began to be used in imitation of the Indian singing style. The same instrument, when introduced to Iran, brought with it the Western sound of violin playing, thus effecting changes in the Iranian notion of how music should sound. Brought to Amerindian peoples in the southwestern United States, it motivated the Navajo and Apache to develop the single-string "Apache fiddle," combining aspects of the violin and the traditional hunting bowlike musical bow.

One of the things that determines the course of history in a musical culture is the method of transmission. In most societies, music lives in oral (or better, "aural") tradition; that is, it is passed on by word of mouth and learned by hearing live performance. It is often assumed that this form of transmission inevitably causes songs to change; each person inevitably will develop his or her own variant, because there is no "notation" (either in print or a sound recording) to remind them of the "original" or "correct" version. Societies differ, however, in their attitude toward musical stability; to some it is important that a song remain stable and unchanged, whereas in others individual singers are encouraged to have their personal versions. In aural traditions, music perhaps cannot go beyond a certain degree of complexity, because limits of memory and the number of different "hands" through which the music passes will probably eventually lead to some change; add to this different performing situations, with more or fewer singers and instrumentalists, and the difficulty of preserving an "original" version increases.

Western academic music is traditionally notated, and there are also notation systems for some Asian musics, although these are usually not as detailed as the Western style and are not normally used by performers while they play or sing. Notated traditions also may be divided into written and printed. Musical notation appeared in Europe long before the development of music printing in the late fifteenth century, but the number of handmade copies of one piece was inevitably small, and they could differ. The change from written to printed music surely led to a different set of ideas about the nature and stability of a musical work. The development of sound recording has affected both aural and written traditions, as a recording allows someone learning a piece to hear it repeatedly in identical form, incorporating those aspects of music often inadequately represented in Western notation, such as tone, color, ornaments, and phrasing. The nature of a musical tradition, then, is affected greatly by the way it is transmitted and by the way its content is taught and learned.

If music has always been changing, since the late nineteenth century it has surely changed more than ever before, especially in the period since 1950. Among the reasons are

1. The colonization of most of the world by North Atlantic nations and, after 1945, the increased political and economic integration of nations that were formerly colonies into a global system
2. The incredible advances in communication by mass media, airlines, and computer networks
3. The dissemination of Western and Middle Eastern cultural values through the diffusion of Christianity and Islam throughout much of the world

The musical world in the late twentieth century is much more homogeneous than it was some three hundred years ago. Musical styles everywhere have begun to partake of the sounds of Western (and often Middle Eastern) music. Western-style harmony, synthesizers, and instrumental ensembles have come to pervade much of the world's music, as have Islamic singing styles and African-derived percussion rhythms. Much of this is a layer of music added to the older traditions, and so the diversity of musics available within each society has increased. One may argue that the musics of the world are becoming more alike, and indeed we now talk about global pop music, but we also need to recognize that because of the globalization of communication, the variety of music available to each individual has increased enormously. Each society maintains, and correctly, that it has a music with at least a certain degree of uniqueness.

For most of human history, the world's musics lived in relative isolation from each other. True, Christianity and Islam spread Western and Middle Eastern musical sounds throughout the world, African musical sounds were spread through the Americas as a result of the slavery system, and in the twentieth century, composers of art and popular music made increasing use of inspirations from the world's musics. Instruments have always traveled from country to country, continent to continent. But these kinds of exchange are modest compared to the ways music from everywhere has become available throughout the world as a result of the ubiquity of CDs, computer technology, and the Internet and also through the increase in international diasporic migration and large-scale tourism. It would seem that virtually all kinds of music are available to peoples everywhere, at least in urban societies. At the same time, the diversity of musical experience of each person has increased enormously, as more of us than ever can now hear recordings (and often live performances) of the world's many musics. It used to be mainly peoples who differed from each other (think "national" musics); now it is just as much the differences among the musical experiences and lives of individuals that characterizes the world's music (think Facebook, Pandora, and YouTube).

MUSICAL INSTRUMENTS

Virtually all cultures have musical instruments. In one sense, there is an infinite variety of instruments, but there is also a good deal of similarity among instruments across cultures. Bowed, stringed instruments held vertically, such as the cello, appear throughout Asia, Europe, and parts of Africa. As we have just seen in the case of the Apache fiddle, they probably developed in the native cultures of the Americas as a result of culture contact with Europeans. Xylophone-like instruments were highly developed in Indonesia, Africa, and Central America. Flutes, drums, and rattles are found throughout the world. Yet each culture has its own version of an instrument type, its own set of ideas about it, and its own terminology. Thus, the African instrument sometimes known as "thumb-piano" or "finger-xylophone"—its metal or reed keys are actually attached to a bridge and plucked, and therefore it is neither a piano nor a xylophone—is known in African languages as *mbira*, *sansa*, *kalimba*, *likembe*, *kasai*, and many other names.

What to call such an instrument in scholarly literature or even in this book? Whenever possible, we use the native designation—*sitar* instead of "North Indian lute," *erhu* instead of "Chinese spike fiddle." In some cases of terminological variety, one term has come to be widely used; for the thumb-piano, for example, *mbira* is now the most common term. But for more general groupings, it is useful to draw on a classification of instruments.

Musicians in the North Atlantic generally use a fourfold grouping—strings, woodwinds, brass, and percussion—that is actually derived not from the nature of the instruments themselves but from their roles in the eighteenth-century orchestras of Mozart and Haydn, as each group fulfilled certain functions in the music. This is a European kind of classification that one needs to know to understand European ideas about music, but most of the world's cultures have their own ways of classifying instruments. To talk about instruments of different cultures comparatively, however, students of world music commonly use a classification system that divides instruments into four main groups on

San women playing *lamellaphones* (thumb-pianos known in Africa as *mbiras* or *sansas*) on the ground. *Source:* Anthony Bannister; Gallo Images/Corbis

the basis of the way in which the sound is produced. Developed by two prominent German scholars of the early twentieth century, Erich M. von Hornbostel and Curt Sachs, the system is actually based on the way a Belgian museum curator, Victor Mahillon, arranged a large and varied instrument collection in Brussels in the nineteenth century, and ultimately it goes back to a way of grouping instruments in philosophical treatises of India.

One of the four classes consists of aerophones, basically wind instruments, subdivided into flutelike, trumpetlike, and reed instruments, among others. A second is chordophones, or stringed instruments. These are divided principally into zithers, which consist of sets of strings stretched in parallel fashion along a board, and lutes, on which strings are stretched along a fingerboard and its attached resonator. Most of the stringed instruments of Western culture—violins, double basses, guitars, and mandolins—are "lutes" that are bowed or plucked. A third group is idiophones, instruments whose bodies themselves vibrate. Among these are rattles, xylophones, bells, gongs, and many other instruments that are struck or rubbed. This is actually the largest group of instruments by far, and there are societies that have representatives of this class only and of no other. Fourth, there are membranophones, instruments in which a membrane vibrates—basically the drums. Each of these classes is elaborately subdivided, so that the system provides a space for each of the world's instruments and perhaps even for instruments not yet discovered. A fifth category, developed long after Hornbostel and Sachs published their scheme, has been suggested: electrophones, instruments that depend on electric power for producing and synthesizing sounds and for amplification. These would include modern synthesizers and computers, as well as electric guitars and electric

CLASSIFICATION OF MUSICAL INSTRUMENTS

Aerophones (Wind instruments)
  Fluelike
  Trumpetlike
  Reeds
Chordophones (String instruments)
  Zithers
  Lutes
Idiophones ("Self" vibrators)
  Rattles/shakers
  Gongs
  Xylophone
Membranophones (Membrane instruments or drums)
Electrophones (Electronic instruments)
  Synthesizer
  Computers

organs, and also older developments such as the theremin, invented in 1920, whose performer moves the hands above the instrument without touching it.

✳ Explore
*the Musical Instrument
Gallery on*
mymusiclab.com

WHY DIFFERENT CULTURES HAVE DIFFERENT KINDS OF MUSIC

Why do different cultures favor different types of music, and what is it that determines the particular type of music? Why indeed do Native Americans of the North American plains sing in a harsh and tense manner, and why did Western music develop its pervasive system of harmony, and why do sub-Saharan African peoples stress rhythmic complexity and the concept of improvised variation? Though these are the questions that we may wish ultimately to answer in this book, we will not be able to do so definitively.

But we can suggest some answers. Some factors should be eliminated from serious consideration at the outset. One is the genetic. There is no evidence that the musical style of a society is determined by heredity. It is true, for example, that black societies in Africa and the New World share certain musical traits; these are not, however, the result of the same factors that determine their physical similarity, but come rather from their common African cultural roots. After all, it has been amply demonstrated by such artists as Zubin Mehta, Yo-Yo Ma, and Seiji Ozawa that members of non-Western societies can become leading musicians in the sphere of Western music, and despite the problems occasioned by exposure delayed until adult life, some Americans and Europeans have become accepted as excellent performers of African and Indian music. As is the case with language, anyone can learn any music, but to become as much at ease and as proficient as a native, to speak musically without accent, requires exposure early in life or special talent and effort.

We should also eliminate the notion that all musics pass through a set of stages, and that we can explain the variety of world musics by suggesting that we are observing each of them at a different stage of the same development. It is possibly true that in a sense musics evolve in a manner similar to that of biological species. But just as it was not inevitable that "lower" species would eventually lead to humans, it is not inevitable (or even likely) that a non-Western music would gradually change to become like Western music. In fact, the very suggestion of this particular trajectory—that is, a narrative of progress moving from simple to complex, the final destination of which is located in the North Atlantic—offers a glimpse into subtly insistent but long discredited Eurocentric habits of thought. For students of the world's music, then, the concept of evolution can make only a small and rather self-evident contribution—that musical systems change in accordance with the needs of the social environment to be able to survive.

Take, for example, the role of music in human migration. In the late nineteenth century, many European peasants moved to North America in search of jobs and a higher standard of living, settling in cities and becoming factory workers. They brought with them their rural folk songs from Poland, Italy, Romania, or Greece to Cleveland, Detroit, and Chicago. But in these cities they no longer needed ritual songs to accompany agricultural festivals, social songs to sing on the village square while courting, or narrative ballads to entertain on evenings, because instead they worked in factories, went to high school dances, and (eventually) listened to radio and watched television. They did need music, however, to help remind them of their European heritage and of their special origins. Therefore, folk songs passed down in aural tradition became national songs learned from songbooks and taught in classes on Saturday mornings and sung at special Polish or Hungarian concerts. In the course of these kinds of performances, they changed from melodies sung unaccompanied to choral settings with harmony, and from songs that existed in many variants to standardized versions. In this way, the music changed to satisfy a new social need. (This, however, is only one of many types of processes that occurred. For example, some immigrants maintained their older song styles and tunes despite the new lifestyles into which they had entered. We may say that in this case, music was used to contradict and balance the prevailing changes in sociocultural organization.)

This suggests that a society develops its music in accordance with the character of its social system. Although such a statement surely does not account for all the aspects of a music or all the differences among musics, it may come closest to answering the general question previously raised. A typical ensemble in South Indian classical music has a clear hierarchy, somewhat along the lines of the Hindu caste system. The solo vocalist is highest and most prestigious, socially and musically; the accompanying drummer is next, followed by the accompanying violinist, the second percussionist, and finally the player of the drone instrument. Among the Mbuti pygmies of Zaire, an egalitarian society with no formal leadership, musical ensembles also have no formal leaders, and the singers in choruses blend their voices.

The European symphony orchestra began to develop seriously about the time of the Industrial Revolution. It is in effect a factory for producing music, in which group precision plays a great role, as does specialization. Each section has its boss, the concertmaster is a kind of factory foreman, and the conductor, who is symbolically different, making no sounds but standing on a pedestal and getting his or her name on the recording package, represents management. In those societies in which the social roles of men and women are extremely different, the genders have separate repertoires and different ways of using the voice. It has been suggested that those societies in which there is good cooperation and relative equality create large ensembles in which this cooperation is reflected, whereas others in which a part of the population is dominated by an elite develop soloistic music.

Let's not carry the argument too far. Surely music is created in part to support and symbolize important aspects of culture, but it also has other functions; for example, it may counteract rather than support the dominant cultural characteristics. There are societies in which one may say in music what one may not express in words and cultures in which music and musicians represent deviation from societal norms. And yet, if we wish to identify what it is that determines the nature of a music, we should look first to the general character of its culture and particularly the types of relationships among people within its society, and to the way the society relates to other societies.

THE FIELD OF ETHNOMUSICOLOGY

The subject of this book properly belongs to the field of ethnomusicology. Ethnomusicology is not the study of particular musics—such as "ethnic" musics—but of all music, from particular perspectives. On the one hand, ethnomusicologists look at any musical culture from a world perspective; they consider the world of musics as a context for the study of any particular music. They are interested in music as it fits into human culture, and as it relates to, affects, and is affected by the other domains of human culture. On the other hand, ethnomusicologists also often pay particular attention to music in political contexts, in music and racial and ethnic identity, music and gender studies, in intercultural relations, nationalism, cosmopolitanism, and globalization. (Examples of these approaches are presented in the chapters that follow.) Ethnomusicologists have also participated in important developments in the biological evolution of music, in psychology of music, and in music education.

Ethnomusicologists customarily regard themselves as either members of the discipline of musicology (the scholarly study of music from historical and social viewpoints) or of sociocultural anthropology (the study of humans with emphasis

Ethnomusicologist Frances Densmore recording an interpretation of a Blackfoot song performed by Mountain Chief. *Source:* Corbis

on culture). Some have, therefore, defined ethnomusicology as the anthropological study of music. But most ethnomusicologists, even those who consider themselves to be anthropologists first, are musicians of some sort; that is, they have studied music formally or informally and have some background as performers.

How and why do people enter the field of ethnomusicology? Typically, because they came into contact with the music of some "other" culture, and fell in love with it and determined to learn how to perform it, study the society from which it came, and figure out—if we can put it that way—how it functions in its society and how it is created and transmitted. Most ethnomusicologists are specialists in one culture, but many eventually study a second culture, in part for comparative perspective. Virtually all who pursue graduate study specializing in ethnomusicology take equal amounts of work in music departments and in departments providing training in the study of culture, history, and the analysis of musical life from the viewpoint of social sciences, such as anthropology and area studies. It is important for them, as well, to attain proficiency in the languages of the cultures in which they will do research. Fieldwork is the most characteristic aspect of ethnomusicological research, but much energy is also devoted to transcribing music from recordings to notation, analyzing interviews, and explicating musical life in the context of theories derived from anthropology and other social sciences.

Fieldwork is a personal activity, but all fieldwork depends on close interaction with members of a society—musicians and others—who become one's teachers and collaborators. The quality of the interaction depends on the type of project and on the fieldworker's personality—whether it is shy or outgoing—the person's gender and age, ethnic background, family status, and much more. But there is no doubt that ethnomusicological research as a whole owes an enormous debt to the musicians of the world who have undertaken to teach their musical system to outsiders, hoping that their students will "get

✳ **Explore**
how to conduct fieldwork in your own community on **mymusiclab.com**

it right" and represent them properly. Field projects vary enormously. Many students of Indian music spend most of their time with one teacher, becoming disciples and learning the musical system through one musician's perspective. Others survey musical life by making large numbers of sound or video recordings. Others spend most of their time interviewing intensively. Detailed description of events such as rituals or concerts may be the focus. Most typically, a fieldworker does all of this. These activities must be carried out at the convenience of the teachers, who have their own lives to lead. At the same time, the fieldworker must cope with practical problems of keeping house, dealing with medical, bureaucratic, and equipment problems, while striving to learn the nuances of a foreign language. Gathering the kinds of information provided in this book required much hard work on the part of many. Yet direct experience in the field provides a depth of understanding unavailable through secondary sources.

In the most recent two or three decades, a few important developments have caused fieldwork to change. Most nations and ethnic groups now produce and market recordings, videos, and DVDs of their own music, and this has changed the role of field recording from broadly documenting everything that may be available to one for accommodating special projects. Increasingly, ethnomusicological research is also carried out by scholars who come from the cultures they study, and there are now ethnomusicologists in virtually all of the world's nations, carrying out studies in their home territory and abroad.

Before c. 1970, most ethnomusicologists—and they were largely North American and European—concentrated on traditional music of non-Western and folk cultures, which had been relatively unaffected by Western music and musical practices. They avoided the many kinds of music in which style elements from various cultural sources were combined; for example, they might avoid Middle Eastern music performed on the piano, or African music using European chordal harmony; as a result, they avoided the study of popular musics in the world's cultures. But now, realizing that most of the world's music is, in fact, the result of cultural mixes, ethnomusicology is perhaps more concerned with popular musics of the whole world than any other music. And finally, North American and European ethnomusicologists have begun to look at their own musical cultures, trying to see what they would learn if they addressed to their own institutions and organizations the kinds of questions that had been helpful to them in learning to understand foreign cultures.

Courses in ethnomusicology in the United States and Canada are most commonly offered in music departments (but in a few cases in anthropology), and most ethnomusicologists who are university teachers serve in departments or schools of music. Since about 1980, ethnomusicologists have begun to participate in recent developments within academic work such as gender studies, critical and interpretive theory, and the study of popular culture, and they have begun, increasingly, to examine their own cultures and to look analytically at the relationship between themselves as scholars and the culture they are observing, realizing that the identity and position of observers are major factors in the resulting interpretation. And although direct analysis of music, beginning with the transcription of recordings into notation and the study of performance in the field, continues to be important, the mainstream of ethnomusicological thought has moved increasingly to the understanding of music and the role it plays in the world's societies and cultures.

With their variety of backgrounds and interests, ethnomusicologists comprise an extremely diverse population of academics. They do have this in common: they try to combine their own, culturally situated observations with the views of a society about its own musical culture in a context of shared social engagement. The chapters that follow attempt to maintain this combination of perspectives.

SUMMARY

✔•⎯Study and Review
on mymusiclab.com

Our introductory excursion into the field of ethnomusicology has reminded us that world music is made up of a diversity of musical cultures. It has also underscored that no music is *intrinsically* better than any other. With this relativistic view as a guide, this chapter introduced us to a three-part approach to studying music; that is, music should be studied as sound, behavior, and idea or conception.

Our excursion also afforded us a glimpse at some universals of music (all societies have something like music; all people sing; music is used in religious rituals, etc.) and suggested a few ways that music is transmitted (e.g., aurally, written, notated), travels (e.g., culture to culture, country to country, etc.), and changes (e.g., mass media and the Internet, globalization, etc.). We also discussed briefly the diversity of the world's instruments and introduced four broad categories for classifying them (aerophones, chordophones, idiophones, and membranophones [along with a newer category called electrophones]).

Our short excursion explored the reasons why different cultures have different kinds of music, and we rejected a few ideas (e.g., genetics and evolution) as discredited and unhelpful on the way to an answer that seems most likely and least problematic—that musical styles appear to develop in relation to the social organization of each culture. Our final topic concerned the field of ethnomusicology itself, and we were reminded that ethnomusicologists study world music from the perspective of both music and culture. They achieve this in large measure through sustained engagement with the communities of practice they are interested in—a methodology most often referred to as fieldwork. Fieldwork—recording and studying, and even learning to perform the music where it is made—is an essential part of the study of ethnomusicology.

BIBLIOGRAPHY

The Field of Ethnomusicology   Bruno Nettl, *Nettl's Elephant* (Champaign: University of Illinois, 2010); Bruno Nettl and Philip Bohlman, eds., *Comparative Musicology and Anthropology of Music: Essays in the History of*

Ethnomusicology (Chicago: University of Chicago Press, 1991); Jennifer Post, *Ethnomusicology: A Guide to Research* (New York: Routledge, 2004); Helen Myers, ed., *Ethnomusicology: An Introduction* (New York: Norton, 1992); Gregory F. Barz and Timothy J. Cooley, *Shadows in the Field: New Perspectives for Fieldwork in Ethnomusicology* 2nd ed. (New York: Oxford University Press, 2008); Bruno Nettl, *The Study of Ethnomusicology*, 2nd ed. (Urbana: University of Illinois Press, 2005); Alan P. Merriam, *The Anthropology of Music* (Evanston, IL: Northwestern University Press, 1964); John Blacking, *How Musical Is Man?* (Seattle: University of Washington Press, 1973); Henry Stobart, *The New (Ethno) Musicologies* (Lanham, MD: Scarecrow Press, 2008); Rolf Bader, Christiane Neuhaus, Ulrich Morgenstern, eds., *Concepts, Experiments, and Fieldwork : Studies in Systematic Musicology and Ethnomusicology* (New York: Peter Lang, 2010).

Surveys of World Music and Musical Cultures   William P. Malm, *Music Cultures of the Pacific, the Near East, and Asia*, 3rd ed. (Englewood Cliffs, NJ: Prentice Hall, 1996); Bruno Nettl, *Folk and Traditional Music of the Western Continents*, 3rd ed. (Englewood Cliffs, NJ: Prentice Hall, 1990); Elizabeth May, ed., *Musics of Many Cultures* (Berkeley: University of California Press, 1980); David Reck, *Music of the Whole Earth* (New York: Scribner's, 1977); Jeff Titon and others, *Worlds of Music*, 4th ed. (New York: Schirmer Books, 2002); Patricia Shehan Campbell, *Lessons from the World: A Cross-Cultural Guide to Music Teaching and Learning* (New York: Schirmer Books, 1991); John E. Kaemmer, *Music in Human Life* (Austin: University of Texas Press, 1993); Bruno Nettl with Melinda Russell, ed., *In the Course of Performance: Studies in the World of Musical Improvisation* (Chicago: University of Chicago Press, 1998); Kip Lomell and Anne Ramussen, eds., *Musics of Multicultural America* (New York: Schirmer Books, 1997); Ellen Koskoff, ed., *Women and Music in Cross-Cultural Perspective* (Urbana: University of Illinois Press, 1989); Lawrence Sullivan, ed., *Enchanting Powers: Music in the World's Religions* (Cambridge, MA: Harvard University Press, 1997); *The Garland Encyclopedia of World Music*, 10 vols. (New York: Routledge, 1997–2001); Philip V. Bohlman, *World Music: A Very Short Introduction* (Oxford: Oxford University Press, 2002); Peter Fletcher, *World Musics in Context* (Oxford: Oxford University Press, 2002); Terry Miller and Andrew Shahriari, *World Music: A Global Journey* (New York: Routledge, 2006); Jennifer Post, ed., *Ethnomusicology: A Contemporary Reader* (New York: Routledge, 2006); Kay Shelemay, *Soundscapes*, 2nd ed. (New York: Norton, 2007); Thomas Turino, *Music as Social Life: the Politics of Participation*, (Chicago: University of Chicago Press, 2008).

Musical Change   Bruno Nettl, ed., *Eight Urban Musical Cultures: Tradition and Change* (Urbana: University of Illinois Press, 1978); Bruno Nettl, *The Western Impact on World Music* (New York: Schirmer Books, 1985); Gerard Behague, ed., *Performance Practice: Ethnomusicological Perspectives* (Westport, CT: Greenwood, 1984); Stephen Blum and others, eds., *Ethnomusicology and Modern Music History* (Urbana: University of Illinois Press, 1991); Charles Keil and Steven Feld, *Music Grooves* (Chicago: University of Chicago Press, 1994);

Ola Johansson, Thomas L. Bell, eds., *Sound, Society and the Geography of Popular Music* (Burlington, VT: Ashgate, 2009).

Instruments   Curt Sachs, *The History of Musical Instruments* (New York: Norton, 1940); Sibyl Marcuse, *Musical Instruments: A Comprehensive Dictionary* (Garden City, NY: Doubleday, 1964); *The New Grove Dictionary of Musical Instruments* (New York: Macmillan, 1984).

Determinants of Music   Curt Sachs, *The Wellsprings of Music* (The Hague: Martinus Nijhoff, 1961); Alan Lomax and others, *Folk Song Style and Culture* (Washington, DC: American Association for the Advancement of Science, 1968); John Blacking, *Music, Culture, and Experience* (Chicago: University of Chicago Press, 1994); Martin Clayton, Richard Middleton, and Trevor Herbert, eds., *The Cultural Study of Music* (New York: Routledge, 2003).

Views of Western Music   Henry Kingsbury, *Music, Talent, and Performance: A Conservatory Cultural System* (Philadelphia: Temple University Press, 1988); Bruno Nettl, *Heartland Excursions: Ethnomusicological Reflections on Schools of Music* (Urbana: University of Illinois Press, 1995); Kurt Blaukopf, *Musical Life in a Changing Society* (Portland, OR: Amadeus Press, 1992); Christopher Small, *Musicking* (Hanover, NH: Wesleyan University Press, 1998); Bruno Nettl, Gabriel Solis, eds., *Musical Improvisation: Art, Education, and Society* (Champaign: University of Illinois, 2009).

Periodicals   These provide articles as well as book and recordings reviews. *Ethnomusicology: Journal of the Society for Ethnomusicology; Asian Music; The World of Music; Yearbook for Traditional Music; British Journal of Ethnomusicology* (now *Ethnomusicology Forum*); *Popular Music.*

The Music of India

CHARLES CAPWELL

ATTENDING A MUSIC CONFERENCE IN KOLKATA (CALCUTTA)

Getting There

As the sun disappeared from the late afternoon sky of a January day, the air hovering above the streets and buildings of Kolkata (Calcutta) thickened with pollution. Ignoring my smarting eyes and abandoning the search for a taxi, I settled on taking a more economical bus ride downtown. The first bus to arrive at the stop, however, was full to overflowing and was besieged by a hardy group, some of whom managed to push their way onto the stair landing or grab onto the rear of the bus for a free but perilous ride. The situation didn't improve with the arrival of the second bus, so when the third one showed up, I joined the siege and succeeded in shoving and elbowing my way onto the first step of the bus. Pressure from those leaving the bus threatened to force me back onto the street, until

the pushing of those boarding behind me propelled me upward into the aisle. Having gotten inside, all of us who had viewed one another as opponents outside suddenly felt a comradely warmth toward our neighbors, and a flurry of apologies and wry comments accompanied the liberties we were compelled to take with each other.

As the bus lurched into traffic, I necessarily struck up an acquaintance with the young man against whom I fell and on whose toes I trampled as I tried to steady myself. My excessive clumsiness tested his fading spirit of camaraderie, but when he learned that we were both headed toward the same "music conference"—series of recitals, that is—he overlooked my assaults and began to chat enthusiastically about the musicians we were going to hear.

When we reached the southeast corner of the Maidan, Calcutta's enormous equivalent of Central Park—Swarup my new acquaintance—and I extricated ourselves from the bus and walked the short distance to the entrance of Rabindra Sadan, the modern concert hall named for Rabindranath

❋─Explore
*Learning Objectives for
this chapter on*
mymusiclab.com

❋─Explore
*the Musical Instrument
Gallery on*
mymusiclab.com

👁─Watch the **Video**
of a sitar and tabla player
on **mymusiclab.com**

Tagore. (Tagore [1861–1941], winner of the Nobel Prize for poetry in 1913, was one of India's greatest artists. Besides being a poet, he was a novelist, dramatist, composer, painter, and educator.)

Preliminaries

Although we had arrived just on time at 6 the hall was sparsely populated because the conference was to run over several days, and the lesser-known artists appear earliest in the series as well as at the beginning of each evening. Swarup had come early because the first performer was a young dancer who was his classmate at the University of Calcutta, where they both studied physics. Many young dancers these days come from the middle class and are well educated, he told me, although traditionally professional performers in music and dance had little education outside their art and held relatively low social positions. His friend Premlata was just about to complete her M.A. and was torn between continuing her studies in physics and trying to establish a reputation as a professional dancer. If she chose the latter, he said, she would face fierce competition and relatively small rewards.

As people milled about in the audience greeting one another and chatting, a few people began to appear on stage adjusting microphones and vases of flowers. At last, a couple of musicians came out, removed their sandals at the edge of the stage, and placed a few instruments on the carpet at the right. Swarup named them for me: there was a *harmonium*, a small box with a bellows and a keyboard; a *sitar*, remotely related to a guitar with a very long, wide neck; a *tambura*, similar to the sitar but with no frets, because its strings are simply plucked to provide a drone (an unchanging pitch to accompany the melody); a pair of small drums called *tabla*; and another drum, barrel-shaped and having two heads, called *pakhavaj*. Because no one paid any attention to the musicians, and they left, once again I started to wonder if something were amiss, but as no one else seemed to be concerned, I relaxed. Soon all the musicians came out, sat on the carpet, and started tuning their instruments. I was a little startled when the tabla player picked up a hammer and started striking his instrument with it; after a few taps at the edge of the skin, however, he tapped the head with his fingers, and I realized he was simply tuning.

The audience still did not seem very interested in the musicians, and even after they started playing, many people continued their conversations while others began to settle down. Not until the dancer made her entrance and gracefully made obeisance to the musicians, the instruments, and the audience in the Indian way by bringing her palms together in front of her face did most of the audience direct their attention to the stage.

Indian Tambura player.
Source: Odile Noel/Lebrecht
Music & Arts

Kathak Dance: **Nritta** (Abstract Dance)

Because everything had struck me as being rather casual so far, I was totally unprepared for what happened next. Premlata suddenly leapt into action, flailing her arms, flicking her wrists in circles, snapping her head from side to side, twitching her brows, and madly pirouetting about, all the while jingling her ankle bells in crisp rhythms that mimicked the drum, which she punctuated by sharply slapping the soles of her bare feet against the floor of the stage. Then in an instant all this dizzying activity was coordinated into one brilliant movement, bringing everything to a complete and astonishing halt, and the dancer froze: one arm straight out and the other arched above her head, fingers twitching and eyebrows quivering as though to express the uncontainable kinetic vitality that the rhythms inspired in her.

A tabla maker lacing a new head to the dahina, or right drum, of the pair. The left drum is called the bayan.
Source: Charles Capwell

Watching her repeat these waves of activity and repose, I began to understand why this music conference had begun with a dancer. It was as though she were simply a physical realization of the musical rhythms that the drummer played, all of which seemed to be magically transmitted to Premlata's feet, while the rest of her body exquisitely ornamented these rhythms. Sometimes the drummer and Premlata would speak to one another in a string of special rhythmic syllables called **bols**, whose rhythms they would then reproduce on the drum and with the feet.

Kathak Dance: **Abhinaya** (Mimed Dance)

There was more to it, I soon discovered. As the harmonium player started to sing, Premlata's physical abstractions of rhythm gave way to mime, and she began to act out the words of his song with gestures and facial expressions but no props. Swarup interpreted for me the words to the beautiful melody, which the sitar and harmonium duplicated, as is customary, without adding any harmony.

It is a very familiar story to many Indians, in large part because it has been retold for many generations in many different media such as **kathak**, the kind of dance we were enjoying. The Hindu god Krishna is said to have been inordinately fond of butter as a child. As the story begins, Krishna's foster mother, Yashoda, is churning butter. When she has finished her tiring household chore, she puts the butter into a clay pot and hangs it from a rafter in her simple cottage out of Krishna's reach.

Then Yashoda leaves the cottage to do some more chores. As the dancer depicts Yashoda's departure, she suddenly twirls about and transforms herself

NRITTA
Abstract Kathak dance.

BOL
Rhythmic syllable in Hindustani music.

ABHINAYA
Gestural interpretation of text in dance.

KATHAK DANCE
Major style of Hindustani dance.

into an impish child to show us the mischievous Krishna intent on retrieving the butter. Frustrated by its being out of reach, he pouts and frets until he thinks of hurling a stone at the pot. At last he succeeds in breaking it and is covered with a torrent of butter, which he greedily licks from hands and arms. Satisfied and very pleased with himself, Krishna quickly realizes he is in trouble as he sees the look on Yashoda's face when she returns home and discovers his mischief. Now Premlata shifts quickly from one character to the other; she shows Yashoda, beside herself with fury, dragging Krishna about by the ear as she scolds him; then the terrified child cowering in expectation of a beating. Just as Yashoda is raising her hand to give Krishna a solid box on the ear, she sees the terror in the little boy's face and comes to her senses; rather than lashing out at the frightened child, she is overwhelmed with motherly protectiveness. Subject to the irresistible charm of childish innocence that Krishna embodies, she scoops him up in a fond embrace and cuddles and fondles him in delight.

Although the audience was small and was a little inattentive at the start, there were many appreciative cries of "*Bah, bah!*" (Bravo!) and "*Bahut accha!*" (Very good!) for her skill both in abstract dance and in mime. Swarup seemed pleased with the response, which he had done his best to encourage as a less-than-impartial critic.

During the brief interval before the next item on the program, we stepped outside for a cup of tea, and I mentioned to him my initial surprise at having a dancer in a music concert.

"Not surprising at all," he replied. "After all, the name of the sponsoring association is 'Kolkata Sangita Mela.' "

"That's the Kolkata Music Festival, right?" I asked.

"Yes, but **sangita**, which we generally translate as 'music,' means not just the melody and rhythm of instrument and voice, but also the embodiment of rhythm in dance and the dramatic expression of story and mood through dance and song as well."

Vocal and Instrumental Performance: **Khyal** and **Gat-Tora**

SANGITA
Music and associated performing arts.

KHYAL
The major vocal style of Hindustani music.

GAT-TORA
The section of Hindustani instrumental performance, accompanied by tabla, in which a short composed melody, the *gat*, is alternated with improvisational passages, *tora*.

Two days later, Swarup and I had tea together again during a break in the last evening's group of performances, which were continuing throughout the night. It was four in the morning, and I desperately needed a pick-me-up; I wished that I had taken the opportunity for a catnap during one of the earlier performances, as some of my neighbors had surprised me by doing. I certainly did not want to fall asleep during the next performance, because the artist was considered among the foremost musicians in India and had been given the position of honor as the final performer. We had just heard a singer, however, who was also considered one of the great musicians performing today, and I wanted Swarup's opinion about his performance. I confessed that I had difficulty keeping awake at the start because the pace seemed so slow.

"Well, that's to be expected, since you don't know what to listen for," Swarup told me. (Rather bluntly, I thought; but of course he was right, I admitted to myself, that's why I wanted his opinion.) "A full-scale performance of khyal, the kind of piece we just heard, begins in *vilambit* **lay**, slow tempo, and concludes—maybe thirty or forty minutes later—in *drut lay*, or fast tempo. You probably found the faster part more enjoyable, right?"

"That's right!" I readily agreed. "I could hardly believe my ears when he sang those rapid passages, the virtuosity was so astonishing."

"Yes, his **tans** are exceptionally clean and precise, but his **alap** is even more satisfying to the connoisseur." "That's the slow part?"

"Right. In the beginning the singer's task is to show subtlety rather than virtuosity in the artistry he employs to reveal the **raga**, the particular set of pitches, that he has chosen to sing." "He must have been very successful, then," I suggested, "because I noticed many people in the audience shaking their heads and making other gestures and comments of approval."

"Oh, yes, he was in particularly good form tonight—but then, artists are often inspired to do their best in Kolkata (Calcutta), because they know the audience is especially sophisticated and demanding here."

We decided to finish our tea quickly and return to the hall in order to not miss the beginning of the final performance. I noticed a palpable air of excitement in the hall as people roused themselves for the arrival of the last star performer just as the dawn was breaking outside. Appreciative applause greeted the famous sitarist's presence on stage, and a murmur of excitement went round the audience as he announced the raga he would play—one that he himself had created, Swarup said.

The sitarist, too, began with an alap that started slowly with a careful, step-by-step revelation of the raga; he began in a low range and slowly worked higher, setting each pitch in its particular melodic relationship to the others. Unlike the singer's alap, however, this one had no drum accompaniment, and the melody seemed to float freely with no awareness of time. Eventually, as Swarup had prepared me to expect, this insinuating melody mysteriously acquired a pulse to which I realized I was lightly tapping my finger—this was the **jor** section. Not long after, though, the pace became so fast I could only listen in amazement as the artist concluded with the **jhala** section. Only after this, did the sitarist begin the gat-tora, joined at last by the tabla player.

I had mentioned to Swarup that in the slow khyal I had been distracted by the drone pitches that were constantly played on the tamburas, but as he had assured me I would do, I was beginning to learn to focus on the melody and to be aware of the drone only subliminally. During the alap, with no other harmony to distract me, I could appreciate the individual pitches of the melody as they stood out against the tonal backdrop of the droning tamburas and began to understand why others would occasionally shake their heads or murmur in approval of something the artist did. Rather than feeling drowsy, I was entranced by the contemplation of these beautiful sounds. This contemplative mood changed, of course, to a more active one, especially with the added interest of tabla accompaniment and **tala**—that is, meter. At the climax, the tabla

LAY(A)
Tempo.

TAN
A rapid and florid kind of improvised melodic passage in Hindustani music.

ALAP(ANAM)
Raga improvisation in free rhythm.

RAG(A)(M)
A scale and its associated musical characteristics, such as the number of pitches it contains, its manner of ascending and descending, its predominant pitch, and so forth.

JOR
The section of Hindustani instrumental performance that follows *alap* and introduces a pulse.

JHALA
The concluding section of instrumental improvisation following *jor* in Hindustani music during which the performer makes lively and fast rhythmic patterns on the drone strings of an instrument.

TAL(A)(M)
Meter.

Watch the **Video** *of a sitar performance* on **mymusiclab.com**

LISTENING GUIDE

MEDIUM AND FAST GATS IN RAGA YAMAN   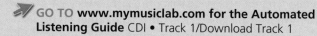 GO TO **www.mymusiclab.com for the Automated Listening Guide** CDI • Track 1/Download Track 1

Performed by Sudhir Phadke (sitar) and Anand Badamikar (tabla)

This performance in Raga Yaman illustrates several of the musical structures introduced in the narrative about the Kolkata Music Conference. Performed by Sudhir Phadke (sitar) and Anand Badamikar (tabla), it includes an example of a short alap, followed by a gat-tora section. The gat-tora section alternates a pre-composed melody (called a gat) with improvised sections (tora). An important component of gat-tora is the **mukhra**—the initial phrase of the gat (melody). The mukhra is used as a way of ending the improvisatory sections and returning to the gat. Another structural feature that you will hear in the gat-tora section is called a tihai. The **tihai** is a pre-composed phrase that is repeated three times to add emphasis to an arrival or to signal a shift to a new section. Following the gat-tora, you will hear a transition to a fast (drut) jhala. A jhala can be performed after a gat-tora, in which case it is accompanied by tabla, unlike the jhala that occurs in the sequence of alap, jor, jhala, each of which is customarily unaccompanied.

The pitches included in the rag performed here—*raga Yaman*—are C-d-e-F#-g-a-b (where C indicates the first note in the rag and does not necessarily match what you might be used to hearing as the pitch "C" in concert tuning). The rag is performed in a tal (meter) called Tintal (4+4+4+4). This sixteen-beat tala is indicated by clapping on beats 1, 5, and 13 and waving the hand on beat 9.

								MUKHRA							
1	2	3	4	5	6	7	8	9	10	11	**12**	**13**	**14**	**15**	**16**
clap				clap				wave				clap			

TIME	SECTION	MUSICAL EVENT
0:00–0:08	**Alap:** Listen for how the performer systematically explores the individual pitches of the raga.	The sitar player strums across the open strings of the instrument as an opening gesture. Listen for the sound of both the melody and the drone strings.
0:09–0:23		The performer begins the alap by moving slowly up the raga, exploring the first few notes.
0:24–0:45		This process continues until the performer eventually reaches the highest note.
0:46–1:10		A zigzag motion back down the raga eventually reaches the original opening pitch.
1:12–1:14		A second open-string strum ends the alap section.

1:15–1:38	**Gat-Tora in Medium Tempo:** Listen for the alternating sections of melody (gat) and improvisation (tora) in this section.	The sitarist plays vilambit (slow) gat, beginning on beat twelve, and repeats the melody twice, concluding with the mukhra (b-a-b-e-d-e-e) ending on **sam** (beat one). If you're having trouble hearing the mukhra, the tabla joins after the very first statement of the mukhra, playing a single stroke at [1:18] before joining in earnest.
1:39–1:44		The sitarist continues without pause into improvisation (tora) for the rest of the tala cycle until mukhra is picked up at beat 12 again, ending on the next sam.
1:45–2:11		Further improvisation in higher range until full gat returns.
2:12–2:22		Restatement of gat.
2:23–2:26		Tora.
2:27–3:44		Mukhra, followed by tora, etc . . .
3:45–3:54		At the close of the gat-tora section, the sitarist performs a tihai leading to sam and a change to fast (drut) gat.
3:55–4:50	**Brisk Jhala in Fast Tempo:** Listen for the increasingly virtuosic melodic and rhythmic explorations on the sitar and tabla.	The sitarist begins to play increasingly elaborate melodic explorations, alternating melody and drone.
4:50–5:55		The transition to jhala is complete and the sitarist signals this with rapid strokes on the drone strings, inserted between melody tones (a hallmark of jhala); the tempo (laya) also increases to about 240 beats per minute at this point.
5:55–6:15		Sitar and tabla join in rhythmic improvisation that takes the raga to a dramatic conclusion.

player, too, displayed an amazing skill that rivaled the soloist's, whereas in the fast khyal, the tabla had only occasionally drawn my attention. At the end, the two performers engaged in a kind of duel in which the intricate rhythms the soloist initiated on the sitar were reproduced by the tabla player as a sort of answer—jawab—to a challenging rhythmic question—sawal. After a while, the patterns of the **sawal–jawab** became shorter and shorter, until the sitar and tabla merged for a hair-raising finish that brought the house down. (Listen to CD I, 1 for an example of alap, gat-tora, and jhala.)

MUKHRA
Initial phrase of a khyal or gat used as a cadence for improvisational passages in Hindustani music.

Ravi and Anoushka Shankar
playing sitars. *Source:* M. Peric/
Lebrecht Music & Arts

TIHAI
A formulaic cadential pattern,
normally repeated three times
with calculated rests between
each statement so that the
performance ends on sam.

SAM
The first beat in a tala.

SAWAL-JAWAB
"Question-answer," rhythmic
challenges between soloist and
accompanist in Hindustani
music.

Leaving the hall thinking we had certainly gotten our money's worth during the previous night, Swarup and I decided to walk home and take advantage of the brisk morning air to refresh ourselves for the long day ahead. Having patiently answered many of my questions during the last few days, Swarup now proceeded to interrogate me about how I perceived the differences between his classical music tradition and my own.

"The most striking difference," I began, "is certainly that every performance we've seen in the last few days has focused on solo performance—vocal or instrumental or dance—with the accompaniment of a drum and the support of a drone. At home, I've attended concerts ranging from true solo recitals to performances by a couple of hundred instrumentalists and singers."

"That's the very thing I like about Western music," Swarup agreed enthusiastically. "There's such a wide range of groups. But you know, when I visited my uncle in London last year and he took me to a performance of Handel's *Messiah*, he complained afterward about it all sounding the same to him, although he's been in London 20 years now! He said, I remember, 'It's all the same raga.'"

Laughing, I nonetheless had to agree with Swarup's uncle, "Yes, I guess he's right. We have a variety of combinations of voices and instruments but are limited in much classical music to major or minor, whereas you use an enormous variety of ragas. How do you remember them all, anyway? We must have heard at least a dozen different ragas in these recitals, and yet you seemed acquainted with them all. For us it doesn't matter whether a piece is in E-flat or C-sharp; it's still the same old scale, just placed a little higher or lower. And for the great majority of music lovers, knowing the difference between one chord and another doesn't enter into it."

"Well, most of the audience here doesn't recognize more than a few common ragas either, but those who've studied music seriously, as I have, eventually come to recognize dozens, while any good performer has to be able to keep a couple of dozen or so active in his performing repertory."

"Without the use of notation, either," I added in admiration.

"Not for performance, no, but students often do write down a short composition they're learning to record a kind of capsule summary of the way a raga should go."

"That can't be too much help," I objected, "because a performance is almost entirely improvised. As you pointed out to me, the composition is simply used as a kind of cadence, an occasional resting place for the soloist to plan what's coming next and to let the tabla player do more than simply keep time."

"Speaking of the tabla," Swarup interrupted, "you've not said anything about tala so far."

"You mean how I feel it is different from Western meter?"

"Yes. You see, I'm afraid that in regard to meter I feel somewhat similarly about Western music to the way my uncle felt about keys or major and minor. Although something like the waltz is very catchy, it's all pretty limited, don't you think?"

Again I laughed and agreed. "Our meters are basically simple and repetitive until the twentieth century, anyway, when all sorts of possibilities have arisen to replace the idea of key as well as regular meter."

By this time we had arrived in front of Swarup's home, and we decided to continue our discussion sometime in the future—when we would, we hoped, be a little less sleepy. As we parted, we thought of the old saying, "Music is a universal language." Perhaps, we agreed, it had started out as something closer to "Music, like language, is universal," because we both felt that, though music might be everywhere, to understand someone else's music was like learning to understand someone else's language.

NATYASASTRA
An early Indian treatise on the performing arts attributed to Bharata and concerned with music, dance, and theater and drama.

Timeline of Indian Historical and Musical Events

2nd millennium BCE	Northwestern India and Pakistan site of Harappan civilization, contemporaneous with Mesopotamian civilization.
2nd–1st millennium BCE	Aryan nomads from further north and west begin to arrive in the region, eventually displacing Harappan civilization. They establish the Vedic religion, predecessor of Hinduism. Its sacred texts, preserved in oral tradition, are the *Vedas*, whose musical chants and melodies influence development of Indian music.
5th century CE	The **Natyasastra** is written, an early treatise on the performing arts
13th century CE	Muslim invaders come to the north, eventually taking over Delhi, but the south remains largely Hindu, and the classical music system bifurcates into Hindustani and Carnatic (Karnatak) systems.

Early 16th century	Northern musician Tansen becomes the official musician of the imperial court near Delhi; becomes model for the master art musician in the north.
Early-to-mid-18th century	New instruments arrive: the violin from Europe and the sarod from Afghanistan.
Later 18th century	Tyagaraja becomes the most famous musician in Carnatic culture, writing many of the kritis that continue to be performed to today. He turns down a court appointment to continue his religious vocation.
Mid-19th century	Christian missionaries bring portable pump organs (known as harmoniums) to India, which rapidly become popular instruments for song accompaniments.
Late 19th–early 20th century	Intellectuals begin a movement to remove the stigma from musical performance, making music and dance acceptable to the middle classes.
1947	India wins its independence from Britain; increased nationalistic feelings lead to renewed interest in native music.
1965	The Beatles' George Harrison becomes interested in the sitar, studying with Ravi Shankar, the great Indian master. Shankar's music is introduced to the West by Harrison, most memorably in the 1971 *Concert for Bangladesh*.

ROOTS

The Vedas

India's civilizations and learning stretch back for millennia, so it is not surprising to find music as one of the key elements in that record. A charming statuette of a dancing girl, for example, is found among the archeological remains of one of the world's oldest civilizations, the Harappan, located in Pakistan and northwestern India, which had connections with the early agricultural theocracies of Mesopotamia in the second millennium BCE. During this period, new people were arriving in the area from further north and west—people who managed through a combination of circumstance and force to supplant the culture of their predecessors. One of the attributes of the Harappan civilization was a writing system, but the newcomers were nonliterate, and for them the power of sound embodied in speech was an aspect of the divine. Speakers of an Aryan language related to most of those spoken in Europe today, the newcomers extolled the power and beauty of their gods in a body of poems they had brought with them that they preserved through oral transmission. Eventually, these poems of the **Rig-Veda** came to be the special responsibility of the top ranking of the four divisions or **varnas** of society, whose many ramifications we call "castes."

The **Brahmins** (also spelled Brahmans), as the members of the top varna were called, were entrusted with supernatural and intellectual matters and were given a long and intensive education from childhood, the purpose of which was to ensure the correct transmission and the correct pronunciation of the Vedic hymns. Particular care had to be taken to preserve these because their very sounds were considered to be the necessary means for coercing the gods to provide for the needs of the people, and after many generations in a new land, the people feared that the archaic language and pronunciation of the Vedas would be lost.

To preserve the accent patterns of ancient Vedic, for example, the Brahmins adopted the practice of associating the three types of spoken accent with a relative pitch level; this gives the recitation of Rigvedic texts the quality of chant, a chant whose melodic contour (or shape) depends precisely on the succession of accents in the sung syllables. A further musical component is found in the durations of the pitches. These too depend on the syllables, because the Vedic language, like classical Latin or Greek, based its verse on the relative length of syllables, rather than on a pattern of accents (or feet), as English verse does. So important was the sound of the text that, long after the enormously elaborate ritual sacrifices of Vedic religion had died out, the Vedas continued to be preserved in oral transmission; the habit of writing them down is relatively recent. Even today some Brahmin boys are trained to memorize the Vedas in chant, although contemporary Hinduism, while venerating the Vedas, has little connection with the ancient ritualistic religion founded on them.

Early Music Theory

A further musical element entered into the preservation of the Rigvedic texts when these were rearranged for use as hymn texts in the *Sama-Veda* and were sung to a collection of special tunes called **Samagana**. The early Sanskrit writers on musical theory and practice refer to these religiously based traditions of chant and song as the source for secular art music. By relating secular music to the intellectual tradition that preserved the Vedas, they were able to provide their own tradition with prestige and dignity. In one early treatise on the performing arts, the *Natyasastra*, written sometime before the fifth century CE, these arts are considered a "new" Veda, more suited for the enlightenment of humankind in a degenerate age than its predecessors. Music, as one of the performing arts, is treated at some length in the *Natyasastra* because it is considered an adjunct of drama, or *natya*. The purpose of drama, according to Bharata, the author of this work, is to create an experience of aesthetic pleasure, or **rasa**, in the spectator. To effect this, the dramatist must use many particular methods in certain ways, which are carefully codified in the *Natyasastra*. Among them, for example, are special types of scales and patterns derived from

Read
*an excerpt from
the Rig-Veda*
on **mymusiclab.com**

RIG-VEDA
Collection of poems that tell the stories of the Indian gods. There are three other Vedic texts, called the Yajur-Veda, Sama-Veda, and Atharva-Veda.

VARNA
Division of society in Indian culture, sometimes translated as "caste."

BRAHMIN (BRAHMAN)
The highest varna or caste in Indian society.

SAMAGANA
Special tunes for singing vedic hymns.

RASA
The affect or emotional state associated with a raga or other artistic expression.

them and distinct types of songs, all of which have prescribed uses for certain types of scenes or situations.

Continuity and Change in Theory and Practice

Although the technical details of the musical discussion in the *Natyasastra* are not entirely clear today, and it is certain that much has changed over the centuries, it is nevertheless evident that some aspects of today's musical practice are related to the treatise. To cite one aspect, the matter of prescribing a variety of scales and their characteristic patterns (that is, the defining of modes, or *ragas*, as they were later to be called in India) continues to be one of the main theoretical concerns of classical music in India. In the *Natyasastra*, the scale that completely filled in an octave was said to contain twenty-two steps, and this continues to influence the way many musicians and theorists think about the octave today, even though for all practical purposes only twelve steps are now used, as in the Western scale. (Play, for example, twelve successive keys on the piano, white and black, and the thirteenth will sound much like the pitch you began with, only higher or lower.) Such is the prestige of ancient theory that, though it may contradict current practice, it is nevertheless accommodated.

But how is it possible to say that twelve and twenty-two are the same? On an instrument like the piano, this is indeed difficult to imagine, because the notes are "fixed." However, these precise pitches of the piano can, when sung or played on a violin, be made to slide from one to another, the space between them being imperceptibly filled. Intonation—how a singer or instrumentalist plays a note—and ornamentation—the subtle additions of other tones "around" the primary note—are key ingredients in how Indian musicians accommodate their theory to practice. This flexibility is used to great advantage in Indian melody, which is expressively ornamented to a much greater degree than is most Western art music. The ornamentation is, therefore, integral to Indian melody and not incidental, and within these ornaments, a musician may claim, are contained the ancient twenty-two divisions of the scale, which have given their names—**sruti**—to the modern subtleties of intonation and ornamentation of the twelve-pitch modern scale. Herein, too, lies the Western misconception that Indian music uses scales constructed on pitches quite different from those of the Western chromatic scale of twelve pitches. A musician of Tehran who uses the piano to play a **dastgah** (see Chapter 3) may, in fact, have to tune it differently from "normal," whereas harmonium players in India find that a single set of twelve pitches suffices to play any raga.

North and South: The Hindustani and Carnatic (Karnatak) Systems

We have used the concept of raga to suggest the continuity of musical thought over many centuries in India, but it may also help us to understand the current split in Indian classical music, which today exists in two related systems,

SRUTI
The twenty-two subdivisions of the octave within Indian classical music theory.

DASTGAH
The mode or scale of a piece in Persian music.

the **Hindustani** system of North India and the **Carnatic** (Karnatak) system of South India. Along the lines laid down over the centuries by theorists, both the Hindustani and Carnatic systems represent ragas as more than just a collection of pitches in a scale. For example, specifying certain pitches for particular emphasis, or forbidding some pitch or pitches from being used in ascending or descending the scale, or requiring that the scale double back on itself before continuing in the original direction, or stating what form a note is to take (sharped, flatted, or natural) in ascent or descent—all these are common features of raga in both systems. Although a raga in the Hindustani system may be essentially the same as its Carnatic counterpart according to these rules and may be recognizably similar in performance, the styles of performance are nevertheless sufficiently different to make it difficult for someone acquainted with one style to appreciate the other. This is a difficulty encountered more, perhaps, by the Hindustani music lover listening to Carnatic music than vice versa; the smoother, more sensuous quality of North Indian performance often seems more melodious and, therefore, more accessible than the intricately ornamented and demanding melodies of the South, which require longer familiarity and attention to appreciate—even for North Indians.

This distinction in style apparently has developed over the last seven centuries. It first appeared in the thirteenth-century treatise **Sangitaratnakara**; most theoretic works that have appeared since have reflected a divergence in musical culture that nevertheless remains founded on a common heritage. As a result, one may now find ragas of the North and South that have a common name—*bhairavi*, to name a popular example—although their different evolutions have resulted in their having quite different musical features, even different scales. Hindu and Muslim Attitudes toward Music and Its Transmission

In part, this divergence in musical culture can be attributed to the fact that North India came under the increasing political and cultural influence of a new group of people: Persians and Turks who practice Islam. They entered the region from the northwest around the thirteenth century CE, following the same basic routes as the ancient Aryan-speaking invaders who brought the Vedas with them. Millennia ago, the Aryan speakers settled in the north and had the profoundest influence there; the Dravidian speakers of the south—although they adopted Vedic practices, the Sanskrit language of learning, and many elements of social culture such as caste—retained their own regional languages and many other aspects of their regional heritage. However, from the thirteenth-century on, the influence of Persian and Turkish culture and of the Islamic religion, which had been sporadically encountered during the previous five centuries, became of singular importance for North India when the foreigners established political control over the area from the city of Delhi.

As the importance of Persian culture and language grew, the significance of Sanskrit learning waned, and expertise in music came largely to mean knowledge of a repertory and style of performance learned through oral transmission in certain families of professional musicians, mostly Muslim. By the early nineteenth century, the lineages, or **gharanas**, established by these families and their students jealously guarded their various musical heritages as trade secrets

Explore
a map of India on the Interactive Globe on **mymusiclab.com**

HINDUSTAN
Region of North India, with a distinct musical tradition—Hindustani.

CARNATIC
Referring to South Indian music.

SANGITARATMAKARA
This thirteenth century treatise on music, the last to be referenced by both Hindustani and Carnatic musical traditions, marks the beginnings of a distinction in style between the Northern and Southern classical traditions.

GHARANA
A school of professional musicians who originally traced their heritage to a family tradition but which now includes nonbiological descendants as well.

to be shared only with talented sons or especially dedicated and loyal men from outside the family. To become the *shagird* (pupil) of an *ustad* (master) was to become an apprentice in a closed guild. Although this apprentice system still exists to a degree in India, and many people feel it is the only proper way to be trained as a professional musician, it is also felt that the remnants of exclusivity and jealousy of the old system of training have hampered the development of Hindustani music.

In Carnatic music, the attitude toward musical preservation and transmission has been somewhat different from that of the north. The gharanas of the north ultimately derive their legitimacy from the famous sixteenth-century musician Tansen, who was brought to the imperial court near Delhi by Akbar at the high point of the Mughal reign. In the south, the most important point of reference is the name and music of Tyagaraja, who is remembered not simply as a great musician but also as a remarkable saint. Unlike Tansen, who during his lifetime accepted positions at various courts, Tyagaraja steadfastly refused an appointment to the southern court of Tanjore, where Carnatic musical culture was flourishing at the end of the eighteenth century. Instead, he composed his songs exclusively for his chosen deity, Rama. Because he was not a professional musician, he was not concerned about keeping these songs as the inheritance of his family tradition alone. Over the last couple of centuries, as the songs of Tyagaraja and his contemporaries came to form the core of Carnatic music and were passed from *guru* (teacher) to *shishya* (disciple), different traditions of repertory and style inevitably arose, but these did not acquire the same sense of familial exclusivity and professional secrecy as did the northern gharanas.

The stories of the careers of Tansen and Tyagaraja reveal some distinctions between Hindu and Muslim attitudes toward music as well. The Hindus viewed music as part of religious rituals, and thus the musician was highly regarded; Muslims feared music because they felt it could draw out man's baser instincts, so musicians were shunned as lower-class citizens. To battle this perception, northern musicians tried to maintain a clear distinction between "art music," which had a rich heritage and connection with centuries of religious thought, and "lower" forms—thus elevating their own status and keeping them from being associated with more common performers. Musicians who were members of Hindustani gharanas, for example, fought to keep exclusive control of their heritage, in part to guarantee them higher status than that accorded to their accompanists, who often accompanied women dancers and served as their teachers.

A similar distinction occurs in dance. The dance we encountered in the Calcutta concert, kathak, began as an elaborate form of storytelling employing music and gesture for the recounting of religious tales. In the nineteenth century, it reached its height as an art form preserved by Brahmin (Hindu) men at the Shi'a Muslim court of Lucknow, where the dance was so admired that even the Shi'a king Wajid Ali Shah was a student of the dance—by all accounts quite a competent one, too! Being based in the Hindu religion and performed by Brahmin men, kathak had as much respectability as a performing art *could* have—which is to say, not a great deal. Other types of dance—or *nautch*, as it was known during the British period—were performed by professional female dancers for the enjoyment of male audiences, who sometimes paid for sexual entertainment as well; naturally these were less respectable.

In the south, trained dancers were required at temples and courts for various rituals and ceremonies. The **devadasis**, or "servants of the gods," were dedicated as children to the service of the temple and received an intensive training in the art of dance. Being "married" to the temple deity, they were not allowed to marry in the usual sense and were therefore not constrained to the limited world of the respectable housewife. Living outside the social role normal for women, they did not have the housewife's "respectability"; but being married to a deity, they could never become widows, who were believed to bring misfortune to all, including themselves. In fact, because of their good fortune in this regard, devadasis were also known as "ever auspicious," and their presence at rites and ceremonies was believed to ensure the welfare of all involved.

Although they were not permitted to marry, the devadasis often became the concubines of prominent men, and the children they had by them often became dancers if girls, or musicians and dance teachers, if boys. These families, having a hereditary association with music and dance, had a lesser status than did Brahmin musicians like Tyagaraja. Thus in South India there was a difference in status among musicians similar to that found in the north between gharana members and the men who accompanied them as well as dancing girls.

In the late nineteenth and early twentieth centuries, some prominent intellectuals sought to remove the stigma associated with the performing arts and to rehabilitate them, so that the growing middle class could take over their patronage and development as the importance of the aristocracy and religious institutions grew weaker. This change is perhaps most noticeable in the dance, where, as we have seen in the description of the concert in Calcutta, women of the middle class may now take up a career in dancing without necessarily losing their status. In the south, too, there are probably more middle-class women dancing *Bharata Natyam*, the classical style of Carnatic dance, than women from the traditional families of performers. The traditional distinction between the high caste of Brahmins and the low castes associated with musical professions has created a social tension in the musical life of South India, as the latter naturally feel they have been the repository for real musical competence, whereas the former feel they have made it possible to continue the heritage of Carnatic music in the new venue of the public concert hall.

THE CARNATIC RECITAL AND TYPES OF PIECES

In our discussion of a concert series in Calcutta, we briefly mentioned some aspects of the performance of dance, instrumental music, and vocal music. Now let us consider the components of a music and a dance recital in South India as we might encounter them in the major South Indian city of Chennai (Madras).

VARNAM

A type of song with which Carnatic recitals generally begin. Sometimes compared to the Western classical "etude" or "study."

KRITI

The major song type of Carnatic music, divided into three parts: *pallavi, anupallavi,* and *caranam.*

RAGAM/ALAPANAM

An improvisation performed before the kriti, that demonstrates the musician's abilities to interpret the ragam (or mode) in which the kriti is written.

In doing so, we can compare what we have learned about Hindustani performance and elaborate on it as well.

Vocal music has a special importance in South India because it also provides the repertory for instrumental music. In other words, instrumentalists play the tunes of vocal music, and in doing so, they generally try to maintain the articulation of the tune as determined by the pronunciation of the words in the original text. Where a syllable of text would be enunciated in a song, for example, a *vina* player (a lute that is somewhat similar to the sitar, but lacks the sitar's sympathetic strings) will pluck a string. Vocal music is important in Hindustani music, too, but instrumentalists rarely reproduce it, and then only as an item of light classical music at the end of a recital.

A Carnatic recital normally starts with a piece called **varnam**, whose purpose is to allow the performer to warm up with a familiar item. Often compared to a Western "etude"—a technical "study," as the name indicates—this is a kind of musical exercise that prepares the musician for the demands of the rest of his or her program.

The major portion of the program normally consists of pieces called **kritis**, which consist of three sections: *pallavi, anupallavi,* and *caranam.* The first portion of the pallavi serves as a refrain, recurring at the end of the pallavi as well as at the end of the anupallavi and of the caranam. The kritis of Tyagaraja and of his contemporaries, Syama Sastri and Muttuswami Dikshitar, all stemming from the late eighteenth and early nineteenth centuries, form a significant part of the repertory of most performers; although these pieces were not written down by their composers, they are "compositions" in the sense of being fixed songs preserved through oral transmission. They have, in fact, been notated in recent times as an alternative to preservation through performance.

In the performance of a kriti, the singer or instrumentalist has several options, despite the "fixed" aspect of the composition. First, he or she may decide to precede the composition itself with an improvised exposition of the **ragam** (as raga is named in the south) in which the kriti is composed. This performance, which is also called ragam or, alternatively, **alapanam**, allows the artist to demonstrate accomplishment in depicting the specific musical characteristics of the ragam in which the kriti has been composed. The audience thereby either learns the nature of the ragam, if it is unfamiliar, or if it is well known, can judge the skill and expertise of the artist in his or her rendition.

The alapanam is in free rhythm; that is, it is without a regular pulse. It is also, therefore, unaccompanied by percussion; only the tambura provides a drone. Eventually the alapanam progresses to tanam when the artist introduces a regular pulsation into the improvisation. Although there is now a pulse, there is no regularity in its arrangement that would produce a meter, or *talam* (the Carnatic version of tala), and the percussion is still absent. The equivalent sections in Hindustani instrumental music—like the sitar performance discussed earlier—are called *alap-jor*; jor is often followed again, as in the sitar recital, with a flashy section of rhythmic drone strumming called *jhala*, but this does not occur in Carnatic music.

Melodic accompaniment of the Carnatic vocalist is generally provided by a violinist who tries to imitate the soloist, immediately reproducing every turn of phrase. The violinist also alternates with the soloist in providing his or her own rendition of ragam and tanam, but during these periods the soloist is silent.

After the ragam-tanam has been concluded, the soloist begins the kriti, which, being in a regularized meter, or talam, is accompanied by percussion. If the artist has preceded the kriti with an improvised ragam-tanam, then he or she will likely insert appropriate kinds of improvisation into the composition as well. There are two types of improvisation: **niraval** and **svarakalpana**. In niraval, the articulation of the melody—derived from the text—is maintained while the pitch content is varied within the prescriptions of the ragam. In svarakalpana, the names of the pitches—sa, re, ga, ma, pa, dha, ni—are sung instead of the text or, if played instrumentally, each pitch is played separately. This practice is somewhat similar to the Western vocal exercises called *solfège* or *solfeggio*, which are sung to the pitch syllables do, re, mi, and so on, in place of words.

One way to determine when improvisation is being used in the kriti is to note when the violinist and soloist no longer perform in unison. During the unison, of course, they both have the composition in mind, but when the soloist improvises, the accompanist must follow as in the alapanam. There will normally be an alternation between soloist and accompanist as well, so that the accompanist temporarily becomes a soloist, too, again as in the improvised alapanam (Listen to CD I, 2 for an example of a kriti).

After the kriti, if the soloist is particularly good at improvisation, ragam-tanam-pallavi may be performed. In this case, the pallavi that follows the ragam-tanam may be the first section of a kriti or may be newly composed by the soloist, but it is merely a composed fragment that is not followed by the remainder of a full-scale composition. Instead, the artist immediately begins to perform niraval and svarakalpana on a more extensive scale than would be usual in a kriti.

Yet a third kind of improvisation may be used called **trikala**, in which the artist will alter the relation of the pallavi to the talam by, for example, doubling, then tripling, and finally quadrupling the duration of its notes, and then perhaps reversing the process to return to the original note values. The purpose of this type of improvisation is to demonstrate virtuosic control over the time component of performance, because the most important feat in any type of improvisation is never to lose one's place in the talam and to be able to conclude precisely at its first beat, *samam*, or at the beginning of the pallavi.

Ragam-tanam-pallavi is considered the ultimate test of a musician, because it requires exceptional training, great confidence, and spontaneous creative ability. Although composed songs play a very great role in Carnatic music, improvisation nevertheless has special prominence. In Hindustani music, both serious vocal and instrumental styles are almost entirely improvised and in this regard are more like pallavi in Carnatic music. Relatively fixed songs are used only in so-called light classical music, the repertory for which derives from regional folk styles, religious devotional music, and lyric songs of an erotic nature associated with dance.

After a performance of ragam-tanam-pallavi, the mood of a Carnatic recital generally changes to something less profound and demanding, and, as in

NIRAVAL
A type of improvisation in Carnatic music that retains the text and its rhythmic articulation but alters the pitches of the melody.

SVARAKALPANA
Improvised singing of pitches using their names in Carnatic music.

TRIKALA
A type of Carnatic improvisation in which the durational values of the notes in a phrase or piece are systematically augmented or diminished.

LISTENING GUIDE

KRITI BY TYAGARAJA, BANTURITI

GO TO www.mymusiclab.com for the Automated **Listening Guide** CDI • Track 2/Download Track 2

Vocal: Seetha Rajan; mridangam: N. Venkataraman; violin: Jayashankar Balan

Let's consider this brief but complete performance of the kriti "Banturiti." Composed by Tyagaraja, this kriti illustrates many of the musical ideas discussed in the section on the Carnatic recital. After the briefest of alapanams in a ragam called hamsanadam (scale C-E-F#-G-B), the singer begins the kriti, which is in the most common talam, called adi. This eight beat talam is indicated by a clap on samam (the first beat) and two other claps on beats 5 and 7; the three beats following samam are indicated by tapping the fingers of the right hand, starting with the little finger, on the palm of the left and "waving" the right hand, that is, turning it palm upward on the palm of the left hand, for beats 6 and 8. These claps and taps are not audible in the recording, but serve as a customary way to orient oneself in relation to the music.

1	2	3	4	5	6	7	8
Clap	Tap	Tap	Tap	Clap	Wave	Clap	Wave

The **eduppu** or opening phrase of this song falls midway between beats 2 and 3—that is, after a clap and a tap of the little finger—and the performer must return to this point accurately whenever finishing a passage of niraval or svarakalpana, improvisation. Alternatively the performer may choose to conclude at samam. In Hindustani performance the eduppu is called the mukhra (see CD I, 1).

In this performance, the singer is accompanied by violin and mridangam (double-headed, barrel-shaped drum); note that these instruments are briefly heard alone after the conclusion of the pallavi and anupallavi. When these instruments are next heard alone, about midway through the caranam, the singer is alternating niraval improvisation with the violinist; then the performance quickly proceeds to svarakalpana as she improvises by singing the note names—sa, ri, ga, ma, pa, dha, ni—before coming to a conclusion by returning to the pallavi theme.

TIME	SECTION	MUSICAL EVENT
0:00–0:03	**Alapanam:** Listen for the way that the performer systematically, though quite rapidly, explores the individual pitches of the ragam, revealing its shape in the process.	Brief drone introduction by the violin.
0:03–0:31		The vocalist begins the alapanam, rapidly introducing the full shape of the ragam.
0:31–0:42		The vocalist and violinist exchange improvised melodic fragments as they complete the alapanam.

0:43–0:49	**Kriti: Pallavi:** Listen for the clear articulation of the eduppu.	Pallavi theme is introduced. The theme includes the melodic fragment called the eduppu that initiates the pallavi theme. The eduppu falls on beat 2.5 and is followed by the whole melodic phrase. (If you're having trouble hearing the eduppu, listen for the return of the first word "Banturiti," for example, at approximately [00:49–00:50], and approximately every 5 seconds thereafter through the pallavi.)
0:49–0:55		The pallavi theme is repeated.
0:56–1:35		Repetitions of the pallavi theme with variations (called sangati).
1:35–1:40	**Kriti: Anupallavi:** Listen for the introduction of the new melodic/rhythmic theme and for the return of the pallavi theme as a refrain.	The first half of the anupallavi phrase is introduced.
1:40–1:55		The full first phrase is introduced and repeated.
1:55–2:14		The second phrase of the anupallavi theme is introduced, followed by a repeat of the first and second phrases.
2:14–2:30		The pallavi theme returns as a refrain (listen for the eduppu beginning with "Banturiti").
2:30–2:53	**Kriti: Caranam:** Listen for the introduction of new caranam text, but sung to the established pallavi and anupallavi melodies. Listen also for the niraval and svarakalpana improvisation so prominent throughout this section of the performance.	Introduction of the caranam text, but performed by using the melodic materials of the pallavi theme.
2:54–3:24		Repeat of theme from the first phrase of the anupallavi, also with caranam text. This is followed by niraval improvisation on this theme.
3:24–4:02		The vocalist and the violinist are alternating their improvisations during this portion of the performance.
4:03–4:21		The niraval section of improvisation is concluded by the vocalist.
4:22–5:15		Introduction of svarakalpana improvisation. The voice and violin again alternate throughout this section.
5:15–5:55		Vocalist returns to anupallavi theme and then concludes with an ornamented pallavi refrain.

PADAM
A lyrical type of Carnatic song that may accompany dance.

JAVALI
A lyrical song form of Carnatic music.

THUMRI
A lyrical type of Hindustani song and a style of instrumental performance modeled on it.

DHUN
A regional song of North India sometimes borrowed for Hindustani performance.

BHAJAN
Hindu devotional song.

EDUPPU
The beginning of a phrase in Carnatic music used as a cadence for improvisations.

✳ **Explore**
the Gallery of Musical Instruments on
mymusiclab.com

Hindustani recitals, pieces of a lyrical, erotic mood may be sung. **Padams** and **javalis** constitute this repertory, associated with the lighter side of the bharata natyam dance style, in which emphasis is placed on mime and gesture for the interpretation of the songs' lyrics. Similar in construction to kritis, padams and javalis also have pallavi, anupallavi, and caranam sections. In performing these, the artist is expected to display a sensitively expressive style, rather than the technical virtuosity of the earlier part of the recital.

In a Hindustani recital, the pieces comparable to padam and javali would be, for example, **thumri**, associated with the female dancers of Lucknow and Benares, or **dhun**, a folk tune from a particular region of India. A Hindu vocalist may also conclude with a devotional **bhajan**, particularly if he or she wants to avoid any stigma of impropriety. The Carnatic recitalist may likewise conclude with songs of a devotional nature. Although the bulk of Carnatic performance is of fixed compositions, improvisation is of great importance. On the other hand, improvisation is central to this type of Hindustani music, because the "fixed" composition is often no more than a tag of recognizable melody. Such a tag—the **eduppu** in Carnatic music, the *mukhra* in Hindustani—is important, however, because it plays a role similar to that of the first beat of the tala, called the *sam*. It is a reference point that the performer must skillfully pick up at the end of an improvisatory passage to demonstrate that he or she has maintained an awareness of the meter during the improvisation. Alternatively, the performer may conclude on sam and in either case may emphasize this arrival point by repeating a phrase three times in succession to conclude at precisely the right place. Called a *tihai* in Hindustani music, the same device in Carnatic music is called *mora*.

In our discussion of Hindustani instrumental music, we have focused on the sitar and tabla for the reason—as many of you may have guessed—that these are the most familiar instruments to non-Indian listeners. Ever since George Harrison of the Beatles became the disciple of Pandit Ravi Shankar in the mid-sixties, these instruments have occasionally cropped up in Euro-American pop music, and their sounds have become relatively familiar to our ears, if not always immediately identifiable. This is a good example of Indian influence on North Atlantic musical life. In our discussion of Carnatic music, on the other hand, you have had a chance to hear a violin accompanying a performance of the famous kriti called "Banturiti." Here, then, we can see evidence of Western influence on musical practice in India. Many other instruments are used in India, of course and, before moving on to a more thorough consideration of the influence of Indian music around the globe, please take a few minutes to explore the gallery of instruments housed on the Web site for this textbook at www.mymusiclab.com.

THE INFLUENCE OF INDIAN MUSIC

Having explored the many instruments used in India, you've no doubt noticed that several of these instruments can teach us about the influence of Western sources on Indian musical practice. However, India itself has had a profound influence on music outside its borders as well. First, we should remember that borders are political entities brought about through circumstances that do not always reflect "natural" linguistic and ethnic groupings. The India that came into existence as an independent state in 1947 when British rule ended, for example, was not the same as "British India." The latter included the present-day countries of Pakistan and Bangladesh but not, technically speaking, the independent princedoms of the Indian subcontinent, which were compelled to join the Indian union only on the dissolution of British India. Not surprisingly, Hindustani music is an important part of the musical life of Bangladesh and Pakistan.

In Afghanistan, too, Hindustani music is viewed as having great prestige. Because in the past the court at Kabul favored Hindustani music, musicians from other areas of Afghanistan as well have come to accept its performance and its theory as a standard of excellence. In this Muslim country, the technical and theoretical apparatus associated with Hindustani music helps to distance it from the stigma of sensual indulgence and thereby to raise the status of musicians. Regional styles still persist, of course, and are generally more favored by the masses of people than the Hindustani genres. Hindustani music performed for the guests at a wedding may lend prestige to the affair, but the familiar **chaharbeiti** songs and **atan**, the national dance, are what get the audience most involved.

The island country of Sri Lanka (formerly Ceylon) has long-standing cultural links with India, and both Hindustani and Carnatic music are to be heard there. The indigenous Sinhalese population, speaking an Aryan tongue, and the Tamil-speaking immigrant community from South India naturally tend to view the difference in musical styles as yet another of the things that separate their unfortunately antagonistic ethnic groups.

Although India's musical links with nearby countries might be expected, we should not overlook the fact that many Indians—and Pakistanis and Bangladeshis—now live abroad and have brought elements of their musical culture with them. In Europe and America, many communities of immigrants from the subcontinent have formed societies for sponsoring musical events that serve as potent reminders to those recently settled abroad of their cultural heritage. They also serve to introduce traditional cultural values to the younger generation born abroad.

Of course, the younger generation, whether born in India or abroad, is often more interested in something more casual than classical music, and there is no doubt that the most widely supported type of Indian music is that associated with the film industry. An Indian film without musical numbers is almost unheard of, and India makes more films than any other country; it stands to reason, therefore, that films are the greatest source of popular music. A **filmigit** ("film song") hit is virtually impossible to escape, even if one does not attend the movies or listen to the radio in India, because it is sure to be broadcast over the public address systems used by neighborhood organizations to help celebrate numerous festivals that occur throughout the year. Many kinds of music provide filmigit with material—from folk songs and classically based melodies to rock and jazz and even various genres of world music—and a variety of instruments and studio recording techniques all help to make it a diverse music, offering something for nearly every taste. Because the early filmmaking practice of dubbing musical numbers has been continued to the present, actors lip-synch to the recordings of famous singers. Dozens of actresses, for example,

CHAHARBEITI
A form of slow, soloistic, unmetered, and improvisatory quatrain singing in Afghanistan.

ATAN
A circle dance considered the national dance of Afghanistan.

FILMIGIT
Popular songs composed for Indian films.

Filmigit singer,
Lata Mangeshkar.
Source: REUTERS/Stringer
JSG/JD

GHAZAL
A form of poetry associated
with Perso-Arabic Muslim
culture enthusiastically taken
up by Urdu speakers in North
India and Pakistan, where it is
often sung.

MUSHAIRA
A traditional poetry-reading
session.

have appeared on the screen, all singing with the voice of the enormously popular Lata Mangeshkar! Lata's voice alone could bring success to a film that might otherwise have been a flop.

New experiments fusing Western popular music and jazz with Indian music are taking place both in India and abroad, with the impetus coming from Western as well as Indian musicians. For example, the late Ananda Shankar, son of the dancer Uday Shankar and nephew of the sitarist Pandit Ravi Shankar, developed a sophisticated stage show of music and dance that is an original amalgam of Western and Indian ideas—not surprising in a man whose father and uncle were already entertaining Europeans with original music and dance in the 1930s. Abroad, the Carnatic violinist L. Shankar (not related) and the tabla player Zakir Hussain have had great success playing a remarkably Indianized jazz with artists like the American jazz-fusion guitarist John McLaughlin.

Perhaps one of the most interesting and successful blends of Indian and Western music is taking place in a type of song with roots in Islamic culture but with a broad appeal to all who appreciate the tradition of romantic Urdu poetry. The **ghazal** is a well-loved poetic form that consists of a chain of related couplets—each of which, however, expresses a self-contained idea—often culminating in a kind of "punchline" couplet that will bring exclamations of appreciation from a group attending a traditional poetry-reading session called a **mushaira**. Ghazals are also sung and may be performed by singers with considerable classical training. In the past, singing ghazals was often one of the accomplishments of courtesans. Although these types of ghazal recitation and singing are at the sophisticated and elegant end of the spectrum, more popular types of ghazal are to be found, for example, among filmigit, in which the form has an important place (Listen to CD I, 3 for an example of a ghazal).

Popular ghazal has reached a new level of sophistication and refinement in its own right in a blend of Western jazz harmony and synthesized instrumentation with more traditional features of ghazal performance produced in modern multitrack recording studios. The flexibility of ghazal has made it an excellent

LISTENING GUIDE

GHAZAL, "BAT KARANE MUJHE MUSHKIL"

GO TO **www.mymusiclab.com for the Automated Listening Guide** CDI • Track 3/Download Track 3

Vocal: Mala Ganguly; tabla: Samar Das; tambura and harmonium (unknown)

This ghazal is sung by Mala Ganguly, who is accompanied here by the traditional ensemble of tabla harmonium and tambura. The ghazal unfolds in rag pahari, a rag considered appropriate for light classical music, and in the eight-beat tal called keharwa.

The music consists of two melodic sections, the first (**A**) providing the melody for the refrain (itself a couplet) and the second providing a contrasting melodic line (**B**) that is used to highlight by means of new melodic contour the first line of each successive couplet. The second line of each couplet is sung to the refrain melody (**A**).

TIME	SECTION	MUSICAL EVENT
0:00–0:21	**Refrain:** Listen for the thorough exploration of the first melodic phrase, used throughout this section to introduce the couplet that serves as the refrain for this ghazal.	The vocalist and harmonium introduce the first phrase of melody (A), performing the first line of the refrain in free rhythm (without tabla).
0:21–0:35		The performers repeat the first line of the refrain, this time with tabla accompaniment.
0:35–1:04		The vocalist moves on to sing the second line of the refrain and then repeats this line.
1:04–1:17		The first line of the refrain returns here, but the vocalist does not complete the line, allowing the harmonium to complete the melody.
1:17–1:49	**First Couplet:** Listen for the introduction of the second, contrasting melodic phrase and the way that the performers work from that melodic phrase back to the, by now, more familiar refrain melody.	The first line of the first (non-refrain) couplet is performed to the second melodic phrase (**B**). Notice that the end of this line is extended with textual repetition and melodic variation.
1:49–2:03		The first line of the couplet is repeated, but without adding the extension with variations.
2:03–2:29		The second line of the first couplet is performed to the refrain melody (**A**) and then repeated.
2:29–2:43	**Return of Refrain:** Listen for "Bat Karane" to orient yourself.	The vocalist returns to the first line of the refrain, treating it in the same manner as she did at [1:04–1:17]. The harmonium completes the melody.

2:43–3:11	**Second Couplet:** The basic pattern for the remainder of the performance is now set. Listen for the repeat of the structure introduced in the first couplet.	The first line of the second (non-refrain) couplet is performed to the second melodic phrase (**B**). Notice that the end of this line is extended with textual repetition and melodic variation.
3:11–3:24		The first line of the couplet is repeated, but without adding the extension with variations.
3:24–3:38		The second line of the second couplet is performed to the refrain melody (**A**) but not repeated.
3:38–3:51	**Return of Refrain:** Listen for "Bat Karane" to orient yourself.	The vocalist returns to the first line of the refrain, treating it in the same manner as she did at [1:04–1:17] and [2:30–2:43]. The harmonium completes the melody.
3:51–4:21	**Third Couplet:** The pattern or the remainder of the performance is now set. Listen for the repeat of the structure introduced in the first couplet. Listen also for the gradually increasing intensity of the tabla during the second line of the couplet.	The first line of the third (non-refrain) couplet is performed to the second melodic phrase (**B**). Notice that the end of this line is extended with textual repetition and melodic variation.
4:21–4:36		The first line of the couplet is repeated, but without adding the extension with variations.
4:36–5:02		The second line of the third couplet is performed to the refrain melody (**A**) and then repeated.
5:02–5:28	**Return of Refrain:** Listen for the return of the full refrain and for the increased intensity of the tabla during this concluding section.	The first line of the refrain is performed and then repeated.
5:28–5:42		The vocalist moves on to sing the second line of the refrain.
5:42–5:56		The vocalist returns to the first line of the refrain, but sings only "Bat Karane" by way of concluding the performance.

medium for experimentation and is sure to guarantee its continued vitality in the musical life of Indian communities throughout the world.

The kind of blend we find in the new ghazal raises the possibility of cross-over from the Indian community to its host environment. There has not been much evidence of this so far, but a type of Indo-British pop music combining aspects of hip-hop, trance, and remix techniques with a folk music and dance style from the state of Punjab called **bhangra** has made some slight inroads in this direction and may point to possibilities for the future. This amalgam of styles has special appeal for urban teenagers of Indian parentage. It allows them to identify themselves ethnically and at the same time to participate in social dancing at clubs, which lets them distance themselves from their parents' heritage and participate in a style of life more similar to that of other young people. In Toronto, where bhangra has also recently become popular, it has been a focus for violent action by conservative elements among the Punjabi Sikh community, who feel it has a deleterious effect on youth—young women in particular. In this context, Bhangra has become more than simply a phenomenon of "world beat," where a new immigrant culture is trying to emerge from old roots in a new environment.

BHANGRA
Pop music of the South Asian diaspora combining aspects of hip-hop, trance, and remix techniques with a traditional folk dance music from the state of Punjab.

PROSPECTS

Indian music has had an enduring influence on international pop styles, offering new sounds and possibilities for popular music and jazz that were initially explored by groups like the Beatles, Oregon, and Shakti. Today, artists like the Sri Lankan-born singer M.I.A., Panjabi MC, and the Raga Bop Trio, among many others, are continuing to draw on this legacy. Western art music, too, has been influenced by Indian music. In the twentieth century, composers like the Frenchman Olivier Messiaen and the American John Cage have found inspiration in the abstract theoretical components of Indian music. The former, for example, found in the theoretical descriptions of ancient talas material that helped him construct his *Turangalila Symphony*, whereas the latter, in his piano sonatas, attempted to write pieces that would reflect his understanding of the theory of rasa, which we encountered in our discussion of the Natyasastra.

During the last twenty to thirty years, recordings of Indian music have become widely available, and ease of travel has allowed Indian artists to appear abroad. The result has been a more readily apparent influence of the sounds and performance practice of Indian music in the works of composers like Terry Riley, Steve Reich, and Philip Glass, many of whom have taken the time to study with musicians from India and other countries (as have, for that matter, a number of pop musicians).

The vitality of Indian music does not depend, however, solely on its vicarious existence in transformation; the latter merely confirms that Indian music is becoming a significant component of world music. The musical traditions of India continue to have a vital role in the cultural life of Indians at home, and despite the influential role of Western music, classical and pop, around the world, it does not yet seem to coexist on an equal footing with, much less be supplanting, filmigit or kriti or khyal in India. Compared with the importance of East Asians in the world of Western classical music, too, the lesser role played by Indians would seem indirectly to imply the strength of Indian musical traditions. Those traditions are undergoing considerable change in the modern world, but their ability to adapt and respond to new circumstances is also an indication of their vitality.

SUMMARY

This chapter has traced the roots of Indian music, which developed over many centuries and was influenced by Indo-Aryan-speaking settlers in the northwest part of the country around the 2nd millennium BCE. Later theorists traced the roots of Indian music to Vedas, a group of religious poems of the Indo-Aryans that were chanted and eventually set to music. A second wave of settlers, peaking in the 13th century CE, brought a new religion—Islam—and new attitudes toward music. At about this time, Indian musical culture began to split into two main parts: northern (Hindustani) and southern (Carnatic). One important reason for this shift toward two traditions is grounded in the differing attitudes toward music expressed by Hindus and Muslims, and this chapter has explored some of the sounds, genres, and performance contexts that have subsequently developed within the Hindustani and Carnatic traditions. Hindustani music tends to be smoother and less ornamented than Carnatic music, but both traditions base melodies on scalar modes called *raga*. Hindustani music is more completely improvised than Carnatic music, which is more based on fixed compositions like the kriti, though improvisation as such is critical to Carnatic performance as well. In Carnatic music, instrumental performance reproduces the melodies of vocal compositions, whereas instrumental music in Hindustani contexts is independent of vocal models. As new influences came to India over the past few centuries, new instruments (e.g., violin, harmonium, clarinet, and saxophone) were incorporated into the music and adapted to local use. Today, Indian music has absorbed much Western influence and, in turn, has influenced Western pop, jazz, and art music.

✓•—[**Study** and **Review**
on **mymusiclab.com**

BIBLIOGRAPHY

Indian Music as a Whole   Peter Lavezzoli, *The Dawn of Indian Music in the West* (New York: Continuum, 2006); Bonnie C. Wade, *Music in India: The Classical Traditions* (Englewood Cliffs, NJ: Prentice Hall, 1979); Bonnie C. Wade, ed., *Performing Arts in India: Essays on Music, Dance, and Drama*, Monograph Series No. 21 (Berkeley: University of California Press, 1983); Peggy Holroyde, *The Music of India* (New York: Praeger, 1972); M. R. Gautam, *The Musical Heritage of India* (New Delhi: Abhinav, 1980); Peter Manuel, *Popular Musics of the Non-Western World* (New York: Oxford University Press, 1988); Lewis Eugene Rowell, *Music and Musical Thought in Early India* (Chicago: University of Chicago Press, 1992); Gerry Farrell, *Indian Music and the West* (Oxford: Oxford University Press, 1997); Selina Thielmann, *The Music of South Asia* (New Delhi: A. P. H. Publishers, 1999); Alison Arnold, ed., *South Asia: The Indian Subcontinent, The Garland Encyclopedia of World Music*, vol. 5 (New York and London: Garland Publishing, 2000).

North Indian Music   Nazir Jairazbhoy, *The Ragas of Northern Indian Music: Their Structure and Evolution* (Middletown, CT: Wesleyan University Press, 1971); Daniel Neuman, *The Life of Music in North India: The Organization of an Artistic Tradition* (Chicago: University of Chicago Press, 1990); Bonnie C. Wade, *Khyal: Creativity within North Indian Classical Music Tradition*

(Cambridge: Cambridge University Press, 1984); James Kippen, *The Tabla of Lucknow* (Cambridge: Cambridge University Press, 1988); Regula Qureshi, *Sufi Music of India and Pakistan* (Chicago: University of Chicago Press, 1995); Charles Capwell, *The Music of the Bauls of Bengal* (Kent, OH: Kent State University Press, 1986); Stephen Slawek, *Sitar Technique in Nibaddh Forms* (Delhi: Motilal Banarsidas, 1987); Walter Kaufmann, *The Ragas of North India* (Bloomington: Indiana University Press, 1968); Edward O. Henry, *Chant the Names of God: Musical Culture in Bhojpuri-Speaking India* (San Diego: San Diego State University Press, 1988); Peter Manuel, *Cassette Culture: Popular Music and Technology in North India* (Chicago: University of Chicago Press, 1993); Ravi Shankar, *My Music, My Life* (New York: Simon and Schuster, 1968); Ravi Shankar, *Raga Mala: The Autobiography of Ravi Shankar* (New York: Welcome Rain Publications, 1999); Allyn Miner, *Sitar and Sarod in the 18th and 19th Centuries* (Wilhelmshaven, Germany: F. Noetzel, 1993); Sunil Kothari, *Kathak, Indian Classical Dance Art* (New Delhi: Abhinav Publications, 1989); Martin Clayton, *Time in Indian Music: Rhythm, Metre, and Form in North Indian Rag Performance* (Oxford: Oxford University Press, 2000).

South Indian Music   Walter Kaufmann, *The Ragas of South India: A Catalog of Scalar Materials* (Bloomington: Indiana University Press, 1976); P. Sambamoorthy, *South Indian Music*, 5 vols. (Madras: Indian Music Publishing House, n.d.); T. Viswanathan, Matthew Harp Allen, *Music in South India: Experiencing Music, Expressing Culture* (New York: Oxford UP, 2003); Ludwig Pesch, *The Oxford Illustrated Companion to South Indian Classical Music* (New Delhi: Oxford University Press, 2009); R. Rangaramanuja Ayyangar, *History of South Indian (Carnatic) Music from Vedic Times to the Present* (Madras: privately published, 1972); Mrinalini Sarabhai, *Understanding Bharata Natyam* (Ahmedabad: Darpana, 1981); Matthew Allen, "Rewriting the Script for South Indian Dance," *The Drama Review*, 41/3:63–100.

DISCOGRAPHY

Anthologies   *A Musical Anthology of the Orient*, vols. 6, 7, 18 (Bärenreiter 30L 2006, 2007, 2018); *Classical Indian Music* (Odeon MOAE 147-9); *Anthology of Indian Classical Music: A Tribute to Alain Daniélou* (Auvldis/Unesco, D8270).

North India   *Parween Sultana* (khyal) (Gramophone Co. of India ECSD 2785); *Ram Chatur Mallick* (dhrupad and dhamar); *Musiques de l'Asie Traditionelle*, vol. 9 (Inde du Nord); *Ravi Shankar* (sitar) (Gramophone Co. of India EASD 1307); *Ananda Shankar and His Music* (modern instrumental pop) (Gramophone Co. of India ESCD 2528); *Begum Akhtar Sings Ghalib* (ghazal) (Gramophone Co. of India ECSD 2399); *Film Hits from Hit Films*, vol. 2 (Gramophone Co. of India ECLP 5470); Joep Bor, ed., *The Raga Guide: A Survey of 74 Hindustani Ragas* (Nimbus Records, NI 5536/9).

South India   *Kaccheri* (vocal) (Nonesuch H-72040); *Vidwan* (vocal) (Nonesuch H-72023); *Dhyanam/Meditation* (vocal) (Nonesuch H-72018); *Musik für Vina* (Telarc MC8); *S. Balachander: Veena Maestro of South India* (Odeon MOCE 1026); *Pallavi* (flute) (Nonesuch H-72052).

Music of the Middle East

BRUNO NETTL

CONCERTS IN TEHRAN

The setting: Tehran, the capital of Iran, a rather modern city of about four million people, close to the last years of the reign of the Shah—that is, about 1970. We are in a modern concert hall, have bought tickets, and sit in the seventh row; there are some twelve hundred seats, only half occupied. The audience is well dressed, in modern Western clothes; we see ladies in fine dresses of Paris fashion, and we recognize academics, professional people, and a fairly large number of foreigners. For a moment, we feel as if we were in a concert hall in a North American city ready to hear a string-quartet concert. On the stage are a few chairs and some music stands.

It seems as if this experience is going to be much like a concert of Western art music, and in some ways that's how it turns out. There are printed programs, an intermission, and ensemble pieces that open and close the program, with a number of solos and duets played in between. The program tells us the names of

the composers of some pieces, and the name of mode—in Persian, **dastgah**— of each piece. A bit late, six male musicians appear on the stage with instruments, are greeted with applause, and sit on the chairs. They are dressed in costumes approximating the clothes one sees on seventeenth- and eighteenth-century Persian miniatures. Shortly, without a conductor, they begin.

The instruments are quite different from each other. There is a heavy-looking lute with long neck and frets, the *tar*, which is played with a pick; also a *kamancheh*, a spiked fiddle with a small round body and four strings, which is held upright on a peg like a miniature cello and bowed with the palm upward. A trapezoidal zither or dulcimer, the *santour*, with seventy-two strings (tuned to twenty-seven different pitches), is played with two small balsa-wood mallets. A fourth player brings a violin, and a fifth, an end-blown, cane flute, the *ney*. Finally there is a drummer, who brings out a goblet-shaped drum with one skin, called *dombak* or *zarb*. These are most of the principal instruments of Persian classical music.

✴ Explore
Learning Objectives
on **mymusiclab.com**

✴ Explore
*the Musical Instrument
Gallery* on
mymusiclab.com

DASTGAH
The mode or scale of a piece in
Persian music.

The program says that the first section of the concert will be in the dast-gah of Shur. I ask my neighbor what that means and am told that there are twelve dastgahs in Persian music, which provide the basic material for all music-making in the Persian classical system. Each has a scale or collection of pitches from which composers or improvisers make selections, and each has a unique configuration of intervals. But each dastgah also has a basic musical motif, a tune consisting of some five or six tones that characterizes it. My neighbor softly sings the main musical motif of Shur in my ear and says, "This is the heart of the dastgah of Shur; when you play Shur, you must always keep coming back to it; otherwise your audience will say you don't really know our music."

In the first piece, all of the musicians sitting behind music stands play together. (I strain to see whether they actually have music, and conclude that they either don't or are just barely looking at it.) They are playing a type of piece called **pishdaramad**, which means "before the introduction," composed by Darvish Khan, who I'm told was a great musician early in the twentieth century. They play in unison, creating a heterophonic texture, and it is easy to pick out the flute's ornamented tune, the nasal voice of the kamancheh, the heavy plucked sounds of the tar, and the brilliant runs of the santour. The drummer keeps meter and tempo, and the piece is obviously in slow triple meter. As I make out the form, I discover that it has a theme that keeps coming back at intervals.

The audience applauds. In the front are a few young men, music students from a conservatory, who move their heads from side to side and cry out gently, "Bah, bah." For the next section all the musicians remain on stage, but the piece is performed by only two of the group, the santour player and the drummer. The santour plays a rapid piece in which a rhythmic pattern keeps being repeated as the basis of a short bit of melody. This melody is, itself, repeated many times with variations, alternates with other tunes, and eventually returns. All this is done with enormous emphasis on virtuosity. The santour player gestures broadly with his arms to show his expertise; halfway through, he takes out a cloth and places it over the strings to show that he can play correctly even without seeing the instrument. It is a great show. In all of this he is accompanied by the drummer, who takes a modest stance musically and physically. At those points when the audience hears something particularly difficult, it bursts into brief applause, while the musicians go on uninterrupted. The name of this kind of piece is **chahar mezrab**, which means "four picks" or "four hammers," possibly because it is so fast that it sounds as if there were four hands flying over the instrument (Listen to CD I, 4 for an example of chahar mezrab).

(Left) Darbucca, the most widely used drum type in the Middle East. (Right) Iranian zarb or dombak.
Source: Wanda Nettl/Bruno Nettl

LISTENING GUIDE

CHAHAR MEZRAB IN MAHOUR (EXCERPT) FROM IRAN

GO TO www.mymusiclab.com for the Automated Listening Guide CDI • Track 4/Download Track 4

Faromarz Payvar, santour
Recorded by Bruno Nettl, 1969

0:00–0:12	Energetic introduction on bass strings establishing regular beat.
0:12–0:13	Short melodic phrase.
0:14–0:15	Bass note figure.
0:15–0:16	Melodic phrase repeated.
0:16–0:17	Bass note figure repeated.
0:18–0:19	New phrase, slightly higher pitched.
0:19–0:21	Bass note figure.
0:21–0:23	Descending phrase back to original starting note.
0:23–0:26	Bass note figure.
0:26–0:31	Repeated, phrase, moving up in pitch, with second ending that drops in pitch, leading to the next phrase.
0:31–0:36	Descending phrase, left unresolved.
0:36–0:40	Repeats and "resolves" to original pitch.
0:41–0:46	Bass note figure.
0:46–0:56	New, rolling melody.
0:56–1:09	Melody repeats as music fades out [0:59–1:09].

PISHDARAMAD

Literally "before the introduction." Introductory piece, composed, metric, and usually played by an ensemble, in a performance of Persian classical music.

CHAHAR MEZRAB

Virtuosic composed metric solo piece in Persian classical music.

AVAZ

In Persian classical music, the improvised, nonmetric section, performed vocally or instrumentally, that is central in the performance.

For the third selection, the group is joined by a female singer, who is greeted with enthusiastic applause. Dressed in modern evening dress, flamboyant and colorful, she sings, accompanied by the tar, music whose words, as my neighbor tells me, are a poem from the fourteenth century by Hafez, "our greatest poet." This section of the performance is called **Avaz**, and it is the part everyone has perhaps been waiting for. She sings short phrases, and I hear the motif of Shur at the beginning, and again at various times moving gradually from the low part of her range to the higher. The music has no beat, it sounds improvised. She has a strong, husky chest-voice, free of vibrato, but she uses lots of ornaments, and as she moves to the higher part of her range, the lines get longer and she dwells for two, three, then fifteen or twenty notes on one

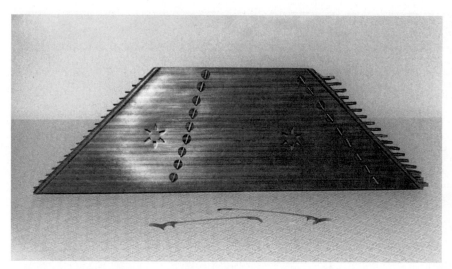

The santour, used in Iran
and neighboring countries.
Source: Wanda Nettl/
Bruno Nettl

syllable. Eventually, she sings lines without using words at all, long passages simply on "Aaah," with a tone that sounds like a combination of yodeling and sobbing, and the audience breaks into applause. Finally, after some fifteen minutes of singing, the performer allows her song to draw to a close, moving to lower pitches and softer sounds. The tar player has been accompanying her improvisation by playing what she sings, but lagging a note or two behind, and at the end of a phrase quickly repeating what she has just sung.

We have heard what is clearly the high point of the performance. The performance continues, with a number of different pieces, solo and ensemble. The instruments, the way the voice is used, the importance of unmetered rhythm, and the obvious importance of improvisation, so expertly on display throughout this concert, illustrate some of the characteristic sounds and aesthetic sensibilities of Persian classical music. The concert runs about ninety minutes and ends in time for the well-dressed middle-class audience to catch buses to their suburban homes.

Before leaving, I tell my neighbor that it has been fun but that I was a bit puzzled. I had been told that Middle Eastern classical music is largely improvised, but here out of some ten movements, only one was clearly in that category. And I had thought that the music would be contemplative, but it struck me as more of a variety show. "Yes," my neighbor agreed, "but that's the modern way of performing Iranian classical music. But perhaps I can invite you to a place where they perform the same music in a much more traditional way."

This concert introduced us to Persian classical music, but events somewhat like the one we've witnessed—traditional music performed in an environment modeled on European art music concerts and performance venues, that is—are also heard elsewhere in the Middle East. There are also many other kinds of formal performances of classical music. So, for instance, in Istanbul, we could attend a Turkish **ayin** in which musicians and dancers interact in a complex spiritual ritual (called **Sema**) belonging to Sufism, the mystical movement of Islam, that benefits themselves as well as the audience, but in different ways. The musicians play a group of composed and improvised pieces, and in several important sections they are joined by vocalists singing in unison. Meanwhile, the dancers, in white robes, whirl ceaselessly, turning and circling, and achieve a state of spiritual ecstasy while the audience looks on calmly and remains essentially passive.

In another kind of classical concert, in Cairo (but it could have been Beirut or Baghdad in its better days), a world-famous singer, singing song after song,

AYIN

A cycle of Mevlevi (Sufi) ceremonial music.

SEMA

A Mevlevi (Sufi) ceremony of mystical ascent involving a whirling dance accompanied by music.

Whirling dervishes dance in circles during a Sema ceremony in Konya, Turkey. *Source:* Chris Hellier/Corbis

liberally amplified, accompanied by a small ensemble with drum, gradually establishes a close relationship with the audience of thousands. Through his emotional vocal passages, he moves them to react, applaud, cry out, respond to his improvisations, his nuanced ornaments, musical sighs and sobs, long virtuosic passages, with volumes from soft to overpowering, and emphases. And he in turn is inspired by these reactions, as performer and audience interact and seem to become unified.

It's interesting to compare these three kinds of concerts, for large audiences, of Middle Eastern classical traditions. Variants of all of them could be heard in many parts of the area. The kinds of music they include do not differ significantly; the social context—a public concert in a large auditorium, performances on stage, and listeners in assigned seats—is essentially the same. But the relationship of musicians and audience, the emotional participation of the audience, and the spiritual interaction of musicians and dancers are different, and they show us some of the great variety of musical experience available in Middle Eastern cultures.

But my neighbor in Tehran had told me, he would take me to an event in which the musical experience was different from that of large concert hall. The invitation was long in coming, but finally I was asked to appear at dinnertime on a particular evening at an address in the wealthier section of northern Tehran. It was made clear that I should not bring along wife, daughter, or date, but that I should come alone, and that being invited to this gathering was a rather special thing. Those who attend this kind of event—called a **majles**, a word that denotes a private concert—don't usually accept outsiders into their midst.

MAJLES
In Persian classical music, a small, informal gathering of men assembled to hear a concert.

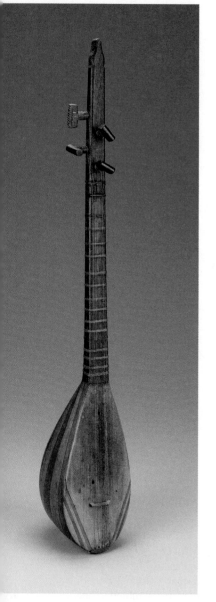

Setar. *Source:* Boston Museum of Fine Arts/Lebrecht

A bit apprehensive, I showed up. It was a modern home, but in the living room there were no chairs, and six men were sitting in a circle leaning against large pillows. Three of them were wearing loose, flowing garments. I recognized two of them, one a physicist and the other a doctor, and it was clear that they were all old friends, although they spoke to each other in rather formal terms. Women's voices were heard—there must have been half a dozen—from the kitchen, but no women were to be seen that evening. Some of the men smoked, a servant brought some wine and brandy, eventually we were served a traditional meal, and as soon as we had finished eating, one of the men present opened an instrument case and began tuning his *setar*. It had not been used in the formal concert but now I was told that it was really the truest, most characteristic instrument of Persian traditional music. It had four strings and frets and was strummed with the forefinger's long nail, melody and drone together. The tone is usually soft, but sometimes it can be loud and vigorous.

The setar player followed the same plan as the ensemble in the first half of the formal concert, but the introductory composed pieces were short, and the improvisations went on at length. The musician paid special attention to the free-rhythm avaz, in which he moved from low pitches gradually up the scale over a good half hour, clearly watching the reactions of his audience and obviously stimulated by it to move gradually into excited and emotional musical statements. In contrast to the public concert, the nonmetric and improvised sections were clearly featured here. During the performance there was a bit of conversation, but usually in the way of comments on the music, such things as "He always does this very well," and "I heard so-and-so play hesar [the section being performed] quite differently last week."

At the end there was a bit of conversation about music, local politics, and the weather, and the guests left, this time bidden farewell at the door by the host's wife. There was a feeling of intimacy between those present and, indeed, between them and the music; these middle-aged men were pleased by what they had heard. But to them it was also, importantly, an intellectual experience, as they commented on what had been played, and how the musician had followed the rules or asserted himself as an individual.

These musical events underscore some of the tensions that appear in Middle Eastern music. We are already familiar with several kinds of opposing relationships: between musicians and audience, soloists and accompaniment, and vocal and instrumental. But there are also other types of sometimes contradictory impulses: between composed and improvised music, music as an ecstatic or a cerebral experience, and—perhaps most characteristic of this culture area—music as a great and wonderful thing compared to something possibly dangerous and, in any event, to be handled with care. While my friend accompanied me to my taxi, he said: "This was really great. I'm glad you got to see this traditional expression of our culture. But don't tell people you were here. A lot of people don't approve of sessions like this." Why would he say this? We'll return to this later.

COMMON FEATURES AND DIVERSITY

Society and Culture

When we speak of the Middle East as a culture area, we think of the heartland of Arab culture—the nations of Saudi Arabia, Syria, Egypt, Iraq, Lebanon, Jordan—and two non-Arab nations, Turkey and Iran, constituting a northern tier. This region is actually quite diverse in culture, religion, and language—for example, Israel, surrounded by Arab nations, is markedly different—but there are some pervasive characteristics of thought and social life that dominate the region and that have radiated for over a thousand years in several directions. Most of North Africa, parts of the Caucasus and Central Asia, and much of the South Asian subcontinent share important features of Middle Eastern culture.

The most important characteristic of the area is the religion and general way of life of Islam. To synthesize a very complex situation, Islamic society may be described briefly as monotheistic and basically egalitarian—all people are equal before God—while insisting on greatly differing cultural roles for men and women. The extended family and, in some more traditional societies, the tribe play a major role in social life. It is important, for consideration of music, that quality of speech, elegance in writing, and direct verbal exchange among individuals play a major role. It is a basis of political life that people in positions of authority—everyone from kings to religious leaders to teachers—should be directly accessible to those under them, as one looks for leadership and guidance directly to the figure of authority, not to intermediaries.

After it was established in 622 CE, Islam was quickly introduced by Arabs to Persia (Iran) and to Turkey and various other Turkic-speaking peoples, and eventually to the Balkans, North and West Africa, and large parts of Asia. With the Islamic religion came the Arabic alphabet, now long held in common by most peoples of the area and adapted to various non-Arabic languages (but abandoned in Turkey after 1922). The Middle Eastern heartland is an area of major literary, and particularly poetic, accomplishments and of great architecture and textile art, such as carpets, as well as grand traditions of miniature painting.

But the Middle Eastern heartland is certainly not completely homogeneous. For sure, peoples who do not feel that they have much in common may be neighbors. Some of the Middle Eastern nations were established by colonial powers without regard to ethnic boundaries; Iraq, for instance, consists of opposing Sunni and Shi'ite Arab populations along with Kurds. Throughout the area, village and nomadic cultures continue to exist alongside heavily urbanized and modernized centers. There is much cultural, linguistic, and religious diversity. To speak simply of "Arab culture" neglects the existence of the many Arabic-speaking groups, from tribal units to urban societies, differences that span the physical distance between Iraq in the East and Morocco in the West. Then there are a number of different Turkic-speaking peoples, beginning with the

Explore
a map of the Middle East on the Interactive Globe on **mymusiclab.com**

Read
Selections from the Qu'ran [Koran] on **mymusiclab.com**

nation of Turkey, as well as Kurds, Armenians, Baluchis, and many more ethnic groups. Furthermore, although most Middle Easterners are Muslims (largely Sunni Muslims in most Arab and Turkish areas, Shi'ites in Iran and much of Iraq), there are also Armenian, Nestorian, and Assyrian Christians, as well as Jews, Baha'is, and Zoroastrians (Zoroastrianism being the original religion of Iran) scattered in small communities. Most members of non-Muslim minorities, however, which once played a prominent role in dominantly Islamic nations, since ca. 1970, have gradually moved to Europe, North America, and Israel.

The Middle East stretches in several directions and has no precise boundaries, and the musical characteristics of its center radiate thousands of miles in all directions. What we label here as the Middle Eastern culture and music area goes beyond the heartland and includes North Africa, all the way to Morocco (a largely Arabic-speaking area); the Caucasus (Azerbaijan, Georgia, Armenia); and Afghanistan and Central Asia, areas with largely Persian and Turkic speakers. Furthermore, some of the characteristics of Middle Eastern music are held in common with South Asia, and it would be difficult to draw a precise line separating the musics of Iran, Afghanistan, and Pakistan. Finally, because of its proximity but also because of a period of some five hundred years of occupation by the Turkish Empire, much of the Balkan peninsula has music clearly related to and often even definitely a part of the music of the Middle East.

This large area of the world—which does not, incidentally, include the entire region of Islam, as Pakistan, Bangladesh, Indonesia, India, and Nigeria are actually nations with the largest Muslim populations—is surely quite diverse musically, but it nevertheless holds in common certain characteristics of musical culture and musical style.

The Middle Eastern Sound

There is enormous variety in Middle Eastern music, but it is fair to say that a typically Middle Eastern musical sound can be identified, just as Western musical performances may have many kinds of singing and instrumental tone color, and yet you can usually distinguish Western music when you've heard it for a few seconds. Whether classical or folk, urban or rural, Middle Eastern music has a unique sound, which comes from a combination of distinctive characteristics.

MONOPHONIC (MONOPHONY)

One melody line is played by all musicians, with no harmonic accompaniment.

PARALLEL POLYPHONY

The same melodic line is played at different pitch levels by two or more performers.

HETEROPHONY

Two or more performers play the same melody, but with small differences in timing or ornamentation.

Fundamentally, and in its older traditions, Middle Eastern music is almost always **monophonic**—which means that there is only one melody, not several melodies proceeding together, as might be the case in a European chorus, and no system of harmony to guide or accompany the melody. This statement is generally correct, but it is important to note members of an ensemble can relate and produce textural variety in a great many ways. Thus, a vocalist improvising may be accompanied by an instrument that follows a note or two behind the vocalist; or there may be **parallel polyphony**, that is, two voices or instruments playing the same melody at different pitch levels, say a fifth apart. Several instruments may play the same tune in basic unison, but each may perform a slightly different version, producing something called **heterophony**. But in principle, Middle Eastern music is monophonic.

CHARACTERISTICS OF MIDDLE EASTERN MUSIC

- Monophony: One melody line is played simultaneously by all performers.
- Ornamentation: Notes are bent or are embellished with trills, glissandos, or short secondary notes.
- Sound Quality (Timbre): Flat, vibratoless tone, with a hard-edged, "raspy" quality.
- Solo, vocal music dominates.
- Improvisation is highly valued.

With this fundamental character goes a prevailingly ornamented style of singing and playing. Many, if not most, tones are "bent" or are embellished with trills, glissandos, or short secondary notes—all kinds of techniques to transcend a simple, straightforward rendering of a pitch. Middle Eastern musicians consider that this ornamentation gives the music its special regional character and accounts for its emotional impact. The more ornamented a passage, the better and more expressive its audience perceives it to be.

Furthermore, there is a characteristic singing style or instrumental tone color. The basic way the voice is used, the kind of sound made by singers and instrumentalists—in other words, the ideal musical sound—is one of the most important characterizing features of any musical style. It is also something that tends to be, on the whole, the same within any one culture, no matter how varied the structure of the music may otherwise be. Thus, the vocal styles of singers of Persian, Arab, and Turkish classical music and of the many regional folk and tribal musics of the area tend to sound rather alike. It is difficult to describe this ideal sound; it is much easier to grasp it by hearing the music. But we might attempt to convey its effect by saying that a lot of it is tense sounding, often with a raspy, throaty, nasal tone, and a certain flatness. Instead of vibrato, it features copious ornamentation. Men often sing high in their range, and women tend to use the lower part of theirs. And the sounds made by instruments often parallel those of the human voice. Thus, players of the traditional spiked fiddle (kamancheh in Persian and Turkish, jouzeh in Arabic), prefer a flat, nasal tone without vibrato, in contrast to the fuller and vibrated sound of the Western violin.

This panorama of musical sound goes with a musical culture in which solo performance dominates, in which singing is central, and in which improvisation plays a major role.

Instruments

But instruments are certainly important as well. Just like musical styles, the entire area shares some dominant instrument types, but each country or culture has its own version or variant. Just

Middle Eastern wind instruments. (Top): two zornahs, double-reed instruments used throughout the Middle East. (Bottom): Arabic Zummarahs, double clarinets with parallel finger-holes. *Source:* Wanda Nettl/Bruno Nettl

Omani musicians play an oud (lute; right) and Arab drum together. *Source:* Charles O. Cecil/Alamy

✳ **Explore**
the Musical Instrument Gallery on
mymusiclab.com

👁 **Watch** the **Video**
of an oud player
on **mymusiclab.com**

as most musicianship involves solo performance and individual improvisation, in the development of instruments, too, regionalism and individualism dominate over widespread standardization.

Speaking generally, the most prominent throughout the Middle East are plucked instruments related to guitars, mandolins, banjos—generically called "lutes"—and a large variety of drums, usually played with the fingers. Other kinds of string instruments are also important, but wind instruments take a back seat.

The most famous of Middle Eastern instruments is the *oud*, a lute with a large body and a short neck and no frets, plucked with a pick made of a feather quill. It looks very much like a European lute and, in fact, is the ancestor of that instrument widely used before 1700, whose name is derived from the Arabic *al-oud*. Many different types of lutes are spread through the region, but the most widespread type has a long neck and frets, despite the fact that the modern oud has no frets (some believe that in the Middle Ages earlier ouds had frets). Beyond that, they vary enormously in size, shape, and number of strings.

The most important bowed instrument type has a small round body with a skin belly and a long fingerboard with three to six strings, which is held vertically, cello style. Used in some classical traditions but most commonly a folk instrument, it has numerous variants and names. Of special interest are instruments generically labeled as "zithers": basically a flat board or box over which parallel strings are stretched. The *qanun* or *kanun*, most important in Turkey, Egypt, and North Africa, is trapezoid shaped or triangular and is plucked as it lies flat in front of the player. The trapezoid santour, considered by many a national instrument of Iran but also found elsewhere, has seventy-two strings and is played with two, very light, wooden hammers.

Three Unities

Three prominent features and beliefs unite Middle Eastern musical culture:

- A vocal and compositional style is derived from the recitation of the Holy Qur'an (Koran in Turkey).
- Music creates a kind of ecstatic, emotional bond between performer and audience.
- The "suite," or collection of individual pieces played together, is the major unifying compositional principle.

Although not classified as "music" in the Middle East and kept separate from secular and even devotional music, the reciting, or chanting of the Qur'an is structurally much like classical nonmetric improvisation. Anyone may recite the Qur'an, but in the mosque professionals render the holy word. Two styles of chanting dominate: *Murattal* is the unembellished, subdued, syllabic, relatively simple style; *Mujawwad* is emotional, ornamented, melodically complicated. Melodies are ruled by a system of modes, similar to the **maqam** system (we will discuss the use of maqams or modes in Middle Eastern music later in the chapter). There are different ways of chanting, schools with different practices, for example, the Meccan, Egyptian, Damascus, and Western North African.

The chanting is improvised, but the Qur'an may be written with a kind of notation that indicates whether a tone is to be ornamented or not, and in which direction the melody should move. Among musicians, the explicitly musical aspect of the Qur'an may ostensibly play a major role, but it is important to remember that the entire system of musical values, the high value of nonmetric, vocal, texted, improvised music and the lower esteem of metric, instrumental, composed music is based on the relative similarity to or difference from the sound of the Qur'an.

Second is the importance of music as a transformer of emotion and mood. According to the musician and scholar A. Jihad Racy in his book *Making Music in the Arab World* "direct association between music and emotional transformation pervades the performers' and listeners' world" (2004:4). The terms *tarab* in Arabic and *hal* in Persian denote the quality in music that affects the listener and that provides a tie between audience and performer. Although in many ways, music is seen as importantly intellectual, or as serving ritual and occupational functions, emotional expression is enormously important to Middle Eastern audiences.

Third, a centerpiece of Middle Eastern classical music systems is the large suite, a composite work consisting, like the Western suite, of several contrasting movements. Their purpose may be just to provide aesthetic and intellectual entertainment, or to evoke a mood or a kind of ecstasy to the listener, or to

MAQAM
Generic term for mode, or system of composing melody, in Arabic classical music. The term is used throughout the Middle East, and the concept occasionally appears with different names such as dastgah and gusheh in Persian, or mugam in Azerbaijan.

TAQSIM
Nonmetric improvised instrumental piece consisting of several short sections, in Arabic and Turkish classical music; spelled Taksim in Turkish.

TASNIF
Type of composed, metric song in Persian music, with words (though sometimes performed instrumentally), and a part of a full classical performance though also found in popular music.

RENG
In Persian classical music, the final piece of a performance, based on the musical traditions of folk dance.

provide background for a ceremony. But although each region of the Middle East has its own form or type, these large works serve as one of several unifying factors in the musical culture of this large area. Each type includes solo and ensemble sections, many include both vocal and instrumental movements, and all have composed and improvised components.

The most common type of suite found throughout the region is known as the **taqsim** (*taksim* in Turkey). It consists of two parts: an improvised, usually nonmetric solo instrumental number and the *beshrav* or *peshrev*, a metric, composed piece usually performed by an ensemble. Other types of suites, such as the Egyptian *wasla*, the *nawbat* found in Morocco, Algeria, and Tunisia, and suites associated with the religious practices of various Sufi sects, feature many more parts, up to 12 sections, with more or less improvisation, some in rhythm and some not, some vocal, and some improvised. The Persian *dastgah* (the same name is used for this extended suite as for Persian modes) is performed in five parts: *pishdaramad* (composed, for ensemble); *chahar mezrab* (composed or improvised, solo); *avaz* (solo, improvised, nonmetric); **tasnif** (metric, composed song); and **reng** (a light, dance-derived instrumental piece). Iraq shares a similar form, known as the "Iraqi maqam," which also centers on an extended avaz.

MUSIC IN CULTURE

Attributes of Music

Middle Eastern culture has a unique view of music. Music is greatly appreciated, but there is also a kind of moral ambivalence or uncertainty about the ways and degrees to which music is acceptable. Music is seen as having a dangerously sensual component that could distract listeners from proper religious and social duties. Just why music should be held in low esteem is not quite clear, as the Holy Qur'an does not direct this attitude, although it cautions believers to avoid the kinds of music that lead to frivolous and lewd behavior. But whatever the roots, in Islamic society in the Middle East, music—other than the liturgical recitation of the Qur'an (which, though sharing many attributes with song in the Middle East, is not classified as music)—must be kept far from the centers of religion. Many believe that devout Muslims should avoid music, and instruments in particular must be kept in their proper context, as must dancing. But these negative aspects of music are lessened by other strands of Islamic thought. Islam holds in high regard scholarly activity, so the study of music—particularly music theory—has a long and rich history. Sung poetry has long been highly valued in Islamic cultures. And, finally, Islamic societies are generally tolerant of non-Muslims, who can have a special role in musical culture. Lois al-Faruqi, examining Arabic legal literature, discovered a strict hierarchy in the types of music and their "acceptability" to society. It begins with music-like utterances that are not music (e.g., Qur'an and religious chants) and goes on to music that is legitimate or *halal:* chanted poetry, music for family celebrations such as weddings, and occupational folk songs, and finally, military music. Her next category consists of a number of genres that are controversial, consisting largely of what we consider to be classical music, followed by music that is illegitimate (*haram*), associated with unacceptable contexts such as nightclubs.

It is a fact that in traditional Middle Eastern cultures, musicians—except for those who had reached fame and stardom—were often held in low esteem. There is no tradition of instrumental religious music, and there are no concerts in the mosques. And whereas Iranians and Turks take their traditions of poetry and visual art, their miniatures, and their carpets very seriously, they usually cannot imagine that music deserves the same dignified treatment. On the other hand, Middle Eastern societies have a lot of what we consider to be music, and they are very good at it. They have found ways to reconcile their religion's ambivalence toward music and their own desire to have music.

Musical activity was often turned over, as it were, to members of non-Muslim minorities, particularly Jews and to a smaller extent Christians. Of course there have always been lots of Muslim musicians, but there have always been a disproportionate number of Jewish musicians. Instrument making and selling, as well, has been in the hands of non-Muslims; for example, in Tehran around 1970, most instrument makers were Armenian Christians.

If music-making was dangerous, the intellectual study of music was not, and thus there developed in Islamic society a tradition of scholarship in music theory that resulted in the writing, between 900 and 1900, of almost two thousand treatises in Arabic, Persian, and Turkish. Among the philosophical and scientific branches of learning, music played a major part, and in fact, the desirability of music, the conditions under which it was socially acceptable, was the subject of many written works.

Defining Music

The very definition of music as a concept is related to the Middle Eastern view of it. In English, it's a broad concept, extending from classical, popular, and folk traditions to idiosyncratic experiments. In Middle Eastern cultures, the definition of music has been narrower and more complex. In Persian, for example, there are two terms to denote music: **musiqi**, derived from Greek and meaning "music," and **khandan**, meaning "to sing, to recite, to read." A particular sound or context of music may be considered one or the other, or in some respect both. Thus, we may say that certain sounds have more "musicness" about them than others. The kinds of music (in our sense) that are socially most acceptable are khandan. Most important, they include the reading of the Qur'an, which in formal situations is always recited (but in a way that emphasizes the words, always in Arabic), is nonmetric, has no instrumental accompaniment, and in accordance with certain rules, is improvised. The more a performance of music is like that of Qur'anic recitation in sound, structure, and social context, the

MUSIQI

Classical and folk forms of music in the Middle East that have less prestige than the religious Khandan.

KHANDAN

To sing, recite, or read, literally. In practice, the highest form of Middle Eastern music, used primarily in chanting the texts of the Qur'an.

LISTENING GUIDE

CHANTING OF THE HOLY QUR'AN

 GO TO www.mymusiclab.com for the Automated **Listening Guide** CDI • Track 5/Download Track 5

Recorded in Chicago, 1973

Note the many silences that break up the phrases as the performer chants the text.

0:00–0:05	Fade in.
0:06–0:13	First phrase, relatively unornamented.
0:14–0:17	Silence.
0:17–0:30	Second phrase; slightly more ornamented.
0:30–0:33	Brief silence.
0:33–0:45	Third line, moving slightly up and then dropping back in pitch.
0:46–0:49	Silence.
0:50–1:06	Higher pitched with much more ornamentation and melisma (one syllable sung over several notes) as the pitch drops.
1:07	Breath.
1:08–1:16	Completion of previous phrase.
1:17–1:38	Leaps up and then descends again as the piece fades out.

ZURKHANEH
Literally "house of strength." Traditional gymnasium in Iran, used by men to exercise, accompanied by a morshed reciting heroic verse with percussion.

MORSHED
Reciter of heroic verse such as *Shahnameh* to accompany exercises in the Zurkhaneh, traditional Persian gymnasium.

less likely it is to be labeled as "music" (Listen to CD I, 5 for an example of Qur'anic recitation).

We can move from Qur'anic recitation along several continuums to arrive at what would be considered "music" (musiqi). These continuums move from vocal to instrumental, from nonmetric to metric, to the use of repeated driving rhythmic formulas, from improvised to composed, from traditional to Westernized. Thus, the music of the **Zurkhaneh**, a kind of traditional gymnasium where men exercise to the chanting of a specialized singer, or **morshed**, who accompanies himself on drum and bells, using the latter also to direct the participants to change exercises, might come next to the religious chanting of the Mosque.

Going further, we have the vocal performance of avaz, the improvised nonmetric section of a classical performance. This is a bit further removed from the ideal of khandan because it is often accompanied, emphasizes some vocal pyrotechnics, and is frequently performed by women. The same kind of music, avaz, but now performed on an instrument, would be next on the scale and definitely called musiqi. The excerpts in CD I, 6, which we will discuss later, illustrate instrumental avaz.

Our continuum then moves on to metric composed songs and then to metric instrumental pieces, such as the introductory pishdaramad in a classical Iranian performance, and eventually to virtuosic instrumental pieces, such as the chahar mezrab (see CD 1, 4), in which rhythmic predictability is greatest on account of the use of repeated rhythmic patterns as well as steady meter. Finally, the popular music performed in music halls and nightclubs, far removed as it is from the ideal of khandan, is the subject of a great deal of religio-conservative ambivalence within Middle Eastern societies. After the Iranian revolution of 1978, for instance, most kinds of music, but particularly those most clearly in the "musiqi" category, were prohibited in public. Importantly, however, these conservative views of "musiqi" are not, by and large, shared by the majority within Middle Eastern societies.

Musicians

It may be hard to accept this concept in a world in which music is pervasive, in the age of star musicians, but in many parts of the world, in traditional societies, musicians were and still are looked down on or regarded as a "special" group of people. In Europe, throughout much of history, one expected foreigners to take the roles of musicians. There are many traditional stories in which the musician is somehow associated with the supernatural, in league with the devil. Musical talent is often described as coming from the supernatural; the famous story of American blues performer Robert Johnson learning the guitar from the devil by traveling to a crossroads at midnight is just one of many such tales. In many folk cultures, musicians were permitted and even expected to engage in unconventional social, sexual, and even religious behavior.

In the Middle East, being a musician meant that you might be a social inferior, but the classification of musicians, like the different classifications of music, balanced the contradictory beliefs that music is dangerous versus supremely desirable. In the classical-music scene of cities, one might be a professional musician or an amateur, but the well-trained and artistic amateur has higher status than the professional. This is based on the high value placed on freedom in the Middle East. Professional musicians may be looked down on because they must perform when ordered and play whatever their patron wishes to hear at whatever length is desired. Amateurs, who play for their own pleasure and for their friends, may make these decisions themselves, particularly those that involve the choice of modal system and improvisation. Considering that in Persian music the selection of mode, maqam, or dastgah, has a lot to do with the musician's mood, as each mode has its own character, the notion of freedom gives amateur status its higher prestige. And because improvised music has the greatest prestige but requires the greatest degree of freedom for the performer, amateurs (assuming they are really as well trained and as knowledgeable as professionals) are able to indulge their own musical desires best, and thus to bring to the audience a feeling of well-being and even ecstasy (tarab in Arabic, hal in Persian).

One group of individuals in Islamic society is particularly associated with music: the Sufis. Sufism is a mystical movement in Islam, which is able to overcome the disapproval of music by saying, in effect, "Music is just another way of knowing and being close to God." Thus many Middle Eastern musicians, if they are Muslims, are members of Sufi sects. In rural or small-town culture of the Middle East, folk songs are not principally performed by the general population (as they are in some of the world's rural societies), but rather by specialist singers and instrumentalists. They are not known as "musicians" per se, but each is a specialist in a particular genre and is thus designated and expects to be paid for performing.

In his study of the Khorasan music, Stephen Blum identified a large number of musician types, recognized as such by society, each of whom specialized in one genre or context. The **naqqal** recited the **Shahnameh** in teahouses. The **darvish** (any of a number of different kinds of individuals all associated with Sufism) might recite the same work, and recent religious poetry, on the streets. The **bakhshi** performed narratives dealing with war and romance at weddings and similar events. The **rouzeh-khan** performed *rouzeh*, songs of the martyrdom of Hossein (grandson of the Prophet Muhammad, d. 680 CE); the **monaqeb-khan** sang about the virtues of 'Ali (cousin and son-in-law of the Prophet Muhammad, d. 661 CE) and his descendants. The **motreb** performed vocal and instrumental music at teahouses; the **asheq** sang romantic narratives in towns and encampments. One person could perform several functions and have several of these designations, but the point was that none of them was associated with the whole of "music" as such; none was a "musician." The relationship between art and folk music is quite different from that found in Western Europe, say, where folk music is ordinarily performed by people who are not specialists. In the Middle East, folk music is the province of the specialist, and art music ideally of the amateur. Looking back to the performances that I attended, the last one—a private concert—is the most socially acceptable, as it was part of a tradition called *dowreh*, a small group of men who meet periodically for a special purpose such as reading the Qur'an or poetry to each other or hearing music. This group is often based on an extended family, and certainly its members belong to the same social class and perhaps even occupation. They feel close to each other and depend on the ambience provided by this sense of belonging and of privacy. In earlier times, music was often heard in these venues, and the notion of music as dangerous accompanies the concept of keeping it within a closed social circle. Traditionally, the most acceptable music was that performed privately, improvised by a soloist, perhaps a highly accomplished amateur, who brings a sense of ecstasy in which the world is temporarily transformed to the music. So, while the improvised sections of a program were very controlled in the public concert and were relatively short compared to the composed materials, improvisation played a much greater role in a small private performance.

NAQQAL

Reciter of the *Shahnameh*, Iranian national epic, in teahouses in small-town Iran.

SHAHNAMEH

National epic of Iran, dealing with mythology and pre-Islamic history, written by Ferdowsi in the tenth century C.E., and ordinarily performed by singing in teahouses.

DARVISH

Leader of a community of Sufis and, in rural Iran, street singer of religious narratives.

BAKHSHI

Iranian folk singer of narratives about war and romance.

ROUZEH-KHAN

Singer of narratives about the martyrdom of the Imam Hossein, in small-town Iranian musical culture.

MONAQEB-KHAN

Singer of narratives about the virtues of Imam Ali, in small-town Iranian musical culture.

MOTREB

Generic name for musician in various Middle Eastern cultures; performer of vocal and instrumental music at teahouses in Khorasan.

ASHEQ

Middle Eastern singer of romantic narratives.

MAKING MUSIC

Melodic Modes: Maqam, Makam, Mugam, and Dastgah

The most important structuring device for composers and improvisers is the modal system. Musicians and musicologists argue unendingly about the definition of "mode," but for our purposes, we may say that it is a pattern or set of rules for composing melody. Modes are found in many of the world's culture areas, but particularly in South and Southeast Asia, Indonesia, European art music of earlier periods, and of course, the Middle East. In the Arab world, the term for mode is maqam (**makam** in Turkish). In the Caucasus, the term for the Azerbaijani version of the system is *mugam*, and in Central Asian Uzbekistan, a more limited body of material called *Shashmakom* (six makams) is used. In Iran, it is the term *dastgah*. A unit like a maqam has a particular scale, that is, a collection or group of pitches from which the composer draws when creating one piece (mode also limits the range of possibilities open to the composer). Generally speaking, the Arab and Turkish manifestations of Middle Eastern classical music constitute one stream, and the forms found in Iran, Azerbaijan, and Afghanistan together form a second stream. The tones are separated by distances in pitch called **intervals**. In Western major and minor scales, the consecutive intervals are major and minor seconds, also called whole- and half-tones. (You can identify them on the piano: Half-tones are made by playing adjacent keys, whole-tones by skipping a key, but be sure to include the black keys in your calculation.) In Middle Eastern music, however, there are, in addition to these intervals, others not compatible with the standard Western system. They are three-quarter-tones, slightly larger than our half-tone, and five-quarter-tones, slightly larger than our whole-tone. The scales of maqams and dastgahs are made up of various combinations of these intervals.

But there is more to a maqam: Along with a scale, there are typical kinds of order in which the tones should appear and short three- or four-note motifs or musical gestures that a composer or improviser must use, bringing them back every ten, twenty, or thirty seconds to maintain the proper character of the mode. To play just anything with the use of a prescribed scale is not enough.

Every Arab or Turkish maqam or Persian dastgah has a name. Some give place of origin. Thus, there is Isfahan (name of a city in Iran), Rak (probably a Persian form of the Indian word "raga," thus indicating Indian origin), Hijaz (a section of Saudi Arabia), Nahawand (a village in Turkey), and so on. The name may instead suggest something of the character of the music: Homayoun (royal), Shur (salty), and the like. In some cases, notions from technical music theory play a role, for example, Mokhalef ("opposite," indicating that the scale is, as it were, turned around), Chahargah ("fourth place," or "fourth fret"), Segah ("third place"), Panjgah ("fifth place"). The systems of Turkish, Arab, and Persian music are quite different, but they share many of these terms, a preponderance of which comes from the Persian language. Although it is impossible to know whether the name of a maqam or dastgah really indicates

MAKAM
Turkish spelling of maqam.

INTERVAL
The distance between two pitches.

LISTENING GUIDE

ILLUSTRATIONS OF MAJOR MAQAMS

⟩ GO TO **www.mymusiclab.com for the Automated Listening Guide** CDI • Track 6/Download Track 6

Performed by A. Jihad Racy on bouzouq and nei

Listen to this recording to hear a number of the most important Arab maqams: Nahawand, Rast, Bayati, Hijaz Kar, Sika, and Saba. Telling them apart is not easy for the uninitiated listener, but one may learn to identify a maqam by its special quirks such as the three-quarter tone that sounds slightly larger than an interval of a half step in Rast; the augmented second of Hijazkar; the compressed diminished fourth in Saba; or the fact that in Sika it is hard to decide which tone is the fundamental tone, or tonic.

TIME	MAQAM
0:00–0:20	Nahawand (Example I, 10 is a longer sampling of Nahawand.).
0:23–1:06	Rast (2 sections).
1:10–2:05	Bayati (3 sections).
2:08–3:16	Hijaz Kar (3 sections).
3:20–4:00	Sika (2 sections).
4:03–4:51	Saba (2 sections), played on the *nei*.

musical relationship to a place or nonmusical character, there is no doubt that Middle Eastern musicians consider each mode to have a particular character. And so, although much of the music of this area is improvised, it is a matter of music-making within rather specific sets of rules and patterns (Listen to CD I, 6 for some examples of Arab maqams).

If you are performing in one mode, you may wish to change, or modulate, to another, and in Arab and Turkish music, each maqam has certain others to which a musician would typically move. Thus, if you perform in Nahawand, you are likely to move to Rast, Hijaz, and Ajam, but not typically to others. In twentieth-century Iranian music, the system has become formalized, with each dastgah including within its purview several **gushehs**, units that are performed one after the other. If, for instance, you want to play the dastgah of Chahargah, you will not only tend to move to particular other modal units as in Arab music, but you must also select your modulations from the gushehs belonging to Chahargah: Zabol, Mokhalef, Hesar, Mansuri, and others (examples of two Persian dastgahs are provided in the accompanying recordings: Mahour [CD I, 4] and Chahargah [CD I, 8 and 9]).

GUSHEH
Subdivision of a dastgah, and smallest constituent part of the radif, in Persian classical music.

Rhythmic Structure

The modal system of Middle Eastern music is complex and fascinating, but rhythm, which usually is harder to explain, is equally complicated. Take the

LISTENING GUIDE

EXAMPLES OF METRIC, NONMETRIC, AND "IN BETWEEN" MUSIC

CD TRACK	TYPE
I, 5	Free rhythm.
I, 7	Sections with regular pulse, but no overall meter.
I, 10	Bits of metric structure.
I, 9, 0:00–0:27	A repeated rhythmic pattern.
I, 4	Regular, driving rhythm.

matter of metric and nonmetric music. Many traditions of music are clearly metric, that is, there is always a metric cycle of beats, possibly with subdivisions, which organizes the rhythmic experience.

In other traditions, there may be no meter at all. And so we are tempted to think of music simply as either metric or nonmetric. But Middle Eastern music actually has a more complicated system of rhythm.

For one thing, it may be metric, or nonmetric, but often is somewhere in between. One can say about the chanting of the Qur'an (CD I, 5) that it is nonmetric, but when we get to singing in the Zurkhaneh, by a morshed who chants epic poetry to percussion accompaniment, we have to admit that although it too is nonmetric, it has more of a metric feel. The same is true of the improvised taqsims of Arab and Turkish music, or the Persian avaz. In a performance of Midddle Eastern music, various degrees of "metricness" can be found at various times, and a performer can switch almost unnoticed between short metric and nonmetric passages (refer to the following listening guide to find excerpts of these rhythmic possibilities).

In Arab and Turkish classical music, metric music is often organized by rhythmic modes of a sort. These are not too different from the talas of Indian music (see Chapter 2) and involve a series of beats—up to twenty-five, but usually from seven to sixteen—some of which are stressed to provide a set of subdivisions. Generically called **iqa'** or *wazn* in Arabic and *usul* in Turkish, these modes have names, like the melodic maqams, and serve as an underlying structure articulated by the drum, which uses different kinds of strokes on the drumhead for stressed and unstressed beats. The melodies that the drums accompany fit in with the rhythmic mode, but sometimes so subtly that one can hardly tell just what the relationship is.

Just as the concept of melodic mode has been widespread, extending from Southeast Asia to Europe (in the Middle Ages), systems of rhythmic modes are

IQA'
Generic name of rhythmic modes, or type of musical meter, in Arabic classical music. Called usul in Turkish.

found in the same area. But they have been abandoned in European music and now play less of a role in the Middle East than formerly; they remain important only in the two classical music systems of India (see Chapter 2).

The Forms and Processes of Improvisation

One of the central features of Middle Eastern music is improvisation, the creation of music in the course of performance. But keep in mind this important distinction: Some Middle Eastern music is improvised, but much of it is composed, without the use of notation, but memorized and handed down through oral tradition. There are also certain kinds of music in which some elements remain the same from one performance to the next, whereas other aspects are created on the spot. A lot of music can be understood as somewhere between absolute improvisation—the performer has "total" freedom, there is no predictability—and absolute restriction by a composer, with the performances being totally identical.

Improvisation is a central feature of many of the world's musics. A great deal of older traditional African music was improvised in the sense that musicians created innumerable variations on a short repeated theme, and possibly no sharp distinction was made between performance of memorized music and the spinning-out of improvised variations (see Chapter 7). In jazz, however, a set of chords, or a popular tune, becomes the basis of improvisation. In the gamelan music of Java and Bali, members of the ensemble improvise variations on a theme that is being played at the same time by other instruments (see Chapter 6). In the classical musics of India and the Middle East, improvised and composed musics coexist, and the two are regarded as distinct processes. The general system of Indian improvisation is related to that of the Middle East, except that different types of improvisation—slow, fast, metric, and nonmetric (alap, jor, jhala in North India; alapana, tanam, trikala in South India)—are recognized (see Chapter 2). Such differences are found in the Middle East as well, but they are not recognized by separate terminology.

As in all musics in which there is improvisation, Middle Eastern musicians do not simply perform anything that comes into their minds. Their improvised pieces have more or less predictable form and musical content. The rules by which one improvises fall into two categories: form and the overall design of a performance. The most widely known Middle Eastern improvised forms are the taqsim of Arab and Turkish music and the Persian avaz. Although it was not possible to provide an entire taqsim among the accompanying recordings, the style is nevertheless illustrated. CD I, 6, introduces several maqams by performing excerpts of Arab taqsims. An entire taqsim is typically five to ten minutes long and consists of six to twelve separate sections. CD I, 7 gives an excerpt from the beginning of a taqsim in the maqam of Nahawand, performed by A. Jihad Racy. The entire performance consisted of six sections (Listen to CD I, 7 to hear this excerpt).

LISTENING GUIDE

TAQSIM IN THE MAQAM OF NAHAWAND

GO TO www.mymusiclab.com for the Automated Listening Guide CDI • Track 7/Download Track 7

Performed by A. Jihad Racy

0:01–0:25	The initial section of the taqsim. The performer begins in the low part of the range, in moderate tempo, and gradually moves higher, and finally moves down to a characteristic closing formula, then pauses.
0:27–0:30 and 0:31–0:34	Two brief groups of transitional, notes which the performer seems to be using to help him create the beginning of the next section.
0:35–1:00	The second main section. Some of the musical gestures of the first section reappear here, but as a whole it is pitched higher, moves a bit more rapidly, and moves between the higher and lower tones more rapidly.
1:00–1:08	Closing formula, similar to that of [0:23–0:25].

An Arab or Turkish taqsim or a Persian avaz—or any of the other improvised genres—is cast in a mode (maqam, makam, or dastgah), which tells the performer the scales, the identities of the pitches, and the typical motifs that must be used. Moreover, the rhythmic structure—not consistently metric, though metric bits may appear—is predetermined. Beyond this, the performer has certain choices, but if we analyze many recorded performances, we see that they follow a limited set of patterns. Performers may decide to move from the main mode into others, and in the case of Persian music, one is almost obliged to do so, moving gradually from a low part of the range to a higher part. They may also decide how many and which secondary modes to modulate into, in what order, and just how long to stay with each one. The overall form is set, but the details are determined by the improviser.

But beyond the matter of overall form, there is a matter of style on a more detailed level. It is this aspect of the music that causes it to sound "Middle Eastern" or "Iranian," or from a particular place or performer. It is the way in which musical materials are handled, repeated, changed, developed, and alternated. In Middle Eastern music, it is important to repeat a motif two or three times but not more. It is important to present a highly characteristic motif occasionally and to surround it with more general material. Most melodic movements should take place in accordance with the scale of the maqam or dastgah, with few large intervals that skip tones. It is expected that the music be ornamented, that one moves from lower to higher areas of the scalar range. These are general rules of style, but how they are applied in detail is up to the improviser. And yet Arab and Persian improvisations have a consistent style, balancing freedom and restriction.

Learning to Improvise

Much of the consistency of a system of improvisation is due to the way it is taught and learned. How does one learn to improvise? In Arab music, many musicians learn by hearing the many variations intoned in Qur'anic recitation and the call to prayer. In music lessons, improvisational bits are offered by the teacher and repeated and memorized by the student. Some Syrian and Iraqi teachers move through the body of music over months or years, maqam by maqam, explaining and demonstrating to the student what is essential, obligatory, and optimal. In South Indian music, a series of exercises that provide the basic musical vocabulary for improvisation are studied and internalized. In jazz, solitary hearing and memorizing of recorded improvisation may alternate with sitting in with and receiving occasional direction and encouragement from masters. In all cases, musicians learn fundamental materials on which improvisation is based and techniques of what one may do with this material to arrive at an acceptable improvised performance. But of course, the outcome is also determined by the individuality of a player's or singer's technique, experience in the world of music, and mood.

Persian music offers an excellent illustration of the relationship between basic material to be learned and the improvised performance. Primarily, Iranian musicians study the repertory of music known as the **radif**, or more properly, the radif of their teacher. A radif consists of some three hundred pieces of music, most of them quite short—thirty seconds to four minutes—and they are organized in the twelve modes, or dastgahs, of Persian music. Thus, each mode has a section of the radif devoted to it. For example, the dastgah of Shur has some thirty pieces. The first is Shur itself, that is, a piece that has the main scalar and thematic characteristics of Shur. Then come others clearly related to Shur, but with their own peculiarities; these are called *gushehs* (see diagram). Some radifs have the same names as Arab maqams, and there is reason to believe that the way Arab musicians combined maqams informally in a performance of a taqsim, for example, was codified by Iranian musicians into the much more formal radif.

RADIF ➔ DASTGAH ➔ MAIN SCALE (in daramad) ➔ PRINCIPAL MUSICAL MOTIF ➔ RELATED GUSHEHS (each with characteristic scale and motif)

A full radif takes some eight to ten hours to play through. A student memorizes it, over a period of maybe four years. The teacher does not directly "teach" improvisation, but the radif itself, having been internalized, teaches a musician *how* to improvise, because it includes the basic materials—scales and requirements of the modes or dastgahs, typical themes, and musical ideas—that are the basis of the musical system, and it repeats and juxtaposes these materials in many ways to provide samples and models for the improviser to use. It provides ideas of how to take a musical motif and transform it into various versions,

RADIF

In Persian classical music, the body of music, consisting of 250–300 short pieces, memorized by students and then used as the basis or point of departure for improvised performance.

LISTENING GUIDE

IRAN: RADIF OF NOUR-ALI BOROUMAND (DASTGAH OF CHAHARGAH)

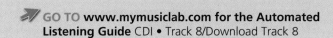

GO TO www.mymusiclab.com for the Automated **Listening Guide** CDI • Track 8/Download Track 8

This recording illustrates the Persian radif; two of the three hundred or so pieces are provided. The first excerpt provides the beginning, or "daramad," of the Dastgah of Chahargah, which provides the musical motif that should dominate improvised performances of that dastgah. This motif begins, and in shortened form ends, the first section ("first daramad," the performer announces) and also begins the second section. Listen to this example several times to gain a bit of familiarity with the motif. It will help you know what to listen for when you get to the examples contained in CD I, 9 and see how the motif appears (and how it is transformed) in improvised performances.

TIME	SECTION	MUSICAL EVENT
0:00–0:06	**Section 1:** Listen for the announcement of the first daramad. Notice the principal musical motif and the way that much of the rest of the excerpt explores similar intervallic relationships.	Announcement of "the first daramad."
0:07–0:12		This opening gesture introduces the principal motif.
0:12–0:49		Continuation of the "first daramad."
0:50–0:54	**Section 2:** Notice here the way that the principal musical motif gets the section started.	Announcement of the "second daramad."
0:54–1:38		The "second daramad" is performed, beginning with the principal musical motif. The recording fades out at [1:27–1:38].

ways of moving gradually from metric to nonmetric rhythm, of repeating and then extending a theme, and of when to present a memorable theme or motif of highly distinct character and when to "noodle around." The content and structure of the radif isn't really different from the improvised avaz, but once you are an accomplished musician, you should not perform the radif in public, but rather practice it and use it as a model, a point of departure, for improvisation (Listen to CD I, 8 and CD I, 9 to hear how the basic motif informs improvisatory possibilities within the Dastgah of Chahargah).

The Persian radif, with its large, formal structure, fits into the Iranian proclivity for complex constructions in the arts. The complicated carpet design; the tendency of literary artists to produce grand, compound works, including a very long national epic; and the complexity of the imperial political system illustrate this tendency. But until the twentieth century, musical performance,

LISTENING GUIDE

SIX EXCERPTS OF IMPROVISATION BASED ON THE DARAMAD OF CHAHARGAH

GO TO **www.mymusiclab.com for the Automated Listening Guide** CDI • Track 9/Download Track 9

This recording includes excerpts from six performances, all based on the bit of music from the radif heard on CD I, 8, showing how several improvisers, all using a part of the radif as a point of departure, can produce quite different kinds of music. The third and fourth excerpts, performed by the same violinist two weeks apart, as well as the fifth and sixth excerpts, played by a famous setar player a decade apart, indicate the range of improvisatory interpretation within the purview of individual musicians.

TIME	INSTRUMENT (PERFORMER)	MAIN MOTIF APPEARS	SPECIAL RHYTHMIC DEVICES	GENERAL DESCRIPTION
0:01–0:35	Santour (Heydari)	[0:01]	Kereshmeh: EQ EQ EEQ Q where E = eight note; Q = quarter note.	Strong, uses kereshmeh rhythm—appears 3 times in a row; deliberate tempo, note pause at [0:24].
0:36–1:15	Kamancheh (Bahari)	[0:36, 0:58]	Metric	Begins slow, lyrical; at [0:58] begins metric rendition of main motif.
1:16–2:01	Violin (Shirinabadi)	[1:16, 1:50]	Nonmetric	Low-pitched, deliberate, rubato, ornamented; note pizzicato or plucked notes [1:25; 1:39]; ascending melodic sequence (a few notes repeated at increasingly higher pitch levels).
2:04–2:58	Violin (Shirinabadi)	[2:05 twice, 2:46]	nonmetric	Slow, deliberate; low-pitched; rubato; note double-stops at approx. [2:12–2:21].
3:02–3:56	Setar (Ebadi)	[3:22]	metric, chahar, mezrab style	Changeable mood; begins metric, moves [3:22] to slow, lyrical, and [3:42] to arapid-fire delivery in style of Chahar mezrab (CD I, 4).
3:59–4:34	Setar (Ebadi)	[3:59, 4:12]	kereshmeh	Strong, rhythmically emphatic. Uses kereshmeh rhythm: at [3:59, 4:12].

which did not enjoy the same prestige as visual art and literature, was an exception to this rule. In the mid-nineteenth century, Iranians became acquainted with European music, as the emperor brought French and Italian musicians to modernize the music of his military establishment. Iranian musicians saw Western music as a grand design—a system with a unified theory, notation, and great control over the listening environment—and they also saw Western musicians as more respected members of their society. This apparently stimulated them to develop the radif, a large, complex work. Organized by musicians who were members of the middle class, it reflected certain important values of Iranian culture: the tension between equality and hierarchy (that is, equality of all before God in Islam and the hierarchy of a political empire), the value of individualism and surprise, and a characteristic way of ordering the smaller parts of an event.

Take an example from traditional Iranian social life as a model. In ordinary relationships between members of a family or close friends, what is important comes first: a father goes through the door before his son, an older friend before the younger, and this is done without much ceremony. In a more formal relationship, people shuffle around deciding who should go first (although it really has been settled in advance that the older, more prestigious, higher placed must precede). In a truly formal event, the amount of introductory behavior preceding the main substance is substantial. A formal dinner, for example, will be preceded by hours of chitchat and tea-with-cookies. The radif is like the family: what is important, main dastgahs, gushehs, motifs, comes first. When the radif is transformed into a more formal performance, the most prestigious part, the improvised avaz, comes later and is preceded by less-prestigious composed pieces. In this way, the radif itself and the music derived from it reflect important values of Iranian culture and principles of social behavior.

HISTORY

Because Middle Eastern music, like most musics, lives in oral tradition, we know much more about its workings in the twentieth century than we do about its history. But as the Middle East generally has long been an area of special interest to Europeans and Americans, its history has been greatly explored by archaeologists and historians. Archaeological sites indicate that the entire area had a large variety of instruments some three thousand years ago. There is evidence that the Sumerians, around 2000 BCE, had a rather complex system of musical notation. The Bible suggests that in ancient Jewish society music was regarded as a joyful activity, and that maybe the ambivalence about music that is characteristic of Islam came to this culture area later on.

We can get some sense of the age of the Middle Eastern system of modes by looking at the modal system of ancient Greece, which was culturally closely associated with Egypt and Persia at that time. The ancient Greek modes—Dorian, Aeolian, Phrygian, Lydian, and so on—whose names are still used in modern modal analysis of Western art and traditional musics, appear to have been units somewhat like maqams or dastgahs. They were scales, but were named after regions and probably derived from local folk-tune types, and they were thought to have some specific character. Though it was only in Greece that theorists and philosophers wrote about the modes, it seems likely that this system of making music was known throughout a far broader area, probably all the way to India, and that the present-day modal systems of South and West Asia are descendants of long-standing traditions.

After Islam became established about 622 CE, empires led successively by Arab, Persian, and Turkish peoples dominated the area for a thousand years. At the courts of these empires, art-music establishments were developed (despite the Muslim ambivalence about music), and famous individual musicians such as Yunus al-Katib (d. 765) and Ibrahim al-Mausili (d. 850) and the Persian Barbod (who lived in the tenth century CE) flourished even during the Middle Ages. Except for verbal descriptions, we have no knowledge of the sound of their music.

But the most important musical heritage of these earlier periods in Islamic history was the immense body of theory and philosophy of music that was produced in many hundreds of treatises written by musicians, scientists, and philosophers, many of them attached to the courts of the Middle Eastern empires. These treatises dealt principally with two topics, the value and acceptability of music and the tuning of the modal scales. Interestingly, however, the precise measurements of pitch that these treatises imply may never have played much of a role in performance, in which intonation is less emphasized than the appropriate musical themes and motifs. Among the authors of these treatises, however, are some of the great names in Arab philosophy—Al-Farabi, Al-Kindi, and Ebn-e Sina (Avicenna)—who included music among the components of a broader system of knowledge.

One important aspect of Middle Eastern music history is its interaction with neighboring culture areas. In the Middle Ages, particularly because of the interaction of Muslims and Christians in Spain, Arab scholars and musicians transmitted Arab (and ancient Greek) ideas and concepts to the Western world. One concrete result was the introduction of the oud, the Arab lute with short neck, to Europe; it became the lute that was so widely used in art music of the Renaissance. Looking in another direction, in the sixteenth century, the Moghul emperor Akbar brought Persian musicians to India, and they are said to have had a major impact, establishing a musical system in north India that was distinct from South Indian or Carnatic music. From the seventeenth to the early twentieth centuries, the dominant power in the Middle East, the Turkish empire centered in Istanbul, had close cultural relations with Europe, and by the nineteenth century, European musical culture began to play a major role. Accordingly, institutions such as public concerts and opera, conservatories of music, notation, and musical technology, along with European ideas about music such as the dominance of composed pieces as compared to improvisations, began to affect the Middle East substantially.

One of the major events in the twentieth century was the establishment of the state of Israel in 1948. The gathering of representatives of Jewish populations from many cultures and countries stimulated the development of a distinctive folk and popular music culture based mainly on a combination of Eastern European and Middle Eastern elements. At the same time, the arrival of many Jewish musicians from Middle Eastern Muslim countries encouraged the preservation and also the interaction of Middle Eastern traditions within Israel.

Vernacular and Popular Music

The Middle East plays host to a wide variety of folk and popular music styles. Perhaps best known in the North Atlantic is the music for belly dancing, performed by a group called *takht* (literally, "platform"), which consists ordinarily of a plucked zither (qanun), a violin, a lute, a goblet-shaped drum, and a tambourine. The music is rapid and is accompanied by fast, complex, but repeated drum figures. Although belly dancing has recently become a genre of popular entertainment, it was traditionally a high art performed by highly trained dancers and musicians.

Many forms of vernacular music combine traditional styles of music with European and North American popular music influences to create new forms. Among the characteristic venues for entertainment in the Middle East is the traditional music hall, as found in some of the large cities in the period around 1970. Here a large audience (mostly of men, and often from the same social or occupational group) may see a long series of entertainment numbers while eating a standard supper and drinking beer. The entertainment may consist of some twenty to thirty acts, some of them political or humorous skits, others folk dances and acrobatics, but the most prominent being musical. Typically, a female singer will be accompanied by a small ensemble of traditional and Western instruments that plays in unison with her while also providing some framing based on Western-influenced harmonies.

Some of these singers have ventured far beyond those music halls. In the period since World War II, a small number of Middle Eastern singers—more women than men—gained great prominence, contradicting the Islamic ambivalence toward music and particularly toward public performance by women. Most famous by far among them was Umm Kulthum (1908–1975). An Egyptian musician who achieved international prominence, Kulthum became a star of radio and film as well as of stage and the record industry. Her songs, composed for her by prominent composers, became widely known throughout the Islamic world and thus qualify as "popular" music. But her singing was based on classical Arab models and included improvisatory passages. At the same time, she was accompanied by orchestras consisting in large part of Western instruments playing in a European-derived style. For almost four decades, she gave monthly concerts lasting four hours (Listen to CD I, 10 for an excerpt of a performance by Umm Kulthum).

LISTENING GUIDE

YA ZALIMNI (EXCERPT)

GO TO www.mymusiclab.com for the Automated
Listening Guide CDI • Track 10/Download Track 10

Sung by Umm Kulthum, with orchestral accompaniment

TIME	SECTION	MUSICAL EVENT
0:00–0:11	First Verse (fade in).	Fade in on first verse; voice paralleled by string section of orchestration with flute. At approx. [0:04], a member of the audience calls out in response to the music.
0:12–0:14	Short instrumental tag.	
0:26–0:27	New verse.	Last word of vocal line is repeated by audience.
0:31–0:32		Again, end of vocal line is repeated by audience.
0:36–0:39		Slightly more ornamentation in vocal line.
0:39–0:52	Same instrumental tag is performed as at [0:11]. Recording fades out [0:42–0:52].	

Other singers, far less well known, such as the Egyptian Abdel-Wahab, the Lebanese Fairuz, and the Iranian Delkash, achieved similar fame on a more local level. The words of these songs are about love, devotion to God, protest against unfairness in society and politics, and the expression of grief. The structure of the poetry greatly affects the rhythmic form of the melodies.

Songs of the sort heard in the music halls could also be heard on radio or bought on 45 rpm disks, and some come from films. They constitute the Middle Eastern version of urban popular music, a type of music that almost everywhere combines indigenous and transnational elements and employs certain instruments and harmonies prevalent in global pop. In general, the popular music of the Middle Eastern cities has a history as a homogeneous style; what one could hear in Cairo, Beirut, and Tehran in the 1970s was very much one kind of music. The culture of the Middle East of centuries past was a relatively unified combination of the confluence of Arab, Persian, Turkish, and other elements, and its popular music in the twentieth century reflects this homogeneity.

In the period after 1980, a number of styles of popular or vernacular music reflected modern social agendas. The genre known as **rai**, found in Algeria and Morocco, combines traditional singing styles, vocal virtuosity, and Arab modes with Western-style chordal accompaniment on synthesizer. In Turkey, a music called *Arabesk* draws young people back from strictly transnational popular musics to a more traditional Middle Eastern sound, as a way of symbolizing

RAI

A modern popular music developed in Algeria and Morocco that combines traditional singing styles and Arabic modes with Western-style synthesized accompaniments.

the Turkish people's association with Islam and to older cultural traditions of the area. Throughout the area, popular music combines Western-derived elements—chordal harmony, tuning of instruments to the European tempered scale, amplification and studio effects, keyboards and synthesizers, guitars, and violins—with traditional Middle Eastern sounds, nonmetric singing with heavy ornamentation usually alternating with metric pieces with a strong beat articulated by traditional hand drums, with words expressing allegiance to traditional cultural values and anticolonial political agendas. Middle Eastern musicians and their music have played a major role in the development of the phenomenon known as "world music" or "world beat," in combination with elements from modern North American and African musics, along with Indian film music. At the same time, music has played and continues to play an important role in anticolonial and nationalistic movements. Despite a growing acceptance of music, certain Islamist fundamentalist movements such as the Taliban in Afghanistan have militated against the practice of music in public.

In the Diasporas

In the history of the world's diasporas—when people in large numbers are forced, usually as a result of poverty or political persecution, to emigrate and settle in foreign "host" countries—music has traditionally played an important cultural role. As illustrated in detail in Chapter 12, the various European ethnic groups who settled in the United States—Italian Americans, Hungarian Americans, and so on—have used their traditional folk music to hold themselves together as communities. The Italian parade in Hartford, Connecticut; the German choir concerts with folk music arrangements in Chicago; the Czech polka bands in Wisconsin all have the purpose of showing their own people—and their foreign neighbors as well—that they have a worthwhile culture. Immigrants who had no interest in music in their home country began to understand its value after they had left home. This applies to Arab Americans and Iranian Americans as well—perhaps even more significantly, even—because music was not necessarily a favored activity until they found themselves living abroad. The Arab American community has many musicians who perform at formal concerts, in night clubs, at weddings and at parties. Although the Arab American community may participate fully in mainstream American culture, it strives to keep the Arab flavor in musical life. Less emphasis is placed on playing only one type of music. Society in Cairo and Beirut emphasized the separation between classical, popular, devotional, and folk music, but these distinctions play a smaller role in North America, where an Arab musician may play classical taqsims in concerts one day and perform in a nightclub for dancing on the next.

The Arab American community was already sizable early in the twentieth century, but Iranian immigrants did not come in large numbers until the 1970s and 1980s. In the cities in which there are many Iranians, nightclubs with popular music abound, and recordings by popular singers who live in America or

Europe, or are able to tour from Iran, are readily available. But the classical music has played a greater role in the Iranian diaspora than in others. Concerts of Persian music—by masters on tour, or by local performers—are important social events. People dress formally, arrive early to socialize, and gladly travel two or three hours for the privilege of attending. Concerts of classical music are the most important ethnic social events in this culture, which, on its home ground, thoroughly de-emphasized music.

✳ **Explore**
the Musical Instrument Gallery on
mymusiclab.com

Iranian immigrant engineers and doctors living in Illinois and California tell a common story: In Iran many of them took no interest in traditional music, but at most, went to hear the Tehran Symphony Orchestra. In North America, Persian music reminds them strongly of home, and they purchase instruments, collect CDs, and try to find opportunities for learning the *radif*. Iranian musicians living in Los Angeles and San Francisco make their living teaching young people *santour*, *setar*, and *kamancheh*, instructing them in the traditional radif, and both immigrants and mainstream Americans have come to learn Arab and Turkish instruments at universities and summer workshops. Traditional music plays an important role, too, in the work of Middle Eastern composers participating in Western art music: in terms of the actual sounds, as they may use the tone system of maqams or dastgahs, and symbolically, as a measure of ethnic identity, by using in their pieces the names of maqams and traditional genres. Alireza Mashayekhi, the first Iranian composer of electronic music, named his first piece "Shur," the name of the first dastgah of the radif. Another piece of his, for computer and flute, is named "Mahur," although its sound has only the vaguest similarity to that dastgah.

In some Middle Eastern nations, the appropriateness of musical activity came into focus again after the 1979 revolution in Iran, when public musical performance—especially by women—was outlawed for several years and continued to be rigorously controlled into the twenty-first century. More radical prohibitions were exercised by the Taliban government of Afghanistan in the 1990s. But the first years of the twenty-first century saw, in the context of political and social reform and the easing of restrictions, a vigorous resurgence of traditional musical life in Iran, Afghanistan, and Azerbaijan. For example, the government of Iran has encouraged the development of Persian as well as Western classical (but not popular) musics, permitting concerts and tours and sponsoring research and attempts at preservation. Music is a subject of intense discussion in the Middle Eastern artistic and intellectual circles, the issues of debate including the concept of authenticity, the recovery and preservation of older folk and classical traditions, the participation of female musicians, and the desirability or avoidance of musical modernization and Westernization.

✔●— **Study** and **Review**
on **mymusiclab.com**

SUMMARY

In this chapter we have encountered the Middle East as a region that encompasses a large, diverse geographical and cultural area and is generally known as the heartland of Arab and Islamic cultures. We've learned a great deal about the musical characteristics that animate the region. Thus, although diverse,

Middle Eastern music generally is highly improvised, with a single melody played by all instruments simultaneously. We've taken several excursions into the musical life of the Middle East and discovered that both vocal and instrumental music is generally highly ornamented, featuring trills, glissandos, or short secondary notes. Although the primary instrument within the region is the oud (a type of lute), vocal music predominates. The most common musical form, moreover, is the suite, within which a grouping of individual pieces and maqams are used as the basis of all melodic creation.

Importantly, we also learned that the best music is thought to inspire a trancelike, higher experience of life. This is a musical ideal deeply connected to religious belief, and we spent some time thinking about the significant role of Islam in society and in musical life throughout the region. Socially, a strict hierarchy is observed between types of music and performers, with talented amateur musicians usually coming from a higher social class. As we have seen, professional or popular musicians are typically not viewed as highly as are talented amateurs. Though this chapter has necessarily left a great deal of the musical life of the Middle East unexplored, the excursions included here point to the rich and diverse range of musical performances and the many ideas about music that continue to animate the region's musical life. As such, this chapter is offered as but a starting point for future encounters with and additional excursions within the music of the Middle East.

BIBLIOGRAPHY

Middle Eastern Music as a Whole V. Danielson, S. Marcus, and D. Reynolds, *The Middle East* (*Garland Encyclopedia of World Music*, vol. 6. New York: Routledge, 2002); Kristina Nelson, *The Art of Reciting the Qur'an* (Austin: University of Texas Press, 1985); Harold S. Powers, ed., "Symposium on the Status of Traditional Art Musics in Muslim Nations," *Asian Music* 12/1 (1980); Owen Wright, *The Modal System of Arab and Persian Music A.D. 1250–1300* (London: Oxford University Press, 1978); Hans Engel, *Die Stellung des Musikers im arabisch-islamischen Raum* (Bonn: Verlag fur systematische Musikwissenchaft, 1987); Amnon Shiloah, *The Dimension of Music in Islamic and Jewish Culture* (Brookfield, VT: Ashgate, 1993); Amnon Shiloah, *Jewish Musical Traditions* (Detroit, MI: Wayne State University Press, 1992); Amnon Shiloah, *Music in the World of Islam: A Socio-Cultural Study* (Aldershot, England: Scolar Press, 1995); Amnon Shiloah, *The Theory of Music in Arabic Writings c. 900–1900* (Munich: Henle, 1979); William P. Malm, *Music Cultures of the Pacific, the Near East, and Asia*, 2nd ed. (Englewood Cliffs, NJ: Prentice Hall, 1977), Chap. 3; Peter Manuel, *Popular Musics of the Non-Western World* (New York; Oxford University Press, 1988), Chaps. 5 and 6; Lois Ibsen Al-Faruqi, "Music, Musicians, and Muslim Law" in *Asian Music* 17, no. 1, 1985, pp. 3–36.

Iran Ella Zonis, *Classical Persian Music: An Introduction* (Cambridge, MA: Harvard University Press, 1973); Bruno Nettl and others, *The Radif of Persian Music: Studies* in *Structure and Cultural Context* (Champaign, IL:

Elephant & Cat, 1987); Stephen Blum, "Persian Folksong in Meshhed (Iran), 1969," *Yearbook of the International Folk Music Council* (1974); Hormoz Farhat, *The Dastgah Concept in Persian Music* (Cambridge, UK: Cambridge University Press, 1990); Jean During and others, *The Art of Persian Music* (Washington, DC: Mage Publishers, 1991); DariushTala'i, *Traditional Persian Art Music: The Radif of Mirza Abdallah* (Costa Mesa, CA: Mazda Publishers, 2000).

Arab Music   Dalia Cohen and Ruth Katz, *Palestinian Arab Music: A Maqām Tradition in Practice* (Chicago: University of Chicago Press, 2006); Amnon Shiloah, *Music in the World of Islam* (Detroit: Wayne State University Press, 1995); Lois Ibsen al-Faruqi, *An Annotated Glossary of Arabic Musical Terms* (Westport, CT: Greenwood, 1981); Jürgen Elsner, *Der Begriff Maqam in Aegypten in neuerer Zeit* (Leipzig: Deutscher Verlag fur Musik, 1973); Henry George Farmer, *History of Arabian Music to the XIIIth Century* (London: Luzac, 1929); Habib Hassan Touma, *The Music of the Arabs* (Portland, OR: Amadeus Press, 1996); Earle H. Waugh, *The Munshidin of Egypt: Their World and Their Song* (Columbia: University of South Carolina Press, 1989); Virginia Danielson, *The Voice of Egypt: Umm Kulthum, Arabic Song, and Egyptian Society in the Twentieth Century* (Chicago: University of Chicago Press, 1997); A. J. Racy, *Making Music in the Arab World* (Cambridge: Cambridge University Press, 2004).

Afghanistan and Central Asia   Hiromi Lorraine Sakata, *Music in the Mind* (Kent, OH: Kent State University Press, 1983); Mark Slobin, *Music in the Culture of Northern Afghanistan* (Tucson, AZ: Viking Fund Publications in Anthropology, 1976); John Baily, *Music of Afghanistan* (Cambridge, UK: Cambridge University Press, 1988); Theodore Levin, *The Hundred Thousand Fools of God: Musical Travel in Central Asia* (Bloomington: Indiana University Press, 1996).

Israel   Amy Horowitz, *Mediterranean Israeli Music and the Politics of the Aesthetic* (Detroit: Wayne State University Press, 2010); Benjamin Brinner, *Playing Across a Divide: Israeli-Palestinian Musical Encounters* (New York: Oxford University Press, 2009); Motti Regev and Edwin Seroussi, *Popular Music and National Culture in Israel* (Berkeley: University of California Press, 2004); Eric Werner, *A Voice Still Heard: The Sacred Songs of the Ashkenazic Jews* (University Park: Pennsylvania State University Press, 1976); Philip V. Bohlman and Mark Slobin, eds., "Music in the Ethnic Communities of Israel," Special Issue of *Asian Music* 17/2 (Spring/Summer 1986); Philip V. Bohlman, *The Land Where Two Streams Flow: Music in the German-Jewish Community of Israel* (Urbana: University of Illinois Press, 1989); Robert Fleisher, *Twenty Israeli Composers: Voices of a Culture* (Detroit, MI: Wayne State University Press, 1997).

Turkey   Laurence Picken, *Folk Music Instruments of Turkey* (London: Oxford University Press, 1975); Karl Signell, *Makam: Modal Practice in Turkish Art Music* (Seattle, WA: Asian Music Publications, 1977); Anders Hammarlund, Tord Olsson, Elisabeth Özdalga, Eds., *Sufism, Music and Society in Turkey and the Middle East* (Istanbul: Curzon Press, 2001); Béla Bartók, *Turkish Folk Music from Asia Minor* (Princeton, NJ: Princeton University Press, 1976); Martin Stokes, *The Arabesk Debate: Music and Musicians in Modem Turkey* (Oxford: Oxford University Press, 1992); Walter Feldman, *Music of the Ottoman Empire* (Berlin: Intercultural Institute for Traditional Music, 1996).

DISCOGRAPHY

Iran   *A Persian Heritage* (Nonesuch H-72060; 1974); *Tradition Classique de l'Iran: Le Tar* (Harmonia Mundi, France HM 1031; 1980); *Iranian Dastgah*, UNESCO Collection Musical Sources (Philips 6586-005; 1971); *Iran*. 2 disks UNESCO Collection: A Musical Anthology of the Orient (Barenreiter Musicaphon BM 30 L 2004; ca. 1965); *The Kamkars: Nightingale with a Broken Wing* (Womad Select WSCDOO9); *Musique Iranienne* [D. Chemirani, M. Kiani, D. Tala'i] (Harmonia Mundi HMA 190391); *Majid Kiant: Santur* (Ethnic B 6756); *Radif: The Integral Repertory of Persian Art Music*, Dariush Tala'i, setaro 5 CDs (AI Sur ALCD 116-120, 1992).

Arab Nations   *Iraq: Ud Classique Arabe par Munir Bashir* (Ocora OCR 63: 1983); *Arabian Music: Maqam*, UNESCO Collection Musical Sources (Philips 6586-0006; 1971); *Taqlisim: The Art of Improvisation in Arabic Music* (Lyrichord LLST 7374; ca. 1984); *The Music of Arab Americans: A Retrospective Collection* (Rounder CD 1122); *Om Kalsoum (Enregistrement Public) Lesa Faker* (Sono Cairo 115); *Mystical Legacies: Ali Jihad Racy Perfonns Music of the Middle East* (Lyrichord LYRCD 7437).

Turkey   *Musik aus der Türkei*, 2 disks (Museum Collection Berlin-West MC1; ca. 1985); *Turkey; An Anthology of the World's Music* (Anthology AST 4003; 1971); *Turkish Village Music* (Nonesuch H-72050; ca. 1969); *The Necdet Yasir Ensemble: Music of Turkey* (Music of the World CDT 128); *Archives des la musique turque* (Ocora C 560082, 1995); *Turquie: Musiques traditionelles vivantes* (Ocora HM 57, 1986); *Musik aus der* Türkei (Museum Collection, Berlin-West LP1, 1985); One *Truth: Omar Faruk Tekbilek* (World Class 11309-2, 1999).

Other Areas   Heritage: *Authentic Songs of Ambience and Ritual from the Musical Heritage of Jewish Communities in Israel* (CBS 63437; ca. 1970); *In the Shrine of the Heart* (Smithsonian Folkways 07470; 2010); *When the Soul is Settled: Music of Iraq* (SFW40533; 2006); *The Silk Road: A Musical Caravan* (SWF 40438; 2002) *Jewish Music*, UNESCO Collection Musical Sources (Philips 6586 001; 1971); *Afghanistan: An Anthology of the World's Music* (Anthology AST 4001; 1969); *Azerbaijani Mugam*, UNESCO Collection Musical Sources (Philips 6586 027; 1975); *Anthologie du Mugham d'Azerbaidjan*, vols. 1 and 2. (Maison des Cultures du Monde, Inedit *W260012J15.*); *Turkmenistan: La musique des bakhshy/Music of the Bakhshy* (Archives intemationales de musique populaire, Geneva CD-651); *Khaled, King of Rai* (NYC Music NYCD1221-2).

The Music of China

ISABEL K.F.WONG

INTRODUCTION

Today's China is the product of more than four thousand years of interaction with many other civilizations around the globe, receiving contributions from these civilizations and in turn enriching them. The population of the People's Republic of China (PRC), established in 1949, exceeds 1.3 billion and includes some 56 officially recognized ethnic groups, known as "nationalities" (*minzu*). Among these, the Han nationality is the largest and is, in fact, the world's largest ethnic group; it comprises more than 93 percent of the country's population. Other major nationalities include the Zhuang, Mongolian, Manchu, Tibetan, and a large group of nationalities who are followers of Islam: the Hui, Uyghur, Kazak, Tartar, Kirgiz, Tajik, and Uzbek, to name a few. Among the Muslim groups the Hui and Uyghur are the largest. The ancestors of the Hui were Arabian, Persian, Central Asian, and Mongolian Muslim merchants, militia, and officials, who first settled in northwest China from the seventh to the fourteenth centuries and later spread all over China. The Uyghur (meaning "united" or "allied") are one of the

ancient Turkic people, who were originally nomads and around the sixth century settled as farmers in what is today's Xinjiang Uyghur Autonomous Region of the PRC, as well as in central Asian countries such as Kazakhstan, Kyrgyzstan, and Uzbekistan. The Uyghur already had high culture and written language in the fifth century. They first practiced Buddhism and served as important transmitters of this religion and concomitant Indic civilization to China prior to the tenth century CE; thereafter, however, they were converted to Islam.

Among the 55 minority nationalities, only the Hui and Manchu use the Han language (Chinese, or *putuaghua*, meaning the national tongue, and known in the West as Mandarin). The others speak their own languages: twenty-nine groups use languages in the Sino-Tibetan language family, and they live in central, south, and southwest China; ten groups use languages in the Altaic language family, and they live in northeast and northwest China; in addition, some other groups speak Indo-European languages. Often, the various minority groups speak each other's languages, as well as the Han language. Tajiks, Uzbeks, and Tartars speak Uyghur, a Turkic language, for instance.

✳ Explore
Learning Objectives on
mymusiclab.com

✳ Explore
*a map of China on the
Interactive Globe* on
mymusiclab.com

BEIJING

Beijing, meaning "capital (*jing*) in the north (*bei*)" is a municipality that serves as the capital of the PRC and hence as its administrative, political, and cultural center. However, prior to the establishment of the PRC in 1949, Beijing had served as the capital city for three dynasties: the Yuan dynasty (1206–1368), established by the invading Mongols; the Ming dynasty (1368–1644), established by the Han, who replaced the Mongols; and the Qing dynasty (pronounced "ching"; 1644–1911), established by the invading Manchu, who destroyed the Ming forces. Yet, first-time visitors to Beijing today who expect to see an ancient city may be surprised to find a brash and modern metropolis crisscrossed by many freeways and flyovers and spiked with high-rises. Between the swaths of concrete and glass, however, visitors may still find some old temples, drum and bell towers, and remnants of traditional quadrangle courtyard housing complexes known as *si he yuan* (four buildings surrounding a courtyard) hidden in old alleyways known by the Mongolian term *hutong*. And certainly, modern visitors to Beijing will visit the grandest remnant of all, the imperial palace of the Ming and Qing dynasties known as the Forbidden City, because common people were forbidden to enter it unless summoned by the emperor. The Forbidden City, which occupies more than three square miles and consists of nearly a hundred grand pavilions with yellow tile roofs, is situated at the central axis of old Beijing. For today's modern dwellers of a much expanded Beijing, the Forbidden City is still regarded as the city's cardinal point.

Just to the north of the city, within a day's trip, visitors can visit the Great Wall (*chang cheng*) nearly 3,000 miles long and extending from east to west China. Begun in the Warring States period (435–221 BCE), the Great Wall was completed by the first king of the Qin dynasty (pronounced "chin"), who reigned during 221–209 BCE. In the subsequent Han dynasty (206 BCE–220 CE), the Great Wall was extended further west. Part of the Han dynasty wall still exists in Gansu province in the west. Most of the Great Wall north of Beijing, where most of today's tourists go, was reconstructed in the Ming period.

Despite its long presence as a capital city for various Chinese dynasties, Beijing is a latecomer in Chinese history. Earlier capitals—Chang'an (today's Xi'an, in Shanxi province) and Luoyang (in Henan province) for the Han and Tang dynasties (618–905 CE) and Kaifeng (in Henan province) for the northern Song dynasties (960–995 CE)—are all situated in north-central China west of Beijing. Prior to the thirteenth century, Beijing was but an insignificant trading center in the north for Mongols, Koreans, and local Chinese people. Its predominance began in the mid-thirteenth century with the formation of Mongol China (Yuan dynasty) under Genghis Khan (c. 1162–1227) and later his grandson Kublai Khan (1215–1294), who took control of the city in 1264 and established it as his capital. Marco Polo (fl. 1254–1324), the Venetian who had worked in Beijing under the Mongol government in the Yuan dynasty, reported that the city had many merchants from all over the world. According to him, a thousand merchants daily arrived in Beijing with camel or donkey carts laden with gemstones, spices, and incense. On their return, they carried with them precious cargos of silk, tea, and porcelain. This international commerce made Beijing very wealthy and cosmopolitan.

Beijing's wealth came from the city's position, beginning in the thirteenth century, as the terminus of the Silk Road, the name given to the ancient caravan trade routes by a German geographer in the 1870s. These routes were first developed by an emperor of the Han dynasty to bring China's capital, Chang'an, in the center of the country, into contact with Central Asian kingdoms (many of which were founded by the ancestors of the Uyghur people), and ultimately several great East-West trade routes joined the many Uyghur oasis cities along the northern and southern rims of the Taklamakan Desert, continuing on to the Middle East and ultimately reaching the Mediterranean.

More than just a series of trade routes, the Silk Road was also an ancient superhighway for cultural exchange. Manicheanism (an early form of Christianity originating in present-day Syria) and Buddhism (originating in India) came to China along the Silk Road. Through it, music and musical instruments and dance from India and the Middle East also came to China. For example, the popular plucked string instrument known as the *pipa* was imported to Tang China from Kucha in today's Xinjiang Autonomous Region of the PRC.

Though today the Silk Road frequently serves as a popular metaphor for East-West cultural exchange (for example, cellist YoYo Ma's Silk Road Project), it no longer functions as the main trade route connecting China with the rest of the world. Beijing, however, continues to be one of several important hubs for international travel and trade, where hundreds of international diplomats, tourists, and businesspeople arrive daily.

Beijing continues to be a cosmopolitan city in a contemporary way. For example, many Western-style nightclubs and bars are found around the city featuring the latest DJs flown in from the West and Japan to cater to an international clientele living in Beijing. Concerts of classical Western music and jazz are a regular feature in Beijing's cultural scene, and appearances on the Beijing concert stage by internationally renowned musicians such as YoYo Ma and Itzhak Perlman are by no means rare. Furthermore, the city boasts two fine music academies. One of them, the Central Conservatory of Music, regularly produces many international award-winning string and piano players and opera singers. For example, the pianist Lang Lang, internationally popular—and perhaps controversial—for his flamboyant virtuosity, is a product of the Central Conservatory of Music, from which he went on to continue his studies at the Curtis Institute of Music in Philadelphia. Less-glamorous career opportunities for students of the Conservatory are offered by the many tourist hotels who desire to create an elegant atmosphere with background music for their guests.

In terms of demography, Beijing is a microcosm of China. Its inhabitants come from every one of the twenty-one provinces of China. People from virtually every of one of the fifty-six nationalities are also well represented. Today's visitors to Beijing can taste many different kinds of cuisine and snacks not only of the Han majority but of other minority nationalities as well. For example, several restaurants in Beijing serve typical Uyghur food, such as lamb kabob,

Read *about the establishment of the Silk Road* on **mymusiclab.com**

Ensemble of Uyghur musicians performing in a restaurant in Urüthe capital city of Xinjiang Uyghur Autonomous Region of China. *Source:* Charles Capwell

flat bread called *nan*, and a delicious *pulao* rice dish mixed with lamb and carrot. A restaurant I enjoy going to in the northwestern part of the city frequently has performances by Uyghur musicians and dancers from Kasghar (or Kashe) of the Xinjiang Uyghur Autonomous Region.

Beijing also has a sizable Mongolian population, and more than 200 of the best musicians from the Inner Mongolian Autonomous Region currently reside in Beijing. Whenever I am in Beijing, I often join my friend, Professor Chogjin, in visiting a Mongolian nightclub, where we can listen to both traditional and popular music performed by these musicians while enjoying a bottle of strong Mongolian liquor with some tasty snacks.

Among the musical attractions of contemporary Beijing is **Peking Opera**. Indeed, a visit to a performance of Peking Opera has become a regular feature for organized group tours to Beijing, together with a dinner of the famous Peking duck. Big tour groups are likely to be taken to the Liyuan Theater (Pear Garden, or Liyuan, is a metaphor for theater). Built inside a modern tourist hotel situated south of the Forbidden City in an area called the Xuanwu district, which was the birthplace of Peking Opera, the Liyuan Theater has an audience capacity of 600 and a modern proscenium stage, but its seating arrangement is modeled after that of traditional Chinese theaters with square tea tables surrounded by several seats facing the stage. Tea and snacks such as peanuts and watermelon seeds are served, in keeping with long-established custom. The usual program for an international audience consists of several scenes with acrobatic displays and mock fighting, but very little singing, which is one of the most important elements of Peking Opera. But because the acrobatic displays are so spectacular in Peking Opera, they provide an attractive introduction to this many-faceted and sophisticated theater.

PEKING OPERA (JINGJU THEATER)

The main type of Chinese popular musical theater that first emerged in the Chinese capital Beijing (Peking) in the later eighteenth century.

When a performance troupe from Beijing, led by China's foremost Peking Opera actor Mr. Mei Lanfang, toured San Francisco, Chicago, New York, and Washington, D.C., in the early twentieth century, reporters named the theatrical style Peking Opera. In China, however, this theater is known as **jingju**, that is, theater of the capital. First formulated in the capital city around the mid-eighteenth century, this theater drew its musical and dramatic elements from several older theaters that were current in Beijing at that time but were first developed in other parts of China. After several decades of performing in Beijing, the actors of these theaters from outside Beijing learned from one another, and after a period of such cross-fertilization, a new theater emerged, which is what we know as jingju today. At first, jingju was shunned by the Han educated class because of its popular origin and its lack of sophistication, but the common people in Beijing took to it right away because of the liveliness of its plots—which are presented in easy-to-understand vernacular language—and the exciting rhythmic drive provided by a battery of percussion that includes drums and clapper, gongs, and cymbals. Soon jingju also gained the favor of the Manchu imperial household, particularly its female members, and this patronage by rulers of the Qing dynasty gave much prestige to jingju and helped to overcome the disdain of the Han intellectual class. With the active participation of educated Han and Manchu men to remold jingju into a more sophisticated theater, it soon gained a dominant position not only in Beijing but also in other parts of China. For more than a hundred years jingju dominated the national theater until the advent of the Cultural Revolution (1966–1976), a complicated, xenophobic, and ultimately ruinous period in modern Chinese history when a group of radicals—encouraged by the late chairman of the PRC, Mao Zedong—ravaged China with continuous and violently destructive political campaigns. This is not the place to discuss the Cultural Revolution; suffice it to say that jingju—together with many other traditional musical genres—was almost destroyed during this period because it was considered to be the cultural product of an old and discredited society. The musicians, actors, and producers connected with these old cultural products became objects of persecution, and many were killed or committed suicide. Although jingju was not completely destroyed by the Cultural Revolution, the end result of its having being silenced for ten years was that the generation who grew up during that period were never exposed to it and hence were totally ignorant of it. Without a knowledgeable audience today, jingju's chances of survival have been greatly weakened.

In 1978, a new, more rational leadership took control of the government, immediately eradicated most of the radical policies, and restored stability to Chinese society. To save China from the danger of bankruptcy brought about by the policies of the Cultural Revolution, the new leadership encouraged foreigners to invest in China by establishing business concerns and manufacturing enterprises. These policies, still in effect today some thirty-five years after the Cultural Revolution, have transformed China, into the world's second-largest and fastest-growing economy. Culturally, this new leadership advocated a

JINGJU

Chinese term for Peking Opera. It means "theater of the capital."

policy of diversity and encouraged a revival of many of the venerable traditions discarded by the radicals, including jingju. This open-door policy has ushered in not only foreign investments but foreign culture as well.

Pop songs, particularly those from the United States, Hong Kong (which became an integral part of China in 1997), and Taiwan, were among the first cultural products to arrive in China. The younger generation of Chinese who came of age after the Cultural Revolution (which makes up more than 35 percent of China's current population) are avid consumers of foreign pop culture. Since the early 1990s, however, homegrown Chinese pop songs have begun to take over a significant part of the pop song market. Today, if visitors to Beijing wander into its record stores, they are likely to find only pop song recordings.

So, imagine my surprise during a visit to Beijing in May, 2006, when I wandered into the New Dongan Mall—a huge complex that would not be out of place in St. Paul, Minnesota—and I heard the sound of drum, cymbals, and gongs that reminded me of the percussion music of jingju. I thought to myself: "Could it really be live music? No, it must be a recording." Nonetheless, I followed the source of the sound and found myself in a little teahouse that also sells souvenirs. Poking my head in, I saw a small stage at one end of the shop on which a man was standing and singing an aria of jingju, although he was in simple street dress and not the elaborate makeup and costume used for theatrical performance. On stage right there was an instrumental ensemble made up of bowed and plucked strings and percussion accompanying the singing. I immediately recognized that this was a traditional *qing chang* (singing without staging, costume, and makeup) performance, which usually includes the participation of talented jingju fans. I could not quite believe what I saw and heard in such an unlikely setting, but I hurriedly went inside, found a chair next to a tea table, and joined about twenty other people who were listening attentively.

Soon a woman came to serve me a cup of tea together with a big thermos of hot water for making more tea and a dish of peanuts and asked me to give her 10 yuan (Chinese currency, 10 yuan being equivalent to about US$1.50) as tea money and entrance fee. I settled down to survey my surroundings and noticed a red-colored wooden board on the back of the stage, with two gold-color Chinese characters "*fu*" and "*shou*" (meaning, respectively, happiness and longevity) engraved on it. A microphone was in the center of the stage, and a half dozen of instrumentalists sat on stage right. Suddenly I heard sounds of enthusiastic applause, as a dignified-looking middle-aged woman stepped onto the stage, followed by a man who carried with him a *jinghu* fiddle, the chief melodic instrument for jingju. As she stepped onto the center of the stage, she pushed away the microphone, walked to the back of the stage, and waited. The jinghu player who was originally among the instrumentalists stood up and deferentially gave his seat to the newly arrived player. I noticed that both the woman and the fiddle player assumed a confident air, and the audience hushed and waited with anticipation.

The fiddle player began an introduction to a jingju aria called *nan ban zi* from the famous jingju excerpt, "*Bawang Bie ji*" ("The King's Farewell to his Concubine"), the signature aria of the famous jingju actor Mei Lanfang, who was a consummate female impersonator for the *dan* role (principal female character). As the fiddle introduction came to a certain point, the woman singer walked toward the front of the stage in elegant, mincing steps typical of the dan role while raising one hand expressively and started to sing. The vocal melody was full of elaborate and subtle ornaments punctuated with irregular syncopated rhythm, but the fiddle matched the intricacy of the vocal line and the articulation of the singer faithfully; periodically the vocal part came to a rest, and the fiddle provided brief interludes until the vocal part resumed. I then noticed that the teahouse had become full—standing room only—and all listened with rapt attention. When the rendition finally came to a close, the audience broke into loud applause and called out "*Hao!*," an equivalent of "Bravo!" in Chinese.

Realizing that the performers must be well known, I leaned over to my neighbor and asked: "Who are the performers?"

"Don't you know?" he replied. "She is a famous professional jingju actress of the dan role, now in retirement, and the fiddle player has been her personal accompanist for years!"

"Who are the usual performers here, then?" I inquired.

"Anybody who loves jingju and can sing its arias or play instruments. Most are just amateurs who are fans of jingju, but occasionally professionals come too, like today. The gathering occurs daily here from 3:00 to 6:00 P.M., and the venue is provided by the city government, which also pays salaries for a group of instrumentalists and for two service persons to take care of the place and audience. This place was just opened six months ago, and I really hope it can be maintained."

The next singer to step onto the stage was a middle-aged man who told the instrumentalists what he wanted to sing, and then the fiddle began an introductory passage. Somewhat bashful and timid at first, he soon warmed up and starting to sing with gusto, if not with expertise. The audience laughed and encouraged him by clapping the rhythm with him; when he got stuck with an intricate rhythmic passage, someone from the audience sang the passage aloud to help him out.

The next person on stage was a fashionably dressed woman with dyed blond hair, wearing high heels. When she opened her mouth to sing, out came a powerful masculine low voice, and I realized that she was a practitioner of the principal old male role called *lao sheng* (old man), and she was good. So the audience rewarded her with "Hao!" In jingju, the gender of the performer is not necessarily the gender of the character he or she portrays.

I stayed for a couple of hours. The teahouse was noisy not only because of the percussion but also because people talked loudly with one another, as it was also a place to socialize. Most of the audience smoked, and cell phones rang incessantly. But I was thankful that I had the chance to experience a piece of old Beijing in New Dongan Mall.

MUSIC OF THE HAN NATIONALITY

Traditional music of the Han nationality includes many types of instrumental music (solo and ensemble), musical narratives, musical theaters, and folk songs of different regions. In the following sections I will discuss a few representative types: music for a seven-stringed zither called the *qin* (pronounced "chin"), one of China's most venerable instruments; music for a four-stringed lute called *pipa*, an instrument imported to China through the Silk Road; and finally, music of the jingju theater.

THE QIN AND ITS MUSIC

The qin is the most highly regarded of Chinese musical instruments because of its antiquity and its rich legacy of associations with scholars and poets. It is made from a hollowed board approximately four feet long and three inches deep with a convex curve to its top. The qin has seven strings of varying thickness stretched over the entire length of the board. Its body is painted with layers of dark lacquer, and although it has neither frets nor bridges, it does have thirteen studs or position markers called *hui*, which are made of mother-of-pearl or other semiprecious material and are embedded along the outer edge of the instrument to indicate finger positions for stopping the strings (i.e., pressing a string against the body of the instrument to shorten its length and thereby change its pitch). The open strings are usually tuned C–D–F–G–A–c–d. The flat, smooth underside of the instrument has two openings called "sound pools," and it is usually engraved with the name of the owner and the given name of the instrument, indicating that the qin is a highly personalized instrument.

Qin playing involves various ways of plucking the strings with the thumb, index, middle, and ring fingers of the right hand (the little finger, which is called *jinzhi*, or "forbidden finger," is not used) and stopping them with the four fingers of the left hand (the little finger is again not used). Using these techniques, a qin player can produce many different types of ornaments, including vibrato (slight rising and falling in pitch), portamenti (slides from one pitch to another), and harmonics (bell-like tones produced when a string vibrates in segments rather than as a single length).

Around the sixth century CE, detailed explanations were written describing the techniques required for producing each and every sound on the qin. This kind of notation, called tablature, is known as **wenzipu** (prose tablature). Later, in the Tang dynasty (618–906 CE), a new type of tablature was created that consisted of clusters of abbreviated symbols derived from Chinese characters; these specified the string number, the stopping positions, and the hand, finger, and direction of plucking. This tablature is called **jianzipu** (abbreviated-character tablature), and its evolved form is still in use today.

Qin. *Source:* Dave King/Dorling Kindersley/DK Images

Throughout Chinese history, the qin has been associated with sages and scholars (male only), giving it a special place in Chinese life and culture. The earliest mention of the qin is found in the *Shujing* (Book of History, compiled c. sixth century BCE). Learning the qin was already a requirement for scholars and gentlemen before the third century BCE. At that time, however, the qin was employed primarily to accompany poetry recitation, as a member of the large orchestra for the court ceremonial music known as **yayue** (elegant music), or to form a duet with the *se* (a twenty-stringed plucked zither). A duo of qin and se symbolized a harmonious spousal relationship or friendship. After the Han dynasty (206 BCE–290 CE), as ceremonial music at court gradually declined, the qin emerged as both a solo instrument and the accompanying instrument for chamber vocal genres. During the end of the Han period and thereafter, the literati initiated the scholarly study of the qin and wrote compositions specifically for the solo qin, and thus its status and prestige were enhanced. In the subsequent periods of the Sui and Tang dynasties and the Five Dynasties (581–618, 618–907, 907–960), the playing of qin and qin scholarship were restricted to court circles only; outside the court, the qin was neglected.

Not until the Song dynasty (960–1027) was there a renaissance of qin music. An ideological system for the qin was developed by fusing Confucian philosophy with Daoist (Taoist) and Buddhist mystical symbolism. According to this ideology, the playing of the qin is an act of contemplation, self-purification, and self-regulation. Hence, it should be played in private, amid charming scenery, under pine trees and beside running creeks, in the privacy of one's garden, or in the cloister of one's own library with incense burning.

The qin vogue among the scholars reached its height in the Ming dynasty (1368–1644), when numerous treatises and handbooks were printed. But in the early twentieth century, rapid social change brought about a sharp decline in interest in the instrument. The number of talented performers dropped to just a handful, and scholarship came to a virtual halt. After the establishment of the People's Republic in 1949, under government encouragement, research in qin music and its history was revived, particularly during the 1950s. In recent years, the qin has been brought into the new context of the modern concert stage, and with the appearance of a younger generation of qin virtuosi, interest in the qin has grown among members of the educated circle. Among the general populace, however, the qin, with its associations with past literary and philosophical traditions, is too exclusive and inaccessible and has therefore been largely neglected.

The earliest extant qin manuscript, dating from the Tang dynasty, contains the composition "*Youlan*" ("Orchids in a Secluded Valley"), which is written in prose tablature. The first printed qin handbook, the *Shenqi mipu* (*The Mysterious Secret Handbook*), compiled by Prince Zhu Quan of Ming, appeared in 1425 and was followed by numerous other woodblock handbooks, together comprising more than three thousand compositions notated in the abbreviated-character tablature. Only about eighty pieces, however, have survived in the oral performance tradition.

In qin handbooks, tempo is indicated by terms such as "Slow down," or "Speed up," but durational symbols are totally absent. These omissions indicate the importance placed on oral tradition and the realization and interpretation

YAYUE
Literally meaning "elegant music," it was Chinese court music of imperial China.

Read
about the chronology of Chinese dynasties on **mymusiclab.com**

of the music by the performing artist. A process of reconstructing ancient pieces from qin tablature through the aid of oral tradition is called *dapu* (literally, "to obtain from the notation"). This process of reconstruction (i.e., realizing the qin tablature into actual sounds by a qin player) has become a venerable tradition. Qin meters vary among free meter, duple meter, and sometimes triple meter, often within the same piece.

Qin notation is very difficult to read, even for those who are literate and cultivate their skills, and this contributes to its exclusive nature. In the famous eighteenth-century novel *The Story of the Stone* (also known as *The Dream of the Red Chamber*) by Cao Xueqin (d. 1763), a passage conveys this well. This greatest of Chinese novels depicts in meticulous detail life in a wealthy and influential family, in particular the love and fate of the hero, Jia Baoyu, and his cousin, Lin Daiyu, two extremely talented, cultivated, and precocious teenagers. In Chapter 86, Baoyu seeks Daiyu out in her quarters and learns something about qin tablature and its philosophy, although his wry concluding comment seems to indicate he takes it all with a grain of salt:

> Daiyu was sitting at her desk reading. Baoyu approached her, saying cheerfully, "I see that you left Grandmother's place early." Daiyu responded with a smile and said, "Well, you wouldn't speak to me, so why should I stay any longer?"
>
> "There were so many people there, I didn't have a chance." As he replied he tried to see what she was reading, but he couldn't recognize a single word. Some looked like the character for "azalea," some looked like the character for "hazy." Another had the radical "big" on the left, the character for "nine" next to it, and a large hook underneath it with the character for "five" written inside. . . .
>
> Baoyu was curious and puzzled. He said, "Sister, I am more and more impressed by you. You must be reading a secret Book of Heaven!"
>
> Daiyu couldn't help laughing. "Here is an educated man! Don't tell me you have never seen a musical score!"
>
> "Of course I have," he replied, "but I don't know any of those characters. Why don't you teach me to read some of it?…For example, what do you make of this character 'big' with that long hook and a character 'five' stuck in the middle?"
>
> With a laugh Daiyu replied, "This character 'big' and the character 'nine' mean that you press on the ninth stud with your left thumb, and this big hook with the character 'five' inside means that you hook inward the fifth string with your right hand. This whole cluster is not a word; it stands for a musical note. There is really nothing to it. You have also many kinds of left-hand techniques such as the quick vibrato, broad vibrato, upward glide, downward glide, trill, quick glide, and so forth."
>
> Baoyu was hopping with joy, saying, "Come on, dear sister, since you know so much about it, why don't we try it out?"
>
> "It is said that the zither is synonymous with the word for self-restraint. The ancients intended it to be used for discipline, for tranquilizing one's emotions, and for suppressing excessive and frivolous desires. In playing the zither, you must select a quiet and secluded place. It could be in the top story of a building, in the forest among the rocks, at a mountain precipice, or at the edge of the water. The weather should be calm, with a light breeze or a clear moon. You have to burn some incense and meditate for a while….
>
> "As to the performance itself, the fingering and the intonation have to be good enough…the position of your heart should be in a line with the fifth stud on the instrument….Now you are ready, bodily, and spiritually."

LISTENING GUIDE

"LU SHUI" ("FLOWING WATER")

GO TO **www.mymusiclab.com for the Automated Listening Guide** CDI • Track 11/Download Track 11

Performed by Professor Wu Wenguang on the qin

"Liu Shui" ("Flowing Water") is a famous composition for the qin. The performer is Professor Wu Wenguang of the China Conservatory of Music in Beijing, the foremost qin player in China today. Wu Wenguang studied the qin under his late father, the famous qin master Professor Wu Jinglue, and his performance is based on his father's 1960 interpretation of the tablature notated in a handbook dated 1876, entitled *Tian Wen Ge Qinpu (Tian Wen Ge Studio Qin Handbook)*. It is a rhapsodic piece of descriptive music portraying a waterfall cascading from a mountaintop, falling through various levels of rock, and then becoming a rapids, eventually running out to the sea.

The composition of "Flowing Water" is attributed to Boya, a great qin master who lived during the Spring and Autumn period (770–476 BCE). Boya's friend, Zhong Ziqi, was an attentive and imaginative listener to Boya's music. As the story goes, when Boya played the piece "Flowing Water" and conjured up the scene of a high mountain in his mind, Zhong Ziqi right away got the idea and said: "Ah! I am thinking of Mount Tai (China's tallest and most sacred mountain)." When Boya thought of flowing water as he played, Zhong Ziqi echoed his thought and said: "How excellent!—broadly flowing rivers and streams." When Zhong Ziqi died sometime later, Boya felt that nobody could match his understanding of the music he played, and so he broke his qin and never played again. Thus, the deeper meaning of this piece is as a symbol of deep friendship. From this story arose the phrase, *"zhu yin,"* literally meaning "a good friend who understands my music," and it is still popularly used today to signify profound friendship.

TIME	SECTION	MUSICAL EVENTS
0:00–0:49	**Sanqi (introduction):** Listen for the way that the **portamento** is used to glide or slide both small and great distances between pitches. Also notice the delicate quality of the harmonics produced by the qin.	The melody is performed with a lot of portamento. Some pitches are reinforced by the lower octave. This section of the piece is in free rhythm.
0:49–1:15		The melody is rendered with harmonics and in a more regular rhythm.
1:16–1:50	**Rudiao (exposition):** Continue to listen for the way that portamento informs the melody. Also notice the degree to which strums across all of the strings add a rich texture to the performance.	The melody is performed in a faster tempo and with wide, sweeping portamenti.
1:50–2:17		In this passage, the tempo is increased yet again.

2:17–3:31	**Ruman (becoming slower):** Notice the extremes of volume and the density of texture that the qin can produce.	Melody and portamenti are embedded in a strumming accompaniment produced by sweeping across all the strings. This portion of the performance culminates at [3:11], after which the strummed portamenti dissipate in a decrescendo and diminuendo to [3:31].
3:32–3:43		A short passage of harmonics.
3:43–4:11		The performance then returns to the strumming style of [2:17–3:31] and again concludes with energetic strumming.
4:11–4:43	**Weisheng (tail sounds):** Notice the delicacy of the harmonics and their slow decay at the end of this performance.	This final section serves as a conclusion and features harmonics again.

PORTAMENTO
A slide or sweep between two pitches.

Baoyu said, "Can't we just do it for fun? It's next to impossible if we have to go through all that rigmarole!" (Adapted from a translation by Rulan Chao Pian)

Practically all qin compositions have programmatic titles either derived from common poetic and mystical images or alluding to Chinese history or legends. The titles evoke a mood or atmosphere familiar to the Chinese.

A typical qin composition usually contains several sections:

1. *Sanqi* (introduction): Begins slowly in free rhythm. Its function is to introduce the principle notes of the mode used in the piece.
2. *Rudiao* (entering the music, or exposition): The meter is established, and the principal motives of the piece are introduced, which are then varied by means of extension, reduction, and changes in timbre, tempo, and register. This part is usually the longest and musically the most substantial.
3. *Ruman* (becoming slower): The principal motives undergo further rhythmic variation, and modulation to other keys may occur. In some larger compositions, motivic materials occurring in the second part may be restated and reinterpreted here; this is called *fuqi* (restatement).
4. *Weisheng* (tail sounds): A short coda concludes the composition. The coda, always played in harmonics and in a slackening tempo, reiterates the important notes used in the composition (Listen to CD I, 11 for an example of the qin and this compositional structure).

THE *PIPA* AND ITS MUSIC

The *pipa* is a four-stringed, fretted lute with a bent neck and a pear-shaped body. The prototype of this instrument, which had five strings, was imported to China from present-day Kucha (known in ancient China as Qiuci), which was one of the largest of the thirty-six ancient Uyghur kingdoms, and in 91 CE it was under the suzerainty of the Han. By the fourth century, the

Kuchan Kingdom of Qiuci had become an important center for Buddhist learning imported from India, as well as the center for Central Asian trade and Indo-European culture, as trade routes running across the Taklamakan Desert intersected with the Silk Road at Kucha. Today Kucha is still a major town in the Xinjiang Autonomous Region in the PRC.

From numerous written accounts (in both Chinese and Uyghur) and the iconographic evidence found in the frescos of many Buddhist grottos along the Silk Road, we can surmise that the five-stringed pipa—which was held horizontally and played with a *plectrum*—originated in Qiuci (Kucha), from where it traveled east to Han China and west to Persia and Arabia. Because of this, it was often called the Qiuci pipa. By the Sui and the Tang periods (respectively 581–618 and 618–905), when Han China entered one of its most cosmopolitan epochs, music and dance from Qiuci—featuring the pipa either as the principal solo instrument or as a member of an instrumental ensemble—formed an important repertory for refined entertainment at court and in homes of aristocrats and wealthy people. The pipa thus became extremely popular in Tang China, and many noted Qiuci musicians gained employment at court and in the homes of the wealthy. After the five-string Qiuci pipa was adapted in China, it underwent transformation and evolved into a four-stringed instrument, although it was still played with the plectrum. This form of Qiuci-inspired entertainment music, known in China as *yan yue* (banquet entertainment music), was imported to Japan around the Tang period. There it became part of the repertory of Japanese court music known as *gagaku* (elegant music), and the four-stringed pipa, played with a plectrum, also went to Japan at the same time and became known as *biwa*.

After the Tang period, the pipa became an instrument for courtesans who were well trained in music and dance, and because of this, the pipa has been associated with artistic entertainments, gaiety, and romance. In a famous long poem entitled "*Pipa Xing*" ("The Song for the Pipa"), the famous Tang dynasty poet Bo Ju-I (772–846) provided a vivid description of a pipa performance by a courtesan:

Yang Jing holding a pipa.
Source: Chris Stock/Lebrecht Music & Arts

Watch the **Video** *of a pipa player* on **mymusiclab.com**

Pipa Xing (Song of the Pipa)

. . . The lowest string hummed like pouring rain;

The higher strings whispered as lover's pillow talk.

Humming and whispering intermingled

Like the sound of big and small pearls gradually falling into a jade plate.

Sometimes it sounded like liquid chirping of orioles hidden among flowers;

Sometimes it sounded like a brook sobbing sadly running through a sand bank.

A strong sweep across the strings sounded as though they had been broken

And the notes suddenly died down.

The music became a lament expressing the deepest sorrow;

The silence revealed more emotion than the actual sound.

Suddenly it sounded as if a silver vase had broken, and the water gushed forth,

Or as if armored horses and weapons were loudly clashing.

Then, before she laid down her plectrum, she ended the music with one stroke

Sweeping all four strings boldly and making a sound like the rending of silk. . . .

(Translated by Isabel Wong)

Chinese written records show that in subsequent periods until the mid-Ming period (around the fifteenth century), the pipa was still played with a plectrum and held horizontally by the player. It was only since the late fifteenth century that the pipa has been held upright on the player's crossed knees and played with the fingers.

The modern pipa has twenty-three to twenty-five frets placed along the neck and the soundboard of the instrument; the four strings are usually tuned to A–d–e–a, and a complete chromatic scale can be produced. The pipa player employs a wide variety of playing techniques, the most distinctive of which are the following:

- Harmonics
- Tremolo, produced by rapidly and continuously plucking a string with all five fingers consecutively
- Portamento (sliding from note to note), produced by deflection of a string before or after it has been plucked
- Percussive pizzicato, produced when a string is plucked violently enough to cause it to snap against the body of the instrument
- Percussive strumming of all four strings

The music of the pipa, characterized by flexible tempi and frequent alternation between softer and louder passages, encompasses many moods ranging from the contemplative and the lyrical to the heroic and even to the comical. Chinese musicians divide the pipa repertory into two categories according to structure: the "big pieces" and the "small pieces."

"Big pieces" are usually quite long and are of three kinds:

1. Continuous (not divided into sections)
2. Divided into many sections that follow a theme and variation structure with themes derived from preexistent materials
3. Divided into many sections that alternate songlike with percussive material

"Small pieces" are usually quite short, each containing about sixty to one hundred beats or so. Most of these pieces are in sectional form.

Pieces in the traditional pipa repertory are also divided into the *wen* (lyrical) and the *wu* (martial) categories. Wen category pieces are expressive in nature and in a slow or moderate tempo, and they tend to employ various kinds of finger techniques to produce embellishments and microtonal ornaments. Wu category pieces tend to be percussive, loud, and in fast tempo—fast strumming techniques are often employed to produce a martial effect.

Sectional pipa pieces, be they "big" or "small," frequently employ a rondo-variation principle in which basic melodic material returns periodically, but in a more improvisational manner than is usual in the Western rondo or variation form.

Pipa pieces often have programmatic titles, and some of these contain clearly descriptive musical elements directly related to their titles; others, however, are more abstract and have only a poetic relationship to their titles.

Notation for the instrument, again a kind of tablature, combines symbols indicating pitches of the diatonic scale and an additional set of symbols indicating various finger techniques. There are approximately a dozen printed collections of music for the pipa, the earliest of which dates from the early nineteenth century. Prior to that time, music for pipa circulated in manuscripts, some of which still exist today. Notation has always been a secondary aid for the transmission of the repertory, as it exists primarily in oral tradition.

In traditional society, the pipa was usually performed in an intimate surrounding, either in a private banquet or in a teahouse. Nowadays, the pipa continues to be a popular instrument, with many young virtuosi being trained in conservatories, but performances usually take place in a modern concert hall.

WINDS AND STRINGS ENSEMBLE IN SHANGHAI

Shanghai, China's commercial capital, is situated south of Beijing at the mouth of the Yangzi River. Part of modern Shanghai was built by the British in the mid-nineteenth century. Today, Shanghai is starting to take on the chic of Paris, the sophistication of New York, and the futuristic vibes of Tokyo. It already boasts the world's fastest train (a magnetic levitation train that takes less than eight minutes to run the thirty kilometers from the Pudong international airport to the city), the longest underwater pedestrian tunnel (under the Huangpu river), and one of the world's tallest hotels—the 88-story Grand Hyatt. However, in some pockets of Shanghai, traditional modes of life are still common, and traditional kinds of music can still be heard there in appropriate surroundings.

One of these is the chamber ensemble of winds and strings called **Jiangnan sizhu**. Jiangnan, meaning "south of the river," which is the designation for the Yangzi Delta region in southeastern China, of which Shanghai is a part. *Si* literally means "silk," and it denotes stringed instruments because strings used to be made of silk (nowadays they are usually made of steel for greater volume). *Zhu* literally means "bamboo," a material from which some wind instruments are made.

Jiangnan sizhu was formerly a favorite pastime of the gentry and educated classes of the urban centers in the Jiangnan region. People gathered at the many private clubs to play and while away a pleasant afternoon or evening. As a rule, the performers of Jiangnan sizhu are amateurs who play for their own enjoyment. In Shanghai today there are still half a dozen or so Jiangnan sizhu clubs whose members are retired urban workers, some of whom belonged to the gentry class before 1949.

Jiangnan sizhu performances generally take place in neighborhood teahouses. The teahouse where I usually go to listen to Jiangnan sizhu is located in the Square of the Temple of the City God in the Old City of Shanghai, a picturesque area lined with many small shops selling all kinds of traditional wares and souvenirs. The old teahouse, always thronged with people, is an elegant structure built on an artificial lake teeming with goldfish, and it is approached via a zigzag footbridge. It is a hexagonal wooden building of two stories, lacquered with dark-brown paint and has intricate latticework windows open on all sides. It has double-tiered black tile roofs with elongated eaves swooping out in a complex pattern of upturned curves.

There is no entrance fee, but customers are required to pay a modest price for a pot of tea. The performance usually takes place in the afternoon when the players arrive one by one, place their instruments on a big table situated at one side of the teahouse, and then sit around it with the string players and the player of the drum and clapper in an inner circle and the rest in an outer one. The player of the drum and clapper (gu ban) serves as a conductor by beating time, and everybody plays from memory.

There is no formal announcement of the program, nor are there program notes, because the audience is familiar with the small, anonymous repertory, which consists of only about two dozen pieces that all have descriptive titles. The first piece for the afternoon—played by the novices—is always short and slow, and more complex pieces are played as the afternoon progresses. Each piece usually lasts ten minutes or more, and some may be played more than once. After one piece is finished, some players may get up from the table, and others sitting among the customers may come up to join the performers, the most skillful and respected players joining in around 4:30 P.M. to perform pieces that are fast and require greater expertise.

When the novices are not playing, they usually sit around the big table listening to and watching the more skilled players. There is no formal instruction, as learning is entirely by imitation, and when novices are considered ready to play, the more skilled players will give them criticism or suggestions.

Jiangnan sizhu pieces always begin slowly and gradually accelerate, ending in a fast tempo. Although the drum-and-clapper player is supposed to provide the beat for the music, the players typically are not overly concerned with rhythmic exactitude. In addition, all the instruments play together most of the time. The overall fuzzy timbral quality of this purely melodic music is attributable not only to the combination of plucked and bowed strings with winds but also to the fact that they play in a relatively high register and use several slightly different tunings.

When I first heard Jiangnan sizhu music, I could discern no break within a given piece. It seemed to me that, once started, it went on without break until the end. I later found out that every piece is divided into sections, but because the end of a section is always overlapped by the beginning of the next, a piece usually gives the impression of being seamless.

Another characteristic of Jiangnan sizhu is the extensive use of improvised embellishments on the basic melody. Every melodic instrument plays the same basic melody, but each player applies the improvised embellishments according to the conventions of his instrument, creating a complicated texture of **heterophony**, which—like the variations in tuning—adds to the fuzzy or thick quality of the melody. Because of this freedom in adding improvised embellishments, no two performances of one piece are exactly alike, and the more skilled the performers, the greater the differences may be.

One of the most important features of Jiangnan sizhu is the use of a technique of structural expansion known as "**fangman jiahua**" ("making slow and adding flowers"), in which the musical materials are expanded by slowing down the tempo of the original melody, and as the notes of the original melody become further apart temporally, other notes are inserted, or interpolated. The result is a new piece that may have sixteen or more notes corresponding to each note of the original melody.

As I mentioned before, the teahouses where Jiangnan sizhu is performed are always noisy, as the customers chat among themselves or come and go. The players are oblivious to the commotion, and in fact, when some of them are not playing, they also chat with their friends! Jiangnan sizhu, like much other traditional Chinese music of a popular nature, is considered a kind of background music to enhance the ambience of a pleasant social environment (Listen to CD I, 12 to hear an example of Jiangnan sizhu).

THE JINGJU THEATER

At the beginning of this chapter I described a performance of the nonstaged variety of Jingju in a teahouse-gift shop in Beijing. Before the Cultural Revolution, staged performances of Jingju by professional actors used to take place

HETEROPHONY
Two or more performers play the same melody, but with small differences in timing or ornamentation.

FANGMAN JIAHUA
Literally "making slow and adding flowers." A technique through which the tempo is slowed to achieve temporal space between the notes of the melody. This space is then ornamented with additional notes.

LISTENING GUIDE

HUA SAN LIU ("EMBELLISHED THREE-SIX")    GO TO www.mymusiclab.com for the Automated Listening Guide CDI • Track 12/Download Track 12

The beginning and conclusion of the first part of this piece are excerpted.

Instruments include *dizi* (transverse flute); *yangqin* (hammer dulcimer); pipa (four-string, plucked lute); and erhu (two-string fiddle).

0:00–0:28	Introduction: Performed here in free rhythm. The dizi stands out because of its distinctive timbre and greater ornamentation.
0:28–1:33	The melody is now performed in regular meter. Listen for the slight differences in ornamentation and tuning among the different instruments. This excerpt fades out at [1:31–1:33].
1:37–2:05	The second excerpt fades in as the performers are approaching the end of first section of the piece. They are playing at a faster tempo than they had adopted at the outset [0:28–1:33].
2:05–2:46	The dizi jumps to the upper register while the other two instruments continue to play the melody in the usual range. The performers execute a ritard (slowing) just before concluding the first section of the piece.

daily, but nowadays, these performances do not take place often, except as tourist attractions, which nevertheless may help stimulate a revival of the art among native connoisseurs.

As theater, Jingju is a conglomeration of the dramatic presentation of plots using music, speech, stylized gestures and dance movements, acrobatics, mock combat scenes, and fanciful makeup and elaborate costumes. Personages of Jingju are divided into four main categories and their subcategories according to sex, age, social status, and character. Each role type is defined by the costume and makeup the actor wears and the prescribed physical movements of each. All the characters sing, but each employs distinct vocal techniques, timbres, and singing styles.

The four main categories of actors are sheng (male role, divided into old male, young male, and warrior subcategories); dan (female role, divided into old female, young refined female, young flirtatious female, and female warrior subcategories); *jing* (painted face, a rough or heroic male role whose face is painted with intricate colored patterns); and *chou* (a male comic role). The basic musical elements of jingju are arias, heightened speech, and instrumental music.

Instrumental music in jingju has many functions. The first and foremost is to accompany the singing and the physical movements and dance. To an audience familiar with the conventional musical code of jingju, it may also describe a dramatic situation and action, indicate the spatial dimension of the setting, convey the moods and psychological makeup of characters, and provide a soundscape or sound effects connected with a particular dramatic moment. With such musical clues, an educated jingju audience will be able to form a mental picture of the temporal and spatial aspects of the drama and respond to them with appropriate emotion and understanding.

The instrumental ensemble is made up of two components: the melodic, or **wenchang** (civic instrumentation) ensemble, and the percussion, or **wuchang** (military instrumentation) ensemble. In the musical communication of information, the percussion ensemble plays a more important function than the melodic group. The percussion ensemble also provides rhythmical punctuation for movements and singing, and it serves to combine all the discrete elements of a play, musical as well as gestural, into a complete whole.

The percussion ensemble is made up principally of five instruments: *danpigu* (a single-headed drum), *ban* (a paired wooden clapper; danpigu and ban are played by one person, who functions as the conductor), *daluo* (a big gong that produces a falling pitch), *xiaoluo* (a small gong that produces a rising pitch), and *naoba* (a small pair of cymbals). In addition, a few other percussion instruments are used for special effects: *datangu* (a big barrel drum), *xiaotangu* (a small barrel drum), several other gongs and cymbals of different sizes, a *muyu* (a "wooden-fish" slit drum), and a pair of small handbells.

The music of the percussion ensemble includes some sixty conventional rhythmic patterns, each of which is identified by a proper name and a specific syllabic pattern. The five principal instruments are combined in different ways to indicate different kinds of dramatic situations, atmospheres, or moods. The three basic percussion combinations are as follows:

1. A trio made up of the big gong, the small gong, and the cymbal, with the big gong as the principal instrument. This combination is usually employed in scenes of pageantry featuring a big crowd of actors and also in dramatic scenes that require strong emphasis.

2. A duo made up of the cymbal, as the principal instrument, and the small gong. This combination usually accompanies tragic scenes.

3. A small gong solo. This is generally used in scenes of a tranquil or lyrical nature.

Besides these basic combinations, other additional combinations include a duo of the big and small barrel drums (used in acrobatic and fighting scenes), a duo of the small gong and the big cymbal (played in a specific way to indicate underwater and thunder sounds), and so forth. The sixty or so named conventional percussion patterns, each requiring different instrumental combinations and varying tempi, perform many functions. These include indicating entrances and exits of dramatic personages and their social

WENCHANG
The instrumental ensemble in Peking Opera made up of melody instruments.

WUCHANG
The instrumental ensemble in Peking Opera made up of percussion.

✳ **Explore**
the Musical Instruments Gallery on **mymusiclab.com**

👁 **Watch** the **Video**
of Chinese percussion instruments on **mymusiclab.com**

Two Peking Opera actresses (dan roles) in a scene from the famous traditional play, "The Story of the White Snake." *Source:* Lebrecht Music & Arts

Beijing resident Wu Xingshui playing the erhu. *Source:* © Lou Linwei/Alamy

❋ **Explore**
The Musical Instrument Gallery on
mymusiclab.com

👁 **Watch** the **Video**
of a sheng player
on **mymusiclab.com**

KUNQU
Classical Chinese musical drama.

status; emphasizing a word, phrase, or name of a person or place; accompanying fights and battles; and producing special sound effects.

The melodic ensemble features mostly strings and winds, as well as a set of ten small, suspended pitched gongs called the *yunluo*. The strings are the *jinghu* (the leading melodic instrument, a two-stringed bamboo, spike fiddle with a very high and piercing pitch), the *erhu*, the *yue qin* (a four-stringed plucked lute with a round sound box), a *sanxian*, and a *ruan* (a large plucked lute with a round sound box). The winds are the *dizi* transverse flute, the *sheng* (mouth organ), and the big and small *suona* (conical double-reed oboes).

The primary functions of the melodic ensemble are to play introductions and interludes for arias, to double aria melodies, and to play incidental music for dance and miming movements, but the strings and the winds perform somewhat different functions. The strings, with the jinghu *as* their principal instrument, accompany the two main types of arias known as the *xipi* and the *erhuang*, which were derived from some folk predecessors of jingju. In addition, the strings play various incidental pieces—all of which have proper names—to accompany some miming movements such as sweeping, changing clothes, putting on makeup, drinking wine, and walking, as well as to accompany scenes of banqueting and general pageantry, celebration, and dance. Each individual piece of named incidental music has an association with specific dramatic situations and moods, and each requires different playing techniques on the various strings for the production of varying volumes and timbres.

The winds—the dizi and the sheng only, without the suona—sometimes in combination with the sanxian and the erhu, accompany arias in scenes derived from the repertory of the older classical theater called **Kunqu**, another predecessor of the jingju, which uses the dizi as its principal melodic instrument. Kunqu-derived scenes are usually lyrical in nature, and in these scenes the yunluo gong set is also used. The winds are also used to accompany arias derived from folk tunes that have been absorbed into the jingju repertory. Furthermore, the winds play specific named incidental pieces to accompany dances derived from kunqu.

Finally, the big and small suona (oboe) are always used in combination with the percussion ensemble exclusively to accompany arias sung by a chorus. Named incidental pieces specially associated with scenes involving military maneuvers, fighting, marching, hunting, or processions are also played by the suona-and-percussion ensemble.

Only nine basic players are in the jingju ensemble, but the performers, who are versatile, usually play more than one instrument. For example, in the percussion ensemble, the conductor, who plays both the single-headed drum and the clapper, also plays the big or small barrel drum. One person plays the various sizes of cymbals, and another plays the various sizes of gongs. In the melodic ensemble, the jinghu and erhu players also play the big cymbals when the music only involves the wind players, and sometimes they may have to play the suona and the dizi as well. The yue qin and sanxian players also play the suona, the dizi, the sheng, and even the yunluo or the barrel drums.

Vocal music in jingju comprises arias, recitative-like short phrases, and heightened speech, which is a type of stylized stage speech having steeply rising and falling contours that exaggerate the natural tonal contours of the Chinese language, in which the meaning of a word depends as much on its melodic contour and relative tessitura as on its particular arrangement of vowels and consonants. The arias express the lyrical sentiments of the character, whereas the recitative-like phrases and the heightened speech propel the narrative of the dramatic action. Heightened speech is used exclusively by important characters and characters of high social status, whereas everyday speech in the Peking dialect is used by the comics and characters of lower social status. In general, arias, recitatives, and speech are performed as solo numbers, but there are exceptions when these are performed by an ensemble.

In jingju, the aural and visual elements are of equal importance. The conventions require that an actor master highly stylized acting techniques as thoroughly as he or she does singing. Just as knowledgeable Chinese audiences would not excuse bad singing, neither would they excuse bad execution of movements on stage. For a jingju actor, the appearance demanded by his conventional role, his capacity for wearing the costume pertaining to it, and the scores of strictly defined movements and gestures are of vital importance. The actor is the focus of attention, the central point of that harmony of movement, which is the essence of a theatrical performance. The costumes are designed to assist and emphasize that movement, together with instrumental music, speech, and arias, all interdependent on one another.

Such a highly stylized and conventional theater requires an audience that possesses "the art of watching and listening" to appreciate it fully. Unfortunately, in recent decades audiences have been rapidly shrinking. The conventions of jingju are deeply rooted in an old society based on Confucian moral precepts and political outlook, and these ideals have been thoroughly discredited by the contemporary socialist state. It is small wonder that young people who have grown up in this state find the art archaic and alien; they prefer programs on television and pop music. In recent years, the government has tried to remedy this situation by taking certain reform measures, which include the creation of libretti with modern themes, reorganizing troupes to streamline the companies, giving more financial incentives to able actors, and introducing electroacoustic instruments, but these measures appear to have met with little success (Listen to CD I, 13-14 for representative examples of jingju arias).

Wind chamber and mouthpiece of a Chinese Sheng.
Source: Philip Dowell/Dorling Kindersley Media Library

LISTENING GUIDE

PEKING OPERA ARIAS

GO TO **www.mymusiclab.com for the Automated Listening Guide** CDI • Tracks 13 and 14/Download Tracks 13 and 14

All jingju arias derive from a group of some thirty preexistent skeletal tune-and-rhythm pattern types called *ban* (literally "beat," but best translated as "melody-rhythmic type"). By setting the same *ban* to a different text, a new aria is produced.

Most arias contain a two-phrase unit that sets a rhymed couplet. The constituent lines, which are of equal length, may have either seven or ten syllables grouped into three prosodic units, 2 + 3 + 2 for seven syllables and 3 + 5 + 2 for ten. The melody for each phrase, however, is always arranged in a five-bar structure, juxtaposed with the three-prosodic-units-per-line textual structure.

Defined in terms of their rhythm, tempo, and corresponding dramatic functions, these are the five main aria types:

1. The narrative aria in 4/4 meter and moderate tempo is usually used to provide narration in an unemotional manner (CD I, 13).

TIME

0:00–0:02	Brief intro on clapper and drum (*bangu*).
0:02–0:18	Instrumental introduction: Strings (jinghu and yue qin) and *bangu*.
0:18–0:45	Voice enters—follows closely melodic line played by strings, with many sliding "leaps" between tones.
0:46–1:08	Instrumental interlude.
1:08–1:29	Voice returns (2nd verse).
1:29–1:48	Instrumental interlude.
1:48–2:07	Voice returns (3rd verse); fades out [1:57–2:07].

---

2. The lyrical aria in 4/4 meter and slow tempo is used at lyrical moments and is usually melismatic.
3. The animated aria in measured rhythm, and fast tempo is used to reveal a character's psychological state.
4. The dramatic aria in free rhythm, always accompanied by a steady beat from the clappers and the fiddle, is used to propel the dramatic action or to add tension to spoken dialogue (CD I, 14).

TIME

0:00–0:27	Dramatic, nonmelodic introduction called "slow, long strokes" (*man chang chui*) indicating entrance of an important character; with cymbals (*naobo*) gongs (*xiao luo*), with high, rising tone; *da luo*, with low, falling tone); and drum (*bangu*) (builds in intensity to dramatic pause at [0:19]).
0:27–0:44	Strings (jinghu and yue qin) and *bangu* perform instrumental introduction.
0:45–1:11	Character (painted-face role) freely sings short melodic phrases with string and drum accompaniment; brief instrumental interludes "reply" to voice.

1:11–1:40	Gongs, drum, and cymbal—reminiscent of opening pattern, starting slowly and building in intensity; drum alone [1:35–1:39] announces transition to next section.
1:40–1:52	Melodic interlude by strings, clapper, and drum.
1:52–2:05	Voice returns for second verse; track fades [1:57–2:05].

5. The interjected aria, usually very short (only one phrase) and in free rhythm, is sung at a highly dramatic moment as a signal or a call.

These five melody–rhythm types are divided into more than ten categories, each of which has different melodic characteristics. The two most important ones are the xipi and the erhuang, which, respectively, derive from a northern and a southern regional theater. In addition, folk tunes of various regions and arias of kunqu have also been absorbed into jingju.

General Characteristics of Music of the Han People

Although the Han people are relatively homogeneous in their cultural outlook and values, and all of them speak a number of related Sinitic languages that are known collectively as Chinese, the various dialects such as Putonghua (Mandarin), Wu, Xiang, Min, Hakka, and Yue (Cantonese) are mutually unintelligible when spoken. However, the use of a common written language and ideographic writing system enables all literate Chinese to communicate with each other. The existence of many regional styles of Chinese music reflects this diversity, too.

Musically, each major linguistic region possesses its own vocal styles and forms. The major types of vocal music of the Han, such as musical narratives and musical theatricals, have been profoundly influenced by the linguistic characteristics of each region. According to Chinese statistics, there are about 317 regional dramatic genres in China today. Instrumental music is also regional in character; for example, the Jiangnan *sizhu* is predominantly a genre of the Jiangnan region, whereas the Fujian province in the south has its own instrumental ensemble style called the Fujian *Nanqu*, and the Guangdong province in the deep south has its own Guangdong *Yinyue*. Some of the same instruments, however, are used in most major instrumental ensembles, such as the dizi and the yangqin (dulcimer).

Despite the regional differences, some common stylistic characteristics result from extensive borrowing of musical styles from region to region. When a particular regional style such as the famous jingju becomes widely adopted throughout the country, a national style is formed.

The Value and Functions of Music

For centuries, the Chinese have equated enjoyment of music with the natural human desire for aesthetic and sensual gratification such as the taste for food, the need for sex, and the satisfaction of seeing beautiful things. Music has traditionally been treated as one of the component phenomena that make up an environment for living. Thus, music has not only served as a means of expressing emotions such as joy and sadness or as a vehicle for spiritual or religious contemplation, but it has also always been integrated into events such as rituals, banquets, weddings, funerals, festivals, harvest celebrations, and so forth. In addition, music has always been conceived of as an integral part of other performing arts such as dance and drama. Furthermore, reference to some types of music has conventionally been used to evoke certain moods and atmospheres in literature, poetry, and painting. This complex and integral view of music and its functions had already become well established in the Zhou dynasty in the first millennium BCE.

Kong Fuzi, or Master Kong (551–479 BCE), known to the West as Confucius, founded the school of philosophy (popularly called Confucianism) that had the greatest impact on subsequent Chinese thought. Confucius maintained that music has positive and negative powers to stimulate related behavior and desire. Positive music, or *shi yin* (proper sound), features the attributes of harmoniousness, peacefulness, and appropriateness; it is an important educational tool capable of inspiring virtue and appropriate attitudes. In contrast, the music he described as negative, or *chi yue* (extravagant music), had the attributes of inappropriate loudness (like thunder and lightning) and wanton noisiness and stimulated excessive and licentious behavior.

Read
*excerpts from
Confucius' Analects*
on **mymusiclab.com**

Confucius lived during the end of the Zhou period in a time of constant warfare and chaos. He hoped to restore China to the peaceful feudalism of the early Zhou years, but felt that the only way the hierarchical system could be made to work properly was for each person to correctly perform his assigned role. "Let the ruler be a ruler and the subjects be subjects," he said, but he added that to rule properly, a king must be a virtuous person, setting an example of proper ethical conduct. To Confucius, social stratification was a fact of life to be sustained by morality, not force. He greatly stressed the possibility of remolding men's minds through education (in which music and dance were important parts of the curriculum) and taught that proper inner attitudes could be inculcated through the practice of rituals (which, to be effective, must have proper ritual music) as well as through the observance of rules of etiquette and decorum.

In the twentieth century Mao Zedong (1893–1976), chairman of the Communist Party from 1949 to 1976, like Confucius, viewed music and the arts as important educational tools. But Mao's practical application of this view was vastly different from that of the Confucianists. To Mao, music and the arts were important tools in the propagation of state ideology. Couched in the language of Marxism–Leninism as interpreted by Mao, the state ideology plays a key political role in the People's Republic; it defines, explains, and rationalizes the whole range of human activities and thinking in the society. Endowed with the sanctity of unchallenged truth, the state ideology constitutes the basis and substance of political values and is buttressed by the fullest extent of coercive power inherent in a sovereign political system. Few in China are able to ignore the all-pervasive influence of ideology. Propagation of ideology is a premier function of the Communist Party acting on behalf of the state, and music and the arts are important components of this propaganda machine.

Mao, like Confucius, differentiated proper and improper kinds of music. The proper or "correct" kinds are those that have been sanctioned by the state and that contain "correct" ideological messages. Improper kinds of music (or politically incorrect music) are those that have been construed by the state to contain "poisonous" influence, either from the discredited "feudal" society of the past or from the capitalistic, decadent West, and as such they must be censored or eliminated.

Authorship and the Creation Process

Before the twentieth century, the idea of an original composition identified with a particular person was foreign to the Chinese, and only a few traditional musical pieces had any attributed authorship. The sources for most traditional Chinese music were anonymous folk or popular materials transmitted orally or through written notation in manuscripts or printed music handbooks. In the traditional method of composition, these were rearranged in different ways, resulting in newly recomposed versions of the older models. The rearrangement process, however, is genre specific; that is to say, each genre has its own procedures and rules regarding rearrangements.

Some genres of music require a measure of improvisation during performance, such as adding improvised embellishments in Jiangnan sizhu. By adding improvised embellishments and varying the dynamics and tempi of the music according to established conventions during a performance and, most importantly, by extending or subtracting portions of the thematic materials in a spontaneous fashion, a performer is in fact acting as a composer as well.

With the introduction of Western ideas to China in the twentieth century came the Western musical repertory, compositional processes and techniques, and the idea of composership. Like their Western counterparts, modern Chinese composers regard themselves as individual creators of original music; the idea and emotion associated with a particular piece of music are regarded as the unique, individual expressions of the composer alone.

Amateur and Professional Musicians

Before 1949 the status of a musician was determined by his education and his occupation. Professional musicians, who relied on music for their livelihood and usually had little formal education, had rather low social status, particularly those who performed entertainment music catering to members of the unlettered class. Unlike the professional musician, the amateur, who did not rely on making music for a livelihood but was accomplished in music, well educated, and cultivated, was regarded as the ideal gentleman. In Chinese history, many distinguished amateur musicians such as players of the qin, who usually came from the leisured class, were given high acclaim as musicians and mentioned in historical documents. Records of professional musicians, on the other hand, were few and far between until the twentieth century.

After 1949, the Communist government hoped to create a classless society, and the stigma on professional musicians was removed. For nationalistic and propagandistic purposes, many forms of traditional entertainment music and folk music that had been frowned on by orthodox Confucians in the past were elevated as China's national heritage, as was the status of their practitioners. The government established many modern conservatories, whose curricula included Western art music as well as traditional Chinese music. Distinguished performers of traditional music, both amateur and professional, were hired as equals to teach in these conservatories.

NEW MUSICAL DIRECTIONS IN THE TWENTIETH CENTURY

In 1911, a Chinese revolution overthrew the Qing dynasty. In its place, a Republic was founded by Dr. Sun Yatsen (1866–1925), a revolutionary with liberal ideas who attempted to model the Republic of China (1912–1949) on the constitutional government of the United States. But China was not yet ready for such an experiment, and Sun's effort was largely a failure. However, the establishment of the Republic of China represented a clean break with old values and practices that had existed for millennia, and in this process traditional music was neglected, and a new type of music was born.

At the beginning of the twentieth century, reformers such as Kang Youwei (1858–1927) and Liang Qichao (1873–1929) advocated the establishment of a new type of school that included in its curriculum practical subjects such as arithmetic, geography, knowledge of the natural world, and classroom music. The reformers contended that traditional Chinese music (such as jingju, Jiangnan sizhu, and music for the qin and the pipa) were unsuitable for modern classroom music. Therefore, a new type of school song was adopted whose melodies, at first borrowed from school songs of the West and of Japan, were given didactic Chinese texts to inculcate a new sense of nationalism in young students. By the end of the first decade of the twentieth century, however, Chinese songwriters, many of whom had received some elementary music training in Japan, began themselves to write didactic school songs. The three most notable were Zeng Zhimin (1879–1929), Shen Xingong (1869–1947), and Li Shutong (1880–1942). The songs they wrote were simple and short, with a limited range and a square, march-like rhythm, and they were predominantly syllabic, reflecting the influence of early Japanese school songs. The song texts were simple and direct messages related to patriotism, self-discipline, military readiness, and civic spiritedness. In the decades that followed, the derivatives of these didactic songs became the main musical diet of the majority of Chinese students.

As the new China faced challenges from the West and from Japan in the early twentieth century, protest songs began to be written. In 1914, at the beginning of the First World War (1914–1917), Japan attempted to seize control of China. Immediately, the Chinese people expressed their outrage in protests, demonstrations, and strikes. Songs denouncing Japanese aggression and the weak Chinese government were part of the protest movement and circulated widely in schools, universities, and nationwide workers' strikes and demonstrations. The musical style of these protest songs resembled that of the school songs, but they were set apart by their texts. Whereas the texts of school songs usually expounded the general principles of good citizenship, discipline, patriotism, and nationalism, those of the protest songs focused on the current political issues and used terse, slogan-like language. These protest songs were the predecessors of the later political songs known as Revolutionary Songs, or "Songs for the Masses," which were developed by the Chinese communists.

During the First World War, Japan formed an alliance with Great Britain against Germany, with the ulterior motive of seizing Germany's colony in China, the Qingdao (Tsingtao) peninsula, as its own colony. China entered World War I in 1917 to declare war on Germany in the hope of recovering Qingdao, then claimed by Japan. But at the Versailles Peace Conference of 1919, the victorious Western powers confirmed Japan's seizure of Qingdao. This act engendered a strong reaction against Japan and the Western allies among the Chinese, who used protest songs to stimulate nationalist sentiment. Then on May 4, 1919, this ferment culminated in a mass student demonstration at the National Peking University. This was the first time that the modern educated class made its mark on Chinese politics, and a precedent was set. The political activities and the intellectual currents set in motion by these students developed into a broad national intellectual awakening known as the May Fourth Movement.

The May Fourth Movement affected the development of modern Chinese music profoundly. The hub of the Movement was Beida (National Peking University) under the administration of its remarkable and liberal chancellor, Cai Yuanpei (1867–1940), who fostered freedom of thought and education. Cai was well versed in the tenets of both Confucianism and Western philosophy, and he wanted to synthesize the Chinese classical tradition and the libertarianism of the modern European West that characterized the May Fourth Movement. When he became chancellor, Cai endeavored to create opportunities for the students to receive an aesthetic education that included music and art, which he maintained were essential subjects in modern education.

Cai felt that the reform of traditional Chinese music was necessary to bring it up to date, by borrowing elements from Western music. In 1916, Cai established an extracurricular music study group at Beida, staffed by both Chinese and Western teachers, which offered students instruction in Chinese and Western vocal and instrumental music; the teachers were also charged with the responsibility of finding ways to modernize traditional Chinese music.

This music group eventually was reorganized and expanded to become China's first academic music department. Under the leadership of the composer Xiao Youmei (1884–1940), who was trained in Japan and Germany, this department offered instruction in music theory, composition, and the academic study of music, in addition to instrumental and vocal instruction. Xiao pioneered the reform of Chinese music by incorporating Western elements, notably harmony. In this way, he put into musical practice for the first time the self-strengthening slogan of 1898, "Chinese culture as the essence, and Western learning for practical use."

Another development initiated at Beida that had significant implications for the future development of the field of Chinese musicology was the Folk-Song Campaign. Inspired by the Russian Narodniki Movement of the 1870s, it called for educated youth to go into the countryside to educate the peasants. Following this philosophy, a group of Beida students encountered folk song and folk art (which were considered unworthy of attention by most of the members of the elites of the old regime) and came to recognize their value. These efforts eventually produced the systematic collection and scholarly research of folk song, which laid the foundation for the future development of Chinese musicology.

The May Fourth Movement also affected the development of modern Chinese music by promoting the use of Chinese vernacular language as a written medium of communication in all fields, including scholarship, in place of the cumbersome literary Chinese that had been the language of literature and scholarship for millennia. Using the vernacular, the young writers introduced a new popular literature that emulated Western forms and spread it through numerous periodicals and newspapers. Inspired by this development, some songwriters began to set new vernacular poems to music. One pioneer was Zhao Yuanren (Y. R. Chao, 1892–1982), a naturalized American who was an internationally known linguist and a composer. Combining elements of traditional Chinese music with Western ones such as harmony, Chao wrote songs with vernacular poetic texts and piano accompaniment. He is now considered the creator of the modern Chinese art song.

One of the most enduring aspects of the May Fourth Movement was the change in the ideology of China's educated class, brought about by the attack on Confucian values. Using newspapers and journals such as *The New Youth*, modern scholars condemned as tyranny the subordination of subject to ruler, wife to husband, son to father, and individual to family, all of which were regarded as remnants of a feudal society. Because the traditional Chinese musical theaters, such as jingju, promoted these feudal values, the merit of such theaters became a subject for debate. Some writers advocated the total elimination of traditional theater, including jingju; others advocated reform by emulating the theater of the West. Though these debates lasted only a few years (mainly from 1917 to 1919) and failed to produce any immediate, tangible reform, they did create a general disdain for traditional music and theater among the modern educated class. Moreover, a lingering sentiment for reform of traditional theater never went away, and when Jiang Qing (1913–1991), wife of Mao Zedong, became the cultural dictator during the Cultural Revolution, she drastically reformed jingju by incorporating elements of Western orchestral and harmonic practice into the music, of ballet into the choreography, and of scenic design into the stagecraft, as well as by replacing the traditional stories with revolutionary plots; this reformed musical drama came to be known in the West as "Model Opera."

At the time of the May Fourth Movement, authoritarian parties were proving successful in Europe, most notably in Russia, where revolution had established the triumph of the Communist Party. The success of the Russian revolution and its Marxist–Leninist political philosophy inspired some of the leading writers and thinkers of the May Fourth Movement, who eventually founded The Chinese Communist Party (CCP) in 1921. It became the major opponent to the ruling Kuomintang (KMT, or Nationalist Party), and the two struggled for control of China for several decades.

By 1923 the impact of Marxism-Leninism on Chinese thought and on Chinese arts and music began to be felt as these came to be viewed as political tools for propaganda. The introduction of the "Internationale" to China in 1923, a song closely identified with the European labor movement of the 1890s and with the Bolshevik Revolution in Russia, came to be regarded as the signal of China's entrance into the world communist movement.

In the ensuing years, the increase of Japanese aggression in China stimulated many more protest songs against Japan, and Russian revolutionary songs began to be heard in leftist circles. The war of resistance against Japan from 1937 to 1945 during World War II stimulated a further outpouring of songs with patriotic themes; composers of all political persuasions joined forces to produce songs in support of the war. Through being used in war films, many of these songs became popular with general audiences, and after the establishment of the People's Republic in 1949, the production of thousands of "Songs for the Masses" became one of the important functions of the propaganda machine.

When I was a young student in the PRC in the early 1950s, the sole musical diet for my contemporaries and myself consisted of nothing but "Songs for the Masses." These songs, whose origins may be traced back to Western Protestant hymns and school songs, modern Japanese and Chinese school songs, Chinese folk songs, and Russian revolutionary songs, are short and simple, use the Western, diatonic scale, and have texts that are slogan-like ideological messages of communism and nationalism. We sang these songs in music classes and numerous political rallies and demonstrations, during the labor sessions in the countryside that every student had to participate in, and in our leisure time to amuse ourselves. One of the outstanding examples from the 1950s is "We Workers Have Strength." In the listening example the song is sung antiphonally between solo and chorus, but when sung in the classroom, the students sing the complete song in unison (Listen to CD I 15, to hear this "Song for the Masses").

LISTENING GUIDE

"WE WORKERS HAVE STRENGTH"

Composed by Ma Ke

GO TO **www.mymusiclab.com for the Automated Listening Guide** CDI • Track 15/Download Track 15

0:00–0:04	Western-style orchestral introduction.
0:04–0:08	Solo vocal line.
0:08–0:10	Choral response.
0:11–0:14	Solo vocal line.
0:15–0:17	Choral response.
0:17–0:25	Chorus sung by all.
0:25–0:36	Rapid back and forth between soloist and chorus.
0:37–0:40	All together.
0:41–0:47	More rapid interchanges between solo and chorus.
0:47–0:51	Final refrain all together.
0:51–0:58	(Track fades as two vocalists begin singing the next verse).

THE RISE OF POPULAR MUSIC

Modern Chinese popular songs, transmitted through recordings, radio, movies, and print, first appeared in Shanghai, China's most cosmopolitan and modern city in the first half of the twentieth century. A port city on the banks of the Huangpu River, an estuary of the Yangzi River, modern Shanghai was built by Europeans in the mid-nineteenth century on a piece of farmland adjacent to the old Chinese walled town. This piece of land had been ceded to the British after the Opium War (1839–1842), and on it the British built a Western-style city to serve as a toehold for commercial penetration to all parts of China. But China also benefited, for from here Western ideas and culture, including music, as well as technology and modern business practice, were disseminated to all parts of the country. Soon after the establishment of modern Shanghai, people from other North Atlantic countries, such as Germany, France, Belgium, Russia, Italy, and the United States, as well as from Asian countries, such as India, Japan, Thailand, Vietnam, and the Philippines, all came to invest, live, and work, thus contributing to Shanghai's commercial and industrial development and to its cosmopolitan atmosphere.

From the beginning, however, Chinese contributions to Shanghai's development were significant, both in the form of capital investment and of manpower. Large numbers of Chinese workers migrated to Shanghai to seek work in Shanghai's factories, providing a labor pool that fueled the city's industrial development. Many could not find work, however, and the women among the unemployed frequently ended up as taxi-dance girls—women paid to dance with customers at cabarets for a short unit of time—or prostitutes. By the early decades of the twentieth century, Shanghai emerged not only as the financial, industrial, and cultural center of China and Asia, but also became Asia's entertainment mecca and a frontier for jazz in Asia. Shanghai also served as the major distributing center of Hollywood movies in Asia, and it was the home of China's domestic movie industry. Cinemas showing Hollywood or Chinese movies were everywhere. Shanghai became a hot tourist stop, and famous jazz musicians from the United States frequently made a stop in its cabarets, which inspired many aspiring jazz musicians from Japan and the Philippines to go to Shanghai for their first lessons in jazz. Already in the 1920s, the city was home to some twenty domestic radio stations, and the number grew rapidly. It was also home to some major Western-owned recording companies.

The bourgeoisie of Shanghai led a hedonistic life style, as vividly described in a 1930s Shanghai guidebook for tourists:

> Whoopee! What odds whether Shanghai is the Paris of the East or Paris the Shanghai of the Occident? Shanghai has its own distinctive night life, and what a life! Dog races and cabarets, hai-alai and cabarets, formal tea and dinner dances and cabarets, the sophisticated and cosmopolitan French Club and cabarets, the dignified and formal Country Club and cabarets, prize fights and cabarets, theaters and cabarets, movies and cabarets, and cabarets—everywhere, hundreds of 'em!
>
> —*All About Shanghai*, Hong Kong: Oxford University Press, 1983 (1934–1935), p. 73.

Shanghai popular song, known in Chinese as **"liuxing gequ,"** is a quintessential product of this environment. This song form arose between the world wars, when Shanghai was at its peak. These songs have lyrics in modern vernacular Mandarin—the universal language of modern China—and melodies and rhythms of a cosmopolitan flavor with traces of Broadway and Hollywood hit tunes, jazz, Latin American rhythms such as tango and rumba, as well as of Chinese folk songs, urban ballads, and modern Chinese school songs.

The melodies of Shanghai popular songs were composed by Chinese, but the instrumentation and orchestration in some recordings was the product of a small number of White Russian musicians who had escaped to Shanghai from Russia during the Bolshevik Revolution and worked for recording companies in Shanghai. These composers, Western or Chinese, drew their sound materials from Shanghai's cosmopolitan soundscape and created a huge repertory of infinite variety catering to a diverse Chinese bourgeois audience with a multiplicity of tastes.

The lyrics of the Shanghai popular song were frequently written by noted popular fiction writers and newspapermen of the day. Drawing on their knowledge of and familiarity with the modern metropolis—both its opulent and seedy sides—these lyricists created a kaleidoscopic picture of modern city life and people, rich or poor, often with wit and verve.

Shanghai popular songs served many functions. They were repertory for nightclub singers in cabarets for dancing, accompanied in these settings by jazz musicians, many of whom were Filipinos. They were used as theme songs for

LIUXING GEQU

Popular song produced in Shanghai since the late 1920s that is a hybrid of various Western and Chinese musical genres. Its lyrics are sung in the Chinese national tongue, the so-called Mandarin.

Chinese song and dance movies, and through such exposure they were transmitted nationwide. At some radio stations, broadcast recordings of Shanghai popular songs made up the bulk of the programming; some radio programs also featured live performances by pop song stars singing audience-requested songs. And, as a source of individual enjoyment, these songs also were printed in the form of inexpensive, pocket-sized booklets that were distributed in neighborhood newsstands, drugstores, and bookstores.

Recordings of Shanghai popular songs were manufactured and marketed primarily by Western-owned recording companies in Shanghai—companies that employed both Chinese and European staff. The most important manufacturer of these songs was the Pathé Recording Company, which eventually monopolized the market (Listen to CD I, 16 for an example of Shanghai popular song).

Popular Music of Today

After the establishment of the PRC in 1949, Shanghai popular song was censored and denounced as "the dregs of imperialism, colonialism, and capitalism," but outside the PRC, fans of Shanghai popular songs continued to enjoy and circulate them. In the 1980s, the EMI Recording Company in Hong Kong reissued many of them on CDs to satisfy popular demand. Also in the 1980s, as China embarked on economic reform and ushered in a more tolerant attitude toward popular art, a small selection of Shanghai popular songs was allowed to be reissued by the government; the original jazzy accompaniments of many songs, however, were replaced by more insipid and square versions for synthesizer. Although technologically more modern, these new versions nevertheless demonstrated the government's continuing suspicion of the original sounds with their cosmopolitan qualities and association with a discredited era.

Coincidently, as Shanghai struggled to reemerge as an international city, a Chinese film about colonial Shanghai, entitled *Night Shanghai*, was produced. The recording of Zhou Xuan's rendition of this song was used extensively as background music. Obviously, the symbolism of this song for Shanghai has not been forgotten as even a CBS news report attested in 1998. When President Bill Clinton visited Shanghai on June 29, 1998, the CBS report began by showing a nightclub scene with many couples dancing to a female vocalist's rendition of "Night Shanghai."

After 1949, new popular songs somewhat reminiscent of Shanghai popular songs were produced in Hong Kong and Taiwan and were sung by local singers. In the 1970s, however, their popularity in Hong Kong was eclipsed by the rise of Cantonese popular songs known in the West as "Canto Pop," which was inspired by White rock of the 1950s and uses synthesizers for accompaniment.

Meanwhile, in 1979, as China emerged from the ruinous Cultural Revolution, the government attempted to transform its centrally planned economy into one that borrowed some measures of a market economy, and it cautiously began to encourage private enterprises. To attract foreign investment, the government pursued an open-door foreign policy. Political pressure on the Chinese people, which used to be quite severe, became somewhat relaxed, and some influences from overseas were allowed to slip in. Beginning in the early 1980s,

LISTENING GUIDE

"YE SHANGHAI" ("NIGHT SHANGHAI")   GO TO **www.mymusiclab.com for the Automated Listening Guide** CDI • Track 16/Download Track 16

One of the most representative Shanghai popular songs is entitled "Ye Shanghai" ("Night Shanghai"); it was the signature song of the most popular star, Zhou Xuan, and ever since its appearance, it has been considered the symbol of colonial Shanghai.

Ye Shanghai

Night Shanghai, Night Shanghai,
A city that never sleeps.
Neon-lights blazing, car horns blaring,
Singing and dancing in blissful oblivion.

Look at her, smiling and welcoming,
Who knows her sorrow and frustration?
Leading a life by night, paying for clothing, food and lodging,

Getting drunk, wasting youth recklessly.
Dawn arriving brings drowsiness, eyes heavy with sleep,
Everyone leaving for home,
The heart churning with the turning wheels,
Then pondering the former night life,
As if waking up from a dream,
Thinking of a new environment.

(trans. Isabel Wong)

In "Night Shanghai," a brief instrumental introduction imitates the sounds of car horns and city traffic, after which comes the vocal part, whose diatonic melody is arranged in the **A–A–B–A** scheme followed by a great deal of North Atlantic popular song of the era. The jazz-like accompaniment is provided by a small band with prominent saxophone and piano parts in the rhythm of the foxtrot, one of the most popular dance steps of the time. In the lyrics, every index of modernity is there: automobiles, traffic, neon lights, and cabarets. A lifestyle that typifies Shanghai nightlife is encapsulated: alcohol intoxication, dancing, and the taxi-dance girl—the many nationalities of women selling sex for a living who personified colonial Shanghai.

In the last two lines the concept of a change to a new environment is introduced, and the song ends with the implication that the taxi-dance girl actually left the metropolis for a new environment—presumably the countryside—as if waking from a bad dream. These two lines touched on two recurrent themes in the cultural imagination of modern China—ambivalence toward colonial Shanghai as both a site of modernity and of corruption and destruction, and the other having to do with the city-country antithesis. The city is often presented in literature as a transient place of dislocation and loneliness, whereas the countryside represents enduring traditional values and a place of continuity. Shanghai popular song truly captures the spirit of its bygone era.

0:00–0:10	Instrumental introduction starts with trumpet fanfare and ends with jazzy saxophone.
0:10–0:27	(**A**) First verse sung to regular 4/4 accompaniment, 8 measures.
0:28–0:44	(**A**) Second verse repeats tune with varied accompaniment, 8 measures.
0:45–1:09	(**B**) Contrasting bridge section, 12 measures.
1:10–1:28	(**A**) Return to opening melody.

pop songs of Taiwan and Canto Pop from Hong Kong took mainland Chinese listeners by storm, particularly among the younger generation, and soon some mainland songwriters began to emulate the style of these imported models.

The transformation and expansion of the Chinese economy also stimulated the growth of China's fledgling popular song industry. Encouraged and controlled by the government until relatively recently, this industry began to recruit and produce its own composers, lyricists, and singers and to manufacture and market its own product. By 1984, Chinese popular music had definitely became commoditized, relying on the government mass media such as radio and television broadcasts and government-sponsored song and dance troupes for its dissemination and marketing, and its dominant concern was profit.

In the ensuing years, Chinese popular music proliferated, grew in strength and complexity, and began to compete for market share with the imports from Hong Kong and Taiwan. Drawing their musical inspirations directly from North American and European models such as jazz, blues, country, rock, and even Baroque music, new styles like *disike* (disco) and *jingge* (energy song) began to appear and gain widespread appeal.

In 1988, another new style called **xibeifeng** (northwestern wind) became extremely popular; its music is a combination of a disco beat and synthesized accompaniment with folk tunes of the Loess Plateau of northwest China, an impoverished region that had once been the cradle of the Communist revolution. Its lyrics are set deliberately in a simple, unsophisticated, and bucolic language addressing issues of feudalism and backwardness in rural northwest China. These songs were appealing to many urban dwellers, who were overwhelmed by rapid changes and inflation resulting from the economic reform and who yearned for the simpler lifestyle of a bygone time evoked in the folk-like music and simple lyrics of the "northwestern wind."

Rock Music

Despite their diversity, these many new styles of popular songs, which the government has labeled **tongsu yinyue** (light popular music), have one thing in common: they are produced by a government-sponsored popular music industry, and the messages they impart are sanctioned by the government. In contrast, there is a small group of underground rock musicians who first appeared on the scene around the mid-1980s. Despite the government's disapproval and its efforts to marginalize rock music and musicians, Chinese rock nonetheless

XIBEIFENG (NORTHWESTERN WIND)
Popular Chinese song genre of the 1980s and 1990s. It combines a disco beat with Chinese folk music, and its lyrics are deliberately artless and simple.

TONGSU YINYUE (LIGHT POPULAR MUSIC)
Chinese popular music of the 1980s and 1990s.

was able to not only survive but attract a significant number of devoted young followers from the urban educated circles. The most famous rock musician, Cui Jian, made his U.S. debut in New York in September 1995.

Chinese rock traces its ancestry directly to Anglo-American rock in terms of melodic styles, rhythms, performing behavior, instrumentation, and ideology. The rock musicians compose their own music and write lyrics that are intensely personal. Although a majority of the lyrics focus on individual expressions of strong inner emotion, others address contemporary cultural and political issues in a deliberately idiosyncratic and ambiguous language.

Rock musicians and their audience form a tight-knit social group. Concerts, never publicized and usually featuring many bands performing together, are named using the English word "parties." There are now about half a dozen bands in existence. Some label themselves as "zhong jinshu" (heavy metal), and others call themselves "benke" (punks) (Listen to CD I, 17 for an example of Cui Jian's music).

MUSIC FOR AND BY MINORITIES

The relationship between Han and non-Han people in the PRC is complicated. Although in recent years the prevalent chauvinistic view of the Han, which tends to regard cultures of non-Han nationalities as somewhat inferior, has abated because of the increasing integration of non-Han nationalities into mainstream Han society. A sense of superiority among the Han, however, still lingers. In fact, through the centuries, Han culture has been much enriched by non-Han culture. This dialectic of power relationships between the Han and non-Han is well reflected in the musical domain.

For a long time the Chinese empire aimed merely to politically control the minorities in its territory and did not try to interfere with their culture and customs. By the time the modern Chinese Republic was established (1911–1949), however, the Republican government, influenced by Western concepts of the nation–state and nationalism, changed the policy toward the minorities to one of aggressive assimilation. The situation changed somewhat under the PRC, which recognized many more official national groups and proclaimed a commitment to protect their rights. But despite this new rhetoric and some real attempts at change, the PRC government neutralized its effectiveness by drawing on Marxist unilinear revolutionary theory, by which the Han were viewed as more advanced in terms of political, economic, technological, and cultural achievements. It thus produced a pseudotheoretical justification for the Han to control and to "help" the minorities.

In the musical domain, the discourse of this power relationship was reflected in the emergence, from the 1950s, of a huge body of revolutionary "Songs for the Masses" based on minority styles as a propaganda tool for legitimizing the PRC among the minority populations and fostering their loyalty to the regime. Distributed through the mass media to the entire nation, these songs were frequently performed by singers selected from the minorities and trained to sing with a vocal timbre that the Chinese call "*mei sheng*" (meaning "beautiful sound," a term translated from the North Atlantic term *bel canto*). This kind of North Atlantic-inspired singing style fostered by conservatories came to be regarded as

LISTENING GUIDE

"HAVING NOTHING"

By Cui Jian

GO TO www.mymusiclab.com for the Automated Listening Guide CDI • Track 17/Download Track 17

One of Cui Jian's most popular songs is entitled "Having Nothing," which he delivers using a somewhat rough vocal quality. Its melody is forceful and direct and effectively projects a lyric expressing alienation and discontent.

By maintaining that he has nothing to his name, Cui Jian is rejecting the new materialism and loss of ideals that had swept China beginning in the late 1980s. The collective "you" points to corrupt officials who were unaware that calamity may happen, as "the ground is moving and water is overflowing." "Having Nothing" was a clarion call by idealistic youths, who were in despair in the midst of widespread corruption in the nation, and who were assuming a pose of nonconformity and detached individualism, protest, and rebellion, Cui Jian injected a whole new ethos into China's cultural consciousness, particularly among university students in the late 1980s, which concluded with the antigovernment demonstrations in Tiananmen Square in 1989.

0:00–0:26	Introduction for synthesizer, guitars, bass, and drum set.
0:26–0:42	**(A)** First verse sung to folk-like melody over continuing accompaniment, 8 measures of 4/4.
0:42–0:58	**(A)** Second verse to same tune with slightly more active instrumental accompaniment, 8 measures of 4/4.
0:58–1:18	**(B)** Contrasting 4 measure melody with overdubbed vocal backing. This is repeated.
1:19–1 34	Return of **A** melody with the addition of a more active role for the drum set.
1:35–1:50	Variation of **A** melody, now with added flute (xiao) accompaniment.
1:51–2:07	Return of **B** melody and fade out [2:05–2:07].

a cultivated professional vocal style. Thus the PRC has created an official representation of what it regards as authentic minority music, which the majority of Chinese people have come to accept and enjoy as such. Mongolian style songs of this sort are particularly popular because of their haunting tunes, and a typical song lyric would usually mention the clear blue Mongolian sky with fluffy white clouds and galloping horses in the great grassland; the Mongolian people, living a happy life, proudly singing praise to the regime and the leadership of Chairman Mao Zedong and the Chinese Communist Party.

During the ten years of Cultural Revolution, music not sanctioned by the radicals who controlled the government was silenced, and this included the previously sanctioned official representation of minority music. Almost everyone suffered during the Cultural Revolution, but minorities suffered most, and this ultimately awakened their ethnic consciousness. When the turmoil ended and the leaders of the Cultural Revolution had been discredited, a new leadership adopted a more conciliatory and sensitive attitude toward minorities and in 1982 enacted more liberal laws to protect minority rights. This greatly encouraged minorities to reaffirm their ethnicity with more determination. Such a development was best reflected by the appearance, in the late 1980s and thereafter, of new cassettes and CDs of pop songs produced by minority singers, who now sang in their own regional vocal styles. This effort was also made possible by the availability of inexpensive means of reproduction and marketing, which has enabled minorities to produce their own music.

Music Performance in a Mongolian Nightclub

Earlier I mentioned that I sometimes visit a Mongolian nightclub in Beijing with my friend, Professor Chogjin, along with his journalist wife, Tana, and a few Han friends who are colleagues of Professor Chogjin at the Chinese Academy of the Social Sciences. The nightclub is situated in a spacious street in the Beijing diplomatic quarters. The inside of the nightclub is decorated like a Mongolian tent known as a yurt (a Turkic word taken into English from Russian; the Mongolian term is *ger*) with Mongolian carpets, furniture, and décor. The waiters and waitresses are dressed in traditional Mongolian costume, a baggy shirt with high collar belted at the waist and loose trousers tucked inside high leather boots.

On one of our visits to the nightclub, while seated around a low table enjoying our food and drink, we chatted jovially in English and Putunghua. Like most educated people from the Inner Mongolia Autonomous Region (in the PRC), Chogjin and Tana are fluent in both Mongolian (belonging to the Altaic language group) and Putonghua of the Han people. A Mongolian colleague of Chogjin in the Academy named Professor Naqin came to join us and told us that we were in luck because Qifeng was singing that night. "Who is Qifeng?" I asked. Naqin pointed at a big poster on the wall, which was a close-up photo of a startlingly handsome young man with long hair, and said: "That's him, the most popular Mongolian pop singer today!"

As we waited for that night's special attraction, a group of young singers stepped onto the stage and began to sing Mongolian pop songs and folk songs to the accompaniment of instruments such as electric guitar and bass guitar, synthesizer, trap set, and several Mongolian instruments such as the *topshuur* (a two-stringed pluck lute), the *morin huur* (a two-stringed spike fiddle with horse-head decoration on the top of the neck), and the end-blown flute *tsuur.* Included in their presentation was a uniquely Mongolian singing style known as *höömii*, which produces a whistle-like melody by changing the shape of the oral cavity to reinforce selected overtones of a sung drone. Popularly known as throat singing in the North Atlantic, the effect of this music is ethereal, and we in the audience stopped talking and listened attentively. Gradually the place filled up, and soon there was standing room only. Most guests seemed to know one another and exchanged greetings in Mongolian. I said to Chogjin and

Explore the musical instruments gallery at **mymusiclab.com**

Naqin: "Popular place, this." Chogjin nodded and smiled: "Yes, we come here to be Mongolians. We need to escape from you Han brothers and sisters every now and then." Chogjin continued: "We Mongolians are very hospitable and always welcome our guests with liquor and songs. Now to be a gracious guest you must drink up. *Gan bei* (bottoms up)!" Mongolian liquor, served in small shallow cups, is rather strong. It is either made of a combination of grains (barley, sorghum, wheat, and corn), which is clear, or of fermented mare's milk, which has a milky color. Jovially we toasted each other while eating noodles and boiled mutton.

Finally, a hush descended on the place as Qifeng entered dressed in a fashionably casual way with a loose shirt and a pair of faded jeans. He first looked around, nodded to a few people, and then came over to give Chogjin a hug and to share a toast. Only then did he walk toward the small stage. Curious about this respectful display, I asked Chogjin about it, and Naqin explained: "The local Mongolians respect him for his scholarly accomplishment and for his ability in gaining respect from the Han academic world!"

As Qifeng stepped onto the stage, the audience applauded. The synthesizer player already on stage started a soft introductory passage, and Naqin whispered to me: "He is going to sing his signature song entitled 'Blessing to My Dear Mother,' which made him a star." Included in the accompaniment were the guitars, the plucked lute (*topshuur*) the flute (*tsuur*), and the horse-head fiddle (*morin huur*). Qifeng's voice was natural, mellifluous, and expressive, quite unlike the nasal and tight-throated timbre used by most current Han pop singers. Although the melody was pleasingly sentimental and simple, Qifeng added lots of subtle ornaments that gave it a distinct Mongolian flavor. He sang two stanzas of the song, the first in the Han Chinese language (*putonghua*), and the second in the Mongolian language. A vocal interlude separated the two stanzas, which was sung in the Mongolian Long Song (*urtyn duu*) style. A Long Song is a traditional Mongolian genre, which in 2006 was declared by UNESCO to be a Masterpiece of the Oral and Intangible Heritage of Humanity. In a traditional setting a Long Song is accompanied by the *morin huur*. But in Qifeng's rendition, the passage was accompanied by the whole ensemble, plus the trap set, giving it a contemporary popular urban twist.

In a Long Song the melody, sung with open throat and at full volume, progresses in wide skips and unfolds in a continuously linear and pulseless fashion; it is characterized by rich and frequent use of ornamentation and of falsetto. Individual pitches, phrases, and text syllables are indefinitely elongated, giving it a rhapsodic quality. It is a demanding vocal style, in which the musical qualities overshadow the text. A Long Song, sung by a skillful vocalist like Qifeng, can transport an audience to the wide-open spaces of the Mongolian steppes and serve as an important reminder of "home" for the urban Mongolians who came to this nightclub for just such an experience (Listen to CD I, 18 for an example of Qifeng's music).

After hearing this song, I asked Chogjin why "mother" was used to represent Mongolia, when I had the impression that Mongol culture is rather male centered. Chogjin said: "Mother is a very important figure in Mongolian culture. She is the custodian of our legends, customs, genealogy, and history. Mongolian written script was invented very recently, and before that, our history was transmitted

LISTENING GUIDE

"BLESSING TO MY MOTHER"

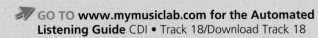
GO TO www.mymusiclab.com for the Automated Listening Guide CDI • Track 18/Download Track 18

Composed by Shienqimud; lyrics in Han Chinese by Han Wei Performed by Qifeng

Do you know, I come from a far away place?
I bring to you fragrance of flowers from the grassland.
Oh, my mother,
Please receive my heart-felt blessing;
Your love is as endless as the grassland.

Why, you gave everything to your children;
Your blood irrigated the pastoral fields where horses graze.

Oh, my mother,
You are the big tree that protects me from storms;
I am the eagle whom you set soaring.

Yet day and night I am nostalgic about the grassland.

When I look back at my native land,
I see your shadow far, far away.

When I see the giant eagle flying to a distant land
I just want to call you, Oh my mother....

(trans. Isabel Wong)

0:00–0:18	Excerpt 1, from beginning of song: Intro for synthesized strings and piano.
0:19–1:18	Vocalist sings using open, mellow timbre; simple melody but with occasional delicate ornaments; piano accompanies.
	[The middle portion of this song (approximately two minutes) is omitted here.]
1:19–2:·45	Excerpt 2, to end of song: Passage of highly ornamented, wordless vocal line, using falsetto voice and glottal ornaments like yodeling typical of "long song" style.

orally, and installed in our mothers' memory. The men were too busy engaging in warfare or animal husbandry. "Mother" is therefore an all-embracing metaphor for the land of the Mongols—not just modern Inner Mongolia, which is now an Autonomous Region in the PRC, or the modern Republic of Mongolia, previously known as Outer Mongolia, but the vast land of Genghis Khan's Mongols. The reference to the endless grassland, the soaring eagle, the nostalgia for a nomadic way of pastoral life, articulate a Mongolian consciousness, which to me is very real. The inclusion of the Long Song style is unprecedented. Partly because few Mongolian pop song singers can sing it, Qifeng learned it from a famous old Long Song singer. It is unprecedented also because Long Song is so unmistakably Mongolia—the yodeling style evokes a life out-of-doors in the grassland. To be frank with you, this very soft and mellow song is chock full of Mongolian nationalistic sentiments. It would not have been tolerated by our Han brothers even ten years ago! Naqin can tell you more about Qifeng because he is part of Qifeng's team. He writes some of the lyrics and is one of his producers."

At my urging, Naqin provided me with the following information: "Qifeng is the first Mongolian popular singer who has not received conservatory style vocal training in the so-called "mei sheng" (bel canto) style, whereas most of the popular Mongolian singers today sing in this academic style. He sings with his natural voice and utilizes indigenous Mongolian folk song vocal style. He is a skillful Long Song singer, having studied for a long time with the King of Long Song, Sularong (transliterated name). He could belt out an extended Long Song whenever he feels like it. In the late 1990s Qifeng first attracted national notice by making an appearance on the government-owned Central Radio Station in Beijing. When he appeared on the government radio and TV stations in 2004 and sang "Blessing to My Mother," it made him a household name, and his records sell in most popular recording stores in some major cities. Since then, he has decided to run his own business, becoming a private entrepreneur. He has gathered around him a group of good friends, both Han and Mongolian, who take care of publicity, arrange for public concerts and recording sessions, and write songs and lyrics for him. In 2004 and 2005 Qifeng sold 200,000 CD copies, which is considered a big figure in China's private enterprise pop music market today. Qifeng's audience comes not only from Beijing, but from other big coastal cities as well, particularly in the south, such as Guangzhou and Hong Kong. Members of his audiences include students and especially businessmen and taxi drivers; most of whom are Han. Of course we Mongols love his songs and are very proud of him, but the Mongol song market is too small. We need to attract the Han market, and therefore most of his songs are sung in Han Chinese, but he is fluent in both the Han and Mongolian languages."

I then asked: "Besides selling records, does Qifeng perform in public?" Naqin replied: "Oh yes, Qifeng constantly travels and gives concerts, usually on temporary outdoor stages, just like those of Western rock music concerts."

"Who decides what song to write, and how a song is produced?"

"Qifeng keeps close ties with his listeners, who write to him telling him what kind of songs they like most. Keeping their requests in mind, we write the lyrics first, and then a composer sets the lyrics to music."

The next day, I went to a record store in Beijing and asked for Qifeng's CDs, which are readily available. I asked the salesperson whether she liked Qifeng's music, and she replied affirmatively and enthusiastically: "Oh yes, we young people like his music very much. It is so different, and so Mongolian. His songs take us away from this congested and polluted city into the clear blue sky of the Mongolian grassland!" I asked: "Have you been to Mongolia?" She said: "Not yet, but I will, one day." I reflected that this is certainly a far cry from the attitude of the older generation. Twenty years ago when I told a friend I was going to the grass-land of Mongolia, she said with shock and dismay, "What? You are going to that wilderness!" Now, through the medium of its haunting melodies and new modes of production, Mongolia has acquired new chic in the Chinese imagination.

In this chapter we have touched on only a fraction of China's enormously varied and valuable musical treasures, many of which have undergone traumatic periods of change, suppression, revival, and renewal in the twentieth century. When I think about the limited musical diet of my high school days in China and compare it to what is once again available today, I am excited by the musical vitality I encounter every time I go back. I feel proud when I see music by Chinese composers on programs of symphony orchestras in the United States or Europe, and pleased when I remember that that UNESCO has recognized the cultural importance and artistic worth of Mongolian Long Song and *Kunqu* opera. We can be assured that music in China will continue to play an important role in the social, political, and everyday world of the Chinese people, as it has been doing for several millennia.

SUMMARY

✓• Study and Review on mymusiclab.com

In our excursions through Chinese musical life we have been reminded that Chinese civilization dates back many centuries and includes many different ethnic groups, cultures, and languages under its umbrella. We have had occasion to encounter key instruments like the qin (zither) and pipa (lute). We've also explored traditional genres of music, including jingju (or Peking Opera), one of China's best-known theatrical/musical styles, featuring elaborate sets and costumes and a richly developed sung repertory. The contexts within which musical performances are held, moreover, led us to investigate traditional venues such as teahouses, where music is played by amateurs and professionals alike. We found that the audience at teahouses comes and goes as it pleases, often talking during a performance. The traditional music played in these venues is often highly improvised, with no announced program.

We also explored the political and philosophical context within which musicians and audiences have had to shape their relationship to performance. So, for instance, drawing on ideas developed within Confucianism, "good music" is understood as maintaining the proper social order and underlining the beliefs endorsed by the state; "bad music," however, leads to improper behavior or to criticism of the status quo. The rise of Communism and the successful 1949 revolution, introduced a new, didactic type of music, expressed well in the many "Songs for the Masses" and meant to instill the government's core message in the citizenry. This music drew on Soviet models. As Chinese society has opened up somewhat following the Cultural Revolution of the 1960s and early 1970s—and this especially in the 1990s and early 2000s—North Atlantic forms of both art music and popular song have become more accepted, though there remains an "underground" of unacceptable musical styles, many of which question the validity of the state's power. Finally, ethnic minorities within China have increasingly found a musical voice through which to assert their unique presence within China.

Though our excursions have been brief, I hope that these encounters with Chinese musical life will inspire you to continued exploration of China's long musical history and its many musical genres, instruments, and ensembles.

BIBLIOGRAPHY

Robert H. Van Gulick, *The Lore of the Chinese Lute*, rev. ed. (Vermont and Tokyo: Charles E. Tuttle, 1969); Fritz Kuttner, *The Archaeology of Music in Ancient China* (New York: Oaragon House, 1990); Su Zheng, *Claiming Diaspora: Music, Transnationalism, and Cultural Politics in Asian/Chinese America* (Oxford; New York: Oxford University Press, 2010); Marc Moskowitz, *Cries of Joy, Songs of Sorrow: Chinese Pop Music and its Cultural Connotations* (Honolulu: University of Hawaii Press, 2010); Frederick Lau, *Music in China: Experiencing Music, Expressing Culture* (New York: Oxford University Press, 2008); Anne Birrell, *China's Bawdy: The Pop Songs of China, 4th-5th Century* (Cambridge, UK: McGuiness China Monographs, 2008); Mingyue Liang, *Music of the Billion: An Introduction to Chinese Musical Culture* (New York: Heinrichshofen, 1985); Mingyue Liang, *The Chinese Chi'in: Its History and Music* (San Francisco: Chinese National Music Association and San Francisco Conservatory of Music, 1972); Bell Yung, *Cantonese Opera: Performance as Creative Process* (Cambridge: Cambridge University Press, 1989); Colin P. Mackerra, *The Rise of Peking Opera, 1770-1870* (Oxford: Clarendon Press, 1972); Kenneth J. DeWoskin, *A Song for One or Two: Music and the Concept of Art in Early China*. Michigan Papers in Chinese Studies No. 42 (Ann Arbor: Center for Chinese Studies, University of Michigan, 1982); Rulan Chao, *Song Dynasty Musical Sources and Their Interpretation* (Cambridge, MA: Harvard University Press, 1967); J. Lawrence Witzleben, *Silk and Bamboo Music in Shanghai: The Jiangnan Sizhu Instrumental Ensemble Tradition* (Kent, OH: Kent State University Press, 1995); Andrew F. Jones, *Like a Knife* (Ithaca, NY: Cornell University Press, 1992); Andrew F., Jones, *Yellow Music: Media Culture and Colonial Modernity in the Chinese Jazz Age* (Durham, NC: Duke University Press, 2001); Frederick Lau, "Forever Red: The Invention of Solo Dizi Music in Post-1949 China,"*British Journal of Ethnomusicology* (1996) 5:113–131; Jonathan P. J. Stock, *Musical Creativity in Twentieth-Century China: Abing, His Music, and Its Changing Meanings* (Rochester, NY: University of Rochester Press, 1996); John E. Myers, *The Way of the Pipa: Structure and Imagery in Chinese Lute Music* (Kent, OH: Kent State University Press, 1992); Stephen Jones, *Folk Music of China: Living Instrumental Tradition* (Oxford: Clarendon Press, 1992); Isabel K. F. Wong, "*Geming Gequ*: Songs for the Education for the Masses," in Bonnie MacDougall, ed., *Popular Chinese Literature and Performing Arts in the Peoples' Republic of China, 1949–1979* (Berkeley and Los Angeles: University of California Press, 1984); Isabel K. F. Wong, "From Reaction to Synthesis: Chinese Musicology in the Twentieth Century," in Bruno Nettl and Philip V. Bohlman, eds., *Comparative Musicology and Anthropology of Music* (Chicago: University of Chicago Press, 1991); Isabel K. F. Wong, "The Incantation of Shanghai: Singing a City into Existence," in Timothy J. Craig, Richard King, eds., *Global Goes Local: Popular Culture in Asia* (Vancouver: University of British Columbia Press, 2003); J. Lawrence Witzleben, ed. "China," in Robert C. Provine, et al. eds., *The Garland Encyclopedia of World Music*, vol. 7: East Asia (New York and London: Routledge, 2002).

DISCOGRAPHY

General   **Anthology of the World's Music: The Music of China**, Vol. 1: Chinese Instruments, ed. and with notes by Fredric Lieberman (Anthology); *Chine Populaire, Musique Classique* (instrumental music) (Ocora); *Chinese Classical Music* (instrumental) (Lyrichord LL 72).

Jingju   **The Chinese Opera** (Lyrichord LLST 7212 sides A & B); *The Peking Opera* (Seraphim SER 60201 sides A & B); *Ruse of the Empty City* (Folkways FW 8882 sides A & B); *Traditional Peking Opera* (Folkways FW 8883 sides A & B).

Kunqu Youyuan Jingmeng   (A Dream in the Garden) (Art Tune Co. CO 228 & 229); *Kunqü Changduan Xuancui* [Selections of Well-known Kunqü Excerpts] (in six cassettes, Shanghai Audio Production).

Qin (Ch'in) Music   **Ch'in Music of Ten Centuries** (Museum Collection Berlin MC7 A & B); *Chinese Master Pieces for the Ch'in* (Lyrichord LLST 7342 A & B); *The Drunken Fisherman* (Lyrichord LL 72 B/3); *"Youlan"* ("Orchids in a Secluded Valley") (Art Tune Co. ATC 73 A/1); *Wumen Qin Music* (Compact disc, Hugo Production, HRP 712-2).

Pipa Music **Floating Petals**...*Wild Geese, Lui Pui-yuen, pipa* (Nonesuch Explorer Series, H-72085); *China, Music of the Pipa* (Complex Disc, Elektra Nonesuch 9 72085-2); *Ambush From All Sides* (Compact Disc, Bailey Record, BCD 90028, band 1); *Autumn Moon Over the Han Palace* (Compact Disc, Bailey Record, BCD 90029, bands 5 & 6); *Autumn Recollection* (Compact Disc, Bailey Record BCD 90030, bands 6 & 7).

Jiangnan Sizhu   **"Chunjiang huasyueye" ("The Moonlit Spring River")** (Art Tune Co. ATC 16 A/1); *"Sanliu" ("Three Six")* (Art Tune Co. ATC 16 B/1); *"Huanlege" ("Song of Happiness")* (Art Tune Co. ATC 16 A/2); *Popular Jiangnan Music* (Hong Kong; under license from China Records Co., Peking).

Regional Ensemble Music   **Music of Amoy** (Art Tune Co. AST 4002 A & B); *Shantung Music of Confucius' Homeland* (Lyrichord LLST 7112 A & B); *Chinese Masterpieces for the Erh-hu* (Lyrichord, LLST 7132 A & B).

"Songs for the Masses"   **The East Is Red** (China Records M 982); *Commune Members Are All Like Sunflowers* (China Records M 2265).

The Legendary Chinese Hits   Vol. 5 Chow Hsuan, EMI FH81005 2.

The Music of Japan

ISABEL K.F. WONG

HOGAKU PERFORMANCE IN TOKYO

Tokyo, Japan's capital, is a crowded, bustling modern city of around 13 million people, nearly 10 percent of the country's population. Although a formidable city at first glance, Tokyo is more like a conglomeration of small towns and neighborhoods clustered together, each with its own shops and narrow, winding streets.

Tokyo is both new and old, Eastern and Western. The variety of Japanese, Asian, and Western musical performances that take place in Tokyo during the concert season (spring to fall) is a reflection of this fact. Any day during the concert season, the visitor is likely to find performances of Western art music or popular music, as well as performances of **hogaku**, Japan's traditional music. Some hogaku performances may take place in the concert halls clustered around

the Tokyo Railroad Station, others in the recital halls inside great department stores in the Ginza area, Tokyo's chic shopping district, and still others in the National Theater, situated across the street from the grounds of the Imperial Palace.

During one of my recent visits, I attended two musical performances at the National Theater, which was opened in 1966 for the promotion and development of traditional Japanese performing arts. It actually comprises two theaters: a large one seating nearly 1,800 people, which is used principally for the performance of **kabuki** musical drama, and a small one seating about 630, which is used to stage a variety of concerts of hogaku music and dance, as well as performances of puppet musical plays known as **bunraku**. Two restaurants are also attached to the National Theater: a larger one on the second floor that serves a set menu for dinner, and a smaller one at the front of the theater grounds that serves snack food.

✳ Explore
Learning Objectives on
mymusiclab.com

✳ Explore
*a map of Japan on the
Interactive Globe* on
mymusiclab.com

HOGAKU
Native Japanese music.

KABUKI
The main form of Japanese popular musical theater.

BUNRAKU
The main form of puppet theater in Japan.

PENTATONIC
Having five pitches.

HETEROPHONY
Two or more performers play the same melody, but with small differences in timing or ornamentation.

A Mixed Concert

One of the hogaku concerts I attended at the National Theater was a gala event commemorating the sixtieth birthday of a respected master. It took place in the small theater and started at 6:30 p.m., but most of the audience arrived before curtain time to have dinner at the restaurants. The concert was sold-out, and I was lucky to have obtained a standing-room ticket—the least expensive kind—at 4,000 yen (equivalent to about $40 U.S. in 1995). The audience was greeted by ushers at the door of the theater and handed program notes (in Japanese) about the four items to be performed; this included song texts and instrumentation and was followed, by many advertisements. The inside of the theater included a proscenium stage and rows of seats. Both the program and the theatre's physical space, then, were similar to what someone attending a concert by the Berlin Philharmonic or the Chicago Symphony Orchestra might expect to encounter. The members of the audience were primarily well-dressed Japanese men and women wearing Western-style clothing, but some older women wore the Japanese kimono.

The relatively long concert, lasting more than three hours, began with three pieces for a chamber ensemble consisting of six musicians. The final piece of the program, which came after an intermission of about twenty minutes, called for a chorus and orchestra, each consisting of a dozen or so performers, as well as dancers. All the performers wore traditional attire and knelt on the floor of the stage with low music stands placed before them.

As each piece began, the performers picked up their instruments from the floor in front of them in a deliberate and uniform fashion. The attentiveness of the audience complemented the erect posture and strict decorum of the performers. At the end of each piece the performers replaced their instruments on the stage floor in the same way that they had taken them up, and only then did the audience applaud. The performers acknowledged the applause by bowing formally and then remained stationary until the curtain had descended completely.

The first piece in the program was an ensemble played by three *kotos* (long, thirteen-stringed zithers) and three *shamisens* (a three-stringed, long-necked,

Yuki Yamada playing the Japanese Koto with the Kifu Mitsuhashi Ensemble at the Japan Society, New York City, 2003. *Source:* Jack Vartoogian/ Front Row Photos

fretless lute, whose sound box is covered with cat or dog skin front and back and whose strings are plucked with a large plectrum). The musicians, who included both men and women, sang as they played. I noticed that the first and last sections were sung with instrumental accompaniment, whereas the middle section, which was the longest, was entirely instrumental. I also noticed that although the music was primarily **pentatonic**, it occasionally used auxiliary pitches. The voice, the kotos, and the shamisens seemed to share a basic melody, but each performed the melody in a somewhat different fashion, rhythmically as well as melodically, resulting in a texture that may be described as **heterophonic**. The second piece was a jiuta (a major koto genre). Broadly speaking, the term denotes a type of vocal piece having a lyrical text that is accompanied principally by the shamisen and sometimes by a koto as well. This performance included both shamisen and koto accompaniment, and the former was supplied by the vocalist herself. Like the previous piece, this too had three sections, of which the middle was a purely instrumental interlude.

The third piece was a trio for solo voice and two shamisens that was derived from a narrative genre called **shinnai-bushi**. The vocalist, who did not play any instrument, sang with a penetrating voice. The type of shamisen used in this piece had a thicker neck than those used in the previous pieces. While one shamisen played the basic melody, the other played a lighter and higher part, heterophonically elaborating the melody. In contrast to the others, this piece was divided into six sections.

During the intermission, people who had not had dinner before the concert—I among them—went to the theater restaurants to have a quick bite. The food was delicious and was served in beautifully decorated lacquered bowls and plates, but when the bell rang indicating that the curtain was about to go up, I hurriedly finished my dinner and returned to the auditorium.

The final piece, featuring some two dozen musicians, made me realize how much of a foreigner I was to Japanese music. Despite the magnificent costumes of the dancers, I had difficulty concentrating on the performance, because I found it disconcerting to have a variety of musical genres and instrumentations mixed in a single modern composition. Yet most of the audience appreciated the piece greatly and even seemed to prefer this composition to the others. The different types of instruments used included a number commonly associated with solo or narrative genres, such as the koto and shamisen, various types of *fue* (horizontal flute), the *shakuhachi* (end-blown, notched flute), and the *nohkan*, the horizontal flute of the Noh theater. Among the other instruments used, some were borrowed from the **gagaku** court music ensemble, such as the *ryuteki* (a horizontal flute), the *hichiriki*, a double-reed oboe, which has

Taiso Yoshitoshi, "Enjoying Herself," 1888. Woodblock print. A music teacher of the Kaei era (1848–1854) smiles as she plays her shamisen. *Source:* Asian Art & Archaeology, Inc./Corbis

✳ **Explore**
the Musical Instrument Gallery on
mymusiclab.com

SHINNAI-BUSHI

A musical narrative form accompanied by the shamisen, found in Shinnai Tsuruga.

GAGAKU

Japanese court orchestral music.

a distinct and penetrating sound, and the *sho*, a mouth organ something like a harmonica. There was also a small percussion ensemble, comprising a small pair of cymbals, a small drum, a wooden clapper, and a small gong. This modern attempt to combine various kinds of traditional music and dance in a single new composition encompassed: fragments of a *jiuta* (played by a trio made up of shamisen, koto, and shakuhachi) an exerpt from the *nagauta* repertory of the *kabuki* theater, a bit of Buddhist chant called shomyo, a shamisen duet, and finally, materials deriving from folk song and dance. At the end of what seemed to this perplexed foreigner to be a tediously long and incongruous composition, the audience surprised me by rising and giving the performers a standing ovation. As soon as the curtain fell, however, the audience disappeared quickly, and clearly no encore was expected.

⊙—Watch the **Video** of a koto and a shakuhachi player on **mymusiclab.com**

A Kabuki Appreciation Class

The second performance I attended at the National Theater was an appreciation class for the *kabuki* theater, which was extremely interesting and educational.

Kabuki, Japan's main popular theater, is regularly performed in several venues in Tokyo; among these, the most famous and best known is the *Kabukiza* (*za* means "seat," but today it has come to mean "theater"), which is situated in the Ginza and contains, aside from the theater, six restaurants. The Kabukiza has about eight or nine kabuki productions a year, each of which runs about twenty-five days. Usually two different programs are performed daily; matinees run from about 11:00 a.m. to 4:00 p.m., and evening performances run from 4:30 p.m. to 9:00 p.m.

The Kabukiza was built in 1887 and has been reconstructed many times since then. It is an impressive theater with more than 2,000 seats, a wide orchestra, and two balconies. The stage, almost ninety-three feet wide, is equipped with revolving platforms and trap lifts. In addition, there is a long runway, the *hanamichi*, connecting the stage with the rear of the theater, which is also part of the stage. In the lobby, various recordings of, and books in Japanese and English, about kabuki are sold along with various souvenirs. Foreigners who do not understand Japanese or are novices to the theater can rent earphones and listen to a simultaneous translation of the libretto.

Kabuki performances are also held several times a year at the larger hall of the National Theater, which also runs a "*Kabuki* appreciation class" for young people every summer. There are two such classes daily at 11:00 a.m. and 2:30 p.m., and I bought a ticket for the morning one.

When it was time for the class to start, all the lights in the theater were turned off except those on the bare proscenium stage, and a man in a kimono appeared on the stage.

"Hello everyone, my name is Iwai Hanshiro, and I am a kabuki actor. I am going to tell you something about the kabuki theater today so that you can appreciate it better. It is a pity that too many Japanese people nowadays cannot appreciate kabuki because they do not understand it. The purpose of this

appreciation class is to tell you some of
the fun and secrets of the kabuki theater,
so you will come to the theater again and
again.

"Let me first tell you a bit of the history of kabuki. The first performance was
done in 1596 entirely by women. The government immediately banned female performance of kabuki, so the stage was taken
over by a troupe of boys, but since 1652,
kabuki has been performed by adult males,
as it still is today, and female roles are impersonated by male actors. In the eighteenth century, when Japan was ruled by
a succession of military strongmen known
as shoguns and entered a long period of
peace, kabuki developed into a definite
cultural form for urban dwellers (*chonin*).
You must remember that kabuki is predominantly a dance theater with musical
accompaniment; it makes use of extensive and elaborate scenery, costumes, and
properties, which I will show you later.

Togashi, a character in the kabuki theatre in a piece called *Kanjincho*. Written
in the 19th century, it takes place in 12th century Japan. *Source:* FRANCE ©
Colette Masson/Roger-Viollet/The Image Works

"Kabuki has borrowed a lot from other types of theater, such as the classical *noh* theater and the puppet theater bunraku. It has also absorbed folk dance
and popular dance. How many of you have been to the noh theater?" Only a
few hands were raised.

"How many of you have seen bunraku?" More hands were raised.

"Let me demonstrate some kabuki gestures that were derived from bunraku and noh."

At this point our lecturer made a vigorous gesture with his arms and legs,
which was masculine, abrupt, and angular. "This gesture is an adaptation of
puppet movement of the bunraku theater, known as *aragoto*, meaning 'rough
business.'"

He then walked in stately, gliding steps, moving without any perceptible
upper-body motion. "This gentle and refined movement came from the noh
theater.

"Dance is very important in kabuki theater. A kabuki actor is primarily a
dancer, and dance is an essential movement toward a climactic static posture."

He now struck and held a dramatic pose, and then turned to us and said,
"Now, this is the time for you to applaud me. We kabuki actors like to know
that you appreciate what we do!" The young audience, encouraged by the lecturer, giggled and applauded enthusiastically. At that moment, a middle-aged
woman sitting next to me shouted, "Bravo!" in Japanese, which was acknowledged by our lecturer with a deep bow in her direction. The young audience
turned to look at her with puzzled expressions on their faces, whereupon our

lecturer said, "This is a very appropriate and common way to give praise to actors. You may try it yourselves!" "Bravo! Bravo!" shouted the audience, greatly energized. Our lecturer bowed graciously to them.

"It is now time to show you something about the kabuki stage. It is equipped with several trap lifts, which are used to bring scenery or musicians from below the stage to the level of the stage floor, and vice versa." As he spoke, several men, who were holding musical instruments in their hands, suddenly rose up through the stage floor. The young audience, obviously loving this, burst into applause.

"There are more fun things to follow. The stage is also equipped with two revolving stages in the center, an outer one and an inner one, which are capable of being moved in opposite directions. These revolving stages are used to change the entire set at once and have been in use since the sixteenth century." As he spoke, a realistic set depicting a large rice field complete with stacks of grain, trees, and thatched huts suddenly revolved into the center of the stage. A few seconds later, this set disappeared from sight, and another one showing the inside of a house, with cooking utensils and straw mats on the floor, appeared in front of us.

Then our lecturer pointed in the direction of the raised runway connecting the stage to the rear of the auditorium, and asked: "How many of you know the name of this runway?" A few treble voices shouted, "*Hanamichi!*" "Good!" our lecturer said. "You have been studying this in school, no doubt! The hanamichi is a unique feature of the kabuki theater. It serves as an additional acting space for the actors and as a more intimate acting area within the audience. There is a passageway built beneath the floor of the theater for actors to go from the dressing rooms behind the stage to the entrance of the hanamichi without being seen by the audience."

Suddenly, a man dressed in the costume of a peasant appeared on the hanamichi at the rear of the theater. He walked a few steps, paused, gently moving his head from side to side as if hesitating, and finally moved forward to the stage proper with an attitude of determination.

"Meet Hayano Kanpei, the hero of the play you are going to see after my lecture! Have you guessed that Kanpei is no peasant? He is really a ronin—that is, a samurai who has lost his master. He is disguised as a peasant to avenge his master's death. If you have been observant, you should have noticed that before he finally proceeded to the stage proper, he moved his head gently from side to side. A peasant does not move in such a refined fashion! The connoisseur would know from this gesture that his real social status is higher than that of a peasant." At this point, the actor who portrayed Kanpei gave the audience a bow and exited.

"Another important element of kabuki theater is music, and it is time to introduce the musicians! In general, there are two groups of musicians: those who appear on the stage, and those who do not. The onstage musician group is called the **degatari**, and the offstage group is called the **geza**." He gave a signal, and a pair of men were elevated from below to stage left. Both were kneeling, and one was holding a shamisen.

"This is the **chobo**, a pair of onstage musicians borrowed from the puppet theater. One is a narrator; the other one accompanies him on the shamisen. Even though they may sometimes participate musically in the events taking place on the stage, the chobo musicians are not actors.

DEGATARI
On-stage musicians in Kabuki theater. This group is divided functionally into two separate ensembles, called the chobo (storytellers) and debayashi (ensemble specializing in performing nagauta, or "long song").

GEZA
The off-stage music of the kabuki theater.

CHOBO
The Gidayu (musico-narrative) duo on the kabuki stage.

"Let me give you an example. Suppose that I am a character in a play who is sobbing. The chobo narrator can take over the sobbing for me without a break, and the shamisen player in turn can imitate the sound of sobbing on his instrument, while all the time the sobbing is supposed to be that of the character onstage, and the accompanists do not participate in the action. The chobo musicians not only participate musically in the events on the stage, they also narrate and explain the plot to the audience; you could say that they are storytellers.

"Sometimes a character in a play may want to sing about his feelings, or another may want to perform a dance. Who will provide musical accompaniment? Another group of onstage musicians is called the **debayashi**, meaning 'coming-out orchestra.' These musicians are singers as well as instrumentalists, and their number varies according to the needs of the drama." He gave a signal, and from the rear of the stage a trap lift raised a two-tiered platform covered with red cloth on whose upper tier knelt six men holding shamisens; below them, on the level of the stage, six singers knelt behind low music stands.

"Let us hear their music!" the lecturer commanded, and the ensemble started to play. "This music is called *nagauta*, meaning 'Long Song,'" our lecturer said. "It is the heart of kabuki music. The music is produced by an ensemble consisting of singers, several shamisen, and sometimes a bamboo flute, plus a percussion ensemble borrowed from the noh theater that includes several drums and the flute called nohkan. Two or three of the singers are soloists; the rest of the singers sing the chorus part in unison." (Listen to CD I, 19 for an example of a debayashi ensemble performing nagauta).

"Now let us bring on the geza musicians." At this moment both the chobo and the debayashi musicians were lowered beneath the stage, and downstage left another group of instrumentalists and a large drum appeared.

"These are offstage musicians called the geza," we were told. "They normally sit in a room situated at stage right, where they can look out to the stage and the hanamichi through a bamboo curtain, and the audience cannot see them. Their job is to provide sound effects for the dramatic action. The instruments are: the *o-daiko* (big drum), shamisen, nohkan, and gongs and bells. Let me show you the strokes of the o-daiko." As he was talking he picked up the two drumsticks and hit the drum with several types of strokes. "Some strokes indicate curtain calls; others create different atmospheres and moods; some strokes represent raindrops, the sound of wind, or thunder, and others represent the appearance of a ghost." When the demonstration was over, the geza musicians disappeared from the stage.

"I know you are very eager to see today's play, but I have yet one more important instrument to show you, and that is the *hyoshigi*." Immediately, a man appeared at the corner stage right, holding two rectangular woodblocks in his hand; he knelt and began playing the blocks in a series of accelerating beats.

"The player is called the *kyogenkata*; he is a stagehand, and the rhythmic pattern he just played announces the rise of the curtain." With this final demonstration, the actor concluded his introduction and called for the play to begin."

DEBAYASHI
The on-stage musicians of the kabuki theater.

LISTENING GUIDE

KABUKI NAGAUTA MUSIC FROM THE PLAY "DOJOJI"

GO TO www.mymusiclab.com for the Automated Listening Guide CDI • Track 19/Download Track 19

This performance illustrates the sound of the debayashi ensemble in kabuki theater. Listen for the way that the vocalist, nohkan (bamboo flute), and shamisen take turns leading the performance.

TIME	SECTION	MUSICAL EVENTS
0:00–0:22	**Introduction:** Listen for the interaction between the shamisen players and the vocalist. They are performing similar melodic material but elaborating it in different ways.	The vocalist and shamisen perform together in this introductory section.
0:22–1:01	**Instrumental Section:** Notice here the sound of the nohkan (bamboo flute) and the drums, both of which join the shamisen. Also listen for the way the nohkan and shamisen take turns leading the ensemble.	The instrumental section gets under way, featuring a melody performed by the nohkan. It is accompanied now by shamisen and drum.
1:01–1:13		The nohkan drops out of the texture, making room for the shamisen to take the lead.
1:13–1:19		The nohkan returns momentarily.
1:19–1:22		The shamisen, once again, takes over the lead role.
1:22–1:41	**Vocal Section:** Listen for the expanded ensemble that accompanies the singer in this section.	The vocalist returns, accompanied here by a much more energetic ensemble including shamisen, nohkan, drum, and a small, bell-like gong.
1:41–2:05	**Instrumental Section:** By now you should be familiar with the sound of the ensemble, so listen now more closely to the way the parts fit together in this performance.	As during the first instrumental section, the nohkan takes the lead at first.
2:05–2:10		The shamisen takes over from the nohkan for a brief moment.
2:10–2:27		The nohkan re-enters as the principal melodic instrument.
2:27–2:40		The shamisen returns once more to lead the ensemble.
2:40–3:02	**Vocal Section:** The vocalist returns, accompanied by the full ensemble heard earlier.	Just as in the section heard at [1:22–1:41], the vocalist returns accompanied by shamisen, nohkan, drum, and bell.
3:02–3:15	**Instrumental Section/Return of Vocalist:** Listen for the short instrumental section here.	A short instrumental section, led by shamisen and then, beginning at [3:04] by nohkan.
3:15–3:35		The vocalist returns, and continues to perform even as the recording fades out beginning at [3:26].

The play, about Kanji's revenge, employed all the devices, mechanisms, and musical groups we had just learned about, and using the simultaneous translation of the dramatic dialogue and explanation of the plot in English transmitted through the headphones I wore, I found that I could easily understand the plot and enjoy the drama.

Vocal and instrumental chamber music recitals and performances of kabuki can be heard and seen in Japan nowadays with some frequency, particularly in the four major cities: Tokyo, Kyoto, Osaka, and Nagoya. These types of hogaku music are essentially products of Japan's most recent "ancient" period—that is, the time from the seventeenth to the nineteenth century known as the Tokugawa or Edo period, when Japan, ruled by the Tokugawa clan in the capital Edo (present-day Tokyo), experienced a period of uninterrupted peace. Cities such as Edo and Osaka grew into populous centers of trade and government, where a large and prosperous bourgeoisie developed, including tradesmen and artisans, who vigorously supported the developing arts and culture. It was under the patronage of this bourgeoisie that the kabuki theater and the many chamber vocal-instrumental genres involving the koto, shamisen, and other instruments came into being and flourished.

Read *about Japan's major historical periods* on **mymusiclab.com**

THEATER MUSIC

The culture of the bourgeoisie, essentially urban and popular, was characterized by a taste for romantic or comic novels, for salacious or witty lampoons, for brightly colored prints and paintings, and above all, for spectacular theatrical entertainment. The kabuki theater, with its lavish costumes and staging, its elaborate stage machinery, and its fondness for plots of romantic love, is representative of this culture.

The Bunraku Puppet Theater

The other important popular theater of the Edo period, which can also be seen today, principally in Osaka and in Tokyo's National Theater, is the puppet theater called *bunraku*. Emerging at about the same time as kabuki and under the same circumstances and patronage—primarily that of the bourgeoisie or chonin of Osaka—bunraku both borrowed from and exerted influence on kabuki theater.

The bunraku puppet, made of wood, is moved by three puppeteers who manipulate its arms, fingers, legs, body, head, eyes, mouth, and even eyebrows. These movements are so realistic that the spectators can easily forget the actor is made of wood, even though the puppeteers are not hidden behind or above the stage. The two junior puppeteers are, however, completely shrouded in black and hooded, and only the senior puppeteer's face is visible.

The narration of the bunraku, both sung and spoken, is provided by a narrator-chanter, who is accompanied on shamisen. This is the same combination as the chobo ensemble we encountered in the kabuki demonstration. When

Bunraku puppeteers operate a warrior puppet during the Kumagai Jinya scene from the play Ichinotani Futaba Gunki. *Source:* Jack Vartoogian/Front Row Photos

a kabuki play is derived from the bunraku theater, the narrative and music accompanying the dramatic actions are provided by the chobo, in the same manner as in the bunraku theater.

The narrative style used in bunraku is called **gidayubushi**, after its developer, Takemoto Gidayu (1651–1714) of Osaka. The vocal style of gidayubushi includes chants, heightened speech, and lyrical songs. The shamisen, whose music is made up of various arrangements of stereotyped patterns, plays preludes, interludes, and postludes to the singing. Bunraku rose to its artistic and popular height when Takemoto collaborated with the famous playwright Chikamatsu Monzaemon (1653–1725).

The Noh Theater

Edo-period musical theatricals are by no means the only kinds of traditional stage genres one can hear and see in Japan today. Among genres originating in other historical periods of Japan, the noh theater is particularly important. Combining various folk dances, musical theatricals, and religious and courtly entertainment of medieval times, noh was transformed into a serious Buddhist art by the performer Kannami Kiyotsugu (1333–1384) and into a refined court art by his son, Zeami Motokiyo (1363–1444). Wearing a mask, brocade robes, and white socks, the chief actor moves and dances slowly on a bare stage with perfectly controlled and restrained movements. Accompanied by a male chorus and a small instrumental ensemble made up of a flute and three drums, he carries the spectator into the austere world of a medieval Japan deeply influenced by Zen Buddhism.

Noh was a product of the Muromachi period (1333–1615), which was marked by continuous military strife among the various clans of warriors

GIDAYUBUSHI
A major Japanese musical narrative style accompanied by the Shamisen created by Takemoto Gidayu.

NOH
Japanese classical drama that originally developed in the early fourteenth century.

(samurai). Exclusively an art of the ruling samurai class from the fifteenth to the nineteenth centuries, noh, with its performing style of elegant simplicity and restraint and its major themes of redemption of human suffering through the love of Buddha, is a direct antithesis of the flamboyant, colorful, and lavish theatrical entertainments of the Tokugawa bourgeoisie such as kabuki and bunraku.

In Zeami's day, a performance of noh consisted of at least five plays—a god play, a warrior play, a female-wig play, a possession play, and a demon play—interspersed with comic plays called *kyogen* for a change of pace. Today the usual program consists of two or three noh plays (each lasting about an hour) and one or two kyogen (lasting about thirty to forty minutes).

Supported mainly by intellectuals now, noh is performed in major cities in special indoor theaters that are owned and operated by five traditional schools of noh performance. In addition, noh plays are performed on various festival occasions throughout Japan on outdoor stages that are built in the compounds of Shinto or Buddhist temples.

The main element and action of a noh play is linked closely with its major actor, the *shite*. The supporting actor, or *waki*, provides a foil for the revelation of the shite's character and the explanation for his actions.

Noh plays are typically in two acts. Thematically, these acts can be organized into five major *dan* (sections or units). The first act comprises the first dan—an introduction—and the second, third and fourth dan—which together make up the exposition of the play—and ends with a dance called *kuse*, the high point of the play. This act provides a full exposition of the spirit of the *shite*. The second act consists of only the fifth dan; in this denouement the shite is transformed into a new character (usually a supernatural being), sings a couple of songs, and performs another dance, called the *mai*, which reveals his new essence after his transformation.

Music for noh consists of songs (solo and choral) sung by the actors or chorus, recitative-like heightened speech for the actors, and instrumental music played by an instrumental quartet (a flute and three drums). The functions of the instrumental ensemble are to play introductory music and interludes, to set the scene or mood of individual units within the two acts, to accompany entrances and exits of actors, to accompany songs and dances, and to provide a rhythmic background for dialogue and action. The songs (*uta*), sung by either the actors or the chorus, are of two types—the **sageuta**, which are short, slow, and in low range, and the **ageuta**, which are longer and higher.

The instruments making up the instrumental quartet for noh are a flute called nohkan and three drums of different sizes. Unlike most bamboo flutes, which consist simply of a tube of dried bamboo, the nohkan is constructed from such a tube split lengthwise into strips that are then turned inside out, wrapped with cherry bark, and lacquered. It has seven finger holes and a mouth hole. Other elements of its construction and playing technique lend this flute a distinctive, piercing sound that helps it retain a strong individuality within the noh ensemble.

The music of the nohkan is made up of various arrangements of a large number of stock patterns. Different pieces are produced by rearrangement of the sequential order of these patterns, and the use of certain sequences is

SAGEUTA
A type of song in lower vocal range used in Noh plays.

AGEUTA
A type of song in higher vocal range used in Noh plays.

HAYASHI
Generic name for ensembles of
flute and drums.

determined by the dramatic conventions of the noh theater. The music for the nohkan serves as a marker for certain subunits of a dan, sets the tempo for the dances and accompanies them, adds a melodic layer to the drum patterns, sets the pitches for the chorus and accompanies it, and provides emphasis for certain lyrical passages of the songs.

The nohkan and the three drums used in noh are collectively called **hayashi** (a generic term for ensembles of flute and drums). The three drums are: the *ko-tsuzumi*, the *o-tsuzumi*, and the *taiko*. The first two are hourglass-shaped drums, whereas the taiko is a shallow barrel drum. Of the three, the smallest but most important is the ko-tsuzumi; although it derives from Chinese and Korean models, the manner of playing it in noh theater is entirely a Japanese development.

The three drums have wooden bodies with two skin heads that are stretched over iron rings and tied to the drum bodies with ropes. The special

✳[Explore
*the Musical Instrument
Gallery* on
mymusiclab.com

Sakiji Tanaka playing the Noh drum Taiko.
Source: Shozo Sato/Isabel K. F. Wong

Sakiji Tanaka playing the Noh drum Kotsuzumi. A kotsuzumi is an hourglass shaped drum held at the shoulder and used in Noh theater. Other instruments include the nohkan (transverse flute), the okawa or otsuzumi (hourglass shaped drum placed on the lap), and the taiko (barrel shaped drum placed on a small floor stand and played with two sticks). *Source:* Shozo Sato/Isabel K. F. Wong

The Noh drum otsuzumi. The otsuzumi is one of four orchestral instruments (three drums and a flute) used to accompany the dances and songs of the traditional Japanese Noh drama. *Source:* Shozo Sato/Isabel K. F. Wong

Sakiji Tanaka playing the Noh drum otsuzumi.
Source: Shozo Sato/Isabel K. F. Wong

tone of the ko-tsuzumi is achieved by carving special patterns on the inside surface of the body and affixing bits of damp paper to the rear head, which is not struck. The ropes holding the heads to the body may be squeezed to increase tension on the heads. The tension of the head of the o-tsuzumi is always at a maximum and thus cannot be altered by further tightening the ropes. In fact, before a performance, the drumhead is heated over a hibachi grill to increase the tension still further, and during a performance a newly heated drum may be substituted. All this tension creates a dry, hard sound that may be increased by the use of hard thimbles on the player's fingers.

The taiko is played with two thick sticks instead of the hands. The drum is placed on a special stand that grips the encircling ropes, lifting the drum off the floor for better resonance. The taiko is used sparingly, normally joining the other instruments for dance sections.

All three drums are capable of producing several basic sounds, and their varying combinations form stock patterns that are identified onomatopoeically.

KAKEGOE
Vocal drum calls used in noh theater.

YOKYUKU
Choral singing in noh.

KOTOBA
A heightened speech style used in the noh theater.

FUSHI
A term for melody in general.

YOWAGIN
Soft-style noh music.

TSUYOGIN
A strong-style noh music.

An additional but integral part of noh drumming is the use of drum calls by the drummers. These **kakegoe**, as they are called, may have originated as practice devices, but they are now part of the overall sound of the music for noh and are certainly one of the distinctive elements that add to its strangely rarefied atmosphere.

Like the chobo ensemble of gidayubushi, the noh hayashi, has been adopted for some kabuki performances, where it always introduces a reference to classical, courtly culture.

The vocal part of noh, called **yokyoku**, is sung by both the actors and the onstage chorus. The melodic style of yokyoku is solemn and spare, betraying its origin in Buddhist chanting of medieval Japan. The articulation of every textual syllable is deliberate and prolonged, and their pronunciation is based on a stage convention different from everyday speech. Together with the actors' stately bodily movements and gliding steps, the music of yokyoku and hayashi contribute to the overall impression that noh theater is ethereal and otherworldly.

Yokyoku has two basic styles: the heightened speech called **kotoba** (words) and the aria called **fushi** (melody). Fushi is sung in two basic ways: the **yowagin** (soft) style, which is delivered softly and is used in lyrical scenes, and the **tsuyogin** (strong) style, which is delivered with strength and is used in masculine and warlike scenes.

The tonal system of the yokyoku is based on the interval of the minor seventh, coinciding with the same interval produced when the uniquely constructed nohkan is overblown. (Most flutes produce the octave when overblown.) Within this minor seventh, three notes making a conjunct pair of perfect fourths provide important tonal centers. If we designate the minor-seventh interval as being from A down to B, then the three tonal centers are A-E-B, in that order of importance. Around each of these tonal centers there is a cluster of notes forming a tonal system for melody.

The rhythmic structure of noh singing, like that for the hayashi, is based on an eight-beat framework, but in a flexible manner. The number of textual syllables in each poetic line to be sung within these beats varies, but a five-syllable line is most common.

The individual musical elements of noh are conceived in a linear fashion, and the key to appreciating noh is to follow the various lines of the voices and the instruments. For example, the chorus and the nohkan may be involved in two completely separate melodic lines, while the drums may be playing a rhythmic pattern of a different length from either. As mentioned, the strong individuality of the components of noh is a characteristic feature, and relying on this, noh can create a complex art from few resources. The center of this art is the poetic text, and the musical elements revolve around it.

Noh plays are produced by a group of people: the poet supplies the text, and the actors, the chorus, and the hayashi compose their own parts according to the text. This creative process works for noh because the music is highly systematized (Listen to CD I, 20 for an example of hayashi and chorus in noh theater).

LISTENING GUIDE

EXCERPT FROM NOH PLAY *HAGOROMO* ("THE ROBE OF FEATHERS")

🖝 GO TO www.mymusiclab.com for the Automated Listening Guide CDI • Track 20/Download Track 20

Hayashi (instrumental ensemble) and chorus

One of the most famous noh plays is *Hagoromo* ("The Robe of Feathers"). Belonging to the category of "female-wig plays," this one-act play in two scenes tells the story of a fisherman (portrayed by the waki) who stole the feather robe of an angel (portrayed by the shite) and thus prevented her return to heaven; however, he was so moved by her distress that he agreed to return it if she would dance for him. The second scene, consisting of a series of dances accompanied by choral chanting and the hayashi, is considered the high point of the play. The excerpt heard here basically alternates rather free-rhythm and ornamented vocal sections sung in the soft style with a more strident vocal and more regular rhythmic accompaniment.

TIME	SECTION	MUSICAL EVENT
0:00–0:25	**Waki sings with accompaniment:** Listen for the distinct contributions of the vocalist and the instruments. Notice the relatively free meter and the kakegoe (vocal calls) inserted by the drummers.	The vocalist opens this recording and is quickly joined by the drums, including the taiko, with its characteristic low, dull pitch. The drummers also intersperse kakegoe throughout this section.
		Notice how the drums are not functioning in this section to create a rhythmically stable backdrop for the vocalist, but rather to introduce their own "voices" into the texture of this free-metered section.
0:25–0:45	**Chorus enters:** Notice that the chorus and drummers settle into a steady rhythmic pulse by the middle of this section.	The chorus takes over the lead role in this section. The contrast between the soloist and the chorus helps delineate sections of the performance.
0:45–1:12	**Waki returns:** Listen here to the vocalist who, although he sings alone, is enveloped in kakegoe and occasional exclamations on the drums.	The waki returns and sings in free meter. He is supported here by intermittent kakegoe and strokes on the drums. Beginning around [1:01] the drummers begin to enter more deliberately into the texture and they also move the performance back toward a rhythmic pulse.
1:12–2:07	**Chorus returns:** Notice the increased activity of the drummers in this section.	The chorus enters and picks up on the regular pulse established at the end of the last section. The chorus continues to perform until the recording fades out, beginning at [1:58].

MIKAGURA
Japanese court religious (Shinto) music.

GAGAKU
Japanese court orchestral music.

SHOMYO
Japanese Buddhist chanting.

TORIMONO
Shinto songs in praise of the gods.

SAIBARI
Shinto songs meant to entertain the gods.

SATOKAGURA
Folk Shinto music.

✳ **Explore**
the Musical Instrument Gallery on
mymusiclab.com

THE RELIGIOUS TRADITIONS
Shintoism and Shinto Music

Among the ancient types of Japanese music that can still be heard today are court Shinto music, **mikagura**; court orchestral music, **gagaku**; and the Buddhist chant, **shomyo**. The latter two were originally Chinese inspired, whereas the first one is entirely indigenous.

The earliest Japanese religion shared many elements with the religions of other peoples of East Asia and only became designated Shinto ("the way of the gods") when confronted with Buddhism and Confucianism. Shinto is a loose agglomeration of local and regional cults with a diversity of gods and spirits, and it includes a variety of religious elements such as nature worship, animism, shamanism, ancestor worship, hero worship, fertility rites, phallicism, fortune-telling, and so on.

Constant change and adaptation is the norm of Shinto. It adopted and adapted gods and cults with ease, and there has seemed to be no clear conception of divinity and no real attempt to articulate a theology on a rational basis, nor is there an organized, hereditary priesthood.

Five elements or objects stand out in Shinto worship: the sun (or fire), water, mountains, trees, and stones. In ritual practice, Shinto ceremony consists essentially of attendance on a god and offerings to him or her, accompanied by invocations and prayers. Festivals represent special occasions for honoring the gods and establishing good rapport with them by offering food, drink, and music and dance. Shinto rituals generally take place during important occasions of life and of the agricultural year, such as birth, marriage (always celebrated at a Shinto shrine), the New Year, plowing, planting, and harvesting. Shinto has nothing to do with death, however.

Until the Edo period, musical creation was regarded as a gift from god and, like the beauty of nature, a miracle. Thus in the Shinto view, an appreciation of music sprang from admiration and awe at what is "natural," pure, and simple, rather than from a rational admiration of the artfully organized.

One type of ancient Shinto music, mikagura, can still be heard today in court Shinto ceremonies. It is performed by a male chorus and accompanied by the *wagon* (a six-stringed zither), the *kagura-bue* (a transverse bamboo flute with six holes), the hichiriki, and the *shakubyoshi* (a pair of wooden clappers). Fifteen songs are still preserved in the present-day repertory, and they are of two main types—the **torimono**, songs paying homage to the gods, and the **saibari**, songs meant to entertain the gods. Since the nineteenth century, mikagura songs have been performed by two choruses, each having its own repertory. The performance is initiated by the leader of each chorus, who sings the initial phrase of a song and accompanies himself on the clappers and is then followed by a unison chorus accompanied by the rest of the instruments. In Shinto ceremonies, dance is an integral part of the ceremony.

In folk Shinto rituals, the music used is called **satokagura**. There are two main types: The one used in shamanistic rituals paying homage to the gods involves a priestess who sings and dances and is accompanied by the *wagon*, the transverse flute, and the *suzu* (bell-tree). The other, used in Shinto festivals and called *matsuribayashi* (festival music), is performed by a hayashi consisting of the o-daiko, two taiko, a transverse flute, and a small gong, *kane*. This music is characterized by a lively syncopated drum rhythm, which accompanies a repeated melodic line played by the flute.

Buddhism and Buddhist Music

Buddhism came to Japan in the sixth century CE from Korea and China. By this time it was already a thousand years old and a highly developed religion. The essential tenet of Buddhism concerns suffering and its elimination through the cessation of desire—the achievement of Nirvana. When it came to Japan, Buddhism gave the Japanese a means of dealing with death and suffering, something that Shintoism had not provided. It affected the Japanese deeply, but their innate delight in the simple joy of life also modified Buddhism by infusing it with an appreciation for life and nature.

During the Nara (553–794) and Heian (794–1185) periods, when Japan's capitals were in Nara and Kyoto, respectively, the great aristocratic clans adopted the Mahayana form of Buddhism. Great monastic systems were established and integrated into the court and its civil administrative system. The theology of Mahayana Buddhism asserted that salvation from suffering and death was open to all, and it attracted a huge following among the populace. The government decreed the building of many great monasteries and demanded religious services praying for peace and prosperity for the state. Scriptural verses called sutras were chanted in these ceremonies to secure good harvests and the welfare of the state.

The chanting of Buddhist sutras is called shomyo; it is performed by a male chorus in responsorial style, and the texts are in several languages. Those in Sanskrit are called *bonsan*; those in Chinese, *kansan*; and those in Japanese, *wasan*. The music consists of a series of stock patterns belonging to two different Chinese-derived scales, the *ryo* and the *ritsu*, each of which has five basic notes and two auxiliary notes. Shomyo chants may be **syllabic** or **melismatic**, and their rhythm may be more or less regular or free. A chant usually begins slowly and gets faster. During the Nara and Heian periods, the aesthetic aspect of Buddhism predominated, not only because of native Japanese sensitivity but also because the aristocrats admired beauty and elegance above all things. Aesthetic cultivation (the playing of music being one of the requirements), together with physical training and psychological discipline—all aspects of one personality—were involved in the attainment of Buddhahood, which was the goal of the Esoteric Buddhism practiced in the Nara and Heian periods. Consequently, ritual, art, and music were as important as scriptures and meditation. It was not just a matter of enlightening the mind but of affecting and transforming the whole world. This view of the world and of man gave great impetus to Buddhist art (including images of Buddha and mandala paintings) as well as Buddhist music.

MELISMATIC-SYLLABIC
Performing a single syllable of text by singing multiple notes or pitches is called a melisma (melismatic). Syllabic singing, by contrast, matches one syllable to a single note or pitch.

The collapse of the Heian court and its civil administration in the eleventh century brought about profound changes in Buddhism. Religious institutions bound up with the fortune of the court nobility declined, while a highly aestheticized and sentimentalized religion, based on the refined enjoyment of beauty, could not meet the challenge of the difficult time ahead. With the constant warfare, famine, pestilence, and social disruption of the ensuing Kamakura (1185–1333), Muromachi, and Azuchi-Momoyama (1333–1615) periods, a new form of Buddhism arose, whose primary mission was to bring salvation immediately within reach. This Buddhism for the masses, called *Amida Buddhism*, had little to do with the arts and aesthetics.

Another form of Buddhism that arose during this difficult period was Zen Buddhism, whose roots were in China and India. Zen emphasizes personal enlightenment through self-understanding and self-reliance by means of meditation, using practices related to the yoga practice of ancient India. In Japan, Zen Buddhism was supported by the military class during the Azuchi-Momoyama period.

Aesthetically, Zen inspired many of the traditional arts of Japan, such as landscape painting, landscape gardening, swordsmanship, the tea ceremony, and noh drama. It was under the patronage of the Ashikaga shogun that Zen and its allied arts, including noh, evolved and developed.

A CONCERT AND A COURT TRADITION

Sokyoku

Popular koto-and-vocal music of the Edo period is known under the generic name of **sokyoku**. The koto is a long zither whose thirteen strings are stretched over movable bridges. The player places the instrument on a mat or low table and plucks the strings using plectra on the thumb and the first two fingers of the right hand. With the left hand, the player presses on the strings to the left of the bridges to create ornaments and new pitches by altering the tension of the strings.

There are two types of sokyoku. The first, **kumiuta**, is a koto-accompanied song cycle; the verses of each individual song, called uta, are derived from preexistent poems whose subjects are unrelated. Typically, an uta has duple meter and is in eight phrases, each divided into four measures. The second type, **danmono**, for koto alone, is in several sections (dan), each consisting of either 64 or 120 beats. The structure of danmono is akin to a loose rondo-variation form. The famous piece "Rokudan" (Six Sections) is a classic example of this form. A basic theme is presented and within each of the six dan the theme undergoes variation with interpolation of new material. "Rokudan" can be played by one koto as a solo piece or by two koto as a duet. Sometimes other instruments, such as the shamisen and the shakuhachi (an end-blown bamboo flute with four finger holes and one thumbhole, with a notch cut in the lip to facilitate sound production) may join in, as they do in the listening example "Rokudan No Shirabe" (Listen to CD I, 21 to hear an example of danmono).

SOKYOKU
Popular koto-and-vocal music of the Edo period in Japan.

KUMIUTA
A suite of songs accompanied either by the koto or the shamisen, or by both.

DANMONO
Sectional form.

JIUTA
A major koto genre that combines techniques of both kumiuta and danmoto. Sometimes also called tegotomono.

TEGOTO
Instrumental interludes in koto music.

LISTENING GUIDE

FIRST TWO DAN OF "ROKUDAN NO SHIRABE"   GO TO www.mymusiclab.com for the Automated **Listening Guide** CDI • Track 21/Download Track 21

Performed by sankyoku trio of koto, shamisen, and shakuhachi by the Zumi-Kan Instrumental Group

This is a recording of the first and second sections, or dan, of "Rokudan No Shirabe," performed by a sankyoku trio of koto, shamisen, and shakuhachi. Each instrument realizes the melody in an idiosyncratic way, resulting in a richly heterophonic texture. The piece begins with a statement of the basic melody in a slow tempo. The performers, however, soon settle into a slightly faster tempo and proceed very gradually to increase the overall tempo of the performance. Listen for the distinctive "voices" of the three instruments. Listen also for the way that the second dan begins to elaborate and extend on the musical and melodic gestures of the first dan.

TIME	SECTION	MUSICAL EVENT
0:00–0:39	**First Dan:** Listen for the distinct contributions of the three instruments. Notice the relatively steady meter and the gradual increase in tempo. Listen also for the way the koto's sustained (ringing) tones carry through while the shamisen's comparatively rapid decay sets it apart from the koto.	The first few melodic gestures of the dan feature the koto and shamisen as lead instruments. The shakuhachi is playing along softly here. (If you're having trouble telling which string instrument is which, listen on a pair of headphones and notice that the koto is mixed more to the left ear and the shamisen more to the right.)
0:39–1:31		The shakuhachi enters more prominently during this part of the dan, mirroring the koto and shamisen.
1:31–2:04		The koto elegantly elaborates on the melody while the shamisen and flute play the basic melodic gestures. This continues until the first dan comes to a close at [2:02].
2:04–3:38	**Second Dan:** Notice that the tempo has increased slightly and that there is more elaboration of the basic melodic gestures in this dan.	The second dan features more frequent elaboration and ornamentation of the main melodic gestures. Notice that the tempo increases slightly here as well and that some new musical ideas are introduced along the way (not heard in the first dan, that is).
		The second dan comes to a close at [3:30] and the recording fades out as the third dan begins.

Jiuta is an important hybrid form of koto music that combines the techniques of both kumiuta and danmono. It is sometimes called *tegotomono*, after the **tegoto**, the important instrumental interludes between vocal sections. Tegotomono usually contain three parts—a foresong (**maeuta**), an instrumental interlude (tegoto), and an after song (**atouta**). This basic structure may be extended (to include an introduction, for instance).

MAEUTA
The first song in a jiuta cycle.

ATOUTA
The last song in the jiuta cycle

LISTENING GUIDE

"CHIDORI"

✈ GO TO www.mymusiclab.com for the Automated
Listening Guide CDII • Track 1/Download Track 22

Performed on two koto and shakuhachi, with voice, by the Zumi-Kan Instrumental Group

One of the most famous koto pieces is called "Chidori." In a full performance, it illustrates well the jiuta form (introduction—song—interlude—song). In this excerpt, we hear only the opening two sections—that is, the introduction and part of the first song (or maeuta). But this is enough to help us think through the alternating structure of the jiuta form (the movement between songs [which are sung] and instrumental sections). Although this particular recording features two koto and shakuhachi, it can also be performed as a solo piece, a koto duet, or a koto and shamisen ensemble.

TIME	SECTION	MUSICAL EVENTS
0:00–1:22	**Introduction:** This recording features two kotos and shakuhachi. Notice the stately tempo set in the introduction. Listen also for the timbre of the koto.	This opening section gives us a glimpse into what the tegoto (instrumental) section following the first song (maeuta) will sound like. Notice the way the kotos and shakuhachi combine to play the melody in heterophonic fashion.
1:22–1:54	**Maeuta (first song):** Notice how the instruments support the vocalist in realizing the melody. Listen for the heterophonic way the ensemble works through the melodic phrases.	The vocalist enters and begins the maeuta (or first song).
1:54–2:03		The vocalist gathers for the next phrase while the instruments provide a brief interlude.
2:03–2:35		The vocalist re-enters and the ensemble continues the maeuta even as the recording fades out starting at [2:30].

SANKYOKU
Jiuta music played by a trio.

Today, jiuta is played by an ensemble called **sankyoku** (trio) consisting of koto, shamisen, and shakuhachi. The koto plays the main melody, while the shamisen and shakuhachi play an elaboration of the main melody, thereby producing a heterophonic texture (Listen to CD II, 1 for an example of jiuta form).

The koto tradition is perpetuated by various schools, the most important of which are the Ikuta School of Kyoto and the Yamada School of Tokyo, whereas the Meian and Kinko schools, also based, respectively, in Kyoto and Tokyo, represent the main traditions of shakuhachi performance. The latter have an interesting and colorful origin. They were founded in the Edo period by masterless samurai, who combined the profession of street musician with that of spy and informer and used their heavy bamboo flutes not just as musical instruments but also as clubs!

The music of the koto and the shamisen best represent the music of the Edo era. Although the shamisen belongs primarily to the world of the theater, with its colorful and exciting entertainments, the koto, by contrast, developed from a court tradition and gradually entered the home, played by members of the rising merchant class as an emblem of cultural accomplishment. In the modern era, the koto maintains a position in Japan similar to that of the parlor piano in nineteenth-century America. It is a popular instrument for middle-class Japanese girls, who play it as a sign of good breeding.

Gagaku

Gagaku, meaning elegant or refined music, is the instrumental and choral music and dance that has been under the continual patronage of the imperial court for more than a thousand years. Influenced by the ancient music of China, Korea, and Sinicized Indian music, it has been carefully transmitted by generations of court guild musicians to the present day and is perhaps the oldest ensemble music in the world. Gagaku is also used to accompany dance; in this role it is called *bugaku*.

Gagaku was first adopted in the Nara period (553–749)—the first major historical period in Japan, during which the Japanese struggled to establish a national government modeled after that of China. Prior to the Nara period, Japan was ruled by various rustic clans, the most dominant of which were the Yamato, who originated on the southern island of Kyushu. Until the Nara period, Japanese history and mythology focused on the gradual northern extension of the imperial Yamato power and the justification for its dominance over other lesser clans of the land.

The construction of the city of Nara was begun in 708, and the court was moved there in 710. Fashioned as a miniature of the Chinese capital of Changan (present-day Xian), it captured perfectly the spirit of an age in East Asian history dominated by the pervasive influence of the great empire of the Chinese Tang dynasty. Nara was the first urban center in Japanese history. Its founding was accompanied by a great burst of economic, administrative, and cultural activities. One of the administrative measures taken was the establishment of a music bureau staffed by musicians from Korea and China. Musicians performed music and dance for court entertainments and rituals.

Nara's founding also ushered in the age of the court nobles, a period that lasted until the later twelfth century. Members of the imperial household, court ministers, and Buddhist priests contended for political power. The constant court intrigues suggest a fundamental instability in the ruling institutions. A century later, this instability was exploited by one court family, the Fujiwara, who were able to dominate the throne and subsequently the political affairs of the country for a long time.

The emperor Shomu and his consort, who was a Fujiwara, were fervent Buddhists, and their influence helped spread this foreign faith. In 737, Shomu ordered the construction of the Todaiji (Great East Temple) in Nara. Housed within the central building of the Todaiji is a huge bronze statue of the Buddha. The casting of the Great Buddha was an impressive technological feat for eighth-century Japan, and it also represented the first Japanese artistic representation of the human form.

At the "eye-opening" ceremony for the Great Buddha in 752, during which the statue was symbolically given life by having the pupils of its eyes painted in, all the great court dignitaries were in attendance. In addition, there were visitors from China, India, and other distant lands and some 10,000 Buddhist priests. It was without doubt one of the grandest occasions in all of early Japanese history. Hundreds of musicians and dancers performed, and many instruments dating from this occasion are still preserved in the imperial treasury of Nara, the Shosoin. Music thus became a part of important rituals pertaining to religious and court affairs.

Nara court music all was of foreign origin and was played primarily by foreign musicians in its original style. The subsequent Heian period (794–1185) showed signs that the Chinese influence was beginning to be assimilated and modified.

Heian (Kyoto), the newly constructed city to which the government moved in 794, remained the capital of Japan for more than a millennium (until the Meiji Restoration in 1868). At the end of the Heian period in 1185, a new military national government was established in Kamakura by the warrior family of Minamoto, bringing an end to the age of the court nobles and ushering in nearly seven centuries of dominance by the warrior class, until the restoration of the Meiji emperor in the late nineteenth century.

During the Heian period, great changes occurred in the governmental system, with the power of the emperor becoming eclipsed by that of the regent, who was controlled by the Fujiwara family. Buddhism continued to flourish in the Heian period, and it had become the principal intellectual system and one of the most important institutional systems in Japanese life. Heian nobles were preoccupied with etiquette and ritual, and they lived in a world governed by formal standards of beauty and the cultivation of poetry and music.

Heian court music still employed a host of Chinese instruments and forms, but the musicians themselves were mostly Japanese. In the ninth century, a standard gagaku orchestra was created under order of the emperor, and a repertory of two main categories was standardized. The **togaku** repertory includes music of Chinese and Indian origin, whereas the **komagaku** includes music of Korean and Manchurian origin. Gagaku music was extremely popular in the Heian court. Not only was it a necessary component of all court ceremonies, but it was also practiced by the court nobles themselves. Amateur gagaku clubs flourished. The famous novel of the Heian period, *The Tale of Genji*, is full of descriptions of musical activities of the noblemen. Today about twenty gagaku musicians who are descendants of musicians of the professional guilds are maintained by the emperor, and amateur ensembles also exist outside the court.

The ensemble for gagaku consists of percussion, strings, and winds. The various instruments used in gagaku are described briefly under separate headings.

TOGAKU
Court music of Chinese and Indian origin in the gagaku repertory.

KOMAGAKU
Japanese court music of Korean origin.

Percussion

1. The *da-daiko*, a huge drum struck by two thick sticks. It is only used in bugaku dance.
2. The *tsuri-daiko*, a suspended two-headed drum, only one side of which is struck with two sticks. It is a **colotomic** instrument—that is, it serves to mark off the larger phrase units.
3. The *shoko*, a small suspended gong played with two sticks. It is usually played on the first beat of every measure.
4. The *kakko*, a small drum whose two heads are struck with thin sticks. The kakko is the leader of the togaku ensemble. Its three basic rhythmic patterns are two types of rolls (a slow roll done with both sticks and a faster roll done on the left skin) and a single tap with the right stick. These patterns are played to regulate the tempo of the piece, and they are found mostly in free rhythmic sections; they are also used to mark off beats or phrases. The kakko is only used in togaku.
5. The *san-no-tsuzumi*, an hourglass-shaped drum with two heads, only one of which is struck. Korean in origin, it is played only in komagaku, by the leader of that ensemble.

Strings

1. The *wagon*, a six-stringed zither used in kagura.
2. The *gaku-so*, a thirteen-stringed zither, a predecessor of the koto. The strings are plucked by the bare fingers or with finger picks. The music for the gaku-so is made up of two basic patterns that are played to mark off sections.
3. The *biwa*, a pear-shaped lute with four strings and four frets played with a small plectrum. It is also used to mark off sections in a piece. The music for the biwa consists primarily of arpeggios, which may end with short melodic fragments. The effect of biwa music in gagaku is primarily rhythmic. This instrument is similar to the old style of Chinese *pipa*.

Winds

1. The *hichiriki*, a short, double-reed bamboo oboe with nine holes, originating from China. Through use of the embouchure and fingering technique, tones smaller than a half-step can be produced. Its tone quality is penetrating and strong, and it is the center of the gagaku ensemble.
2. The *kagura-bue*, a six-holed bamboo flute that produces a basic pentatonic scale; other pitches may be produced by using special fingerings. The length of this flute varies, and thus also its actual pitch. It is used for Shinto ceremonies.
3. The *ryuteki*, a seven-holed bamboo flute of Chinese origin used for togaku music. It is the largest of the gagaku flutes.
4. The *koma-bue*, a six-holed flute of Korean origin used for komagaku music. It is the smallest of the gagaku flutes.
5. The *sho*, a mouth organ with seventeen reed pipes (two of which are silent) in a cup-shaped wind chest with a single mouthpiece. Its predecessor was the Chinese *sheng*. Chords are produced by blowing into the mouthpiece

✳ **Explore**
the Musical Instrument Gallery on
mymusiclab.com

COLOTOMIC

Marking or delineating major phrases in a musical composition. Used to describe percussion instruments that have this function.

and closing holes in the pipes. Its primary function is harmonic. Typically, each chord is begun softly and gradually gets louder, whereupon the next chord is produced with the same dynamic swelling; this process is repeated continuously by inhaling and exhaling air.

The wind instruments are the heart of the gagaku ensemble; they play roles analogous to those of the strings in a Western symphony orchestra.

Different instrumentations are used for togaku and komagaku. The former uses three sho, three hichiriki, three ryuteki, two biwa, two gaku-so, one kakko, one shoko, and one taiko. Instrumentation for komagaku is similar in many respects but, nonetheless, distinctive. The *koma-bue* is used instead of the ryuteki, the san-no-tsuzumi instead of the kakko, and the strings are not used.

The musical style of gagaku is characterized by smoothness, serenity, and precise execution without virtuosic display. The melody, played on the hichiriki and the flutes, is supported by chords produced on the sho. An abstraction of this melody is played on the gaku-so in octaves and on the biwa in single notes. Although smaller sections of a piece are marked off by a biwa arpeggio, larger sections are delineated by tsuri-daiko and shoko strokes. Drum patterns played by the kakko or san-no-tsuzumi serve similar colotomic functions and also regulate the tempo of a piece. When a chorus joins in performing the melody of gagaku, it sings in a natural voice using very little ornamentation.

The melodies of gagaku use six modes theoretically based on the Chinese-derived ryo and ritsu scales. The rhythm is organized so that slow pieces have an eight-beat rhythm, moderately fast pieces have a four-beat rhythm, and fast pieces have a two-beat rhythm.

Gagaku music, like most Japanese music that came after it, was conceived in an aesthetic scheme of introduction–exposition–denouement known as **jo-ha-kyu**, which has also influenced the aesthetic of noh. In gagaku, jo is the *netori*, a slow prelude that introduces the musical mode in which the piece is written. In a full-blown gagaku piece, the sho generally starts the netori, followed in turn by the hichiriki, the flute, and finally the kakko. The mood of the netori is generally subtle and serene and has a tentative feeling like a warm-up.

During the ha section, the rhythm becomes regular. Here the main body of the composition begins. The hichiriki and flute play the basic melody, the sho provides a harmonic background, and the percussion provides accompaniment; shortly, the strings also join in. Once the entire ensemble is playing together, there is no further change in the full ensemble sound.

Kyu is the rushing to the end. Here the tempo becomes fast. Toward the end, the pace slackens once again, and the instruments drop out one by one as the texture becomes thinner. Finally, only the biwa and the gaku-so are left. They play two or three slow notes, the biwa ending by plucking the dominant or the tonic of the mode, and the gaku-so completing the composition with one stroke on the tonic. Listening to the archaic sound of the gagaku, one may imagine going back into the rarefied time of the Heian court nobles and

JO-HA-KYU
A basic aesthetic concept in Japanese music. Jo denotes "introduction"; ha denotes "development"; kyu denotes the final section of a composition.

LISTENING GUIDE

EXCERPT FROM A GAGAKU PIECE: ➤ **GO TO** www.mymusiclab.com for the Automated
NETORI (PRELUDE) AND ETENRAKU IN HYOJO **Listening Guide** CDII • Track 2/Download Track 23

Performed by Nippon Gagaku Kai (Gagaku Society of Japan)

Etenraku is the most famous instumental piece in Gagaku and has no dance accompanying it. It was imported from Tang dynasty China, but over the centuries various tunings have been developed, so there are now three versions. The excerpts here introduce many of the instruments discussed in our text within a concrete musical example. This recording, performed in a pentatonic mode called hyojo, also gives a glimpse of the first two parts of the jo-ha-kyu scheme so central to the aesthetics of gagaku. Notice the continued accumulation of energy and volume during Etenraku, achieved, at least in part, by gradually adding more and more instruments into the texture.

TIME	SECTION	MUSICAL EVENTS
0:00–0:08	**Netori (prelude):** In this short opening prelude corresponding to the "jo" or introductory section of the jo-ha-kyu scheme, listen for the distinct "voices" of the six instruments that gradually enter.	The sho (mouth organ) opens the performance.
0:08–0:27		The hichiriki (bamboo oboe) enters, following the prescribed order of entries in netori.
0:27–0:36		The kakko (small drum) is added to the texture. And the ryuteki (bamboo flute) enters subtly in support of the hichiriki.
0:36–1:01		The ryuteki now takes a more prominent role and the hichiriki drops out.
1:01–1:30		The gaku-so (zither) and biwa (lute) enter and the ryuteki drops out. (If you're having trouble telling them apart, listen on headphones, where the gaku-so will be primarily on the left side and the biwa primarily on the right.)
1:30–1:36	**Etenraku:** This is the main portion of the performance, and you should continue to listen for the distinct instruments that continue to enter the ensemble. You might also want to think about this section as the "ha" (or development) section of the jo-ha-kyu aesthetic scheme.	The ryuteki returns and begins to introduce the Etenraku melody in a slow tempo, beginning the "ha" section of the composition.

1:36–2:17	The kakko returns and is joined by the shoko (small gong). At [1:41] these two percussion instruments are joined by the daiko (a larger drum). At [1:53] the kakko performs an extended roll.
2:17–2:37	The sho and hichiriki reenter at this point.
2:37–4:57	Gaku-so and biwa reenter, playing intermittently and completing the ensemble. This texture remains in place until the recording fades out beginning at [4:52].

sharing with them, for a brief moment at least, their profound preoccupation with aesthetic self-cultivation (Listen to CD II, 2 for an example of jo-ha-kyu in a gagaku performance).

GENERAL TENDENCIES AND CHARACTERISTICS OF HOGAKU

Before closing, it may be helpful to provide some summary observations on the general tendencies and characteristics of traditional Japanese music, hogaku.

The rise and fall of a particular style of music through Japanese history has been closely linked with changes in political life, social conditions, and religious developments. For example, the gagaku of the Nara period was regarded as a symbol of the authority and power of the newly evolved imperial and national government, and no effort was spared to increase its grandeur.

The noh theater, with themes of redemption of human suffering through the love of Buddha, was exclusively an art of the ruling samurai during the long ages of military strife. It is, in particular, an expression of the samurai class's preoccupation with Zen Buddhism, which emphasizes simplicity and personal enlightenment through self-understanding and self-reliance. Noh was also a political symbol of the samurai class. During the Edo period, it continued to be performed in the Edo castle, the political center of the Tokugawa military government. Finally, the popularity of the kabuki and the bunraku theaters was due entirely to the rise of the urban bourgeoisie and their patronage. As the bourgeois arts par excellence, they represent a fondness for popular entertainments and, in particular, lavish theatrical entertainments.

Japanese music is closely tied with ritual, literature, and dance, and these ties have remained unbroken through the ages. It was said that in ancient times, when the emperor or his courtiers asked for the pronouncement of an oracle, it was habitual to offer a musical performance first; therefore, the court has always kept musicians in its service.

In hogaku, vocal music predominates. Music serves primarily as a vehicle for words and literature. All Japanese instruments were developed to emulate the human voice. It is noteworthy that the first significant instrumental solos, the tegotomono, were created to serve as interludes to the verses of songs.

Among Japanese music genres, theatrical music is the most important. The course of Japanese music history is marked by a steady growth of theatrical music. This is due again to the Japanese love of storytelling and preoccupation with ritual.

Finally, we have noted the basic Japanese aesthetic concept of jo-ha-kyu (introduction–development–denouement) and the application of this concept in various kinds of music. We have also noted the propensity of the Japanese to use stock melodic patterns in creating new compositions. It remains to be noted that Japanese music is predominantly a chamber music in its conception; even the gagaku ensemble is essentially a chamber orchestra.

SUMMARY

Study and Review on mymusiclab.com

Our excursion into the music of Japan has illustrated that Hogaku, or traditional Japanese music, comprises many different styles, from religious and dramatic music to court and popular genres. We learned that the earliest known Japanese musical style is gagaku, the traditional music of the court. Also fairly ancient are the religious Shinto music and the chanting of Buddhist monks, known as shomyo. The major Japanese theatrical styles we encountered are the kabuki drama; bunraku puppet theatre; and the earlier noh theater. We also learned that typical Japanese instruments include the shamisen (plucked lute), koto (plucked zither), shakuhachi (end-blown flute), and sho (mouth organ), along with various drums.

This chapter has only begun to explore the rich musical heritage of Japan and we have not had occasion to explore the popular music of Japan. That said, this chapter has opened a window onto the long and complex history of Japanese musical life and offers some guidance for those interested in exploring it further.

BIBLIOGRAPHY

William P. Malm, *Japanese Music and Musical Instruments* (Rutland, VT: Charles E. Tuttle, 1959); David Hughes, *Traditional Folk Song in Modern Japan: Sources, Sentiment and Society* (Folkestone: Global Oriental, 2008); William P. Malm, *Six Hidden Views of Japanese Music* (Berkeley: University of California Press, 1986); Carolyn Stevens, *Japanese Popular Music: Culture, Authenticity, and Power* (London: Routledge, 2008); William P. Malm, *Nagauta: The Heart of Kabuki Music* (Rutland, VT: Charles E. Tuttle, 1963); Alison Tokita and David W. Hughes, *The Ashgate Research Companion to Japanese Music* (Aldershot, Hampshire, England: Ashgate, 2008); Francis Taylor Piggott, *The Music and Musical Instruments of Japan.* 2nd ed. (London: B. T. Barsford, 1909; repr. New York: Da Capo, 1971); Eta Harich-Schneider, *A History of Japanese Music* (London: Oxford University Press, 1973); Robert Garfias, *Music of a Thousand Autumns: The Togaku Style of Japanese Court Music* (Berkeley: University of California Press, 1975); Willem Adriaansz, *The Kumiuta and Danmono Traditions of Japanese Koto Music* (Berkeley: University of California Press, 1973); Bonnie C. Wade, *Togotomono: Music for the Japanese Koto* (Westport, CT: Greenwood, 1975); James R. Brandon, William P. Malm, and Donald H. Shively, *Studies in Kabuki: Its Acting, Music, and Historical Context* (Honolulu: University Press of Hawaii, 1978); Kunio Komparu, *The Noh Theater: Principles and Perspectives* (New York, Tokyo: Westherhill/Tankosha, 1983); Christine Reiko Yano, *Tears of Longing: Nostalgia and the Nation in Japanese Popular Song* (Cambridge, MA: Harvard University Press, 2002); Shuhei Hosokawa, et al., eds., Mitsui Toru, trans., *A Guide to Popular Music in Japan* (Kanazawa: IASPM-Japan, 1st printing, 1991; 2nd printing, 1993). Bonnie C. Wade, *Music in Japan* (New York, Oxford: Oxford University Press, 2005).

DISCOGRAPHY

General   *Nihon No Ongaku*, 2 disks (Polydor MN-9041–9042) (notes in Japanese).

Instruments   *Traditional Music of Japan*, 3 disks, with notes in English and Japanese by Shigeo Kishibe (Nihon Victor, JL 52–54); *Japan: Semi-Classical and Folk Music*, with notes in English, French, and Italian by Shigeo Kishibe (Odeon 3 C064–17967); *Classical Music of Japan* (Elektra EKS 7285).

Shomyo   *Shomyo-Buddhist Ritual from Japan, Dai Hannya Ceremony-Shigon Sect* (UNESCO Collection Musical Sources, Philips); *The Way of Eiheiji, Zen-Buddhist Ceremony* (Folkways FR 8980) (everyday chanting of shomyo).

Shinto Music   *Edo No Kagura To Matsuri Gayashi* (Nihon Victor SJ 3004) (shinto festival and dance music).

Gagaku   *Gagaku Taikei* (Nihon Victor SJ 3002) (instrumental gagaku; another disc (SJ 3003) contains vocal gagaku); *Gagaku: Ancient Japanese Court Music* (Everest 3322); *Gagaku* (The King Record KC 1028).

Noh   *Noh*, 2 disks (Nihon Victor SJ 1005, 1006) (the most complete albums for noh; with history, music theory, libretti, photographs, and explanatory commentaries for each piece); *Hogoromo and Kantan* (Caedmon TC 2019) (contains two major noh dramas, sung and performed by players of the Komparu and Kanze School of Noh, Tokyo); *Japanese Noh Music* (Lyrichord LL 137).

Koto Music   *Sokyoko To Fiuta No Rekishi*, 4 disks (Nihon Victor SLR 510–513); *Japanese Koto Music, with Shamisen and Shakuhachi* (Lyrichord 131) (performed by masters of the Ikuta School).

Music of Indonesia

CHARLES CAPWELL

JAVANESE MUSIC IN CHICAGO

A subtly glowing array of bronze ingots, pots, and gongs in intricately carved wooden cases painted indigo and red with flashes of gold leaf—this was the dazzling sight that greeted us, a small group of university students and faculty who had come to the Field Museum in Chicago for an afternoon's introduction to the performance of **gamelan** music. Gamelan—an Indonesian word meaning "musical ensemble"—can be variously constituted, but the one at the Field Museum is representative of those used at the princely courts on Java, the most heavily populated island in the nation of Indonesia. Nowadays, similar gamelan can be found in many universities and colleges in the United States and Europe. The Field Museum gamelan, however, has a special history: a couple of Dutchmen who owned coffee and tea plantations on Java brought the gamelan to Chicago, along with a group of Javanese musicians and craftsmen, for the

Columbian Exposition of 1893, a great world's fair. The same entrepreneurs had arranged similar contributions to an exposition in Amsterdam a decade earlier and to another in Paris in 1889. At the latter, the composer Claude Debussy was enchanted by the music he heard and later tried to capture what appealed to him in pieces of his own such as some in his *Prélude*s and *Images* for piano.

Now that dozens of Indonesian gamelan of various types are to be found scattered around the United States in private and institutional collections, dozens of Americans have become competent performers and scholars of different types of Indonesian music. At the time of our visit to the Field Museum, Dr. Sue Carole DeVale, an ethnomusicologist with a special interest in the study of musical instruments (organology), took charge of our instruction. She had been fundamental in getting the museum to restore the gamelan, which had been more or less forgotten in storage for many decades, and had convinced them to make it available for use under her direction.

✳ Explore
Learning Objectives on
mymusiclab.com

✳ Explore
*a map of Java on the
Interactive Globe* on
mymusiclab.com

GAMELAN
An ensemble of instruments
such as those found in the
central Javanese courts.

METALLOPHONE
An instrument classification
term for idiophonic instruments
made of metal.

CHORDOPHONE
Scientific term for all types of
string instruments, including
violins, guitars, and pianos.

Balinese gamelan.
Source: Johann Scheibner/
Peter Arnold

THE JAVANESE GAMELAN

Instruments in the Javanese Gamelan

Like most high-quality gamelan, this one consists largely of
metallophones—in this case, instruments of gleaming bronze—but it
also includes a **chordophone** (*rebab*, a two-stringed fiddle), a xylophone
(*gambang*), an **aerophone** (*suling*, a notched vertical flute), and a couple of
membranophones (*kendang*, drums).

Sitting among the metallophones, we became aware that the bronze
had been fashioned in several different ways to make the various types of
instruments. The *saron*s, for instance, had keys shaped like rounded ingots.
These were pinned through the holes in their ends to the edges of a shallow
trough made in a wooden case that served both to hold them in place and to
increase their resonance. There were three different sets of sarons, each in
a different octave. The highest, the *peking*, had a delicate but piercing tone;
that of the middle range, *barung*, was mellower and longer-lasting; and the set
in the lowest range, *demung*, had a powerful clang. The peking was sounded
by striking the keys with a mallet of water-buffalo horn, but the others were
played with heavier and less bright-sounding wooden mallets.

A similar three-octave range was found in the differently constructed
*bonang*s, although there were only two of these. The lower-pitched bonang
barung and the higher bonang *panerus* each spanned two octaves, with the
higher octave of the lower instrument duplicating the lower octave of the
higher one. The "keys" of the bonangs resembled overturned bowls with
knobs protruding from the tops, which is where they were struck with a pair

of baton-like mallets wrapped with string. Each instrument had two rows of bowls resting on strings that were stretched in wooden frames.

The *kenong* also had bowl-like individual components, but these were fewer and much larger than those of the bonangs, and each one was supported in its own case on a web of string. A single bowl, closer in size to one from the set of bonangs but flatter in contour, sat by itself and contrasted with all the other instruments because of its curiously dull-sounding "clunk"; this was the *ketuk*.

The most impressive bronze instruments, for both their size and their sound, were the hanging gongs. ("Gong," by the way, is a Malay—that is, Indonesian—word.) The largest, gong *ageng*, was nearly a meter in diameter, and its slightly smaller mate, gong *siyem*, hung by its side. A smaller gong, named kempul, was suspended on the end of the same rack that holds the two large gongs. Like other names such as gong or ketuk, kempul is onomatopoetic and calls to mind the sound of the instrument it names.

In addition to these common instruments, the Field Museum gamelan also contained two others—the *jenglong*, similar to the kenong, which is found in gamelan from Sunda, the western part of Java, and the gambang *gangsa*, similar to the wooden gambang but with bronze keys like those of the saron instead of wooden ones. All in all, this original group of about twenty-four instruments was as impressive for its size as for its beauty; nevertheless, at the time of its use at the Columbian exposition, it lacked certain other instruments that have since been added.

Of the instruments that were lacking, perhaps the most important is the *gender* (pronounced with a hard "g" as in "good"). They come in two sizes (gender panerus and gender barung, like the bonang) and group thin, slab-like bronze keys in a slightly larger range than the saron. Much thinner than the ingots of the saron, the keys of the gender are struck with a pair of mallets with padded disks at their ends, and they produce a delicate, muffled ringing that makes up for their soft volume with longer-lasting resonance. The secret to the long-lasting sound is that each key has its own individually tuned amplifying resonator in the form of a tube. The key is suspended above this tube by strings, so that it is not damped by resting directly on the case (the saron keys rest on pads of rubber or rattan to lessen the damping). Another instrument similar in construction to the gender is the *slentem*, but it is struck with a single mallet and is similar in melodic function to the saron.

Originally, the kempul in the Columbian Exposition gamelan, as described, had been a single hanging gong, but additional gongs have been added to complete a full scale, as was also done for the kenong. Although the two-stringed fiddle, the rebab, was part of the original ensemble, the plucked string instrument *celempung*, a type of zither, was among the additions.

Tuning and Scales

Having familiarized ourselves a bit with the components of what at the start had seemed a bewildering array, we still had one further thing to learn before taking up our mallets to attempt our first piece: the instruments came in

AEROPHONE
Scientific term for all types of wind instruments, including trumpets, flutes, and the organ.

MEMBRANOPHONES
Scientific term for all instruments using a stretched membrane for sound production, that is, all true drums.

Explore *the Musical Instrument Gallery* on **mymusiclab.com**

Javanese gamelan instruments.
Source: Chris Stock/Lebrecht
Music & Arts

pairs. A complete Javanese gamelan is in fact two orchestras in one, for there are two different types of scales used in Javanese court music, one of five tones (pentatonic) and another of seven tones (heptatonic). Because the gaps (intervals) between pitches in one scale are different from those of the other, it is not possible to select five tones from the heptatonic scale to produce the pentatonic, and therefore there is a separate collection of instruments for each tuning system (**laras**). To play in laras *slendro* (pentatonic system), for example, the saron players faced front, and to play in laras *pelog* (heptatonic system) they had to make a quarter-turn to the left. (You could get a general idea of the contrast between these by playing on the piano **C-D-E-G-A** as 1–2–3–5–6 of slendro and **E-F-G-Bflat-B-C-D** as 1–2–3–4–5–6–7 of pelog.)

Although the Western scale, like that of the white piano keys, is heptatonic, too, we soon discovered that the seven pitches in pelog formed a different set of intervals from the regular half and whole tones on the piano. The difference was not so simple as merely being one between Javanese and Western scales, however, because each gamelan has its own unique slendro and pelog scales, unless it has been constructed purposely on the model of an existing gamelan. It is as though each symphony orchestra in the West used slightly different forms of major and minor scales, and as a result their performances of standard works like Beethoven's Ninth Symphony would all sound subtly distinct from one another.

LARAS

Javanese tuning system; there are two primary types (1) slendro (with a five-note scale) and (2) pelog (with a seven-note scale).

Instrument Functions and Formal Principles

When we finally took up our mallets to play, we began with a **gendhing** (a piece of music for gamelan) in pelog called "Golden Rain." As the sarons attempted the first section of their melody, we sang along with them using numbers for the pitches and following our instructor: 6–5–3–2 we sang out as the sarons sounded the tones, all of equal duration. After repeating this phrase, we learned the next one, 3–3–2–3, and then returned to the original for the conclusion. On the last tone, the player of the gong ageng was given the signal to strike, and the awe-inspiring sound left little doubt that we had arrived at an important juncture. The role of the gong was just to furnish this most important punctuation at the end of every completed melody—a melody, in this case, with sixteen beats, with a single pitch on every beat. Two distinct musical functions were illustrated in this beginning: the sarons provided a "skeletal melody" (**balungan**) whose periodic punctuation (the **colotomic structure**) was provided by other instruments like the gong ageng.

The other colotomic instruments were the next to join in as the sarons grew more confident: the kenong sounded the appropriate pitch at the end of every group of four beats (**gatra**), and so every fourth kenong stroke sounded with the gong. In the same manner, the kempul sounded the pitch every fourth beat midway between strokes of the kenong, omitting the second beat, however, so as not to interfere with the continuing resonance of the gong. Finally, on every odd-numbered beat, the "clunk" of the ketuk was heard, so the beats in between kempul and kenong were marked, too.

The next instruments to join in were the bonangs, which added a third functional component to the music, that of elaboration of the balungan. Because their music was more elaborate, they required more dexterity and skill than the other instruments. Although we had been pleased at the ease with which we initially had picked things up, it became clear as we patiently waited for the bonang players to start mastering their parts that things were getting rapidly more complicated and demanding. Although the bonangs required more skill to play, the principle behind their basic method of melodic elaboration was easy enough to understand: As the kenong and kempul played every fourth beat, the bonang barung did the opposite and divided the beat in two, and the boning panerus divided it into four, doubling or quadrupling each pair of balungan pitches. The peking (highest-pitched saron) was also told to double the number of pitches to a beat by anticipating each balungan note. Thus, the first gatra (four-beat phrase of the balungan) came out like this:

bonang panerus	6	5	6	.	6	5	6	5	3	2	3	.	3	2	3	2
bonang barung		6		5		6		5		3		2		3		2
peking		6		6		5		5		3		3		2		2
Saron				6				5				3				2
kempul								5								
kenong																2
Gong																X

GENDHING
A piece of Javanese music for gamelan.

BALUNGAN
Skeletal melody in Javanese music.

COLOTOMIC STRUCTURE
The marking of fixed beats within the metric structure of a musical piece by particular instruments; in gamelan music these include gong, kenong, kempul, and ketuk.

GATRA
A four-beat phrase in Javanese music.

GONGAN
A phrase concluded with a stroke on gong ageng or siyem.

KENONGAN
A colotomic phrase in Javanese music marked by a kenong stroke.

BUBARAN
A small-scale Javanese gendhing having sixteen beats.

GERONGAN
A male chorus that sings with Javanese gamelan.

PESINDHEN
Javanese female vocal soloist.

When we got the whole sixteen-beat phrase together, it sounded like a marvelous clock whose music was the actual time-keeping mechanism. Just as with a clock, the sounding of the gong signaled a conclusion that could also be the taking-off point for another cycle.

The drum player, our instructor, indicated whether or not we were to repeat this phrase. In regulating and supporting the pulse and rhythm of the music, the drummer fulfilled the fourth function in the ensemble so that the melody, its elaboration, and its punctuation were controlled from this instrument rather as the conductor in a Western orchestra controls the rest of the group. (In the eighteenth-century Western orchestra, in fact, the "conductor" was actually a performer, too—usually the first violin or the harpsichord player.)

When we had at last become comfortable with this first phrase, we went on to complete the piece with a second, similarly constructed phrase (7567 5672 2765 6765), which we now learned to call a **gongan**, that is, a phrase punctuated with a stroke of the big gong. As we have seen, each gongan was divided into four four-beat **kenongan** (punctuated with a kenong stroke), and each of these was further subdivided by a kempul stroke on the second beat and ketuk strokes on beats 1 and 3. Because this colotomic pattern is a fixed structure, it is common to a number of pieces differentiated from one another by, for example, their balungan, but similar in their colotomy. These make up a general category of small, simple pieces called **bubaran**.

The piece we had learned, as was mentioned, has the title "Udan Mas" ("Golden Rain") and is used to send people off at the end of a ceremony or concert. It served as our farewell too, as we had used up most of the afternoon and decided not to press our luck in attempting another piece (Listen to CD II, 3 to hear a performance of this piece).

The Variety of Styles and Forms

Although we came away feeling we had accomplished quite a bit in one afternoon, we had, of course, barely scratched the surface of this one type of Indonesian music. We hadn't even touched some of the instruments such as the genders, for example, because we played a "loud-style" piece in which gender, rebab, celempung, gambang, and suling do not participate. These difficult instruments are used for the elaboration of "soft-style" pieces, which may also include singing by a chorus of men (**gerongan**) and one or two female soloists (**pesindhen**).

We had naturally learned to play a short, simple type of piece, but among the types of other pieces for gamelan are some whose gongan, for example, have sixteen times as many beats as our sixteen-beat bubaran. And instead of playing just twice for each beat, the saron peking might play four times to fill in the great gap between one beat and another—so it might be as much as ten minutes between strokes of the gong ageng instead of the approximately ten seconds of our bubaran.

LISTENING GUIDE

BUBARAN "UDAN MAS" (GOLDEN RAIN)

➷ **GO TO** www.mymusiclab.com for the Automated
Listening Guide CDII • Track 3/Download Track 24

Paku Alaman Court Gamelan in Jogyakarta

This recording illustrates the main formal and rhythmic structures of a category of short gamelan pieces called bubaran. Bubaran are based on a sixteen-beat colotomy and "Golden Rain" incorporates two sixteen-beat phrases (gongan) punctuated at the end by the largest gong. Each gongan makes use of a balungan (skeletal melody) performed on saron and consisting of one pitch per beat. The following schematic representations of pitch contour and relative beats should assist you in picking out the two distinct melodies, and to see how they unfold within a sixteen-beat gongan structure.

Gongan 1:

Pitch (sarong)																
Pitch number	6	5	3	2	6	5	3	2	3	3	2	3	6	5	3	2
Beat	1	2	3	4	5	6	7	8	9	10	11	12	13	14	15	16

Gongan 2:

Pitch (sarong)																
Pitch number	7	5	6	7	5	6	7	2	2	7	6	5	6	7	6	5
Beat	1	2	3	4	5	6	7	8	9	10	11	12	13	14	15	16

TIME	SECTION	MUSICAL EVENT
0:00–0:07	**Introduction (Buka):** Notice the rounded tone and rapid decay (i.e., the notes fade out quickly without ringing out or sustaining their sound over time) of the bonang. Also listen for the sound of the kendang, the drum that guides the performance and cues the performers.	Introduction (buka) on bonang, joined by kendang and leading to first gong and first saron note at [0:07]. (The gong accents beat 16 in the colotomic cycle. You'll notice that the saron enters at the same time. It will be tempting to hear that as the first beat, but it's actually the last in the cycle, so count 16, 1, 2, 3, 4, etc. from the gong stroke.)
0:07–0:16	**First gongan:** Notice how much brighter and more sustained the sound of the saron is in comparison to the bonang. See if you can hear the melody clearly and follow along with the colotomic structure.	The first gongan, with balugan melody played on saron and marking one pitch per beat, is performed. Notice that the low gong is struck on the 16th beat. (If you're having trouble hearing it, listen for the most prominent instrument and follow along with the pitches indicated in the preceding schematic.)

0:17–0:26		The first gongan is repeated.
0:26–0:35	**Second gongan:** Listen for the new melodic content and for the way the colotomic structure remains stable. The gong is still articulating the 16th beat.	The second gongan is performed.
0:36–0:44		The second gongan is repeated.
0:45–1:03	**First gongan with repeat:** By now you should be familiar with the melody of the first gongan. This time see if you can hear some of the distinct rhythmic layers being performed by the gamelan. Notice, for instance, the rapid playing on the boning panerus (it generally plays four notes for every one note struck on the saron).	First gongan with repeat, beginning at [0:54].
1:03–1:20	**Second gongan with repeat:** Listen here for the way that the kendang drum interacts with the colotomic structure. Try to hear both the melody and the rhythmic and timbral complexities surrounding that melody.	Second gongan with repeat, beginning at [1:12]. Notice the gradual increase in tempo (accelerando) toward the end of the repeat.
1:20–1:34	**Repeat of both gongans:** Notice that the first gongan is played significantly faster, this time.	First gongan with repeat, continuing at the increased tempo achieved by the accelerando.
1:34–1:46		Second gongan is performed and a decelerando begins the process of slowing the tempo before the second gongan is repeated. The ongoing performance fades out during the repeat even as the decelerando continues.

As an example of a small-scale, soft-style piece, we could consider *ketawang "puspawarna" laras slendro pathet manyura*. This is a work entitled "Kinds of Flowers" ("Puspawarna") that has a gongan of sixteen beats, like a bubaran, but it is divided into only two eight-beat kenongan, and therefore it falls into the class of **ketawang**. It employs the scale of the pentatonic tuning (laras slendro) in one of three particular ways or **pathet**, that is called "peacock" (manyura). (There are also three distinct pathet for laras pelog.)

"Puspawarna" is a popular piece played not only on the precious gamelan of princes but also on the modest two- or three-piece ensembles of itinerant street musicians. Despite its wide use for a variety of circumstances and audiences, however, it is not merely a piece intended for listening pleasure. It also has particular associations and prescribed uses, and even its title can tell us something about the political and cultural history of Java.

KETAWANG
A type of Javanese gendhing having thirty-two beats.

PATHET
A particular way of using a scale or laras in Javanese music.

THE CULTURAL AND HISTORICAL SIGNIFICANCE OF JAVANESE GAMELAN MUSIC

Ketawang "Puspawarna": A Piece for the Prince

Just as "Hail to the Chief" played by the Marine Band is often used to announce the arrival of the president at a function or ceremony, "Puspawarna" was played by the gamelan of the two subsidiary central-Javanese courts to announce the presence or the arrival of their respective princes. The main courts of the Sultan of Yogyakarta and of the Susuhunan of Surakarta (Solo) were established in the mid-eighteenth century when the Dutch succeeded in supporting their trade interests by asserting political control over much of the Indonesian archipelago. The central-Javanese kingdom of Mataram was divided at that time between two ruling families centered at Yogyakarta and Solo, with a secondary court, the Mangkunegaran, attached to Solo. Later, in the early nineteenth century, the Paku Alaman court was established as an adjunct to Yogyakarta, and the various princes had their own particular identifying pieces of music, with "Puspawarna" serving both of the subsidiary courts and symbolizing a family connection between them.

Because political power was largely in the hands of the colonial overlords, the wealth and energy of the courts was expended on the development of cultural matters such as music and dance as a means of both establishing and justifying their precedence and prestige. Mataram had been the last great native power in Java, a Muslim kingdom in a land where Islam had steadily been increasing its influence for several centuries. As the Sanskrit words in the title "Puspawarna" and in the name of pathet "Manyura" reveal, however, the culture of India and its Hindu and Buddhist religions had considerable influence on the elite and ruling classes in Java and other parts of the Indonesian region for a millennium or so before the establishment of Islam, which itself had been introduced in large part by traders from northwestern India. Although a segment of Indonesian society may follow a strict and conservative Islam that, among other things, condemns most musical and performing arts, the aristocracy of Java, while accepting the "new" belief, continues to prize the older spiritual and cultural concepts and also to accommodate indigenous practice and beliefs that antedate any of the imported ones (Listen to CD II, 4 to hear a performance of "Puspawarna").

Some Spiritual Aspects of Javanese Gamelan Music

We may discover something of the complex relationship between Islam and music in Java by citing some observations made about seventy years ago by the ethnomusicologist Jaap Kunst (1973, 266–67):

> The gamelan, found by the Islam on arrival in Java as an indispensable element of all Hindu ceremonials, has never become . . . an integral part of Mohammedan religious rite. Accordingly during the month of fasting, as well as on Fridays, all orchestras in the whole of the Javanese territory are expected to remain silent.

LISTENING GUIDE

KETAWANG "PUSPAWARNA"

GO TO www.mymusiclab.com for the Automated **Listening Guide** CDII • Track 4/Download Track 25

Paku Alaman Court Gamelan in Jogyakarta

This recording illustrates the main characteristics of a soft-style piece. Included here are a solo female vocalist (pesindhen) and a male chorus (gerongan). The structure of ketawan pieces revolves around sixteen-beat gongan, and these are subdivided into two eight-beat kenongan. In addition to the introductory **buka**, this particular kenongan also incorporates two common structural components: an **ompak** ("bridge") which is repeated and precedes a contrasting **ngelik** section. A ngelik is usually longer than one gongan and, usually also where the gerongan (the male chorus) sings the main melody of the ketawan composition. Thus, the formal structure of the piece unfolds over the course of five gongan as follows: Gongan **A** (ompak); gongan **A** repeated (ompak); gongan **B, C,** and **A** (ngelik). This entire structure is then repeated.

TIME	SECTION	MUSICAL EVENTS
0:00–0:07	**Introduction (buka):** The rebab (string instrument), joined by the kendang (drum), open this performance and lead up to the first gong	Introduction (buka) on rebab, joined by kendang and leading to first gong at [0:07]. (The gong accents beat 16 in the colotomic cycle. It is tempting to hear that gong stroke as the first beat, but it's actually the last in the cycle, so count 16, 1, 2, 3, 4, etc. from the gong stroke.)
0:07–0:22	**Ompak section (Gongan A):** Notice the entrance of the pesindhen (female vocalist) and also the dramatic slowing of tempo.	Gongan **A** is introduced at a brisk tempo but the tempo begins to slow almost immediately. At [0:18] the female vocalist (pesindhen) enters.
0:22–0:46		Gongan **A** is repeated with a continuing decelerando and reaches a settled tempo at the end of this gongan. Notice the continued presence of the female vocalist as well as the stylized male vocal cries that enter at colotomic points.
		During the repeat of Gongan **A**, you can find your bearings within the colotomic cycle by counting one beat for every four strokes on the drum, starting with 16 at the sound of the low gong at [0:22]. At beat eight, you will hear a particularly rich, sustained note in medium register (usually played just slightly after the beat), played on the kenong. This note cuts through the texture of the other instruments, and when you hear it once or twice, you'll be able to hear it every time. On beat sixteen, the lowest gong sounds out.

0:46–1:13	**Ngelik section (Gongan B, C, and A):** Listen for the entrance of the gerongan (male chorus) and the melody that stretches across the three gongan (B, C, and A).	Gongan **B** is introduced and the gerongan enter between beats 5 and 6 of the colotomic cycle (the second syllable they sing is on beat six).
1:13–1:41		Gongan **C** is introduced and the gerongan enter here on beat 3. Notice the continuation of the melody. Notice also the continued presence of the pesindhen in the texture.
1:41–2:09		Gongan **A** returns, but as a vehicle to complete the gerongan melody. The chorus again enters at beat 3.
2:09–2:36	**Ompak section repeated:** By now you should be familiar with the overall structure of the piece. See if you can hear the contrasts between the Ompak and Ngelik sections. Also try to hear the gerongan melody as a whole statement across multiple gongan.	Gongan **A**
2:36–3:04		Gongan **A** repeated.
3:04–3:32	**Ngelik section repeated.**	Gongan **B**.
3:32–3:59		Gongan **C**.
3:59–4:44		Gongan **A**.
		Notice the brief accelerando at [3:55] followed by a dramatic decelerando, initiated at beat 1 of the concluding gongan [3:59], but put to especially dramatic use after beat 8 [4:12], such that the last half of the gongan unfolds ever more slowly until the last gong stroke serves as a powerful concluding gesture.

(This rule is not strictly adhered to in the kraton [court]. All that is done there is to avoid beating the gong ageng, and to play the gong kemodong [a substitute gong] instead. The princes, for that matter, are regarded as above the adat [customary law]. When, for example, one of their memorial days falls in the fasting month, then the prohibition of gamelan-playing, it seems, is raised entirely. Then, however, a sum of money is paid into the mosque cashbox as a compensation of this breach of the religious adat.)

MUSIC IN JAVA: ITS HISTORY, ITS THEORY, AND ITS TECHNIQUE, Jaap Kunst. © 1973 Martinus Niljhoff Publishers. With kind permission from Springer Science+Business Media B.V.

Princely privilege was partly related to the use of music in rites and ceremonies, and to do away with music altogether would have undermined it; yet acceptance of Islam required some recognition of its precepts. So a fine was paid to the mosque when a princely anniversary requiring musical performance

BUKA
Introduction to a Javanese gendhing.

OMPAK
Refers to the opening, usually repeated gongan in ketawang pieces.

NGELIK
A section in ketawang pieces that contrasts with the surrounding material (ompak) and is usually longer than one gongan. It is also usually where the gerongan sings the melody of the ketawang composition.

to ensure its success violated the prohibition against playing the gamelan, or alternatively, the most imposing and important instrument in the ensemble was silenced, and a simpler substitute was used. In the latter case, the gong ageng no doubt stood as a metonymical symbol for the whole ensemble that could be considered silent, too, if it were absent.

The Power of the Gong

But another reason for silencing the gong might also be offered. In many cultures the blacksmith has held a special position, not simply because of his technological expertise but also because of his spiritual power (Eliade 1978, 238). Metallurgical skill was considered to require supernatural cooperation, and the smith, therefore, had to be possessed with special powers to accomplish his extraordinary task of converting earth and stone into metal. In Java, the smith in charge of forging a new gamelan used to prepare himself by fasting and other acts of purification, so that he could become fit for possession by the spirit of Panji, a culture hero who figures in many traditional Javanese stories. If the forging of the instruments were successful, they too would become the abode of a spirit, and the gong ageng, the most difficult instrument to make, would contain the greatest spiritual power.

Especially fine old gamelan—or their spirits—have even been ennobled. One at the Yogyakarta **kraton**, for example, that actually antedates the founding of the Sultanate in 1755 and that is used for special celebrations, such as those accompanying the birthday anniversary of Mohammed, is referred to as "Kangjeng Kyai Guntur Madu," or "Venerable Sir Torrent of Honey." For this reason, it remains proper etiquette when entering the gamelan to remove one's shoes and to avoid the rudeness of stepping over an instrument. Further, the spirit of the gamelan, embodied in the gong ageng, is paid homage with offerings of food, flowers, and incense. A rigidly orthodox Muslim might find such behavior to be verging on idolatry, so it is not surprising that even in the more flexible attitude found at the kraton, the gong ageng should be singled out for silencing on days of heightened religious significance within Islam.

A Christian, too, might object to venerating the spirit of the gong, but just as different attitudes prevail among the Muslims, Christians can also accommodate old patterns of behavior. Consider a story told to me by a dancer whose family had been performers connected with the Yogyakarta kraton and whose father had converted to Christianity. Once when he was rehearsing with a gamelan, he was disturbed by the gong's poor tone quality, even though it was supposed to be a very fine instrument. It was suggested that the spirit of the gong was disturbed and that an offering of incense and flowers should be made to it; when this was done, the dancer was pleased and surprised to notice that the gong began to sound resonantly and clearly again.

The spiritual power that is invested in old gamelan by tradition in turn invests power in their owners, for which reason they are important components of princely regalia (**pusaka**), over which battles have been fought in the past. The *gendhing* (musical work) played on these gamelan, too, may have such power that, for example, it was in the past forbidden to hum them casually. When transcribing

KRATON
Javanese royal court.

PUSAKA
Javanese royal heirloom.

them into notation—a practice initiated as a result of European influence in the nineteenth century—it used to be considered advisable to make an occasional mistake to prevent the power of the tune from being used inappropriately.

The Sacred Dance *Bedhaya*

The tunes accompanying the sacred dance **bedhaya** are considered especially powerful because of the reputed origin of the music and dance and their association with kingship, as illustrated in this paraphrase of a story from the *History of Gamelan* by Warsadiningrat:

> One night in the year 1643, Sultan Agung (the last great ruler of the kingdom preceding the establishment of Yogya and Solo) was meditating when he heard music that was so beautiful it gave him goosebumps. The next day he decided to form a dance troupe and called together musical experts to arrange the melodies for the accompaniment. Suddenly Kanjeng Sunan Kalijaga appeared; one of the nine saints legend credits with introducing Islam into Java, he was a noble Hindu by birth, who first became a notorious bandit and then converted to Islam after a lengthy period of continuous meditation in the manner of a Hindu holy man. Kalijaga congratulated the Sultan on his plans to create the gendhing bedhaya, for it was clearly a gift from He Who Is Great and Holy and meant to be a pusaka for the kings of Java that would bring blessings of peace, supremacy, and strength until the end of time.
>
> Nine young girls from noble families were selected for their beauty and grace to dance the bedhaya. The bedhaya dance is important because (1) it contributes to an understanding of Javanese culture by providing a guide to meditation; (2) it explains certain strategies of war; and (3) it contributes to an understanding of music that portrays deep and noble emotions.
>
> Just as the dance lessons were to begin, Kanjeng Ratu Kencana Sari, queen of all spirits, good and evil, suddenly arrived from her palace in the South Sea, in the dress and make-up of a bride. She appeared every day at dusk for three months to teach the dance, because she loved the noble and majestic melodies, and she still appears for this reason. Because of this, when the bedhaya is performed, complete offerings of many kinds are prepared and a great deal of incense is burned continuously throughout the performance, and all the performers—dancers, singers, and musicians—must be pure and clean (Becker 1987; Gertz 1973, 25–29).

As we see in this story, bedhaya is a remarkable example of the eclectic nature of Javanese elite culture and the way in which it is used to assert status. Music and dance that conjure an indigenous Javanese goddess from her home in the sea and receive the blessing of a legendary Muslim saint, whose conversion was accomplished through yogic meditation, constitute one of the special heirlooms that buttress the powers of the king.

The Shadow Play: *Wayang Kulit*

The shadow-puppet theater, or **wayang kulit**, is another Indonesian performance medium using music that has achieved special prominence in Javanese culture and that may also be associated with extraordinary power. Whereas stories of Javanese and Islamic origins are performed in shadow plays,

BEDHAYA
Sacred court dance of Java.

WAYANG KULIT
Indonesian shadow play accompanied with gamelan music.

DALANG
Master puppeteer of the Javanese shadow-puppet play.

KARAWITAN
Learned music in the Javanese tradition.

the stories derived from the Indian epics the *Mahabharata* and the *Ramayana* have the greater popularity and prestige, particularly the Mahabharata. Performed over the course of a whole night, the plays generally depict a battle whose turmoil is reflected in a disturbance of nature that, toward morning, is resolved when order is restored to human society and the world.

The stories of the wayang kulit revolve around Indic characters, but they have been Javanized by the introduction of a number of comic characters, who act as servants to the protagonists and incidentally serve as translators for the audience, because their masters speak a Sanskritized and poetic Javanese that is not commonly understood. This problem reflects the situation in contemporary Javanese, which has many styles of speech based on social class distinctions. (In Indonesia, whose motto is "Unity in Diversity," the Indonesian language—Bahasa Indonesia—has rapidly gained acceptance throughout the country as the lingua franca because it helps to overcome regional, ethnic, and class differences.) The chief of the clowns, Semar, is a fat, lazy, wily, lascivious, and obstreperously flatulent fellow, but he is also a mysteriously all-knowing sage who even takes precedence over the Hindu god Siva himself. Java may have been awed by exotic Indian culture, but it seems that autochthonous wisdom still earns the greater respect. Because Semar speaks colloquially, he has the advantage not only of entertaining the audience with his wit and shenanigans but also of giving good advice and wise counsel.

Wayang Shadow puppet.
Source: Doug Steley A/Alamy

In fact, all the familiar characters in wayang communicate, at least by their actions, the various modes of human existence and manners of behavior. The shadow play has thus long been a medium for moral and ethical instruction and for discussion of contemporary events, and today it is often a medium for explaining government social programs as well.

All the different skills and knowledge needed to perform the shadow play come together in the **dalang**, the puppeteer, a man (rarely a woman) who commands a thorough knowledge of **karawitan** (musical repertory and practice). He is familiar with the many different stories of the plays and their appropriateness for particular occasions, speaks with a host of voices suited to everyone from the most refined gentleman to the crudest villain, and can skillfully move his puppets to convey an equal range of refinement and crudity. The dalang knows archaic languages and the full range of contemporary social dialects, is a repository of spiritual and cultural values, and is acquainted with the latest political events and social problems. No wonder he is often thought to be a kind of superman!

Seated between a light source and a thin screen, the dalang casts the shadows of flat leather puppets against the screen, all the while giving the appropriate signals to the gamelan for the pieces of music needed to accompany the scene, be it a moment of comic relief with Semar dancing, or a tremendous battle between the forces of good and evil. To set the mood for an upcoming scene, he sometimes sings, too.

Now that dalangs can learn their art in schools (just as gamelan musicians do), an abbreviation and standardization of the wayang stories and of the puppeteers' skills is occurring. This inevitably lessens the special aura of the wayang and of the dalang but helps to ensure them a continuing role in the cultural life of modern Indonesia.

MUSIC IN BALI

The arts of Indonesia, especially music and dance, have undergone many changes over the centuries as political and social circumstances have created different requirements and possibilities for performance. Among recent influences, the impact of tourism is certainly one of enormous significance, particularly for the arts of Bali, the small island just to the east of Java in the Indonesian archipelago. A jet airport that was opened there in 1969 has made Bali easily accessible to tourists from around the world, and they have been coming in ever-increasing numbers. Not that tourism is new to Bali: Some of its most famous visitors—painters, composers, anthropologists—arrived there in the decades prior to World War II and often stayed long enough to leave their indelible imprint on Balinese life.

Some Historical Events Influencing Balinese Culture

Before we discuss the impact of tourism on the music of Bali, we will first consider a couple of political events of singular importance in the history of Bali. Earlier, we mentioned the Islamic kingdom of Mataram in the discussion of ketawang "Puspawarna." This kingdom was the predecessor of the central Javanese courts founded in the eighteenth century through intervention of the Dutch, which still continue to exist in a ceremonial way in the present-day Republic of Indonesia. Mataram itself had earlier displaced the Hindu kingdom of Majapahit, whose refugees migrated to Bali in the fifteenth century. The elite Hindu-Buddhist-based culture of Majapahit introduced a new layer into the cultural fabric of Bali, and those who resisted its caste-based hierarchy and monarchical organization retreated to remoter areas of the island, where so-called Bali Aga or "old Bali" villages continue many of the pre-Indo-Javanese ways.

The other overwhelming event in Bali's history took place in 1908, when the kingdoms that had dominated the island for the previous several centuries were finally dissolved by the Dutch, who invaded the island and took over its administration. The effect of Dutch intervention on Bali was quite different from that on Java. In Java the newly established courts, provided with financial resources but given limited responsibilities of governance, evolved an elegant way of life that fostered the development of the arts as the most effective means of retaining exalted status. In Bali the courts were dissolved, and the descendants of nobles, who were often employed as agents of Dutch rule, rarely had the financial resources to maintain the elaborate musical establishments associated with courtly life.

✳ Explore
a map of Bali on the Interactive Globe on **mymusiclab.com**

Music in the Balinese Courts

Among the several different ensembles maintained by Balinese kings, with their different instruments, musicians, repertories, and functions, was the **gamelan gambuh**, a kind of opera derived from Majapahit models. Quite unlike the large gamelan of metallophones we encountered in Java, this one is smaller and consists of several extraordinarily long, vertical flutes (suling gambuh) and a rebab, with a few percussion instruments for punctuation and rhythmic control. The melodies of the flutes and fiddle are elaborately ornamented like those of the corresponding instruments in the Javanese gamelan, but rather than being part of a much denser and richer texture that competes with them, these flute melodies are the sole focus of attention. The flutes, whose tones have an ethereal quality, are played in such a manner that the melody is never interrupted when the player takes a breath. Using his cheeks as a kind of bellows, he inflates them before taking a breath so that he can continue to sound the flute with air from his cheeks while breathing in.

The long-winded melodies and unfamiliar orchestra, the stately progress of the action, and the archaic language of the actors and general lack of comic episodes have given gambuh the status of a venerated relic of the past, even though it has recently undergone something of a revival. Much more popular today is the **gamelan arja** theater, another type of operatic performance not associated with courtly ceremony. Although it is also accompanied by a small ensemble with flutes (of a shorter, more common type) and a few percussion instruments, it employs a greater variety of stories (including some on modern, topical subjects), female as well as male actors, and a lot of comedy.

Now rather rare, the "gamelan with the big gongs" (**gamelan gong gede**) is another ensemble that played an important role in the old courts. In its construction, it is more similar to the large instrumental gamelan of central Java than the gamelan gambuh. For instance, it incorporates colotomic instruments similar to those of the Javanese ensemble, such as gong, *kempur* (kempul), and *kempli* (ketuk). The *gangsa*, instruments responsible for playing the core melody called *pokok* in Bali (balungan in Java), share similarities in construction and musical role with their Javanese counterparts, the saron and slentem. The *trompong*, an important lead instrument with structural similarities to the Javanese bonang, functions both to introduce pieces and elaborate the pokok, The gamelan gong gede was regularly played for public ceremonies and temple festivities and performed

GAMELAN GAMBUH
An archaic type of Balinese court opera and its accompanying orchestra.

GAMELAN ARJA
A type of Balinese opera.

GAMELAN GONG GEDE
Older Balinese court music, used for court and temple rituals, similar in sound and style to the Javanese gamelan.

pieces with regular structures whose melodies, elaboration, colotomy, and rhythm were realized in ways broadly similar to those discussed earlier for Javanese gendhing. An important difference, however, is the fact that, like the majority of Balinese ensembles, the gamelan gong gede is a single orchestra with but one tuning system, pelog. Further, the version of pelog used is pentatonic—a selection of five pitches from the heptatonic pelog system scale. Like gambuh, this gamelan has a more popular and modern counterpart that we will discuss later.

A third court ensemble, **gamelan Semar pegulingan**, is a sizeable orchestra consisting largely of metallophones that was used to play purely instrumental arrangements of gambuh for the private enjoyment of the court. Because gambuh melodies use heptatonic scales, some gamelan Semar pegulingan used to have fully heptatonic instruments, but others played pentatonic versions of the melodies. Today this ensemble, with its peculiarly delicate sound, has been revived to play a variety of old-style, classically structured pieces as well as new compositions and arrangements.

A very modest ensemble, the **gender wayang**, has not suffered a loss of popularity or needed revival because of its association with the shadow play based on stories of the Mahabharata and Ramayana. This quartet of gender, similar in construction and playing technique to the gender of Java and tuned in laras slendro, is the sole accompaniment, other than the voice of the dalang, for the Mahabharata; some percussion and colotomic instruments are added to it for the stories of the Ramayana. The quartet consists, in fact, of two pairs of gender distinguished from one another by being in different octaves. Each instrument pair is also gendered, that is, a pair of instruments includes a male and female instrument. Within each pair, moreover, one instrument is distinguished from the other by being slightly "out of tune," that is, a particular key on one instrument is purposely made slightly higher or lower than its twin to create a sensation of acoustical beats that gives a shimmering quality to the pitch when the keys on both instruments are struck simultaneously. As the instruments of a pair are often played in unison, the result is a constantly throbbing resonance that almost seems to be breathing. Although particularly effective in the Balinese wayang quartet, this principle of purposeful "mistuning" is evident in other bronze ensembles as well and is especially noticeable when an octave is played.

The gender wayang continues to be a vitally important component of Bali's musical life, but the gamelan gambuh, Semar pegulingan, and gong gede have lesser roles as reminders of the past. With the passing of the courts, the patronage needed for the maintenance of the large numbers of instruments and for the support of the musicians, actors, and dancers disappeared. The common people of Bali, however, responded by filling the gap left by the absence of noble patrons, and this provided the impetus and stimulus for developing new types of performing arts. When Western intellectuals began to discover Bali between the World Wars, there was an efflorescence of the arts as they adjusted to the passing of old forms while accommodating new influences from the people and from contact with foreigners.

GAMELAN SEMAR PEGULINGAN
Large, Balinese court orchestra that plays instrumental versions of gamelan gambuh melodies.

GENDER WAYANG
Four-piece ensemble of genders that typically accompanies the Balinese shadow play.

Musicians in Gamelan orchestra play their instruments in a procession at a Hindu cremation ceremony in Bali, Indonesia. *Source:* Paul Souders/DanitaDelimont.com/ Newscom

A Modern Form of Dance and Music: Kebyar

Explore
the Musical Instrument Gallery on
mymusiclab.com

GAMELAN GONG KEBYAR
A modern type of Balinese music and the dance it accompanies, which is noted for its virtuosic and unpredictable playing style.

KOTEKAN
Often virtuosic and rapid interlocking rhythms important within gamelan kebyar performances and consisting of two parts (a lower part and a higher part) played on two separate instruments. Generally, multiple pairs of instruments are simultaneously involved in performing kotekan.

The most vibrant of the new styles was the result of the reshaping of the gamelan gong gede into the **gamelan gong kebyar** by dropping some instruments and modifying and borrowing others. The *trompong*, for example, was dropped because its function as the introducer of pieces and as elaborator of melodies became less important when gender-like instruments called *kantilan* started playing virtuosic interlocking patterns (**kotekan**) as the elaboration for kebyar. And the gangsa, the main melody instruments of the gamelan gong gede (responsible for the pokok, that is), yielded their role to other gender-like instruments with lower ranges than the kantilan.

Village gamelan clubs often bought older-style gamelan no longer maintained or needed by the courts and recast them into the new form, and the new music developed for these was a revolutionary departure from the sedate and majestic pieces of the repertory for the gamelan gambuh or gamelan gong gede. In the latter, predictably familiar formal structures, conventional instrumentation, stable rhythms, and relatively unvaried dynamics created a sense of classical elegance; but the music of kebyar was a revolutionary change—virtuosic, mercurial, flashy, and unpredictable (Listen to CD II, 5 for an example of gamelan gong kebyar).

In an old-style gendhing for the gamelan gong gede or Semar pegulingan, the introduction would normally be a somewhat tentative solo on the *trompong*, an instrument similar to the Javanese bonang. Kebyar music, on the other hand, immediately asserts its independence from older formal traditions by beginning with a loud, confident unison for the whole ensemble. Instead of the classical elegance and refinement of former times, it displays a willful exuberance, progressing in fits and starts with sudden dynamic contrasts, jerky syncopations,

LISTENING GUIDE

GAMELAN GONG KEBYAR "KEBYAR TERUNA" 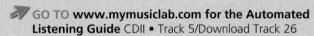 **GO TO www.mymusiclab.com for the Automated Listening Guide** CDII • Track 5/Download Track 26

Performed by Gamelan Gong Kebyar of Pliatan

This recording is characteristic of Balinese gamelan gong kebyar performances. It incorporates many passages of kotekan, brilliant changes in tempo, dynamics, and texture that distinguish it from the older, more stately gamelan gong gede style, and produces the shimmering quality associated with the slightly different tunings achieved between the male and female counterparts of the various pairs of instruments in the gamelan.

TIME	SECTION	MUSICAL EVENTS
0:00–0:38	**Introduction:** Listen for the intense character of this introduction. Notice especially the sound of the ceng-ceng cymbals.	Introduction featuring almost the entire gamelan playing in unison. Typical of kebyar style, the introduction incorporates varied dynamics and tempi and irregular rhythms and syncopations.
0:38–0:42	**Passages featuring reyong and gangsa:** Take note of the different sounds produced by these two instruments.	Passage for reyong with kotekan (interlocking patterns). This passage introduces the reyong theme that will reappear in the next section.
0:42–0:48		Passage for gangsa with kotekan, introducing the patterns that will return in the calung-jegogan section.
0:48–1:24	**Section for reyong:** Listen for the way that the reyong plays kotekan within the structure provided by the gamelan. Notice also the dynamic shifts (changes in volume [loud-softer-loud]) in this section. Finally, notice that the kotekan being performed on the reyong are drawn from the patterns established during the reyong passage at [0:38–42].	The reyong is featured in this section. Notice that the lowest gong sounds consistently throughout this section. The kempli, which is struck but dampened with the other hand, and therefore sounds a bit dry and percussive, plays eight strokes per gong stroke. This underlying structure will help keep you oriented given the speed at which the kotekan moves.
1:24–2:00	**Section for calung/jegogan:** Notice the slower, lower-pitched melody emerge in the calung-jegogan. These instruments are in the same family group as the high-pitched gangsa, heard at [0:42–0:48]. Notice also that the kotekan played on the gangsa during that earlier passage reappear in this section.	The lower-pitched calung and jegogan are featured, but they are accompanied by kotekan in the higher-pitched gangsa. It is hard not to focus only on the dazzling figurations of the gangsa, but see if you can attend to the musical activity simultaneously unfolding in the other instruments. Again, you can orient yourself by listening for the 8/1 ratio of kempli to gong.

2:00–2:06	**Cadential pattern:** Listen for the way a syncopated, repeated figure brings the section to a close.	The cadential pattern, driven by the kendang (drums) and ceng-ceng (cymbals), is repeated once and then extended with a sustained stroke (not dampened, that is) on the reyong.
2:06–2:22	**Increased tempo and intensity:** Notice the dramatic and sudden increase in tempo here. Listen for the increasingly syncopated strokes on the reyong.	This section of increased tempo and intensity affords the most virtuosic drumming and ceng-ceng playing in the performance.
2:22–3:01	**Return of calung/jegogan section:** Listen for the return of the material used earlier at [0:48–1:24].	The material presented in the earlier calung-jegogan section returns here at a faster tempo and with more intensity. This section, because it is faster, provides for the most virtuosic kotekan passages. The performance continues as the recording fades out, beginning at [2:56].

Balinese Kebyar dancers in performance. *Source:* Paul Kennedy/Lonely Planet/Newscom

and breathtakingly rapid figuration. No wonder many older connoisseurs found kebyar a disturbing phenomenon when it first took Bali by storm around the time of World War I (Listen to CD II, 6 for an example of gamelan gong gede).

Originally a purely orchestral music ideally suited for musical competitions among different villages, kebyar was given a new twist when it began to accompany dance. About 1925, a young dancer named Maria made a particular impression with his version of a dance to go with this exciting music. Like the fixed structures of the classical gendhing, the various dances performed by

LISTENING GUIDE

GAMELAN GONG GEDE "TABUH EMPAT PENGAWAK"

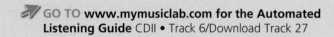 GO TO www.mymusiclab.com for the Automated **Listening Guide** CDII • Track 6/Download Track 27

Performed by Gamelan Gong Gede "Sekar Sandat" of Bangli

This recording, excerpted from a typical old-style piece for gamelan gong gede, well illustrates the kind of music to which the new kebyar style presented such a startling contrast. The meandering trompong introduction is starkly different from the explosive beginning of "Kebyar Teruna" (CD II, 5), and the stately progression of the melody when the whole ensemble enters (at [2:00]) is rigidly organized with a regular tempo and equally regular ornamentation and orchestration.

TIME	SECTION	MUSICAL EVENTS
0:00–1:05	**Introduction:** Listen for the slow and deliberate way the trompong handles the introduction.	Introduction, featuring the trompong and performed in free meter.
1:05–1:23		The gong enters, marking both an end to the solo introduction and the beginning of a transition to metered, colotomic performance.
1:23–1:29	**Drums and remaining instruments enter:** Notice how the drums introduce a regular pulse and that, shortly thereafter, the entire ensemble joins the trompong. This is due, in part, to the fact that the tempo of the performance is now clear and the colotomic parts can be slotted into place.	The drums enter and immediately establish a regular beat.
1:29–2:00		The entire ensemble joins the trompong, regularly subdividing the beat in the colotomic fashion that should sound familiar to you by now.
2:00–2:29	**The main melody (pokok) enters:** Listen for the slow manner in which the pokok unfolds.	The pokok enters, performed on the gangsa at the rate of about one note every two seconds. The subdivided beat is emphasized by the ceng-ceng cymbals. The recording rapidly fades out at [2:28].

trained court dancers or by people making offerings at the temple were based on traditional movements and gestures, and the stock characters of dramas like gambuh were confined to expressing the limited range of moods suited to them. But Maria's kebyar mirrored the fleeting moods and unpredictable contrasts of the music. The dancer performed in an unusual crouched position that was on the same level as the seated musicians with whom he sometimes interacted directly, seeming to tease and cajole. Alternately rising onto his knees and squatting, playing with a fan, flashing a bizarre series of glances that registered astonishment, pique, enticement, and fury in rapid succession, the dancer would interpret the music's every change. To top things off, he might conclude by joining his accompanists in a choreographically performed solo on the trompong (an instrument not much used in kebyar but symbolic of Balinese musical heritage), all the while continuing to bob up and down and back and forth on his knees, twirl his mallets like a drum major, and register a bewildering series of moods on his face. Although originally danced by boys or young men, today kebyar is also danced by young women dressed as men. This kind of cross-dressing in dance performance is nothing new, however.

The individual nature of kebyar gave a new importance to the role of the composer and choreographer, and for a while compositions were jealously guarded as the special property of a particular club. The concept of the "composition" in the view of the Balinese gamelan club, however, is quite different from how a piece, by Beethoven, for instance, is generally understood by orchestras in the North Atlantic. We can get an idea of how a Balinese composition is realized and treated from a memoir written by John Coast, an impresario who arranged the first world tour of the gamelan from Pliatan village in 1951. For this occasion, Coast wanted a special new piece, and he commissioned Maria to choreograph a new dance to go with it. Here is his account of how the gamelan learned the piece.

> When we arrived about nine o'clock that night in the village we found the gamelan well into the first melody of the new dance [which they were learning by having each part demonstrated, as is customary, rather than from a score]; and it was Kebiar music, though new, Maria [*sic*] told us, having been composed originally by Pan Sukra for a club in Marga, near Tabanan, but it had never been used. And anyhow, these tunes were arranged for a girl dancer, while the original ones had been for a man.
>
> It took about three weeks for the thirty minutes of music to be perfectly mastered by Pliatan, and at the end of that time Pan Sukra went home to his village. Then Anak Agung, Made Lebah, and Gusti Kompiang grinned freely. "Now it is our turn," they said.
>
> "What do you mean?" we asked.
>
> "Aggh! This is crude music. Now it is a matter of tabuh—style. You will see. It must be rearranged and polished by the club (Coast 1953, 109).

From DANCERS OUT OF BALI, John Coast. GP Putnam & Sons, 1953. Used with kind permission of Laura Rosenberg at the John Coast Foundation for the Performing Arts in Bali.

As a comparison, we might think of the Boston Symphony Orchestra playing a composition originally composed for the New York Philharmonic and, when the composer had turned his back, rewriting it according to their own tastes! No doubt some instrumentalists in Boston would respond with that expressive "Aggh!" to a newly commissioned work, but it is highly unlikely they would have the temerity to suggest altering the piece once it was completed, even if the composer had once asked for their advice on how to arrange the parts for their particular instruments.

Even in matters of interpretation, the initiative is apt to come from the music director or conductor rather than of the rank-and-file instrumentalist.

But in Pliatan, as in other Balinese gamelan, the repertory was shaped by the contributions of all the club members, although decisions may have been made by acknowledged leaders like Anak Agung, a nobleman, and Made Lebah, a commoner, both of whom were respected performers and teachers.

In his account of the creation of the dance to go with the new music, Coast (1953) again reveals the cooperative nature of the work.

> And we saw the story of the dance unfold, as Maria had told us it would, creating itself bit by bit, with ideas thrown in from us all. We saw Raka as the little bumblebee sunning herself in a flower-filled garden, in moods of surprise, delight and fear; we saw the gaudy male bumblebee enter, and Sampih could pick up Maria's ideas with the speed with which a western ballet dancer follows an enchainement in class; we saw him spy the delectable little bee, zoom toward her, court her, frighten her by his advances till she fled from him. Then Sampih danced alone in baffled fury as the Kebiar music raged around him, and in the last rollicking melody he danced a Kebiar of sheer frustration around the whole gamelan, flirting desperately with its members. This was a development out of Maria's original Kebiar, and he called it now: Tumulilingan Mengisap Sari—the Bumblebee Sips Honey.
>
> Luce was meanwhile busy with the costumes. . . . All our Pliatan family [*sic*] were engrossed in this dance, for it was a new thing and it was ours. (110).

To the creation of this new piece—which soon became a standard item in the repertory of the gamelan gong kebyar—even Coast and other members of the entrepreneur's retinue were able to make contributions as part of the "Pliatan family."

THE INFLUENCE OF FOREIGN ARTISTS AND TOURISTS

A Ramayana Performance: Kecak

Coast and his entourage were hardly the first outsiders to have an influence on Balinese arts. Two examples should suffice to illustrate this point. Walter Spies, a visual artist and musician who toured Indonesia (playing two-piano recitals) with the Canadian-American composer, Colin McPhee, in 1938, was involved in the development of **kecak**. This unusual performance medium is of particular interest because it has become a "must-see" item for tourists, who are often unaware that they are witnessing an art form specifically created to satisfy them. Because it is strange and disturbing in terms of Westerners' usual experience of performing arts, kecak has indeed satisfied millions of tourists as an experience of something powerfully exotic, without which the time and money spent in getting to new and distant places might seem poorly spent.

The kecak takes its name from the brusque, staccato monosyllables shouted by a large chorus of men in rapid and intricately interlocking rhythmic patterns. A few other men use their voices to imitate the sound of a small gamelan, and these two elements accompany a drastically shortened version of the Ramayana

KECAK
A type of dance drama accompanied by a large male chorus that chants rhythmically, usually performed for tourists.

acted out by a few actor–dancers. The basic story is this: Sita, wife of King Rama, an incarnation of the god Vishnu, has been abducted by the demon Ravana, who carries her off to his palace in Sri Lanka, but Hanuman, general of the monkey army and devotee of Rama, pursues them and rescues Sita. Because the chorus of men intermittently takes on the role of Hanuman's monkey army and sounds like chattering monkeys, the performance is sometimes also called the "Monkey Chant."

The rhythmic shouting of the men is traditionally associated with rituals of divination, in which young girls are entranced so questions can be put to the spirits (*sanghyang*) that take possession of them. Although music and dance are frequently part of these rituals, dramatic stories from the Ramayana are not. Thinking that the kecak was an exciting and unusual kind of music, Spies suggested using it as the foundation for a concise presentation of the Ramayana that would give tourists, who were already discovering Bali before World War II, a professionally arranged and attractive means of experiencing it.

A Trance Dance: *Barong*

Like kecak, **barong** is another kind of trance ritual that has been adapted as a regular performance medium for tourists. It is a kind of dramatic presentation accompanied by the gamelan gong or kebyar that represents the struggle between Good (in the being of the barong, an awesome but benevolent lion) and Evil (impersonated by a horrendous and malevolent witch). At the high point of the story, the supporters of the barong attack the witch with their *krises* (wavy daggers) and are forced by the witch's magic to turn them instead upon their own bodies, but the magic of the barong protects them from injuring themselves. During performances at village temples, many participants may fall into trance during and after the battle. Indeed the spirits that are normally thought to reside in the masks of the barong and of the witch may possess the men who wear them as well.

In temple rituals for the Balinese themselves, the barong is certainly an event of supernatural import, but that does not prevent it from being an entertainment as well. One village, in fact, may visit another to perform its particular version of the barong and be appreciated for the style with which it performs as well as for the evident power of its barong and witch. There are, in fact, trance performances in Bali and elsewhere in Indonesia in which the trancers are said to be possessed by animals or even inanimate objects and that seem to have the presentation of a type of entertainment as their sole or main purpose. In such circumstances, the entertainment of tourists with a barong performance seems to fit in with the Balinese view of things, but such a performance cannot mean the same thing as one in which the primary object is to create a sense of well-being and security for the community, rather than, for economic gain, to satisfy the curiosity of outsiders. Although many of the tourists may regale their friends back home with stories of the "authentic" rituals they witnessed, the Balinese probably have a clearer idea of the distinction between the different types of "authenticity" involved in the performance of barong for themselves and for tourists.

Changes in the motivations and presentation of performances of kecak or barong may bother those whose original associations with the performance have strong meaning. However, this is surely an inevitable part of human experience, because no society is static, and all culture must evolve and change or cease to exist. Just as the Sun Dance and other festivities of the Plains Indians in North America developed into pan-Indian powwow celebrations, and like the Medicine Dance of the San people of Botswana, which has evolved into a performance for others as well as for the San themselves, barong, too, may be undergoing a shift from an organic and vital part of specific Balinese communities to a "cultural performance" meant to help shape the idea of "Baliness" for the modern Balinese and for the outside world. Musical performances like barong, after all, can help mediate not just the contact between the human and the otherworldly but also the contact between groups of human beings, and we may hope that this latter role is no less powerful a validation of an art form than the former.

FOUR KINDS OF POPULAR MUSIC IN JAVA

Gambus

Entertainment and monetary gain are often thought of as the only reasons for the existence of many types of popular music. But when we think, for example, of how some people enjoy hip hop and willingly pay for the pleasure of listening to it, whereas others dislike it but are vehemently devoted to reggae or heavy metal, it becomes clear that more powerful motivations must also be involved. Like barong, popular music can shape an identity—for an individual or a group—and present it to the world.

In Indonesia, one of the pop musics that succeeds in doing this as well as providing its consumers a good deal of enjoyment is **gambus**, a genre named for an Arabic instrument that signifies connection with the homeland of Islam. Nowadays the gambus may be present only by virtue of having lent its name to the genre, the instrument itself having been replaced by the 'ud, which has wider currency in the music of the Middle East.

Not just the instruments of gambus—which may include, for example, *marawis* (sing. *mirwas*), small double-headed drums from Yemen—but the musical style itself reflects Middle Eastern origins, with its short, often sequentially repeated phrases and simple, catchy, and danceable rhythms. Even the vocal timbre is often more that of Middle Eastern than of Indonesian singers although so-called modern gambus (*gambus moderen*) may use Indonesian lyrics. The dress of the performers as depicted on the sleeves of cassettes and CDs may include such articles as the kaffiyeh and agal, the Arab headdress worn by men. Although the texts of gambus may have Islamic subject matter, the songs are much appreciated for their musical qualities—too much so in view of the more puritanical Muslims who feel that music is not conducive to leading a proper Islamic life, because it directs the listener to focus on the sensual instead of on the spiritual. Perhaps one could imagine

GAMBUS
A type of Islamic song having Arabic influence; the name of the plucked lute originally used to accompany this song.

LISTENING GUIDE

GAMBUS "CARI HABURAN"

✈ GO TO **www.mymusiclab.com for the Automated Listening Guide** CDII • Track 7/Download Track 28

TIME	MUSICAL EVENTS
0:00–0:21	Improvised prelude on gambus ('ud) and violins. One violin plays sustained bass notes while the other elaborates the melody.
0:22–1:23	Free rhythm rendition of first verses.
1:24–1:50	Voice concludes, and instruments continue melody with cadential accompaniment of interlocking drums (mirwas [pl. marawis]) At this point, the violin responsible for the bass notes becomes more actively involved in elaborating the melody as well.
1:50–2:48	Previously heard verses sung in free rhythm, now sung in 4/4 meter.
2:48–3:09	The interlocking drum cadence continues in similar fashion until the recording fades out at [3:00–3:09].

a similar confrontation in the United States between supporters of Christian rock and their adversaries (Listen to CD II, 7 for an example of gambus).

Dangdut

Dangdut is another popular music that is an extraordinary mix of Western rock and Indian film song. Its Indonesian texts have usually dealt with homiletic advice about leading a better, more productive, and uprightly Islamic life, although secular love lyrics are becoming increasingly common now. Its infectious rhythms have earned it the onomatopoetic name dangdut, which represents its characteristic drum sounds and, for those who deride it, its suspiciously worldly appeal. Dangdut was transformed into a popular medium for broadcasting Islamic values to the public in the seventies under the influence of the superstar Rhoma Irama. He was originally called Oma, but he added the "R" and "h" from Raden Haji, a title given those Muslims who, as he did, perform the pilgrimage to Mecca. Dangdut became the dominant pop music in the '90s, and like the Indian songs from which it borrowed so much, it has been featured heavily in films (Listen to CD II, 8 for an example of dangdut).

Kroncong

Dangdut, a relatively recent phenomenon, has had a fairly swift rise in popularity in the manner of many kinds of commercial pop, but **kroncong**, another popular style, has a long history in Indonesia stretching back to the first contact with European colonialism. The Portuguese ports in the

DANGDUT
Popular Indonesian musical style that combines Western rock and Indian film music influences.

KRONCONG
A type of popular Indonesian music originating from Portuguese-derived sources.

LISTENING GUIDE

"CURAHAN HATI"

Grup Tanjidor Kembang Ros
Sophia Welly, vocal

GO TO **www.mymusiclab.com for the Automated Listening Guide** CDII • Track 8/Download Track 29

This example of dangdut is performed by a **tanjidor** group—a kind of ensemble from the more rural outskirts of Jakarta. Unlike the heavily commercialized, professional, rock ensemble sound popularized by Rhoma Irama, tanjidor ensembles are comprised of amateur musicians and blend European-derived band instruments with local instruments. This recording features saxophone, clarinet, trumpet, a fiddle of Chinese origin (called a tehyan), and several local percussion instruments. Importantly, tanjidor groups do not generally focus on dangdut as a major component of their repertory. It is a testament to the immense popularity of the commercialized dangdut songs of artists like Rhoma Irama and Elvy Sukaesih (among many others) that these songs are being incorporated into the repertories of regional ensembles like the tanjidor. A song with lyrics about the complications of love, "Curahan Hati" means "From the Heart."

TIME	SECTION	MUSICAL EVENTS
0:00–0:33	**Introduction**	The ensemble plays a melodic theme twice through in heterophonic fashion. This theme becomes the basis for interludes later in the performance.
0:34–0:58	**Verse 1:** Vocalist enters and sings the first verse.	Notice the **A** [0:34–0:46] **B** [0:47–0:58] structure of the melody and that it differs from the theme played by the instruments. You'll notice that the **B** melody functions almost like a tag refrain in subsequent verses.
0:58–1:13	**Instrumental interlude**	The ensemble returns to the opening melodic theme.
1:13–1:59	**Verse 2:** Vocalist introduces new melodic content.	Notice that the first melodic phrase, which is repeated after a short instrumental break, **C** [1:13–1:26 and 1:33–1:45], is comprised of new material. This is followed by a move back to a variation of **B**, heard most clearly in the last line of text.
2:00–2:28	**Interlude:** This time the vocalist performs the opening theme with instrumental accompaniment.	After the vocalist sings the opening theme through once, the instrumentalists play a variation on that theme, closing with the familiar melodic material [2:16–2:28].
2:29–3:14	**Verse 3:** Vocalist introduces new text but follows melodic pattern established in verse 2.	
3:15–3:52	**Conclusion:** The vocalist sings the opening theme twice through as the song comes to a close.	As before the instrumentalists accompany the vocalist as she sings the opening melody [3:15–3:29]. During the repeat, however, the instrumentalists join the vocalist in performing the melody, adding a bit of energy as the piece concludes [3:29–3:52].

East—such as Goa in India, Macao in China, and Malacca in Malaysia—and the Portuguese areas of southern Africa and the Azores linked Europe of the sixteenth and seventeenth centuries to the spice-growing areas of Indonesia. Before the Dutch established colonial hegemony in the Indonesian archipelago, the Portuguese outposts on the islands served as centers for the shipment of

TANJIDOR
Musical ensemble from the outskirts of Jakarta that blends European-derived band instruments with local instruments.

KETUK TILU
A small, Sundanese ensemble
consisting of rebab, gong,
three ketuk, and drums.
This ensemble accompanies
a female dancer/singer.

spices to Europe. These communities of mixed ethnic and racial background nevertheless maintained aspects of Portuguese culture such as the Christian religion and some types of folk music. In Indonesia, this music came to be called kroncong. During the late nineteenth and early twentieth centuries it had a somewhat unsavory reputation associated with urban violence and glamorous toughs called *buaya kroncong* (kroncong crocodiles), who were like the Malay pirates of some Hollywood movies in the twenties and thirties.

The typical instruments accompanying kroncong are of European derivation: violin, cello, flute, and plucked strings of various types; one of the strings, similar to a ukulele, has given its name to the genre. These provided a simple, harmonically based accompaniment to vocal melodies sung with a mellifluous sweetness Americans might think characteristically Hawaiian. When kroncong began to attract the interest of a more polite section of middle-class Javanese society in the twenties and thirties, it underwent a kind of acculturation to central Javanese style, and although the instruments were the same, they took on functional qualities similar to those of gamelan music. The flute and violin became like the suling and rebab, providing free, heterophonic elaboration of the melody. The cello, while continuing to provide a foundation for the harmony, was played pizzicato in rhythms resembling kendang-like drum patterns; and the kroncong, with its regular offbeat plucking, had a resemblance to the ketuk.

Some kroncong during this period also took on the typical 4 × 8-bar structure of Tin Pan Alley ballads, with a repeated first phrase that also returned after an intervening and contrasting second phrase: **AABA**. They also acquired a jazzy feeling with the addition of "blue notes." What had been an indigenously evolved, traditional popular music, based on very old importations, had evolved into a more internationalized commercial music at the same time that it was becoming more "Javanized."

With a variety of styles appealing to different ethnic groups and social strata, kroncong became a music of broad appeal. Its popularity was consolidated during World War II when the Japanese banned foreign popular music, thereby helping it become a vehicle for the expression of national solidarity and nationalist sentiment. Although newer styles like the rock-oriented kroncong pop have developed more recently, the powerful nostalgia evoked by the music from the war and prewar period gives it a strong appeal for an older audience, even as the young continue to turn toward music like dangdut (Listen to CD II, 9 for an example of kroncong).

Jaipongan

The *jaipongan* style of pop music has the unique characteristic of being derived from a type of professional folk entertainment of Sunda (West Java) and does not betray the foreign derivations or influences of gambus, dangdut, or kroncong. The Sundanese **ketuk tilu** (three ketuk) is a small ensemble of musicians playing rebab, gong, three ketuk, and drums, who accompany a female dancer-singer (and sometimes prostitute) in a kind of audience-participation performance during which various men get up to dance with her. Many similar types of dance

LISTENING GUIDE

KRONCONG "MORISKO"

↗ GO TO www.mymusiclab.com *for the Automated* *Listening Guide* CDII • Track 9/Download Track 30

Performed by Orkes Kroncong Mutiara, vocal: Suhaery Mufti

TIME	MUSICAL EVENTS
0:00–0:12	Introduction in free rhythm on flute.
0:13–0:37	Plucked strings set up accompaniment patterns regularly subdividing beat in a manner reminiscent of gamelan practice over which flute continues its ornamental floating melody.
0:38–1:20	Voice takes over melody of song, and flute adds ornamental flourishes in manner of gamelan suling at ends of vocal phrases.
1:20–1:23	Fades out.

entertainments exist or existed in Java and Bali as well as other parts of Indonesia, and troupes were often hired for private parties or for celebrations connected with occasions like weddings or circumcisions.

Like dangdut, the word **jaipongan** was made up from syllables represent-ing drum sounds, and flashy Sundanese-style drumming is basic to this style. A saron is generally added; to the instruments derived from ketuk tilu. This adds another characteristic equally as attractive as the drumming and as typi-cally Sundanese, because the saron is in slendro while the singer and rebab usually perform in another tuning such as pelog, adding ornamental pitches as well. According to Philip Yampolsky (in his liner notes for *Tonggeret*, None-such 79173-2), a young musician named Gugum Gumbira was responsible for introducing the amalgamation of various Sundanese musical components that started the jaipongan craze in 1974. Its popularity soon caused it to spread be-yond his original troupe to other parts of Java outside Sunda, as well as to take on the nature of a popular dance fad for couples.

Although the social-dance fad has waned in recent years, Gugum Gumbira has concentrated on creating staged performances, and as Philip Yampolsky remarks: "Today, Jaipongan is accepted as a 'national' stage dance." It is even included in cultural performances by Indonesian students in the United States for national-day celebrations (Listen to CD II, 10 for an example of jaipongan).

UNITY IN DIVERSITY

"Unity in Diversity," as we pointed out earlier, is the national motto of Indonesia, a nation created within the memory of many of its present-day citizens. Creating unity is a primary concern in any attempt to form a nation,

JAIPONGAN
Popular Indonesian music that is derived from the native folk entertainment of Sunda (West Java).

LISTENING GUIDE

JAIPONGAN, "DAUN PULUS KESER BOJONG"   GO TO **www.mymusiclab.com for the Automated Listening Guide** CDII • Track 10/Download Track 31

Performed by Gugum Gumbira and his Jugala Group, singer Idjah Hadidjah

TIME	MUSICAL EVENTS
0:00–1:14	Extended introductory passage highlighting the virtuosic and flashy Sundanese drumming style in which the drums are struck with the hands and even manipulated with the feet. Melody on rebab, and regular clacking of cymbal-like kecrek. Periodic shouts from the performers add to the raucous and rowdy atmosphere typical of jaipongan performance.
1:14–1:45	The performers yell the name of their group JU—GA—LA alternating with the leader who sort of groans it in a gruff voice.
1:45–2:13	Introduction concludes with entrance of sarons playing phrase with an answer by drums, both then repeated.
2:13–3:00	Singer briefly introduces song unaccompanied and is joined by other performers starting at [2:20]. Her highly elaborate melody is heterophonically accompanied by the rebab and progresses with occasional, startling comments from the drum.
3:00–3:03	The recording fades out.

and is equally important to sustaining one. But the chore is a remarkably daunting one in a country with the topography of Indonesia and a population ranging from the industrialized city dwellers of Java to recently contacted groups of former headhunters in Papua (the Indonesian part of New Guinea) and Kalimantan (the Indonesian part of Borneo). In the scholarly view of music, the unity of the area is often related to the use of bronze-casting technology and cyclical musical structures that also link Indonesia to the Southeast Asian mainland, southern China, northeastern India, and the Philippines. Valid and interesting as this system of relationships is, it does not accommodate many other types of musical phenomena in Indonesia such as, for example, the various pipe ensembles of people in Kalimantan, whose music might be reasonably discussed in comparison with that of similar ensembles among the Andean Aymara or South African Venda.

The necessity of national "unity," evidenced in music by the establishment of government conservatories with standardized curricula, will present a challenge to the more marginal components of Indonesian society and to their cultural forms. These components of Indonesia's "diversity" will likely be neglected—as they have been in this chapter—but their lack of importance for the national scene does not necessarily indicate the inevitability of their disappearance or impoverishment. Thanks to the inexpensive and widespread technology of recording, many types of regionally circumscribed musics find a locally supportive market that helps to perpetuate them and at the same time alter their uses and associations. Rather than propagating a narrow range of musical product, the cassette, CD, and VCD industry in Indonesia has in effect created the audio equivalent of the country's motto, a wide range of music in a uniform medium.

Recorded sound has demonstrated the variety of Indonesia's music today, but it has also preserved the sound of its past: The gamelan brought to the Columbian Exposition of 1893 was recorded not only on film but also on wax cylinders, the audio-recording medium of the day. Although these are not the first recordings of an ethnomusicological nature—some earlier ones were made of Native Americans—they are among the earliest, and they help to lend a special aura to the instruments now housed in the collection of the Field Museum. What would those musicians recorded in 1893 have thought, I wonder, if they had been able to hear the performance of bubaran "Udan Mas" that was described at the start of this essay?

SUMMARY

✓•— Study and Review
on mymusiclab.com

Gamelan is an Indonesian term for musical ensemble. In central Java, these are usually instruments of bronze—gongs and keys—with the addition of drums, a flute, a fiddle, a xylophone, and a zither.

As we have heard, the kinds of ensembles that are referred to as gamelan are diverse, indeed. The occasions during which gamelan becomes important to the event at hand are similarly diverse. In fact, Gamelan music serves ritual and spiritual, governmental, dramatic, and social functions. The shadow-puppet play—Wayang Kulit—in particular, is one of the major theatrical forms that uses gamelan accompaniment. We have also encountered some specific and characteristic musical ideas within Indonesia. So, for instance, we learned that Indonesian music is generally based on repeated musical phrases of varying length. We also learned that Javanese music uses two scales—a five-note (slendro) and a seven-note (pelog) one. In Bali, pelog predominates, but the important gender wayang ensemble for accompanying the shadow play uses slendro.

Our encounter with the music of Indonesia has also pointed out some of the differences between Javanese and Balinese gamelan music. So, for instance, Balinese gamelan sound is distinguished from its Javanese relative by the use of paired, gendered instruments that are tuned slightly differently, creating a shimmering or pulsating effect. Additionally, a type of gamelan music, called kebyar, is distinguished from its Javanese and Balinese antecedents by the virtuosic performance of kotekan and by the sudden rhythmic and dynamic shifts that characterize the style. As we have seen, the emergence of performance styles such as kecak and barong in Bali point to the ways that music can change and take on new forms and meanings in response to factors such as tourism. Finally, many newer popular styles (such as gambus, dangdut, kroncong, and jaipongan) combine outside influences—ranging from Arabic pop, Western rock, and Indian film music—with traditional Javanese musical instruments and ideas.

BIBLIOGRAPHY

Java   Judith Becker, ed., *Karawitan: Source Readings in Javanese Gamelan and Vocal Music*, 3 vols., Michigan Papers on South and Southeast Asia No. 29, 30, 31 (Ann Arbor: Center for South and Southeast Asian Studies, University of Michigan, 1984, 1987, 1988); Henry Spiller, *Erotic Triangles: Sundanese Dance and Masculinity in West Java* (Chicago: University of Chicago Press, 2010); Mantle Hood, *The Nuclear Theme as a Determinant of Patet in Javanese Music* (New York: Da Capo, 1977); Susan Pratt Walton, *Mode in Javanese Music*, Monographs in International Studies Southeast Asia Series No. 79 (Athens, OH: Ohio University Center for International Studies, 1987); Andrew Wintraub, *Power Plays Wayang Golek Puppet Theater of West Java* (Athens, OH: Ohio University Press, 2004); Claire Holt, *Art in Indonesia: Continuity and Change* (Ithaca, NY: Cornell University Press, 1967); Sarah Weiss, *Listening to an Earlier Java: Aesthetics, Gender, and the Music of Wayang in Central Java* (Leiden: KITLV, 2006); Judith Becker, *Traditional Music in Modern Java: Gamelan in a Changing Society* (Honolulu: University of Hawaii Press, 1980); Jaap Kunst, *Music in Java: Its History, Its Theory and Its Technique*, 2 vols., ed. Ernst Heins (The Hague: Martinus Nijhoff, 1973); Mircea Eliade, *The Forge and the Crucible*, 2nd ed. (Chicago: University of Chicago Press, 1978); Peter Manuel, *Popular Musics of the Non-Western World* (New York: Oxford University Press, 1988); Bronia Kornhauser, "In Defence of Kroncong," in Margaret J. Kartomi, ed., *Monash Papers on Southeast Asia No. 7* (Clayton, Victoria: University of Monash, 1978); Ward Keeler, *Javanese Shadow Puppets*, Images of Asia (Singapore: Oxford University Press, 1992); Jennifer Lindsay, *Javanese Gamelan: Traditional Orchestra of Indonesia*, Images of Asia, (Singapore: Oxford University Press, 1992); Michael Tenzer, *Balinese Music* (Berkeley, CA: Periplus Editions, 1991); Ernst Heins, *Music in Java: Current Bibliography, 1973–92* (Amsterdam: Institute of Musicology Ethnomusicology Center, 1993); Bernard Arps, ed., *Performance in Java and Bali: Studies of Narrative Theatre* (London: School of Oriental and African Studies, 1993). Ben Brinner, *Knowing Music, Making Music* (Chicago: University of Chicago Press, 1995); Sumarsam, *Gamelan: Cultural Interaction and Musical Development in Central Asia* (Chicago: University of Chicago Press, 1995); R. Anderson Sutton, *Traditions of Gamelan Music in Java: Musical Pluralism and Regional Identity* (New York/Cambridge: Cambridge University Press, 1991); Sean Williams, *The Sound of the Ancestral Ship: Highland Music of West Java* (Oxford: Oxford University Press, 2001).

Bali   Colin McPhee, *Music in Bali: A Study in Form and Instrumental Organization in Balinese Orchestral Music* (New York: Da Capo, 1976); Henry Spiller, *Gamelan: the Traditional Sounds of Indonesia* (New York: Routledge, 2008); Brita Renée Heimarck, *Balinese Discourses on Music and Modernization Village Voices and Urban Views* (New York: Routledge, 2003); Colin McPhee, *A Club of Small Men* (New York: John Day, 1948); Colin McPhee, *The Balinese Wajang Koelit and Its Music* (1936; repr. New York: AMS Press); John Coast,

Dancers of Bali (New York: Putnam, 1953); I Made Brandem and Frederik deBoer, *Kaja and Kelod: Balinese Dance in Transition* (Kuala Lumpur, New York: Oxford University Press, 1981); Urs Ramseyer, *The Art and Culture of Bali* (New York: Oxford University Press, 1977); Michael Tenzer, *Gamelan Gong Kebyar: The Art of Twentieth-Century Balinese Music* (Chicago: University of Chicago Press, 2000); Michael B. Bakan, *Music of Death and New Creation: Experiences in the World of Balinese Gamelan Beleganjur* (Chicago: University of Chicago Press, 1999); Britqa Renee Heimarck, *Balinese Discourses on Music and Modernization* (London: Routledge, 2002); Edward Herbst, *Voices in Bali* (Hanover, NH: University Press of New England, 1997).

DISCOGRAPHY

Java   *Java Palais Royal de Yogyakarta: Musiques de Concert* (Ocora 558 598); *Java Historic Gamelans*, Art Music from Southeast Asia IX-2 (Philips 6586 004); *Musiques et Traditions du Monde: Une Nuit de Wayang Kulit Légende de Wahju Tjakraningrat* (CBS 65440); *Java Court Gamelan from the Pura Paku Alaman Jogyakarta* (Nonesuch H-72044); *Java Court Gamelan Istana Mangkunegaran Surakarta* (Nonesuch H-72074); *Java Court Gamelan Kraton Yogyakarta* (Nonesuch H-72083); *Sunda: Musique et Chants Traditionnels* (Ocora 558 502); *Tonggeret* (Jaipongan) (Nonesuch 79173-2).

Bali   *From Kuno to Kebyar: Balinese Gamelan Angklung* (Smithsonian Folkways SFW 50411); *Semar Pegulingan: Golden Gong of Bali* (Grevillea Records GRV 1020); *Gamelan of the God of Love: Gamelan Semar Pegulingan* (Nonesuch H-72046); *Bali: Musique et Théâtre* (gender wayang, gambuh) (Ocora OCR 60); *Golden Rain* (kebyar) (Nonesuch H-72028); *Bali: Le Gong Gede de Batur* (Ocora 585 510); *The Balinese Gamelan: Music from the Morning of the World* (Nonesuch 72015); *Gamelan Music of Bali* (Lyrichord LLST 7179).

General   *Music of Indonesia*, series of twenty compact discs issued by Smithsonian Folkways.

The Music of Sub-Saharan Africa

THOMAS TURINO

A SHONA MBIRA PERFORMANCE IN ZIMBABWE

Heading toward the roundhouse after dark, I heard the powerful sound of people playing *hosho* (large maraca-like shakers) from some distance down the path. As I entered the dimly lit kitchen hut where the ceremony was being held, I could make out people clapping, singing, talking, and drinking; one frail old woman was dancing by herself in the center of the room. Beneath all of this there was still another sound, soft yet deep and moving like the combination of water and bells. This was the *mbira*. Two men, leaning against the far wall, sat with their hands hidden inside large calabash gourds playing mbira. They were the foundation of the musical activity, and the singers, dancers, and hosho players created their rhythmic patterns and improvised vocal parts based on the many simultaneous melodies that the mbira played.

CHAPTER 7

During a break in the music, I asked the mbira players to show me their instruments. Twenty-two slightly rusted metal keys were tightly fastened over a metal bridge on a wooden soundboard, with bottle caps attached to a metal plate on the board. A necklace of bottle caps was also strung around the gourd resonators, creating the buzzing sound a torn stereo speaker makes. The musicians explained that without the gourds, the mbiras were too soft to be heard in occasions for communal music making, such as the *bira* (ceremony) that we were attending, and without the buzzing of the bottle caps, they would not sound like mbira.

The mbira belongs to a general class of instruments known as **lamellaphones** (plucked tongues or keys mounted on a soundboard or soundbox). It is sometimes referred to as "thumb piano" and thought of as a toy in the United States. Yet the mbira that these men were playing is one of the most highly developed classical instruments of the Shona, a Bantu-speaking people of Zimbabwe in southeastern Africa. Although different types of lamellaphones are played all over Africa, this class of instruments has been most highly developed by the Shona and other

Shona instruments (left to right): karimba, hosho rattle, 22-key mbira in calabash gourd, 22-key mbira, side view. *Source:* Thomas Turino

✳ **Explore** *the Learning Objectives* on **mymusiclab.com**

👁 **Watch** *the video of a mbira player* on **mymusiclab.com**

groups in southern Africa. The Shona play a variety of lamellaphones associated with different regions of Zimbabwe, including the *karimba*, the *njari*, and the *matepe*, but presently, the twenty-two key mbira is the most popular type. Shona mbira players often specialize on one variety of instrument, each with its own distinct scale pattern and playing techniques; changing from a karimba to an mbira or njari is like switching from a guitar to a mandolin or a banjo.

The musicians sat down and began playing another piece. Listening more closely to the mbira players this time, I could hear distinct bass, middle, and high melodic parts coming from the two instruments. I watched their hands closely. They played the same patterns for a long time before changing perhaps only one or two pitches by striking different keys and then repeated the new variation many times. But even when they were playing the same patterns, I sometimes thought that I heard changes in the melodies.

During their next break the musicians explained that it was always like that. Even simple mbira pieces contained many inner melodic lines that resulted not from changes in the keys played but rather from the particular combination of right- and left-hand parts that were played. They explained that mbira music was an art of creative listening as well as playing, and that the mbira itself seemed continually to suggest new inner melodic lines to the musician even when his hands continued to play the same keys. They told me that this was one reason why mbira players can perform the same pattern for a long time without getting bored or feeling the need to create constant contrasts. It was almost as if the mbira itself magically created its own variations; one simply had to have patience and learn to hear what it had to offer. I enjoyed talking to these musicians and was learning something of the art of listening to Shona music, but it was time for them to return to playing for the ancestral spirits in the *bira* ceremony.

LAMELLAPHONE
A general class of musical instruments that have tuned metal or reed tongues set on a bridge mounted to a soundboard or box; it is played by striking the keys. The mbira is but one example of this instrument type. Other lamellaphones used in Zimbabwe include the karimba, njari, and matepe.

The Bira

The Shona believe that their ancestors continually interact with and affect the lives of the living. As in many places, Shona people emphasize maintaining good relationships with their parents, grandparents, and other elder relatives; for the Shona, however, such relationships do not cease when someone dies. Interactions with deceased relatives take place through spirit possession when an ancestor enters and speaks through the body of a living person—a spirit medium. Not everyone who dies comes back as a spirit. However, those who do return select one person to be their medium for life. (Family spirits are usually within the past three generations.) Once spirits make themselves known in this way, family members can call them back to speak with them at a family-sponsored ceremony known as the **bira**. Misfortunes such as illness or losing a job are sometimes interpreted as the result of offending a particular ancestor. People also commonly turn to their ancestors for advice during times of trouble. Even when there is no specific problem, some families periodically hold ceremonies to honor an ancestor or simply to keep in touch (just as we might feel the need to call our parents when living away from them). In the central and some northern parts of Zimbabwe, these ceremonies often involve mbira music and dance to call the ancestors; in other Zimbabwean regions drums are used instead of mbira.

As the *bira* begins people arrive gradually; those already present casually talk and joke together to the music of the mbira and hosho, which will play all night. Mbira players are musical specialists who are invited to perform at the ceremony. They supply the musical foundation, but as the evening progresses,

BIRA
A Shona religious ceremony involving spirit possession.

Shona mbira players Emmanuel Chidzere and David Mapfumo with singer and hosho player Pyo Murungweni, Murehwa District, Zimbabwe. *Source:* Thomas Turino

Shona women of Mhembere singing and playing hosho, Murehwa District, Zimbabwe. *Source:* Thomas Turino

family and community members join in by clapping different patterns and dancing in the center of the room. Men and women also may contribute to the performance by singing melodies that weave in and out of the mbira's bass part or by performing in a high-pitched yodeling style. (Instead of singing actual words, the singers use **vocables**, rhythmic syllables that have no semantic meaning.) Both well-known verses and improvised words are also sung to fit the occasion, and the poetry moves people as do the dance and the music at this participatory event. After one piece has ended, the two mbira players begin again, each with his specific part, and again the different participants add what they will, until the performance becomes a dense, rich fabric of sound, movement, and feeling. As the spirit medium shows subtle signs that the ancestor is coming, the rest of the participants often begin playing, dancing, and singing more intensely. This collective energy helps to bring on possession.

Good mbira playing and concentrated communal effort are essential for the success of the bira because music is one of the main attractions that call the spirit into the ceremony. As the intensity mounts and the energy within the room becomes right, the spirit enters the body of the medium. Spirits are particularly attracted by the music that they enjoyed while they were living. Thus, playing the right tunes is important for bringing on possession. Once possessed, the spirit medium is usually dressed by an attendant in a special robe. The medium who now has become the spirit may continue singing and dancing, or may become quiet and withdrawn. After the spirit has participated in the event for a brief time, the music comes to a halt. The host of the bira welcomes the spirit, now sitting in the center of the room, with a formal greeting. He also offers special beer, brewed by the family for seven days, and snuff. The participants then consult the ancestor about the problem or issues that occasioned the bira,

VOCABLES

Nonsemantic syllables that are sung; "nonsense syllables."

and a discussion ensues between the spirit and the concerned participants. After the consultation, the music, singing, and dancing start up again and continue until morning, even if the spirit decides to leave the medium some time during the night.

THE MBIRA AND SOME GENERAL PRINCIPLES OF AFRICAN MUSIC

A closer look at Shona mbira performance reveals a series of features and aesthetic preferences that are common to many sub-Saharan musical traditions. These include the practice of **interlocking**—fitting your pitches and beats into the spaces of other parts or alternating the pitches or phrases of one part with those of another to create the whole. As we will see, this occurs at a variety of levels in mbira performance and in the other African traditions we will study. **Call-and-response**—the alternation of leader and chorus parts or of a vocal and instrumental part—illustrates the principle of interlock at the highest level of musical organization. Call-and-response is a common practice all over sub-Saharan Africa.

A second general feature of African music is the aesthetic preference for dense overlapping textures and buzzy timbres that contribute to a dense sound quality. Third, African music is often cyclical and open-ended in form involving one or more repeated melodies or rhythmic patterns (**ostinatos**) as the basic foundation of a performance. These repetitive, cyclical pieces are often performed for a long time with gradual variations added as a performance progresses. Community participation is valued in many African musical traditions. Repetition and long performances facilitate participation by giving nonspecialized participants a chance to get their bearings and to enter the performance.

African music is famous for its rhythmic complexity. At the most basic level, this involves the juxtaposition or simultaneous performance of duple and triple rhythmic patterns (patterns of two against patterns of three). The multiple layering of different rhythmic patterns creates a tension and, at times, an ambiguity such that a listener can hear and feel the same music in a variety of ways depending on which rhythmic part or pattern he or she is focusing on. Another typical African musical trait is that melodies often descend (start high and end with lower pitches). A final general characteristic is that African music, and musical ensembles, often involve "core" and "elaboration" parts. The "core" musical roles and parts are those that must be in place for a performance to go forward. Core parts are the foundation that make other contributions, variations, and improvisations possible. In mbira performance, core roles include the basic rhythmic flow maintained by the hosho and the basic melodic–harmonic ostinato played in the midrange and bass of the mbira. The "elaboration" parts, no less essential to an artful performance, include clapped patterns, vocal lines, high mbira melodies and bass variations, and dancing.

INTERLOCKING
The practice of fitting one's pitches and beats into the spaces of other parts, or alternating the pitches or phrases of one part with those of others to create the whole; also called *hocket*.

CALL-AND-RESPONSE
The alternation or interlocking of leader and chorus musical parts or of a vocal and instrumental part.

OSTINATO
A repeated or cyclical melody or rhythmic pattern.

GENERAL CHARACTERISTICS OF AFRICAN MUSIC

- Interlocking melodies and rhythmic parts
- Preference for dense, overlapping textures and buzzy timbres
- Cyclical forms (based on melodic/rhythmic ostinatos)
- Flexible approaches to rhythms often combining or juxtaposing units of twos and threes
- Descending melodic shape
- Musical roles including "core" and "elaboration" parts

Interlocking

The longest, lowest keys on the mbira are found in the center; the metal keys become shorter and higher as they fan out to each side. On the left side of the instrument, a row of longer bass keys are set directly below the midrange keys, with the row of the highest keys on the right side of the instrument. The keys on the left side are played by the left thumb, and the right thumb and forefinger play the keys on the right side. Mbira pieces are constructed so that the left thumb interlocks with the right thumb and forefinger to play a single midrange melody. On many pieces, the left thumb also alternates between the midrange keys of the upper-left row and the bass keys of the lower-left row to produce an independent bass line that interlocks with the midrange melody. Finally, the right forefinger plays the smallest, highest keys (far right) to produce additional descending high melodic lines. These pitches again are alternated with the left-hand part in interlocking fashion. The bass, midrange, and high melodies create a variable contrapuntal texture, and a listener's perception of the piece can change substantially by shifting attention from one line to another or to the resultant melodic patterns that emerge from the relations between different parts.

The hand-clapping patterns, dance movements, and vocal melodies performed by participants at a bira and other occasions frequently do not simply reproduce the basic beat and, typically, are not performed in unison. Rather, each participant may add his or her own clapped patterns, sung parts, or dance movements, so that they fall in between or around central beats and pitches—in the spaces—of other people's parts, thereby providing another series of interlocking aspects. A basic musical value among the Shona, and in many African societies, is the ability to add one's own distinctive part to the ensemble while making it blend with the whole. Call-and-response singing, an obvious form of interlocking, is also common in Shona music-making.

Density

The final contrapuntal, multirhythmic character of a communal Shona performance results from the interlocking and dense overlapping of the participants' contributions. The Shona, like many African peoples, prefer dense, rich sounds. Bottle caps or shells attached to gourd resonators and mbira sound-boards create a buzzing aura around the discrete pitches that contrast with the clear, "pure" instrumental timbres (tone qualities) preferred in the European classical tradition. The multiple layers produced in a communal performance also add to the density of sound, as does the very nature of the mbira, on which keys previously struck continue to ring through the following pitches sounded, with each key producing multiple overtones.

Cyclical Form and Variation

The typical form of classical mbira music is a melodic–harmonic cycle, or osti-nato, of forty-eight quick beats. The particular ostinato of most classical mbira pieces is divided into four twelve-beat phrases in 12/8 meter. As an mbira performance progresses, small variations, including traditional formulas and improvised lines, are gradually added to, and over, the basic ostinato. Mbira players say that a skilled musician must have patience and not rush the varia-tions. It is not considered good playing to use overly apparent or dramatic con-trasts; rather, one variation must be built on the last and subtly lead to the next within the ostinato cycle. Usually, each variation will be repeated a number of times before further development is attempted.

Conceptions of Music

The very definition of what constitutes a musical "piece" in Shona society, and in many sub-Saharan societies, suggests another characteristically African feature. Although mbira pieces have titles, the composition is conceived as an aggregate of musical resources that may be put together in different ways, making each performance recognizable as "the piece" and yet unique. These resources include the harmonic, temporal, and melodic character of the basic ostinato; a series of stock variations and motifs associated with the piece; and certain sung melodies and lines of text. The length of a given performance, the number of variations used and the order in which they are performed, the speed and character of development, and the improvisations on the basic pat-terns, however, make each performance distinct. This approach resembles that of jazz, blues, and some rock performers, indicating one way that people work-ing in these styles may have been influenced by the African heritage.

In Shona villages, "the piece" and music itself are conceptualized as a process linked to specific people and particular moments or contexts, whereas for some musical traditions in the West, music has become a reproducible sound object that can be, and is, isolated and abstracted as a thing in itself. Record-ings and written scores perhaps facilitate thinking about music as an object that can be purchased, consumed, collected, and copyrighted. It is significant that the Shona words for the two basic parts of a mbira piece—**kushaura** and **kutsinhira**—are not nouns, referring to things, but rather are verbs ("kushaura" means literally "to lead the piece"), underlining the notion of music as an interactive process (Listen to CD II, 11 for an example of the general characteristics of African music as illustrated through an mbira performance).

KUSHAURA
"To lead the piece"; the first part, or lead part played by one Shona mbira player.

KUTSINHIRA
"To accompany"; the second accompanying part played by a second Shona mbira player.

LISTENING GUIDE

MBIRA MUSIC: "NHEMAMUSASA"

GO TO **www.mymusiclab.com for the Automated Listening Guide** CDII • Track 11/Download Track 32

Chris Mihlanga and Bernard Matatfi, mbiras, Tom Turino on hosho
Recorded by Tom Turino in Harare, Zimbabwe, July 1993

Although the mbira can be played solo, a piece is not really considered complete unless two players are present to play their separate, complementary parts that interlock to create the whole. One part is called the *kushaura* ("to lead the piece," to play the basic piece), and the other is called kutsinhira. The *kutsinhira* consists of a second, accompanying part. On many pieces the kutsinhira part is almost exactly the same as the kushaura, but it is played a beat behind so that each pitch played by the first part is doubled by the second. This doubling effect produced by the two instruments can be heard on the high descending lines of *Nhemamusasa*, which means "cutting branches for a shelter." This happens for the first time around [0:40] in the recording. With the exception of the high melodies, however, Nhemamusasa involves a second type of kushaura-kutsinhira relationship in which a completely different accompanying part is composed to interlock with the kushaura part. Listen especially to the ways that you can orient your listening to attend to either duple or triple meter throughout this performance.

You can follow the basic ostinato melody in the kushaura by counting one beat per note. Twice through this pattern constitutes one 48-beat cycle. Remember that this is very schematic and that small variations to the melody occur consistently throughout the performance:

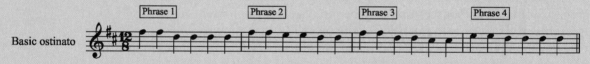

In this example, each of the melody notes played on the kushaura counts for two beats. This can be represented rhythmically as follows:

Phrase 1

Beat	1	2	3	4	5	6	7	8	9	10	11	12
Kushaura melody	x		x		x		x		x		x	

The high descending melody can be represented as follows. Listen for the "echo" effect of the kutsinhira doubling the kushaura:

The hosho provides a particularly good way of beginning to hear the interplay between duple and triple meter. The following representation of phrases 1 and 2 of the basic ostinato can help you orient yourself. If you listen to the hosho and count it as 123 456, 123 456 (or 1 - - 2 - - 1 - - 2 - -), then the melody played on the kushaura unfolds in triple meter against the hosho (three melody notes for every two strong beats on the hosho, or 1 - 2 - 3- 1- 2- 3). The numbering above the notation is intended only to help you count the duple and triple feel. The smaller numbers underneath the notation reference the actual eighth note count in 12/8 meter.

Again, this can be rhythmically represented as follows (just the first phrase). In order to help you hear the 3 against 2 rhythms, I highlight duple and then triple division of the twelve beat cycle in two successive tables:

Phrase 1 (triple meter)

Triple	1		2		3		1		2		3	
Beat	1	2	3	4	5	6	7	8	9	10	11	12
Kushaura	x		x		x		x		x		x	
Hosho	X	x	x	X	x	x	X	x	x	X	x	x

Phrase 1 (duple meter)

Duple	1			2			1			2		
Beat	1	2	3	4	5	6	7	8	9	10	11	12
Kushaura	x		x		x		x		x		x	
Hosho	X	x	x	X	x	x	X	x	x	X	x	x

TIMING	SECTION	MUSICAL EVENTS
0:00–0:05		The recording fades in, playing the third phrase of the basic ostinato and completes the fourth phrase.
0:05–0:40	**Basic ostinato:** Try to hear the two mbiras and the hosho as distinct contributors to the overall texture. Notice the buzzing quality of the mbiras. Focus in on the melody being played on the kushaura.	Basic ostinato pattern begins. The 48-beat cycle consists of four 12-beat phrases. Try to follow along as the complete cycle is repeated four times. If you're having trouble hearing the phrases, you can use the timings below (for each phrase of the first cycle), to get your bearings:

[0:05–0:07] Phrase 1
[0:07–0:09] Phrase 2
[0:9–0:011] Phrase 3
[0:11–0:13] Phrase 4

Different players "hear" the beginning of the cycle in different places. This aspect is not fixed, thus my designation of phrase numbers is somewhat arbitrary.

0:40–0:57   **High descending variation:** Notice the close imitation of the kushaura melody by the kutsinhira. Notice also how this high melodic variation provides contrast to the basic ostinato.

The high descending melody, also based on a 48-beat cycle, is introduced here and played twice. The timings for the first four phrases of the first cycle are given below:

[0:40–0:42] Phrase 1
[0:42–0:44] Phrase 2
[0:44–0:46] Phrase 3
[0:46–0:48] Phrase 4

0:57–1:15   **Basic ostinato returns:** Listen for the overall melody contained within the 48-beat cycle. Try to hear it as a total statement.

The basic ostinato returns and is repeated twice. To help you hear the overall melodic shape, listen this time for the whole cycle (instead of for the shorter phrases):

[0:57–1:05] Cycle 1
[1:06–1:15] Cycle 2

1:15–1:32   **High descending variation:** See if you can begin focusing on the hosho here. Try to hear the faster (123 456) rhythm, and notice how the melody played on the kushaura now takes on a triple feel (3 melody notes for every 2 accented notes played on the hosho).

Two cycles of the high melodic variation.

1:32–1:57   **Basic ostinato:** Continue to focus on the hosho. Try to hear the 3 against 2 texture. Also attend to the "inside and inner" voices (i.e., not melody and not bass, but in-between) that animate this performance. The interlocking parts played on both mbiras can help you hear the duple and triple meters. Try to listen to these instead of the melody and you'll hear the piece differently.

Three cycles of the basic ostinato, played with increased bass note accents. These bass notes should help you hear the 3 against 2 because they line up with the accents played on the hosho.

1:58–2:23   **High descending variation:** Now try to listen in duple again, that is, try to hear the melody independently of the hosho.

Three cycles of the high descending melody. Remember that one of the aesthetic principles at play here is being able to orient yourself as a listener and performer in either duple or triple meter.

2:23–2:48	**Basic ostinato:** Another exercise that will help you hear these ideas is to tap one hand to the accented hosho beats and your other hand to the melody notes played on the kushaura. Practice this and you'll be able to internalize the 3 against 2 rhythms at play in this example.	Three cycles of the basic ostinato.
2:48–3:04	**High descending variation:** Listen to the overall performance and work your focus between the various melodic and percussive parts.	Two cycles of the high descending melody.
3:05–3:28	**Basic ostinato**	Two full cycles of the basic ostinato are followed by a fade out during the third cycle.

AFRICA GENERAL AND AFRICA SPECIFIC

To this point, I have tried to link certain features of Shona mbira playing with more widespread African musical characteristics. Indeed there is a tendency among North Americans and Europeans to think of Africa as *one* place and African music as a single, identifiable phenomenon. The continent of Africa has over fifty countries, however, and linguists have identified at least 800 ethnolinguistic groups. In Nigeria alone, 386 different languages have been identified. The organization of sub-Saharan Africa into modern nation–states is primarily a colonial legacy based on the way the continent was divided by the European powers at the end of the nineteenth century. It has little to do with internal social divisions within these territories or with the linguistic groups that cross national borders. (Mande societies, for example, span parts of Senegal, Gambia, Mali, Burkina Faso, Côte d'Ivoire, Guinea, and Sierra Leone.) Because many musical traditions are linked to specific ethnolinguistic groups, it is often better to think about African music in these rather than in national terms.

In contrast to the stereotypic vision of small, so-called primitive tribes in Africa, various kinds of traditional political organization include (1) complex, hierarchical, centralized states with political authority vested in the hands of hereditary rulers; and (2) more decentralized, smaller-scale societies where political power was regulated by interactions between kinship groups such as clans or lineages. Centralized kingdoms with highly developed political organization have existed in Africa from early times. One example is the state of Zimbabwe (the modern country was named after this early empire), which was thriving by the twelfth century. On the other hand, small egalitarian bands of hunters and gatherers such as the BaMbuti Pygmies have lived for centuries in the central African rain forest. Hunter-gatherer groups such as the Pygmies and the San (Bushmen) are in a small minority, however. The majority of African

✳ Explore
a map of Africa on the Interactive Globe on **mymusiclab.com**

societies depended on agriculture and animal husbandry for subsistence—stable agriculture being important for state formation. Just as political and economic systems differ widely between specific African societies, family and social structures are also diverse.

Sometimes there are important correlations between economic modes of production, social structure, and musical practices and style. Given the socioeconomic diversity among African societies, we would expect musical diversity as well. Indeed, there are important differences in the styles, processes, and functions of music-making among different African societies, just as there are differences in conceptions about music, the role and status of musicians, and the types of repertory, instruments, and dances performed. As I suggested earlier, however, some basic similarities in musical style, practices, and aesthetics span the sub-Saharan region, even among such diverse groups as the Shona in southeastern Africa, the BaMbuti Pygmies in the central rain forest, and the Mande peoples in the northwestern savanna region. Taken at the most general level, these similarities allow us to speak of "African music" (much as the European harmonic system, among other general traits, allows us to identify mainstream "Western music"). Nonetheless, it is the facets that distinguish the different African musical cultures, rather than the similarities, that will probably appear as most significant to Africans themselves.

In the sections that follow, similarities with the major characteristics outlined for Shona mbira music will serve as a focus for the discussion of several specific African musical cultures. At the same time, differences among the musical cultures will be emphasized, and these differences will be considered in light of the distinct ways of life and worldviews that characterize different African societies.

MUSICAL VALUES, PRACTICES, AND SOCIAL STYLE

The Pygmies

The word *Pygmy* is an outsider generic term applied to social groups found in the equatorial forest area stretching from Gabon and Cameroon in the west to Uganda, Rwanda, and Burundi in the east. People in these groups self-identify by more specific terms such as BaMbuti, Bibiyak, and Baka. The Ituri Forest, bordering on Uganda to the east and Sudan to the north, remains a major stronghold for Pygmies, and about 40,000 live in this region. The majority of groups maintain a semiautonomous hunting-and-gathering existence. Centuries ago, the Pygmies found their central forest region invaded from the north by Bantu (a major linguistic category in sub-Saharan Africa) and Sudanic groups, who were cultivators and pastoralist. The Pygmy languages were abandoned for those of the neighboring groups, with whom they entered into types of patron-client relationships. The anthropologist Colin Turnbull, however, suggests that the BaMbuti Pygmies of the Ituri Forest lead a kind of double life, maintaining their own traditional ways (with the exception of language) when alone in the forest and taking part in Bantu ritual and musical life on their visits to the villages. Here we will concentrate on Pygmy life and music in their forest home.

The BaMbuti net-hunters maintain a nomadic existence, setting up camps for a month or so in different places in the forest as they continue their search of game. Net-hunting, like most aspects of Pygmy life, is a communal affair, with male family members stringing their nets together in a large semicircle and the women and children beating the brush to scare game into them. The catch is shared. Bands are composed of nuclear families, and although certain individuals are considered to have more expertise in some realms of activity than in others, there is little specialization of social and economic roles within age and gender categories. A formalized hierarchical system of leadership is not present. Because survival depends on cooperation rather than competition, the keystones of Pygmy society are egalitarianism, consensus, and unity. Because of their nomadic existence, the ownership of goods and property is minimal among most Pygmy groups.

All these aspects strongly influence their musical activities. The Pygmies have few musical instruments of their own. Pygmy instruments include whistles and end-blown flutes made from cane. They may be used to accompany singing or in duets for informal music-making. In flute duets, one instrumentalist plays a repeating ostinato pattern, while the other plays a part that interlocks and overlaps with the first, reminding us of the basic principles of Shona mbira performance. Rhythm sticks and rattles are found, as are several trumpet types such as the long, end-blown molimo trumpet. Some Pygmy bands also use a musical bow. A few other instruments, such as small lamellaphones and drums, may be borrowed from their Bantu neighbors.

Vocal music is at the core of Pygmy musical life. Some songs are sung by individuals informally such as lullabies and game songs; however, communal singing for collective ceremonies and occasions is considered much more important. Like most aspects of Pygmy life, musical performance is a non-specialized activity. As in net-hunting, where men and women fulfill different roles, musical participation may be differentiated by gender, depending on the context. For example, men are the primary singers for the **molimo** ceremony, through which the benign relationship with the sacred—and living—forest is maintained. Women are the primary singers for the **elima**, a puberty ceremony. On other occasions—for instance, before almost every hunt—men and women sing together (Listen to CD II, 12 for an example of BaMbuti singing during the *elima*).

Except for ritual occasions, when gender and sometimes age distinctions are made, musical performance involves anyone in the band who wants to sing. Song forms are varied but follow two basic principles that we have already encountered in the Shona mbira music and the Pygmy flute duets—the use of ostinato and interlock. A standard organizational feature found among the BaMbuti Pygmies and in many other African societies is the use of a leader and chorus in call-and-response format. The leader, or one group of people,

MOLIMO

A Pygmy ceremony for the forest; a straight valveless trumpet used in the ceremony.

ELIMA

A Pygmy puberty ceremony for which women are the primary singers.

LISTENING GUIDE

BAMBUTI VOCAL MUSIC: "ELIMA GIRLS INITIATION MUSIC"

⫸ **GO TO** www.mymusiclab.com for the Automated Listening Guide CDII • Track 12/Download Track 33

Recorded by C. Turnbull and F. Chapman

This listening selection is divided into two excerpts ([0:00–1:48] and then [1:52–end]). In the first song, the "chorus" provides an eight-beat ostinato over which one—at first— and later several lead singers provide higher-pitched descending melodic variations (entering at approximately [0:06]). The leader-chorus relationship can be heard as an interlocking or call-and-response arrangement, but in illustrating the preference for density, the two parts continually overlap and are offset. The second song is performed in this same way. Note in both performances how individual singers provide slight variations on the chorus and lead parts adding to the density of the whole.

sings a melodic phrase and is immediately answered by a second group singing another phrase so that the two interlock to create the entire melody. Pygmy vocal practice frequently uses the **hocket** technique (singers alternating short melodic fragments to create a melody), reproducing the same practice of interlocking parts. Yodeling is also frequently practiced by some Pygmy groups and is often considered a hallmark of their vocal style.

In its simplest form, the call-and-response phrases are simply repeated continually, creating a cyclical ostinato pattern like that described for Shona mbira music. People within an Mbuti chorus help to create a dense, layered sound by simultaneously singing a number of individual variations of the basic melodic parts. Among the Pygmies of the Central African Republic, ostinatos without call-and-response organization constitute a basic structure. On top of the basic ostinato, singers may add a second complementary ostinato, and others will perform variations on both melodies, thereby creating a dense, overlapping contrapuntal texture (a texture consisting of different simultaneous melodic lines). The time span of the basic ostinato serves as the reference point for various clapped and percussion parts. Thus, one percussion part may be a six-beat pattern and another may last eight beats, dividing the overall time span of the song, say of twenty-four beats, into different-length cycles.

Certain individuals may begin or lead a song, just as different individuals are considered to have particular expertise in other realms of life. Once a performance is in motion, however, musical roles and leadership may shift, and different voices may move in and out of the background. Hence, Pygmy musical style and practice grows from, and reflects, the specific egalitarian nature of Pygmy social and economic life, just as certain features (e.g., ostinatos, density, and interlock) are consistent with African musical practice in other societies.

As in Shona societies, Pygmy musical performances often involve communication with the spiritual world. However, they have different ideas about

HOCKET
Interlocking pitches between two or more sound sources to create a single melody or part.

the nature of the spiritual world and their own interaction with it. According to Colin Turnbull, the Pygmies recognize that they cannot see, truly comprehend, or give a single name to God. Because they view the forest as the benevolent provider of their lives and livelihood, however, they associate divinity with the forest, itself living and divine. They believe that the world and the forest are basically good, and if misfortunes—such as a bad hunting period, sickness, or death—come, it is because the forest is sleeping. Their response is to wake it by singing to it every night during a ceremony known as the molimo, which may last several months. The long, tubular, end-blown trumpet known as molimo is used to create the sounds of the forest and answer the men's singing, thereby realizing, through ritual, the relationship the Pygmies feel with their natural surroundings and the divine.

Unlike the Shona, who use elaborate and varied sung poetry in performances for the ancestors, communicating with the divine occurs among the Pygmies primarily through musical sound alone. Song texts are kept to a minimum, even to a single line such as "The forest is good." Because the Pygmy conception of the divine cannot be formulated with words, it may be that music, whose existence and meaning are likewise both concrete and diffuse, provides a more direct mode of relating to and representing God. Nonetheless, it is interesting that the Pygmies emphasize singing much more than instrumental music and yet grant so little attention to sung poetry and the power of the word. In this and other important respects, these people of the forest are very different from the Mande on the savanna in West Africa.

The Mande of West Africa

The Mande represent one of the most important ethnolinguistic groups in sub-Saharan Africa. A number of Mande subgroups, including the Mandinka of Senegal and Gambia, the Maninka of Guinea and Mali, the Bamana (or Bambara) of Mali, and the Dyula of Côte d'Ivoire, all claim a common descent from the thirteenth-century Mali empire. Connected historically to the Mali state, Mande societies are characterized by a social hierarchy as well as by occupational specialization. Although slavery once existed, the two main social categories in contemporary Mande societies are **sula** and **nyamalo**. Sula refers to "ordinary people," farmers, merchants and people in urban occupations, and it includes the aristocracy as well. According to Roderic Knight, who has studied Mande music for many years, the term nyamalo designates those who rely on a specialized craft as a profession. In Mande societies these crafts include metalsmiths, wood and leather workers, and musicians, known by the term **jali**. The "material" that the musician works with is not the musical instrument (although they do typically make their own), but the *word*, whether spoken or sung.

In the traditional hierarchy, the craft specialists, as "service providers" to the king and the general population, occupied various slots below the general populace, but as the sole providers of goods and services needed for both

SULA
Social category in Mande societies, referring to "ordinary people" in contrast to craft specialists.

NYAMALO
Craft specialists in Mande societies, a category including professional musicians.

JALI
The term for a hereditary professional musician in Mande society, who serves as an oral historian and singer/performer.

Mande kora player, Kunye Saho, of the Gambia. *Source:* Roderic Knight/ Thomas Turino

DONKILO
The basic sung melody of Mande jali songs.

SATARO
A speechlike vocal style performed by Mande jalolu.

✳ **Explore** *the Musical Instrument Gallery* on **mymusiclab.com**

👁 **Watch** *the video of a kora player* on **mymusiclab.com**

agriculture and war, they were at the same time regarded with awe and respect. All the nyamalo, by virtue of their specialized knowledge, were regarded as having access to a special life force (the nyama) that gave them a certain power over others. The jali, with the power to manipulate words, had the greatest power. He or she (women being the prime singers) could praise when praise was due, or criticize if necessary, incorporating oblique commentary and poignant proverbs into their song texts if a public figure exhibited lackluster behavior.

At the present time the distinction between the sula and nyamalo social groups are not as strictly maintained as they once were. Yet the jali (pl., jalolu) still maintains many of his or her traditional roles as oral historian, musician, praise singer, genealogist, announcer for the aristocracy, and diplomat, and they still perform at important social events such as weddings, child-naming ceremonies, religious holidays, and affairs of state.

The Mande case clearly differs in some ways from conceptions about music and musicians within Pygmy society, where music-making is a nonprofessional, largely nonspecialized activity. In contrast, the jali is a hereditary specialist working as a professional musician and verbal artist, whose status position derives from hierarchical rather than egalitarian social relations.

Another distinction between these two societies regards the power of the word and the importance of song texts. Although vocal music is important in both societies, jali performance often emphasizes verbal artistry and elaborate texts, whereas some of the most important Pygmy music such as singing for the molimo ceremony involves very little text. Nonetheless, certain features of Mande musical style are consistent with the general traits discussed for the Pygmies and the Shona.

The main instruments played by the Mande jali to accompany singing are the *balo* (a xylophone), the *kora* (a bridge harp), and the *kontingo* (a five-stringed plucked lute with a skin face like the banjo); male jalolu specialize on one instrument. The kora is unique to the Mande. It has twenty-one strings and a range just over three octaves. Cowhide is stretched over the gourd sound box, and strings come off the neck in two parallel rows perpendicular to the face of the sound box. The scale series alternates for the most part between the two rows and the two hands (right hand—do, left hand—re, right hand—mi, left hand—fa, etc.). The basic playing technique for the kora often involves plucking alternate notes by the right and left hands so that the melody results from the interlocking of these two parts, similar in principle to mbira playing and the principle of interlocking parts in general. Another similarity between the kora and the Shona mbira is the attachment of a metal plate with jangles to the bridge of the kora. This produces the buzzing timbral effect favored in so many sub-Saharan societies.

Mande music performed on the kora consists of several components. Each piece has a basic vocal melody known as **donkilo** and a second kind of improvised, declamatory singing style called **sataro**. Sataro sometimes receives major emphasis in jali performance, as does text improvisation and the insertion of proverbs and sayings appropriate to a given context. It was traditionally through the performance of formulaic praise and proverbs for a given occasion that the jali earned a living—praising a patron, telling a story, or recounting history. The use of songs to fulfill these social functions is widespread throughout West Africa and in other parts of the sub-Saharan region.

The jali accompanies his singing with the **kumbengo** part—a short ostinato, the most basic organizing feature of a performance—played on the kora. The kumbengo is played for long periods during which subtle variations may gradually be introduced, as in Shona mbira playing. Improvised instrumental interludes known as **birimintingo** are inserted between the long ostinato sections. The nature of the four components of a jali performance—kumbengo (K), birimintingo (B), donkilo (D), and sataro (S)—will become clearer by listening to "Ala l'a ke" and following along with the text (Listen to CD II, 13 to hear this example).

On this recording one can clearly hear the metal jangles buzzing and the relatively soft volume of the kora compared to the voice. As is apparent here, the birimintingo sections provide a greater degree of musical contrast, departing from the basic kumbengo ostinato. This type of instrumental interlude that alternates with the basic ostinato is distinctive from Shona mbira performance or a Pygmy song, where variations and improvisations are added to and over the basic cycle. Nonetheless, the conception of what constitutes a "piece," that is, a series of stock resources that are uniquely arranged and improvised on according to the needs of a given performer and occasion, are similar between the Mande and the Shona.

The Ewe of Ghana

North Americans often have the general impression that African music primarily consists of drumming. As we have seen, vocal music, strings, and other types of melodic instruments such as the mbira may have equally, or more, prominent positions in certain contexts. One of the most famous sub-Saharan regions for drumming, however, is the West African coast. Among the Anlo-Ewe of Togo and the southeastern coast of Ghana, dance drumming is the most important type of musical activity.

The Anlo-Ewe, who remain musically and socially distinct from other Ewe groups farther north and inland, work primarily as farmers and fishermen. Southern Eweland is divided into autonomous political districts, with the Anlo district having the largest population and cultural influence. This district, which traditionally functioned like an independent state, was ruled by a paramount chief, whose status was mainly ceremonial and sacred, although he had the important role of mediating disputes. The chief stands at the pinnacle of a political hierarchy over geographically organized territorial and town chiefs and finally over clan, lineage, and ward (village subdivision) leaders. The clans and lineages (tracing descent to a common male ancestor) and wards thus form an important basis of the social system. Age sets (groups of people of similar age who identify with each other on this basis) are another

KUMBENGO

The basic instrumental ostinato, which serves as the foundation for Mande jali performance.

BIRIMINTINGO

An instrumental interlude or "break" during which a Mande jali departs from the basic ostinato.

LISTENING GUIDE

MANDE KORA MUSIC: "ALA L'A KE"

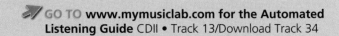
GO TO www.mymusiclab.com for the Automated
Listening Guide CDII • Track 13/Download Track 34

Kunye Saho, kora, and voice
Recorded by Roderic Knight, 1970

The text, designation of parts, and translation were kindly provided by Roderic Knight.

TIME	KORA	VOICE	
0:00	K		(Instrumental introduction.)
0:10			Kumbengo.
0:21	K	D	*A, Ala l'a ke, silan jon m'a ke* (Ah, God has done it, now it was not a man)
0:37	K	D	*Kuo bee kari bai.* (all things can be delayed.)
0:40	K	D	*Kunfai kuno te baila.* (but not the wishes of God.)
0:47	K	D	*Ala ye men ke te baila.* (What God has done can't be delayed.)
0:55	K	D	*Kori bali ku la manso le.* (The omnipotent king.)
0:58	K	D	*Kun fara kina ngana nin tabisi nani . . .* (head-splitting celebrity and . . .)
1:06	K	S	*N'ali be nganalu lala, nganalu man kanyan.* (If you are calling great people, they're not all equal.)
1:11	K	S	*Damansa Wulandin nin Damansa Wulamba* (Damansa Wulan the small, and Damansa Wulan the big)
1:13	K	S	*Moke Musa nin Moke Dantuma* *(Moke Musa and Moke Dantuma)* *Tarokoto Bulai bangeta.* (Tarokoto Bulai was born.)
1:16	B		*Birimintingo.* (Instrumental interlude, with vocable singing.)
1:44	K	D	*Ala ye men ke te baila* (What God has done can't be delayed) *Dula be ngana juma fanan kilila* (This song is calling the other celebrities too) *Somani Tamba, a Bajo bane.* (Somani Tamba, ah, only child.)
2:01	K	S	*N'ali be nganalu la la, nganalu man kanyan* (If you are calling great people, they're not all equal) *E, nafa a barika. Sidi nuku makoto nin.* (Eh, thanks for profit. Sidi the greedy one and buyer of gold, ah, king now.[?])

2:17	K	D	*Dua le jabita, ban in fa dua le jabita.*
			(Prayers have been answered, mother's and father's prayers have been answered.)
			Lun min na nte lota julo da la
			Wori jula nin sanu jala.
			(On the day I stood at the trader's door traders of silver and gold.)
2:31	B		Instrumental interlude with singing in parallel.
3:44	K	D	*Suoluo, Samban Jime!*
			(The horses, Samban Jimeh!)
			Suoluo, Samban Jime!
			(The horses, Samban Jimeh!)

important feature of social organization. Social organization is often a key to understanding basic aspects of music-making, because the formation of ensembles, the definition of genres, and even the organization of musical events are frequently shaped by local conceptions of social hierarchy as well as according to the groups (e.g., gender, age, lineage) that people use to define their social identity.

Among the Anlo-Ewe, voluntary dance clubs, organized by individual villages, wards, or age groups, are the primary institutions through which the all-important dance-drumming traditions are performed. As villagers migrate to the cities, new dance clubs are often created on the basis of hometown identity, and these clubs may serve as the basis for social networks and support

Ewe Drum Ensemble: Gideon Foli Alorwoyie of Ghana. Lead drummer for the Yewe Cult, funeral music. *Source:* Art Davis/Thomas Turino

systems in the urban environment. According to David Locke, an ethno-musicologist and performer of Ewe music, the organization of some dance clubs traditionally reflected the political structure of the ward and lineage, although European influences have also by now been incorporated.

The dance-drumming clubs are generally led by a committee of men and women consisting of a chairperson, a secretary, and the leaders of different sub-groups within the institution (i.e., dance leaders, and leaders of the drummers and the singers). Club organization may be seen as resembling the broader Ewe political hierarchy, which involves a paramount chief who presides over the leaders at the more specific levels of social organization (territorial, village, clan, etc.). Living in a hierarchical society ourselves, this might appear as a normal way to organize things, and yet we must remember that to the egalitarian Pygmies this might seem strange. Besides the officers already mentioned, another key figure in the club is the composer, who is responsible for creating the distinctive music and song texts that serve as identity emblems for his institution.

Unlike the Pygmy band, where some kind of music is likely to be performed almost daily, musical performance is less frequent among the Ewe. Occasions for club performance include the welcoming of government officials, the promotion of a political party, the formal presentation of a new club, or occasions for recreation. One of the primary functions of the clubs is to support its members during crises and especially on the death of a family member. Like the Shona, the Anlo-Ewe place great religious importance on the ancestors and the spirits of the dead, who are believed to intervene in the lives of the living. The Ewe thus place major emphasis on providing honorable funerals for the new spirits, and it is considered extremely prestigious to have a dance club perform at these events.

In terms of musical specialization and professionalism, we might think of the Ewe dance clubs as midway on a spectrum between the highly trained, specialized, and professional jali and the nonspecialist, nonprofessional Pygmy musician. For example, rehearsing is an important part of an Ewe club's activities, and learning to perform the dance and music is relatively rigorous, whereas among the Pygmies learning to sing, like learning to talk, is a normal part of socialization. Where the jali is a full-time musical professional, most members of the Ewe dance clubs can be thought of as semiprofessional at best. That is, except when fulfilling personal obligations to club members—such as performing for a funeral or for recreation—the organizations expect payment for their musical presentations, but the members usually only derive a small portion of their income in this way.

As Alfred and Kobla Ladzekpo have suggested, the drumming, dancing, singing, and hand clapping in an Ewe performance must be thought of as a unified whole. If any individual part is modified, the perception of the whole changes, because each part is heard as relative to and dependent on the others, as in a mbira performance. This characteristic, common to many African musical traditions, is a result of the practice of interlocking multiple parts.

Ewe dondo drum player of Ghana, member of the Brekete Cult. *Source:* Art Davis/ Thomas Turino

The Anlo-Ewe perform a number of different dances. Depending on the specific dance tradition, each club uses various types of music. For example, clubs involved in the *takada* tradition have different genres for processions, more leisurely types of dancing, and the vigorous styles of dancing that are accompanied by the full drum ensemble. The specific instruments used also depend on the dance traditions performed by a given club, although certain instruments are widespread (Listen to CD II, 14 for an example of Anlo-Ewe dance drumming).

Typically, Ewe drum ensembles include a double-bell (*gankogui*), which often plays a repeated ostinato within a twelve-pulse cycle, serving as the organizational point of reference for the rest of the instrumental parts. A gourd shaker (*axatse*) performs a similar role. In addition, a series of four or more different-sized barrel-shaped drums (made of wooden staves and hoops, ranging from 55 cm to 124 cm in length) may be used for a variety of functions. The large drums (e.g., *atsimevu*, *gboba*) are used by lead drummers to create music from a repertory of established and improvised patterns. The middle-sized drums (*sogo* and *kidi*) serve the function of a chorus, playing a more limited variety of patterns in call-and-response fashion with the lead drummer, and they interlock their patterns with other percussion parts. In the takada tradition, the smallest drum (*kaganu*) plays a single repeated ostinato, which in combination with the bell and rattles creates the ground of the overall rhythmic organization that consists of the combination of the different parts.

*❋Explore
the Musical Instrument Gallery on*
mymusiclab.com

LISTENING GUIDE

EWE DANCE DRUMMING: "GADZO,"
A THEATRICAL DANCE

GO TO **www.mymusiclab.com for the Automated**
Listening Guide CDII • Track 14/Download Track 35

Two small drums, a mid-sized drum, bell, and several rattles.
Recorded by S. K. Ladzekpo

In the Ewe Gadzo dance, the singers begin the piece, and then the bells and shakers establish the basic time cycle before three drums enter with their interlocking parts to create a rich texture and rhythmic excitement. The hand clapping that remains consistently part of the texture offers a great way of switching perception between duple and triple meter. As the performance unfolds, identify and focus on the hand clapping to frame first two and then three claps of your own. This can be represented as follows:

Hand clapping	X					X						
Duple	x			x		x			x			
Triple	x		x		x		x		x		x	

TIME	SECTION	MUSICAL EVENTS
0:00–0:02	**Vocal introduction.**	The leader opens the performance with a speech-like call that is immediately answered by the chorus.
0:02–0:08		The leader then introduces the basic lead melodic part (**A**).
0:08–0:20	**Entry of bell, shakers and hand clapping:** Notice how the bell, shaker, and hand clapping set the basic time cycle and groove for the performance. Listen for the hand clapping in particular, because you'll use this later to explore the 3 against 2 rhythms of the performance.	The leader and chorus then introduce the main call-and-response interchange melody (**B**). While they do this, the bell, shaker and hand clapping are added to the texture. At [0:12] the lead drum begins to add sparse patterns to the texture.
0:20–0:27	**Lead vocal section (A):** Compare this repetition of the lead melody to the first instance [0:02–0:07] and notice how different it feels in terms of accents and structure now that it is accompanied by the percussion instruments.	The lead vocal section **A** returns, this time firmly embedded into the time cycle set by the percussion instruments.
0:27–0:49	**Entry of supporting drums:** Notice the return of the leader-chorus melody and the way the supporting drums intensify the rhythmic drive of the performance. Try to attend to the hand clapping in the background of the texture.	The leader-chorus call-and-response interchange returns **B**. The supporting drums enter at [0:28], playing interlocking patterns that strengthen the rhythmic drive. Once the entire drum ensemble is playing, the groove remains constant until the "coda."

0:49–0:56	**Lead vocal section (A):** Continue to listen for the hand clapping and prepare to tap along in duple and triple meter.	The lead vocal section (**A**) returns, this time carried along by the entire ensemble.
0:56–1:11	**Lead/chorus interchange (B):** Try to tap your hand along in duple time with the hand clapping (i.e., two times for every one hand clap on the recording).	The leader/chorus call-and-response interchange returns.
1:11–1:21	**Instrumental section:** Listen for the yodel-like vocalizations and shouted interjections by the singers. Keep trying to tap along in duple meter.	A short break in the **A–B** alternation creates an instrumental section.
1:21–2:47	**A–B alternation:** Listen to the overall flow of the leader-leader-chorus sections and attempt to tap along to the hand clapping in triple meter (i.e., three taps for each hand clap).	The **A** and **B** sections continue to alternate as follows: [1:21–1:27] A [1:27–1:48] B [1:48–1:54] A [1:54–2:15] B [2:15–2:21] A [2:21–2:47] B
2:47–2:58	**Coda:** Listen for the short instrumental break, followed by a vocal interjection by the leader, which is then repeated several times by all.	Notice the interjection by leader at [2:48] followed by the chorus as the recording fades out.

Within these ensembles we thus find musical principles and aesthetic values that have already been discussed for other African societies: call-and-response, interlock, ostinato organization, improvised variation based on stock formulaic patterns, and density in the resulting sound of the entire ensemble. The drum ensemble accompanies both the dancing and the singing, and it is the songs themselves that are considered particularly important to Ewe participants for expressing the distinctive identity of the club. As elsewhere in Africa, the dance steps performed can be considered integral to the polyrhythmic fabric of the total performance.

The Buganda Kingdom

Buganda is the name of the country that was formerly the most powerful independent kingdom in the Lake Victoria region in East Africa; *Baganda* is the term for its Bantu-speaking people. The kingdom was particularly well off economically thanks to favorable conditions for agriculture, particularly to the raising of bananas, the staple crop. Unlike many African kingdoms, the Ganda king, or kabaka, did not have "divine" or sacred status. His notably strong, centralized power was supported by a system in which the king directly appointed and could remove subordinate chiefs and by his ultimate control over many estates. (This contrasts with other African kingdoms, where middle-level chiefs could appoint their own subordinates, thereby creating an independent power base.) Although individual citizens belonged to clans and other social groups, primary allegiance was to the state and to the kabaka himself.

The kabaka's court was a major center for musical activity. The kabaka supported a number of different ensembles, and the musicians lived as retainers on land granted by the king. One important court ensemble consisted of at least five side-blown trumpets made of bottle-shaped gourds. The different gourd-trumpets each produced different pitches necessary to complete a melody and were thus played strictly in interlocking fashion. Like most of the Buganda instruments, the trumpets were associated with a specific clan. Another court ensemble, of less prestige than the trumpets, consisted of five or six end-notched flutes accompanied by four drums. An instrument specific to the court was the *akadinda*, a large twenty-two-key xylophone in which the keys were freely set on two supporting logs running perpendicular to them. A single akadinda was played by six different musicians, three sitting on each side of the instrument. The most important royal ensemble of all was the *entenga*. This consisted primarily of twelve drums carefully graded in size and tuned to the local pentatonic (five-tone) scale, thus actually serving as melodic instruments. These were played by four musicians; they were accompanied by three other drums played by two drummers. The performance of the entenga was strictly limited to the royal enclosure.

The same principles of interlocking parts and ostinato organization that have been described for the Shona, Ewe, Pygmies, and Mande are also basic to entenga and akadinda performance. Each piece contains two distinct melodic rhythmic parts known as *okunaga* (meaning "to start") and *okwawula* ("to divide"), each of which is composed of two or more phrases. On the akadinda xylophone, the three players for one of the parts sit across the keys facing the three musicians who play the other. The pitches of the starter and divider parts literally alternate, thereby reproducing the basic hocket or interlocking technique between the players on opposite sides of the keys. The parts themselves involve ostinato patterns. A third part comprising only two pitches, called the *okukoonera* (or "binder"), emphasizes composite patterns formed by the interaction of the okunaga and okwawula. The okukoonera helps the players orient themselves within the dense ensemble texture.

The political importance of the royal drums is dramatically illustrated by the story of the Buganda kingdom. During the colonial period, African kingdoms were often left in place within the European colonies, because the native political systems could be used to rule African populations indirectly. Under an agreement with the British colonizers, the kabaka of Buganda was officially recognized in 1900 as the ruler of his semiautonomous state, with the provision that he obey the British governor of the Uganda Protectorate.

However, after independence, many new African states had to deal with the threat to state sovereignty that independent kingdoms within their boundaries

Watch *the video of the akadinda* on **mymusiclab.com**

might pose. Although such problems have been handled variously in different African countries, in Uganda violent means were used to suppress the powerful Ganda king. Only a few years after gaining independence in 1962, troops under Uganda's first leader, Apollo Milton Obote, stormed the kabaka's palace and sent him into exile in an effort to stamp out the independent kingdom.

It was no accident that the royal drums were among the things destroyed in the attack on the palace. Traditionally, the drums were such central emblems of the kabakaship that potential heirs to the throne were known as the "Princes of the Drum." In *Desecration of My Kingdom* (London: Constable, 1967), a book written in exile by the last kabaka, Mutesa II, he notes that

> Among the sad news of who is dead, who is in prison and what is destroyed comes the confirmation that the Royal Drums are burnt. I saw this work begun and feared that it must have been completed. These drums, of which there are more than fifty, are the heart of Buganda, some of them hundreds of years old, as old as the Kabakaship. To touch them was a terrible offense, to look after them a great honour. A Prince is not a Prince of the Blood but a Prince of the Drum and his status is determined by which Drum. They all had separate names and significance and can never be replaced. (p. 193)

With the destruction of the former political system and way of life in the name of nationalism came the demise of musical traditions that were central symbols of that kingdom. Although often less dramatic in nature, transformations of African musical life have taken place, and are still occurring, throughout the sub-Saharan region under the pressures of capitalism, nationalism, urbanization, and influences of cosmopolitanism.

A SAMPLING OF INSTRUMENTS

Judging from the few societies already touched on, we can see that African musical performance includes all the major instrument types (percussion instruments, skin-headed drums, winds, and strings), and the importance of given instruments may vary from one society to another. Vocal music, however, seems to be emphasized by a great majority of African societies, with the sung poetry often considered as important as the musical accompaniment—if not more so.

We have also seen that aspects of the social and economic organization influence the number and types of instruments used within a given society. For example, the Pygmies and the San of the Kalahari Desert have relatively few permanent instruments and a minimal material culture generally because of their nomadic way of life. In societies where the royal court was an important site for musical performance, the number, size, and complexity of instruments may be greater because of both available wealth and a more stable environment for performance. This was the case for the large Ganda drum-chime *(entenga)* and xylophone (akadinda) ensembles as well as for court traditions of other East and West African kingdoms.

The tremendous variety of African musical instruments, either played solo or combined in various types of ensembles, makes even a partial list difficult. It may be useful to highlight some of the most important instrument types as well as some that are less well known.

✳ Explore
the Musical Instrument Gallery on
mymusiclab.com

Percussion Instruments

Classified as percussion instruments, lamellaphones (known as *mbira*, *karimba*, *kisaanj*, *likembe*, and many other names, depending on the region) and xylophones are two of the most widespread and important instrument types in the sub-Saharan region. Although they have diffused to the Americas, lamellaphones like the mbira are instruments uniquely of African origin. Rattles, bells, cymbals, rhythm sticks, stamping tubes (hollow tubes with an open end made to sound when struck against the ground), and scrapers are also among the most common instruments found. For each of these general types, however, there are many different varieties, each with a specific local name. For example, there are rattles with the seeds inside the gourd (the *Shona hosho*) and those on which beads are sewn into a net stretched around the outside of the gourd (the Ewe *axatse* and the *sèkèrè* of the Yoruba of Nigeria). New materials such as soda bottles and cans are becoming increasingly important for the construction of percussion instruments.

Although percussion instruments such as bells, scrapers, and rattles primarily serve rhythmic functions, the aspects of pitch and timbre are important considerations in their construction and incorporation into a given ensemble. The parameters of pitch and timbre allow the given percussion instrument to contrast with and complement the other instruments used. For instance, the clear, high-pitched, metallic bell in Ewe ensembles contrasts in both pitch and tone quality with the drums, and the *hosho* both provides a timbral contrast and serves to augment the density in mbira performance.

Drums and "Drum Languages"

The variety of African drums and their social importance in many societies is striking. In Ghana, for example, the relative status of Akan chiefs of different communities and regions is indicated by the size of their *atumpan* drums. A subordinate chief cannot have drums larger than his superior's drums. Among the many Yoruba kingdoms of Nigeria, each court was said to have its own dance rhythms provided by a special set of royal drums. The very power of the drum music—and the styles played—were supposed to express the elevated nature of the aristocracy. Also among the Yoruba, some of the most important orisas (deities) have specific types of drums and repertories associated with them. Drumming is used to call the gods into their mediums during Yoruba spirit-possession ceremonies, much as was described for Shona ceremonies. Thus, in these societies, drums are tied to both political and spiritual sources of power.

African drums are usually carved from a single wooden log (e.g., the Ganda *entenga*, Yoruba *dundun* and *igbin*, and Akan *atumpan*, and the Shona *ngoma*) but may also be constructed with wooden staves and hoops, as described for the Ewe. Drums are also made from ceramics, gourds, and even tin cans and oil drums. Both double- and single-headed types are found in hourglass, conical, cylindrical, and bowl shapes, among others. Metal jangles, shells, or seeds are attached to drums among West African groups such as the Hausa, Dagbamba, Yoruba, and Akan peoples to create the same type of buzzing effect described for the kora and mbira.

The attention paid to the pitch of drums is notable in many African societies, and it may involve the combination of different-sized, fixed-pitch drums in ensemble. Some drums, like the Yoruba dùndún and the lunga of the Ghanaian Dagbamba, however, are used to produce multiple pitches. With these hourglass-shaped tension drums, the different pitches are produced by squeezing the lacing that connects the two drumheads under one arm while the other hand beats it with a curved stick. The importance of pitched drums goes beyond merely creating contrasts; as we have seen, it is sometimes extended to making tuned drums serve as melodic instruments (e.g., the entenga). More interesting still, pitched drums are used in many African societies to imitate speech.

👁 Watch *the video of a* dùndún player *on* **mymusiclab.com**

Many languages in the Niger-Congo family, including the Bantu languages, are tonal; that is, the meaning of a word depends on the relative pitches applied to given syllables. Drums, lamellaphones, and even instruments such as the guitar are used by the Yoruba of Nigeria to articulate verbal formulas—for example, proverbs or praise names—by imitating the tonal patterns of the words. Longer messages can be played by drumming the tonal contour of different well-known stereotypic verbal formulas. Because many words may share the same number of syllables and tonal contours, the meaning of a given "word" (drummed tonal pattern) can be clarified by following it with a formula of its own (e.g., "cat" might become "cat walks quietly at night"), the tonal patterns of the whole phrase being easier to recognize. The social and "linguistic" contexts are crucial to interpretation. The Akan atumpan, a set of two large tuned drums, are used as speech surrogates, as are the Dagbamba lunga, drums of the Yoruba dùndún family, and wooden slit drums and paired skin-headed drums in the Congo region, among other examples (Listen to CD II, 15 for an example of how the Yoruba dùndún is used as a "talking drum").

Wind Instruments

In some societies, wind instruments, especially horns, are also used for signaling. Trumpets, made from metal or animal horns and often side blown, are particularly prevalent throughout the sub-Saharan region and are frequently played in interlocking fashion, as was described for the Ganda. Side-blown and vertical flutes are widespread African wind instruments. It is perhaps less well known that panpipes are also found in different parts of Africa, including among the Venda of southern Africa, the Soga of Uganda, the Yombe of Zaire, the Shona, and in Mozambique. Ranging from a single tube closed at one end and blown like a bottle to instruments with multiple tubes and pitches, panpipes are usually played collectively in interlocking fashion, with the tones of the scale divided among the various instruments of the ensemble, so that each performer inserts the pitches that he or she has with those of others to create a complete melody.

LISTENING GUIDE

GREETINGS AND PRAISES PERFORMED ON THE YORUBA DÙNDÚN DRUM

GO TO **www.mymusiclab.com for the Automated Listening Guide** CDII • Track 15/Download Track 36

Recorded by William Bascom

This excerpt illustrates how the dùndún is used as a "talking drum." The drummer first plays a pattern, and then another drummer recites the corresponding verbal phrase. Included are common greetings like "Good morning" as well as brief praises that would have been played in honor of a chief. The dùndún is an hourglass-shaped pressure drum. When the player squeezes and pulls the ropes that bind the heads on both ends of the drum, increased tension is created so that the pitch is raised; when the cords are relaxed, the tension lessens, and the pitch drops.

Stringed Instruments

Although we usually think of the banjo as the most American of instruments, its prototype was brought by slaves during the colonial period. The banjo was modeled on West African lutes, which are known by various names, depending on the linguistic group and region (e.g., *tidinit* in Mauritania, *halam* among the Wolof in the Senegambia area, *kontingo* among the Mande). The sound box is made from a gourd or a carved wooden back with a stretched skin for the face. A neck is attached, and these instruments have between two and five strings, depending on the region.

A wide variety of harps exist in different African societies. The kora, which we have already discussed, combines features of the lute (with a sound box and neck) and the harp. Instruments of this type with both straight and curved necks are found all over the sub-Saharan region. Single- or multiple-string fiddles made with round sound boxes and skin faces are also important in West Africa (e.g., the *goge* of the Hausa people of Nigeria) as well as in central and eastern Africa.

The oldest and one of the most widespread stringed instruments of Africa is the musical bow. Like the bows used to shoot arrows, it consists of a single string attached to each end of a curved stick. Depending on the tradition, either a gourd attached to the stick or the mouth cavity of the player serves as a resonator. The string is either plucked or, alternatively, struck with another stick; it is sometimes stopped with a hard implement to raise the pitch. The playing technique results in a percussive and yet beautiful and delicate sound. One of the newest and most widespread stringed instruments is the guitar. Local acoustic guitar traditions exist all over Africa, and electric guitars have become central to the new urban styles (Listen to CD II, 16 for an example of the musical bow).

Watch *the video of a musical bow player on* **mymusiclab.com**

LISTENING GUIDE

MUSICAL BOW PLAYED BY A NDAKA MAN

GO TO www.mymusiclab.com for the Automated **Listening Guide** CDII • Track 16/Download Track 37

Recorded by Colin Turnbull

We have already discussed the society and music of the BaMbuti pygmies. One of the most important scholars who studied and recorded their music and way of life was Colin Turnbull. He recorded this BaNdaka pygmy playing his musical bow, in this case made from a bent sapling, with a thin section of vine used for the string. The player holds one end with his toe against the ground, and the other against the edge of his mouth, which serves as a sound resonator. By flexing the bow, he shortens the string and raises the pitch. So pleased was he with his performance that he shouts "Budah!" in the middle of it, an expression of joy.

POPULAR MUSIC IN THE TWENTIETH CENTURY

Over the course of the twentieth century, new popular music styles emerged in countries throughout the sub-Saharan region alongside the indigenous musical traditions that continued to be performed. African musicians combined European, North American, and Latin American musical instruments, scales, harmonies, rhythms, and genres with local musical instruments and styles to create their own distinctive forms of popular music. Local elements and musical sensibilities made each emerging style unique, whereas the cosmopolitan elements served as a kind of common denominator among them. During the first half of the twentieth century, European colonialism generated institutions and social attitudes that led to the emergence of new musical styles. Midcentury, African nationalism became a primary force for local musical creativity. By the 1980s, in the context of the "worldbeat" or "world music" phenomenon, African musicians were attracted by international markets and thus shaped their styles to cater to cosmopolitan audiences in Europe, North America, Japan, Australia, and elsewhere.

Through military conquest, various European powers colonized the sub-Saharan region to control resources and labor for production and ultimately to expand capitalist markets. Along with the use of force, colonial governments and missionaries also used legislation and education to teach Africans to accept European "civilization" as superior to their own ways of life and thus to accept their own subservient position. Through colonial education, a small African middle class began to emerge in the various colonies. Serving as clerks, teachers, foremen, and in other low-level administrative positions, this group understood European education as the means to upward social mobility within the colonial order. In the process, middle-class Africans internalized colonial values and aesthetics and became attracted to European and cosmopolitan music and dance styles.

European musical instruments and styles were first taught to Africans through two colonial institutions—military bands and schools. Particularly in the British colonies, Africans were trained in military band music, and these musicians often went on to form dance bands that played cosmopolitan styles such as European popular music and jazz; it was often these musicians who also created new local popular styles. In the process of Christian conversion, missionaries taught schoolchildren religious songs and hymns, which were sometimes translated into their own languages. Through singing in school and church, Africans learned how to read music, and they became accustomed to European diatonic melodies (i.e., melodies based on the standard do-re-mi scale) and harmonies with basic Western chords (I, IV, V). They also learned very different aesthetic values. For instance, instead of the dense overlapping sounds typical of indigenous performance, schoolchildren were taught to value clear, precise phrasing (e.g., everyone singing the same notes at exactly the same time) and precise vocal diction. These values influenced certain urban popular styles such as highlife in Ghana, and "concert" music in Zimbabwe that especially appealed to the African middle class.

In addition to schools and the military, commercial interests also played a key role in diffusing cosmopolitan instruments and styles in Africa. By the 1920s, a variety of relatively inexpensive instruments such as mass-produced guitars, harmonicas, concertinas, accordions, autoharps, and banjos became available in dry good stores in larger towns, cities, and mining centers. These instruments became popular among the emerging working class who, through wage labor, had some money to spend. Commercial recordings of European popular music, Latin American and Caribbean styles (especially Cuban son, and Trinidadian calypso), and U.S. popular music, including jazz, country and western, and popular groups such as the Mills Brothers, became available by the 1930s and 1940s, as rock 'n' roll, soul, and rap would become later.

By mid-century, local acoustic guitar styles had emerged in many parts of sub-Saharan Africa. Sometimes the guitar was simply adapted to styles formerly played on local indigenous instruments. For example, in Zimbabwe and South Africa, the guitar was used to play mbira and bow music or in West Africa to play music formerly performed on indigenous lutes (e.g., *halam*, or *kontingo*). In other cases, African musicians used the guitar to play foreign styles. Surprisingly, early American country and western performers such as Jimmie Rodgers and Tex Ritter were popular models for African guitarists in many regions. The acoustic guitar, usually accompanied by percussion instruments, was also used to play new styles that were fusions of foreign and local musical elements. Examples include West African "palmwine" guitar music and various acoustic guitar styles in the Congo region and in southern and eastern Africa. Common to African guitarists in many places, a two-finger (thumb and index) picking style was used to play independent bass and melody lines within simple chord progressions (e.g., I, IV, V; I, V; I, IV, I, V; I, IV, ii, V) in first position (on the first three frets of the guitar). By the 1960s, electric guitars had begun to replace acoustic instruments in popularity.

West Africa

In West Africa, dance-band **highlife** music originated on the Ghanaian coast, where the training of local African musicians in the brass-band idiom had begun as early as the eighteenth century and where port life had introduced the locals to many international musical styles. By the 1920s, big bands using brass instruments and playing European popular dance genres like the waltz and fox-trot began performing at upper-crust social affairs for the Westernized African elites and Europeans. During this period local Akan melodies and rhythms began to creep into the highlife repertory, thereby Africanizing what was more or less a Western musical style in terms of rhythm and orchestration.

It was not until after World War II, however, that the fusion of Western and African elements became more integral in big-band highlife. According to David Coplan, E. T. Mensah, the "King of Highlife," was the first to orchestrate both traditional themes and indigenous rhythms for dance band in conjunction with the use of North and Latin American genres, such as swing and samba, and Caribbean genres like the Cuban son, and calypso (see chapter 10). By this time, the electric guitar had been incorporated, and Mensah's group used that instrument as well as trumpet, trombone, saxophone, string bass, and a Cuban-style percussion section. While these groups were playing for higher-class patrons, a parallel development of "guitar-band" highlife grew up among the lower classes in urban centers. This style fused the techniques and repertories of local Ghanaian instrumental traditions with those of the guitar and songs learned from sailors. The music of West Indian sailors, whose rhythms were originally based in African lamellaphone and string techniques, came full circle and began to influence West African highlife. "Palm-wine" music, played on acoustic guitar and accompanied by various percussion instruments, spread throughout British West Africa in informal settings. In Lagos, palm-wine and other syncretic urban working-class styles served as a basis for **jùjú** music among the Yoruba of Nigeria. During the 1930s performers such as Tunde King performed a small-ensemble style with guitar-banjo (banjo body with a six-string guitar neck) accompanied by a tambourine player and *sèkèrè* (rattle with beads on the outside of the gourd). Christopher Waterman suggests that after World War II, the use of amplification influenced jùjú's evolution to increasingly include both more cosmopolitan and indigenous African features simultaneously and to expand the size of the ensembles. With the use of amplified guitars and vocals, it became possible to introduce larger and more complex percussion sections using the Yoruba

HIGHLIFE
A form of urban-popular dance-band music of Ghana; also played in Nigeria and elsewhere in West Africa.

JÙJÚ
A form of Nigerian popular music associated with the Yoruba that combines electric instruments with indigenous drums and percussion.

LISTENING GUIDE

I. K. DAIRO AND THE BLUE SPOTS, "SALOME."
RECORDED IN LAGOS, 1962

GO TO www.mymusiclab.com for the Automated Listening Guide CDII • Track 17/Download Track 38

After an accordion introduction, Dairo sings the text followed by a brief accordion solo (**A** section). The accordion then drops out for a new section (**B**). This section involves a percussion break in which the talking drum takes the lead playing verbal phrases that a unison vocal chorus repeats. At approximately [1:18], the talking drummer plays a short vocal phrase that is immediately repeated by the chorus in call-and-response, making the melodic (speech-song-like) quality of the talking drum particularly apparent. The **B** section ends with a bongo solo. A shortened accordion introduction and vocal material from the **A** section then comes back to conclude the piece, creating an overall **A B A'** structure. In addition to the combination of Yoruba and Cuban instruments, the piece incorporates the "clave" rhythmic pattern of the Cuban son (played by the "rhythm sticks," see chapter 10), which has influenced cosmopolitan music around the world. The text itself illustrates a combination of Yoruba and cosmopolitan elements—much of the text that Dairo sings falls squarely within the style of pop love songs. The texts drummed and sung in Section **B**, however, include Yoruba proverbs.

TIME

00:0   **Accordion introduction**

0:16   **Dairo singing:**
   Sú sú sú bebi-o   (Shoo, shoo, shoo baby)
   Bebi Salome mi-o   (My baby Salome)
   Mo fé lo rí bebi-o Salome mi   (I want to go see my baby Salome)
   Mámá Bekun mi   (Mother of Bekun)
   Salome ó wùn mí-o   (Salome, she attracts me)
   T' ó bá jé t' owó,   (If it is a matter of money)
   màá tepá mó sé owó mi-o,   (I will work hard to make money)
   Salome
   Salome ó dára l' óbìnrin iwa re l'ó wùn mi-o   (Salome, she is a fine woman, it is her character
   Salome   that attracts me)
   Eléyin'jú egé
   Eyín fún j'owó Salome,   (She has [egg] eyes that can trap)
   Eyín m'énu gún-o   (Teeth whiter than cowries, Salome)
   Oyínbó Salo, Salome   (Teeth that shape the mouth)
   Salome, Salome, Salome, etc.   (Light-skinned Salo, Salome)

0:51   **Accordion solo**

1:10   **Percussionists' break**

1:18   **Dùndún talking drum:**
   Emí ò ní sí níbè, émi ò ní sí níbe   (I will not be there, ×2)
   Níbi wòb gbé sorí burúkú èmi ò ní sí níbè   (Where they have bad destiny, I will not be
                                                              there)

1:26	**Vocal chorus:**	
	Emí ò ní sí níbè, émi ò ní sí níbe	(I will not be there, ×2)
	Níbi wòb gbé sorí burúkú èmi ò	(Where they have bad destiny, I will not be
	ní sí níbè	there)
1:37	**Dùndún talking drum:**	
	Ire gbogbo kò ni s'èyìn mi, ní lé ayé ayé	(All the good luck will not happen when I am not present, in this life)
1:41	**Vocal chorus:**	
	Ire gbogbo kò ni s'èyìn mi, ní lé ayé ayé	(All the good luck will not happen when I am not present, in this life)
1:45	**Dùndún talking drum:**	
	Yes, ké, o béréfe	(Yes, you start to love)
1:47	**Vocal Chorus:**	
	Yes, ké, o béréfe	(Yes, you start to love)
1:48	**Dùndún talking drum:**	
	Yes, ké, o béréfe	(Yes, you start to joke)
1:50	**Vocal Chorus:**	
	Yes, ké, o béréfe	(Yes, you start to joke)
1:53	*O béréfe*	(You start to joke)
	O béréfe	(You start to joke)
	O béréfe	(You start to joke)
1:58	**Bongo solo**	
2:06	**Accordion reenters**	
2:10	**Dairo sings:**	
	Sú sú bebi Salo	(Shoo, Shoo, baby, Salo)
	Bebi Salome mi-o, bebi-o, bebi	(Baby Salome, my baby, etc.)
	bebi-o, Salo, Salome-o	

sèkèrè and the hourglass-shaped "talking drum," as well as other instruments often of Cuban derivation, such as bongos, congas, maracas, and *claves* ("rhythm sticks"). I. K. Dairo was a major juju star of the 1960s. At the height of their popularity, his group, The Blue Spots, included nine members and instrumentation typical of bands at that time: guitar, talking drum, bongos, congalike drums, claves, maracas, and agogo (double-bell); Dairo also occasionally performed on a single-row button accordion instead of guitar (Listen to CD II, 17 for an example of jùjú music).

Now associated with the names Ebenezer Obey and King Sunny Ade, jùjú has become one of the internationally best-known "African-pop" styles. Ade has added the pedal steel guitar to the two or more electric guitars, bass, and large percussion section of his band. The highly polished "studio" sound of contemporary jùjú bands is also aided by the use of synthesizers. Jùjú groups combine the traditional functions of praise singing and social-dance drumming and perform both at urban bars and neotraditional Yoruba ceremonies (naming ceremonies, weddings, funerals). Although Western harmonies are used, jùjú music is organized around a series of interlocking ostinato parts played by the guitars and drummers and leader–chorus call-and-response singing.

Congolese Guitar Music

Within sub-Saharan Africa, the urban-popular guitar music of the Congo region has had a more profound impact on musicians and audiences than any other single African style. Leading exponents of the style include Franco and his band O.K. Jazz, Docteur Nico, and Kanda Bongo Man, among others. Local likembe (lamellaphone) dance music (accompanied by struck bottles and a drum) and Afro-Cuban music, especially the Cuban son, served as the foundations of the Congolese style. By the mid-1950s, some musicians replaced the role of the likembe with acoustic guitar, and by the late 1950s Caribbean music became a primary model, with electric guitars as well as saxophones, trumpets, clarinets, and flutes sometimes being used. Different international "dance crazes" involving Afro-Cuban music were fueled throughout the Americas, Europe, Asia, and Africa by the recording and movie industries. The Afro-Cuban son, often referred to internationally as rumba, and the distinctive Cuban son clave pattern (heard in the I. K. Dairo example) took hold in the Congo region.

At first, Congolese "rumba" groups copied the Cuban recordings to the extent that some even imitated the original Spanish texts. As time went on, however, the Congolese bands began to develop their own distinctive sound as well as to incorporate new foreign influences such as riffs from North American soul music. Less rhythmically complex than jùjú, the Congolese style is organized around one or more guitar ostinatos, which serve to accompany the high, sweet singing style of performers like Franco. This style is now known internationally as soukous. A performance usually includes long improvised guitar solos as well as the sparse, orchestrated entrances of the horn section over a danceable rhythm in duple meter. Perhaps inspired by the Congolese "rumba" sound, the use of Cuban-style rhythms and rhythm sections can be heard in East and West Africa as well as in the modern music of Mali where, as in the music of the Super-Rail Band, such elements are fused with electric guitar ostinatos and solos that are clearly based on kora music.

South Africa

The urban-popular music of South Africa—a particularly early European settlement—differs in various ways from the styles created in other countries. The traditional music of the Nguni (Zulu-, Swazi-, Sotho-, Xhosa-speaking) peoples of the region is itself stylistically distinct from the music of other African areas. For example, in contrast to all the African musical styles that we have discussed so far, Nguni music is a predominantly choral-vocal style using slower tempos and lacking the polyrhythmic percussion accompaniments found in, say, West Africa. The music taught by Christian missionaries, also a choral tradition, had a particularly strong impact in South Africa, as did North American urban-popular music.

Various related syncretic choral styles were created using these sources in the context of the dismal living conditions of rural African migrant workers, who were forced by harsh circumstances to seek employment in the mines and cities. Within the workers' compounds, vocal-dance groups formed and participated in competitions, which became a primary social outlet. The competition song-dance genre known as isicathamiya blended the harmonies taught by missionaries with the slow Zulu choral style characterized by multiple overlapping ostinatos and an emphasis on the outer voices (low and high). The music of Ladysmith Black Mambazo and the earlier 1939 hit "Mbube" ("Lion," or "The Lion Sleeps Tonight") of Solomon Linda (popularized internationally by Pete Seeger) are examples that came from this line of development.

In addition to Christian vocal traditions, urban-Black South African music was also highly influenced by American popular styles, including that of minstrel shows, ragtime, jazz, and more recently soul, rock, and hip-hop artists. In the 1960s and 1970s, Zulu "jive" or mbaq'anga bands blended electric guitars, traps, and a particularly prominent electric bass line variably with accordions, violins, pennywhistles, and saxophones for a straight ahead, driving dance beat in 4/4 time. These bands also backed up vocal groups, such as the Mahotella Queens, with a male singer ("growler") and female singer–dancers. Black jazz, rock, and hip-hop groups continue to flourish in South African cities, and Capetown still celebrates carnival with a performance tradition directly based on the American minstrel show of the nineteenth century.

Zimbabwe

Like elsewhere in Africa, Congolese rumba has been popular in Zimbabwe since the late 1950s, and South African styles such as mbaq'anga have also been influential among local musicians, as have North American rock and soul and Jamaican reggae. Two urban-popular guitar genres, however, stand out as unique to Zimbabwe. The most famous of these involves the performance of classical mbira and dance-drumming music by electric dance bands. The second genre, known as *jit* or jiti, is associated with dance drumming and songs performed in informal gatherings in Shona villages. Both mbira music and jit were played by solo itinerant acoustic guitarists by at least the late 1940s (at the time jit was called marabi, tsaba, and by other South African names). Similar to much Shona village music (but unlike mbira music), jit has a two-phrase ostinato, each phrase being twelve quick pulses with beats 1, 4, 7, and 10 receiving equal accents. These characteristics remain regardless of whether jit is performed by village drummers and singers, solo acoustic guitarists, or electric dance bands.

By the mid-1960s, young Zimbabwean rock bands began to add a few Shona village songs to their typical repertoires of Congolese rumba, South African mbaq'anga, and North American rock and soul. It was in the 1970s, however, during a period of heightened African nationalism and the violent war to end white rule, that urban audiences began responding to electric band renditions of Shona village music. Inspired by positive audience reactions, a number of Zimbabwean guitar bands increasingly began to play more local Shona music, including dance-drumming genres, mbira-based songs, and jit, in response to the social climate of the time. This original "neoindigenous" Zimbabwean guitar style continued to be refined throughout the 1980s by artists such as Thomas Mapfumo, an artist whose style has been called chimurenga music (a Shona word for "struggle").

Mapfumo's music is a wonderful example of the blending of indigenous African and cosmopolitan-popular musical elements. He began his professional career in the 1960s playing cover versions of English and American rock and soul music, as well as some Shona village songs. He recorded his first song based on classical mbira music in 1974. On this recording and throughout the 1970s, his bands played mbira, dance-drumming, and jit songs, as well as other genres, with electric guitars, bass, drums, and horns. In the mid-1980s, when he began to tour abroad, however, Mapfumo added an actual mbira player to pique the interest of cosmopolitan audiences; by the early 1990s he had three mbira players in the band.

Classical mbira pieces like "Nhemamusasa" are used as the basis for some of Mapfumo's pieces. Electric guitars might play the basic four-phrase kushaura ostinato as well as melodic lines that would be on the higher mbira keys; the electric bass plays the part of the lower mbira keys of the kushaura. In recent recordings, according to Mapfumo, the keyboard often plays the kutsinhira mbira part, and the mbiras divide these parts as they normally would. The drummer plays a rhythm on the highhat that sounds like the hosho (gourd shakers) used to accompany the mbira, and Shona hand-clapping patterns and an actual hosho are also added. Mapfumo sings in Shona village style, including the high yodeling technique and low-pitched singing of vocables; he also sings traditional lyrics as well as texts of his own composition. Although Shona people who remain in the villages and who have migrated to the cities still play mbira and hosho, or drums, at spirit-possession ceremonies, Mapfumo's music, like that of urban-popular bands all over Africa, illustrates the creativity and adaptability of African musicians in the context of ever-changing social conditions (Listen to CD II, 18 for an example of Thomas Mapfumo's music).

LISTENING GUIDE

"CHITIMA NDIKATURE" (EXCERPT)

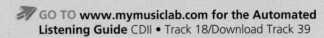 **GO TO www.mymusiclab.com for the Automated Listening Guide** CDII • Track 18/Download Track 39

Performed by Thomas Mapfumo and The Blacks Unlimited

This track is an example of Mapfumo's mature style, which features one electrified mbira (bottle caps removed) with electric guitar, keyboards, bass, drums, hosho, and congas along with two female vocalists. This piece is based in the classical mbira repertory using a forty-eight-beat cycle (four twelve-beat phrases) and is related to the "Nymaropa tune family." Mapfumo performs with a softer, smoother vocal style here, as compared to his earlier recordings, but still uses indigenous Shona vocal techniques such as the singing of vocables with the lower lines of the mbira part. The allusive imagery of the sung poetry and its mosaic quality are also typical of indigenous Shona songs.

TIME	MUSICAL EVENTS	
0:00	Solo mbira plays the entire 48-beat mbira kushaura cycle.	
0:06	Trap drummer leads the rest of the band in beginning on the fourth phrase of the mbira cycle.	
0:10	Full band enters on the second phrase of the cycle, the electric guitar taking the lead.	
0:28	Mapfumo enters singing:	
	Ho yarira amai vemwana	(It has now started, my wife)
	Ho yarira mucherechere	(It has sounded now)
	Ho yarira ndisina kudya	(It has started before I've even eaten)
	Ho yarira mucherechere (stanza ×2)	(It has started now)
1:00	Guitar solo.	
1:07	*Iye zvandanga ndaona—Haa-a* (×3)	(What I had observed—vocables)
	Hona bhurukwa remwana rabvaruka	(The child's shorts are now torn)
	Hona mazuva angu asare mana	(I'm now left with four days)
	Hona vakomana mandiregerea—I yaa hoo	(You have let me down—vocables)
	Hona ndofa zvangu ndimire kani	(I am going to die without dignity
	—Iya hoo	—vocables)
2:02	*Hona musikana ndanga ndichikuda*	(Girl I loved you—vocables)
	Iya hoo	
	Hona ndakurarmbira mai varoyi	(I've changed my mind because your mother is a witch)
	Hona vanofamba nezizi mutswanda—Haa o	(She goes about with an owl in a basket)
	Hona vane mhungu inobika sadza—Haa o	(She has a mamba [snake] that cooks food)
2:34	*Hona nyamafingu ichiuhenekera—Haa o*	(While a viper holds a torch for it)
	Hona kwedu kure handingakusvike—Haa o	(I come from afar, I can't reach it)
	Hona ndotosvika mvura yanaya—Haa o	(I can only reach it after the rains)
	Hona chitima nditakurewo—Haa o	(Train carry me)
	Haa o, Haa o	

3:06	Women singers enter with vocables:
	A ye iye ye (×2)
	Haa owoye o vakuru woye (×4)
4:01	Mapfumo enters singing:
	Ho chitima nditakurewo (×5) (Train carry me)
	Fade out.

Thomas Mapfumo performing with his band, The Blacks Unlimited, in a nightclub in Harare, Zimbabwe.
Source: Thomas Turino

✓•─ **Study** and **Review** on **mymusiclab.com**

SUMMARY

Sub-Saharan Africa is a vast area with many different societies, each with their own distinctive music; however, we have identified some common general musical characteristics and approaches that pertain to many African societies. African music favors ostinatos (repeated rhythmic and melodic cycles), polyphony (multiple melodic parts performing at once), and interlocking parts. Musical performance, moreover, is often a communal participatory activity, and pieces often comprise a collection of melodic or rhythmic formulas that are subject to group variation and thus differ from one performance to another. In addition, we have discovered that many musical performances accompany religious or civic rituals.

Social structure and conditions influence music and performance. For example, the nomadic BaMbuti pygmies use fewer instruments and favor vocal performance. Those instruments that they do use tend to be smaller and lighter, fitting their traveling lifestyle. On the other hand, the Buganda kingdom, with a highly organized, centralized government, developed elaborate court music ensembles. The wide range of musical instruments used throughout sub-Saharan Africa include lamellaphones (for example, the mbira), strings (the kora and kontingo), xylophones, trumpets, flutes, musical bows, and drums.

During the twentieth century, cosmopolitan musical influences from the United States, Latin America, the Caribbean, and Europe, have been incorporated into the African musical scene and have been combined with local styles and practices for the creation of new, vital African musical styles. These styles include highlife, juju, soukous, and mbaq'anga, among many others. It should be clear that this chapter has only addressed a small fraction of the musical life of sub-Saharan Africa. That said, it provides a point of departure for further exploration.

BIBLIOGRAPHY

African Music, General   Robert Kauffman, "African Rhythm: A Reassessment," *Ethnomusicology* 24 (3), 1980; Alan P. Merriam, "Traditional Music of Black Africa," in Phyllis M. Martin and Patrick O'Meara, eds., *Africa* (Bloomington: Indiana University Press, 1977); Stig-Magnus Thorsén, *Sounds of Change Social and Political Features of Music in Africa* (Stockholm: Sida, 2004); J. H. Kwabena Nketia, *The Music of Africa* (New York: W.W. Norton, 1974); Ruth Stone, ed., *Garland Encyclopedia of World Music, vol. 1: Africa* (New York: Routledge, 1998).

Ewe and Ghana   Jacqueline Cogdell DjeDje, *Fiddling in West Africa: Touching the Spirit in Fulbe, Hausa, and Dagbamba Cultures* (Bloomington: Indiana UP, 2008); John Miller Chernoff, *African Rhythm and African Sensibility: Aesthetics and Social Action in African Musical Idioms* (Chicago: University of Chicago Press, 1979); Alfred Kwashie Ladzekpo and Kobla Ladzekpo, "Anlo Ewe Music in Anyako, Volta Region, Ghana," in Elizabeth May, ed., *Musics of Many Cultures* (Berkeley: University of California Press, 1980).

Ganda Music   Lois Ann Anderson, "Multipart Relationships in Xylophone and Tuned Drum Traditions in Buganda," *Selected Reports in Ethnomusicology* [vol. 5:] *Studies in African Music* (Los Angeles: Program in Ethnomusicology, Department of Music, UCLA, 1984); Peter Cooke, "Canada Xylophone Music: Another Approach," *African Music* 4 (4), 1970.

Mande Peoples   Roderic Knight, "Music in Africa: The Manding [Mande] Contexts," in Gerard Béhague, ed., *Performance Practice: Ethnomusicological Perspectives* (Westport, CT: Greenwood, 1984); Eric Charry, *Mande Music* (Chicago: University of Chicago Press, 2000).

Pygmies   Colin Turnbull, *The Forest People: A Study of the Pygmies of the Congo* (New York: Simon & Schuster, 1962); Michelle Kisliuk, *Seize the Dance! BaAka Musical Life and the Ethnography of Performance* (New York: Oxford University Press, 1998).

Shona of Zimbabwe   Paul F. Berliner, *The Soul of Mbira* (Chicago: University of Chicago Press, 1993); Thomas Turino, *Nationalists, Cosmopolitans, and Popular Music in Zimbabwe* (Chicago: University of Chicago Press, 2000).

Studies in African Urban-Popular Music   John Collins, "Ghanaian Highlife," *African Arts* 10 (1), 1976; John Collins, *African Pop Roots* (London: Foulsham, 1985); David Coplan, *In Township Tonight! South Africa's Black City Music and Theatre* (London: Longman, 1986); David Coplan, "Go to My Town, Cape Coast! The Social History of Ghanaian Highlife," in Bruno Nettl, ed., *Eight Urban Musical Cultures* (Urbana: University of Illinois Press, 1978); Veit Erlmann, *African Stars: Studies in South African Performance* (Chicago: University of Chicago Press, 1991); Ronnie Graham, *The Da Capo Guide to Contemporary African Music* (New York: Da Capo, 1988); Christopher Waterman, *Jùjú: A Social History and Ethnography of an African Popular Music* (Chicago: University of Chicago Press, 1990).

DISCOGRAPHY

Anthologies   *Musical Instruments 1: Strings*, Music of Africa Series No. 27 (GALP 1322); *Musical Instruments 2: Reeds (Mbira)*, Music of Africa Series No. 28 (GALP 1323); *Musical Instruments 3: Drums*, Music of Africa Series No. 29 (Kaleidophone KMA 3); *Musical Instruments 4: Flutes and Horns*, Music of Africa Series No. 30 (GALP 1325); *Musical Instruments 5: Xylophones*, Music of Africa Series No. 31 (GALP 1326); *Musical Instruments 6: Guitars 1*, Music of Africa Series No. 32 (GALP 1327).

Ewe and Ghana   *Folk Music of Ghana* (Folkways FW 8859); *Drums of West Africa: Ritual Music of Ghana* (Lyrichord LLST 7307); *Ewe Music of Ghana* (Asch Mankind Series AHM 4222); *Songs of War from the Slave Coast: Abutia-Kloe Ewe* (Ethnic Folkways FE 4258).

Ghana   *Uganda 1*, Music of Africa Series (Kaleidophone KMA 10).

Mande   *Kora Manding: Mandinka Music of the Gambia* (Ethnodisc ER 12101); *Mandinka Kora par Jali Nyma Suso* (Ocora OCR 70); *Rhythms of the Manding Adama Drame (Jembe)* (UNESCO Collection, GREM DSM 042); *Malamini Jobarteh & Dembo Konte, Jaliya* (Rounder 5021); *Sounds of West Africa: The Kora & the Xylophone* (Lyrichord LLST 7308).

Pygmies   *Music of the Rain Forest Pygmies* (Lyrichord LLST 7157); *Pygmies of the Ituri Forest* (Folkways FE 4457); *Music of the Ituri Forest* (Folkways FE 4483).

Shona   *The Soul of Mbira: Traditions of the Shona People of Rhodesia* (Nonesuch H-72054); *Africa: Shona Mbira Music* (Nonesuch H-72077); *The African Mbira: Music of the Shona People of Rhodesia* (Nonesuch H-72043); *Rhodesia I*, Music of Africa Series (Kaleidophone KMA8); *Ephat Mujuru: Master of Mbira from Zimbabwe* (Lyrichord LLST 7398).

Urban-Popular Music   *Ju Ju Roots: 1930s–1950s* (Rounder 5017); *King Sunny Ade and His African Beats; Juju Music* (Mango 9712); *Zulu Jive* (Earthworks ELP 2002); *Viva Zimbabwe* (Earthworks ELP 2001); *Voices of Africa: Highlife and Other Popular Music by Saka Acquaye and His African Ensemble from Ghana* (Nonesuch Explorer H-72026); *Black Star Liner: Reggae from Africa* (Heartbeat 41556); *Mbube Roots: Zulu Choral Music from South Africa, 1930s–1960s* (Rounder 5025); *Thomas Mapfumo and The Blacks Unlimited;* Corruption (Mango MLP 9848).

The Musical Culture of Europe

PHILIP V. BOHLMAN

MUSIC IN THE LIFE OF MODERN VIENNA

Streets and Stages: A Musical Stroll

As we stroll through the streets of Vienna on a June evening, the sounds and symbols of music envelop us. Music is everywhere, and Vienna has derived ways to make its own musical persona obvious. Grandiose edifices, monuments, and statues attest to great musicians of the past and the extravagant performances of the present. The sounds of street musicians intermingle with insistent scales wafting from an open window in a music academy. Wall placards announce many upcoming concerts, and musicians with violin cases or armfuls of musical scores scurry into buildings on the way to rehearsals or concerts. Even restaurants and the foods they serve bear the names of composers and musicians. This is an image of Vienna as the quintessentially musical city in a fundamentally musical nation in the heart of Europe, an image to which we are well accustomed. It is an

image underscored by recordings and movies, history books and tourist literature, all conspiring to convince the world that Vienna is, above all, a musical city.

Continuing our stroll, we begin to see that the larger image of Vienna as a musical city is considerably more complex than its surface suggests. The map of Vienna in our hands tells a great deal about the interaction between the cultural core—symbolized by the city center (First District), which the Ringstrasse, with its governmental and cultural buildings, surrounds and the concentric ring streets that ripple outward toward the Alps in the west, the Czech and Slovak Republics in the north and east, and Hungary and Slovenia in the east and south. The major highways radiating from the center connect it with these other countries and cultures, which until little less than a century ago constituted an empire ruled by Austria. The Habsburg Monarchy is no longer a political reality, but Vienna still has the look and the sound of an imperial capital: We see many cars from the countries of Eastern Europe, and we hear street musicians singing in Hungarian or playing Slovak instruments. After the transition from communism to newly

Staatsoper (State Opera House).
Source: Lazar Mihai-Bogdan/
Shutterstock

STAATSOPER
The National, or "State," Opera
of Austria, serving the Habsburg
court during the Austro-
Hungarian Empire, until World
War I.

**GESELLSCHAFT FÜR
MUSIKFREUNDE**
"Society for the Friends of
Music"; institutional home
to concert halls, archives,
and artistic monuments that
recognize the past history of
Austrian music.

independent nation-states in the early 1990s, Austria's borders opened again, and musicians were among those who took advantage of the cosmopolitan musical life of its capital. As we listen to the many contrasting musics, it is apparent that Vienna attracts musical diversity and provides it with ample opportunities to express itself.

The annual Vienna Festival is in full swing during June, so it is hardly surprising that, as we head in the direction of the **Staatsoper**, many people are funneling into the front doors to see the nightly performance. Opera is an elegant affair, and many attend this evening's performance, dining before the 5:30 P.M. curtain and going to the nearby Mozart Café for drinks and desserts between acts. We check a kiosk to see what opera is on this evening, thinking it might be *Le Nozze di Figaro*. It is instead Richard Strauss's *Rosenkavalier*, although we see from the schedule of Vienna Festival events that *Figaro*, a Viennese favorite, will be staged later in the month.

Many symbols of Vienna's musical past lie within a few blocks of the State Opera. We walk a few blocks to the **Gesellschaft für Musikfreunde**, a large building with several halls for musical performances, a library, archives, and even a showroom for the distinguished Austrian piano manufacturer Bösen-dorfer. We pass along Bösendorfer Street (the Austrians have a habit of giving musical names to just about everything) and enter the piano showroom. It is an imposing, even daunting, place, filled with pianos so highly polished that one hesitates to touch them and draped with huge posters of great Austrian pianists (and a few non-Austrians) staring or smiling down at us. Somehow, we get the impression of music that we should see and respect, even worship, but touching and playing seem out of the question just now.

We consider attending a concert in the Society for the Friends of Music—it hosts several evening concerts during the Vienna Festival—but everything is sold out, and, anyway, we are a little underdressed. Still, it is early summer, and our disappointment fades quickly as we resume our walk through Vienna. Many people are walking toward St. Stephen's Cathedral, the middle of Vienna's downtown. Kärntner Street, Vienna's main shopping thoroughfare, leads in that direction, and it is not long before we encounter numerous street musicians. They are of many types, and accordingly they are performing a remarkable variety of musical repertories. Flower vendors are selling an array of plants from the countryside and some imported from Italy and Spain, and they hawk their wares with a singsong style characterizing work songs. Several groups of street musicians have come to Vienna from Hungary, including a folk-dance troupe from a single village, whose performances are narrated by the local priest. The Hungarian musicians perform an amalgam of styles, mixing rural folk songs with contemporary popular hits. The young dancers even perform entire rituals, for example, a mock wedding. Everything, however, bears the stamp of the Hungarian language and an awareness of Hungarian instrumental styles (Listen to CD II, 19 for an example of the work songs described above).

We also encounter the rather raucous sounds of a young American singing chestnuts from the folk-music revival of the 1950s and 1960s, and with some embarrassment we throw a few coins into his guitar case. At the edge of the square surrounding St. Stephen's, we pause to listen to an Andean panpipe ensemble, performing songs of political protest in Spanish and attracting the largest crowd of all the street musicians. Whether or not anyone understands the lyrics, the Andean ensemble (no one seems to know whether they are Peruvian or Bolivian) obviously earns a considerable amount of money, probably enough to draw them back to this square through the rest of the summer. We conclude our excursion by entering St. Stephen's itself and are greeted by the magnificent sounds of an organ on which Bach is being played, the music of a North German Protestant in the cathedral of this largely Catholic Austrian city. The other visitors in St. Stephen's seem rather unsure whether the music accompanies a religious service, but they respond meditatively, remaining silent or only whispering nervously to their neighbors.

Just as nervously, we leave the cathedral and decide to spend the rest of the evening at a local wine garden, a so-called **Heuriger**, where we will enjoy the wine of the season and the urban music called **Schrammelmusik**, named after Johann and Josef Schrammel, two nineteenth-century musicians who made this style of "folk-like" (**volkstümlich**) urban music famous and contributed to the compositions and performance practice of the tradition. By the end of the evening, we wonder whether there is any music that we did not encounter, and if so, whether we might have happened on it had we chosen a different route. Rumors fly about that there is good country-western music at a club called "Nashville." We hear, too, that some bands from the Celtic and

HEURIGER
Austrian wine garden, which is often a site for traditional music.

SCHRAMMELMUSIK
"Schrammel-music"; urban folk-like music of Vienna, named after a family of musicians.

VOLKSTÜMLICH
"Folk-like" music of Central Europe, in which traditional folk and modern popular musics are often mixed.

LISTENING GUIDE

SPANISH WORK SONG: "LA TRILLA"   ➤ GO TO **www.mymusiclab.com for the Automated Listening Guide** CDII • Track 19/Download Track 40

This work song from the Andalusia region of Spain reveals many of the region's historical connections to the Muslim culture of North Africa, the Mediterranean, and the Iberian Peninsula. The song itself would traditionally accompany grain threshing, and it therefore reflects periods of repetitive movement and repose. The bells that begin the example and keep a steady sense of rhythm and meter are here more stylized because of the nature of recording in a studio, but originally they would have been attached to the animal assisting in the threshing.

The alternation between speaking voice and singing voice determines the structure of the song itself. The speaking voices communicate more directly to animals assisting in the work, whereas the singing voice employs melisma, the extensive performance of melody that creates the feeling of arabesque in this example. Witness, then, a shift between speech and song, hence the threshold between the use of voice in music and in communication that borders on music. Though used for a work song, the melody is very complex, showing a tendency to move between one mode, or collection of pitches, and another.

TIMING	SECTION	MUSICAL EVENT
0:00–0:06	**Intro:** The song is ushered in by the bells, accompanying the movement of work.	Traditionally these bells would have been attached to the animal assisting in the threshing.
0:06–0:13	**Communicative Speech:** The song gets under way with speaking. Speech will alternate with sung sections for the remainder of the song.	Speaking initiates the song as communication between the worker and the animal.
0:13–0:36	**Melismatic Singing:** This is the first section of the melody. The melody consists of several of these sections, and they are each bounded by communicative speech.	The first section of the melody is sung in **melismatic** style. Notice the subtle shifts in mode that signal deep historical connections to the Muslim culture of North Africa, the Mediterranean, and the Iberian Peninsula.
0:37–0:43	**Continued alteration between speaking voice and singing voice:** Notice the back-and-forth established between speech and song here, and remember that the whole song was historically accompanied by the physical work of threshing.	Communicative speech returns, punctuating the sections of song.
0:43–1:11		The second section of the song is performed in melismatic style.
1:12–1:24		Communicative speech returns, followed by a long break during which all we hear are the bells.

1:24–1:42	Return to melismatic singing (third section of song).
1:42–1:53	Speech returns to punctuate the section.
1:54–2:23	Return to melismatic singing (fourth section of song).
2:24–2:31	Speech returns to punctuate the section.
2:32–2:44	Return to melismatic singing (fifth section of song). Here we have evidence of the approaching conclusion because of the brevity of the section.
2:44–2:50	Communicative speech brings the song to its conclusion.

klezmer revivals are playing in the city this evening. Just where are the limits of Vienna's musical life? (Listen to CD II, 20 for an example of this "*volkstüm-lich*" urban music).

The Many Musics of Vienna

The musical life that we discover during an evening's stroll through Vienna sharply contrasts with many descriptions of this quintessentially Central European city. Music-history books, for example, contain labels for musical styles that are distinctively Viennese, such as "Viennese classicism," "Viennese waltzes," and even the "Second Viennese School" of avant-garde composers in the early twentieth century. Could we also observe a similar "Vienneseness" in our encounter with the vibrant musical life of the city on a summer evening? Surely there was no question that our expectation that Vienna would be a "very musical" city was fulfilled. It would hardly be an exaggeration to say that music—its presence as sound and idea—was everywhere. And yet it is not that easy to pin down what was especially "Viennese" about it or even any unequivocally Viennese trait connected to style, repertory, or performers. The street performers were often not even Austrian, and the multitude of musical sounds was more often mixed than identifiably of Viennese origin. Vienna's presence, nonetheless, was essential to our musical encounter. The city attracted these musicians, sanctioned their performances, and brought together the conflicting histories and cultural contexts in a unique way. What we heard during our stroll—indeed, what we would have heard on any stroll—*was* Viennese music.

Our firsthand encounter with Viennese music reveals that there are many possible ways of understanding just what it is. One view seems anchored in the existence of a historical canon, a series of repertories created by gifted composers who lived in Vienna because of the ideal conditions it provided for both the creation and performance of music. Music symbolizes something unbroken and persistent in the history of the city, and the language used to describe music's historical role—notably the stubborn word *classical*—tells us that the past has been important in the present.

MELISMATIC
Performing a single syllable of text by singing multiple notes or pitches is called a melisma (melismatic). Syllabic singing, by contrast, matches one syllable to a single note or pitch.

KLEZMER MUSIC
Jewish instrumental musicians, active in social events and rites of passage in Eastern Europe prior to the Holocaust and revived in Europe and North America at the end of the twentieth century.

LISTENING GUIDE

"DAS WIENER FIAKERLIED" ("THE VIENNESE COACHMAN'S SONG"), COMPOSED BY GUSTAV PICK.

GO TO www.mymusiclab.com for the Automated **Listening Guide** CDII • Track 20/Download Track 41

Performed by Stewart Figa, baritone, and the New Budapest Orpheum Society, Philip Bohlman, Artistic Director.

"The Viennese Coachman's Song" (1884) was the biggest hit from turn-of-the-century Vienna. The song tells a rags-to-riches tale of a simple coachman who was able to offer rides to the most prominent citizens of the day. The journeys in the song, therefore, follow the city streets, and they also map the cultural history of a changing world, one in which the coach would eventually become obsolete as Europe modernized. The song, too, crosses a border between folk styles—it begins as a march from the country, and then the refrain is a waltz from the city. It uses urban dialects and the sounds of popular songs from the day, not unlike those that might have been flowing into and out of Strauss operettas and cabaret.

Stewart Figa sings in a style with the German inflected by Yiddish, signifying the growing immigration of Jews from rural Eastern Europe into modern Vienna (the composer, Gustav Pick, was an example of such immigration). Figa's performance career ranges from his profession as a Jewish synagogal cantor to work on the Yiddish stage, and with the revival cabaret ensemble, the New Budapest Orpheum Society.

TIME	MUSICAL EVENT
0:00	Introduction, cabaret-style band.
0:14	Verse one, in rural march style, evoking the horses who bear the coach.
1:19	The refrain begins, employing an urban waltz style.
1:50	Verse two begins.
2:53	Refrain of verse two.
3:25	Verse three begins, with the narrative bringing the coachman's life to a close.
4:26	Refrain of verse three.

Translation of "The Viennese Coachman's Song"

1. I drive two midnight horses.
   They pull my fancy coach.
   They're stronger than a Norse's,
   And far beyond reproach.
   It doesn't do to strike them.
   I never use a whip.
   I murmur, "Giddy-up, you two.
   Let's take another trip."
   In less than fifteen minutes,

   From Lamb Street to the club.
   We don't attempt a slow gallop.
   I push them faster, clop, clop, clop.
   They sound like shooting rifles.
   Then all at once I feel
   I'm not in charge of trifles.
   I'm a coachman, I mean real.
   Now, anyone can drive a hack,
   But Vienna calls for quite a knack.

Refrain
I'm proud to be Viennese. Life suits me fine.
I serve as a coachman, the top of the line.
I fly through streets with speed like none other can.
I'm truly a Viennese man.

2. *To be the perfect driver,*
You must be like a god,
A silent, strong provider,
You listen, think, and nod.
I often take the rich men
To visit "Number One."
In fact, last night, Count Lamezan
Stopped off to have some fun.
I might pick up two lovers,

Improper true, I know.
If later someone asks me, "Who
Those lovers were?" What do I do?
I never stop to answer.
I glide on down the street.
It's safe for each romancer,
'Cause the horses are discreet.
If grandpa wants to have a fling,
That's fine with me, and I just sing.

Refrain

3. *I'm turning sixty Monday.*
I've worked for forty years.
But I would not trade one day
For other bright careers.
A coachman and his carriage
Are mated well by fate.
And when I die, hitch up my team,
And mention heaven's gate.
Just let my horses canter

As I go to my grave.
Direct them to the heart of town,
The smart, expensive part of town.
And though it's rather tiny,
I want the town to see,
My carriage black and shiny
Is the final ride for me.
Upon my gravestone, don't forget,
I would like this simple epithet.

Refrain
He was proud to be Viennese. Life suited him fine.
He served as a coachman, the top of the line.
He flew through streets with speed like none other can.
He was truly a Viennese man.

Another view of Viennese music concentrates not on the central core but rather on the periphery, on Vienna's tendency to attract outsiders. Relatively few of the composers generally associated with Vienna were originally from the city or received their musical education there; Mozart, Haydn, Beethoven, Brahms, and Mahler were all outsiders, and their biographies demonstrate vividly that being accepted as an insider was no easy task. Clearly, the modern street musicians are not so different from the pantheon of Viennese composers in their relation to the city; the outsider status of the Hungarian folk singers or the Andean panpipe ensemble at once privileges and impedes, while making their presence almost unexceptional.

A third view of Viennese music challenges the historical nature of the first two and poses what we might call postmodern arguments. According to this view, Vienna forms a sort of cultural backdrop that permits unexpected—even jarring—juxtapositions. Accordingly, certain conditions foster Viennese musics at particular moments, but these are almost random. Such a view helps to explain why the old and the new, the classical and the avant-garde, opera and street music exist side by side. Vienna is no less important to the various juxtapositions, because it provides a cultural template that encourages them. Its concert halls, music academies, and streets all become the stages for a music that, whatever else it might be, is unassailably Viennese.

EUROPE AS A MUSIC CULTURE

Europe as a Whole

There is no more commonly held assumption about music's relation to cultural and geographical areas than that something called "European music" exists. Other categories are created to contrast with European music, for example, Middle Eastern music, whose position in a world culture is determined by Europe's geography, not its own. Throughout the world, students study European music; they call it by other names at times, perhaps "Western music" or "Euro-American music," but generally "European" became common parlance in the twentieth century.

Just what European music is, of course, is another question. Despite the lack of consensus, relatively few writers on music concern themselves with stating the limitations of European music or defining what it is. It might be easiest to suggest that it is the music of Europe or the music created in Europe. Would, then, the Andean panpipe ensemble we heard in Vienna be European music? And would the music of Islamic Spain in the Middle Ages be European music? If we answer "no," we argue that Europe is more a shared culture than a unified geographic entity. If we answer "yes," we place greater importance on what happens within the geography, allowing even that the geography shapes the culture.

Europe is indeed unified in several ways. For example, it is a continent, largely though not completely bounded by water. Linguistically, most peoples of Europe are related, closely in several cases and more remotely in others. Those languages not related to the larger Indo-European family, such as Hungarian and Finnish, may demonstrate European interrelations of their own. The cultural history of the continent has a sort of unity, although sometimes that unity results only from barricading the continent from Asia and Africa. Religion unifies Europe. Europeans were historically largely Christian, certainly to a degree that distinguishes certain aspects of shared culture; to travel from Europe toward Asia, the Middle East, or North Africa brings one immediately into contact with peoples who are not primarily Christian. In Europe, the growing number of non-Christians today, particularly Muslims from the Middle East and South Asia, is seen by many as a fundamental transformation of Europeanness itself. At the beginning of the twenty-first century, more nations are joining the European Union, thereby responding to calls for political and economic unity. All these cases for unity contain exceptions, but together they justify studying Europe as a whole.

✳ **Explore**
a map of Europe on the Interactive Globe on **mymusiclab.com**

Multicultural Europe

Despite the acceptance of Europe's cultural wholeness, individuals do not always—or even most of the time—identify with it. Instead, individuals identify more often with the culture of the town, region, or nation in which they live. Similarly, at the individual level, most identify more closely with a regional musical style than with an abstract European unity. It has been characteristic of music in Europe that patterns of regional and cultural identity have remained especially pronounced, even as mass culture encroaches in the twenty-first century. The geographic area surrounding Lake Constance in Central Europe, for example, belongs to a single cultural area in which a single dialect of German is spoken, and its musical styles and repertories are related by a long history. This small area nevertheless includes parts of four nations (Germany, Switzerland, Austria, and Liechtenstein). Even though the folk musics of Germany, Switzerland, and Austria are distinct at a national level, the Lake Constance region plays the decisive role in determining musical unity.

The musical areas of Europe also result from groups of people who share a way of life and a distinctive music, even when these have little to do with national and political boundaries. Jewish, **Saami**, and **Roma** (Gypsy) music cultures in Europe, for example, are circumscribed primarily by boundaries that arise within these communities. Roma communities exist throughout Europe, having adapted to many different socioeconomic settings. Roma musicians have traditionally adapted to the music in countries where they settled, often fulfilling specialized roles as performers in non-Roma society. This adaptability has not erased a distinctively Roma musical life. Bolstering that musical life have been the customs, languages, and social functions that are unique to the Roma community. It is not quite proper to speak of "Roma"—and surely not "Gypsy"—culture as a homogeneous whole. Instead, we must always keep in mind the distinctive linguistic and cultural communities that make up the whole.

If we were to generalize about the music of Roma and **Sinti** in Europe, we would need to take into consideration a process of negotiation between the community and the larger nation or cultural area of which it was a part. We would also need to incorporate the ways in which Roma and Sinti make distinctions among their own musics. The Saami in northern Europe have traditionally responded relatively little to the music cultures of Norway, Sweden, Finland, and Russia, whereas Jewish musicians have often been active participants in the musical life outside the community, so much so that certain differences of style and repertory have disappeared. The Roma musicians, for their part, often borrow from Jewish styles and repertory previously performed by Jewish musicians in northern Romania (Listen to CD II, 21 to hear an example of this centuries-long negotiation of musical style).

European Unity in Modern Europe

Many genres of European music reflect an underlying belief that unity of musical style is important. Hungarian and German folk-music scholars have created classification schemes that assert the historical presence and importance

SAAMI
Circumpolar peoples, living in northern Norway, Sweden, Finland, and Russia, whose musical practices in Europe mix indigenous and modern sounds.

ROMA
Transnational communities of people pejoratively referred to as Gypsies; active participants in Europe throughout history and across the continent.

SINTI
One of the largest communities of Roma, with a particularly strong presence in Central Europe.

LISTENING GUIDE

"KHUSED" (CHASSIDIC DANCE)

GO TO www.mymusiclab.com for the Automated Listening Guide CDII • Track 21/Download Track 42

Performed by Gheorghe Covaci, Sr., and Gheorghe Covaci, Jr.

Recorded by Rudolf Pietsch and Philip V. Bohlman, February 23, 1996, Vadu Izei, Romania

Two Roma musicians, a father and son renowned throughout the Transylvanian Carpathian Mountains near the Ukranian border, perform a wedding dance from the Jewish repertory that had wide currency in Romania prior to the Holocaust. The dance itself is strophic, here with four verses, each increasing in tempo from its predecessor and revealing the generally ecstatic nature of the wedding celebrations of Chassidic Jews, observant communities following the spiritual traditions of the Baal Shem Tov, a rabbi from the eighteenth century.

The Covacis play a violin and a guitar, mixing Roma styles (e.g., playing the guitar upright in the lap) with Romanian styles. These musicians reveal the ways in which earlier Jewish repertories have come to serve other ethnic communities in Eastern Europe, and they particularly illustrate the centuries-long exchange between Roma and Jewish neighbors. The musicians play other repertories as well, for other ethnic and religious groups in the multicultural area of Transylvania.

TIME	SECTION	MUSICAL EVENTS
0:00–0:12	**Verse 1:** Listen to the three-part melody that makes up the verse (**AABBCC**).	The violin performs the first section of the melody. Notice that it consists of two short phrases that form a complete statement (**AA'**) [0:00–0:06]. The guitar joins shortly after the opening gesture on the violin and the melody is repeated [0:06–0:12].
0:12–0:23		The second section of melody, again consisting of two short phrases, is introduced [0:12–0:18] and repeated [0:18–0:23].
0:23–0:34		The third section of the melody is introduced [0:23–0:28] and repeated [0:28–0:34].
0:34–0:44	**Verse 2:** Listen for the tempo increase that pushes up the intensity of the performance.	(**A**) section.
0:45–0:55		(**B**) section.
0:55–1:05		(**C**) section. Notice the rhythmically more complex strumming on the guitar during this section.
1:05–1:15	**Verse 3:** Now that you have heard the melody twice, listen for the increased tempo and intensity, and notice the nuanced strumming on the guitar in the (**C**) section.	(**A**) section.
1:16–1:26		(**B**) section.
1:26–1:36		(**C**) section. Notice, again, the rhythmically more complex strumming on the guitar during this section.

1:36–1:46 **Verse 4:** Listen for the increasingly ecstatic performance. In addition to the slightly increased tempo, the violinist plays more forcefully than in previous verses and the guitarist, for the first time, incorporates more complex rhythmic strumming into the (**A**) section of the melody, adding intensity to the performance.	(**A**) section. Notice the rhythmically more complex strumming on the guitar during this section.
1:46–1:56	(**B**) section.
1:56–2:08	(**C**) section. Notice the double stop (two notes bowed at once) on the violin to conclude the dance song.

of these folk musics. European folk music in general falls into repertories that have national, linguistic, or cultural designations, suggesting that those who describe these repertories feel that unity is fundamental to what folk music really is. Scholars in several countries have gone so far as to recognize patterns of unified history in their national folk musics. This is particularly evident in Hungarian and English folk music; but elsewhere, too, we encounter the belief that the music of the past is related to the music of the present.

Folk music can reveal and articulate history in both musical and cultural (or, better, political and nationalistic) ways. The classification of Hungarian folk song is based on claims about whether the progression of musical style has been relatively unbroken since the time Hungarian people lived in Asia (old style) or whether it has absorbed influences from surrounding European peoples (new style; see chart on page 251). Figure 8-1, from Béla Bartók's collections of Hungarian folk song, demonstrates the characteristics of the old style in every way. Each characteristic is bracketed and numbered according to the chart on page 251 to help you identify the musical arguments that Bartók and other Hungarian scholars brought to their understanding of history (Listen to CD II, 22 for an example of the "old style" of Hungarian folk song).

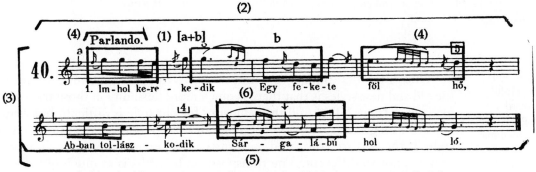

Figure 8-1 "Imhol kerekedik"—Hungarian Folk Song in the Old Style. *Source:* Bartók, Béla. *Das ungarische Volkslied.* Berlin: de Gruyter, 1925, p. 11, Example No. 40.

LISTENING GUIDE

"THE OWL WOMAN'S BALLAD"

➤ GO TO **www.mymusiclab.com for the Automated Listening Guide** CDII • Track 22/Download Track 43

Kati Szvorák, singer, and Ferenc Kiss, Jew's harp

"The Owl Woman's Ballad" is a clear example of the "old style" of Hungarian folk song. It has a four-line structure, (**ABAB**), in which the contour of the (**B**) lines are similar to those of the (**A**) lines, only at an interval of the fifth lower. The slow tempo and elaborate style are characteristic of what Béla Bartók called **parlando rubato**, a speech-like melody with much give-and-take in the rhythmic structure. The words are clearly important also because this is a ballad, in which a story is being told.

Kati Szvorák is one of Hungary's foremost singers of several styles of folk song. She has an immense command of traditional repertory, from which "The Owl Woman's Ballad" comes, but she also sings in the Hungarian "new folk" style, a hallmark of the ensemble, the Stonemasons, who often accompany her. She began her career singing with army folk ensembles, and then after the end of state socialism in Hungary, she branched into other styles, among them religious folk song from the countries surrounding Hungary.

TIME	SECTION	MUSICAL EVENTS
0:00–0:07	**Verse 1:** Listen to the four-line structure and for the melodic relationship between the (**A**) and (**B**) lines. Line (**B**) completes the melody initiated by line (**A**).	Line (**A**). Notice the melodic contour and see if you can hear it reappear in line (**B**).
0:07–0:15		Line (**B**), transposed down a fifth, as in the "old style."
0:15–0:22		Line (**A**).
0:22–0:28		Line (**B**) concludes the verse.
0:29–0:43	**Verse 2:** Listen to the melody and see if you can hear it as two statements of (**ABAB**).	Lines (**A**) and (**B**).
0:43–0:56		Lines (**A**) and (**B**) repeat.
0:56–1:10	**Verse 3:** Now that you have heard the melody twice, listen for the subtle accompaniment provided by the Jew's harp.	Lines (**A**) and (**B**). Song concludes without completing the four-line structure.

PARLANDO RUBATO
Identified by Béla Bartók and characterized by a speech-like style that stresses the words while incorporating a great deal of give-and-take in the rhythmic structure. It is associated most closely with "old style" Hungarian folk song.

One of the first things we notice when we compare the musical traits of the old and new styles is that there is much more flexibility in those traits recognized as "new." To fulfill the requisites for old style is difficult, but virtually any Hungarian song—folk, popular, or even religious—fits into the new style. If the two are compared even further, we realize that in certain ways they are not so different. The transposition by fifths is as much old as it is new style, excluding the fact that a falling melody should somehow be older.

Comparison of Old- and New-Style Hungarian Folk Song

Old style	New style
1. A five-note, or pentatonic, scale, in which no half-steps were found.	Whereas pentatonic scales are occasionally found, more common are the so-called church modes or major mode.
2. Melodies or phrases that started high and ended lower.	Melodies are repetitive, and they form arches rather than descending contours.
3. A melody in two halves, in which the second half repeated the first, only at the interval of the fifth lower.	Four-line verses like the following (A^5 designates a phrase transposed a fifth higher); A A^5 A^5 A; A A^5 B A; A B B A.
4. A steady rhythmic style Bartók called parlando rubato (speech-like).	Rhythm is not "speech-like" but rather "dancelike," demonstrating what Bartók called tempo giusto.
5. Only Hungarian musical elements are heard.	Non-Hungarian musical elements have been incorporated.
6. No influence of popular song or other "outside" genres.	The influence of popular song, particularly Hungarian popular genres from the nineteenth century, is evident.

Pentatonicism, too, is not excluded from the new style, and one might argue that the ornamentation in the old style has a tendency to fill in the gaps in its characteristic five-note scale. Figure 8-1, for example, is pentatonic when we consider only the main notes, but it has a seven-note scale when we add the ornaments, marked in Bartók's transcription with small noteheads.

The Hungarian construction of history from folk-song style has clear nationalistic implications, and these are important to understand as ideas about European music. Transposition by fifths was important to Bartók because it was quite rare in Western and Central European music, but more common in Central and East Asian traditions. A style of music that utilized transposition by fifths, therefore, proved that the integrity of the Hungarian people had been maintained to some measure, at least since they left Asia to settle in Europe. The close relation of the old style to speech (*parlando*) also reveals an attempt to link music to the uniqueness of Hungarian culture, because the Hungarian language is not a member of the Indo-European family. Clearly, identifying songs in the old style provided a strong argument for Hungarian nationalism. Recognizing that songs in the new style had been influenced from the outside—that their rhythms were regularized and loosened from their connection to language—made an equally strong nationalistic appeal. This interweaving of musical style, national history, and cultural ideology is such that we find it difficult to determine which characteristic of a song was determined for musical reasons, which for ideological for musical reasons, which for ideological reasons, and which for both (Listen to CD II, 23 to hear two of Bartók's own compositions based on folk music).

PENTATONICISM
Melodic structure based on scales with five pitches, often revealing an historically early stage of folk-music style.

Read
a biography of Bartók
on **mymusiclab.com**

LISTENING GUIDE

BÉLA BARTÓK: TWO DUOS FROM THE 44 VIOLIN DUOS, "LULLABY" AND "DANCE FROM MARAMOROS"   GO TO www.mymusiclab.com for the Automated **Listening Guide** CDII • Track 23/Download Track 44

Performed by Andrea F. Bohlman and Benjamin H. Bohlman. Recorded by Philip V. Bohlman

These two violin duos illustrate the contrastive styles of Hungarian folk music, the *parlando rubato* style of "Lullaby" and the **tempo giusto** style of "Dance from Maramoros." Parlando rubato is speech-like, and it follows the nuances of song and evokes in an instrumental piece the contours of language through embellishment. Clearly, a lullaby would be speech-like. A dance, in contrast, has a quick tempo that allows for rapid and coordinated movement on the dance floor. "Maramoros" is the Hungarian designation for Transylvania, which indicates that Bartók composed this dance to reflect characteristics of the region (the Roma musicians featured on CD II, 21 live in this region). In the "Lullaby" the two violins might represent a child and a parent at bedtime, one singing gently, the other declaiming forcefully that it might be time to go to sleep. In the "Dance from Maramoros" the variety of string sounds in Hungarian folk music is clear, from the percussive sound of the second violin to the plucking of the same instrument toward the end of the brief dance.

The two violinists, Andrea and Benjamin Bohlman, are young American musicians who specialize in the performance of chamber music for strings. Like the Roma musicians performing on CD II, 21 they are from the same family, in fact, that of the author of this chapter.

"Lullaby"

TIME	MUSICAL EVENTS
0:00	Solo voice, with gentle melody begins.
0:09	The other voice enters, showing firmness.
0:31	Dialogue, or conversation, begins between the two voices.
0:47	Gentleness increases in both voices.
0:53	The voices succumb to fatigue.

"Dance from Maramoros"
This dance is fast and through-composed, evoking the sound of a Hungarian string band.

TEMPO GIUSTO
Identified by Béla Bartók and characterized by a dance-like style that stresses strict adherence to meter. It is associated most closely with "new style" Hungarian folk song.

The concept of "music history," itself a particularly European notion, asserts that unity is somehow central to the formation of musical repertories. French music, then, is more than just music that utilizes the French language or music created or performed in France; rather, it is music that occupies a position within French music history, maintaining an essential style that is French. Whether the patterns of stylistic unity sought by European scholars are real or not is open to question. They have sometimes produced rather unfortunate historical distortions, for example, when some German musical scholars sought to equate pockets of German folk-music style (in French Alsace-Lorraine or in the so-called German **speech islands** of Eastern Europe) with colonialist expansion in the late nineteenth and early twentieth centuries. Nonetheless, the need to equate musical style with national and regional unity in Europe remains one of the most noticeable traits of the continent, even at the end of the twentieth century.

The "Europeanness" of music assumes many forms in modern Europe. However, motivations for retaining and expressing nationalistic or regional musical qualities have changed, as have the audiences who listen to popular and classical musics. A Polish popular singer must sing part of her repertory in English to ensure success in Warsaw, but that success allows her to sharpen the bite of the political message in her songs, both Polish and English. The mass media link the different linguistic regions of Europe in new ways, thereby empowering indigenous languages to claims of greater importance while permitting international languages to encroach at an increasing pace.

The Europeanness of music today is not unlike the attributes we observed during our stroll through Vienna. Seemingly unrelated traditions are juxtaposed in unpredictable ways. Elements of indigenous and foreign music commingle, and in some cases they demonstrate an affinity for each other. Revitalizing old folk music is not an uncommon way of highlighting contemporary political issues. The old and the new coexist. Just as Vienna shaped its conflicting musical parts into a unity that reflected the history and contemporaneity of Vienna, so too does the Europeanness of music today assert itself so that the changing complexion of Europe has a powerful musical presence. That European music so often combines such diverse parts is, as we shall see, fundamental to the basic ideas that Europeans hold about music.

SPEECH ISLANDS

Sprachinseln, or the German-speaking cultural islands in Eastern Europe, given nationalist significance by Germany prior to World War II.

IDEAS ABOUT MUSIC

The Concept of "European Music"

Music is many different things to Europeans. Still, we recognize that certain qualities make music "European" and enable us to discuss a European music culture. We commonly employ the term "European art music" to describe the classical music of the Western concert hall. "European folk music," too, provides a way of classifying shared musical activities.

Earlier in the history of ethnomusicology, music outside of Europe was defined by contrasting it with European music, calling it simply "non-European." Implicit in such terms was not the notion that all European music was the same, but rather that certain experiences, both historically and culturally, had produced musical activities and ways of thinking about music that were more similar to each other than to those elsewhere in the world. Hungarian and Norwegian folk musics, therefore, do not sound like each other, but both fulfill certain expectations of what folk music should be in rural European society and in the construction of national cultures, musical styles, and art musics.

Music in Peasant and Folk Societies

European ideas about music have a great deal to do with shared historical experiences and the ways these experiences have formed modern European societies. Early in European history, social relations were relatively undifferentiated and rural, and yet a common culture—consisting of language, folklore, and belief system—provided cohesion. Music played a role in expressing the common culture of a people because it was in a language shared by the people and was a part of their daily lives and rituals. Music was thought to be inseparable from the essence of a culture. As such, it could express the culture's past, share traits of a language, and articulate religious belief. In doing so, music differentiated one society from another on the basis of national, regional, and linguistic styles.

This type of music is, of course, what we call "folk music." Folk music is a particularly European concept. Johann Gottfried Herder, a German who grew up in the Baltic area of Eastern Europe, coined the term **Volkslied** in the late eighteenth century, and the collection and study of folk music spread throughout Europe by the end of the nineteenth century. The gap between a village folk song and a symphonic poem using it was massive, but it is significant for our consideration of European music that folklorists, composers, and many other intellectuals found it vital to bridge that gap. Folk music provided a means for understanding both the essence of, say, the Polish people and the ultimate expression of that essence in a national art music. Many twentieth-century European composers, such as Béla Bartók and Ralph Vaughan Williams, combined collecting and writing about folk music with composing in nationalistic styles.

Music in Urban Society

Most European concepts of folk music portray it as the product of rural life. A certain irony lurks behind the need to privilege the music of rural life, because European society has a long history of extensive urbanization. Markets, seaports, monasteries, courts, and fortifications all served as the kernels from which great European cities developed during the Middle Ages. European cities have often served as the gathering points for people from other places, that is, people singing in different languages and performing on different instruments. As we might expect, musical "trade" has been as common in the city as mercantile trade. During the Middle Ages, troubadours, **minnesingers**, and minstrels emerged as highly skilled musical specialists who traveled to urban centers, courts, and fairs, picking up new styles and repertories. Urbanization has also affected the manufacture of musical instruments and the mass production of music in all forms, ranging from printed broadsides in early modern Europe to recordings in the twenty-first century.

Cities may bring the musics of many different groups together, but by no means do they eliminate the distinctive qualities of these musics. This is particularly true of communities that were relatively independent of national folk music or European art music. Roma and Sinti musicians not only have a distinctive music culture, but they also perform as musical specialists in a variety of settings outside their own society, such as in the small courts of southeastern Europe prior to the twentieth century. Similarly, a wide variety of musical styles and repertories exist in European Jewish communities, while Jewish musicians are known for the specialist roles they play in non-Jewish society. Even the klezmer ensembles that performed widely for the rites of passage in the Jewish shtetls of Eastern Europe occasionally traveled to play at Christian celebrations.

Music Within the Nation, Music Outside the Nation

Music cultures such as those of the Saami and Jewish communities illustrate yet another characteristic of European music, namely the persistence of repertories that cross national borders. The boundaries of Saami music culture mirror the reindeer-herding routes in far northern Scandinavia and Russia. The Celtic folk-music traditions of Western Europe—traditions unified by the Gaelic languages and related stylistic traits, among them the harp and bagpipe—stretch from Brittany (western France) north through Wales and Ireland to Scotland. These traditions, moreover, have remained a vital part of the musical practices of Celtic communities living abroad—in places such as the United States, for instance. Modern political boundaries have failed to eliminate these traditions, and in fact their unity of musical style characteristic has ensured their cultivation during periods of revival (Listen to CD II, 24, for an example of the Celtic folk-music tradition).

The twentieth-century political state has become a significant force shaping modern ideas about music in Europe. Governments have been particularly supportive of music, providing financial support for folk as well as classical music and supporting festivals and broadcast media. When Bulgaria sought to create an international image of Bulgarian music in the 1980s, it toured its Bulgarian State Women's Chorus throughout the world. State choral ensembles from the Baltic countries of Lithuania, Latvia, and Estonia tour widely, promulgating an officially sanctioned national sound. It is hardly surprising that there is no single model for national music in Europe. A national music may have a style that results from a unified history, or it may combine rather disparate styles from different parts of a country, symbolizing modern unity. Whatever the reasons for associating music with the state, politics have come to play a powerful role in twentieth-century ideas of European music.

Music and Religion

Religious concepts and experiences often provide keys for understanding music in European society. Both folk and scholarly classifications include categories that specify some forms of religious music, not infrequently relying on just two large categories, "sacred" and "secular" music. These broad classifications

LISTENING GUIDE

"BLACK IS"

GO TO **www.mymusiclab.com for the Automated Listening Guide** CDII • Track 24/Download Track 45

Performed by Anish (Ned Folkerth, Aileen Dillane, Kevin Moran, Aidan O'Toole, Brendan Bulger).

In this contemporary version of "Black Is the Color of My True Love's Hair," folk music and popular music interact in complex ways. The text of the lyrical song is well known in Irish American traditions, and it has circulated through various folk and even country-music versions. In this performance, there is a healthy tension between the text and the instruments of a traditional Irish band, which improvise and vary in contrasting ways.

Anish is an Irish American band, with a shifting membership. It draws primarily on traditional repertories, but seeks new sounds and contexts in which to present them. The changing styles in the performance, therefore, reflect the changing landscapes of the Irish diaspora.

TIME	MUSICAL EVENTS
0:00	Introduction, with instruments entering to add new layers and dimensions.
0:35	First verse of "Black Is the Color of My True Love's Hair" begins, followed by multiple verses.
2:21	Instrumental interlude, with traditional and more contemporary improvisation.
2:57	Return of "Black Is the Color of My True Love's Hair".
4:16	Final vocal riffing on "Oh, I love the ground whereon she stands".

COUNTER-REFORMATION
A period of Catholic revival (mid-16th to mid-17th centuries), energized in response to the Protestant Reformation.

POLYPHONIC
Generic term referring to all music in which one hears more than one pitch at a time, for example, songs accompanied by guitar, choral music, orchestral music, or two people singing a round together. Refers more specifically to music which incorporates two or more simultaneous melodic lines or parts.

tend to mask a far more complex presence of religion in European ideas about music. If we consider the larger historical impact of Christianity on European culture, we see that systems of musical patronage often reflect the structure and hierarchy of the church. Indeed, much of the music studied as European art music was created for specific use in religious services. It was not uncommon for musical style to respond to the requirements of the church hierarchy, for example, the call during the sixteenth-century **Counter-Reformation** for a **polyphonic** style that rendered text as audible as possible.

Folk music that accompanies ritual or that embodies spiritual themes is overwhelmingly religious in many communities. A harvest or wedding song, for example, may articulate a community's most fundamental sacred beliefs. Not only are Norwegian folk songs predominantly religious in thematic content, but many are actually variants of hymns that have entered oral tradition. Religious pilgrimages have generated new songs and formed new communities that give these songs special meaning and function. During the Cold War, religious music became a primary voice for resistance, especially in Eastern Europe. In the political transition in Eastern Europe, the music of pilgrimage has mobilized villages and nations alike as they sought new identities in shared religious experience; a recent example is the foot pilgrimage

Pilgrims arriving at the basilica of the Black Madonna of Czçestochowa, July 2005. *Source:* Philip B. Bohlman

from Pope John Paul II's home village of Wadowice, whose participants sang on their way to the Black Madonna of Czçestochowa in the summer of 2005. Most recently, religious music has created venues for protesting violence against foreign workers and asylum seekers in Central Europe.

Concerts and Concert Stars

When most of us think about European music, we think also about how and where it takes place. In short, we equate European music with concerts. The concert is a specialized musical event, one in which the difference between performer and audience is very great, and the focal point of most activity is the singing or playing of music. At one level, the concert suspends the ritual of folk or sacred music by privileging the music itself, and social behavior dictates that one listen carefully to a particular musical text. At another level, concerts have generated their own rituals in European society, and audiences behave according to social requirements specific to the concert setting—dressing in a certain way, refraining from conversation, and listening attentively.

Concerts have become a form of musical ritual particularly suited to modern Europe. Some concerts may preserve one type of musical ritual, whereas others become the moment for radical innovation. The European concert empowers musicians to recontextualize music, to bring rural folk music to the streets of the city, or to relocate sacred music in a public auditorium. Though an idea shared by all Europeans, the concert has nevertheless remained one of the major sources of musical diversity in modern times.

Concerts inevitably shift a certain degree of attention to the performer as a result of splitting musical participation into the two groups of music makers and audience. The performer acquires importance because of the skill he or she possesses and the role the audience wants the performer to play. Virtuosity often becomes one of the markers of this role, and outstanding musicians become extremely important in European ideas about music. The virtuoso has taken many forms. We think first of the performer who plays the most difficult passages in a concerto cadenza faster than anyone else—the early-nineteenth-century Italian violinist Nicolò Paganini, for example. Some in the nineteenth century speculated—a few even seriously—that Paganini's virtuosity resulted from otherworldly influences, perhaps some sort of pact with the devil. Stories about the nineteenth-century piano virtuoso Franz Liszt chronicle his amorous skills, which were linked to his ability as a performer when he tossed broken piano strings to adoring women in the audience.

Although many stories about virtuosi are apocryphal, they reveal a great deal about European ideas about music. The virtuoso is somehow superhuman and can achieve things that no mortal is able to achieve. A sort of cult-figure worship develops around this superhuman quality. We find these ideas embedded elsewhere in European music, such as the association of certain instruments, particularly fiddles, or musical structures, especially the "devilish" interval of a tritone, with supernatural forces. The German philosopher Friedrich Nietzsche canonized these ideas in his writings about cultural superbeings, and music historians have applied them to virtuosi—composer, conductor, and performer alike. European music has been inseparable from the presence of individuals who stood out from the rest of society.

The Individual and Society, Creativity and Community

As a social counterpoint to the musicians who stand out as exceptional, more communal forms of music-making continue to thrive in European society. Musical ensembles in which the total musical product depends on a group's willingness to subsume individual identity into that of the ensemble reflect many ideals that Europeans associate with folk music. In the idealized folk society, all music theoretically belongs to the community, and because the means of producing music—family traditions, group interaction, community ritual—are shared, music becomes an aesthetic metaphor for communality. We recognize that this notion of communality is idealized, and yet we need not look far before discovering similar metaphors for other types of European music-making. The four voices of a **string quartet**, one of the most common ensembles, interact so that competition to make one voice dominate the others would undermine the performance. To symbolize this social equality, the chamber orchestra, the largest chamber ensemble in the classical tradition, often performs without a conductor. Not only does this avoid the symbol of power accruing to an individual, but it also assures the performers that their musical and social survival depends on functioning as a whole with interacting parts (Listen to CD III, 1 for an example of a folk-music ensemble functioning in this fashion).

STRING QUARTET
The ensemble of European chamber music that idealizes the social and musical equality of the modern era—two violins, viola, and violoncello.

LISTENING GUIDE

"STEIRISCHER MIT GESTANZLN" ("DANCE FROM STYRIA, WITH STANZAS")

GO TO www.mymusiclab.com for the Automated Listening Guide CDIII • Track 1/Download Track 46

Performed by Die Tanzgeiger ("The Dance Fiddlers")

Performed by Austria's premier folk-music ensemble, "The Dance Fiddlers," this dance moves across the cultural landscape of Austria and its changing history. The dance starts in Styria, the mountainous area with Graz as its provincial capital, and it eventually ends up in modern Vienna, the cosmopolitan world of the capital on the Danube. A "Steirischer," or "Styrian," is in this case a *Ländler*, a slow rural dance in triple meter, often used for social rituals and courting. Once the waltz begins about one-third of the way through the dance, the style changes. A "Gestanzln" is a style and genre with improvisatory verses, punctuated by instrumental interludes. There is much humor in the verses, actually a kind of jousting between the singers, each one trying to show that he is cleverer than his predecessor.

The traditional is relocated in the modern world in the style of performance championed by "The Dance Fiddlers." They collect many of the songs and dances they use as sources and then transform them to bridge the cultural worlds at the center of Europe.

TIME	SECTION	MUSICAL EVENTS
0:00–0:08		The ensemble sets the key and prepares for the Ländler.
0:29–1:00	**Ländler:** Listen to the melody and see if you can hear it in triple meter (**1**, 2, 3, **1**, 2, 3).	The Ländler begins. It is a slow dance in triple meter. The form of the dance tune is (**AABB**).
1:00–1:16	**Waltz with Stanzas:** Now that you have heard the slow Ländler, listen for the increased tempo of the waltz and how the Gestanzln, or stanzas, are alternated with short interludes played by the ensemble.	Waltz begins. It is a fast dance in triple meter.
1:17–1:24		The first vocal stanza enters. Notice that it is sung as a trio (that is, three singers are harmonizing with each other).
1:25–1:32		Instrumental interlude.
1:32–1:40		Second vocal stanza enters, responding to the first.
1:40–1:47		Instrumental interlude.
1:47–1:55		Third vocal stanza.
1:55–2:02		Instrumental interlude.
2:03–2:10		Fourth vocal stanza.
2:10–2:17		Instrumental interlude.
2:17–2:25		Fifth vocal stanza, incorporating nonsense text of counting forward and backward.

2:25–2:33	Instrumental interlude.
2:33–2:40	Sixth vocal stanza, incorporating a joke about the nuclear disaster at Chernobyl.
2:41–3:07	Final instrumental section, transposed to a higher key for effect.

TAMBURITZA

String ensemble of southeastern Europe and in the diasporas of ethnic and national groups from the Balkans, with distribution of voices from low to high.

The folk-music or chamber ensemble may appear as idealized models for European society, but the complexity of European society, in which the parts do not always function as a whole, can also be symbolized by the musical ensemble. Folk-music ensembles—the **tamburitza** of southeastern Europe, for example—derive their structure in part from the soprano-alto-tenor-bass structure of choirs. European classical music ensembles became relatively fixed in this format in the late eighteenth century, and so we see that the tamburitza and the string quartet both symbolize a perception of gender roles in an otherwise egalitarian society.

German male choruses in the nineteenth century became a symbol for the power of nationalism embedded in and expressed by the *Volk*, the German people. Similarly, large choruses in socialist Eastern Europe during the second half of the twentieth century symbolized the achievement of the modern socialist state. Even though musical ensembles function in vastly different ways, their connection to the people as a collective society pervades European ideas about music. We witness a vivid portrayal of this in Mozart's opera, *Le Nozze di Figaro*, in which the peasant folk together constitute the choruses, who gather on the stage at the culmination of significant scenes to serve as the final arbitrators of the actions of peasant, specialized laborer, and noble alike. In the end, the chorus is what symbolizes the communal underpinnings of European society (see introduction for more information about this opera).

MUSICAL INSTRUMENTS

If we reflect back on our stroll through the streets of Vienna and take stock of the instruments we observed musicians playing, we might be struck both by the importance and variety of musical instruments. The pianos in the Bösendorfer showroom were displayed as if in a museum, untouchable and expensive symbols of an elite. No less untouchable was the organ in St. Stephen's, whose sounds filled every corner of the Gothic cathedral, yet failed to help us locate the organist tucked away in a loft somewhere. The instruments of the street musicians were equally symbolic of identity and social function. The distinctiveness of the Andean panpipe players comes most directly from their instruments; once considered a measure of music's universality, panpipes now serve as markers of a few musical cultures, especially those of the South American highlands (see chapter 9).

Musical institutions in Vienna also bear witness to the importance of instruments. Museum collections juxtapose the so-called "period instruments" of early music with the experimental models of more recent times, and folk-music archives assemble folk instruments. The music academies are metaphors for the learning and specialization that musical instruments demand. Musical instruments are inescapable symbols of the unity and distinctiveness of European musical life. They may tell us that a musical style or repertory is European on one hand but Austrian, Hungarian, Sicilian, or Macedonian on the other. Instruments act as a vital material representation of musical life in Europe and as such embody its history and its great diversity.

Folk Instruments

Musical instruments have long served as some of the most commonly employed criteria for classifying music. Folk instruments were constructed within the society or community where the particular musical repertory was performed. Indeed, many thought that a folk instrument was one built by its player, therefore functioning ideally for the player's needs. An instrument imported from elsewhere, even a neighboring village, did not belong to the musical life of the community in quite the same way. In the idealized folk society of Europe, an instrument is somehow the extension of the individual musician and yet a marker of the community's musical identity. It is a specific product that we should be able to trace to its maker and the particular roles it plays in a given community.

Some folk performers do make their own instruments, but today the norm is that instruments come from elsewhere and are probably the product of an unknown maker or an industrial manufacturer. The willingness of European musicians to borrow an instrument from elsewhere is by no means a modern phenomenon. Instrument types and names reveal a long history of instruments traveling both within Europe itself and across its borders. European instruments such as the lute and the guitar came originally from Islamic North Africa, and the Ottoman presence in southeastern Europe induced a particularly rich exchange with Turkey. The **saz** has long been no less Balkan than Turkish. Instruments like the bagpipe and the violin exist in countless variations in folk-music cultures throughout Europe; local communities everywhere have adapted these instruments to their own music cultures, and individual musicians have personalized them. The Hardanger fiddle of Norway, a fairly recent adaptation of the violin, is indisputably Norwegian; a Swedish *hummel* is as likely to bear witness to the individual who performs it as is the *gusle*, or bowed lap fiddle, of a Montenegrin or Serbian epic singer. The ubiquity of such instrument types notwithstanding, they show that the tendency to use instruments to express individuality and community identity has not abated in modern Europe (Listen to CD III, 2 for an example of the gusle).

Explore
the Musical Instrument Gallery on **mymusiclab.com**

SAZ
Lutelike instrument used widely in Turkish art music and spread throughout the regions of southeastern Europe, into which the Ottoman Empire extended.

LISTENING GUIDE

"TZARINA MILIČA UND DUKE VLADETA,"
BORO ROGANOVIĆ, *GUSLE* PLAYER

GO TO **www.mymusiclab.com for the Automated
Listening Guide** CDIII • Track 2/Download Track 47

Recorded by Philip V. Bohlman

The Montenegrin American *guslar*—a player of the bowed spike fiddle, called the *gusle*—performs a traditional Balkan epic song from the *Kosovo Cycle*. The songs in this cycle move between oral and written traditions, and they describe, in a series of different accounts about historical events, the struggle between the Ottoman Empire and Christians for southeastern Europe.

The style of the song is typical of an epic song, with single lines of melody unfolding one after the other. The *guslar* performs this song more or less as he has his entire life, but he also introduces elements of improvisation, especially when accompanying himself. Boro Roganović immigrated to the Chicago area in the late 1980s, and he performs primarily for cultural events in the large ethnic communities of Slavic language-speaking residents.

After a brief gusle solo, the singer begins at approximately [0:30] and then continues through a series of melodic variations until the song ends at approximately [6:28]. This is relatively short for this type of epic song, which can extend as long as necessary to tell a story.

When Instruments Tell Stories

Europeans tend to anthropomorphize instruments and regard them as music makers with human qualities. We refer to the parts of an instrumental piece as its "voices," and it is fairly common to relate these directly to human vocal ranges. Europeans, like peoples throughout the world, ascribe human qualities to instruments (think of how many instruments have "necks," that part of the human body in which the vocal cords are located) and decorate instruments with human or animal figurations. Instruments become the musician's partner in music-making.

Musical instruments in Europe often assist in telling a story, which is one of the functions that makes them human-like. Among the earliest specialists who performed secular narrative song in Europe were those who sang by accompanying themselves on an instrument. The medieval *minnesinger*, for example, recounted tales of history and great heroes, encounters with lovers and with enemies, all the while relying on the narrative assistance of the lute. The importance of the lute to the German song tradition appears in a nineteenth-century interpretation in Richard Wagner's *Die Meistersinger von Nürnberg*, in which the mastersingers must prove themselves by playing the lute according to the rigorous rules imposed on the tradition.

Whereas Wagner's vision was particularly Romantic and German, the narrative epic traditions in southeastern Europe predate medieval Europe,

"Klezmer House" in Kazimierz, the Former Jewish Quarter of Krakow, Poland. *Source:* Philip B. Bohlman

evolving from the Homeric epic traditions of ancient Greece. The epic is a narrative genre in which the poet–singer performs tales from the life of a hero or heroine. The singer's instrument, the gusle, has become so closely identified with the genre that the singer's name, guslar (player of the gusle), is derived from the instrument itself (see CD III, 2).

The instruments of classical European music also demonstrate narrative functions, often in such ways that we recognize a close relation to rural society and folk beliefs. The twentieth-century composer Igor Stravinsky used the narrative potential of the orchestra to transform the pagan ritual of *Le Sacre du Printemps* (*The Rite of Spring*) and the Shrovetide folktale of *Petrushka* into classical ballets. The narrative power of the piano, too, marks the work of many composers; for example, Robert Schumann told the tale of attending a pre-Lenten party (again Shrovetide) in his *Carnaval*. Narrativity also distinguishes the symphonic tone poems of late nineteenth-century composers and the nationalistic works of composers seeking to use the orchestra to tell the stories most characteristic of their own history.

The stories told by musical instruments often acquire sweeping symbolic power. The revival of *klezmer music* has, for example, served as a powerful reminder of the destruction of European Jewry during the Holocaust, especially in countries such as Poland and Germany, where that destruction was extreme. Traditionally, klezmer ensembles comprised a group of instrumentalists—the Hebrew words *kleh* ("vessel") and *zemer* ("song") form the contraction, klezmer—who accompanied weddings, dances, and other events where strictly sacred music would be inappropriate. In the twenty-first century, klezmer ensembles play and record regularly in the cities that lost their Jewish populations, such as Kraków, where klezmer clubs even appear in the former Jewish quarter of Kazimierz.

Musical Instruments in an Industrial Age

Although personal, communal, and human qualities continue to influence European concepts about musical instruments, modern European music would be inconceivable without technology. Technology's influence is evident in the development of new areas of musical life—for example, the dependence of rock-music instruments on mass-produced sound and dissemination. Perhaps less evident is the previous development of new instrument types during the rapid industrialization of European society from the end of the seventeenth century on, when instruments we now regard as standard—the piano, for instance—were invented and reinvented. The technology of musical instruments is also one of the primary musical exports from Europe, and we can recognize European influences on non-European musics by the adaptation of certain types of technology, such as the *harmonium* in North India and Pakistan. Moreover, technological developments have directly affected the reception of music, making it possible for larger audiences to hear a piano with a more powerful cast-iron frame or the amplified sounds of a folk-music ensemble using microphones.

No instrument symbolizes the impact of technology on European musical instruments as fully as the piano. Invented at the beginning of the eighteenth century in Italy, piano makers transformed the direct striking or plucking action of the clavichord and harpsichord into a more powerful action by employing a series of levers connected by joints. The piano's new design not only allowed a broader palette of sound colors but also made it possible for the piano to dominate the other instruments with which it was played. As the piano grew larger, so did its sound; as its machinery grew more complicated, the factories that manufactured it became more sophisticated and efficient. The technology to create pianos kept pace with the demand for an instrument that had its own solo repertory and a role in many other repertories. The piano both appeared on the stage of the largest concert hall and stood in the parlor of the bourgeois home.

A product of technology, the piano became the preferred instrument of the European "everyperson" by the mid-nineteenth century. It was an instrument that resulted from mass production and was capable of attracting mass audiences. Pianos followed Europeans as they settled elsewhere as both immigrants and colonizers. Yet the piano did not lend itself particularly well to other musics. Its technology was so highly developed that it could not be easily adapted to non-European scales. It stood apart in non-Western societies, effectively symbolizing the hegemony of European music in the colonial era.

Instruments and Musical Professionalism

Musical instruments often represent complexity, which is a musical quality highly valued in European society. Whereas both singers and instrumentalists generally practice and study to acquire their skills, playing an instrument is often regarded as less natural, less a product of pure gifts than singing. The distinction between vocal and instrumental forms of music is, in fact, universal, and in many societies, such as those of the Islamic world, instrumental music may be criticized or even prescribed because it is less human, that is, not directly tied to words. Restrictions on instrumental music are not unknown in Europe, where periodic attempts to keep instruments out of Christian religious music are among the hallmarks of conservative religious movements. When they ascended to power in 1649, forming the English Commonwealth, the Puritans inveighed against instruments in churches and ordered that organs be destroyed.

Instrumentalists therefore acquire the status of specialists and, very often, professionals. They stand out as exceptional in society because of the skills they command, and the best—that is, the most skillful—receive financial rewards for their labors. The exceptional role of instrumentalists does not always reflect public sanction; instrumentalists like the **becar** in southeastern Europe are sometimes regarded as ne'er-do-wells or troublemakers (and, not insignificantly, attractive lovers). The outsider status of the instrumentalist also empowers one to move with ease from community to community, or even to perform within several distinct societies. We have witnessed this already with Roma and Sinti musicians. Medieval minstrels, generally instrumental musicians, were also distinguished by relative mobility. In more modern times, the klezmer ensembles of European Jewish society have also been recognized as traveling performers. Increased mobility ensured the profitability of the instrumentalist's trade. We see again the European willingness to view music as a product, indeed one that a consuming society is willing to pay to hear.

BECAR
Instrumentalist and musical specialist in southeastern Europe, often distinguished by great mobility.

HISTORY AND SOCIAL STRUCTURE IN EUROPEAN MUSICAL LIFE

The Underlying Historicism of European Musical Thought

Throughout this chapter, we have seen that history is one of the primary forces unifying European concepts of music. Just as Europeans are aware of larger historical forces and moments—whether wars, religious transformations, or responses to other parts of the world—they also share a sense that a historical unity characterizes the musics of Europe. We witness such unity in phrases like "European art music" or "European folk music" (and conversely in phrases like "non-European music").

MENTALITÉ
A collective way of thinking, expressed in the cultural activities of a group or community.

BROADSIDE BALLAD
A printed version of a folk song, usually combining a well-known melody with a topical text; printed on large sheets and sold inexpensively.

At least since the Renaissance, those who have written about music have largely concerned themselves with some musics of the past and the relation of these musics to a more recent time. It is hardly surprising that we commonly refer to scholars who write about European art music as music historians.

Individuals and Collectives in the History of Music

History takes a number of distinctive forms in European concepts of the relation of music to a given community, society, or nation. Music may be a part of and serve as a voice for a people's **mentalité**. In contemporary usage, the mentalité of a people is that cultural profile existing apart from the actions of armies and political figures; instead, it forms from the everyday acts, aspirations, and belief systems of an entire society. The concept applies particularly well to an interpretation of musical life that emphasizes folk music as a body of expressive activities shared by an entire cultural group; in effect, folk music becomes the product of the group's mentalité.

We find a similar sense of collectivity in Johann Gottfried Herder's eighteenth-century model for the shared music of a people, *Volkslied*. Herder and nineteenth-century folk-music scholars steeped their concept of Volkslied in historical potential. The "everyperson" in European society, therefore, continued to contribute to music history by sharing in a musical collective. Even attempts to reformulate the concepts of folk music into "people's music" (in Marxist thought) or "group song" (a formulation associated with the German scholar Ernst Klusen) retain the basic premise that it is a collective that shapes the formation, transmission, and history of music.

Few modern scholars accept the notion that a folk song or any other form of popular music came into existence simply because of the will and collective action of the community. Instead, an individual, usually a musician with some specialized role in the musical life of the community, creates a piece of music, "composes" it, and establishes its position in a particular music history. Folk songs might begin their history in oral tradition by first being printed on a broadside and sold on the street, largely to earn profit for the composer, printer, and hawker. The **broadside ballad**, which often appeals because it captures the news of the moment, is only possible if it embodies certain aspects of the community's mentalité and relies on the community's knowledge of common melodies, yet it is the individual who composes these relations in the ballad.

The broadside composer is often anonymous and represents one end of a continuum of individuals in music history. At the other end, we find the twentieth-century recording virtuoso, whose status as a cult figure would seem to stand outside of history (fans will regard the virtuoso's interpretations as superior to those fixed or limited by historical performance practice). The history of European music has gradually shifted more emphasis toward the individual. The notion of the individual musician standing out from his or her community was virtually unknown in the Middle Ages, but it began to form in the fourteenth century, when minstrels acquired names such as "Fiddler" or

"Pfeiffer" (Piper) that help us to understand the relation between the musical specialist and the community. The designation of the individual as potentially exceptional, a musical genius, began only in the late Renaissance, but quickly became a primary impetus in European music history, and by the nineteenth century music historians were using "great composers" to mark the epochs of historical change (e.g., the "Age of Bach").

Modern Nations, Modern Histories, Modern Musics

Twice during the twentieth century, world wars radically redrew the map of Europe, creating new political entities while splitting and eliminating many old ones. The new face of Europe has had a profound effect on musical life in the continent. Just as new nations and cultural boundaries have developed, so too have new music histories emerged to interpret and, in some cases, to justify the widespread change. More than at any previous moment, the diversity of Europe's music at the beginning of the twenty-first century is a result of conscious historicism—the revitalization of a musical past in the present. On one hand, historicism interrupts the path of steady historical development by altering traditional social contexts. On the other, it collapses the differences between past and present, making it possible to combine musical styles and repertories in ways particularly appropriate to the political reality of modern Europe. Musical historicism recaptures the past in distinctly modern ways.

Just what can musical historicism capture from the past? In what ways do elements from the past effectively serve as the music of the present? There are no simple answers to these questions. Modern European musical cultures have employed historicism with quite different motivations. One of the most common motivations is nationalism. This reflexive impulse explains the urge to search for Czechness in the music of the Czech Republic. A nation of quite distinctive regional and minority cultures, the Czech Republic has nevertheless endeavored to establish the criteria that make music Czech, finding little consensus among composers or folk-music styles of the past. If Czechness in music is itself elusive, the motivation to discover a distinctive nationalism is not unique to the Czech Republic.

We find similar tendencies among the inhabitants of Southern Tyrol in Italy, who have carved out repertories of music that consist entirely of German-language songs and pre-Italian Latinate dialects, called **Ladino**, which also survive in the region today. Songbooks in the region simply do not contain songs in Italian, and the examples in German, Ladino, and English (the last usually from the American folk-song revival) reveal a clear pattern of choosing selectively from the past to build the repertory of the present. European institutions of classical music also arise because of the historicist impetus. The state or national academy of music, orchestra, or chorus has become normative throughout Europe. The new map of modern Europe has relied on the historical underpinnings of musical life to reformulate that life, to modernize it, and to link it to new historical conditions.

LADINO
The pre-Italian Latinate dialects of the southern Alps in Italy and Switzerland. Ladino is also the Romance vernacular language historically spoken by Sephardic Jews.

EUROVISION SONG CONTEST

The largest popular-song contest in the world, established in 1956 by the European Broadcasting Union and pitting national entries against each other in an annual spectacle judged by telephone voting from the entering nations.

Explore
the history of the Eurovision Song Contest on **mymusiclab.com**

EUROPEAN MUSIC AT THE BEGINNING OF THE TWENTY-FIRST CENTURY

The Eurovision Song Contest

The spectacle of European nationalism is nowhere greater than during the annual **Eurovision Song Contest**, the largest popular-music competition in the world. The national entries, reaching forty by 2005, represent some aspect of the amalgam of cultures and the mixes of the local and the global that will appeal to the ultimate jury, European citizens themselves, who vote by cell phone through their national committees.

The Eurovision Song Contest is a moment when Europe turns to popular song as a means of performing its national and global identities. On the Saturday evening each May when the Grand Prix ceremonies are broadcast by the member networks of the European Broadcasting Union, hundreds of millions of Europeans find themselves glued to their television sets to watch the national entries perform and to root for their favorite songs and national musical heroes. In many cities, crowds of fans flood the main public squares to watch the Eurovision on massive screens and to root not only for their national entries but also for the entries from nations regarded as cultural and political allies. Scandinavians vote heavily for other Scandinavians; the Balkan countries of Southeastern Europe back each other; even historical foes—the United Kingdom and Ireland, Greece and Turkey—trade votes; the former republics of the Soviet Union rarely give support to Russia.

In the world of popular music, the professional stakes for a good showing at the Eurovision are very high. The Eurovision played a signal role in launching the careers of the Swedish group Abba, the Canadian singer Céline Dion (performing and winning for Switzerland in 1988), the Israeli worldbeat star Ofra Haza, and the Celtic music phenomenon Riverdance, which was catapulted to prominence after its Eurovision intermission performance in 1993. Winning, or even doing well, in front of an international audience can mean lucrative recording contracts and a string of appearances for the European media who sponsor the Grand Prix.

All this sounds more like media hype and crass commercialism than a response to the Cold War, the reunification of Europe, and the countercurrents of old and new nationalisms. Once the different singers and groups start performing, the evidence for national identities becomes even more perplexing. European popular song at the Eurovision may not look particularly European, and it often does not sound European. In 2000 and 2001, African American styles were particularly prominent among the national entries, ranging from the blues to Motown to hip-hop. The entries from Southeastern Europe draw heavily on folk traditions, whereas former colonial nations, especially France, allow minority voices to emerge.

Ideology may be musically nationalist, for example, in countries with Muslim majorities, or internationalist. In 2006, Finland's heavy metal band,

Street musician at the 2005
Kyiv Eurovision Song Contest.
Source: Philip B. Bohlman

Lordi, won with the song, "Hard Rock Hallelujah," a throwback to a metal
style of the 1980s, which on its surface had no more to do with Finland than
Nokia telephones, Finland's internationally consumed gift to globalization.
Lordi emerged, however, from a competitive field that included the Armenian
singer André, whose entry, "Without Your Love," as the inaugural entry for
Armenia, was politically innocent on its surface, but circulated in advance on
a video that included overt references to a contested century of struggle with
Turkey. Such mixes of the national and the international have spread across
the face of the Eurovision Song Contest for a half-century, from its earliest
years after 1956, when popular song voiced a response to the Cold War, to
2006, when the national entries reached farther into the politics of the European Union and the cultural struggle between Christian Europe and Muslim
North Africa and the Middle East.

Why should this surprise us? we might ask, for other international and
hybrid popular styles also dominated previous periods during the half-century
history of the Eurovision Song Contest. Celtic influences were most palpable
in the 1990s, and before that Mediterranean song dominated, following on
the era of rock 'n' roll and French chanson. Turkey and several nations from
Southeastern Europe, wishing to draw attention to historical and musical connections to Islamic traditions, often combine Middle Eastern instrumental and
vocal improvisatory styles.

Lest we think there is conformity, we find ourselves confronted by alternative styles as the gala performance moves from group to group. The entries

Ukrainian Folk Chorus during the 2005 Kyiv Eurovision Song Contest, performing before the statue of the nineteenthcentury national poet, Taras Shevchenko. *Source:* Philip B. Bohlman

from Southeastern Europe seem unwilling to buy into the prevailing musical fashions. The entries from Bosnia-Hercegovina, Croatia, Macedonia, and Romania have something else to say about the history of Europe during the dozen years of its reunification efforts. Regional and local politics find their way into national entries, such as Norway's 1980 entry, the Saami Mattis Hætta, who, together with Sverre Kjelsberg, performed the song, "Saamiid Ædnan," which was based on a Saami yoik and included extended passages of yoiking. In 1999, Germany's Sürpriz, herself Turkish-German, sang "Journey to Jerusalem," an acknowledgment of the cultural debt to and political difficulties of Germany's so-called guest workers from Turkey, who had historically been denied German citizenship. Eurovision entries that make political statements rarely win the contest or even place particularly high, but they are able to seize one of the most visible forums in the continent at a highly charged public moment. Eurovision songs produce controversy and create new possibilities for dialogue, and in so doing, they speak powerfully and globally for Europe today.

That song—popular and folk, local and global—engages directly with the New Europe, and its contradictions could not have been more evident in the 2005 Eurovision Song Contest in Kyiv, Ukraine. Following the winter of 2004–2005, when the Orange Revolution shook Ukraine, Eurovision echoed the struggle on the streets and gave voice to the movement to align the nation with Western Europe, particularly through eventual membership in the European Union. The Eurovision winner from 2004, Ruslana, lent her voice to the Orange Revolution, going on a hunger strike, while the 2005 Ukrainian entry, Greenjolly, openly called for revolution in its hip-hop entry, "Razom Nas Bahato, Nas Nye Podolaty" ("Together We Are Many, We Cannot Be Defeated"). The images from the 2005 Kyiv Eurovision reveal the extraordinary reach of national politics. Ukrainian popular musicians took to the streets of Kyiv, with folk accordionists providing counterpoint to workers' choruses at the feet of the nineteenth-century national poet, Taras Schevchenko. Other national entries took up the banner of the revolution, such as Norway's Wig Wam, calling for a "rock 'n' roll revolution." As the contest itself was broadcast on the final evening of the contest, 30,000 gathered in Independence Square, creating a sound mix of their own.

Depending on our musical preferences and political predilections, we can understand a Eurovision song as folk, popular, or classical, typically European or cosmopolitan, socially conservative, or liberal. As a juxtaposition of all these traits, it reflects a balance, and it is the nature of that balance that eventually establishes the relation of the Eurovision song as a musical symbol for Europe

The Norwegian Entry, Wig Wam, at the 2005 Kyiv Eurovision Song Contest, waving the symbol of the Orange Revolution. *Source:* Philip B. Bohlman

Crowds gathered to watch the 2005 Eurovision Song Contest in the host city of Kyiv, Ukraine, May 21, 2005, Independence Square. *Source:* Philip B. Bohlman

in the twenty-first century. That balance—struck and forged among the conditions of history, society, politics, geography, language, style, performance, musical instruments, and repertory—assumes myriad forms while charting the path of European music history. That balance, in fact, provides the dynamic tension that makes it possible to understand the music of Europe as a whole that achieves its identity only from its diverse, composite parts.

SUMMARY

✓•⎯Study and Review on **mymusiclab.com**

European music, as we have discovered, is a complex combination of different musical styles, created by many different peoples. It is used both to highlight individual experts (virtuosos, for example) and to affirm communal bonds (as is the case with folk ensembles). Music is mobilized by various European countries as a means of defining themselves and creating a unified culture, often resulting in articulations of musical nationalism. The story of Europe's music is, moreover, closely related to its history. European folk music, for instance, is often associated with a specified cultural group or regional area—determined, that is, by the long history of social and political interaction within Europe. The mobility of Roma and klezmer musicians is a stark reminder that musical interaction across national borders has a rich and deep history in Europe.

Urbanization, beginning in the Middle Ages, introduced a wider variety of musics and musical instruments to performers and audiences. As industrialization spread throughout Europe beginning in the eighteenth century, new instruments were invented—notably the piano—that revolutionized how music was performed. How people listened to music also shifted over time, and the formal concert developed in Europe as the primary way of hearing musical performance, with set rules for both the performers and the audience.

In the contemporary moment, the Eurovision Song Contest is an annual event that, since the middle of the twentieth century, has reflected the tensions between local and international musical styles and continues to underscore the diversity in European music today. The diversity represented in the Eurovision Song Contest also illustrates one of the central ideas of this chapter—the idea that the music of Europe achieves its identity only from its diverse, composite parts.

BIBLIOGRAPHY

Europe as a Whole Bruno Nettl, *Folk and Traditional Music of the Western Continents*, 3rd ed. (Englewood Cliffs, NJ: Prentice Hall, 1990); Timothy Rice, James Porter, and Chris Goertzen, eds., *Europe*, vol. 8: *The Garland Encyclopedia of World Music* (New York: Garland, 2000).

Cultural Life in Vienna and Austria Walter Deutsch and others, eds., *Volksmusik in Österreich* (Vienna: Österreichischer Bundesverlag, 1984); Carl Schorske, *Fin-de-Siècle Vienna* (New York: Alfred A. Knopf, 1980).

Folk Music Ralph Vaughan Williams, *National Music* (New York: Oxford University Press, 1954); Walter Wiora, *European Folk Song: Common Forms in Characteristic Modification* (Cologne: Arno Volk, 1966); Philip V. Bohlman, *The Study of Folk Music in the Modern World* (Bloomington: Indiana University Press, 1988).

Music of Eastern and Southern Europe Béla Bartók, *Hungarian Folk Music*, trans. M. C. Calvacoressi (London: Oxford University Press, 1931); Béla Bartók and Albert B. Lord, *Serbo-Croatian Folk Songs* (New York: Columbia University Press, 1951); Philip V. Bohlman and Nada Petković, eds., *Balkan Epic: Song, History, Modernity* (Lanham, MD: Scarecrow Press, 2011); Timothy J. Cooley, *Making Music in the Polish Tatras: Tourists, Ethnographers, and Mountain Musicians* (Bloomington: Indiana University Press, 2005); Albert B. Lord, *The Singer of Tales* (Cambridge, MA: Harvard University Press, 1960); Bernard Lortat-Jacob, *Sardinian Chronicles* (Chicago: University of Chicago Press, 1995); Svanibor Pettan, ed., *Music, Politics, and War: Views from Croatia* (Zagreb: Institute of Ethnology and Folklore Research, 1998); Timothy Rice, *May It Fill Your Soul: Experiencing Bulgarian Music* (Chicago: University of Chicago Press, 1994); Mark Slobin, ed., *Retuning Culture: Musical Changes in Central and Eastern Europe* (Durham, NC: Duke University Press, 1996); Jane C. Sugarman, *Engendering Song: Singing and Subjectivity at Prespa Albanian Weddings* (Chicago: University of Chicago Press, 1996).

Music of Central Europe Philip V. Bohlman, *Central European Folk Music: An Annotated Bibliography of Sources in German* (New York: Garland, 1996);

Celia Applegate and Pamela Potter, eds., *Music and German National Identity* (Chicago: University of Chicago Press, 2002).

Music of Western and Northern Europe   Frances James Child, *The English and Scottish Popular Ballads*, 5 vols. (Boston: Houghton Mifflin, 1882–1898); James R. Cowdery, *The Melodic Tradition of Ireland* (Kent, OH: Kent State University Press, 1990); Chris Goertzen, *The Normal Fiddle in Norway* (Chicago: University of Chicago Press, 1997); James Porter, *The Traditional Music of Britain and Ireland: A Research and Information Guide* (New York: Garland, 1989); Cecil J. Sharp, *English Folk Song: Some Conclusions* (1st ed., 1907), 4th ed., rev. Maud Karpeles (Belmont, CA: Wadsworth, 1965).

Music of Ethnic Groups or Communities Stretching across Several Nations   Samuel G. Armistead, Joseph H. Silverman, and Israel J. Katz, *Judeo-Spanish Ballads in Oral Tradition* (Berkeley and Los Angeles: University of California Press, 1968); Philip V. Bohlman and Otto Holzapfel, eds., *The Folk Songs of Ashkenaz* (Middleton, WI: A-R Editions, 2001); Bálint Sárosi, *Gypsy Music*, trans. Fred MacNicoll (Budapest: Corvina, 1978); Mark Slobin, *Old Jewish Folk Music: The Collections and Writings of Moshe Beregovski* (Philadelphia: University of Pennsylvania Press, 1982); Martin Stokes and Philip V. Bohlman, eds., *Celtic Modern: Music at the Global Fringe* (Lanham, MD: Scarecrow Press, 2003); Barbara Rose Lange, *Holy Brotherhood: Romani Music in a Hungarian Pentecostal Church* (New York: Oxford University Press, 2002).

European Musical Genres   Rolf Wilhelm Brednich, Lutz Röhrich, and Wolfgang Suppan, eds., *Handbuch des Volksliedes*, 2 vols. (Munich: Wilhelm Fink, 1973, 1975); Richard Middleton, *Voicing the Popular: On the Subjects of Popular Music* (New York: Routledge, 2006); Leslie Shepard, *The Broadside Ballad: A Study in Origins and Meaning* (Hatboro, PA: Legacy, 1978); Lajos Vargyas, *Hungarian Ballads and the European Ballad Tradition*, 2 vols. (Budapest: Akadémiai Kiadó, 1983).

Instruments   Erich Stockmann and Ernst Emsheimer, ed., *Studia instrumentorum musicae popularis* (Stockholm: Musikhistoriska Museet, 1969–present; currently 11 vols.).

Nationalism and Music   Sidney Finkelstein, Composer and Nation: *The Folk Heritage in Music*, 2nd ed. (New York: International Publishers, 1989); Philip V. Bohlman, *Focus: Music, Nationalism, and the Making of the New Europe*, 2nd ed. (New York: Routledge, 2011).

DISCOGRAPHY
Discographical Note

Among the best surveys of national folk musics are those released on the Folkways label and rereleased on the Smithsonian label, with extensive critical notes geared toward students among others. A particularly good selection of

Eastern European traditions is to be found on the Nonesuch Explorer label. The European recordings of the "Alan Lomax Collection" have been steadily appearing since the mid-1990s on the Rounder label, each of them with notes by well-known ethnomusicologists. The Rounder Lomax collections for Italy, Romania, Spain, and Yugoslavia are fairly extensive.

European academies of science and ethnological museums often produce recordings of extraordinarily high musical and educational quality, reproducing both modern field recordings and rereleasing historical collections from the first era of recorded sound. During the 1970s and 1980s, a period of widespread folk-music revival in Europe, and during the 1990s, when the European Union's political and economic influence spread, voluminous recordings of local, regional, and national folk-music traditions have appeared on CD.

The most comprehensive discographical guide to national and ethnic popular music is Simon Broughton, Mark Ellingham, and Richard Trillo, eds., *World Music: The Rough Guide*, vol. 1: *Africa, Europe and the Middle East* (London: The Rough Guides, 1999). The *Rough Guides* also have published CDs of national and regional music in Europe, emphasizing ethnic and national styles of popular music.

Students will also wish to consider recordings of European art music and popular music, which are available in large numbers in libraries and record stores. When studying and listening to these recordings, however, the student may wish to make comparisons in new ways and to examine new issues that their mass production reveals—for example, just how are these genres marketed in different ways, or how do different nations produce the "same" music but in different ways?

Deutsche Volkslieder, 2 discs (DGG 004-157, 004-160); *Electric Muse: The Story of Folk into Rock*, 4 discs (Folk 1001); A. L. Lloyd and Ewan MacColl, *English and Scottish Popular Ballads* (Washington 715–723); *Folk Music of France* (Folkways P 414); *Folk Music of Hungary*, collected by Béla Bartók (Folkways 1000); *Folk Music of Portugal*, 2 discs (Folkways 4538); *Folk Music of Rumania*, collected by Béla Bartók (Folkways 419); *Islamic Ritual from Yugoslavia: Zikr of the Rafa'i Brotherhood* (UNESCO Collection, Philips 6586 015); *Le mystère des voix bulgares*, 3 vols. (Electra/Nonesuch 79165-2); *Liturgical Chant for Lent and Easter: Armenian Mekhitarist Community of Venice* (UNESCO Collection, Philips 6586 025); *Songs and Dances of Holland* (Folkways 3576); *Songs and Dances of Norway* (Folkways 4008); *Songs and Dances of Spain*, 5 discs, with notes by Alan Lomax (Westminster WF 12001-5); *World Collection of Recorded Music*, 6 discs, based on collections of Constantin Brăiloiu (VDE 30-425-430); *Dancing on the Edge of a Volcano: Jewish Cabaret, Popular, and Political Songs, 1900–1945* (Cedille Records CDR 90000 065); *The Rough Guide Music of the Gypsies* (The Rough Guide RGNET 1051 CD); *Unblocked: Music of Eastern Europe*, 3-CD set (Ellipsis Arts CD 3570).

Music in Latin America

THOMAS TURINO

AN ANDEAN MESTIZO FIESTA IN PAUCARTAMBO, PERU

Most of the year the rural Andean town of Paucartambo seems almost empty. Many people have migrated to the nearby city of Cuzco, the ancient capital of the Incas, or to larger cities on the Peruvian coast in search of employment and a different way of life. However, in the weeks before the festival for Paucartambo's patron saint, the Virgen del Carmen (July 15–18), the place begins to stir in preparation. All the houses are freshly whitewashed, the streets are cleaned, and people who have moved elsewhere begin returning home. The fiesta organizers visit the homes of relatives and friends who have promised financial contributions. Through generous support, the main sponsor hopes that his lavishness will make this a fiesta that people will always remember. Meanwhile, food, liquor, beer, and fireworks arrive in truck after truck—there is never enough.

The primary participants in the fiesta are **mestizos** (people of mixed Spanish and indigenous cultural heritage) from the town itself. The people of the surrounding Quechua-speaking indigenous communities are excluded from taking part, and come mainly to watch. In the weeks before the fiesta, the members of the various dance ensembles begin to rehearse for long hours on patios behind closed doors. They practice so that they may please the Virgin with their dancing and so that, this year, their group will be considered the finest. Meanwhile, the women sew the elaborate costumes and older men make the ceramic masks.

Twelve or more costumed dance ensembles perform during the fiesta, and each one tells part of the story of the town and its people. The heroes of the fiesta drama are a dance group known as the *Qhapaq Chunchos*, the "rich and powerful jungle Indians." (Paucartambo is located in a beautiful river valley on the eastern slopes of the Andes near the jungle region.) Their costume includes the feathered headdress associated with Peruvian jungle Indians and spears indicating their role as warriors. Within the fiesta drama, the Chunchos represent heroes, the

✳ **Explore**
Learning Objectives on
mymusiclab.com

✳ **Explore**
a map of Latin America on
mymusiclab.com

MESTIZO

A relative term referring to people and a social identity involving the blending of European and Amerindian beliefs and cultural practices. Although in the past used as a racial category, it now more accurately denotes the variable incorporation of Iberian (Spanish and Portuguese) and indigenous cultural heritages.

Chuncho Dancers, Paucartambo, Peru. *Source:* Thomas Turino

"home team." Throughout the fiesta the Chuncho king and his soldiers express the nobility of the town through dignified behavior and disciplined martial dance. The Chunchos open the festivities by dancing for the Virgin on the church steps. During the processions of the statue of the Virgin, the Chunchos dance around her litter serving as an honor guard.

The other main protagonists of the fiesta drama are the *Qollas*, representing uncivilized outsiders, the traders of the high plateau of southern Peru. These mestizo dancers act out their part as "savages from the *puna*" (places of extremely high altitude) in various ways. They lead their llama (loaded with the goods that actual Qolla traders would carry) in and out of stores, upsetting things as they go. They whip each other in one part of their dance; and they conduct themselves in an unruly manner throughout the fiesta days. Their dramatic persona thus contrasts fundamentally with the reserved, disciplined, dignified behavior of their rivals, the Chunchos.

According to one legend told in Paucartambo, the statue of the Virgen del Carmen originally belonged to the Qollas of Puno, Peru, but through battle the Chunchos won her and brought her to Paucartambo, where she remained as the provider of prosperity, health, and all good things. In another version, I was told that the Virgin originally belonged to Paucartambo. On one occasion, the Qollas tried to steal her (the statue) away, but were attacked by the Chunchos, who defended her and, by winning the battle, kept her safe in Paucartambo. As a reminder of these and other legends surrounding the Chunchos, the Qollas, and their special relationship to the Virgin, a dramatic mock battle is fought during the fiesta, and each year the Chunchos win.

Qolla Dancers, Paucartambo, Peru. *Source:* Thomas Turino

The *Saqras* (or "devils," in the native Quechua language) are also central to the meaning of the fiesta, because they serve as foils to the holy saint. The Saqras' costumes include clothing representing the colonial Spanish, blonde wigs alluding to Europeans, and ceramic animal or monster masks. Their choreography is reminiscent of a genteel European **contra dance**, and this fortifies the satiric portrayal of Europeans. These devil dancers combine imagery that expresses Peruvian attitudes about the evil that comes from beyond this world, as well as the evil that arrived in ships from beyond the Andean world beginning in the 1500s. During the two fiesta processions, the statue of the Virgin is carried through the streets accompanied by dancers, music, and the people of the town. At these times, the Saqra dancers climb onto the red-tiled roofs and, as the saint passes, shield their eyes from her brightness and slowly disappear behind the rooftops. Both in the drama and according to local beliefs, the Virgin blesses each house, ridding it of evil, as she passes during the processions.

Most of the other dance groups in the fiesta also represent and parody outsiders. The *Doctores*, for example, represent lawyers and government officials who are known for their exploitation of rural Peruvians. As the Doctores move through the streets, they frequently "capture" people of the local indigenous communities who have come to town to watch the fiesta. Once the dancers have encircled an unfortunate man, they begin beating him with the heavy law books that they carry as a part of their costume while shouting insults and abuses. The image of the law book used as a weapon against common people is enacted by making it a concrete weapon—much to the hilarity of onlookers lucky enough not to have been caught.

CONTRA DANCE
A type of partnered line dance in which couples arrange themselves in two facing lines.

Saqra (Devil) Dancers,
Paucartambo, Peru.
Source: Thomas Turino

The cast also includes the *Qhapaq Negros*, a dance ensemble representing black slaves brought during the colonial era; the Chilenos, expressing
the enmity toward the devastating Chilean army of the War of the Pacific
(1879–1884); the *Chuk'chus*, or malaria carriers from the jungle; the *Majeños*,
exploitative liquor traders from the city of Arequipa; and the *Maqtas*, or clowns,
who serve as the policemen during the fiesta, among other dance ensembles.
As a wonderful addition, some dancers have lately begun to dress up as young
hippie tourists. They wear backpacks and floppy hats and stick toy cameras
into people's faces as they move through the streets, thereby commenting on
the most recent invasion of outsiders and demonstrating the ongoing creativity
of these fiesta dancers.

Each dance group is accompanied by its own band and a series of distinctive pieces that, through association over the years, have become as important
to the characters presented by the groups as their costumes, choreography, and
dramatic behavior. Some of the music is particularly pictorial, such as the stag-
gering melody played by a brass band to fit the Majeño liquor traders' drunken
dance. The Chunchos' music, played on flutes and drums, is reminiscent of
nearby lowland Indian styles and thus, like the dancers' feathered headdresses,
adds to their portrayal of jungle Indians. Although the dancers are mestizos
from the town of Paurcartambo, this dance group hires indigenous musicians
to accompany them.

Much of the music in the fiesta is based on major local genres, such as the
mestizo wayno, or is more European in form like the contra dance music used
by the Saqras and other groups. The fiesta includes indigenous-styled flute
and drum bands, like the one that accompanies the Chunchos; brass bands;

and a type of local dance band (**orquesta tipica**) that combines indigenous, end-notched flutes (called *kenas*) with European instruments such as violins, harp, and accordion. These orquestas are thus a microcosm of the European-indigenous mix that characterizes the fiesta and a mestizo cultural orientation more generally. Unlike the dancers, who are mestizos from Paucartambo, the bands are hired by the dance groups and usually comprise semiprofessional musicians from elsewhere (Listen to CD III, 3 for an example of indigenous-styled flute and drum bands).

Upon entering the town of Paucartambo during the fiesta days, one is struck by the apparent chaos and intensity of multiple bands playing simultaneously while strange costumed characters roam the streets as if they had taken over the town. The plaza is filled to capacity with drunks, dancers, fighters, lovers, and spectators. Beneath the surface, many stories are being told, woven together, by the dance groups and their musicians, who are essential to the meaning and the very existence of the festival. The townspeople say, "Paucartambinos were born to dance," and for four days a year they do little else—in honor of their beloved saint and simply for the joy of it. For four days a year, the plaza and cobblestone streets are transformed into a stage for a music drama that turns the normal order of daily life upside down, but that at the same time expresses some of the most important things that Paucartambinos have to say about themselves. These things are too old or too complicated or too deep to say directly with words, and so they dance.

SOCIOCULTURAL HERITAGES AND HISTORICAL BACKGROUND

Within the Latin American region are many radically different lowland and highland Native American societies. There are African American cultural enclaves where African beliefs, practices, and styles are primary models for social and artistic life. There are also social groups, especially in major cities, predominantly characterized by European and cosmopolitan social and cultural style. The worldview, lifestyle, and artistic practices of a lowland Amazonian Indian in Brazil may bear little or no relation to those of a member of the cosmopolitan elite in Rio de Janeiro, or to those of the members of an Afro-Brazilian religious **candomblé** cult house in Bahía, northeastern Brazil. This diversity, even within a single country, makes it difficult to talk about Latin America as a single unified cultural or musical area.

At the same time, the common historical experiences of Iberian (Spanish and Portuguese) colonialism since the sixteenth century, the formation of contemporary nation–states in the nineteenth century, and North American economic and cultural domination in the twentieth have resulted in certain widely diffused cultural and musical features. Iberian influence is the oldest and most profound common denominator in Latin America. This is exemplified by the wide diffusion of the Spanish language (Portuguese in Brazil), Catholicism, and a number of musical characteristics. Iberian cultural elements, however,

ORQUESTA TIPICA
A mixed ensemble of European instruments and indigenous Andean flutes.

CANDOMBLÉ
An Afro-Brazilian religion heavily involving West African religious beliefs and musical practices.

LISTENING GUIDE

TRADITIONAL DANCE, CHUNCHOS OF PAUCARTAMBO

GO TO **www.mymusiclab.com for the Automated Listening Guide** CDIII • Track 3/Download Track 48

Two wooden transverse flutes, snare/bass drums
Recorded by T. Turino

This dance tune is played by two flutes in a loose heterophonic texture. That is, each flautist simultaneously plays variations of the same melody, rather than performing in strict unison, to produce the richer sound that indigenous Andeans prefer. The melody consists of two asymmetrical parts: a short Part **A** (8+4 beats), and a slightly longer Part **B** (8+8 beats).

If we think of this whole melody as having a range of a bit more than an octave, then Part **A** generally involves pitches in the higher half of that octave, whereas Part **B** mainly explores pitches in the lower half of the octave. Part **A** and Part **B** of the melody also include a shared melodic phrase. The melody can be represented somewhat schematically, as follows:

	PART A		**PART B**			
Upper half of octave:	**A1**					
Lower half of octave:		**A2**	**B1**	**B2(= A2)**	**B1**	**B2(= A2)**
Length in Beats:	8	4	4	4	4	4

The drums, for their part, repeat a simple rhythmic accompaniment throughout the performance.

TIME	SECTION	MUSICAL EVENTS
0:00–0:04	Part **A**: Listen for the way this melodic part initially explores the upper half of the octave. Also notice the descending melodic gesture that completes this part and will reappear in Part **B**.	The flutes and drums initiate the dance tune and perform the first melodic gesture (eight beats) of Part **A**—exploring the upper half of the octave. (If you're having trouble counting the beats, listen for the bass drums. They are striking the drums on the beat fairly consistently [though sometimes they play two notes per beat]. With a little practice you'll hear the beat clearly.)
0:04–0:06		The flutes then complete Part **A** by performing a second, descending melodic gesture (four beats), this one exploring the lower half of the octave.
0:06–0:08	Part **B**: Listen to how this section is created from the combination and repetition of two, short melodic gestures. Listen also for the return of the second gesture introduced in Part **A**.	The first melodic gesture of Part **B** (four beats) explores the lower half of the octave.
0:08–0:10		The second melodic gesture from Part **A** is reintroduced here (four beats).

0:10–0:14		The first and second melodic gestures are repeated, completing Part **B**.
0:15–0:20	Parts **A** and **B**: Listen to the whole melody and see if you can hear and feel the asymmetrical parts against each other. Part **A** consists of 12 beats, whereas Part **B** is fully 16 beats long.	Part **A** (twelve beats).
0:21–0:28		Part **B** (sixteen beats).
0:29–0:34	Continued alternation between Parts **A** and **B**	Part **A** (twelve beats).
0:35–0:42		Part **B** (sixteen beats).
0:43–0:48		Part **A** (twelve beats).
0:48–1:00		Part **B** extended here (twenty-four beats).
1:01–1:06		Part **A** (twelve beats).
1:06–1:15		Part **B** (sixteen beats).
1:15–1:21		Part **A** (twelve beats).
1:21–1:28		Part **B** (sixteen beats).
1:29–1:40	Conclusion	The conclusion consists of the first melodic gesture of Part **A**, after which the performance comes to a close.

have been combined with regionally specific indigenous lifeways to form local mestizo cultures in some regions and with African heritages to form African American cultural enclaves in others. The mestizo fiesta in Paucartambo is one example of the result.

Various indigenous groups of the Amazon and other lowland forest areas have maintained the greatest distance from European and North American lifeways. Contact with missionaries, white settlers, and capitalists, however, has had a long and in many cases disastrous effect on these peoples, on the rain forests, and thus on the planet as a whole. The major pre-Columbian states of the Aztecs and Mayas were located in Mesoamerica and the Incas in the Andes. The large native populations in these regions supplied much of the necessary labor for the Spanish colonizers. In these areas, highland Amerindian cultural styles, values, and practices remain vibrant in some communities or have combined with Iberian elements to form particularly distinctive examples of Latin American mestizo musical styles. African influences remain the strongest and have fused most prominently with the Iberian in the Caribbean and along the coasts of Venezuela, Colombia, Ecuador, the Guiana region, and northeastern Brazil, where slave labor supported the plantation economy.

Other Latin American countries, such as Argentina and Chile, are characterized by the predominance of European heritage and cosmopolitan cultural style, as are the middle-class and elite populations in most major Latin American cities. Because of intense rural-to-urban migration throughout the twentieth century, however, the capitals of Latin American countries have typically become heterogeneous social and musical microcosms of their countries as a whole.

Given this social diversity, it is best to study Latin American music through a consideration of the different types of cultural groups in specific locations—with the understanding that it is the Native American, mestizo, and African American cultures that have generally produced the most unique Latin American musical styles and practices. We will begin with some widespread characteristics of Latin American music that largely pertain to mestizo music-making.

MESTIZO MUSICAL VALUES AND MUSICAL STYLE

Devil Dancers in Michoacan, Mexico. *Source:* Thomas Turino

General Features of Mestizo Music

The term *mestizo* is a relative concept that indicates a blending of European with local Native American cultural heritages and worldviews; in some cases African elements may be included as well (e.g., the marimba in Central America). As we shall see, cultural distinctions between indigenous and mestizo social groups are often a matter of degree rather than kind, as well as a matter of how local peoples define their own social identities.

General features of mestizo musical life include costumed dances similar to those described for the Paucartambo festival. During the colonial period, missionaries used music and costumed dances to attract indigenous peoples to Christianity. Costumed dances have been performed in Catholic festivals from Mexico to Chile since that time. Characters brought to life through dance—old men; soldiers; devils, monsters, and other supernatural beings; figures from Biblical stories; animals; Spaniards; Africans—are widely portrayed in mestizo festival dance dramas. Nonetheless, the music used to accompany the dances and the stories told through them varies widely from one country, region, and even community to another. Moreover, a region's repertoire of dances changes over time, as we saw with the recent addition of "hippie-tourist" dancers in Paucartambo.

In the colonial era, missionaries taught European stringed instruments, especially an old type of European diatonic harp and violin. Along with harps and violins, guitars and mandolin-type instruments, such as the *bandúrria*, are central to music-making among both indigenous and mestizo musicians in many areas. As far as we know, stringed instruments did not exist in pre-Columbian Central and South American societies, but once European models for these instruments were available, they spurred tremendous creativity. The centuries following the colonial conquest gave rise to a dazzling array of local variations of stringed instruments, especially the guitar; Latin America has more unique variants of the guitar than any other region on earth.

Based on the military band tradition, brass bands became part of mestizo town and village festivals throughout Latin America beginning in the nineteenth century. Town and village bands play local dance music and song genres as well as more cosmopolitan religious, nationalistic, and popular music. In some places, band instruments (e.g., trumpets, saxophones, clarinets, trombones) are found in novel combinations with local indigenous flutes and percussion instruments; harps, violins, and guitars; and marimbas. In the twentieth century, diatonic button accordions as well as piano accordions have come to be widely used in many local mestizo ensembles and urban bands. More recently diffused from North America, electric guitars, electric keyboards, and synthesizers have attracted Latin American musicians and have been incorporated into, in some cases, very distinctive local styles.

European scales and harmony were widely taught by missionaries throughout Latin America, and they became commonly incorporated within local mestizo musics. The seven-note (do-re-mi) scale, minor

Latin American diatonic harp played by a street musician in Cuzco, Peru. *Source:* Thomas Turino

Indigenous Quechua bandúrria players accompanying a Carnival Dance in Canchis, Cuzco, Peru. *Source:* Thomas Turino

COPLA
An Iberian-derived verse form with four octosyllabic lines per stanza.

SESQUIALTERA
The combination or juxtaposition of duple and triple rhythmic patterns, both simultaneously in different instrumental parts, or sequentially in the same part; *hemiola*.

scales, and other older European scales are commonly used, as are European-based chord progressions. An especially common trait in mestizo instrumental performance and singing is the use of parallel thirds (e.g., the interval from do to mi) or sixths (do to la). Strophic form (the music stays the same while the lyrics change from stanza to stanza) is a common characteristic of mestizo music. Iberian verse types such as the **copla** (a four octosyllabic-line stanza) are widespread; six-line stanzas and many other varieties are also often found.

A common form of rhythmic–metric organization in mestizo music results from the combination of duple and triple rhythms—as if musicians were playing in both 3/4 (waltz time) and 6/8 (jig-time) meters within the same piece. Known as **sesquialtera** (or *hemiola*), duple and triple rhythmic patterns can be juxtaposed sequentially by the same instrument or are played simultaneously by different instruments within an ensemble. Thus, a bass instrument might emphasize a triple (3/4) feeling against the duple feeling played by a guitarist, with the maraca player moving back and forth between duple and triple patterns. The tension that results from juxtaposing duple and triple rhythms creates a wonderful excitement in the music. In addition to sesquialtera rhythmic organization, local variants of the waltz in 3/4 time are widespread as are variants of the European polka, marches, and other genres in 2/4 and 4/4 time.

Return to Paucartambo

The Fiesta of the Virgen del Carmen in Paucartambo clearly illustrates the nature of mestizo culture. At the most concrete level, the townspeople define who and what is mestizo by excluding the active participation of people from nearby indigenous Quechua communities. (Restricted participation distinguishes mestizo and indigenous status, rather than residence, because mestizos who have moved elsewhere can still return to dance in the fiesta.) In other ways the event reflects the complex combinations of indigenous and European heritages and worldviews that are the hallmark of mestizo culture. In regard to religious meaning, for example, the festival celebrates the Catholic saint, but for many people in the town her significance is fused with that of Pachamama (Earthmother, provider of life), an indigenous divinity. The Catholic festival also combines elements of indigenous harvest rituals with local mestizo merchants' more immediate desires to attract people to their stores. Nowhere is the blending of cultural heritages and values more evident than in the bands that perform music for the event.

Three types of ensemble are heard. Several brass bands are hired—for the Majeños dancers, the processions, and sometimes for other dance groups. Because of their volume and the expense of hiring brass bands, they are the most prestigious type of ensemble. The Chunchos and several other groups use side-blown flute and drum ensembles (CD III, 3); the combination of flutes (of many different types) with drums is a tradition that hails from pre-Columbian times in the Andes, Mexico, and other regions of Latin America.

The major ensemble type used to provide mestizo dance music in Paucartambo, however, combines European and pre-Hispanic Andean instruments within the same band. These groups, known simply as orquestas tipicas (typical orchestras), feature a large diatonic harp, violins, accordion, and sometimes mandolin. Indigenous vertical end-notched flutes known as *kenas*, however, are also included, as are drums. Along with panpipes and trumpets, kenas were one of the main wind instruments played in the Andes before the Spanish arrived (Listen to CD III, 4 for an example of the *orquesta tipica* sound).

Other music heard during the fiesta is representative of the major mestizo genres of Peru: the wayno, the **marinera**, the **yaraví**, marches, and religious hymns. Not tied to specific contexts, the first three popular genres are performed in all types of social gatherings and private music-making occasions ranging from serenades and family birthday parties to drinking bouts with friends and theater stage performances.

The **wayno (or huayno)**, the most important Peruvian mestizo genre, is best recognized by its rhythm, which varies between a ♫♫ figure and an eighth-note triplet feel within a 2/4 or 4/4 meter (sometimes three-beat measures occur at the end of phrases). The mestizo wayno is a social couple's dance involving fast foot tapping, subtle flirtatious movements, and sometimes the use of a handkerchief waved in the hand; in these general traits it resembles many other mestizo social dances of Latin America. Like much Latin American mestizo music, the wayno is strophic with usually two, three, or four text lines within short repeated melodic sections (e.g., **AABB, ABAB)**. Texts on a variety of joking, romantic, political, or topical themes are, like the Qollas' songs, in Spanish, Quechua, or a combination of the two. My friend and teacher Julio Benavente, a mestizo musician from Cuzco, Peru, once told me that when he really wanted to speak his mind and heart through a song, he would compose a wayno because it can encompass any topic and is a genre of profound feeling. The song texts frequently use nature imagery and in this, the use of Quechua, and the rhythm, the wayno is closest to indigenous roots of all the major Peruvian mestizo genres (Listen to CD III, 5 for an example of wayno).

The marinera is also a couples "handkerchief" dance. It is typically set in the European major scale with European tonal harmony and is characterized by sesquialtera (duple-triple hemiola) rhythm in moderate tempo. The form is typically **AABBCC**, and this is repeated twice with a short break in between as "La Primera" (first) and "La Segunda" (second) parts. The song texts are almost always on light romantic themes, sung in Spanish. In many social situations, such as at a private evening party at the fiesta sponsor's house in Paucartambo, marineras are coupled with a faster wayno to animate the dancers.

Unlike the marinera and wayno, the yaraví is not danced; rather, it is used to serenade a lover, for a serious moment at social gatherings, or to express

MARINERA
Mestizo song-dance genre of Peru in sesquialtera rhythm.

YARAVÍ
A slow, sad, lyrical mestizo song genre from Peru.

WAYNO, OR HUAYNO
The most widespread Andean mestizo song-dance genre in Peru, also performed by some indigenous musicians. The song texts are strophic, and the tunes comprise short sections in forms such as **AABB**. Waynos are in duple meter with a rhythmic feel varying between an eighth-and-two-sixteenth-note figure and an eighth-note triplet.

LISTENING GUIDE

**TRADITIONAL DANCE AND SONG:
"QOLLAS DESPEDIDA"**

**GO TO www.mymusiclab.com for the Automated
Listening Guide** CDIII • Track 4/Download Track 49

Qollas of Paucartambo: Two metal kenas, (flutes), violin, mandolin, harp, accordion, and drum
Recorded by T. Turino

This syncopated melody is carried by the violins, kenas, mandolin, and accordion, producing a densely blended timbral quality. After the upward leap in the opening phrase, the melody settles into a descending pattern (moving generally from higher to lower pitches). Descending melodies of this sort are a feature common in both mestizo and indigenous Andean music. The song is strophic, with six lines per stanza and is structured around three short, repeated melodic Sections in **AA BB B'B'** form. The **A** and **B** Sections each comprise two short melodic phrases (**A = a, b; B = c, d**), each with its own text. The two **B'** Sections consist of the single text lines "Ay Señorallay" (sung to melodic phrase **"d"**) and "Ay Ñuest'allay" (also sung to melodic phrase **"d"**), and serve as a repeated melodic-text refrain at the end of each stanza (**B' = d**). In this performance, the dancers sing as a unison chorus and their vocal rendition of the entire (**AA BB B'B'**) form is alternated with instrumental renditions of the melody. Songs sung to the Virgin by the Qollas and other dance groups are performed in Spanish, Quechua (the indigenous language), or, as in this performance, in both languages, clearly illustrating the complex blending of European and indigenous cultures that defines Andean mestizo identity generally.

TIME	SECTION	MUSICAL EVENTS
0:00–0:04	**Instrumental performance of the melody:** Listen for the way this melody is structured into a short (17 seconds), **AA BB B'B'** form. Listen also for the descending melody in all but the opening gesture of **"A."**	A
0:05–0:09		A repeated.
0:09–0:11		B
0:11–0:13		B repeated.
0:14–0:15		B' (notice that it consists of melodic phrase **"d".**)
0:15–0:17		B' repeated.
0:17–0:20	**Sung performance of the text/melody:** The **A** and **B** sections are sung in Quechua, but the refrain (**B'**) is performed in Spanish.	A (Quechua).
0:20–0:24		A repeated (Quechua).
0:24–0:26		B (Quechua).

0:27–0:29	**B** repeated (Quechua)	
0:29–0:32	**B'** and **B'** repeat (Spanish)	
	(d) *Ah, Señorallay*	(Oh my Lady)
	(d) *Ay Ñust'allay*	(Oh my princess)
	Both of the lines of text in **B'** are referring to the Virgin.	
	AA BB B'B'	
0:32–0:47	**Instrumental performance of the melody:** Listen for the richly heterophony texture and the densely blended timbral quality produced by the ensemble.	
0:48–0:51	**Sung performance of the text and melody:** This time the entire text is sung in Spanish.	**A**
	(a) *Adiós Adiós*	(Goodbye, goodbye)
	(b) *Compañeros míos*	(Companions of mine)
0:52–0:55	**A** repeated	
0:56–0:58	**B**	
	(c) *Hasta el año*	(Until the year)
	(d) *Del tres mil*	(Until the year 3000)
0:59–1:01	**B** repeated	
1:01–1:04	**B'** and **B'** repeat	
	(d) *Ah, Señorallay*	(Oh my Lady)
	(d) *Ay Ñust'allay*	(Oh my princess)
1:04–1:20	**Sung performance of the text/melody:** The vocal chorus repeats the stanza they just performed.	Same as previous stanza
1:21–1:44	**Instrumental performance of the melody:** In this final repetition of the **AABBB'B'** melody, listen for the richly heterophony texture and the densely blended timbral quality produced by the ensemble.	**AA BB B'B'**

deep feelings when one is alone. It is a slow lyrical song, usually on sad themes of unrequited love, leaving family or home, or the absence of loved ones; yaravís are almost always sung in Spanish. The genre features the sesquialtera combination of 3/4 and 6/8 meters, but because of its slow tempo, the sesquialtera does not create the same excitement as when used in faster genres such as the marinera, the Venezuelan *joropo*, and the Mexican **son**. Musically and historically, the Peruvian marinera is closely related to the Chilean and Bolivian

SON

Mexico's most important song-dance genre, a strophic song usually on romantic themes and in many regions characterized by sesquialtera rhythm.

LISTENING GUIDE

POPULAR WAYNO (HUAYNO) MUSIC: "QUISIERA OLVIDARTE"

GO TO www.mymusiclab.com for the Automated Listening Guide CDIII • Track 5/Download Track 50

Performed by La Pastorita Huaracina (Maria Alvarado)

This classic recording was a hit record in Peru and is representative of the commercial wayno music that gained tremendous popularity in the 1950s and 1960s. Maria Alvarado, a long-time resident of Lima, is accompanied by a string band in the style of her native highland department of Ancash. The group comprises several guitars, mandolins, violins, and accordions. This is a strophic song in **AA BB'** form, with an animated closing section known as **fuga** (labeled Section **C**, melodic phrases **e** and **f**). As in the Qollas' song (CDIII, 4), each section comprises two short phrases (**A = a, b; B = c, d; B' = c, d'**) and each phrase features its own text line. The length of these phrases is also important to note. The **A** Section contains two asymmetrical phrases (4+6) whereas the **B** section includes two symmetrical phrases (4+4). Section **B'** is, once again asymmetrical (4+6). The ensemble adds a three-beat extension to several of the phrases. The phrase structure of verse one can be sketched as follows:

Section:	A			A			B		B'		
Phrase:	a	b	Ext.	a	b	Ext.	c	d	c	d'	Ext.
Beats:	4	6	3	4	6	3	4	4	4	6	3

Once the performance reaches the fuga, the length of phrases changes yet again. This time the predominant length is three beats. The fuga unfolds as follows:

Section:	C		C'	
Phrase:	e	f	e	f'
Beats:	3	3	3	4

Note the quick, high vocal ornaments (e.g., on the words "*he* podido" and "mald*i*to" so characteristic of highland women singers. Note also the humorous insults hurled at her lover in the final lines of the fuga.

TIME	SECTION	MUSICAL EVENTS
0:00–0:08	**Instrumental introduction**	The performance is initiated by guitar.
0:09–0:15		The ensemble joins the guitar in preparation for the first verse.
0:16–0:23	**Verse 1:** Listen for the overarching structure **(AA BB').** Listen also for the way the **"b"** and **"d'"** phrases are extended by the ensemble.	**A (a)** *Quisiera olvidarte* (I would like to forget you). **(b)** *Pero no he podido* (but I can't)
0:24–0:31		**A** repeated.

0:31–0:35		**B (c)** *Este amor maldito*	(This wicked love)
		(d) *Rendida me tiene*	(has conquered me)
0:36–0:43		**B'** (lyrics repeated).	
0:44–1:11	**Instrumental interlude:** Listen for a repeat of the entire melody, including the extensions at the end of phrases **"b"** and **"d."**	**AA BB'** Notice the words, clapping, and vocal sounds of animation included here. This is how it would be done to inspire dancers.	
1:12–1:20	**Verse 2:** This time, see if you can hear the way the **"b"** and **"d'"** phrases are extended by the ensemble.	**A (a)** *Quisiera morirme*	(I would like to die)
		(b) *Para no olvidarte*	(rather than forget you)
1:20–1:27		**A** repeated.	
1:27–1:32		**B (c)** *Luego sepultarme*	(then bury myself)
		(d) *Dentro de tu pecho*	(in your chest)
1:32–1:39		**B'** (lyrics repeated).	
1:40–1:43	**Fuga section begins:** Listen for the shift to three-beat phrases and for the new melodic content.	**C (e)** *Anda vete cholo*	(Go away boy)
		(f) *Ya no te quiero mas*	(I don't love you anymore)
1:43–1:47		**C' (e)** *Por más que te quiero*	(For me to love you)
		(f) *Te haces de rogar*	(you will have to beg)
1:47–1:51		**C** repeated.	
1:51–1:54		**C'** repeated.	
1:55–2:10	**Instrumental interlude:** Listen for a performance and repeat of the entire fuga melody.	**CC' CC'** (repeated). Notice the words, clapping, and vocal sounds of animation included here. This is how it would be done to inspire dancers.	
2:10–2:13	**Fuga section with new lyrics**	**C (e)** *Anda vete cholo*	(Go away boy)
		(f) *Ya no te quiero mas*	(I don't love you anymore)
2:13–2:18		**C' (e)** *Por más que te quiero*	(For me to love you)
		(f') *Te haces de rogar*	(you will have to beg)
2:18–2:21		**C (e)** *Anda vete sucio*	(Go away dirty boy)
		(f) *Ya no te quiero mas*	(I don't want you anymore)
2:21–2:33		**C' (e)** *Hasta que te bañes*	(Until you take a bath)
		(f) *Ya no te vuelvo a querer*	(I couldn't return to loving you)

FUGA
A term used throughout Peru to indicate an animated concluding section to a dance piece.

JAROCHO ENSEMBLE
Musical group from the rural, southern coastal region of Veracruz state. It includes a large diatonic harp, a four-string guitar (requinto), and one or more jaranas (a small guitar with eight strings).

HUASTECA REGION
A Mexican region including northern Veracruz State and Tamaulipas, and the musical style from that region.

MARIACHI
Ensemble type originally from Jalisco, Mexico, consisting of two or more violins, vihuela, guitarrón, two trumpets, and various guitars.

CONJUNTO NORTEÑOS
Popular dance bands originally associated with northern Mexico and southern Texas, featuring three-row button accordion, bajo sexto (12-string guitar), bass, and drums.

cueca and the Argentine *zamba*; the *triste* in Bolivia and Argentina is kin to the Peruvian yaraví.

Mestizo Music in Veracruz, Mexico

Throughout Latin America regionalism is extremely important for understanding musical styles as well as the ways people conceptualize their own identities. In Mexico, mestizo musical styles are strongly identified with their regions of origin, yet because of the mass media and tourism, many of the most important regional musics can be heard presently in any major city of the country, along with the most popular international Caribbean, Latin American, and North American styles. A visit to the city of Veracruz will introduce us to the vast array of mestizo musics of Mexico.

Like other Mexican cities, Veracruz has several areas where outdoor cafes line the street or plaza. These social centers attract a host of full-time professional strolling musicians who perform different Mexican regional styles at patrons' tables for a fee. At other restaurants, loudspeakers blare international popular music, such as old recordings of Cuban dance music, contemporary salsa, and other Caribbean styles. As a seaport on the gulf coast, Veracruz has long-standing musical ties with the Caribbean, particularly Cuba, which has produced some of the most successful, widely diffused popular music in the world. During a single night in the cafes of Veracruz, I heard in addition to this recorded music, local **jarocho ensembles**, a **huasteco** trio from the northern gulf coast region, several **mariachi** bands associated with the state of Jalisco, a *marimba* group from southern Mexico, and several norteño accordion groups (**conjunto norteños**).

The local mestizo jarocho ensemble, associated with the rural southern coastal region of Veracruz state, consists of a large diatonic harp with between 32 and 36 strings, a *requinto* (a small four-string guitar), and one or more *jaranas* (a small guitar type with eight strings in five courses) for the fast, rhythmic, strummed chordal accompaniment. These groups specialize in a regional variant of Mexico's most important mestizo song–dance genre: the *son*. The famous 1950s rock 'n' roll song by Richie Valens, "La Bamba," is, in fact, a son jarocho that has been played in Veracruz since at least the turn of the nineteenth century.

Sones in the jarocho and other Mexican regions are typically strophic songs. Sung verses are alternated with instrumental interludes, which in some regions are variations or improvisations on the sung melody or a set instrumental melody. Individual musicians also have their own repertoire of instrumental "riffs" (melodic formulas) that they can plug into a given performance. Sones in most regions are played with duple and triple rhythmic patterns juxtaposed within a quick 6/8 (or in some regions 12/8) metric frame (sesquialtera). There are sones in both major and minor modes, and basic European chord progressions, for example, the use of I, IV, and V chords played in repetitive patterns, are common.

The song texts are frequently about women and romantic love, but may also be playful, joking songs, expressions of regional pride, or simply about music and dance occasions. A stanza from "La Bamba" includes a typical type of word play:

> *En mi casa me dicen*
> (In my house they call me)
> *En mi casa me dicen el inocente*
> (In my house they call me the innocent one)
> *Porque tango muchachas (×2)*
> (Because I have girls)
> *Entre quince y viente*
> (Between fifteen and twenty)
> *Y arriba arriba,*
> (and upward and upward)
> *Y arriba arriba, arriba-ré*
> *Yo no soy marinero (×2)*
> (I'm not a sailor)
> *Por tí seré, por tí seré*
> (For you I'll be, for you I'll be).

The texts of sones are often set in four- or six-line stanzas, although there is flexibility such that longer stanzas (as in "La Bamba") are sung, and verses of unequal length may even be included in the same song. Some texts are fixed, but frequently performers have a wide repertory of different stanzas that they can choose from and order at will. New stanzas may also be improvised so that no two performances of a son will be alike; this is certainly true for the classic son jarocho, "La Bamba." Unlike the bilingual mestizos of Paucartambo, Peru—who may sing songs in both Spanish and the indigenous language, Quechua—mestizo sones in Mexico are typically sung only in Spanish. As this example shows, Native American elements are less pronounced in Mexican mestizo culture than in mestizo culture in southern Peru and Bolivia. The stronger European orientation of Mexican mestizo culture is the more typical case for mestizos in Latin America generally.

After the jarocho ensemble moved away from my cafe table in Veracruz, I was treated to the music of a **huasteca ensemble**, one of the most virtuosic styles Mexico has to offer. Typically, these professional strolling musicians would be heard at cafes, restaurants, parties, and festivals in their own native huasteca region of northern Veracruz and the state of Tamaulipas. Specializing in sones huastecos, the trios consist of violin as the lead instrument accompanied by two local guitar variants: the *huapanguera* (larger than a guitar with eight strings in five courses) and the smaller five-stringed jarana. These instruments are strummed, ambiguously mixing duple and triple (sesquialtera) rhythms within 6/8 meter (Listen to CD III, 6 for an example of a son huasteco).

Mariachi groups, Mexico's most famous type of ensemble, are also heard in the cafes and on the streets of Veracruz as well as all over the country.

HUASTECA ENSEMBLE
Mexico group hailing from Northern Veracruz and Tamaulipas state, featuring violin accompanied by two types of guitars.

Explore
the Musical Instrument Gallery on **mymusiclab.com**

LISTENING GUIDE

TRADITIONAL SON HUASTECO

GO TO **www.mymusiclab.com for the Automated Listening Guide** CDIII • Track 6/Download Track 51

Performed by Los Caporales de Panuco

Violin, huapanguera (or guitarra quinta), jarana huasteca (smaller guitar), and two vocalists

Recorded by Chris Strachwitz in Tampico, Tamaulipas, Mexico, January 1978.

On this recording, the violinist is at the center of the ensemble, his playing rich with powerful, syncopated rhythmic bowing, slides and other ornaments, double stops (bowing two strings at once), and extremely quick finger work. The vocals are traded back and forth between the two lead singers, who frequently use falsetto singing to create an exciting effect that distinguishes this style from jarocho and other regional son styles.

Sesquialtera is created by the fact that 3/4 (triple) and 6/8 (duple) meters are both present at the same time. The easiest way to hear this is to listen for the (relatively consistent) eighth-note strumming pattern established by the hurapanguera and jarana and attempt to count it in both meters. The strumming pattern can be sketched as follows, with the "x" indicating the muted, percussion-like sound of the strings being plucked but prevented from vibrating:

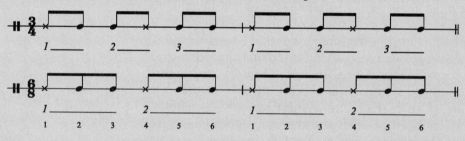

TIME	SECTION	MUSICAL EVENT
0:00–0:04	**Introduction:** Listen for the strumming pattern established by the huapanguera and jarana.	A brief violin introduction opens the performance.
0:04–0:20		The huapanguera and jarana enter. Notice how the violin plays over the accompaniment, rendering short phrases that cut across the regular strummed rhythm (see notation above).
0:20–0:30	**Singer 1, Verse 1**	Singer 1 introduces the basic melody while singing verse 1.
0:30–0:39	**Singer 2, Verse 1:** Listen for the second singer's more liberal use of falsetto.	Singer 2 repeats verse 1 but in more ornamented style.
0:40–0:49	**Singer 1, Verse 2**	Singer 1 moves on to verse 2, performing in a style less ornamented than that of singer 2.

0:50–1:08	**Instrumental interlude 1:** The violin takes the lead here. Notice also that the huapanguera plays a bass line consisting of eighth notes underneath much of the violin improvisations. Try to begin hearing the duple and triple meters embedded in the performance.	As the violin plays, the huapanguera performs an active bass line. Meanwhile, the jarana continues to maintain the basic strumming pattern.
1:08–1:17	**Singer 2, Verse 3:** The singers switch their order of entry, with singer 2 taking the lead for verses 3 and 4.	Singer 2 performs verse 3.
1:18–1:28	**Singer 1, Verse 3**	Singer 1 returns, repeating verse 3.
1:29–1:38	**Singer 2, Verse 4**	Singer 2 moves the song forward, singing verse 4.
1:38–1:56	**Instrumental interlude 2:** The violin takes the lead here. Notice also that the huapanguera again performs a bass line consisting of eighth notes underneath much of the violin improvisations.	This interlude mirrors in many respects the first interlude that occurred at [0:50–1:08].
1:56–2:05	**Singer 1, Verse 5:**	Singer 1 performs verse 5.
2:05–2:14	**Singer 2, Verse 5:** Listen for the second singer's more liberal use of falsetto.	Singer 2 repeats verse 5.
2:15–2:24	**Singer 1, Verse 6:**	Singer 1 completes the vocal component of this performance with verse 6.
2:24–2:46	**Instrumental conclusion**	The instrumentalists play one more improvisatory section that serves as a conclusion to the performance.

The mariachi tradition originated as a local string band style in the western Mexican state of Jalisco. In the early decades of the twentieth century, rural mariachi groups were small string bands with several violins accompanied by the percussive strumming of a *vihuela* (small five-string guitar type with a convex back) and *guitarrón* (large acoustic bass guitar with a convex back) or harp. Band instruments like a trumpet, trombone, or flute might have been occasionally added to the basic string quartet.

Feelings of nationalism spurred the glorification of Mexican peasants and local rural culture around the time of the Mexican Revolution (beginning in 1910). This led to a greater interest in rural music within urban higher-class circles. During this time, and through the 1920s, a few mariachis from Jalisco began to gain popularity in Mexico City playing at parties, cafes, and occasionally at theaters. It was the mass media, however, that acted as the springboard to national prominence for this type of regional ensemble. Mariachis began

RANCHERA
A Mexican song genre with rural and working-class associations.

to be featured on radio and, after 1931, in Mexican movies—just as singing cowboys were becoming popular figures in Hollywood movies around the same time.

With their entrance into mass popular culture, mariachis evolved into their current form: They grew in size; their repertories became more diverse; fancy "Mexican cowboy" costumes (*trajes de charro*) became standard; and the music became increasingly more arranged and polished. One, and later two, trumpets were added as standard instruments, violin sections were enlarged, and guitars were added to the vihuela and guitarrón as additional rhythm instruments. Although originally specializing in sones from Jalisco, after mariachis entered the national arena, they also began to play sones from other regions as well as polkas, *canciones* **rancheras** (popular "country" songs), *corridos* (Mexican ballads usually on historical or topical themes using the copla text form), marches, and other genres.

In the restaurants and cafes of Veracruz one can also hear conjuntos norteños and marimba groups. As their name implies, conjuntos norteños are associated with northern Mexico and southern Texas. Currently a three-row diatonic button accordion serves as the lead melody instrument and provides extended "fills" between sung lines. The accordion is backed by a large twelve-string guitar (*bajo sexto*), and when playing in stationary locations such as bars and nightclubs, electric bass and drums are standard. These conjuntos perform corridos, waltzes, and boleros (a relatively slow romantic song-dance genre from Cuba), but polkas and canciones rancheras often make up a large portion of their repertories. Like the norteño style itself, canciones rancheras have working-class and romanticized-rural associations. Rather than being defined by particular musical characteristics, the particularly popular ranchera genre is best defined by its sentimental aesthetic and crying-in-your-beer, truck-driving, hard-drinking, cantina imagery. In many ways, ranchera songs are the Mexican equivalent of North American country and western.

Sitting in a cafe in Veracruz, it is almost comical to watch the marimba layers struggle with their heavy table-like instrument as they move about competing for patrons with the other strolling musicians. In the south of Mexico, throughout Guatemala, and in many Central American countries, the marimba is a primary musical instrument. This xylophone has wooden keys tuned to the Western scale and hanging resonators that produce the marimba's characteristic buzzing sound. Various ethnomusicologists have shown that the marimba originally came to the Americas from Africa, and the marimba's buzzy timbre is similar to many African instruments (see Chapter 7). Although marimbas are still played by African American communities on the Pacific coast of Colombia and Ecuador, in southern Mexico and Central America the instrument has been adopted both by indigenous and mestizo musicians. In the mestizo traditions of southern Mexico and Guatemala, and as I saw it performed in Veracruz, several musicians play lead and accompanying parts on the same large marimba. Although marimba groups in Veracruz could play a wide range of Mexican genres and international pop songs, local sones are the standard fare in its traditional home in southern Mexico. Unlike the sones from the other regions we have discussed, in southern Mexico, as in Guatemala, many sones are in a moderate 3/4 waltz time. This feature, like the many types of ensembles encountered in the city of Veracruz, illustrates the tremendous regional diversity of mestizo music in Mexico.

NATIVE AMERICAN MUSICAL VALUES AND MUSICAL STYLE

Highland Indians in Mexico, Guatemala, and the Andean highlands of Ecuador, Peru, Bolivia, and Northern Chile have interacted with mestizos and people of European heritage for centuries. Hence, they have been involved in the same processes of musical syncretism that characterize mestizo music. Cultural differences between indigenous highland peoples and mestizos are often more a matter of degree than of kind. Yet even after centuries of contact, indigenous communities, especially in the southern Peruvian and Bolivian highlands, have maintained their own languages and a distinct social ethos and have continued to develop their music along their own aesthetic lines to a significant degree. The Aymara-speaking people of southern Peru offer one example.

Aymara Pinkillu (Flute) Ensemble in Huancane, Puno, Peru. *Source:* Thomas Turino

The Aymara of Southern Peru

Quechua and Aymara speakers comprise the two major indigenous groups of the Andean highlands, with Quechua speakers in the majority. Aymara communities are located around Lake Titicaca in Peru and Bolivia and further to the south in Bolivia and northern Chile. We will focus on Aymara musical life in Conima, a district in the Province of Huancané (like a county), on the north side of Lake Titicaca in the state of Puno, Peru.

Like indigenous highland and lowland communities in other parts of Latin America, the Aymara of Conima emphasize the importance of collective community life. As highland agriculturalists and herders of llamas, sheep, alpaca, and some cattle, Aymara peasants are tied to their land, and they depend on good relations with their neighbors for support in labor exchanges and communal work projects, as well as for social and moral support. Reciprocity, egalitarian relations, and community solidarity have come to constitute core values for ordering the Aymara social world. It is not surprising that ways of making music emerge from these same principles of collective social life.

PACHAMAMA
Earthmother, an Andean concept of the living, spiritual earth.

Although there are two small village brass bands in the district of Conima (the indigenous musicians having learned these instruments during military service), Aymara musical life revolves around the performance of local indigenous wind instruments and drums. Men play *siku* (panpipes) and, historically, end-notched vertical cane flutes (kenas) in dry-season festivals (April–October); these instruments are of pre-Columbian origin. Aymara musicians also play cane *pinkillus* and wooden *tarkas* (vertical duct flutes with a recorder-like mouthpiece) during the rainy season. Side-blown cane flutes (pitus) are played all year-round. Panpipe ensembles are typically accompanied by large double-headed drums known as *wankara* or *bombos*, pinkillus are accompanied by large indigenous snare drums known as *cajas*, and tarkas are accompanied by Western snare and bass drums. The different wind instruments are not mixed in ensembles (sikus are played only with sikus, tarkas with tarkas, etc.). Different size instruments are used in siku, tarka, and pitu ensembles to create parallel harmonic lines.

Stringed instruments were not played in the Andes before the Spanish arrived, and they have not been incorporated into Aymara music-making in the Province of Huancané. Stringed instruments such as the harp and violin, however, have been adopted by indigenous Quechua communities and by Indian musicians in many Latin American regions. Elsewhere in southern Peru and Bolivia, the *charango* (a ten-string Andean guitar variant the size of a ukulele) has a special place in both Quechua and Aymara communities. Unlike Andean Quechua culture, vocal music is relatively rare in Aymara festivals.

Explore
the Musical Instrument Gallery on
mymusiclab.com

Aymara Sikuri (Panpipe) Ensemble in Huancane, Puno, Peru.
Source: Thomas Turino

In the district of Conima, community and intercommunity festivals may be held as often as once a month. Many festivals are connected to the agricultural cycle and to local Aymara deities. Aymara communities also collectively celebrate life cycle events (weddings, first haircutting ceremonies for babies) and collective work projects (e.g., roof raisings) with music and dance. Some festivals may be linked with Catholic celebrations, although usually Aymara deities will be granted greater prominence than Catholic imagery. For example, in Conima, the festival called Fiesta de la Virgen de la Candelaria, or simply Candelaria (February 2), is actually an agricultural ripening festival in which prayers and rituals are offered for **Pachamama** (Earthmother), the ancestors, and local mountain deities.

This festival is Christian primarily in name, not in substance, whereas the mestizo fiesta in Paucartambo is *really* dedicated to the Catholic saint (Virgen del Carmen) with only a few indigenous elements included.

Aymara peasants in Huancané generally play music only in large community wind ensembles for these public communal festivals; even practicing music by oneself is rare. During festivals any man is welcome to play with his community regardless of his musical knowledge or ability. Also, Aymara musicians do not usually comment on or correct other players in their group so as not to offend them. In keeping with their egalitarian values, there is no formal ensemble leader who has the power to direct others or restrict participation. Music is performed so that the community can come together in dance, music, and celebration. Music is judged on the quality of the social relations and the total experience that it engenders as much as on the quality of sound produced. From this perspective, to ask a less-skilled person not to play, or to embarrass him by correcting him publicly, would do more damage to "the music" than any inappropriate sounds he might make.

In Aymara communities in Conima, individuals generally do not like to stand out or be singled out in social situations, both because the group is granted greater importance than individual identity and perhaps for fear of arousing jealousy. Likewise, there is no place for soloists in ensemble performance. Rather, the primary aesthetic ideal expressed by Aymara musicians is that ensembles should "play as one" or sound like a single instrument, and no individual's instrument should stand out from the dense sound of these Andean wind ensembles. The preference for a dense, well-integrated sound is also reflected in Andean instrumental performance techniques and instrument construction. Flutes and panpipes are blown to create a breathy sound, which aids group blending, and instruments are tuned slightly differently so that a rich combination of overtones will result. The act of "playing as one" and creating a thick, well-blended sound with no soloists thus becomes a clear musical articulation of the central ways of being for this egalitarian, collectively oriented society.

The Aymara siku (panpipe) tradition also illustrates this cooperative style of performance. Panpipes are constructed with two separate rows, the seven-tone pitch series alternating between them. The rows are divided between two musicians who, having only half the pitches needed to make a melody, must interlock their notes (**hocket**) with those of their partner to perform a piece. Aymara panpipe ensembles, which sometimes have up to fifty players, are actually made up of these paired musicians who must interact reciprocally and blend with the whole.

Approaching music and dance as a collective activity that fosters community participation and unity is common to many highland Indian communities in Latin America. Yet, the Aymara of Conima represent the extreme case where music is *only* performed in large community ensembles during public festivals. Native Americans in other regions also perform music solo for enjoyment or other purposes. For example, a Quechua boy in the Andes might play his kena flute for solitary entertainment while herding llamas or his charango to court a girlfriend; a Quechua woman might sing to her children or while working in

HOCKET
Interlocking pitches between two or more sound sources to create a single melody or part.

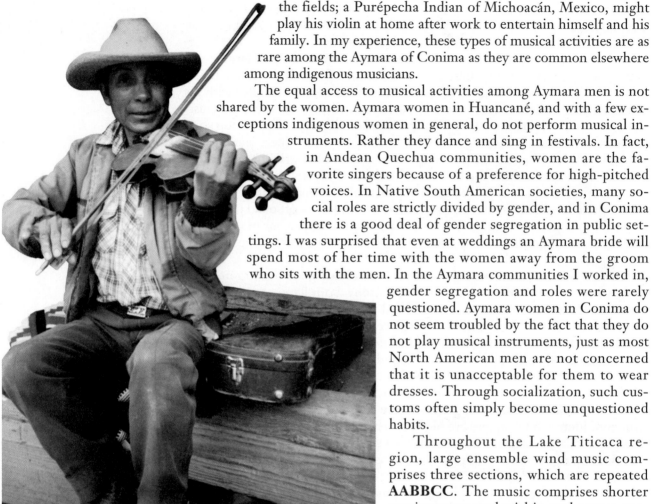

José Romero, Purepecha violinist from Michoacan, Mexico. *Source:* Thomas Turino

the fields; a Purépecha Indian of Michoacán, Mexico, might play his violin at home after work to entertain himself and his family. In my experience, these types of musical activities are as rare among the Aymara of Conima as they are common elsewhere among indigenous musicians.

The equal access to musical activities among Aymara men is not shared by the women. Aymara women in Huancané, and with a few exceptions indigenous women in general, do not perform musical instruments. Rather they dance and sing in festivals. In fact, in Andean Quechua communities, women are the favorite singers because of a preference for high-pitched voices. In Native South American societies, many social roles are strictly divided by gender, and in Conima there is a good deal of gender segregation in public settings. I was surprised that even at weddings an Aymara bride will spend most of her time with the women away from the groom who sits with the men. In the Aymara communities I worked in, gender segregation and roles were rarely questioned. Aymara women in Conima do not seem troubled by the fact that they do not play musical instruments, just as most North American men are not concerned that it is unacceptable for them to wear dresses. Through socialization, such customs often simply become unquestioned habits.

Throughout the Lake Titicaca region, large ensemble wind music comprises three sections, which are repeated **AABBCC**. The music comprises shorter motives repeated within and across sections, especially at section cadences. Scales differ. Tarka music in Conima uses five- and six-tone scales, whereas panpipe, pinkillu, and side-blown flute music also feature seven-tone scales. The lion's share of music has syncopated rhythms set in a duple meter with drum parts either playing a rolling repeated pattern (pinkillu music) or following the rhythm of the melody of panpipe, tarka, and side-flute ensembles. In Conima, ensembles create new pieces each year, and musical composition takes place in collective "brainstorming" sessions at rehearsals the night before a given fiesta. In contrast to stereotypes of Indian or "folk" music being old and unchanging, Aymara musicians in Conima, Peru, emphasize new compositions using these set forms, scales, and rhythms for the different genres they have fashioned. (Listen to CD III, 7 for an example of Aymara panpipe music.)

LISTENING GUIDE

PANPIPE MUSIC: "MANUELITA"

GO TO **www.mymusiclab.com for the Automated Listening Guide** CDIII • Track 7/Download Track 52

Sikuris Centro Social de Conima
24 sikus (panpipes) of six different sizes; 2 bombos (drums)
Recorded by Thomas Turino in Lima, Peru, June 1986

Like the vast majority of music in Conima, this sikuri piece is in **AA BB CC** form. It is a slow piece in a genre simply referred to as *lento* (slow). The long-held chords at the beginning of the piece and at section endings are typical of all pieces in this genre. Note that this cadence formula is heard at the end of all sections except the second **B** and between the two **C** Sections. The accented strokes of the drumming pattern are designed to fit with the melody. Note the overlapping and blending of instruments to create a dense texture.

TIME	SECTION	MUSICAL EVENTS
0:00–0:03	**Introduction:** Listen to the long-held chord at the opening of this performance.	Long-held chord, a standard introduction for the lento genre.
		Try to remember the pitch of the highest panflute, because it is the highest note played throughout the performance and will help you identify the chord when it returns at the end of sections.
0:03–0:14	**"A" Section:** Listen for the breathy sound that the performers are producing on their flutes. Listen also for the syncopated melody (against the rather uniform beat provided by the drums).	The performers introduce Section **A**. Listen for the reappearance of the opening, long-held chord at the end of this section [0:12–0:14].
0:14–0:24		Section **A** is repeated. Listen again for the cadential (concluding) use of the introductory chord [0:23–0:24].
0:24–0:35	**"B" section:** Listen for the contrasting melody in this section.	The performers introduce Section **B**. Listen for the reappearance of the cadential chord you heard at the end of the **A** Sections [0:33–0:35].
0:35–0:44		Section **B** is repeated. This time, however, notice that the cadential chord is not used to transition to the next section.
0:44–0:52	**"C" section:** Notice that the melody is similar to that of Section **A**, but that the long-held chord that characterizes the opening gesture of the melody in the **A** Section is not part of the **C** Section.	The performers introduce Section **C**. Notice that the cadential chord is again left out in transitioning to the repeat of Section **C**.

0:52-1:01		Section **C** is repeated. Here, the cadential chord reappears in preparation for the return of the A Section [0:59–1:01].
1:01-2:00	**Repeat of AA BB CC:** Listen again for the overall form of the piece.	The performers repeat the entire song in the same fashion.
2:00-2:56	**Final repeat of AA BB CC:** Listen for the overall form of the piece, and see if you can begin to hear how the cadential chord helps mark the transitions from one section to the next.	The performers again repeat the entire song in the same fashion.
2:56-3:06		The song concludes with two long-held chords.

A Lowland Indian Case: The Suyá of the Brazilian Amazon

Musical aesthetics and conceptions about music among lowland Amazonian Indian groups share some of the elements described for Conima but differ radically in other ways. Whereas Aymara musical culture centers around wind instruments and drums, and singing is unimportant, the music of the Suyá Indians of the Brazilian Amazon is predominantly vocal, sometimes accompanied by rattles. As with the Aymara, collective participation in musical performances during Suyá festivals is a vital way to represent and maintain social unity within a village, and the blending of voices in unison singing embodies an important aesthetic value. But the Suyá also have songs that are individually owned and sung, indicating that there is more room for individual expression than among the Aymara of Huancané, where solo performance is basically nonexistent.

To take this one step further, although the Aymara stress "playing as one," ethnomusicologist Anthony Seeger has shown that some Suyá performances include a variety of individuals singing their own, different, **akía** songs simultaneously, along with shouts, laughter, and other vocal sounds. This type of Suyá performance results in what to our—or Aymara—ears would be cacophony. Yet for the Suyá all these simultaneous songs and sounds contribute to the total creation of a performance. The Suyá aesthetic often favors the dense combination of multiple, relatively independent sounds to form the whole. It reflects a different conception, relative to the Aymara, of the relationship of individuals to the community.

The Suyá believe that songs come from and are learned from animals, insects, fish, and plants of the forest. As with other Amazonian groups, important Suyá festivals and song types are named for and involve the representation of natural species. These have symbolic importance in relation to the ecological environment that sustains the Suyá through hunting, fishing, and agriculture.

AKÍA
An individually owned and sung song of the Suyá Indians of Brazil.

Many indigenous Andean festivals and song types are similarly related to the specific environment and Andeans' occupations as agriculturalists and herders. In addition to ecological-economic issues, musical styles and genres are used almost universally to distinguish and represent distinct groups within societies. For the Suyá, gender and age are central criteria for delineating important social categories and status within a village, and musical genres and singing styles are similarly differentiated according to gender and age.

Although musical instruments are not prominent in Suyá society, they have a wealth of distinct vocal genres that range from everyday speech to more formalized genres of political, historical, and artistic oratory; chantlike performance genres; and finally, a variety of different singing styles. The prominence of vocal music among the Suyá is typical for lowland Indian societies. However, some lowland Indian groups also play panpipes, side-blown and vertical flutes, valveless trumpets, drums, and various types of percussion instruments. As with many native lowland and highland groups, dance is a central aspect of most musical festival occasions and is a deeply integral aspect of musical life.

AFRICAN AMERICAN MUSICAL VALUES AND STYLES

After reading about African music in Chapter 7, we can appreciate the influence of the African heritage in Latin America. The use of cyclical forms, call-and-response, interlocking melodic and percussion parts, and an appreciation of dense overlapping textures are all part of Afro-Latin American music making, as is the use of African musical instruments.

For example, along the Pacific coast of Ecuador and Colombia, an area with an African American population, historically the marimba was used for the **currulao**, a community dance in which women and men may meet and form new relationships. A currulao performance exemplifies a variety of African musical features. The marimba (twenty to twenty-eight wooden keys with bamboo resonators, played by two musicians) is accompanied by single-headed conical drums (like conga drums) of two different sizes, which are classified as male and female, as is often the case for African instruments. The currulao ensemble also includes two deeper double-headed drums (*bombos*) and bamboo shakers, which add rhythmic-timbral density, much like *hosho* in a Shona mbira performance (see Chapter 7).

Like most sub-Saharan African music, the basis of this marimba music is an ostinato with improvised variations. The drums and shakers play separate but interlocking rhythmic parts, often in duple and triple meter simultaneously. This African-derived style of ensemble performance is used to accompany a solo singer, who interlocks his or her vocal part with a female chorus in call-and-response fashion. The vocal quality of the singers is distinctly African and contrasts with indigenous and mestizo singing styles in Latin America. It is also striking that the women singers yodel in a style somewhat reminiscent of Shona and other African singing traditions (Listen to CD III, 8 for an example of *currulao*).

CURRULAO
Afro-Colombian, Afro-Ecuadorian dance context in the Pacific Coast region in which marimba is featured.

LISTENING GUIDE

MARIMBA DANCE: "CURRULAO BAMBUCO"

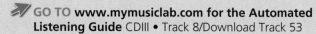

GO TO www.mymusiclab.com for the Automated **Listening Guide** CDIII • Track 8/Download Track 53

Two-person marimba, drums, shakers, male and female voices
Recorded by N. E. Whitten in Buenaventura

You can clearly hear the African influences on this recording of "Currulao Bambuco." The instruments play interlocking duple and triple rhythms; the vocal parts are organized in leader-chorus, call-and-response patterns; melodies and rhythms are based on short, repetitive phrases (ostinatos); and the vocal style features yodeling and other vocal sounds. The primary ostinato on which this piece is grounded is supplied by the marimba, which with some variations continues throughout the performance. As the performance progresses, a female lead vocalist takes over from the male lead singer who is heard early on.

The following reductions are designed to help you key in on the simultaneous presence of duple and triple meters and to hear it with reference to several of the instruments performing on this recording. The marimba and one of the drums play rhythmic patterns that fall into duple meter, whereas the shakers and a separate drum perform patterns that are best heard in triple meter. See if you can follow along with one instrument at a time, first counting it in duple and then counting it in triple while listening to the song.

Aligned in duple meter (6/8):

Count	1			2			1			2		
Beat	**1**	2	3	**4**	5	6	**1**	2	3	**4**	5	6
Marimba, duple		x	x	**X**		x		x	x	**X**		x
Drum, duple		x	x	**X**	x	x		x	x	**X**	x	x
Shaker, triple	**X**	x	**X**	x	**X**	x	**X**	x	**X**	x	**X**	x
Drum, triple	**X**		**X**		**X**		**X**		**X**		**X**	

Aligned in triple meter (3/4 within 6/8):

Count	1		2		3		1		2		3	
Beat	**1**	2	3	4	**5**	6	**1**	2	**3**	4	**5**	6
Marimba, duple		x	x	**X**		x		x	x	**X**		x
Drum, duple		x	x	**X**	x	x		x	x	**X**	x	x
Shaker, triple	**X**	x	**X**	x	**X**	x	**X**	x	**X**	x	**X**	x
Drum, triple	**X**			**X**			**X**			**X**		

As this song develops, listen for the marimba, which supplies the basic ostinato: two short six-beat phrases (in 6/8 meter). One of the drums reinforces this duple feel. Notice also that the shakers emphasize a triple pattern. One of the drums strongly reinforces this triple feel. Attempt to hear the performance as unfolding in triple meter and tap your foot or hand in duple meter. Now try hearing the performance in duple meter and tap your foot in triple meter. See if you get one foot or hand to mark time in duple meter while the other foot or hand marks triple meter.

0:00–0:04	The ensemble is already in full swing when the recording fades in.
0:04–0:16	A male vocalist enters, singing a short phrase, and a female chorus responds [0:08–16]. The male leader uses a falsetto voice often throughout the performance.
0:16–0:21	The vocalists give way to the instrumentalists.
0:21–0:32	The male singer rejoins the ensemble, and the female chorus responds [0:28–032].
0:32–0:44	The vocalists give way to the instrumentalists again.
0:44–0:57	The male singer rejoins the ensemble again and the female chorus responds [0:48–0:57].
0:57–1:03	The vocalists give way to the instrumentalists yet again.
1:03–1:14	The vocalist rejoins the ensemble, and the male-call and female-response patterns become shorter.
1:14–1:29	The female chorus introduces a new melodic motif in yodeling style.
1:29–1:45	A female vocalist enters and sings a series of short calls, and the female chorus quickly responds with the new yodeling motif.
1:45–2:15	The yodeled motif is repeated numerous times by the female vocalists, who introduce some subtle individual variations.
2:15–2:37	The female vocalist reenters and sings a series of short calls, and the female chorus quickly responds with the new yodeling motif.
2:37–2:52	The female chorus continues to perform the yodeled motif.
2:52–3:09	The female singer adds a new, higher variation over the rest of the female chorus, and the track fades out even as the performance continues.

Along with the marimba, a wide variety of African-styled drums, the musical bow (e.g., the berimbau of Brazil), and various lamellaphones ("thumb piano") were diffused to the Americas from Africa. In the Caribbean, a large box lamellaphone (*marímbula*) serves a bass function in a variety of ensembles. A smaller hand-held lamellaphone of Angolan character was used in Brazil in the last century, and the smaller type is still played among the Saramaka of Surinam. Runaway slave communities established in the forests of Surinam maintain their own amalgamation of African cultural practices to this day. Among these is the playing of *papai benta*, a lamellaphone with reed keys mounted on bridges on a flat board. Held between the knees and played with the index fingers, the instrument is used to perform pieces that are ostinatos with variations, as is the case with Shona mbira music. Drums are also prominent among the Saramaka of Surinam, used to accompany dancing and historical songs and to call the gods and ancestors.

Afro-Brazilian Music

The use of African-derived musical styles, concepts, and instruments is perhaps best exemplified in Latin America by certain religious traditions in the Caribbean and Brazil. In the Candomblé religions of Bahía, northeastern Brazil, music and

ORIXA
A spirit or deity in the Yoruba
religion of Nigeria.

dance are fundamental to worshiping various **orixas** (deities) hailing largely from
the Yoruba religion of Nigeria. The songs, often in call-and-response, are accompanied by a trio of different-sized single-headed drums (*atabaques*), also of
Yoruba origin, and a West African styled double bell (*agogô*). Strikingly, the roles
of the double bell and of the different drums in the trio mirror those for the
same instruments in Yoruba musical performance. The bell plays an ostinato
pattern that orients the other musicians, the two smaller drums interlock to play
the ground ostinato part, and the largest, or "mother," drum is used by a lead
drummer for improvisation and to interact with the dancers. Even West African
words are retained in the songs, although their meanings are largely forgotten.

African rituals such as "the baptism of drums" (drums being considered sacred instruments and dedicated to the deities) are practiced in Bahía. Candomblé
activities are organized within specific religious centers (cult houses), each of
which has its own religious and musical leaders and group of religious initiates.
The initiates undergo special training and rituals to become the mediums of
specific deities. At ceremonies, the music is played for dancing, for invocations
to the gods, and in the context of spirit possession among the initiates.

Brazil's most famous musical event is carnival in Rio de Janeiro with its long
parades, floats, huge percussion ensembles, and multitude of elaborately costumed
dancers and singers. Samba, Brazil's most famous musical genre, is associated with
this carnival although, in fact, samba has a number of rural and urban variants and
is performed in a variety of settings. For example, beginning after World War I,
but especially during the 1930s and 1940s, an urban ballroom type of samba became popular in Brazil and internationally through such singing stars as Carmen
Miranda. This type of samba was performed by Western-style dance orchestras
or smaller string ensembles with a small Afro-Brazilian percussion section.

✳ Explore
*the Musical Instrument
Gallery* on
mymusiclab.com

The special kind of urban samba heard at a carnival comes from the hillside
Afro-Brazilian neighborhoods of Rio that grew through urban migration from
northeastern Brazil and elsewhere during the twentieth century. In keeping
with its Afro-Brazilian roots, this type of samba is accompanied by massive
percussion ensembles in which the different instruments—for example, *surdos*
(large bass drums), agogós (double bells), *pandeiros* (tambourines), *tamborím*
(small hand-held drum played with a single stick), *reco-recos* (pronounced
heco heco) (metal spring scrapers), and *cuícas* (friction drums) and *cavaquinhos*
(small four-string guitar variant)—all play their own syncopated interlocking
parts. The samba songs accompanied by the percussion ensemble are sung in
Portuguese in call-and-response fashion, also illustrating an Afro-Brazilian
source.

Since the 1920s, carnival performance in Rio—percussion music, song, choreographed dance, and parading—has been organized by the *escolas de samba*
(samba schools). Samba schools are not formal educational institutions. Rather,
they emerged as grassroots Afro-Brazilian neighborhood institutions largely
from the poorer black areas of the city. They were primarily carnival performance ensembles that represented their neighborhoods during the celebration.
Over the years the samba schools have grown tremendously. Nowadays they
have bureaucratic leadership structures and are divided into separate specialized

"wings," including wings for samba composers, for dancers, and for percussionists. During carnival, the different samba schools compete against each other, and they spend much of the year preparing for the event. Numerous songs are composed and the best selected, costumes and floats have to be designed and made, and as the carnival approaches, different wings rehearse intensively.

Rio's carnival has grown to become the country's largest musical spectacle, and it has become big business. The costs for samba schools to launch a competitive performance are enormous and require major sponsorship; the stakes for doing well in the competition are also high. Critics claim that as the carnival has become increasingly commercialized and controlled by outside economic and media interests, it has lost much of its original grassroots basis. Yet Afro-Brazilians from the neighborhoods still join in the dance and percussion ensembles with a pride in this tradition and simply for the exhausting joy of participating in one of the world's largest parties.

SUMMARY

✓• Study and Review on mymusiclab.com

As we have seen, the Latin American continent encompasses many different types of societies, each with their own musical traditions. Mestizo cultures—resulting from the mixing of Spanish or Portuguese and Native Latin American lifeways—have become a common denominator influencing many forms of Latin American music. In each country or region, different combinations of European and Native influences occurred, with one or the other being more or less predominant. Mestizo music is characterized by European scales and harmonies, strophic song forms (the melody of each verse is the same, but the words change), and complex rhythms created by playing duple (two- or four-beat) and triple (three-beat) rhythms sequentially and simultaneously.

The guitar—in many variants—is the most common stringed instrument, along with violin, harp and mandolin. Various types of indigenous flutes, pan-pipes, and drums are still in use throughout Latin America. Brass band instruments, too, were popularized in the nineteenth century, followed by accordions in the early twentieth century, and electric guitars and keyboards in the second half of the twentieth century. Native American musical performances tend to be group events, without focusing on individual musicians (e.g., the Aymara), and musical performances are tied to specific rituals and events.

Afro-Latin American music is a combination of African, European, and Native influences. In instrumentation, composition, and performance, Afro-Brazilian music and performance traditions like the currulao of the Pacific coast of Colombia exhibit strong influences from African heritage. Though this chapter could not address them, many other musical styles—styles such as *vallenato*, *tango*, *cumbia*, *forró*, *champeta*, *bossa nova*, and *chamamé*, to name but a few—are actively practiced in and around Latin America and in places where Latin American communities live throughout the world. The case studies explored in this chapter, then, are best understood as but a starting point to engaging the sound worlds and musical communities of Latin America.

BIBLIOGRAPHY

General Gerard Béhague, "Folk and Traditional Music of Latin America: General Prospect and Research Problems," *The World of Music* 25/2 (1982); Dale A. Olsen, "Folk Music of South America—a Musical Mosaic," in Elizabeth May, ed., *Musics of Many Cultures: An Introduction* (Berkeley: University of California Press, 1980); Dale A. Olsen and Daniel E. Sheehy, eds., *The Garland Encyclopedia of World Music, vol. 2: South America, Mexico, Central America, and the Caribbean* (New York: Garland Publishing, 1998); Dale A. Olsen and Daniel Sheehy, eds., *The Garland Handbook of Latin American Music* (New York: Routledge, 2008); John M. Schechter, ed., *Music in Latin American Culture: Regional Traditions* (New York: Schirmer Books, 1999).

Highland Indigenous and Mestizo Music Max Peter Baumann, "Music of the Indios in Bolivia's Andean Highlands (survey)," *World of Music* 25/2 (1982); Henry Stobart, *Music and the Poetics of Production in the Bolivian Andes*. Aldershot, (Hants, England: Ashgate, 2006); Robert Garfias, "The Marimba of Mexico and Central America," *Latin American Music Review* 4/2 (1983); Karl Gustav Izikowitz, *Musical and Other Sound Instruments of the South American Indians* (Göteborg, Sweden: Elanders Boktrycheri Aktiebolag, 1934); Manuel Peña, *The Texas-Mexican Conjunto: History of a Working-Class Music* (Austin: University of Texas Press, 1985); John Schechter, *The Indispensable Harp: Historical Development, Modern Roles, Configurations, and Performance Practices in Ecuador and Latin America* (Kent, OH: Kent State Press, 1991); Thomas Stanford, "The Mexican Son," *Yearbook of the IFMC* (1972); Robert Stevenson, *In Aztec and Inca Territory* (Berkeley: University of California Press, 1968); David Stigberg, "Jarocho, Tropical, and 'Pop': Aspects of Musical Life in Veracruz, 1971–1972," in Bruno Nettl, ed., *Eight Urban Musical Cultures* (Urbana: University of Illinois Press, 1978); Thomas Turino, *Moving Away from Silence: Music of the Peruvian Altiplano and the Experience of Urban Migration* (Chicago: University of Chicago Press, 1993); Raul Romero, *Debating the Past: Music, Memory, and Identity in the Andes* (New York: Oxford University Press, 2001); Helena Simonett, *Banda: Mexican Musical Life Across Borders* (Middletown, CT: Wesleyan University Press, 2001); Zoila Mendoza, *Shaping Society Through Dance: Mestizo Ritual Performance in the Peruvian Andes* (Chicago: University of Chicago Press, 2000).

Amazonian Cultures Anthony Seeger, *Why Suyá Sing: A Musical Anthropology of an Amazonian People* (Cambridge: Cambridge University Press, 1987); Jonathan David Hill, *Made-from-Bone: Trickster Myths, Music, and History from the Amazon* (Urbana: University of Illinois, 2009); Anthony Seeger, "What Can We Learn When They Sing? Vocal Genres of the Suyá Indians of Central Brazil," *Ethnomusicology* 23/3 (1979): 373–94.

African American Traditions Gerard Béhague, "Patterns of Candomblé Music Performance: An Afro-Brazilian Religious Setting," in Gerard Béhague, ed., *Performance Practice: Ethnomusicological Perspectives* (Westport, CT: Greenwood, 1984); Timothy Brennan, *Secular Devotion: Afro-Latin Music and Imperial Jazz.* (New York: Verso, 2008); Harold Courlander, "Musical Instruments of Cuba," *Musical Quarterly* 28 (1942); Luis Heitor Correa de Azevedo, "Music and Musicians of African Origin in Brazil," *World of Music* 25/2 (1982); Larry Crook, "A Musical Analysis of the Cuban Rumba," *Latin American Music Review* 3/1 (1982); Chris McGowan and Ricardo Pessanha, *The Brazilian Sound: Samba, Bossa Nova, and the Popular Music of Brazil* (Philadelphia: Temple University Press, 2009); Alma Guillermoprieto, *Samba* (New York: Vintage Press, 1990); Peter Manuel, *Popular Musics of the Non-Western World* (New York: Oxford University Press, 1988); Susan Thomas, *Cuban Zarzuela: Performing Race and Gender on Havana's Lyric Stage* (Urbana: University of Illinois, 2009); Peter Manuel, ed., *Essays on Cuban Music: North American and Cuban Perspectives* (Lanham, MD: University Press of America, 1991); Charles A. Perrone, *Masters of Contemporary Brazilian Song: MPB 1965–1985* (Austin: University of Texas Press, 1989); Alison Raphael, "From Popular Culture to Microenterprise: The History of Brazilian Samba Schools," *Latin American Music Review* 11(1), 1990; Norman E. Whitten, Jr. and C. Aurelio Fuentes, *Black Frontiersmen: A South American Case* (New York: Schenkman, 1974); Katherine J. Hagedorn, *Divine Utterances: The Performance of Afro-Cuban Santeria* (Washington, DC: Smithsonian Institution Press, 2001); Robin D. Moore, *Nationalizing Blackness: Afrocubanismo and Artistic Revolution in Havana, 1920–1940* (Pittsburgh, PA: University of Pittsburgh Press, 1997).

DISCOGRAPHY

Highland Indigenous and Mestizo   *Mountain Music of Peru*, vol. 2 (Smithsonian Folkways CD 40406); *Musik im Andenhochland/Bolivien* (Museum Collection Berlin [West] MC 14); *Huayno Music of Peru*, vol. 1 (Arhoolie CD 320); *The Inca Harp: Laments and Dances of the Tawantinsuyu, the Inca Empire* (Lyrichord LLST 7359); *Your Struggle Is Your Glory: Songs of Struggle, Huayno and Other Peruvian Music* (Arhoolie 3025); *Kingdom of the Sun: Peru's Inca Heritage* (Nonesuch H-72029); *Music of Peru* (Folkways FE 4415); *Mexico: Fiestas of Chiapas and Oaxaca* (Nonesuch H-72070); *Texas-Mexican Border Music* [vol. 24]: *The Texas-Mexican Conjunto* (Folklyric 9049); *Marimba Music of Tehuantepec* (University of Washington Press UWP 1002); *Music of the Tarascan Indians of Mexico: Music of Michoacán and Nearby Mestizo Country* (Asch Mankind Series AHM 4217); *Music of Mexico: Sones Jarochos* (Arhoolie 3008); *Music of Mexico* [vol. 2]: *Sones Huastecos* (Arhoolie 3009); *Amerindian Ceremonial Music from Chile* (Philips 6586026).

Amazonian Cultures   *Why Suyá Sing* (cassette, Cambridge University Press); *Indian Music of the Upper Amazon* (Folkways FE 4458).

African American   *La História de Son Cubano, Sexteto Boloña* (Folklyric 9053); *In Praise of Oxalá and Other Gods: Black Music of South America* (Nonesuch H-72036); *Afro-Hispanic Music from Western Colombia and Ecuador* (Folkways FE 4376); *Afro-Brazilian Religious Songs: Cantigas de Candomblé* (Lyrichord LLST 7315); *An Island Carnival: Music of the West Indies* (Nonesuch 72091); *The Sound of the Sun: The Westland Steel Band* (Nonesuch H-72016); *Meringues and Folk Ballads of Haiti* (Lyrichord LLST 7340); *Cult Music of Cuba* (Folklways FE 4410); *Music from Saramaka: A Dynamic Afro-American Tradition* (Folkways FE 4225).

Music in the Caribbean

TIMOTHY ROMMEN

CAT ISLAND, JUNE 2, 2006. NINTH ANNUAL RAKE 'N' SCRAPE FESTIVAL

It's pushing 8:00 P.M. on a Friday in June, and the crowd is packed into virtually every nook and cranny of the improvised fairground—a fairground erected next to the Arthur's Town airport especially for this event. The revelers have gradually assembled here over the past day or two, and although the crowd is predominantly Bahamian, a small handful of tourists and a group of folk music aficionados from Atlanta have joined the celebration. Cat Island is one of the many "Family Islands" in the Bahamas, and Arthur's Town is located on its northern end. For most of the year, Arthur's Town is a small village on a relatively small island (the entire population of Cat Island stands at about 1,600 people), but during the Rake 'n' Scrape festival, which was first held in 1998, the island is bursting at the seams with people. As the festival weekend draws near, guest houses and private homes throughout the sixty-mile-long island are filled

to overflowing with visitors. If you want to attend, then you'd better have made reservations a few months in advance.

The overwhelming majority of Bahamians live on New Providence and Grand Bahama (in the cities of Nassau and Freeport, respectively). The Family Islands have historically, and somewhat paradoxically, been touted as the greatest cultural repositories of the nation while, at the same time, receiving very little financial attention from the government. This state of affairs—which has led to increased migration out of the Family Islands in search of employment and educational opportunities—has been changing in recent years, though, and the Festival is a good example of current efforts to bring the Family Islands into the national limelight in tangible (and material and financial) ways.

The stage, set up at the far end of the fairgrounds, is flanked on either side by a giant tower of speakers, and several cabinets of subwoofers line the foot of the stage. The stage itself is arranged to accommodate both a full house band and a range of smaller ensembles. The perimeter of the fairgrounds, meanwhile, is completely

✳ Explore
Learning Objectives
on **mymusiclab.com**

✳ Explore
*a map of the Bahamas on
the Interactive Globe*
on **mymusiclab.com**

RAKE 'N' SCRAPE
A traditional Bahamian music, usually played on accordion, saw, and goatskin drum.

QUADRILLE
A dance, originating in Europe and adapted to Caribbean contexts. It was historically performed by couples arranged in a square formation and following a series of set dance figures.

Ophie and the Websites, Saturday, June 3, 2006, in Arthur's Town, Bahamas. *Source:* Timothy Rommen

overtaken by shacks (small temporary booths made of plywood) out of which Cat Islanders are serving food, straw work (for which Cat Island is famous), and other handmade souvenirs. I arrived here this afternoon from Nassau and am looking forward to hearing some of the very best rake 'n' scrape bands in the Bahamas perform. Ophie and the Websites are here, as are Bo Hog and the Rooters.

Rake 'n' scrape is a traditional music of the Bahamas, today usually played on accordion (most commonly on a two-row button accordion such as the Hohner that Ophie plays), saw (literally a carpenter's saw), and goatskin drum. Rake 'n' scrape ensembles traditionally accompanied **quadrille** dancing, and although quadrille is not as popular today as it was even twenty-five years ago, rake 'n' scrape artists have continued to play their tunes outside of that social context. Perhaps equally important, the rhythms and sounds of traditional rake 'n' scrape provide the foundation for a great deal of the popular music being performed in the Bahamas today. Musicians are increasingly exploring ways of incorporating rake 'n' scrape into the context of full dance bands, adding saw, accordion, and goatskin drum to ensembles that already feature at least drum kit, bass, and electric guitar, and, sometimes, also keyboards and a horn line. In fact, one of the most exciting of these popular rake 'n' scrape singers is going to be performing tonight. His stage name is Ancient Man, and his songs, along with those of a few other rake 'n' scrape–influenced artists, including the Lassido Boys, Elon Moxey, and Ronnie Butler, are leading what might be considered a revival of sorts in Bahamian popular music—rake 'n' scrape style.

But this night isn't just about rake 'n' scrape; storytellers will precede the musical entertainment, and the audience has packed in to hear them. Storytelling was, not so long ago, a major pastime and an art form in its own right throughout the Bahamas (and the rest of the Caribbean, for that matter).

Today, few can still tell the stories the way they used to be told, but there are active attempts to keep the oratory arts alive in the Bahamas, and the fact that it has been programmed into the festival is a good indication of that initiative.

The fairgrounds are cooling off nicely from the oppressive heat of the day, and the festival gets under way in earnest at about 9:30 P.M. After several rounds of storytelling by both children and adults, the sounds of rake 'n' scrape take over. First on stage are the Lassido Boys (a Cat Island band). They perform for nearly an hour, heating up the crowd before handing over the stage to Ophie and the Websites. In contrast to the Lassido Boys, who incorporate electric guitar, bass, and an additional percussionist into their rake 'n' scrape sound, Ophie and the Websites are a traditional ensemble consisting only of accordion, saw, and drum, and their set highlights many of the traditional tunes that Bahamians associate with rake 'n' scrape (Listen to CD III, 9 for an example of rake-n-scrape music).

Ophie and the Websites's set is dominated by tunes that, not so very long ago, would have accompanied quadrille dancing. Although there isn't any organized quadrille dancing on stage this evening, something else is happening. Here and there around the fairgrounds, in small groups of two, three, and four dancers, the quadrille is being taught and danced. Mothers are teaching daughters, grandchildren are copying their elders. Rake 'n' scrape and quadrille dancing are, among other things, about being together—about enacting community—and tonight's festivities are providing a forum for doing just that.

Ancient Man in Concert at the Cat Island Rake-n-Scrape Festival, Friday, June 2, 2006. *Source:* Timothy Rommen

OBEAH
Bahamian folk belief and practice derived from African models and concerned with controlling and deploying powers in service of both good (i.e. healing) and evil (i.e. vengeance).

As night turns to morning, Ancient Man takes the stage, singing his current hit single, entitled "I Ain't Asking for Much." He is wearing a scarf that bears the word "Kuumba." (Kuumba is the name of the sixth day of Kwanzaa and it means "creativity.") The scarf, moreover, is woven in Rastafari colors. By wearing this scarf, Ancient Man is simultaneously affirming his affinity for African American cultural symbols and his solidarity with his Caribbean neighbors. And this is not surprising, for he very deliberately foregrounds Bahamians' African heritage through his music, fashion, and spirituality. Earlier this afternoon I asked him why he chose to call himself Ancient Man, and his response was, "I didn't name myself. The spirits [specific to **obeah**, and pronounced "sperrets"] named me." Embracing and valuing African heritage is, for Ancient Man, an important key to thinking about identity in the Bahamas—a key that he embodies in his performances.

Ancient Man performs a half-hour set backed up by the house band, and the band remains on stage to accompany the evening's remaining headliners, including Sparkles and Nita. The Lassido Boys come back on stage at about 1:45 A.M. and they play a short set to finish things off. The first night of the festival comes to an official close at about 2:30 A.M. The music continues, however, because many of the artists, along with a few hundred festival-goers, retire to a nearby nightclub, owned and operated by the Lassido Boys—a club called "Dis We Place." The festivities finally lose steam sometime around 4:30 in the morning, and I retire for a few hours of sleep.

For two nights (and well into the mornings) the audience at the festival is treated to both traditional rake 'n' scrape bands and to popular music heavily influenced by the rhythms and sounds of that musical tradition. On the third night, however, rake 'n' scrape takes a backseat to gospel music. All the performances this night are focused on sacred music traditions, from traditional anthems to songs influenced by African American gospel and R&B. Once again, traditional and popular forms share the stage, juxtaposed to highlight both distinctly Bahamian sounds (such as the anthems) and connections to broader musical and religious trends and sensibilities (like African American gospel music).

I should note here that Cat Island is, in Bahamian lore, a center not only of rake 'n' scrape, but also of obeah. Obeah is associated in the Bahamas with folk magic and (at times) with black magic. There are so many well-known tales about obeah on Cat Island, that, in the weeks leading up to the festival, I have been regaled with stories and by turns solemn and joking warnings anytime I mentioned that I was going to be attending the rake 'n' scrape festival. The juxtaposition of Christianity with obeah—in this case by singing gospel music in what is considered by many to be quintessential obeah country—is a powerful reminder of the various negotiations that Bahamians (and inhabitants of the entire Caribbean region) have found necessary to make sense of their spiritual histories and futures. The gospel concert marks the end of the Festival, and along with a great many other visitors, I plan to make my way back to Nassau the following day.

The festival illustrates at multiple levels the simultaneous presence of unmistakably local characteristics and of elements drawn from (or present in) regional

dancer uses surprise, stealth, and grace to get close enough to the female dancer to thrust his pelvis at her in a move called a *vacunao*. She in turn evades his moves, improvising her own playful dance steps in the process. As you might imagine, rumba caused a great deal of hand-wringing among the middle and upper classes, and it was banned or severely limited on several occasions throughout the late nineteenth century (Listen to CD III, 11 for an example of rumba guaguancó).

Bèlè and Bomba   Rumba is not an isolated phenomenon within the Caribbean (though it certainly is uniquely Afro-Cuban). Indeed, rumba is one among a *series* of drumming traditions with accompanying dance that emerged throughout the Caribbean during the nineteenth century. It is important to think about these styles because of the significant, even foundational, role they have played in the development of popular musics throughout the region. Let's briefly explore just two of them: *bèlè* and *bomba*.

Bèlè drumming (also called belair) developed in rural Martinique and is played on a drum of the same name (a variant of this drumming tradition, played on a drum called a gwo ka also emerged in Guadeloupe). The drum is played by two performers: one straddles the drum, playing on the drumhead with both hands and a foot (which is used to dampen and undampen the drumhead to produce different pitches); the other performer uses a pair of sticks (called *tibwa*) to beat out characteristic and intricate cross-rhythms on the side of the drum. Bèlè is accompanied by call-and-response singing and by dancing. The dancers focus particular attention on close coordination between their steps and the improvisatory drum strokes (they have to pay attention to keep up with the drummer as opposed to dancing somewhat independently from the lead drummer as they do in rumba guaguancó).

This practice of West African origins was once prevalent throughout the Eastern Caribbean, but is today limited to folkloric exhibitions or to isolated revival movements (such a revivalist movement took place in rural Martinique in the 1980s). Although there are several different ways and styles of playing bèlè, one of the central rhythmic ideas of Martinician and Guadeloupean bèlè—the **cinquillo**—also provided serious inspiration first for *biguine* and then for *zouk* (two Antillean popular musics). In bèlè, the cinquillo is beat out by the tibwa, but it translates very well to shakers (called *chacha*) when the rhythms are applied to playing biguine. In zouk, as we shall see, the rhythm is often simplified to an almost-constant 3+3+2 motive and played with rim shots on the snare while shakers or hi-hats play the cinquillo rhythm. Another interesting aspect of the cinquillo is that it turns up over and over again throughout the region. As such it is not unlike the rake 'n' scrape rhythm—flexible and useful in a variety of musical contexts. For instance, the cinquillo, which came to be a central and defining feature of the light-classical Cuban salon music called *danzón*, is prevalent in popular genres like Haitian *meringue*, and even makes its way into other popular musics like calypso.

CINQUILLO
A rhythmic cell common throughout the Caribbean, containing five separate articulations and organized into a long-short-long-short-long pattern.

LISTENING GUIDE

RUMBA GUAGUANCÓ: "CONSUELATE COMO YO" GO TO **www.mymusiclab.com for the Automated Listening Guide** CDIII • Track 11/Download Track 56

Carlos Embale Ensemble: Clave, Palitos, Congas, Leader, and Chorus

This recording illustrates the main formal and rhythmic structures of rumba guaguancó. The narrative section (canto) is followed by the montuno (beginning at [2:47]) and the clave, palitos, and congas all provide an interlocking, rhythmic foundation for the dancers. The quinto, or lead, conga, improvises over the top of the texture.

The song's lyrics are an encouragement to give up on love because it only leads to heartbreak.

Console yourself like me, because I also had a love that I lost.
And for this (reason) I say now that I won't love again.
Because what good was love to you if that love betrayed you like it did me
O my negra I love you but now I don't love anymore
Hear me . . . Hear me well

(trans. Jodi Elliott)

The clave, palitos, and congas play the following rhythms fairly consistently throughout the performance as shown here. Try to hear them individually. Although the clave in this performance follows a 3/2 pattern (that is a group of three strokes, followed by a group of 2 strokes) another very common clave pattern in rumba is the 2/3 pattern.

Clave:

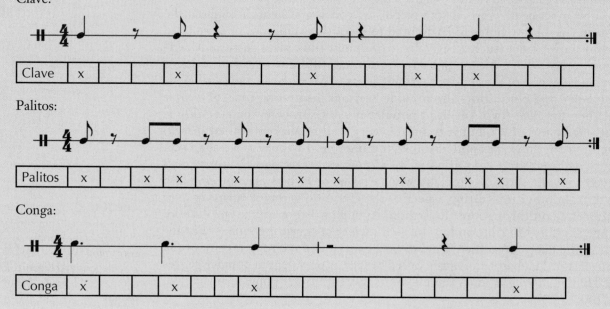

The whole rhythmic texture looks like this:

Clave	x			x			x		x		x			
Palitos	x		x	x		x		x	x		x	x		x
Conga	x			x			x						x	

TIME	SECTION	MUSICAL EVENTS
0:00–0:06	**Canto:** Listen to the way this narrative section features the soloist/leader and his interactions with the chorus, who always sing the main melodic phrase with him. Listen also for the individual percussion instruments and see if you can hear their unique contributions to the overall rhythmic texture of the performance. Listen to this section multiple times. The first time, focus on the melodic and textual organization. Next, listen for the congas (the lowest-pitched of the percussions instruments). Then listen for and clap along with the clave (3 strokes, then 2 strokes). Finally see if you can hear and clap along with the palitos (the highest-pitched of the percussion instruments).	The clave, palitos, and congas open this performance, getting their interlocking rhythms set and preparing for the vocalists entry.
0:06–0:32		Lead vocalist improvises an introductory melody using vocables.
0:32–0:43		Chorus responds to the leader with the first phrase of the canto (and also the first phrase of the melody). *Consuelate como yo ...*
0:43–0:59		The lead vocalist returns with another improvisatory flourish.
1:00–1:13		The chorus returns, repeating the melody and text. *Consuelate como yo ...*
1:14–1:36		The chorus, now augmented by additional singers, repeats the first phrase of melody and text twice more.
1:36–2:00		The lead vocalist again improvises a text-less melody.
2:01–2:24		The smaller version of the chorus sings the second and third phrases of the melody, complete with new text, revealing the overall structure of the canto melody to be **ABA**.

2:25–2:46		The expanded chorus takes up the second and third phrases of the melody as well.
2:46–3:14	**Montuno:** Notice the slight increase in tempo and the new melody. Listen for shorter intervals between the lead vocalist and chorus here and for the quinto solo.	Chorus and lead vocalist take turns singing short phrases.
3:14–3:33		The quinto, or lead conga, plays a solo. This is a good moment to see if you can hear the individual percussion instruments in addition to the solo.
3:34–4:00		The lead vocalist and chorus reenter, continuing their call-and-response interaction until the performance comes to an abrupt end.

✳ Explore
the Musical Instrument
Gallery on
mymusiclab.com

Bomba is a Puerto Rican tradition that emerged from the slave barracks, probably during the early decades of the eighteenth century. It is relatively rare to hear bomba today—it is preserved primarily in staged renditions and performed by folkloric groups. Nevertheless, there are places like Loiza, where young players are mounting a revival of the genre. The bomba was traditionally danced on special days—to mark the end of harvesting, for birthdays, christenings, and weddings. Bomba is a generic name that, like bélé, encompasses a wide range of rhythms and subtypes. The bomba ensemble generally includes dancers, a lead drum (*primo*), a second, lower pitched drum (*buleador*), sometimes a third drum (also called *buleador*), *cuá* (sticks), maracas, singer, and chorus (*coro*). The dance is essentially a challenge pitting the virtuosity of the dancers against the skill and speed of the lead drummer. Bomba dancing incorporates two levels of call-and-response: between the lead singer and the coro and between the lead drummer and the dancers.

Although bomba has declined in popularity over the course of the last century, the rhythmic ideas and aesthetic values embedded in the practice have found expression in Puerto Rican dance band music (notably in the repertories of performers such as Cortijo and Ismael Rivera during the 1960s). Bomba rhythms have also found their way into *salsa*, and bomba remains (along with *plena*) a firm part of Puerto Rican musical identity.

The Twentieth-Century Rumba   At the turn of the twentieth century, according to Robin Moore (*Nationalizing Blackness*, 1997), Cuban elites were looking for a musical identity for their newly independent nation. European-derived forms, including operettas (called *zarzuelas*), burlesques, and light classical salon and dance musics, all of which were common in Cuba at the time, were too European to offer a distinct national sound. There were, to be sure, Cuban elements that stood out. The habanera rhythm (from the *contradanza*) and the cinquillo (already discussed) were very popular both within

Cuba and abroad. And yet, there was some concern that the musical genres within which these rhythms operated were, in the end, still too European to serve nationalist purposes. On the other hand, Afro-Cuban musics like rumba were considered too "primitive," too drum-oriented, and not modern enough for the new nation.

The central paradox was how to create a national culture (a project virtually inconceivable without incorporating Afro-Cuban expressions) and present it as civilized and modern (for which it seemed necessary to marginalize "blackness"). In short, how to find a way to "browning" Afro-Cuban music? Mirroring the state of affairs in Trinidad, members of the black middle class did not object to this project because they were attempting to distance themselves from their own cultural heritage to obtain a greater measure of acceptance within Cuban society. They resented the "blackness" of rumba as much as, if not more than, did the elite.

While elites were busy looking for their answers within Cuba, the World's Fair of 1889 in Paris had illustrated quite clearly the marketability of the primitive and of *negritude*. Composers like Debussy were fascinated by Indonesian gamelans, artists were thrilled by African masks, and a bit later, audiences went wild over Josephine Baker's revues. Jazz was beginning to make inroads in Europe and, by 1920, a tango craze hit all of Europe. People turned to *l'arte negre* for a variety of reasons, both aesthetic and philosophical, and the stage was set for a new dance craze to hit the streets. A few Cuban entertainers who had been performing rumba in a "cleaned-up," staged form in Havana found their way to Paris, where, in 1927, they performed with great success.

By the 1930s, this cleaned-up, commercial rumba was being danced all over Europe and in the United States—ironically solidifying precisely the "exotic" image from which Cuban elites were trying to distance themselves. While rumba swept through Paris and the world, the rumba of the urban lower class was still quite maligned in Cuba. When tourists became increasingly interested in rumba, however, things gradually changed. The top-tier clubs began hiring more Afro-Cuban musicians (in order to claim greater authenticity). Rumba found acceptance abroad and this led, at least in part, to its subsequent repositioning at home despite the fact that it was still symbolically tied to the legacy of slavery and to Africa.

A parallel development had, nevertheless, taken place within Cuba itself during these years. Elements of the traditional rumba had also become firmly entrenched in the formal structure and instrumentation of a new genre called *son*—the dance band tradition that gradually became the international face of Cuba. The clave and the two-part formal structure of *canto* (called *largo* in sones) and montuno, to name but two aspects of traditional rumba, became central to the sound of *son*, and *sones* rapidly became extremely popular in Cuba and abroad. So, rumba found its way into the world and into a more benign local genre (son), and the combination of these two processes made it possible for elites to embrace it—outside recognition, inside redefinition (Moore 1997).

"Wie Tanzt Man Rumba?" Reproduction of a how-to guide for German-speaking rumba dancers, created by dance instructor Walter Carlos. Initially printed in the October 1931 edition of *Wintergarten* Magazine. Photographer: Timothy Rommen. Used by permission, Biblioteca Nacional Jose Marti with thanks to Robin Moore.

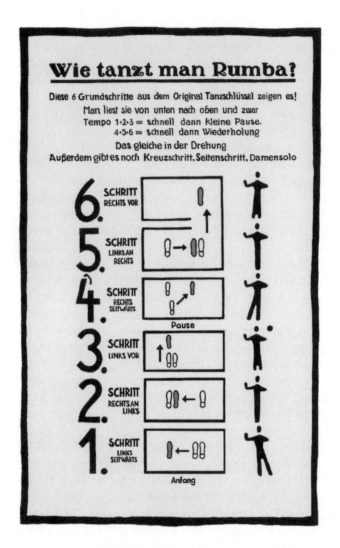

The popularity of son was such that the sounds traveled throughout the region, contributing to the incorporation of elements like the clave into Trinidadian calypsos, Jamaican mento bands, and George Symonette's cover-tune, "Love Alone." By contrast to son, which has remained popular, rumba is today no longer widely popular in Cuba. However, several ensembles specialize in performing it, a fact that keeps rumba from becoming merely a folkloric music. This has also meant that rumba continues to serve as a source of musical inspiration for Cuban dance bands playing styles like son and, more recently, *timba*. This is another example in which questions and issues related to class, cultural politics, travel, tourism, and national identity all contribute to the ways that a musical practice is received and rethought. And, in similar fashion to calypso and steel pan, the sounds of rumba, and especially of son, had an effect beyond Cuba's borders as the music was "exported" through recordings, radio, and performing groups.

WE, THE PEOPLE: NATION AND IDENTITY IN THE CARIBBEAN

A second theme in Caribbean musics concerns how musical style reveals national or communal struggles with identity. The Bahamas offer a case in point. As the country moved to majority rule in 1967 and then achieved independence from Great Britain in 1973, a concomitant cultural negotiation was taking place. As in our example from Cuba, middle-class Bahamians felt that the island's cultural icons were too backward for mobilization in service of national identity. The long history of colonialism had ingrained a certain predilection for British culture, resulting in a parallel silencing of Bahamian culture. Significantly, musicians played an important role in bringing Bahamian customs, foods, clothing, language use, and musical traditions back into the public eye, both through their lyrics and by means of performance. In fact, **junkanoo**, a carnival-like festival celebrated on Boxing Day (December 26) and New Year's Day, gradually came to serve as an icon of Bahamian identity.

In the Bahamas, junkanoo developed during the nineteenth century and took the form of a nighttime festival during which slaves would get together to visit, celebrate, and socialize. After emancipation in 1838, however, it came to be associated in the minds of elites with loud revelry and violence (more imagined than real) and was generally disparaged. Junkanoo gradually became associated with a particular rhythm, performed on goatskin drums and accompanied by whistles, cowbells, and whatever other instruments people could get their hands on (bugles, bicycle horns, etc.). The characteristic rhythms of junkanoo developed over the course of some decades, but by the early twentieth century, they had codified to some degree into roles for the various drums and bells.

JUNKANOO
A Bahamian festival, celebrated on Boxing Day (December 26) and New Year's Day and including music, costume arts, and dance.

Bahamas, New Providence Island, Nassau, Junkanoo Festival. *Source:* Bob Thomas/ Stone/Getty Images

The festival was variously banned, threatened, and limited throughout the nineteenth and early twentieth centuries. Just as with carnival in Trinidad, elites felt threatened by junkanoo and passed injunctions, such as the Street Nuisance Act of 1899, that severely limited the festival (in this case by prohibiting junkanoo during the late nighttime hours when it was customarily celebrated). However, as tourists began to frequent the Bahamas more regularly in the years following World War II, they began to express real interest in junkanoo. Merchants along Bay Street in Nassau seized the opportunity and began to institutionalize the festival. During the 1950s there was a gradual recognition that this festival could generate tourist revenue. The drive toward independence began in earnest around the same time, and junkanoo thus began to factor as a marker of Bahamian identity.

By the time independence became a reality in 1973, junkanoo was a very different festival than it had been prior to World War II. It now took place in a centralized location with a set parade route (along Bay Street), had been recognized as an official competition (with rules, judges, and prizes), was broadly "Bahamian" and sponsored by the state (the Masquerade Committee had been absorbed into the Ministry of Tourism). Most importantly, junkanoo had become a positive source of identity for Bahamians (including elites). Junkanoo illustrates how a festival tradition gradually came to define for a nation–state an important aspect of its identity leading up to and in the wake of independence.

But the Caribbean also plays host to other political arrangements. The next two case studies consider what happens when identity is being negotiated in the context of a foreign *departmént* (that is, within the French Antilles, which are foreign *departménts* of France) and—more drastically still—when it is being negotiated by people who do not have any way of constituting themselves within the geographical boundaries of a nation–state (as is the case with the Garifuna).

Zouk

The French Antilles were not particularly active in the popular music scene during the early 1970s. *Biguine*, the local dance band music, had been a hugely successful genre earlier in the twentieth century and had, in fact, been one of the first Caribbean musics to attract early and sustained interest by recording companies (along with calypso). But biguine had gradually lost much of its popularity to other regional styles. George Decimus, a founding member of the band called Kassav', came to believe that this void—which was filled by nonlocal musics like merengue (Dominican Republic), cadence-lypso (Dominica), and *konpa-direct* (Haiti)—was a result, ultimately, of a lack of confidence in Antillean identity. This belief led in 1979 to the birth of Kassav', a band explicitly committed to producing technically flawless, rhythmically complex, unquestionably Antillean music for world consumption.

The band implemented several strategies of representation, starting with its name. "Kassav'" is a local dessert that is made from manioc and needs to be carefully prepared, because if made improperly, it can result in a toxic cake.

ZOUK
Popular music style of the French Antilles, popularized in the 1980s by the band Kassav'.

The band thus claimed local cuisine and folk knowledge as their own. Kassav' also decided that its lyrics would be sung in the local language, *creole*. Among Antilleans, creole had for the longest time been considered the language of the poor and uneducated, whereas French was considered proper and refined. The band featured the gwo ka (Guadeloupean bèlè drum) and foregrounded local rhythms to instill a sense of pride in Antillean sounds and instruments. The rhythms of the gwo ka were soon transferred to the drum kit, but nevertheless remain the basis for the music that came to be called **zouk**. Kassav' recorded in Paris to have access to the best equipment possible and was extremely sensitive to international sounds (especially to those of the World Beat craze of the late 1970s and early 1980s). In 1984 Kassav' released the song "*Zouk-la se sel medi-kaman nou ni*" ("Zouk is the only medicine we have"), and it was a huge success. Having gained traction on the international market, the band was forced to articulate their ideology more clearly to the public both at home and abroad. Among these ideas were: They wanted to create a music that would be picked up and understood by non-Caribbean ears, to write music that would defend the sounds of the Antilles and of the black diaspora on the international market, and to craft a current translation, with the available means, of the Caribbean musical sensibility, which enters into contact with all cultures. It is important to note also that the band boasted a broadly international membership. Originally a Guadeloupean band, the membership quickly expanded to include Martinician, Belgian, Cameroonian, French, and Algerian musicians. Finally, one of the remarkable aspects of Kassav's membership is the union of Guadeloupe and Martinique, a remarkable union because of the strong, long-standing mistrust and competition that has divided these two *départménts*. So Antillean unity is a particularly salient message—a message that the band literally embodies.

As Jocelyne Guilbault (1993) noted, Kassav' foregrounds its hybrid nature and, in so doing, proposes a new vision of Antilleans as mixed and hybrid, culturally rich, and modern world citizens. There is also a peculiar logic to challenging the métropole with creole by so carefully appealing to the exoticism that drives the world music industry. In the end, Kassav' was able to turn both Paris and Fort-de-France in a big way—Fort-de-France, because creole thumbed its nose at Paris, and Paris because creole had found a space outside French national culture (the world music market) that could then be reabsorbed as French diversity by the urban elite.

Punta and Punta Rock

Garinagu is the name of the people of West African and Amerindian descent who settled along the Caribbean coast of Belize, Guatemala, Honduras, and Nicaragua during the nineteenth century. Garifuna is another, more common name for this people—a term that serves also to refer specifically to their language. The beginnings of the Garifuna trace to the island of St. Vincent, one of the few places in the Caribbean where Amerindians were able to successfully resist the colonial encounter well into the eighteenth century. On St. Vincent,

PUNTA ROCK
Popular music style developed by the Garifuna, featuring call-and-response vocals and a rich percussion accompaniment derived from traditional punta music.

the Amerindians met and intermarried with two shiploads of Africans, who had reached shore after their slave ships were wrecked in a storm on the way to Barbados around 1635. The Garifuna, known in St. Vincent as the Black Caribs, eventually found themselves at war with and technologically outmatched by the British, who had become increasingly interested in St. Vincent during the course of the eighteenth century. The Garifuna, led by a chief named Chatuye, were eventually defeated in 1796—a defeat that prompted a massive (and forced) Garifuna migration with eventual resting points in places like Guatemala and Nicaragua. This migration began with the exile in 1797 of some 2,000 Garifuna to Roatan Island off the coast of Honduras. The dispersal of the Garifuna from St. Vincent has led many to refer to themselves as the Garifuna Nation throughout the diaspora.

In 1802, Garifuna from Honduras began settling in Belize (then British Honduras), and on November 19, 1832, many of the exiles from Roatan Island joined the Garifuna who had already settled there, a day that, since 1977, has been recognized as Garifuna Settlement Day. There are six major Garifuna settlements in Belize today, but beginning in the middle of the twentieth century, large numbers of Garifuna have been migrating to the United States, where there are now sizable communities in New York, Los Angeles, and Chicago. Oliver Greene has pointed out (2002) that in 1993 there were an estimated 225,000 Garifuna in Central America and about 90,000 in the United States. The difficulties of maintaining identity across several host nations and between multiple languages (Spanish, English, and Garifuna) has led many Garifuna to focus careful attention on preserving language, customs, music, and other traditions. This concern is illustrated in the creation of **punta rock**.

To understand the ideology and sound of punta rock, though, it is necessary to offer a brief introduction to its musical antecedent—punta. Punta is a song genre that symbolically reenacts the cock-and-hen mating dance and is usually composed by women. Punta is performed during festivals, at wakes, and at celebrations that follow *dugu* ceremonies (religious ceremonies during which a family appeals to the ancestors for help in solving a given problem). It is a secular, duple-meter genre, and the lyrics are often cast in the vein of other regional genres such as calypso, giving expression to strong currents of social commentary and political consciousness. It's a couples dance that features rapid movement of the hips and a totally motionless upper torso. Punta usually involves call-and-response singing, drums, rattles, and sometimes conch shell trumpets. The drums used in punta are called the *primero* and the *segunda*. As you might imagine, the primero improvises over a steady ostinato (repeating motive) laid down by the segunda (Listen to CD III, 12 for an example of punta).

"Punta" (recorded in 1982), illustrates both the extent to which children were still being taught Garifuna musical practices at that time and the increasing need for renewed attention to Garifuna language and identity. It reminds us that Garifuna were actively passing on traditions despite the rhetoric that accompanied the rise of punta rock while simultaneously offering a bit of perspective on the ideological position that artists took with respect

LISTENING GUIDE

"PUNTA"

GO TO **www.mymusiclab.com for the Automated Listening Guide** CDIII • Track 12/Download Track 57

Performed by Henry, Bobsy, and Lena Nuñez

TIME	SECTION	MUSICAL ELEMENTS/LYRICS
0:00–0:20	Listen briefly for the three main elements: the vocals, the primero, and segunda drums.	This song is being performed by three children. The lyrics of the song are mostly in English: *When the teacher speaks I don't like it. Hey Dandi (Mountain Cow or Tapir) walking away.* *Hey, Tiligad's sister is walking away.*
0:20–0:40	The vocals: Listen for the English content in the lyrics.	The children are singing in a mixture of Garifuna and English. Recorded in 1982, at the very moment that the first punta rock artists were gaining popularity, this performance illustrates both the continuation of traditional forms of tutelage (these children learned how to drum and sing punta from their elders) and offers some sense of the felt need for a revitalization of Garifuna language (the children sing mostly in English).
0:40–1:00	The segunda pattern: Listen for the repeating ostinato in the segunda drum.	The rhythm that drives this song is played on the segunda. It consists of the following pattern: You can hear it in 2/4 or as a 6/8 pattern, but the actual feel is somewhere between these two:

2/4 feel

Segunda	x				x		x	x
Pulse	x				x			

6/8 feel

Segunda			x			x	x	x
Pulse			x			x		

TIME	SECTION	MUSICAL ELEMENTS/LYRICS
1:00–1:30	The primero: Listen for the improvisatory and virtuosic role of the primero.	The primero is free to improvise over the segunda pattern. In this sense, it fulfills a role not unlike the quinto drum in rumba ensembles.

to their project—not enough was being done to promote Garifuna lifeways. Accordingly, the late 1970s found a new musical approach gaining momentum among Garifuna. Indeed, punta was being consciously revitalized as popular music through a genre called punta rock. Punta rock is an adaptation of punta and to a lesser extent of *paranda* (a folk-song genre for voice and guitar) and is very popular in Belize and in places like Guatemala and Honduras (where only *cumbia* outstrips it in terms of popularity). The language of punta rock is Garifuna, a major marker of ethnicity and of identity for performers and fans alike. There are, to be sure, punta rock songs with English or Spanish lyrics, but Garifuna, along with the rhythms of punta, remain major markers of identity. Unlike punta, however, punta rock is composed and performed largely by men instead of women.

The shift from punta to punta rock was motivated in part by concern over the degree to which young Garifuna were identifying with the musical styles they were hearing primarily over the radio. Sounds from Bob Marley to James Brown were floating across the airwaves, and traditional punta simply couldn't compete. Initially (in the late 1970s) the traditional punta ensemble was merely augmented with a lead guitar and a turtle shell (to approximate a snare drum sound). Performers gradually added keyboards and drum machines (which replaced the segunda) in the 1980s, and the basic tempo of punta was increased, leading to a radio-friendly and ethnically marked popular music. One of the ways that the sound was adapted to more modern-sounding arrangements was to split the traditional punta rhythm (the segunda part) between kick drum and snare.

Garifuna continue to face significant challenges to their identity. They live in modern nation–states of which they form but a small minority. They share a common heritage, but are spread over several national borders, including the United States, making large gatherings for reunions or *dugu* ceremonies quite difficult to realize. Finally, they continue to eat, dance, sing, and speak in ways not recognized as mainstream within their respective nation–states, making it tempting for some to entertain the thought of blending in. These challenges, however, have been confronted with a focus on the shared history of the Garifuna—by a renewed interest, growing during the 1970s and 1980s, in preserving language, customs, and rites and by new artforms that include the creation and dissemination of punta rock. This is a story of identity quite different from zouk or junkanoo, but it offers another example of the challenges to identity that confront peoples living in the Caribbean region.

"All O' We Is One": Class and Cultural Politics in the Caribbean

Junkanoo also serves as an excellent introduction to the next theme in Caribbean music—class and cultural politics within the region. Junkanoo is touted as the great, national unifier by the Bahamas Ministry of Tourism and by participants alike. All Bahamians, whether day laborers or prime ministers, participate in the festival. For these two parades (Boxing Day and New Year's Day), at least, Bahamian society dissolves ethnic and class issues and celebrates together—so the argument goes. And yet, a closer examination reveals some very interesting trends within the structure of junkanoo groups themselves. Each junkanoo troupe is made up of a front line and a back line. The front line includes dancers (both choreographed and free dancers) and a range of set

MUSIC IN THE CARIBBEAN

pieces designed to illustrate and explore the group's chosen theme. The back line consists of the instrumentalists: brass players, bellers (cow bell players), lead drummers, and bass drummers. Bellers and drummers also blow whistles along the parade route. The number of people who participate in these troupes is quite considerable. The largest groups, like the *Valley Boys, Saxons, Roots*, and *One Family*, for example, can bring as many as one thousand junkanooers to Bay Street for a given parade.

Vivian Nina Michelle Wood has pointed out that women generally gravitate toward the costume arts while men play instruments, and that drums are generally the domain of the grass roots while local whites play *mas* (i.e., masquerade). In other words, junkanoo groups tend to preserve an internal division of labor that traces some of the historical fissures within Bahamian cultural and social life. Metaphors of unity, then, only go so far toward explaining junkanoo. When subjected to a bit of analysis, it becomes clear that some of the struggles related to cultural politics within the Bahamas continue to rest uneasily at the very heart of this most powerful of national symbols. Junkanoo illustrates gender, ethnic, and economic fissures within Bahamian society and offers an introduction to a theme that plays out musically in powerful ways throughout the Caribbean.

Chutney and Chutney-Soca

An example of cultural politics as it relates to ethnicity can be found in Trinidad, where East Indians and Afro-Creoles continue to work out just what sounds and tastes should represent the nation. East Indians, the descendants of indentured laborers brought to the region from South Asia, are present in large numbers in Trinidad, Guyana, and Suriname. They arrived first in Guyana, where some 250,000 disembarked between 1838 and 1917. Suriname, getting a rather late start, imported some 37,000 East Indian laborers between 1873 and 1916. Trinidad followed Guyana's example more quickly and began importing indentured laborers in 1845. By 1917, some 144,000 East Indians had arrived in Port of Spain, and the resulting East Indian community has since grown to comprise approximately 41 percent of Trinidad's population.

Hindu and Muslim religious beliefs and practices were added to the growing number of religious systems in Trinidad, and the government's Population and Housing Census of 2000 suggests that approximately 30 percent of the population claims Hindu or Muslim faith. East Indians, of course, brought with them not only religious beliefs, but also ways of living, making music, and speaking, all of which added layers of complexity to Trinidadian society. Dr. Eric Williams, Trinidad's first prime minister, attempting to find a way of uniting Trinidadians toward the common goal of nation building in the early 1960s, tried to do away with this complexity by reconfiguring the way people thought about their place in Trinidadian society. In a now-famous address he suggested, "There can be no Mother India, for those whose ancestors came from India . . . there can be no Mother Africa, for those of African origin. . . .

The only Mother we recognise is Mother Trinidad and Tobago, and Mother cannot discriminate between her children" (Williams, *Forged from the Love of Liberty*, 281).

And yet, Dr. Williams's attempt at using familial metaphors to unify a society splintered along ethnic fault lines foundered. One reason for this failure was that the cultural productions that the government chose to represent the way that Trinidad looked, sounded, and tasted, were, almost without fail, of Afro-Creole extraction. We have already seen that calypso, steel bands, and carnival came to hold a special place in terms of Trinidad's national identity. East Indian musical traditions, like Tan-singing, tassa drumming, and chutney, were not equally promoted. Although Dr. Williams's address posited Mother Trinidad as the only mother for all Trinidadians, the terms of *inclusion* into the ostensibly multicultural nation did not change appreciably for East Indians.

Added to this political dimension of interethnic relations in Trinidad has been the increasing economic success of East Indians. Afro-Creoles have found themselves increasingly economically outstripped by East Indians, whether in small business ventures or in terms of employment. By the mid-1980s, this growing East Indian economic power had translated into burgeoning political power. When, in the 1990s, East Indians succeeded in turning the political tables on Afro-Creoles, electing Basdeo Panday prime minister in 1995, there was a great deal of worry among Afro-Creoles that the cultural tables would be turned as well.

Musical style plays a major role in these cultural politics, each style carrying an extra measure of weight as an expression of a particular identity and subject position within the nation. Styles such as calypso and soca continue to be tied to the Afro-Creole community in Trinidad, whereas chutney and tan-singing are understood as "authentically" East Indian forms of expression. And although there were artists and fans who broke through these categories of musical ownership to explore mixtures or simply to sing or participate in a different style, these artists were the exception rather than the rule. It is predictable that these artists were often roundly criticized for these breaches of artistic (read cultural) propriety.

Even as recently as the 1990s, controversy raged over musical styles. A case in point is **chutney-soca**, which blends aspects of both *soca* and *chutney* to produce a hybrid drawing on both Afro-Creole and East Indian musical styles. As musicians began to sing chutney-soca in the tents during carnival and in the Soca Monarch competition, both Afro-Creole and East Indians raised concerns. Afro-Creoles were unsure how to judge chutney-soca in a competition designed to deal only with soca. East Indians were by turns aggravated at the fact that East Indian musicians and musical characteristics were even participating in carnival and upset at those Afro-Creole musicians who chose to perform "their" music—a musical blend that they had vigorously opposed in the first place. To satisfy both groups, a new category for competition, called the "Chutney-Soca Monarchy," was created in 1996. This move, although certainly making the job of judging the soca competition more clear-cut (a happy development for Afro-Creoles), continued to legitimize and further

CHUTNEY-SOCA
Popular music style of Trinidad that combines elements of two earlier styles, soca and chutney.

institutionalize the "separate but equal" policies for which East Indian leaders had been pushing (see Edmondson 1999; Manuel 2000). Musical ownership thus remains a major component of cultural politics in Trinidad.

Two other East Indian musics—Tan-singing (now on the verge of falling out of use) and chutney—further illustrate Caribbean cultural politics. *Tan-singing* is a light-classical tradition and features several different genres, the most important of which is Thumri. *Thumri* is, for many East Indians, a tangible link to South Asian musical practices, and although it is certainly indebted to South Asian models, it has developed as a uniquely East Indian musical practice. Thumri is a vocal genre accompanied by *dholak* (drum), *dhantal* (metal clapper), and harmonium, which doubles the vocal line in heterophonic style. And yet, this musical style is gradually passing from active performance into folklore. Most performers no longer can speak Hindi, and the tradition seems to be dying a slow death at the hands of chutney and Bollywood film music.

Chutney is a folk music of South Asian origin, usually sung by women for women at celebrations such as weddings. The lyrics are often humorously educational with regard to domestic and marital subjects. Traditional instrumentation for these songs is not unlike that for Tan-singing, employing a harmonium, dholak, and dhantal, although the performance style is no longer touched with the virtuosity of Tan-singing. This tradition continued through the 1960s, but starting in the 1970s, male East Indian singers like Sundar Popo began to explore chutney as a popular genre, performing it in public and even in carnival tents and adding other instruments to the ensemble, including keyboards, drum kits and drum machines, bass, and electric guitars. This move from the private to the public sphere—and from folk to popular status—caused a great deal of concern among East Indian leaders and was only exacerbated when women performers began to experiment with the style as well. And yet, chutney grew in popularity and, in the 1980s, helped to launch the hybrid I discussed earlier: chutney-soca. Both performance styles continue to be popular, and East Indian leaders seem to have resigned themselves to the fact that East Indian culture and social structures can no longer remain isolated from Trinidadian national culture. And yet, the separate but equal policies continue to be attractive, and Trinidadians continue to face serious challenges in the realm of cultural politics.

Merengue

Merengue music of the Dominican Republic offers a very different example of class and cultural politics. During the mid-nineteenth century, merengue developed from the salon-type music popular throughout the region at the time (*danza* and *contradanza*). It was gradually picked up as a folk music, and this style came to be played far away from the dance halls and salons of Santo Domingo. It should come as no surprise that those in positions of power denounced this rural merengue as vulgar and primitive. The early merengue ensemble usually included *guira*, guitar/*quatro*, *marimba* (like the *marímbula*), and *tambora* (a double-headed drum), and by 1870, the button accordion took the place of the

MERENGUE
Popular dance music of the Dominican Republic.

string instruments. Merengue was quite varied from region to region, but the style of the Cibao valley was most influential. By the 1920s merengue *típico* of Cibao had become somewhat standardized and could even include a saxophone playing melodies and countermelodies alongside the accordion. In contrast to many of the genres explored earlier, merengue focuses a great deal of its rhythmic intensity in emphasizing on-beats. So merengue is in 2/4 meter, and the "one, two, one, two" of each measure is pounded out by the kick drum and by the bass guitar (in contemporary ensembles), making this feel a prominent feature of the genre. The structure of these songs is similar to Cuban rumba/ son in that there is a narrative section (called merengue) followed by a more syncopated call-and-response section (called *jaleo*). Early merengues also often included a short, march-like introduction, called a *paseo*, during which the dancers would make their way to the dance floor. This introductory section is rarely played in the contemporary moment. In the 1930s, nation, music, and ideology were linked by Rafael Trujillo, who rose to power in 1930 and remained in power until his assassination in 1961. Merengue was re-urbanized under Trujillo, who championed it as the national music (starting in 1936), using it not only to solidify his own dictatorial power, but also to posit a Dominican Republic distinctly different (in every possible respect) from Haiti. If Haiti was African, then the Dominican Republic was Iberian, and merengue from the cibao region appeared to support that claim. That merengue was already a thoroughly creole musical tradition, developed in and through negotiating both African and European influences, was expressly denied by Trujillo. This was to be a musical genre that countered Haitian musical styles, emphasized European aesthetic ideas, and would, so Tujillo hoped, unify the country with regard to class relations. He mandated that urban dance bands take up the merengue, and not a few merengues were composed in his honor. That lower-class, rural music was now being performed in elite ballroom settings was not a particularly satisfying turn of events for Dominican socialites, and yet Trujillo's mandates managed to firmly install merengue at the heart of Dominican national identity. The lower-class roots of merengue were resounded, in part through the use of swing bands, complete with trumpets and especially saxophones, that came to play a type of merengue called *orquesta* merengue. The piano accordion, moreover, became the instrument of choice in these orchestras because of the increased flexibility that it offers over the button accordion (which can play in only a few keys).

During the middle years of the twentieth century, both urban and rural styles of merengue existed side by side and were played on national radio, and although both remained tied to their class roots, both also served as markers of Dominican identity. The merengue típico of the Cibao has come to be called *perico ripiao* and remains the "roots" version of merengue. Following Trujillo's assassination in 1961, the orquesta merengue style gradually evolved into the popular, commercialized merengue (utilizing fairly typical electric dance band ensembles) that took the international scene by storm in the 1980s and 1990s and remains popular today (Listen to CD III, 13 for an example of neo-traditional merengue típico).

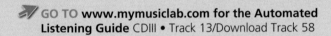

LISTENING GUIDE

MERENGUE TÍPICO: "CONSANGRACIÓN DE CARIÑA"

GO TO **www.mymusiclab.com for the Automated Listening Guide** CDIII • Track 13/Download Track 58

Accordion, saxophone, bass, guira, tambora, congas

La India Canela

This recording illustrates the old three-part structure of merengue that used to be standard for merengue típico. It begins with a short, march-like paseo, which would have been used to give dancers enough time to escort each other to the dance floor. This is followed by the merengue section. At about [1:17], the performance moves into the third section, called *jaleo*. It is more improvisatory, more syncopated, and even moves between duple and triple meter toward the end. In the contemporary moment, most merengues will simply start with the merengue section, creating a two part merengue/jaleo structure not unlike the rumba/son structure explored earlier. The lyrics are an expression of true love:

> *You are so beautiful and so pretty that I love you.*
> *I love all of you now and forever.*
> *I dedicate to you my affection and help*
> *and I'm thinking of loving only you eternally.*
> *Yes! Before getting married, stop by here.*
> *You belong to me and I will make you happy.*
> *Before getting married, think it over.*
> *Mami, you don't know how much I love you.*
> *Listen beautiful negra, how do you know . . . how much I love you?*
> *Nobody loves you like I love you!*

(trans. Jodi Elliott)

TIME	SECTION	MUSICAL ELEMENTS
0:00–0:09	**Paseo:** This opening section presents only the accordion, bass, and guira. Notice the march-like quality, and think about how this short section provides just enough time to grab a dance partner and make your way to the dance floor.	The opening paseo melody is played by the accordion and accompanied by bass and guira.
0:9–0:18		The paseo is repeated.
0:19–0:32	**Merengue:** Notice the dramatic increase in tempo and the straight-forward 2/4 meter, emphasized by the bass, which plays on one and two consistently throughout this section. Listen also for the nimble counter-melodies and harmonies played by the saxophone in response to the accordion.	The merengue gets underway, and the accordion and saxophone set the stage for verse one.

0:32–0:48		Verse one, delivered by two vocalists, is sung over an accompaniment accented by accordion and saxophone riffs at the end of phrases.
0:48–1:01		The accordion and saxophone take over and play an interlude.
1:01–1:17		The vocalists return and sing verse two.
1:17–1:36	**Jaleo:** This is the most syncopated, energetic section of the performance. Listen for the improvisatory explorations by all members of the ensemble and, in particular, for the sections, toward the end of the jaleo, during which the ensemble switches back and forth between 2/4 and 6/8 meter, creating sections during which 3 against 2 rhythms are prevalent.	The jaleo begins, and it is signaled by both a new melodic theme and by the shift in the bass guitar. Instead of playing on beats 1 and 2, the bass now intones notes on the off-beats of each measure (playing on the AND of 1 and the AND of 2). Notice that the end of this subsection ends in a repeated formula that signals the vocalists.
1:36–1:51		The vocalists take over, singing another verse.
1:51–2:10		The instrumentalists play another interlude, concluding with the repeated formula introduced earlier.
2:10–2:25		The vocalists take over again.
2:25–2:42		The instrumentalists return, this time playing in 6/8 time so that the rhythm shifts to 3 eighth notes per beat instead of 2 per beat as has been the case throughout the performance to this point. This 3 against 2 is heard most easily by listening to the bass guitar line. This shift to 3 against 2 heightens the intensity of the improvisations.
2:42–3:03		The instrumentalists return to the repeated formula that signals the return of the vocalists and also shift back to 2/4 meter in the process. Instead of bringing the vocalists back immediately, however, the accordion performs a solo over the repeating formula.
3:03–3:19		The vocalists return for a final verse.
3:19–3:44		The instrumentalists move again to a 3 against 2 feel in 6/8 meter. Listen for the bass guitar here, which improvises a bit within the harmonic framework.
3:44–3:52		The instrumentalists return to 2/4 meter and play a concluding figure to bring the performance to a close.

Travel and Tourism: Reconfiguring Home and Away

As we have already seen, travel and tourism are important themes throughout the Caribbean—themes that play out in both centripetal (inward-moving) and centrifugal (outward-flowing) patterns. The musical styles that are created at "home" are affected by travel and tourism even as these creations, in going abroad, affect other places and musical practices. We will explore some of the other ways that travel and tourism can help us think about musical practices both within and outside the Caribbean by considering the several types of travel (both actual and imagined) with which the growing Caribbean diasporas in many locations throughout North America and Europe continue to negotiate their understandings of home and away, illustrating that Caribbean musics have participated in significant ways in globalized networks of music-making, and exploring several of the religious practices that have historically emerged in response to travel in the Caribbean. The emergence of major carnival festivities in New York (Labor Day Carnival), London (Notting Hill Carnival), and Toronto (Caribana) reminds us to think about globalization as a double-edged and uneven process that globalizes the local while localizing the global. When we think about patterns of reception within the Caribbean, we also need to keep in mind that the movement outward from the Caribbean of these various musical styles and festival traditions does, in fact, affect in a tangible way the life of people in the métropoles even after it has returned "home." And this not least because many of these urbanites are Caribbean nationals who for educational or employment reasons have found themselves "abroad." The Labor Day Carnival works in large part because of the enthusiastic support of the Caribbean community in New York. Caribana represents not merely a chance to get together and play mas or to hear great artists, but also a means of recognizing publicly the twice-diasporized nature of life in a city like Toronto. That non-Caribbean participants gain exposure to and often appreciation for Caribbean Carnival arts and musical life is, of course, an important motivating factor and source of pride for those who are representing, say, Barbados at Notting Hill Carnival in London.

But travel and tourism also suggest the possibility of considering new relationships to the past and to "home" that are coming to characterize communities living abroad as well as those who have stayed behind. Nostalgia, for example, drives perceptions of home and away in significant ways. Take the lyrics of a Bahamian song entitled "Island Boy," and written by Eric Minns, which repeatedly assert: "Island Boy, you've got your mind on your job in New York but your heart's in the Caribbean." The new diasporas of the Caribbean configure themselves not only around family networks and everyday concerns related to employment and education, but also around memory and particular views of history that allow narratives of the past to be woven into a more nuanced sense of place in the present.

One strategy is to configure home as an idealized place that exists in the past (not just the good old days, but also that good old *place*). This process allows diasporic communities to view their "home" (say, Port of Spain) as simply a stopover on the road toward the "real home," but not really all that much better than their present physical location (say, London). This affords a new relationship to identity forged through recovering a way of being in the world (and of being in the present) that works toward that "good old place" (with all of the cultural and social implications that this idea entails), regardless of one's actual physical location. Importantly, this approach to home and away means that new traditions in new places not only become possible but desirable, and carnival celebrations in cities like London, New York, and Toronto are merely the most obvious examples of this trend.

Another example of this tendency is the musical effects that follow from the artistic interactions that occur between musicians from various locations throughout the Caribbean in places like New York. For instance, *salsa* is an example of how travel has influenced the music of the Caribbean and of Latin America. Salsa, which grew out of experiments by Latino musicians in New York during the 1960s, variously combined elements of Cuban and Puerto Rican musical styles (the principal, if not the only musical influences) to create a hybrid, flexible style that swept to popularity during the 1960s and 1970s. The presence of musicians from various locations throughout the Caribbean in New York and their musical interactions and negotiations led to a new genre that has since found a home (and legions of fans) in most urban centers of Spanish-speaking Latin America. Travel and tourism have led to new trends of music-making (salsa) and to new cultural practices (various carnivals) in those places outside the Caribbean where Caribbean nationals make their homes.

Caribbean musics have also had a global effect quite independent of Caribbean communities living abroad. Evidence of this can be seen in the immense global popularity of reggae, which took the world by storm during the 1970s and 80s, But reggae represents only one of the chapters of Jamaica's engagement with North American and globalized music markets. Jamaican popular dance music, in fact, has a long history of reciprocal exchanges with North American popular music. R & B heavily influenced the early history of ska in the 1950s and into the 1960s. While reggae was being sold to worldwide audiences by artists like Bob Marley, Peter Tosh, and Bunny Wailer (to name only three of the most iconic performers), *dub music* (versions of recorded reggae manipulated by engineers in ways that created new aesthetic visions of reggae) was beginning to influence the early explorations of hip hop in New York City. Dancehall, itself heavily influenced by hip hop, represents only the latest example within in a long history of these musical exchanges. Artists like Beenie Man, Sean Paul, Lady Saw, Buju Banton, Bounty Killer, and Elephant Man, to name just a few, are variously benefiting from collaborations with North American artists and finding it possible to

Baju Banton, 2002. *Source:* Jack Vartoogian/Front Row Photos release their own, very successful, records. It is important to recognize, then, that sound travels in different ways and along different routes than do people, but that both of these patterns continue to create new and powerful musical practices that afford individuals, whether living within or without the Caribbean and irrespective of citizenship, new means of constructing their identities.

Some sacred musics offer another range of responses to questions of travel in the Caribbean. These musics are tied quite closely to diasporic narratives, growing from the need to address fundamental spiritual concerns in new contexts. Other sacred practices are clearly predicated on travel to the region by missionaries and, more recently, on the role of the mass media. All Caribbean sacred musics, however, give expression to the variety of ways that beliefs and cosmologies have been negotiated within the region. Catholic, Protestant, Hindu, Muslim, Jewish, and African religious contexts were all brought to the region during the colonial encounter. Of these religious systems, Catholicism and Protestantism were imposed on a great many people for whom these religions represented primarily another register of colonial control. One of the main results of these traveling (and imposed) religious practices has been religious syncretism, a strategy whereby elements from two or more religious traditions are combined into new practices. Stuart Hall (2001:35) has remarked, "It is impossible, in my experience, to understand black culture and black civilization in the New World without understanding the cultural role of religion, through the distorted languages of the one book that anybody would teach them to read." His assertion rings true without regard to whether that one book was being taught by Baptists, Anglicans, or Catholics.

That said, African-derived drumming is a major component of the ceremonial music central to syncretic religious systems such as Cuban *santería*, Trinidadian *shango*, and Haitian *vodoun*, all of which have found ways of combining African deities and cosmologies with Catholic saints and doctrines. In santería the drums are called *batá*, and there are three main instruments in a batá ensemble: the *iyá* (largest drum), *itótele* (midsized drum), and *okónkolo* (smallest drum). The drums are considered sacred, and important rules and rituals circumscribe their construction, care, and use. Only initiated drummers may touch these drums, and the drums are imbued with a spiritual force, usually called *Añá*, upon their initiation. The drums are played without the improvisational elements present in genres such as rumba, bélé, and bomba. Instead, each drum plays more-or-less set rhythms that are associated with individual **orisha** and that also correspond, in part at least, to patterns and inflections particular to Yoruba language. These rhythms provide the foundation that the lead singer builds on in invoking the particular orishas toward which the batá drums are directed.

In Jamaica, a particularly rich range of responses to Protestant missionizing was deployed, including a practice called dual membership, whereby an individual could claim to be, say, Baptist, but would also participate in myal or convince rituals (both of which are local, African-derived religious practices). Rastafarianism, which developed in the 1930s, is significant in that it managed to link, albeit for a short time, its theological and social message to the soundtrack of reggae (thanks in large part to artists like Bob Marley).

ORISHA
A spirit understood as one of the manifestations of God within Yoruba and Yoruba-derived religious practice.

BHAJAN
Hindu devotional song.

CHOWTAL
A form of folk music associated with phagwa (holi) in Trinidad and having roots in Indian (Bhojpuri) folk music.

The message and the sound have been split from one another in recent years (especially with the rise of dancehall in the mid-late 1980s). Niyabinghi drumming, however, continues to be an important component of Rastafarian religious life. The *Niyabinghi* ensemble consists of three drums—*bass*, *funde*, and *askete* (which improvises over the solid rhythms performed on the other two drums)—an ensemble of instruments and an associated set of rhythmic ideas adapted from Jamaican Kumina rituals and from Burru drumming. Niyabinghi drumming is an excellent example of the ways that African-derived instruments and traditions can be "retuned" in the process of searching out and refashioning African roots.

During the middle decades of the twentieth century, Pentecostalist missionaries made significant inroads throughout the Caribbean (and in Latin America), as a result of which gospel music and contemporary Christian musical styles are now very prevalent in the region. Beginning in the 1970s, local genres have also been identified as potential evangelical tools, leading to new styles like *gospelypso* (calypso and gospel dancehall). These musical traditions often illustrate the complex ways in which church communities are utilizing regional and transnational styles both for their own local purposes and to participate in globalized forms of Christianity (see Rommen 2007).

Finally, there are also sacred musics that participate in religious networks separate from those that trace European and African religious travels. *Tassa drumming*, for example, accompanies the Hosay festival in Trinidad. *Hosay* is a Shia Muslim festival commemorating and celebrating the martyrdom of Husayn ibn Ali (the Prophet Muhammad's grandson). Ensembles include two primary kinds of drums—lead and second drums—and hand cymbals, but the number of players can vary greatly. Significantly, the Hosay festival has, in Trinidad, become a site of potential interethnic and interreligious participation. Hindu East Indians also contribute to the range of sacred musics circulating in the Caribbean. Two of the principal genres include bhajans and chowtal. A **bhajan** is a devotional song almost always incorporating a text dealing with a spiritual topic. In Trinidad, the bhajan is usually accompanied by a harmonium and sometimes by a violin, but because of the devotional nature of the material, virtuosity is consciously downplayed in bhajans.

One of the major Hindu festivals on the Trinidadian religious calendar is called *phagwa*, or *holi*. This festival is held in March and celebrates the victory of good over evil. Groups of East Indian men play and sing a style called **chowtal** during this festival, and there are often competitions during the *phagwa* season. Chowtal is usually accompanied by percussion (including hand cymbals, dholak, and dhantal).

The complex colonial encounter, coupled with the continued presence of missionaries, has created within the Caribbean a wide range of religious practices, each deployed to make sense of histories and futures, and each reflecting the need to make meaningful the present. Music has accompanied these travels and continues to offer audible and tangible support to people of faith throughout the region.

SUMMARY

✓●─[Study and **Review**
on **mymusiclab.com**

Cat Island, Monday June 5th: I am waiting at the Cat Island Airport, along with several dozen other late-departing festivalgoers, shooting the breeze and reliving some of the great moments of the weekend. We've heard storytelling, seen quadrille dancing, experienced traditional, popular, and sacred musics. In short, the festival provided a glimpse at many of the registers of musical life I have discussed in the preceding pages. In offering these short vignettes, I have juxtaposed each of these musics and themes to suggest ways they overlap, draw on each other, interact, and in general offer inspiration to each other. The unifying themes are powerful—rhythms like rake 'n' scrape and cinquillo, formal patterns like canto/montuno, ensemble aesthetics (like the predominance of three interlocking drum parts), and patterns of religious life, to name just a few possibilities, appear and reappear throughout the region. And yet, these common musical threads are highly individuated in terms of their local instantiations, accruing different meanings, diverse social functions, and new sounds, depending on where (and when) they happen to be performed. The cinquillo finds expression in rural, lower-class bélé drumming and in the elite spaces of Cuban danzón. The habanera rhythm finds itself equally at home in nineteenth-century Cuban contradanza and in today's reggaeton. Caribbean musics thus reflect the challenges of shared history while simultaneously reworking the present into sounds and shapes that offer new ways of making meaning and creating community. This holds true for nation–states and festivals like junkanoo, for the Garifuna Nation and genres such as punta rock, and for Arthur's Town, Cat Island, and that one rake 'n' scrape band: Ophie and the Websites.

BIBLIOGRAPHY

General   Ray Allen and Lois Wilcken, eds., *Island Sounds in the Global City: Caribbean Popular Music and Identity in New York* (New York: New York Folklore Society: Institute for Studies in American Music, Brooklyn College, 1998); Peter Manuel, ed.,*Creolizing Contradance in the Caribbean* (Philadelphia: Temple University Press, 2009); Sandra Pouchet Paquet, Patricia J. Saunders, and Stephen Stuempfle. *Music, Memory, Resistance: Calypso and the Caribbean* (Kingston, Jamaica: Ian Randle, 2007); David Moskowitz, *Caribbean Popular Music: An Encyclopedia of Reggae, Mento, Ska, Rock Steady, and Dancehall* (Westport, CT: Greenwood, 2006); Susan, Thomas, *Cuban Zarzuela: Performing Race and Gender on Havana's Lyric Stage* (Urbana: University of Illinois Press, 2009); Frances Aparicio and Cándida F. Jáquez, eds., *Musical Migrations: Transnationalism and Cultural Identity in Latin/o America* (New York: Palgrave Macmillan, 2003); Kenneth Bilby, "The Caribbean as a Musical Region" in Sidney W. Mintz and Sally Price, eds., *Caribbean Contours* (Baltimore, MD: Johns Hopkins University Press, 1985); Richard D. E. Burton, *Afro-Creole: Power, Opposition, and Play in the Caribbean* (Ithaca, NY: Cornell University Press, 1997); Belinda Edmondson, ed., *Caribbean*

Romances: The Politics of Regional Representation (Charlottesville: University Press of Virginia, 1999); Stuart Hall, "Negotiating Caribbean Identities" in Brian Meeks and Folke Lindahl, eds., *New Caribbean Thought: A Reader* (Kingston: University of the West Indies Press, 2001); C. L. R. James, *Beyond a Boundary* (Durham, NC: Duke University Press, 1993 [1963]); Peter Manuel with Kenneth Bilby and Michael Largey, eds., *Caribbean Currents: Caribbean Music from Rumba to Reggae*, 2nd ed. (Philadelphia: Temple University Press, 2006); Dale A. Olsen and Daniel E. Sheehy, eds., *The Garland Encyclopedia of World Music, vol. 2: South America, Mexico, Central America, and the Caribbean* (New York: Garland Publishing, 1998); Eric Williams, *Forged from the Love of Liberty: Selected Speeches of Dr. Eric Williams*, edited by Paul Sutton (Port of Spain: Longman Caribbean, 1981); Kevin Yelvington, ed., *Trinidad Ethnicity* (Knoxville: University of Tennessee Press, 1993).

Monographs and Articles   Frances Aparicio, *Listening to Salsa: Gender, Latin Popular Music, and Puerto Rican Cultures* (Hanover, NH: University Press of New England, 1998); Francio Guadeloupe, *Chanting down the New Jerusalem: Calypso, Christianity, and Capitalism in the Caribbean* (Berkeley: University of California Press, 2009); Rebecca Miller, *Carriacou String Band Serenade Performing Identity in the Eastern Caribbean* (Middletown: Wesleyan University Press, 2007); Shannon Dudley, *Music from behind the Bridge: Steelband Spirit and Politics in Trinidad and Tobago* (New York: Oxford Univeristy Press, 2008); Paul Austerlitz, *Merengue: Dominican Music and Dominican Identity* (Philadelphia: Temple University Press, 1997); Gage Averill, *A Day for the Hunter, A Day for the Prey: Popular Music and Power in Haiti* (Chicago: University of Chicago Press, 1997); Brenda Berrian, *Awakening Spaces: French Caribbean Popular Song, Music, and Culture* (Chicago: University of Chicago Press, 2000); Curwen Best, *Culture @ the Cutting Edge: Tracking Caribbean Popular Music* (Kingston: University of the West Indies Press, 2004); Kenneth Bilby, *True-born Maroons* (Gainesville: University of Florida Press, 2005); Samuel Charters, *The Day is So Long and the Wages So Small: Music on a Summer Island* (New York: M. Boyars, 1999); Carolyn Cooper, *Sound Clash: Jamaican Dancehall Culture at Large* (New York: Palgrave Macmillan, 2004); Carolyn Cooper, *Noises in the Blood Orality, Gender, and the "Vulgar" Body of Jamaican Popular Culture* (London: Macmillan Caribbean, 1993); John Cowley, *Carnival, Canboulay, and Calypso: Traditions in the Making* (New York: Cambridge University Press, 1996); Shannon Dudley, *Carnival Music in Trinidad: Experiencing Music, Expressing Culture* (New York: Oxford University Press, 2004); Juan Flores, *From Bomba to Hip-Hop: Puerto Rican Culture and Latino Identity* (New York: Columbia University Press, 2000); Henry Frances, *Reclaiming African Religions in Trinidad: The Socio-Political Legitimization of the Orisha and Spiritual Baptist Faith* (Barbados: University of the West Indies Press, 2003); Oliver Greene, "Ethnicity, Modernity, and Retention in the Garifuna Punta" in *Black Music Research Journal* 22/2 (2002); Jocelyine Guilbault, *Zouk: World Music in the West Indies* (Chicago: University of Chicago Press, 1993); Katherine Hagedorn, *Divine Utterances: The Performance of Afro-Cuban Santeria* (Washington, DC: Smithsonian Institution Press, 2001); Dick Hebdige, *Cut 'n'*

Mix: Culture, Identity, and Caribbean Music (New York: Routledge, 1987); Donald Hill, *Calypso Calaloo: Early Carnival Music in Trinidad* (Gainesville: University Press of Florida, 1993); Michael Largey, *Vodou Nation: Haitian Art Music and Cultural Nationalism* (Chicago: University of Chicago Press, 2006); Timothy Rommen, *Funky Nassau: Roots, Routes, and Representation in Bahamian Popular Music* (Berkeley: University of California Press, 2011); Peter Manuel, *East Indian Music in the West Indies: Tan-Singing, Chutney, and the Making of Indo-Caribbean Culture* (Philadelphia: Temple University Press, 2000); Elizabeth McAlister, *Rara! Vodou, Power, and Performance in Haiti and Its Diaspora* (Berkeley: University of California Press, 2002); Robin Moore, *Nationalizing Blackness: Afrocubanismo and Artistic Revolution in Havana, 1920–1940* (Pittsburgh, PA: University of Pittsburgh Press, 1997); Robin Moore, *Music and Revolution: Cultural Change in Socialist Cuba* (Berkeley: University of California Press, 2006); Viranjini Munasinghe, *Callaloo or Tossed Salad? East Indians and the Cultural Politics of Identity in Trinidad* (Ithaca, NY: Cornell University Press, 2001); Helen Myers, *Music of Hindu Trinidad: Songs from the India Diaspora* (Chicago: University of Chicago Press, 1998); Tejaswini Niranjana, *Mobilizing India: Women, Music, and Migration Between India and Trinidad* (Durham, NC: Duke University Press, 2006); Deborah Pacini Hernandez, *Bachata: A Social History of Dominican Popular Music* (Philadelphia: Temple University Press, 1995); Timothy Rommen, *"Make Some Noise:" Gospel Music and The Ethics of Style in Trinidad* (Berkeley: University of California Press, 2007); Norman Stolzoff, *Wake the Town and Tell the People: Dancehall Culture in Jamaica* (Durham, NC: Duke University Press, 2000); Stephen Stuempfle, *The Steelband Movement: The Forging of a National Art in Trinidad and Tobago* (Philadelphia: University of Pennsylvania Press, 1995); Ned Sublette, *Cuba and Its Music: From the First Drums to the Mambo* (Chicago: Chicago Review Press, 2004); Lise Waxer, ed., *Situating Salsa: Global Markets and Local Meanings in Latin Popular Music* (New York: Routledge, 2002); Vivian Nina Michelle Woods, *Rushin' Hard and Runnin' Hot: Experiencing the Music of the Junkanoo Parade in Nassau, Bahamas* (Ph.D. diss. Indiana University, 1995).

DISCOGRAPHY

General   *Caribbean Beat*, vols. 1 and 2 (Intuition INT 3112 2 and INT 3126 2); *Caribbean Island Music* (Electra Nonesuch 72047-2); *Caribbean Voyage: Brown Girl in the Ring* (Rounder CD 1716); *Caribbean Voyage: Caribbean Sampler* (Rounder 11661-1721-2); *Caribbean Voyage: Carriacou Calaloo* (Rounder CD 11661-1722-2); *Caribbean Voyage: Dominica* (Rounder 11661-1724-2); *Caribbean Voyage: East Indian Music in the West Indies* (Rounder CD 11661-1723-2); *Caribbean Voyage: Grenada* (Rounder CD 11661-1728-2); *Caribbean Voyage: Martinique* (Rounder 11661-1730-2); *Caribbean Voyage: Nevis & St. Kitts* (Rounder CD 82161-1731-2); *Caribbean Voyage: Saraca* (Rounder CD 11661-1726-2); *Caribbean Voyage: Tombstone Feast* (Rounder CD 11661-1727-2); *Caribbean Voyage: Trinidad* (Rounder CD 11661-1725-2); *West Indies: An Island Carnival* (Electra Nonesuch 9 72091-2).

Bahamas   *Joseph Spence: The Complete Folkways Recordings, 1958* (Smithsonian Folkways CD SF 40066); *The Bahamas: Islands of Song* (Smithsonian Folkways SF 40405); *The Bahamas: The Real Bahamas in Music and Song* (Nonesuch 79725-2); *The Bahamas: The Real Bahamas, Vol. II* (Nonesuch 79733-2). *BELIZE: Belizean Punta Rockers, Vol. 1* (Stonetree STR06); *Traditional Music of the Garifuna of Belize* (Folkways FW 04031).

Cuba   *A Carnival of Cuban Music* (Rounder CD 5049); *Afro-Cuba: A Musical Anthology* (Rounder CD 1088); *Afro-Cuban All Stars: A Toda Cuba le Gusta* (World Circuit/Nonesuch 79476-2); *Buena Vista Social Club* (World Circuit/Nonesuch 79478-2); *Cuba I Am Time* (Blue Jackel CD 5010-2); *Cuba in Washington* (Smithsonian Folkways SF CD 40461); *Cuban Counterpoint: History of Son Montuno* (Rounder CD 1078); *Cuban Dance Party* (Rounder CD 5050); *Folk Music of Cuba* (UNESCO D8064); *Havana & Matanzas, Cuba ca. 1957: Batá, Bembé, and Palo Songs* (Smithsonian Folkways SFW 40434); *Sacred Rhythms of Cuban Santeria* (Smithsonian Folkways SF CD 40419); *The Cuban Danzón: Before There Was Jazz, 1906–1929* (Arhoolie CD 7032).

Dominican Republic   *Merengue Típico from the Dominican Republic* (Smithsonian Folkways SF 40547); *Quisqueya en el Hudson: Dominican Music in New York* (Smithsonian Folkways SF 40495); *Essential Merengue: Stripping the Parrots* (Corason CORA122); *Merengue: Dominican Music and Dominican Identity* (Rounder 1130); *Juan Luis Guerra: Areito* (Karen CDK 146); *Sergio Vargas: 15 Exitos* (Sony SMK 84949).

French Antilles   *Biguine, Valse et Mazurka Creóles, 1929–1940* (Fremeaux & Assoc. CD FA 007); *Caribbean Revels: Haitian Rara and Dominican Gaga* (Smithsonian Folkways CD SF 40402); *Dance! Cadence!* (CDORB 002); *Konbit: Burning Rhythms of Haiti* (A&M CD 5281); *Rhythms of Rapture: Sacred Musics of Haitian Vodou* (Smithsonian Folkways SF 40464); *The Best of Kassav'* (Olivi Musique OLI2-1325).

Jamaica   *Bob Marley: Songs of Freedom* (Tuff Gong CD 314-514 432-2); *Bongo, Backra, and Coolie: Jamaican Roots*, vols. 1 and 2 (Smithsonian Folkways F-4231 and F-4232); *Drums of Defiance: Jamaican Maroon Music from the Earliest Free Black Communities of Jamaica* (Smithsonian Folkways CD SF 40412); *Explosive Rock Steady: Joe Gibbs' Amalgamated Label 1967–1973* (Heartbeat CD HB 72); *Mento Madness* (V2 Records 638812720122); *Ska Bonanza: The Studio One Ska Years* (Heartbeat CD HB 86/87); *The Harder They Come (Soundtrack)* (Island CD 314 486 158-2).

Puerto Rico   *Ballet Folklorico Hermanos Ayala: Bomba de Loíza* (Blue Jackel 54527-2); *Cuarteto Mayarí, 1941–1942* (Harlequin HQ CD 134); *Jíbaro Hasta El Hueso: Mountain Music of Puerto Rico* (Smithsonian Folkways SFW 40506); *Pedro Flores, 1935–1938* (Harlequin HQ CD 72); *Pedro Padilla y Su Conjunto: Return on Wings of Pleasure* (Rounder CD 5003); *Puerto Rico in Washington* (Smithsonian Folkways SF 40460); *Rafael Hernandez, 1932–1939* (Harlequin HQ CD 68); *Somos Boricuas/We Are Puerto Rican* (Henry St. HSR 0003);

The Music of Puerto Rico (Harlequin HQ CD 22). *Salsa: Spanish Harlem Orchestra: Un Gran Dia En el Barrio* (ropeádope 0-7567-93135-2-2); *The Best of Fania Allstars* (Columbia/Legacy CK 85871).

Trinidad   *Calypso After Midnight* (Rounder CD 11661-1841-2); *Calypso at Midnight* (Rounder CD 11661-1840-2); *Calypso Awakening: From the Emory Cook Collection* (Smithsonian Folkways SFWCD 40453); *Calypso Breakaway, 1927–1941* (Rounder CD 1054); *Calypso Carnival, 1936–1941* (Rounder CD 1077); *London Is the Place for Me: Trinidadian Calypso in London, 1950–1956* (Honest Jons HJRCD 2); *Lord Invader: Calypso in New York* (Smithsonian Folkways SFW CD 40454); *Mighty Sparrow, Volume 1* (Ice Records CD 691302); *Pan All Night: Steelbands of Trinidad and Tobago* (Delos DE 4022); *Peter Was a Fisherman: The 1939 Trinidad Field Recordings of Melville and Frances Herskovitz, Vol. 1* (Rounder 3719); *Shango, Shouter, & Obeah: Supernatural Calypso from Trinidad, 1934–1940* (Rounder CD 82161-1107-2); *The Golden Age of Calypso: Dances of the Caribbean Islands* (EPM Musique 995772); *The Heart of Steel: Featuring Steelbands of Trinidad and Tobago* (Flying Fish CD FF 70522); *The Sweet Groove of Phase II Steelband* (Rituals CO 796).

West Indian Rhythm   *Trinidad calypsos on world and local events featuring the censored recordings—1938–1940* (Bear Family BCD 16623 JM).

Native American Music

BRUNO NETTL

"NORTH AMERICAN INDIAN DAYS"

A Modern Ceremony

The scene is the town of Browning, Montana, in the middle of the Blackfeet Native American Reservation. To the west are the rugged mountains of Glacier National Park, and in all other directions one sees the yellowish look and the curved contours of the high plains in late afternoon. We are on the edge of the small town with its handful of stores, boarded-up businesses, and streets with potholes, and have gone to the center of a large circle of tents. Some are the kind you can buy at any camping store, but others are canvas versions of the grand tepees of the Plains tribes with their ceremonial painted decorations. We are entering a kind of miniature stadium with entrances on four sides and an expanse of grass in the middle.

Some three hundred people are sitting on benches or folding chairs; about half of them seem to be Native Americans, the rest whites, many with cameras

and cassette recorders. There is a podium on one side, and a master of ceremonies (MC) is speaking over a loudspeaker, asking dancers (who are not visible just yet) to prepare for the grand entry. Around the edge of the grassy center several bass drums are spaced, each representing a singing group of a half-dozen men that seems to be setting up amplification equipment. Eventually, eighteen singing groups take their places; a few of them include one or two women, but one of them is entirely made up of women. The MC proceeds to call the roll, naming and locating each group and giving it a number; each responds with a stroke on the drum. It turns out that the groups (also called drums) come from various locations on the reservation or from the Blackfoot reserves in neighboring Alberta. About half of them are from other tribes, from Eastern Montana, the Dakotas, Arizona, and Washington. Their names indicate locations or family names, and it becomes clear that the members of a "drum" are often members of an extended family.

✳ Explore
the Learning Objectives
on **mymusiclab.com**

Grand Entry

The MC, who happened to be the chief of the tribal council and a well-known politician in the Native American world of the 1970s, engaged in a bit of light-hearted banter and then called on one of the "drums" to sing the song for the "grand entry." Throughout the song, and, indeed, throughout most of the **powwow**, the members of the singing group sit in a circle, facing each other but essentially looking at their drums or the ground, bent forward, singing with great concentration, ignoring the audience and also the dancers when they finally enter the enclosure.

Then, rather suddenly, we see dancers in flamboyant costumes entering from all four sides of the enclosure, each group in single file, moving to the right and steadily clockwise around the center of the circle, eventually making a wide stream of bodies, perhaps 150, moving rhythmically to the drumming. The men wear brightly colored cloth-and-feather outfits, each unique; the women wear long dresses decorated in various ways with beads and colored cloth, simpler and more modest than the men's costumes. Each dancer, however, has a costume in some sense of the word, while the singers wear blue jeans, T-shirts, and farmers' caps. From one entrance emerges a line of male dancers moving athletically, with large steps and jumps; on the opposite side, men with more restrained movements enter the enclosure. These two types of dancers are called fancy and traditional dancers, respectively. The women, though with much more restrained motions, divide themselves along the same lines in the other two entrances. All dancing is "solo." Couples do not dance, but while the men move singly and idiosyncratically, some of the women dance slowly, grouping themselves two or three abreast.

POWWOW

Tribal or intertribal gathering in twentieth-century Native American culture, a principal venue for performance of traditional and modernized music and dance.

Powwow Festival: four Sioux male dancers with feather staffs dance in grand entry. *Source:* Tony Freeman/ PhotoEdit

The song ends after seven or eight repetitions. The MC indicates that the next one will be sung by Drum no. 7 from Heart Butte (a small town thirty miles south of Browning) and that it will be (as most turn out to be) a type of song called **intertribal**,. The singing and dancing begins again. It goes on like this for several hours, each drum or singing group taking its turn. The series of songs are frequently interrupted by related events such as a song and brief procession to mourn a recently deceased member of the community, different dances such as circle and owl dances (the latter danced by couples), dance contests, and brief ceremonies. The style of the music is much the same throughout, and the singing groups from all locations sound similar and share a repertory. Members of the audience talk, walk in and out, speak with dancers and singers, take photos, and record the singing on cassettes. The scene is similar to that of a small-town sports event (Listen to CD III, 14 for an example of a Blackfoot Grass Dance song).

Ancillary Events

Although the main events of North American Indian Days take place in the dance enclosure, other activities with music are worthy of attention. In a small hut, a traditional gambling game, played by two teams facing each other and hiding a bullet or stick, is in progress. The team hiding the object sings constantly, songs with a limited melodic range consisting of the alternation of only two brief musical phrases, all the while beating rhythmically and rapidly on a plank. But the high, intense, pulsating singing of the dance songs is here replaced with a lower, more relaxed style. A couple of blocks away, a kind of barn dance is taking place in a parking lot, with a country-and-western band composed of members of the Blackfoot tribe singing old Nashville favorites. A half-mile further, south of the town, a small rodeo is in progress. It is billed as an "Indian rodeo"; its content is like that of other small-town rodeos in Montana, but the participants are all Native Americans. Before and between the events recorded music is played over a loudspeaker and attracts little attention; it is patriotic music, such as the national anthem, "America, the Beautiful," and also Sousa marches. The next morning there is a parade with many dozens of floats representing businesses and institutions of the area—some are Native American, others white—this is a central event in North American Native American Days. Some of the floats have music, live or recorded, and for once one hears traditional Native American music—the modern intertribal songs—along with rock, jazz, and Christian hymns.

North American Indian Days is a spectacle that characterizes Native American culture in North America in several ways. First, it is a successor of the midsummer religious ceremonies that were held traditionally by many Native American societies. Furthermore, as an intertribal event, it symbolizes to both Native Americans and whites the broad Native American identity that is important to them. The fact that the same songs are known to singing groups from all over, that the same style (with some regional diversity) is used by many tribes, and that linguistic differences are submerged as the songs have no words

INTERTRIBAL
Songs or dances based on the Plains styles with which traditions of various other tribes are combined, developed for performances at modern powwows.

LISTENING GUIDE

BLACKFOOT WAR OR GRASS DANCE SONG   GO TO **www.mymusiclab.com for the Automated Listening Guide** CDIII • Track 14/Download Track 59

Performed at North American Indian Days, Browning, Montana, 1966
Sung by Heart Butte Singers (7 men)
Recorded by Bruno Nettl

This recording illustrates many features of the "plains" music area. The track fades in while the performance is in the middle of a stanza. We can clearly hear how the singers set up a steady rhythm by beating on the edge of their bass drum. When the first full stanza begins, the drum's leader sings an initial phrase in a falsetto voice—tense, harsh, loud, and ornamented [0:37–0:44]. This is often called the "push up" or "lead." The phrase is then repeated by a second singer. The whole group enters during this repetition, still singing softly. This portion of the strophe is called the "second." After this repetition, the whole group sings a stately melody, consisting of several short phrases and moving down the scale until it flattens out an octave below the beginning. The stanza comes to a close after this longer melodic section is repeated. This section is called the "chorus." The whole stanza is then repeated several times. Note that the first two stanzas are sung and drummed softly, and then tempo, intensity, and loudness increase rapidly (at about 1:30). The song has no words; only **vocables** or meaningless syllables are sung, but all of the singers perform these in unison. The overall form of the song can be represented as **AA BCDE BCDE**, with **BCDE** noticeably longer than **A**. In fact, **E** is a variation of **A**, an octave lower. This kind of song structure is called **incomplete repetition**. This type of melody, which begins high and gradually "steps" down to a low ending pitch, is often referred to as a "**terraced melody**."

TIME	SECTION	MUSICAL EVENTS
0:00–0:05	**Stanza 1:** The performance is already underway as the recording fades in. Listen for the clicks of the drumsticks on the side of the drum throughout this section. Listen also for the "hard beats" or "honor beats" toward the beginning of the second **B** Section.	The recording fades in as the repeat of Section **A** is under way (the "second").
0:05–0:22		Section **BCDE** (called the "chorus") is performed. Notice the clicking of the drumsticks on the side of the drum and the way the melody descends almost stepwise to its lowest notes at the end of the section.

[0:05–0:08] **B**
[0:09–0:12] **C**
[0:12–0:16] **D**
[0:17–0:21] **E**

0:22–0:37	Repeat of Section **BCDE**. Notice the incorporation of "hard" or "honor" beats at [0:27–0:29].
	
	   [0:22–0:25] **B**
	   [0:25–0:29] **C**
	   [0:29–0:33] **D**
	   [0:34–0:37] **E**

0:37–0:44 **Stanza 2:** Listen to the short **A** Sections, and notice the way that the melody is incorporated into the end of the "chorus" (phrase **E**), but sung an octave lower.	Section **A** begins the second stanza. This is sung by the lead singer. This is called the "push up" or "lead.'
0:44–0:50	Section **A** is repeated, this time by a second singer. That singer is accompanied by the other performers (singing softly). This portion of the strophe is called the "second."
0:50–1:06	The "chorus" is sung by the whole group. Notice the melodic gesture toward the end of the section [0:57–1:01, phrase **E**] that mirrors Section **A** an octave lower.
1:07–1:23	The "chorus" is repeated, again incorporating "hard" or "honor" beats at [1:12–1:13].
1:24–1:30 **Stanza 3:** Listen for how the singer transitions the group from beating on the side of the drum to beating on the skin itself. Notice that the intensity increases markedly as all the performers begin to play on the skin of the drum.	"Push up" or "lead."
1:30–1:37	"Second," but this time the second singer begins to beat his drumstick on the skin at [1:33–1:37], signaling the whole drum to do the same. A crescendo (gradually increasing volume level) accompanies this shift and accomplishes a transition into the "chorus."
1:37–1:52	The crescendo carries into the "chorus." Notice that the intensity of the performance also increases at this juncture.
1:52–2:06	Chorus is repeated.
2:06–2:46 **Stanza 4:** Listen to the whole melody, and see if you can hear and feel it as a whole musical statement.	[2:06–2:11] "Push up." [2:11–2:16] "Second." [2:17–2:32] "Chorus." [2:32–2:46] "Chorus" repeated.
2:47–2:59 **Beginning of Stanza 5:** The recording fades out just as the repeat of Section **A** is begun.	[2:47–2:51] "Push up." [2:51–2:59] Fade out during the "second."

VOCABLE

Nonsemantic syllables that are sung; "nonsense syllables."

INCOMPLETE REPETITION

A song structure common in intertribal and Plains style and consisting of two sections. The first section includes a short melodic phrase, called a "push up" or "lead," followed by a repetition of that melody by another singer. This repetition is called the "second." The second section, called the "chorus" generally consists of two or more phrases and is, itself, repeated.

TERRACED MELODY

A melody structured so that it begins in a high register and "steps" or "cascades" down to a low concluding pitch.

(or occasionally English words) underscores that function of the powwow. The coexistence of several events, each with different music—gambling games from an ancient tradition, dancing from a modern Native American one, other events with Western music performed by Native Americans—symbolizes the present life of Native Americans as a separate population that nevertheless participates in the mainstream culture. The comparison of traditional and fancy dancers reflects the dual role of the event—traditional ceremony and modern entertainment. What is important for us to note is the way in which traditional Native American music is used to exhibit the old tradition but also to tie the various strands of the culture, old and modernized, to each other.

SOME OLDER CEREMONIAL TRADITIONS

The concept of "song" in most Native American cultures is a relatively short unit, rather like our nursery rhyme or hymn. Songs are ordinarily presented, however, in large groups and sequences as parts of elaborate ceremonies and rituals. Most religious ceremonies are elaborate affairs, lasting many hours or even several days. In many ceremonies, the songs to be performed and their order are specifically prescribed. In others they are not. In the **Peyote** ceremonies of Plains tribes, for instance, each singer must sing four songs at a time, but they may be any songs from the Peyote repertory, and only at four points in the ceremony must particular songs be sung.

Thus, the "Night Chant" (**Yeibechai**) of the Navajo, a curing ceremony, requires nine days and nights and includes hundreds of songs and their poetic texts. The **Hako**, a Pawnee ceremony of general religious significance, required several days and included about one hundred songs.

Native American drummers form a drum circle at the Cheyenne Arapaho powwow in Oklahoma. *Source:* Allen Russell/Alamy

The medicine-bundle ceremonies of the Northern Plains peoples might consist of several parts: narration of the myth explaining the origin of the bundle, opening the bundle and performing with each of the objects in it, a required activity (dancing, smoking, eating, praying), and the singing of one or several songs (usually by the celebrant, sometimes by him and others present) for each object. The Blackfoot Sun Dance, the largest and most central of the older tribal ceremonies of this culture, required four preparatory days followed by four days of dancing. The Peyote ceremony, which became a major religious ritual in many tribes of the United States in the course of the late nineteenth and twentieth centuries, consists of a night of singing. Each participant—there may be from ten to thirty sitting in a circle—sings four songs at a time, playing the rattle while his neighbor accompanies him on a special drum.

Secular events, too, are structured so that songs appear in large groups. The performance of a Stomp Dance, a social dance of southeastern origin performed by a line of dancers moving in snakelike fashion with responsorial singing, leader and group alternating, includes a dozen or so songs. The North American Native American Days powwow, described earlier, takes four days (Listen to CD III, 15 for an excerpt of a Creek Stomp Dance Song).

THE WORLD OF NATIVE AMERICAN CULTURES AND MUSIC

Native American Societies Past and Present

American Indian life today is highly variegated. Some tribal societies maintain their special identity; other groups of tribes were, through happenstance or force, obliged to share a reservation and have somehow fashioned a unified culture. Some activities and ceremonies, such as the powwow we have described, are of an essentially intertribal nature. Native Americans from various tribes find themselves in large cities and join together to establish for themselves a common identity. In most respects, of course, they share the culture of their non–Native American compatriots, speaking English or Spanish. It is largely in music and dance that their Native American background is exhibited to themselves and to others.

Most of what is known about Native American music comes from the last hundred years, when recording techniques and ethnography were developed. Native Americans had, of course, already experienced much negative and positive contact with whites by this time, but in the early part of that period (late nineteenth and early twentieth centuries) one could still get a picture of what Native American music and musical culture may have been like before contact. It is clear, first of all, that each tribe had its own musical culture, repertory, musical style, uses of, and ideas about music. There were between one and two thousand tribal groups in North America, almost all speaking distinct languages. The average population of a tribe was around

PEYOTE MUSIC

Songs, in a characteristic style, accompanying a ceremony surrounding use of peyote, a drug derived from a cactus. The peyote religion is a major component of twentieth century Native American culture of the Plains and Southwest.

YEIBECHAI

A major curing ceremony, lasting nine days, of the Navajo; also known as "Night Chant."

HAKO

A complex ceremony of the Pawnee, carried out for the general welfare of the tribe and the world, requiring four days of singing, dancing, and ritual.

LISTENING GUIDE

"CREEK STOMP DANCE SONG"

Song leader, John Mulley

GO TO **www.mymusiclab.com** for the Automated **Listening Guide** CDIII • Track 15/Download Track 60

"Stomp Dance Song" is really a series of songs to accompany a line dance, sung by the dancers. The dance leader is the song leader, and the form is responsorial, that is, the leader sings a short call or phrase, and the group responds by simply repeating what the leader has sung **(A)**, or something to complete his phrase **(B)**. This "call-and-response" is repeated a number of times until a high-pitched call ends the song and a new one begins. Ordinarily the first song consists of a call on one tone, the second expands the range, and others provide a slightly more complex melody. The singers accompany themselves with rattles. In form, melody, and rhythm the songs tend to become increasingly complex. The singers draw on a stock of traditional musical motifs whose content, variations, and order they improvise. This recording illustrates many characteristics of the "Eastern" music area.

TIME/SECTION	RHYTHM	FORM		MELODY
		Solo	*Group*	
0:07 **Beginning call**				
0:13 **Song no. 1**	Duple meter.	**A** (with variations)	**A**	Mostly on one tone.
0:30		**B**	**B**	Higher.
0:38		**C**	**C**	Triadic tune (like C–E–G).
0:47 **Song no. 2**	Triple meter (Beats: solo 1, 2; group, 3).	**D**	**E** (with many variations)	Higher. Note triadic melody throughout. Note the arc-shaped melodic contour, as the pitch gradually rises in the middle of the song and then descends.
1:07 **Song no. 3**	Five-beat meter (Beats: solo, 1, 2, 3; group, 4, 5).	**F**	**G**	Both F and G have more elaborate melodies than Song no. 2. Note the pentatonic bits of melody.
1:32 **Song no. 4**	Complex and varying meter. Sometimes solo has 8 beats, and group, 5.	**H**	**I** (much variation)	Melodic material more elaborate; scales are pentatonic, range over an octave.
1:46 **Rattle begins to be audible.**				
2:10 **End of excerpt.**				

a thousand, but some were much larger, and others had only one hundred to two hundred persons. Each tribe, however, had a large number of songs and used them in many ceremonies, for curing, to accompany dances, and to draw boundaries between subdivisions of society such as age groups, clans, and genders.

Anthropologists have classified these cultures into six to eight groups called culture areas, each with characteristic types of housing, ways of acquiring and preparing food, clothing, religion, and economic and political structure. Thus, for example, the peoples of the North Pacific Coast fished, built wooden houses, had a rigid class structure including slaves, fashioned complex ceremonial sculpture such as totem poles and masks, and held special **potlatch** ceremonies to exhibit personal and family wealth and status. The Native American people of the Plains specialized in hunting buffalo as the prime source of food, housing, and clothes, first on foot with the help of dogs and later on horseback. They were nomadic, lived in tepees, and had a rather informal and egalitarian political structure. Their religion was based on guardian spirits that were acquired by men in dreams, and their ceremonial life included many kinds of acts that showed personal courage. The Pueblo Native Americans of the Southwest, on the other hand, lived in towns of cliff dwellings, grew corn and other plants, and had an extremely complex ceremonial life. In California, a great many very small tribes lived seminomadically, with complex ceremonial life, but subsistence based on hunting small animals, including insects, and gathering plants.

Unity and Diversity in Native American Music

Comparing the sound of North American Native American music with that of Africa or Japan shows that Native American music is relatively homogeneous. It is almost always **monophonic**, and with few exceptions it is vocal. Although there are a number of distinct singing styles, they have in common a tense sound and the use of pulsations on longer notes. Two or three types of forms predominate. There are strophic songs, rather like folk songs or hymns in that a stanza of several lines is repeated several or many times: some very short songs consist of one or a pair of lines repeated many times; and there are forms in which two contrasting sections of music, one usually higher than the other, alternate. Almost all the singing is accompanied by percussion, usually drums or rattles. Thus, the many Native American musical cultures have a good deal in common.

But if we were to go into great detail, analyzing hundreds of songs and making a statistical study of their characteristics for each tribe, we would discover that each group has a unique musical repertory and style. There are differences even between neighboring tribes. The picture is not totally confusing, however, as there are units, which we might call **music areas**, that coincide roughly, though not always precisely, with the culture areas. It is worth mentioning that they do not coincide well at all with language areas; that is, societies speaking related languages often do not share either cultural or musical characteristics.

POTLATCH

A ceremony once common among the peoples of the North Pacific Coast, held to exhibit personal wealth and family status, and often commemorating important events in the life of the host (i.e., marriage, death, birth of a child, etc.). Potlatch ceremonies usually included a feast and the giving of gifts.

MONOPHONIC

Referring to music comprising a single melody; without chords or other melodic or harmonic parts.

MUSIC AREA

A group of Native American tribes who share similar musical styles, roughly corresponding to the cultural areas (but not by language).

Music Areas

The seven music areas are:

1. Plains
2. Eastern United States
3. Yuman (Southwestern United States and parts of Southern California)
4. Athabascan (Navajo/Apache; also Southwestern U.S.)
5. Pueblo (Papago; Southwestern United States)
6. Great Basin (Nevada/Utah)
7. Northwestern Coast (Oregon, Washington, and also some tribes in Alaska)

The Plains area coincides well with a culture area. It has the singing style most distant from standard Western singing, emphasizing high pitch, rhythmic pulsations on the long tones, tension, and harshness. Its characteristic form consists of stanzas internally arranged as follows: a short phrase is presented and repeated; there follows a descending line of three or four phrases ending with a low, flat cadence that is sometimes a version of the initial motif an octave lower; this long second section is repeated, so that the total may have the following scheme: **AA BCD BCD**. The Blackfoot song already discussed in connection with the great powwow (CD III, 14) is a typical Plains song.

The Eastern part of the continent has a greater variety of forms, which usually consist of several short phrases in different arrangements; a rounder and more relaxed vocal sound; some singing in which a leader and a group alternate brief bits of music, the so-called call-and-response pattern; and resulting from this, occasional bits of polyphony. The Creek Stomp Dance Song (CD III, 15) is typical of Eastern U.S. song.

A group of cultures representing the Yuman-speaking peoples of the southwestern United States and some cultures in southern and central California specialize in a form in which one section, a phrase or short group of phrases, is repeated several times but is interrupted occasionally by another, slightly higher and definitely contrastive section, called by some Yuman peoples and also by ethnomusicologists the "rise." Here also we have a relaxed kind of vocal style. The Walapai, a Yuman culture, are representative of this music area (Listen to CD III, 16 for an example of Yuman style song).

Also in the southwestern United States we have the Athabascan style of the Navajo and Apache peoples. Its typical traits are a large vocal range, a rather nasal-sounding voice, and even rhythms that can almost always be written by using only quarter- and eighth-notes.

The style of the Pueblo Native Americans shares features with those of both the Athabascan and the Plains peoples but has a low, harsh, pulsating vocal style and long, complex forms. Related to both Plains and Pueblo songs are those of the Papago people. The Great Basin style, found in Nevada and Utah as well as northern California, and also in the **Ghost Dance** songs of the Plains people, has songs with small vocal range and with a characteristic form

GHOST DANCE
Native American (principally Plains) religious movement of protest against U.S. government excesses of the 1880s.

LISTENING GUIDE

WALAPAI FUNERAL SONG

GO TO www.mymusiclab.com for the Automated
Listening Guide CDIII • Track 16/Download Track 61

This Walapai funeral song illustrates two of the most prominent features of the Yuman music area. First, notice the relaxed vocal quality that the singers bring to the performance. Compare this, for instance, to the much more intense example of Plains style heard on CD III, 14. Second, the song structure incorporates a "rise." The overall structure combines two related melodic phrases (**A A'**) and repeats the pair four times before being interrupted by the "rise," which is higher in pitch and contrasting in character. After the rise is repeated, the performers return to singing **A A'**.

TIME	SECTION	MUSICAL EVENTS
0:00–0:03	**Fade in and A A':** Listen for how the two short melodic phrases are paired together to create a repeating **A A'** structure.	The recording fades in as the performers complete Phrase **A'**.
0:04–0:08		Phrase **A**. Listen for the relaxed vocal quality of the performers.
0:08–0:12		Phrase **A'**.
0:13–0:17		Phrase **A**.
0:17–0:21		Phrase **A'**.
0:22–0:26	**Rise:** Listen for how the performers introduce a higher-register melody, the contours of which also contrast with the more static **A** and **A'** phrases.	The rise interrupts the lower-register melody, introducing a whole new range of higher pitches and a much more active melody line.
0:26–0:31		The rise is repeated.
0:32–1:17	**A A' and Rise:** This time see if you can hear how these two, lower-pitched and more static melodic phrases work to set up the "rise." You'll hear four repetitions of the **A A'** pairing, followed by the rise. When the rise bursts onto the scene, listen for how much energy it injects into the song, not only because of the higher pitches and the more active melody but also because it takes a while to arrive.	[0:32–0:35] Phrase **A**. [0:35–0:40] Phrase **A'**. [0:40–0:45] Phrase **A**. [0:45–0:49] Phrase **A'**. [0:50–0:54] Phrase **A**. [0:54–0:58] Phrase **A'**. [0:59–1:03] Phrase **A**. [1:03–1:08] Phrase **A'**. [1:08–1:12] Rise. [1:13–1:17] Rise Repeated.
1:17–1:31	**Back to A A' as a conclusion:** Listen for how a final statement of the **A A'** pairing brings the song to its conclusion.	[1:17–1:21] Phrase **A**. [1:22–1:31] Phrase **A'** and end of song.

POLYPHONIC
Generic term referring to all music in which one hears more than one pitch at a time, for example, songs accompanied by guitar, choral music, orchestral music, or two people singing a round together. Refers more specifically to music which incorporates two or more simultaneous melodic lines or parts.

in which each of a group of phrases is repeated once, for example, **AABBCC**. This style is illustrated in the Pawnee Ghost Dance recording (CD III, 18).

The Northwest Coast peoples and some of the Inuit share a typical singing style and complex rhythms, often pitting patterns in voice and drum against each other. The Northwest Coast is also the area richest in wind instruments and has a well-documented, if not prominent, **polyphonic** tradition.

IDEAS ABOUT MUSIC
What It Is and What It Does

For all their interest in music and their large repertories, Native American peoples did not develop longer, more complex forms with greater interactions. There are three main reasons why this didn't happen:

1. Oral tradition places some limitations on the complexity of materials to be remembered.
2. There is really quite a lot more complexity, at a microscopic level, than the listener may at first perceive.
3. Most important, the idea of technical complexity has never been a criterion of musical quality to Native American peoples. Rather, music is measured by such things as its ability to integrate society and to represent it to the outside, its ability to integrate ceremonial and social events, and its supernatural power. The rather athletic view of music taken in Western culture, where star performances by individual composers and performers and their ability to do difficult things is measured, is replaced in Native American cultures by quite different values.

Music has supernatural power. In Blackfoot culture, it is the songs that, as it were, hold the power. Thus, each act must have its appropriate song. In a ceremony in which a medicine man is trying to influence the weather, he will have a bundle of objects, which he opens and displays, but their supernatural power is not activated until the appropriate song is sung. In many Native American cultures, songs are thought to come into existence principally in dreams or visions.

Composition and Creativity

In the Plains, a man has visions in which powerful guardian spirits appear to him, and these are validated by the songs they sing to him. As many songs have no words, it is clearly not simply the texts but the act of singing—producing a kind of sound that has no other function in life—that embodies spiritual power. The strong association with religion, unusual even when we consider that religious music is a cultural universal, is characteristic of Native American music.

NATIVE AMERICAN MUSIC   **367**

Beyond the composition of songs in visions by Plains people, the creation of songs is viewed differently in Native American traditions than in most European and Asian cultures. It may be that songs are thought to exist in the cosmos and need to be brought into human existence through dreams. In some tribes songs are extant in the supernatural world but need to be "unraveled" by humans in dreams to be realized. In an Inuit culture, there is a finite quantity of songs, and new ones can be made up only by combining elements of extant ones. In some tribes, making up songs is associated with emotional or mental disturbance. Except in modernized musical contexts, one rarely finds a situation in which humans are given credit for creating music. Specialists in making up songs are usually also experts in religious matters, and their technical competence or aesthetic creativity seems not to be an issue.

Music, a Reflection of Culture

In Native American cultures even more than others, the musical system is a kind of reflection of the rest of culture. A Blackfoot singer said, "The right way to do something is to sing the right song with it"; and indeed, in theory at least, the Blackfeet have particular songs for all activities. The more an activity is subdivided—as, for example, a ceremony—the more specific the association of songs with its various parts. For example, in the Beaver Ceremony, the ceremonialist has a bundle of 168 objects, mostly dressed skins of many birds and animals of the environment but also some handmade objects, rocks, and sticks. For each he must sing the appropriate song. Traditionally, the men of the tribe divided themselves into seven societies by age, and a man was initiated successively into them roughly every four years. Each society had its ceremonies and certain duties in social life and warfare, and each had its separate group of songs. There were special songs for warfare, riding, and walking. The most important social division, between men and women, was also reflected musically. Women had, so it seems, a separate and much smaller repertory, although they might join in singing certain men's songs; but more important, their singing style was different, with a smoother and more nasal tone than the men's, and with the pulsations being not rhythmic stresses but melodic ornaments. In many Native American cultures, the major divisions in society are paralleled in musical repertory and style.

MUSICAL INSTRUMENTS

Types of Instruments

In North America, the Native American music is prevailingly vocal. Almost all instruments are percussive, and their function is to provide rhythmic accompaniment to singing. Solo drumming is actually rare. But there is a great variety of drum and rattle types. Large drums with two heads or skins, small hand-drums with a single skin, kettledrums filled with water for tuning, and pieces of rawhide simply suspended from stakes are examples of drum types widely distributed. There are container rattles made of gourds, hide pieces sewn together, or a turtle shell; others fashioned of strings of deer hooves; and more. Although the musical function of these instruments is essentially the same, a culture may have many types, distinguished in the details of decoration with beads, feathers, animal skins, carving, and painting, each type associated with a particular ceremony. There are other idiophones as well such as notched stick scrapers, clappers, beaten planks, stamping tubes, and jingles. Small metal bells, introduced centuries ago by Europeans, have become established and incorporated in some of the cultures.

The most widespread melody-producing instrument is the flute. Various kinds of flutes are found, including true end-blown flutes in which the player's pursed lips direct a ribbon-shaped column of air against an edge of the blow-hole, as well as duct flutes rather like European recorders. In some tribes, the repertory of flute music consists simply of songs that may also be sung. Elsewhere, particularly in the southwestern United States, there is a separate repertory of flute music, although its style is not markedly different from that of the songs.

Among the instruments found in small numbers among a few tribes, we should mention the use of simple reeds and trumpets for recreational and ceremonial occasions on the North Pacific Coast. The musical bow, similar to or identical with a hunting bow, appears to have been used as an instrument in the southwestern United States and has been succeeded by the "Apache fiddle" or Navajo violin, a bowed instrument with one horsehair string and a cylindrical body about twelve inches in length, probably created as a combination of the bow and the Western violin.

Plains Indian hand drum with drumstick covered with rawhide. *Source:* Wanda Nettl/ Bruno Nettl

Northwest Coast Indian drum. *Source:* Wanda Nettl/Bruno Nettl

Blackfoot ceremonial objects: Two medicine bundle rattles, pair of gambling bones. *Source:* Wanda Nettl/Bruno Nettl

Instruments, Singing, and Words

Most important, however, the instruments of Native Americans are largely nonmelodic percussion instruments, and melody-producing instruments have special and restricted functions. In this respect Native Americans are similar to other cultures with small populations such as the tribes of Australian aboriginals, whose main instruments are percussion sticks of eucalyptus, struck against each other, and the *didgeridoo*, a long trumpet used mainly to play a single-tone drone. It is important to know, however, that the didgeridoo requires complex playing techniques such as circular breathing and changes in the shape of the mouth cavity for varying the tone color. In Polynesia, instruments are used mainly to accompany singing, and in Melanesia and Micronesia the principal instruments are panpipes.

If the relative dearth of melody-producing instruments is noteworthy in Native American cultures of North America, it is important to keep in mind that, in many of them, songs may not be primarily a vehicle for words. Although some Native American song texts, like those of the Navajo and Pueblo peoples, are often highly elaborate poems, in Plains people culture songs may have no words at all but only *vocables*. Where there are words, they are usually brief and occupy only a short portion of the melody. Here are the *complete* texts of two Blackfoot songs: "Sun says to sing" (song of the Sun Dance ceremony); and "It is spring; let others see you" (sung at the beginning of a medicine-bundle ceremony, before the bundle is opened). In a sense, we could conclude that songs without words substitute for the absent instrumental music.

ASPECTS OF THE HISTORY OF NATIVE AMERICAN MUSIC

Reconstructing Prehistory

There is little direct or written information about the history of Native American music, yet various kinds of circumstantial evidence permit reasonable guesses toward a rough reconstruction. Though there is still considerable

✳ **Explore**
the Musical Instrument Gallery on **mymusiclab.com**

debate about the early history of Native American presence in the Americas, most scholars agree that they originally arrived, probably in waves, from Asia at least 14,000 years ago and possibly much earlier. If there are musical styles and practices that Native Americans share with Asian cultures, they would have to be very ancient. The only musical material to which one can reasonably point is the existence, in many Indian cultures, of a stratum of short, simple songs consisting of one or two repeated lines and built on a scale of three or four tones, associated with children, games, and love charms. Among these, it is game songs, usually called gambling songs, that remain most widespread today (Listen to CD III, 17 for an example of a game/gambling song).

This type of music, consisting of short tunes with few pitches repeated or varied many times, is found in many parts of the world and may possibly be a remnant of a highly archaic stratum of human music. Comparison of North and South American Native American music may also reveal some clues. There are musical styles shared by the two regions. For instance, peoples of the Gran Chaco, a region in the Rio de la Plata basin, South America, have forms and a singing style not too different from that of the North American Plains. Ideas about music—the reflection of cultural categories in modes of performance, music's central role in myths about the origin of culture, music as a way of communicating within and with the supernatural world—often seem similar in the two regions. On the other hand, South American Native American music is, in most respects, very different from North American: there are more instances of major participation by women, and there is much more instrumental music. This suggests that the musical styles of North America developed independently and perhaps later. As cultures tend to hold on to their languages more tenaciously than to other things, and as language groupings do not often coincide with musical areas, the music of one society may have changed rapidly and frequently. If so, the picture of Native American music history must have been quite variegated, with tribes adopting new music as they changed important aspects of their culture.

It is assumed that large ceremonies and massed populations generally give rise to complex musical structures, and thus Aztec and Mayan societies had choral music and probably polyphonic structures. But this kind of correlation is not found in East Asia, and as few instruments were either extant or preserved in archeological sites, little can be known about the music of the classical Mexican cultures. Similarly, archeological sites in the United States and Canada give us little information about musical life.

Modern Music History

Since the Coming of White People   Native American history is better documented, and aspects of it have been widely studied since the coming of white people. The tragic social and political history is accompanied by a great reduction in the content of musical culture. Clearly, as entire tribes were wiped out and virtually all Native American peoples were relocated, suffering cultural

LISTENING GUIDE

LUMMI (WASHINGTON STATE) STICK GAME SONG

GO TO www.mymusiclab.com for the **Automated Listening Guide** CDIII • Track 17/ Download Track 62

Performed by Joe Washington and family

Although this example is performed by the Lummi, who represent a Northwest Coast culture, this gambling song does not illustrate that music area's general song style or musical characteristics but belongs, rather, to the special style of game songs, which is distributed widely throughout the continent. This is a song which accompanies a game in which one team hides sticks, singing while the other team tries to locate them. Notice the subtle **A A'** form of the melody. The rough sketch of the contour of each melodic section that follows points out the main differences. The melody is also mirrored in parallel fourths (an interval). You can hear this by listening for a higher-pitched voice in the background, singing along with the main vocalist. Finally, notice that the song utilizes only four notes. You can see this in the representations shown here.

Compare the notation shown previously to this textual representation of the contour and follow along as you listen.

Section	A						
Highest pitch	long,	long,	short, short, short				
				short,	long		
					short,	long,	
Lowest pitch							long (x2)
Section	A'						
Highest pitch	long						
	short, short,		short, short, short				
		short,		short,	long,		short, short
Lowest pitch				long	long,	long,	

TIME	SECTION	MUSICAL EVENTS
0:00–0:03	**A:** Listen for the melodic contour of the **A** Section. Notice also that the melody is being mirrored in parallel fourths by another vocalist (quite far in the background of the mix).	Steady drums provide a foundation for the song.

0:04–0:10		Section **A** is performed.
0:10–0:12		Notice that the vocals drop in volume once the lowest note is reached, thereby foregrounding the drums.
0:12–0:18	**A'**: Listen now for the ways that the **A'** section differs from section **A**. The second highest note becomes more important here than the highest note (which drives section **A**). The melody is also slightly more ornamented, with more neighboring notes incorporated into the contour. Finally, the section is slightly longer than Section **A**.	Section **A'** is performed, also ending on the lowest note.
0:18–0:21		The drums again take precedence as the vocalists end the phrase on the lowest note and prepare to transition to Section **A**.
0:22–0:39	**A and A'**: Listen to the whole melody again and see if you can hear and feel it as a whole musical statement.	[0:22–0:28] Section **A**. [0:28–0:30] Transition to **A'**; the drums are foregrounded here. [0:30–0:35] Section **A'**. [0:36–0:39] Transition to **A**; the drums are foregrounded here.
0:40–1:04	**A and A' and fadeout**: Listen to the whole melody again and this time see if you can hear and feel it as a whole musical statement without following along with the time markers. Can you hear the transition from section **A** to **A'**?	[0:40–0:46] Section **A**. [0:46–0:48] Transition to **A'**; the drums are foregrounded here. [0:48–0:53] Section **A'**. [0:53–0:57] Transition to **A**; the drums are foregrounded here. Fadeout begins. [0:57–1:04] Fadeout completed as Section **A** begins again.

disintegration through devastating famines and epidemics, knowledge of ceremonies and rituals as well as social repertory decreased, and much was simply forgotten. As Native Americans were motivated to take up Western lifestyles and religion, they also began to participate in Western music and sometimes to adopt Western conceptions of music for their own musical culture. So in the Plains, for example, the notion that all songs have a supernatural origin has been replaced by the acceptance of human composition. And to the original emphasis on music as a carrier of supernatural power has been added the European concept of music as entertainment.

But the tragic history of the Native Americans also brought with it, as a happier kind of by-product, interesting new developments in music, as Native American people came to use music as a weapon to fight back against total absorption and to preserve their cultural identity.

A tribe of Sioux Indians perform a Ghost Dance, a traditional dance thought to bring peace, prosperity, and a return of lost lands from The *London Illustrated News,* published in 1891. *Source:* MPI/Getty Images

The Ghost Dance   The modern music history of Native Americans may be said to begin after the great tragedy of the massacre at Wounded Knee in 1890, which resulted in part because Sioux and Arapaho people had taken up the practice of the Ghost Dance religion. This messianic cult began in the Great Basin area (Utah and Nevada) and was taken up by the Plains tribes, who hoped that it would help them in combating and defeating the white people, bringing back the dead, and restoring the buffalo—in other words, bring back the good old days. As these Plains people learned the Ghost Dance ceremony, they learned its songs, which were composed in a simple style that also made them think of a simpler, better time. But these songs and their style also enriched Plains music. Typical Ghost Dance songs consist of a few short phrases, each of them repeated once: **AABBCC**. This style of music, taken up by many tribes—thus, an intertribal style—was superimposed on the older song traditions (Listen to CD III, 18 for an example of a Ghost Dance song).

Peyote Music   The songs of the Peyote religion (already mentioned in our discussion of ceremonies), like the Ghost Dance songs, are an intertribal overlay on the individual tribal and area styles. Although Ghost Dance songs are hardly ever sung any more, Peyote songs are a major element in the contemporary Native American music scene. Based on the hallucinogenic buttons of a cactus native to Mexico, the Peyote religion spread through much of the Native North American world between 1700 and 1940. Peyote religionists developed a distinct song repertory; you can easily recognize a Peyote song regardless of the singer's tribal identity. Their singing style is probably derived from that of the Navajo. The rhythmic structure uses elements of Apache rhythm—the "incomplete repetition" type of form and the descending melodic contour come from the musical practices of the Plains (and can be heard in CD III, 14), and the percussion accompaniment is a kettledrum filled with water that possibly originated in the southeastern United States.

LISTENING GUIDE

PAWNEE GHOST DANCE SONG:
"THE YELLOW STAR"

GO TO www.mymusiclab.com for the Automated
Listening Guide CDIII • Track 18/Download Track 63

Sung by Wicita Blain, c. 1919
Recorded by Frances Densmore

Frances Densmore was among the first to record Native American performers. She did so on an early recording device—called a phonograph—that used wax cylinders to record the sounds. You can see a photograph of Densmore sitting behind her phonograph, recording a Blackfoot singer called Mountain Chief in 1916, in the Introduction (on page 21). You'll notice that the sound quality on this selection is somewhat muffled and that you can hear a pulsing hissing or scratching in the background. That pulsing is caused by the way the needle amplifies the rotation of the wax cylinder during playback. This recording thus affords us a chance to hear both the machine and the performer, as it were. More importantly, because this recording is so early, we are afforded a chance to hear a Native American performer before the influence of twentieth-century mass media came to exert as great an impact as it would over the coming decades.

This recording is a Ghost Dance song in the style of Great Basin music, but it is sung by a Plains Pawnee singer. Its form is typical of Ghost Dance repertory, in that it consists of three short phrases, each of which is repeated before moving on to the next phrase; **AABBCC**. The phrases are, in fact, very short. Note, for example, that two repetitions of the "A" phrase take only about six seconds to perform.

TIME	SECTION	MUSICAL EVENTS
0:00–0:03	**Phrase A:** Listen for the distinct contour of this short phrase. Notice the repeat.	Phrase **A**.
0:04–0:06		Phrase **A** repeated.
0:06–0:09	**Phrase B:** Listen now for the ways that Phrase **B** is distinct from Phrase **A**, in both melodic contour and length (slightly longer).	Phrase **B**.
0:09–0:12		Phrase **B** repeated.
0:13–0:15	**Phrase C:** Listen for the unique character of Phrase **C**.	Phrase **C**.
0:15–0:17		Phrase **C** repeated.
0:18–0:31	**AABB:** Here, listen for the how phrase **A** and **B** complement each other. Phrase **A** includes the highest pitches in the whole song. Phrase **B** moves through a middle register to the lowest note in the song. Phrase **C** is not performed in this repetition.	[0:18–0:23] Phrase **A** and repeat. [0:23–0:31] Phrase **B** and repeat.

| 0:32–0:48 | **AABBCC:** Having listened for the way that phrase **A** and **B** complement each other, now listen to how phrase **C** completes the structure. Phrase **A** includes the highest pitches in the whole song. Phrase **B** moves through a middle register to the lowest note in the song. Phrase **C** reinforces this low note and sets up a return to the higher register of phrase **A**. | [0:32–0:37] Phrase **A** and repeat. [0:37–0:43] Phrase **B** and repeat. [0:43–0:48] Phrase **C** and repeat. |
| 0:49–1:14 | **AABBCC:** Listen here for the slight variations that are introduced especially in the **B** and **C** phrases. | [0:49–0:53] Phrase **A** and repeat. [0:54–1:01] Phrase **B** and repeat. [1:01–0:08] Phrase **C** and repeat followed by several seconds of silence at the end of the performance. |

You can identify a Peyote song by its words—or, rather, "meaningless" vocables or syllables sequences, as they are quite unique; examples are "heyow-itsinayo," "heneyowitsine," and "heyowanene," and each song ends with an amen-like "heneyowe." The origin of these vocable patterns is not known, but conceivably they came from the Comanche language of the southern Plains. This is a religion that tries to tie Native American peoples together and takes a conciliatory position toward Christianity, and thus Christian texts in English are occasionally used. Here, too, we see forced culture change resulting in new musical style and the broadening of Native American musical culture.

Peyote songs must be sung at certain structural points in the nightlong ceremony, at the beginning, and at sunrise; most songs can be selected by the singers at their discretion, as long as they are Peyote songs. The Peyote religion has some Christian overtones; the name of Jesus appears occasionally among the vocables. Some religionists claim that "Indians know Jesus better than do white people," and the Peyote organization is known generally as a "church." Quite apart from Peyote music, there is also a body of Christian hymnody based on traditional Native American music, with hymnals that include traditional Anglo-American hymn tunes and monophonic songs in traditional style with Christian words (Listen to CD III, 19 for an example of Peyote song).

The Powwow Culture   In the second half of the twentieth century, the most significant trend has been the development of the powwow culture. This is the most visible strategy for building an intertribal Native American culture and the consciousness of ethnic identity that goes with it, and it is joined by the establishment of a Native American popular music whose sound is clearly in the mainstream of American popular music styles, but that is still recognizably native. In a related development, Native American artists have made significant contributions to the world of concert music and dance.

LISTENING GUIDE

KIOWA PEYOTE SONG: OPENING PRAYER SONG GO TO www.mymusiclab.com for the Automated **Listening Guide** CDIII • Track 19/Download Track 64

Performed by David Apekaun

This example illustrates the intertribal Peyote style and is sung by a Kiowa singer. This "Opening Prayer Song," using the syllables "he-ne-ne-ne-ha-yo-wi-tsi-na-yo," has a two-part structure in which a line is sung, repeated, and then replaced by another. A concluding line is then sung, followed by the closing formula "he-ne-yo-we." This pattern is then repeated with slightly different melody and a new line **(D)** and without the repeat of the **A** line, making the second part of the structure shorter than the first. The complete form of a verse can be sketched as **AABCX** (closing formula), **A'DCX** (closing formula). You'll notice that the last line and the closing formula remain constant in both parts of the verse structure.

It is best to listen by following the vocables or syllable sequences of this recording in order to hear the structure. I've indicated the syllables as they are sung. The syllables are also a guide to the rhythm. Shorter notes and syllables are combined with hyphens; longer notes and syllables stand on their own.

TIME	SECTION	MUSICAL EVENTS
0:00–0:03	**Introduction:** Listen for the opening gestures on the kettledrum (often called a water drum) followed by the entrance of the singer.	Drum enters. The recording fades in as the repeat of Section **A** is under way.
0:03–0:07		Introductory vocal: *he ne he ne he ne he ne ne.*
0:08–0:24	**Stanza 1:** Listen for the overall structure of the song by following along the vocables or syllable sequences.	[0:08–0:11] **First Section:** Line **A**. *ha (he) ne ne ha-yo-wi-tsi na yo* [0:12–0:15] Line **A** repeated. *ha he ne ne ha-yo-wi-tsi na yo.* [0:15–0:18] Line **B**. *ha na-yo-wi-tsi na hi-ya no ha wa.* [0:19–0:20] Line **C**. *ha hi-yo wa ne.* [0:20–0:24] Line **X** (closing formula). *ha-yo-wi-tsi na he ne yo we.*
0:24–0:34		**Second Section:** Line **A'**. Notice the same syllabic sequence as **A** in the first section, but a different melody here. *ha he ne ne ha-yo-wi-tsi na yo.* [0:27–:029] Line **D**. Here both melody and syllable sequence are new, so a new letter is assigned **(D)**. *he-ya-na-yo-wi-tsi na yo.*

[0:29–0:31] Line **C.**

ha hi-yo wa ne.

[0:31–0:34] Line **X.**

ha-yo-wi-tsi na he ne yo we.

First Section: Listen for the closing formula [0:47–0:50]:

ha-yo-wi-tsi na he ne yo we.

0:35–0:50 **Stanza 2:** This time see if you can hear the closing formula at the end of the first and second sections of the stanza. This will help you get a feel for the shape of this song.

0:50–1:01 **Second Section:** Again, see if you can hear the closing formula [0:57–1:01]:

ha-yo-wi-tsi na he ne yo we.

1:01–1:26 **Stanza 3:** Listen to the whole melody and see if you can hear and feel it as a whole musical statement.

[1:01–1:16] **First Section.**

[1:16–1:26] **Second Section.**

1:27–1:57 **Stanza 4:** Now try once more to hear as many structural details as you can, including the closing formula at the end of the first and second section.

[1:27–1:41] **First Section:** Listen for the closing formula [1:38–1:41]:

ha-yo-wi-tsi na he ne yo we.

[1:41–1:57] **Second Section** Again, see if you can hear the closing formula [1:48–1:52]:

ha-yo-wi-tsi na he ne yo we.

Notice that the drum speeds up during the closing formula, thereby emphasizing the conclusion of the song.

This intertribal style, based on Plains music and forming a common song repertory for the powwow culture, was illustrated in our description of the Blackfoot North American Native American Days. However, powwows take place throughout the United States and Canada, in places of concentrated Native American population, where they celebrate ethnic identity and intertribal unity. Where there are few Indians, powwows are used to make nonnatives aware of Native American culture. Native Americans have used the powwow as a powerful wedge for making themselves—but also, it's important to note, others—aware that they are no longer the "vanishing American."

A celebration on the campus of the University of Illinois in Urbana dramatically illustrated the use of the powwow for education and empowerment. It was presented by a small number of Native Americans, largely visitors from out of town, with the main purpose of instructing local people in the structure, content, and functions of intertribal powwows. The visitors received pamphlets on "Powwow Etiquette" with instructions that included certain ritual actions: times to stand, to sit, to remove hats, to dance or not to dance, to take pictures and to refrain, but above all, to follow the directions of the master of ceremonies. All this was justified by reference to unspecified older sacred Indian traditions, but the main purpose of the rules was to create a situation in which a distinction between whites and natives was drawn—a distinction defined by the natives, but also intended in certain respects and at some moments, to be ignored or overcome. Music and dance were used to negotiate and symbolize, to establish times in which whites were to stay out of the native business, and other times in which they were to participate. As in the powwow at Browning, discussed at the beginning of this chapter, music and dance were used to cope with the nonnative "other" in a number of ways.

A part of the powwow repertory is the body of so-called forty-nine songs or forty-niner songs, which ordinarily have mildly romantic or amusing (and sometimes considered by powwow dancers as uproariously funny) words in English, such as "I don't care if you're married sixteen times, I will get you," or "When the Dance is over, sweetheart, I will take you home in my one-eyed Ford," or "My sweetheart, she got mad at me because I said hello to my old-timer, but it's just OK with me" (Listen to CD III, 20 to hear two examples of the forty-nine songs).

A Native American record industry marketing native music—primarily the intertribal powwow repertory—to Native Americans emerged in the 1950s (with the label North American Soundchief) and flourishes yet today. Clearly, many young Native Americans spend much of their music listening time with these CDs and tapes. The concept of music as mainly ritual and communication with the supernatural has given way to one of music as entertainment and an expression of ethnic identity. There are now virtually countless singing groups, or "drums," some known only on their own reservation, others traveling widely, following the powwow circuit, entering contests that provide substantial monetary prizes.

Women in Native American Music   It is widely stated, and perhaps even true, that women's role in Native American musical activity before about 1900 was restricted and, at any rate, quite different from that of men. But surely the many tribes differed greatly in this regard. In some California tribes and among the Navajo, women played important ceremonial roles. In Plains cultures, they were restricted to private events, whereas musical performances in public or for addressing the supernatural were men's activity. In modern Native American culture, women have played increasingly prominent roles. For one thing, they have often held onto older traditions better than men. Judith Vander found that Shoshone women knew and could sing old songs, including those of the Ghost Dance, better than men. My male informants among the Blackfoot sometimes turned to their wives for jogging their musical memories.

The matter of gender sometimes played a special rule in musical life. In some Plains cultures, Berdaches—men who dressed as women and did women's work and might be homosexual—were sometimes extolled as great singers. And among the Blackfoot, women identified as "manly-hearted," often daughters of influential men, associated themselves culturally with men, could be heterosexually promiscuous, and carried out the male roles in ceremonies, singing men's songs in men's singing styles.

As observed at North American Indian Days in Montana, women have increasingly become active as members of drums, or powwow singing groups. In the powwow tradition of 1960, a drum was usually based on the men of

LISTENING GUIDE

TWO MODERN POWWOW LOVE SONGS   *GO TO* **www.mymusiclab.com for the Automated Listening Guide** CDIII • Track 20/Download Track 65

Recorded by Willard Rhodes

Both of these songs alternate vocable verses with English language words. They are composed in a simple strophic format, **AABC** (first excerpt) and **AABB'** (second excerpt). The English language lyrics are introduced into this structure with a different melody, but they are worked into the overall form of the stanzas as follows: **DD'BC** and **CCBB'**, respectively.

TIME	SECTION	MUSICAL EVENTS
0:00–0:09	**SONG 1, Stanza 1:** Listen for the overall structure of this short verse—**AABC**.	[0:00–0:04] **A** [0:04–0:08] **A** repeated.
0:09–0:14		**B**
0:14–0:18		**C**
0:18–0:22	**Stanza 2:** Listen for the English language lyrics, sung to a new melody, but connected back into the structure of the stanza in the **B** and **C** phrases (sung, again in vocables).	[0:17–0:21] **D** (new melody). *When the dance is over, sweetheart.*
0:22–0:26		**D'** (**D** melody extended). *I will take you home in my one-eyed Ford.*
0:26–0:30		**B**
0:30–0:33		**C**
0:34–0:52	**Stanzas 3 and 4:** This time see if you can hear the way that these two, slightly different melodic shapes work together in alternation. The **A** phrase is sung with vocables and incorporates the highest pitches in the song. The **D** phrase contrasts with this because of its lower register and incorporates English language text. Both are unified by the **B** and **C** phrases.	Stanza 3: all vocables.
0:52–1:10		Stanza 4: English and vocables.
1:11–1:20	**SONG 2, Stanza 1:** Listen for the overall structure of this short verse—**AABB'**.	[1:11–1:15] **A** [1:16–1:20] **A** repeated.
1:20–1:26		**B**
1:26–1:33		**B'**
1:34–1:43	**Stanza 2:** Listen for the English language lyrics, sung to a new melody. There are more lyrics here than in the first song, but the performers still manage to get back to the structure of stanza 1 by the **B** and **B'** phrases.	**C** (new melody). *My sweetheart, hey-a-hey-a.*

1:37–1:43		**C** repeated and **B** (melody folds into **B** at the end of the line).
		She got mad at me because I said hello to my old-timer.
1:43–1:50		**B'**
		But it's just ok with me, oh wey-a-wey… hey.
1:51–2:12	**Stanzas 3 and 4:** This time see if you can hear how these two, slightly different melodic shapes work together in alternation. The **A** phrase is sung with vocables and incorporates the highest pitches in the song. The **C** phrase contrasts with this because of its lower register and incorporates English language text. Both are unified by the **B** and **B'** phrases.	Stanza 3: all vocables.
2:13–2:34		Stanza 4: English and vocables.

an extended family—father, sons, nephews, sons-in-law—along with some close friends. Occasionally a woman of the family might sit in. Gradually, however, the participation of women increased, to the extent that many drums have several female members, and a number of drums traveling the powwow circuit consist entirely of women. Some drums consisting largely of men have female leaders.

Popular Music Of particular interest is Native American music's entry into the mainstream of American popular music. There is a genre known simply as "Indian rock music," which combines the use of some traditional tunes, the percussive sound of Native American songs, and texts derived from or referring to Native American culture. Among the famous exponents of this music in the 1960s and 1970s was the jazz-rock musician Jim Pepper, a Native American musician performing with a multiracial ensemble. His popular "Newly-Wed Song" uses material from the two forty-nine songs that we previously heard. As early as the mid-1960s, rock groups devoting themselves more explicitly to protest, such as XIT, came to the fore, along with Native American singers, such as Buffy Sainte-Marie and Peter LaFarge, who performed Western-style popular music with words about Native American issues.

GO TO CDIII • Track 21/ Download Track 66

In the 1990s, the Navajo flutist Carlos Nakai developed a variety of styles based on, or referring to, Native American culture, composing for traditional, popular, and classical music contexts, performing solo and with Western instruments. The ensemble Ulali, led by a female singer, performs music syncretizing Western and Native style, singing Plains-like tunes but in vocal harmony and backed by chords on synthesizers and guitar. Flutes, which played a modest role in many Native cultural traditions, have increased in importance, to the extent that flute music accounts for perhaps half of the Native music recordings produced for the mass market. This shift in emphasis probably results from the importance of instruments in Euro-American culture.

These recent developments in musical sound and in ideas about music as well as contexts for performance show that Native American music is very much alive. Native American peoples use it, and dance, more than anything else to show to each other and to other Americans that they are a distinct ethnic group. To them, music functions both as a way of maintaining their cultural integrity and as a form of mediating between themselves and other culture groups. In this sense it continues a tradition, for in earlier times, too, its function had been that of mediation, but between humans and the forces of the supernatural.

In historic times, Native American tribes were probably concerned about their natural environment, as is evident in the attention to wildlife as natural phenomena in their traditional ceremonies. No doubt, however, they sometimes also violated the environment, taking occasion, for example, to slaughter more buffalo than needed for survival. In the second half of the twentieth century, they became increasingly involved in preservation and protection, as their areas of residence were affected by large-scale industry, mining, fishing, and agriculture. Much of the modern popular music produced by Native American musicians speaks to environmental issues, and Euro-Americans have increasingly interpreted Native American culture as symbolic of environmental and spiritual concerns and made it part of the "New Age" cultural movement. Native American musicians have sometimes accepted these attitudes, seeing the New Age movement as an ideological ally as well as a market for Native art and music. Thus, for example, one can find numerous CDs of Native American flute music labeled as appropriate for meditation.

Much of the Native American popular music does not differ in its musical style and sound from mainstream rock, blues, and pop, but its words deal with social, economic, and political issues faced by American Indians. Traditional-sounding music such as the powwow repertory, but also including other nonceremonial genres, continues to be hugely popular in Native American communities as indicated by the thriving CD and prerecorded cassette market. Recent surveys uncovered twenty-three different tapes and CDs of Blackfoot music in a shop frequented by Blackfoot customers in Montana and thirty-three CDs of older traditional, modernized, New Age, and popular Native American music in a large bookstore in a Midwestern college town.

SUMMARY

✓•—⎡**Study** and **Review**
on **mymusiclab.com**

Our explorations conclude with a brief review of the main sounds of and ideas about music in Native American life. Native American songs tend to be very short, and are generally sung in large groups for specific rituals. Individual skill is not valued as highly as group participation in performance. The voice, moreover, is the primary instrument. Drums, rattle, scrapers, and flutes are the most widespread percussion and wind instruments. Native American singing style usually features a tense, pulsating voice, though this does vary a bit among the seven "music areas" that we have identified as having common musical cultures. The Yuman music area, for instance, is known for a more relaxed vocal quality than is the Plains musical area.

In traditional Native American culture, music serves as a mediator between humans and the supernatural world. In recent memory, music has continued to serve a mediating function in this way (i.e., Peyote Songs), but has also been used to mediate representations of Native American culture to non-Native American listeners and to their fellow Native Americans. Since the coming of white people, new forms—such as the Ghost Dance and Peyote Song—have developed, and intertribal musical styles have become prevalent. Today, Western pop influences—including rock and hip hop—have led to a new type of intertribal popular music. The vitality of Native American popular music continues to suggest creative ways of addressing Native American concerns about the environment and related to presenting Native American history to new audiences.

BIBLIOGRAPHY

North America as a Whole   Marcia Herndon, *Native American Music* (Hatboro, PA: Norwood, 1980); Bruno Nettl, *North American Indian Musical Styles* (Philadelphia: American Folklore Society, 1952); Helen H. Roberts, *Musical Areas in Aboriginal North America* (New Haven, CT: Yale University Press, 1936); Tara Browner, ed., *Music of the First Nations: Tradition and Innovation in Native North American Music* (Urbana: University of Illinois Press, 2009); John William Troutman, *Indian Blues: American Indians and the Politics of Music, 1879–1934* (Norman: University of Oklahoma Press, 2009); Michael Pisani, *Imagining Native America in Music* (New Haven: Yale Univeristy Press, 2005); Bryan Burton, *Moving Within the Circle: Contemporary Native American Music and Dance* (Danbury, CT: World Music Press, 1993); Richard Keeling, ed., *Women in North American Indian Music: Six Essays* (Bloomington, IN: Society for Ethnomusicology, 1989); Victoria Lindsay Levine, *Writing American Indian Music: Historic Transcriptions, Notations, and Arrangements* (Middleton, WI: A-R Editions for the American Musicological Society, 2002); Tara Browner, *Heartbeat of a People: Music and Dance of the Northern Pow-wow* (Urbana: University of Illinois Press, 2002); Luke Eric Lassiter, Clyde Ellis, and Ralph Kotay, *The Jesus Road: Kiowas, Christianity, and Indian Hymns* (Lincoln: University of Nebraska Press, 2002).

Plains Cultures   Bruno Nettl, *Blackfoot Musical Thought: Comparative Perspectives* (Kent, OH: Kent State University Press, 1989); Frances Densmore, *Teton Sioux Music* (Washington, DC: Bureau of American Ethnology, 1918); Robert Witmer, *The Musical Life of the Blood Indians* (Ottawa: National Museum of Man, 1982); Alan P. Merriam, *Ethnomusicology of the Flathead Indians* (Chicago: Aldine, 1967); William K. Powers, *War Dance: Plains Indian Musical Performance* (Tucson: University of Arizona Press, 1990); James Howard and Victoria Levine, *Choctaw Music and Dance* (Norman: University of Oklahoma Press, 1990); Luke E. Lassiter, *The Power of Kiowa Song* (Tucson: University of Arizona Press, 1998).

Other North Native American Peoples   Charlotte Frisbie, ed., *Southwestern Native American Ritual Drama* (Tucson: University of Arizona Press, 1980); David P. McAllester, *Peyote Music* (New York: Viking Fund Publications in Anthropology, 1949); David P. McAllester, *Enemy Way Music* (Cambridge, MA: Peabody Museum of American Archeology and Ethnology, 1954); Judith Vander, *Songprints* (Urbana: University of Illinois Press, 1988); Judith Vander, *Shoshone*

Ghost Dance Religion: Poetry, Songs, and Great Basin Context (Urbana: University of Illinois Press, 1997); Frank Mitchell, *Navajo Blessingway Singer*, ed. Charlotte J. Frisbie and David P. McAllester (Tucson: University of Arizona Press, 1978); Thomas Johnston, *Eskimo Music by Region: A Comparative Circumpolar Study* (Ottawa: National Museum of Man, 1976); Beverley Cavanagh, *Music of the Netsilik Eskimo: A Study of Stability and Change* (Ottawa: National Museum of Man, 1982); Ruth Murray Underhill, *Singing for Power: The Magic of the Papago Indians of Southern Arizona* (Berkeley: University of California Press, 1938); Richard Keeling, *Cry for Luck: Sacred Song and Speech Among Yurok, Hupa, and Karok Indians of Northwestern California* (Berkeley: University of California Press, 1992).

Instruments   K. G. Izikowitz, *Musical and Other Sound Instruments of the South American Indians* (Götesborg, Sweden: Kungl, Vetenskap-och Vitterhets-Samhälles and lingar, 1935); Thomas Vennum, Jr., *The Ojibwa Dance Drum* (Washington, DC: Smithsonian Institution Press, 1982); Beverley Cavanagh Diamond and others, *Visions of Sound* (Chicago: University of Chicago Press, 1995).

DISCOGRAPHY

Anthologies   *A Cry from the Earth: Music of the North American Indians* (Folkways FC 7777; 1979); *An Anthology of North American Indian and Eskimo Music* (Ethnic Folkways FE 4541; 1973).

Blackfoot   *An Historical Album of Blackfoot Indian Music* (Ethnic Folkways FE 4001; 1979); *Blackfeet* (Indian IR 220; ca. 1980); *Blackfeet Pow-Wow Songs* (Canyon C-6119; 1974).

Other North American Peoples   *American Indians of the Southwest* (Ethnic Folkways P 420; 1951); *Music of the Sioux and Navajo* (Ethnic Folkways P 401; 1949); *Kiowa Peyote Ritual Songs* (American Indian Soundchief Kiowa-590; ca. 1970); *The Great Plains* (Canyon ARP 6052; 1966); *Indian Music of the Canadian Plains* (Ethnic Folkways FE 4464; 1966); *Papago Dance Songs* (Canyon 6098; 1973); *Popular Dance Music of the Indians of Southern Arizona* (Canyon C-6085; 1972); *Inuit Games and Songs* (UNESCO Collection Musical Sources, Philips 6586 036; 1978); *Indian Songs of Today* (Library of Congress AFS L36; ca. 1960); *Omaha Indian Music* (American Folklife Center, Library of Congress AFC L71; 1984); *Inuit Games and Songs* (Auvidis Unesco AD 090); *Native American Traditions: Music of New Mexico* (Smithsonian/Folkways SF 40408); *Creation's Journey: Native American Music* (Smithsonian/Folkways SF 40410); *Heartbeat: Voices of First Nations Women* (Smithsonian/Folkways SF 40415); *Dancing Buffalo: Cornel Peewardy and the Alliance West Singers;* Dances and Flute Songs from the Southern Plains (Music of the World CDT-130); *Talking Spirits: Native American Music from the Hopi, Zuni, and San Juan Pueblos* (Music of the World CDT-126).

Recent Developments   *Spirit Horses: The Music of James Demars* [*Concerto for Native American Flute and Chamber Orchestra*] (Canyon CR 7014); *Solo Flights: Various Native American Artists* (Soar 1245-CD); *Ulali: Mahk Jchi* (Thrush Records CD 0605287581); *Walela: Unbearable Love* (Triloka 7930185209-2); *Northern Wind: Jingle Dress Songs* (Arbor Records AR-11282).

Music of Ethnic North America

BYRON DUECK

MUSIC, ETHNICITY, AND POLITICS IN PUBLIC PERFORMANCE

On a cold October day in 2002, the city of Winnipeg in the western Canadian province of Manitoba welcomed Queen Elizabeth II. She was touring the country as the nominal head of state—Canada is, unlike the United States, a constitutional monarchy—to commemorate the fiftieth year of her reign. Two public concerts were organized for the occasion, the first in the afternoon at a park in the city center, the second in the evening on the grounds of the provincial legislative buildings.

At the first event, the queen and Prince Philip strolled through the grounds of the Forks Historic Site at the juncture of the two rivers that meet in the center of the city. The afternoon was devoted to performances by young amateur musicians and celebrated the ethnic diversity of the province. When immigrants began to pour into Manitoba from around the world in the late nineteenth century,

they often came in large groups and settled in geographic blocs, inspiring early twentieth-century commentators to remark on a patchwork ethnic "mosaic" in the western provinces. Fittingly, then, the visitors were met on their walk by performers who represented some of these historical communities, including a Ukrainian dance troupe and Mennonite and Icelandic youth choirs.

Upon reaching the shore of the Red River, the royal guests were seated for a short program of performances. A choir of students from the northern port town of Churchill sang the national anthem in French, English, Cree, and Inuktitut (the country's official languages and two indigenous ones). A group of young French Canadian women presented an exhibition of folk dancing in the distinctive Franco-Manitoban style, the dancers doing an animated "jig" step while moving through intricate ensemble patterns. A high-school dance group performed "Cabaret" from the musical of the same name, and there were speeches from a number of politicians. The program culminated in a performance of *Spirit of the Rivers*, a work for choir, narrator, dancers, and prerecorded musical accompaniment.

Spirit of the Rivers festival, October 2002, Manitoba, Canada. *Source:* ADRIAN WYLD/AFP/Newscom

The event organizers had clearly put a great deal of thought into how this concluding performance might represent the cultural diversity of the province. *Spirit of the Rivers* had lyrics in English and French, but also in Cree. The music was in a contemporary Western choral idiom, but the prerecorded accompanying track incorporated a number of prominent elements that suggested indigenous music: rattle, drum, and a series of high-pitched cries of the kind sometimes heard in the pow-wow singing of the northern plains (see Chapter 11). As the piece moved into an untexted instrumental coda, dancers from various traditions joined in: a group of young ballet dancers occupied the center of the stage, while dancers representing the province's Scottish, Irish, Portuguese, Ukrainian, and Afro-Caribbean communities performed behind them.

The performance synchronized through music and dance the various social groups that are often held to comprise Canada as a nation. The languages sung corresponded to the three populations that have been most active in negotiating their sovereignty relative to one another throughout the country's history: anglophones, francophones, and indigenous Canadians. Meanwhile, diverse dance styles represented other immigrant ethnic groups. In short, the event brought together members of the communities whose interrelationships and integration have long been the subject of national political discussions. (Political philosopher Will Kymlicka, for instance, describes the historical development of Canada as involving "the federation of three distinct national groups (English, French, and Aboriginals)" supplemented by a fourth, "polyethnic" population of immigrants [1995: 12–13]). Dance and song made the national mosaic visible and national polyphony audible.

And yet a second welcoming concert, held at the provincial legislative grounds later that day, occasioned a decidedly less consonant display of national coexistence. In the period leading up to the queen's visit, spokespeople from a number of First Nations groups had voiced concerns about the federal government's failure to live up to the obligations outlined in the treaties signed with indigenous communities in what is now the province of Manitoba. The living conditions in these communities, which were generally much poorer than anywhere else in the province, were a particularly sharp grievance, as was recently proposed legislation perceived to threaten indigenous sovereignty.

maintain distinct and particular musical traditions even as they borrow musical elements from other communities and groups; and consider musical phenomena that seem, by contrast, to be shared across many boundaries, whether of community, ethnic group, or region. We will then spend some time examining the special contribution of African American music to North America. Finally, we bring our excursions to a close by considering, not how music helps to convey cultural concepts, but rather how music is itself conceptualized.

Three broader questions underlie these investigations. The first concerns difference and similarity. Many North American ethnic, religious, regional, and community groups have their own unique musical styles and practices. At the same time certain widespread cultural elements play a significant role in shaping North American musical life, even across social boundaries. These include Christianity, the legacy of slavery, economic structures such as labor specialization and capitalism, and widespread musical forms such as the two-part fiddle tune and common-practice harmony. One challenge for this chapter (and for ethnomusicology more generally) involves accounting for these widely distributed aspects of North American musical life, while also recognizing the ways they are complicated and challenged by ethnic, religious, and regional particularities and local practice.

A second broad question has to do with the differences between professional and nonspecializing musicians, and between everyday musical activity and more extraordinary moments of performance. Consider the performances by the schoolchildren at the afternoon welcoming ceremony previously described. To prepare for such events, "ordinary" children have to spend long hours practicing on their own and rehearsing with colleagues in classrooms, community halls, church basements, and other spaces of assembly. Calendars have to be coordinated and money spent on travel and costumes. In short, ethnic performance is a special, passing moment made possible by a much longer engagement with ethnic community. And thus ethnicity is not experienced solely in moments such as the one just considered. It is also lived in everyday interactions that prioritize certain groups of people, specific ways of interacting, and particular musical activities.

A third broad question involves the concept of performance, broadly conceived: what do musical acts accomplish? Here again, it is useful to refer back to the opening vignette. Ritual festivity in this case presented national unity from a certain perspective——but from another it made apparent deep differences of opinion about the government's right to represent certain constituencies. Ethnic music and dance were not simply "symbolic" expressions of unity or diversity here. They actively made these abstractions concrete——or, from another perspective, failed to do so. The performance of *Spirit of the Rivers* did not only represent unity: it integrated participants in collective activity. Conversely, the singing protest at the evening concert did not simply symbolize aboriginal difference, but rather actively produced it. In launching a welcome that competed with the one on the main stage, the protesters brought their difference into being as a social and musical fact—a difference that would not otherwise have been audible within the unity being showcased.

SOUNDLY ORGANIZED TIME

The winter holiday season in North America is distinguished from other, more ordinary times of the year by music above all else. On tinny-sounding outdoor speakers, on the radio, and especially in stores and shopping malls, pop songs celebrate snow, reunions with loved ones, the giving of gifts, and a certain jolly elf. Many of these songs were composed in the 1930s and 1940s and resemble other Tin Pan Alley tunes from that era: they have catchy, singable melodies and make frequent use of the 32-bar **AABA** form ("Santa Claus Is Coming to Town" and "Rudolph the Red-Nosed Reindeer," for example). Alternating with the pop songs are Christmas carols and hymns: pieces that make explicit reference to the birth of Jesus and its theological implications. These are, predictably, especially prevalent at the church services and devotional events that lead up to Christmas and on the day itself. Also parts of the annually transformed soundscape are pieces from the world of art music: here an excerpt from Handel's *Messiah*, there a piece from Tchaikovsky's *The Nutcracker*. Yet the seeming ubiquity of Christmas music masks a North American musical life that is anything but unified. Those who observe Christmas do so through widely varying repertories: songs, melodies, lyrics, and performance styles differ from community to community and ethnic group to ethnic group. Not all Christians even observe holidays at the same time: Old Calendar Orthodox Christians, for instance, celebrate Christmas in early January. And, of course, as the success of Adam Sandler's "The Chanukah Song" suggests, there are many who do not observe Christmas, whose year is structured around quite different celebrations and solemnities, and who perhaps feel a sense of distance from these annual musical transformations.

Music shapes the experience of passing time, and does so at a number of different levels. For instance, people have an innate ability to follow regular patterns of pulsation (see Clayton, Sager, and Will 2004). This universal ability is expressed through a wide range of culturally specific rhythmic and metrical practices: for instance, the interlocking patterns of sub-Saharan African music (see Chapter 7) or the complex structures of Indian tal (see Chapter 2). But "slower" levels of temporality are likewise shaped by musical experience, and human societies around the world have imbued the daily, monthly, and yearly cycles with various, culturally specific musical associations. In Chapter 9, for example, we saw how an Andean community marks each year with a fiesta, celebrated through music, dance, costuming, and extraordinary forms of behavior.

Similar structures of temporal organization are evident in North America. As might be expected on a continent of such ethnic and regional diversity, social groups establish commonalities and differences in part through distinctive ways of organizing time. Ethnicity and identity come into being through the temporal and musical division of life, in both its everyday aspects and its more memorable and festive ones. Let's explore a few of these.

Liturgical Cycles

The cultural organization of time is perhaps most evident in religious liturgies, where music and various forms of heightened speech (for instance, chant and sacred readings) establish and consecrate daily, weekly, and annual cycles. Sacred time is organized on a weekly basis in a number of traditions, of course: Christian churches privilege Sunday as a day of worship, Jewish congregations meet on the Sabbath (from sunset on Friday to sunset on Saturday), and Muslim congregational prayer occurs on Fridays. In all three religious traditions, these meetings incorporate the reading, recitation, or singing of special and sacred texts. Not all of these practices are considered to be "music" by practitioners (see Chapter 3); in most cases, however, the texts are declaimed using some form of heightened speech (an intoned or cantillated vocal delivery in some cases, and song in others).

Sacred liturgies also articulate daily cycles. Some Christian traditions observe the **Office** (based on the canonical hours), a set of daily worship services in which certain prayers, readings, and chants are performed at fixed times: matins in the morning and vespers in the evening, for instance. The Islamic call to prayer, heard five times a day, is another example. At a more mundane level, the largest and loudest musical instruments in many cities are the bells in church steeples. Their hourly or even quarter-hourly pealing might be heard to do the ongoing work of sacralizing passing time, albeit in a manner that has become so familiar it often goes almost unnoticed. Occasional controversies over the public broadcast of the Islamic call to prayer tend to ignore that the pealing of church bells is an even more prevalent example of religious expression being publically broadcast.

Turning to longer cycles of temporality, liturgy also shapes the organization of the year. For instance, the Christian year begins with Advent (the four Sundays preceding Christmas) and progresses through the celebration of the Nativity to Epiphany. After a period of "ordinary time" comes the second major period of special observance, beginning with Lent, reaching a peak during Easter celebrations, and moving through to Pentecost. These events are associated with particular kinds of music; many hymnals, for instance, contain sections devoted to Advent, Christmas, and Easter. And as the opening of this section suggests, some of these songs—Christmas carols, most notably—are heard well outside the confines of liturgical practice.

In Jewish and Islamic practice, too, congregations and communities mark the passing of the year through ritual, moving through sequences of holy days and associated observances. In Judaism, the most important events are the High Holy Days: Rosh Hashanah (the New Year Festival) and Yom Kippur (the Day of Atonement), which arrive in autumn. The central holiday in Islam is the month of Ramadan, which occurs in the ninth month of the lunar year (accordingly, a few days earlier every solar year). In both Jewish and Islamic practice, these events are observed in part through special assemblies and the recitation of special texts.

OFFICE
Organized to correspond to the canonical hours, the Office (also called the Divine Hours) is a set of daily worship services in which certain prayers, readings, and chants are performed at fixed times. The services include matins, vespers, and compline, among others, and the practice is generally associated with Catholic, Orthodox Christian, and Anglican/Episcopal traditions, though other traditions include these services in their worship as well.

A rabbi blows the shofar to signal Rosh Hashanah, the Jewish New Year. *Source:* World Religions Photo Library/ Alamy

Although musical articulations of time are most extensively connected to liturgical practice, there are also more secular manifestations. Some are connected to the standardized work week that holds for many North Americans (although this work week, too, has its origins in the religious calendar). For example, special radio programs of talk and music accompany morning and evening commutes. On Friday and Saturday nights some radio stations play nightclub-like dance mixes, acknowledging the arrival of the weekend and its pleasures. It could be suggested that music helps to mark and consecrate the distinctions between productive but onerous work and pleasurable but prodigal leisure. Again, as in the case of sacred music, sounds do not simply reflect the social division of time but rather actively help to shape it: North Americans' work and leisure are experienced and organized through the sounds and silences associated with them.

Music is coordinated with temporal cycles and religious structures in societies around the world, although rarely in the same ways. North American society is distinctive in part because of the great variety of ways of organizing temporality. Yet this diversity should not obscure certain larger trends. The prevalence, indeed the near ubiquity, of Christmas carols and church bells in public spaces attest to the significance of Christianity in shaping North American soundscapes and musical temporality.

Music and Age Categories

If the daily, weekly, and yearly rounds are organized by music, so too is the life cycle. Certain genres of music are associated with social categories, including age and gender. Of these, children's music is perhaps the most readily distinguished. In North America, there are significant bodies of repertory that are closely associated with children—particularly girls—of elementary school age (Listen to CD III, 22 for an example of children's song).

LISTENING GUIDE

"MISS SUE FROM ALABAMA"

Recorded by Edna Smith Edet in New York City

GO TO www.mymusiclab.com for the Automated **Listening Guide** CDIII • Track 22/Download Track 67

These game songs were recorded in New York, probably in the 1970s, where they were sung by what sounds like a chorus composed largely of girls. In performances of the songs, according to the notes of the recordist, Edna Smith Edet, the children move in a circle and perform actions that are coordinated with the words. In the first version of "Miss Sue from Alabama," they move their hands to the words "chicka boom," move their feet on "tic, tac, toe," and "waddle and shake shoulders on 'boom tick a wally wally.'" In the second version, which emerges from the first, they mime "curl," "toy," "wrap," and "down," stopping all motion on "stop." The circle game ends with the children tickling each other.

[0:00] Miss Sue from Alabama (1)

Miss Sue (clap clap), Miss Sue (clap clap),
Miss Sue from Alabama;
Now let's have a party,
Chicka boom, chicka boom,
Chicka boom boom boom.

[0:13] Now let's have a tic tac toe,
A tic, a tac, a tic tac toe.

[0:19] Now Mama's in the kitchen
Peeling white potatoes,
Father in the alley
Drinking white ladle [?White Label?],
Brother in the [playpen],
Waiting for the clock to go,
Boom tick tock, boom tick a wally wally

[0:51] Miss Sue from Alabama (2)

Miss Sue, Miss Sue,
Miss Sue from Alabama,

[0:57] [Now let's,] My mother had a baby
And father's going crazy.
But if it's a girl,
I give it a curl
And if it's a boy,
I give it a toy,
Wrap it up in toilet paper
Send it down the elevator

[1:19] First floor, stop, ticking over,
Second floor, stop, think it over,
Third floor, you better watch out,
'Cause S T O P spells stop.

The performances of "Miss Sue from Alabama" present fragments of everyday life for children in the New York of the 1970s and perhaps today, too: mama, father, brother, and a new baby; the somewhat obscure world of adult life, where fathers drink in the alley and mothers have babies; locations both familiar (the elevator and its floors) and imagined (Alabama). There are hints of simmering sibling antagonism: just what is being sent down the elevator in this song, for instance? Present too are many of the elements Kyra Gaunt

(2006) identifies in her book on African American girls' games: quotations from popular culture alongside other orally circulating elements, and above all a playful, musical physicality. What is also highlighted in this pair of examples is the diversity and particularity of children's musical games. Edet describes finding ten different versions of another song, "Here We Go Willoughby," in an eight-block radius. As this suggests, children's games differ from playground to playground and community to community, reflecting locality, but also the creative work of young innovators and improvisers.

Other forms of musical activity tend to be associated with certain social categories as well, although perhaps not quite so exclusively. Young people, and especially young men, invest immense amounts of energy learning to perform genres such as rock, metal, and hip-hop. Youthful pop singers and boy bands are marketed aggressively to adolescent girls. And it is a North American commonplace that paired adults often take up couple dancing in later life—for instance, learning ballroom dancing or Chicago stepping—while younger singles are more likely to dance apart, to genres such as rock and roll and electronic dance music. But these generalities are complicated by ethnic, regional, and class variations, which give particularity to musical and choreographic experiences of age and gender. For some young North Americans, youthful musical experiences probably do involve dancing in highly individuated styles suited to electronic dance music, and adulthood and committed partnership are embodied in the dance lessons they take to prepare themselves for wedding receptions and similar occasions. But for many others, couple dances may be the very form in which youthful good times are experienced: in dancing the country two-step or *pasito duranguense* (see below), for instance.

Music and Rites of Passage   Music is not only connected to particular stages of life, but also and especially to ritual undertakings that mark and effect movements from one stage or state of social life to another. Through these rites of passage, communities imbue the life cycle with meaning in a way similar to how they organize the passing of time through liturgy. Birth rites—for instance circumcisions and baptisms—commemorate the moments when new persons join communities, whereas funerary rites—wakes, funerals, viewings, and memorial services—mark departures. Other rites of passage accompany and affirm transformations from childhood to adolescence and adolescence to adulthood, or various stages of educational achievement; for instance, bar and bat mitzvahs, *quinceñeras*, confirmations, and various graduations. Still others perform marriages. Music plays an important role at many such events.

Take, for instance, wedding ceremonies. In the late 1980s and early 1990s I occasionally accompanied weddings at a Mennonite church in a small western Canadian town. Observant Mennonites are Christians who tend to practice adult baptism, nonresistance (for many this means refusing to do military service), and, in many cases, a wariness of ideas and practices deemed too worldly. The rejection of worldliness has had musical implications: in some Mennonite churches instruments have been disallowed. The church where I played was relatively liberal, however, and, in addition to the piano, there were amplified guitars and even a drum set. Indeed, weddings made extensive use of instrumental music. At the opening of a service, the pianist typically performed pleasant music—nothing too showy or harmonically unusual—as wedding guests moved to their seats. Once everybody was in place, the bridal party processed in, not uncommonly to an arrangement of Pachelbel's Canon in D. The length of the processional was often worked out the night before the wedding so that there would be exactly enough music to get the parents, bridesmaids, groomsmen, and groom down the aisle to the front of the church. There was no telling, however, whether nerves or mistakes would change the speed of the procession on the actual day of the wedding, so whoever was playing had to be prepared to cut things short. The entrance of the bride required special music, of course, and this was typically picked with care and in consultation with her in advance. During the service itself, the congregation sometimes sang a hymn, and there was typically a song on the themes of love and marriage, performed by a friend or relative of the bride or groom. After the pronouncement of marriage, the pianist played a recessional as the couple went back down the aisle. This last, obviously, had to sound grand and joyful, and it was usually showier than the music played at other points during the service.

Music served a number of purposes at the ceremony. First, it demonstrated the taste of the bridal couple and their families and reinforced the grandness and consequentiality of the event. The quality of the music was important for some of the same reasons that the quality of the food and the clothing of the bridal party were concerns. This said, the music was by no means the most important element of the service. It tended to occupy a moderate sonic and emotional register, without drawing too much attention to itself, and it had to be timed correctly to accompany the movements of the ritual participants into the sanctuary and out of it. In fact, there were only two moments when the music was the primary focus of attention: during the congregational hymn and the solo song. At both of these moments, the texts sung expressed important beliefs shared by the bridal party and the assembled witnesses: concerning, for instance, the love between God and humanity, or the loving relationship between a married couple.

All in all, these ceremonies progressed like many North American Christian weddings, and stood in a reasonably close relationship to the continental mainstream. In other ways they were quite distinct. For instance, the ceremonies were typically followed by a reception, but rarely by a dance. The community and the church were conservative in a number of respects, and many disapproved of drinking and dancing. In other nearby communities and congregations, drinking and dancing were important parts of the wedding reception, and hosts hired a DJ or even a full band to perform at the function. Indeed, there existed a widespread tradition in the region of the pre-wedding social: engaged couples raised money for their nuptials by holding a dance at a community hall. But the congregation I played for eschewed such activities, or at least the majority of its members (those who wanted them as part of their wedding typically held a reception in a neighboring town). By excluding drinking and dance from weddings, the church actively distinguished itself from surrounding communities and from the worldly North American mainstream. Nevertheless, to characterize these differences in behavior simply as boundary maintenance (that is, a way of separating one's own community from others) does not do them justice: they were also a creative way to address a theological imperative to moral behavior. Thus, although church services incorporated a piano, amplified instruments, and worship songs that drew upon pop precedents, they nevertheless avoided certain equally common North American musical behaviors deemed morally problematic. Evident here too is an inventive, selective engagement with the world beyond the community.

The place of music in this wedding ceremony certainly cannot be generalized to all of North America—it is rooted in a specific place and time. Neighboring communities celebrated weddings in different ways, depending on their own cultural and religious particularities. Neither is ritual practice historically stable. When I worked as a pianist in the 1980s and 1990s, weddings only occurred between men and women: today of course it is possible for same-sex couples to be wed in Canada and a number of states in the United States, opening up possibilities for creative elaborations of ritual and musical practice. A quick perusal of wedding videos on the Internet suggests both continuity and change. Music continues to play processional and recessional roles in many ceremonies, both traditional and new: a lesbian couple walks down the aisle to Pachelbel's Canon in one video; in another, a chorus sings "San Francisco" as a postlude at a wedding between two men in that city in 2008. So it is that specificities of history and place intersect with widely distributed musical practices in shaping North American ritual life.

To sum up, North American ethnicity is performed and experienced through musical practices that coincide with and effect transitions between, temporal divisions and life stages. Christian and English-speaking traditions enjoy particular prominence, whereas others stand outside this mainstream. The preceding accounts demonstrate that ethnicity is lived not only at moments of solemnity and festivity, but also during the everyday stretches these punctuate. Moreover, it is performed into being through the ongoing musical organization of life and passing time.

MUSICAL PARTICULARITY AND HISTORICAL CONTINUITY

Social groups value those practices that distinguish them from one another. Perhaps particularly important for many ethnic communities are the practices that connect them to their original homelands. Yet in many cases these traditions are quite different from what arrived with the original immigrants. Subsequent generations have modified them in ways that acknowledge a new, North American, context. Moreover, musicians, instruments, genres, and practices have in the intervening generations moved among groups. Hence many communities have a complicated relationship to their valued musical traditions, which may have come to them well after their arrival in North America. All of this suggests two key characteristics of North American musical life identified by Philip V. Bohlman (2008): its simultaneous adaptability and particularity. On the one hand, musical practices and technologies move between communities, regions, and ethnic groups. On the other hand, community members feel a strong sense of ownership of, and connection to, these practices, no matter how recently they have been adopted. Some of the complexities of these musical movements and senses of ownership are explored in the following case studies.

Anglo-American Ballads   Clarence Ashley first recorded "The House Carpenter" for Columbia Records in 1930 (Smith [1952]: 3), and then again after he was "rediscovered" during the 1960s. The song is an example of American music from Appalachia (the highlands that extend from Pennsylvania to Alabama). It is a ballad: that is to say, a song that tells a story. Straightforward musical structures reinforce the centrality of the narrative element in this performance. The song has a basic strophic form, all verses being set to the same repeated melody. Supporting this structure, the banjo accompaniment ticks along in the background, rarely drawing attention to itself (Listen to CD III, 23 to hear this ballad).

This ballad seems to have originated in England and been brought to North America by immigrants from Great Britain, Northern Ireland, or both, sometime between the late seventeenth and early nineteenth century. It proliferated in the North American context, and regionally differentiated versions of the song emerged in Newfoundland, New England, the Midwest, the West, and especially Appalachia (Burrison 1967: 282, Gardner-Medwin 1971: 426). In fact, this particular ballad seems to have flourished much more widely in North America than on its island of origin (Burrison 1967).

Legendary banjo player/singer Clarence "Tom" Ashley at his home in North Carolina. *Source:* BenCar Archives

So, immigrants brought "The House Carpenter" with them to North America from their original homeland and preserved it in their new one. Yet Ashley's recording suggests transformation as well as perpetuation. For instance, the ship carpenter in the British version of the song has become a house carpenter in the American one. This reflects a new performance context: ship carpenters were rarer in Appalachia than in Britain, whereas house carpenters were well known in the highlands, where the wood construction of houses was quite common (Gardner-Medwin 1971:421).

But the instrumentation of the recording reveals something even more telling about the new American musical context. Clarence Ashley accompanies himself on the banjo in the recording, which has its roots in an instrument of African origin, brought to the Americas by slaves (Epstein 1975). Banjo-type instruments are documented amongst Caribbean blacks in the [late] seventeenth century and African

LISTENING GUIDE

"THE HOUSE CARPENTER"

GO TO www.mymusiclab.com for the Automated Listening Guide CDIII • Track 23/Download Track 68

Clarence Ashley, vocals and banjo

The House Carpenter

1. *"Well met, well met," said an old true love,*
   "Well met, well met," said he.
   "I'm just returning from the salt, salt sea
   And it's all for the love of thee."

2. *"Come in, come in my old true love,*
   And have a seat with me.
   It's been three fourths of a long, long year
   Since together we have been."

3. *"Well I can't come in or I can't sit down,*
   For I haven't but a moment's time.
   They say you are married to a house
   *   carpenter*
   And your heart will never be mine."

4. *"[Now I saw] I could have married a king's*
   *   daughter dear.*
   I'm sure she'd have married me.
   But I've forsaken her crowns of gold
   And it's all for the love of thee."

5. *"Now will you forsaken your house carpenter*
   And go along with me?
   I'll take you where the grass grows green
   On the banks of the deep blue sea."

6. *She picked up her little babe,*
   And kisses gave it three,
   And said, "Stay right here, my darling little babe
   And keep your papa company."

7. *Well, they hadn't been on ship but about two*
   *   weeks,*
   I'm sure it was not three,
   And his true love began to weep and mourn
   And he [???] most bitterly

8. *Says, "Are you weeping for my silver or my gold,"*
   Says, "Are you weeping for my [store]
   Are you weeping for that house carpenter
   Whose face you never see any more?"

9. *"No, it's I'm not a-weeping for your silver or*
   *   your gold,*
   Or neither for your [store].
   I am weeping for my darling little babe
   Whose face I'll never see any more."

10. *Well, they hadn't been on ship but about*
    *   three weeks,*
    I'm sure it was not four,
    And they sprung a leak in the bottom of the
    *   ship*
    And it sunk for to rise no more.

This song is a version of a ballad for which there is printed evidence dating back to the seventeenth century. It seems particularly close to a variant first published in London around 1785, entitled "The Distressed Ship Carpenter" (Burrison 1967: 271–2). Compare the first two verses of the following ballad with the first and fourth of the previous.

The Distressed Ship Carpenter

1. *Well met, well met, my own true Love*
   Long time I have been seeking thee,
   I am lately come from the salt, salt Sea,
   And all for the Sake, Love, of thee.

2. *I might have had a King's Daughter,*
   And fain she would have married me,
   But I've forsaken all her Crowns of Gold,
   And all for the Sake, Love, of thee.

3. *If you might have had a King's Daughter,*
   I think you much to blame,
   I would not for Five Hundred Pounds,
   That my Husband should hear the same.

4. *For my Husband is a Carpenter,*
   And a young Ship Carpenter is he,
   And by him I have a little Son,
   Or else, Love, I'd go along with thee.

Americans by the middle of the eighteenth (ibid.). They were initially played by black musicians but eventually adopted by whites, first it seems in the course of local music making, and later in the context of minstrelsy (see below for a description of this musical style).

Ashley's instrument points to a social and musical context unique to the United States, where black slaves and free white men historically played similar music on similar instruments. In fact, as work by Alan Jabbour and others suggests (Jabbour 2001, Epstein 2003, Wells 2003), much of the instrumental music that today is widely associated in the popular imagination with white musicians was also historically played by blacks, as is evidenced by the fact that many American fiddle tunes employ complex rhythmic syncopations that suggest the influence of African musical traditions (see Chapter 7).

Tecnobanda, Quebradita, and *Duranguense*: Other Migrating Musical Styles

Similar developments have occurred in the more recent past. For instance, the early 1990s and 2000s saw a surge in the popularity of a number of musical styles on Spanish-language radio stations in the United States——namely, **tecnobanda** and **música duranguense**——and the related **quebradita** and *pasito duranguense* dance crazes (see Hutchinson 2007, Simonett 2001). In these genres, singers perform in close vocal harmony, in alternation with melodic fills by brass, reed, and electronic keyboard instruments, and dramatic bursts of sound from the kit drum and tamborón (a combined bass drum and cymbal). Much of the music makes use of dance rhythms—including the polka, waltz, and cumbia—that are common enough in North America, but quite different from those that are prominent in mainstream dance music oriented to young people. Singers and the instrumentalists accompanying them sometimes stray from the center of the pitch, performing on what some listeners would consider the "sharp" (high) or "flat" (low) side of the notes. Given that some of these genres came to prominence at a moment when producers of English-language popular music were enthusiastically embracing electronic methods of pitch correction to ensure vocal and instrumental parts were "in tune" with each other, the discrepancies in some tecnobanda songs stand out dramatically on the radio dial and in urban public spaces. Thus, through instrumentation, dance rhythms, and tuning, this music establishes a marked difference from the anglophone popular musics that otherwise dominate the soundscapes of American cities. In so doing, it also establishes a certain kind of Mexican-American musical ethnicity.

TECNOBANDA
A popular dance music derived from blending the instruments and repertory of traditional banda ensembles (brass bands) with electronic instruments.

MÚSICA DURANGUENSE
A popular dance music that developed in Chicago. A variant of tecnobanda, the musical style is derived from blending banda with electronic instruments. It is notable for it's emphasis on percussion lines and for the generally faster tempos at which the repertory is performed. The accompanying dance is characterized by western attire and a typical dance step, called pasito, derived from the traditional dancing in Durango, Mexico. Duranguense is popular in both Mexico and the United States.

QUEBRADITA
A dance craze, accompanied by tecnobanda ensembles and privileging cumbia dances, which became especially popular in Los Angeles, northern Mexico, and throughout the Southwest. Characterized by western attire, hat tricks, and flips.

Many elements of tecnobanda can be traced to longstanding rural Mexican musical traditions. The genre emerged as an updated and electrified version of traditional village banda (band) music from the northwestern Mexican state of Sinaloa, as Helena Simonett (2001) and Sydney Hutchinson (2007) explain. The Sinaloan banda traditionally incorporated melodic wind and brass instruments, a tuba to play the bass line, and the tamborón and snare drum as percussion instruments. (The mariachi ensembles discussed in Chapter 9 represent another example of the importance of brass instruments in Mexican music cultures.) To this, the newer genres added instruments like the electric guitar and electronic keyboards.

A closer look at banda and its descendents, however, reveals that its history is not simply that of a rural Mexican genre carried northward to American cities by Mexican immigrants. Rather, a long history of border crossing and musical borrowing is evident. Musicians have long moved back and forth between the northern Mexican states and Texas, establishing rich musical connections between Spanish-speaking communities on both sides of the border (Peña 1985). Moreover, the polka and waltz rhythms that are common in tecnobanda and related genres (on both sides of the border) point to an important German influence in that region. Both polka and waltz were popular in Europe and North America in the nineteenth century, but their popularity in northern Mexico probably was due to the presence of German immigrants in Texas and in the city of Monterrey in the state of Neuvo Leon. These immigrants brought dances and instruments—particularly the accordion—with them when they settled in these areas, making a significant impact upon the music culture of the border area (Hutchinson 2007: 27).

This cross-border borrowing and migration is just as complicated in the case of two dance crazes growing out of the banda tradition: quebradita and pasito duranguense. Duranguense, most dramatically, emerged in Chicago, led by the ensemble Grupo Montéz de Durango (see the discography for a short list of recordings and performers in the various tecnobanda genres). The style incorporates some elements that can be found in music and dance from Durango and evidences the influence of previous Mexican popular styles. In other ways it is innovative, however; for instance, women musicians contribute on a previously unprecedented scale. Crucially, duranguense was not "brought along" by migrants from Mexico but rather emerged in the United States. And from the beginning it addressed a transnational audience on both sides of the border.

As in the case of "The House Carpenter," the model of immigrants preserving old traditions in a new country does not seem adequate. Immigrant communities borrow instruments and stylistic elements from one another, they adapt musical practices to suit new social circumstances, and the resulting transformations sometimes double back to impact musical practices "back home."

Not all practices undergo dramatic developments and transformations; nor do all musicians appropriate elements from neighboring music cultures upon arrival in North America. In some instances old repertories continue to be practiced, often in similar circumstances to those in which they originated, and within communities that have retained quite strict boundaries. But even in these situations, musical activity and discourse frequently reflects the new North

American context. For example, the Hutterites, a Protestant group whose members live communally, abide by strict guidelines concerning comportment and dress, speak a relatively rare Central European language, and maintain a conservative musical tradition. Hutterite music tends to be **monophonic** and unaccompanied, eschewing instrumental accompaniment and especially secular subjects (Wulz 2002). Yet even these musically conservative communities occasionally borrow sacred songs from other communities, import new melodies, and engage in discussions about introducing certain new practices. Thus the everyday production of ethnicity involves, at some level, an acknowledgment of neighboring communities and broader mainstreams. Sometimes this means borrowing genres, stylistic elements, and technologies from neighbors, and sometimes it involves the explicit rejection of their musical practices.

PARTICULAR AND GENERAL MUSICAL PRACTICES

The "mosaic" metaphor introduced at the beginning of the chapter is one of the ways that North Americans characterize the cultural diversity of their countries. Another metaphor, perhaps more closely associated with the United States, is the "melting pot"—the idea of a national culture that emerges as various contributing traditions blend together. These characterizations are familiar and comfortable but not entirely accurate: musically speaking, evidence of both "melting" and "sustained" difference can be found in North American music. There is on the one hand a tendency toward distinctiveness: ethnic groups, regions, and communities actively differentiate themselves through musical means. On the other hand, there is a tendency towards musical borrowing, seemingly even in the most conservative music cultures. Communities appropriate musical sounds and technologies from one another, and these sometimes change hands altogether. As we've seen, music that is frequently associated with white Appalachian musicians is in fact a hybrid music, making use not only of British songs and genres but also of traditional African-American instruments. Meanwhile tecnobanda, quebradita, and duranguense are often associated with a northern Mexican identity, but they draw upon German rhythms and instrumentation, and they reflect years of interaction between Mexican and Texan musicians. Thus the paradox: musical materials circulate, but the resulting hybrid practices are nevertheless held to belong quite closely to particular communities, regions, and populations (see Bohlman 2008).

A similar tension emerges when we explore the relationship between stylistic particularities and generalized practices in North American fiddle traditions, where numerous regional styles are distinguishable from broader national or international ones. In fiddling from Cape Breton in the Canadian maritime province of Nova Scotia, fiddlers are typically accompanied by pianists, who play in a unique syncopated style. The **strathspey**, a dance tune of Scottish origin in duple time, is particularly prominent, as are patterns of melodic embellishment that are borrowed from bagpipe traditions. By contrast, in Quebec (but also in many Canadian indigenous communities) fiddlers perform rhythmic "clogging"

MONOPHONY
One melody line is played by all musicians, with no harmonic accompaniment.

STRATHSPEY
A dance tune, associated with Scotland, in 4/4 meter. Characterized rhythmically by dot-cut, or Scotch "snaps" (a short note followed by a dotted note).

Unidentified fiddler and banjo player, c. 1910. Amateur musicians like these two men performed throughout the United States for local parties and gatherings during the 19th and early 20th centuries. Notice the single-row melodeon in front of the banjo player's chair. *Source:* BenCar Archives

patterns with their feet as they play. And the fiddle style of the "upper South" in the United States is characterized by a distinctive syncopated bowing style that reflects the influence of African American musicians (Jabbour 2001).

Thus, a great deal of regional and ethnic musical diversity can be catalogued based on musical particularities. But it is just as important to acknowledge that certain musical structures are widely distributed, and even normative (if not universal), in North American musical practice. Fiddling traditions incorporate at least two such generalized musical structures: the standard **AABB** dance form, and a standard harmony pattern, using the tonic, dominant, and subdominant chords as described in the discussion that follows. Both of these structures are evident in Dwight Lamb's performance of "Rocky Road to Jordan."

Lamb is an American fiddler and accordionist of partial Danish descent. His musical repertory was shaped by both family connections and engagement with mass media: his maternal grandfather was an accordionist and his father was a fiddler, but he also learned tunes by listening to musicians who performed on the radio, particularly a fiddler named Uncle Bob Walters, who later in life became a personal friend (Lamb 1999). Lamb's repertoire reflects a diverse array of fiddling and dancing practices— the fiddlers in his circle played Danish, German, Scottish, American, and Canadian fiddle tunes. And yet, his varied repertory makes frequent use of the formal and harmonic patterns just mentioned (Listen to CD III, 24 to hear an **AABB** fiddle tune).

The formal and harmonic structures of fiddle tunes typically reinforce one another. Experienced musicians are aware of this correspondence at some level (in many cases probably unconsciously) and gauge their activity to the 32-bar form so that everything more or less matches up. A general feel for these forms helps fiddlers to learn new tunes and remember old ones, and it allows accompanists to play along with tunes they don't recall particularly well or have not

LISTENING GUIDE

"ROCKY ROAD TO JORDAN"

GO TO **www.mymusiclab.com for the Automated Listening Guide** CDIII • Track 24/Download Track 69

Dwight Lamb, fiddle; Lynn Holsclaw, guitar

If you listen closely, you should be able to hear that the tune has two sections that alternate throughout the piece. The first, labeled **A**, begins in a lower range and lasts until about [0:17] into the track. At that point, the second part, labeled **B**, begins, marked by a shift into a higher register. Further close listening will reveal that the melodic material in both **A** and **B** is repeated; so, for instance, [0:09–0:17] is a repetition of [0:00–0:09]. For this reason, the tune is said to be in **AABB** form. This structure is carefully synchronized with the underlying pulse. If you count along with the music, which ticks along at about 120 beats per minute, you should be able to hear that there are exactly 16 beats in each of the four sections of the tune, for a total of 64 in each iteration. In 2/4 meter (two beats per measure, or bar) these 64 beats translate to 32 measures or bars. This 32-bar **AABB** dance form and other closely related ones are used throughout North America. To be sure, these forms are broken or elaborated by fiddlers, and in certain fiddling traditions they are treated much more freely than in others, but they are nevertheless very widely practiced.

0:00	**A** Section.
0:09	**A** Section repeated.
0:17	**B** Section.
0:25	**B** Section repeated.
0:33	**A** Section.
0:41	**A** Section repeated.
0:49	**B** Section.
0:57	**B** Section repeated.
1:05	**A** Section.
1:13	**A** Section repeated.
1:21	**B** Section.
1:29	**B** Section repeated.
1:37	**A** Section.

Close attention to the melody and the guitar part reveals another element of musical structure, equally important but somewhat more abstract: harmony. Each section of the tune moves through a harmonic progression, evident in chord changes in the guitar part and in changes of pitch content in the fiddle melody. It might be difficult to hear these progressions if your ears are not attuned to them, but if you listen closely you should notice that there are three different harmonies in play in total. North American music theorists—and many musicians—call these harmonies the tonic, subdominant, and dominant, or alternately, chords I, IV, and V. Each of these comprises three simultaneously sounding pitches drawn from the seven-note diatonic scale, and each is named for the lowest of those three pitches. In the diagram that follows, chord I is associated with D, the first note in the D major scale, chord IV with G, the fourth note, and chord V with A, the fifth.

Harmonic structure of "Rocky Road to Jordan"

	Bar 1	Bar 2	Bar 3	Bar 4	Bar 5	Bar 6	Bar 7	Bar 8
A section	I	I	V	V	I	IV	V	I
B section	I	I	V	V	I	IV	V	I

Harmonies in the key of D major

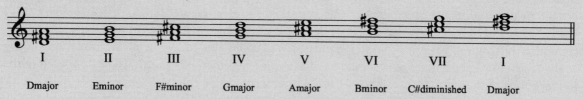

I	II	III	IV	V	VI	VII	I
Dmajor	Eminor	F#minor	Gmajor	Amajor	Bminor	C#diminished	Dmajor

Harmony can be a complex business, and many North American music scholars devote entire careers to unlocking its secrets and structures. A few key points can be suggested here. First, this piece stands in dialogue with the most central or dominant structure of harmonic organization: the common practice system, which is organized around a fundamental opposition between tonic and dominant, chords I and V. In common practice music, the fundamental motion is from I to V and back to I again. Two variations of this pattern are evident in Section **A** of "Rocky Road to Jordan," one in each four-bar half. In the first four bars, the harmony moves from I to V (I–I–V–V), where it is interrupted. The second four bars introduce the tonic again and, this time, articulate a complete version of the fundamental pattern, moving from I to V to I via IV (I–IV–V–I). The completion of the I–V–I pattern creates a sense of musical closure, especially because it coincides with the end of a rhythmic and formal grouping.

heard before. As long as a tune follows the standard form and uses the common harmonic practice, fiddlers and accompanists can, so to speak, slot melodic patterns and chord progressions into appropriate places within the structure. In short, these patterns help make everyday music making possible, because they provide a basic, agreed upon framework. It should not be surprising that structures such as the common practice system have informed some of the most widely distributed folk and popular music practices in North America, including fiddling, gospel song, country music, and some forms of the blues and jazz. Indeed, common-practice harmony is also a default in duranguense, música norteña, and other Mexican-American genres.

But, again, there are many other options for harmonization—if none so widespread and well established as common-practice ones. Some tunes, genres, and performers draw upon a wider harmonic palette, incorporating a broader range of chords than those used in "Rocky Road to Jordan." In others, the dominant-tonic relationship is not as central as it is in common-practice harmony. In still other cases, tunes are based upon scales or modes that are not easily harmonized using I, IV, and V. For instance, on the same album from which the preceding example was drawn, Dwight Lamb plays a tune in the Dorian mode (a seven-note mode distinct from both major and minor); it is harmonized by two chords, I and II rather than I and V.

Though slightly less widespread, these alternative harmonic structures are themselves musical commonplaces, known to, and practiced by, musicians across North America. And as in the former case, when they are employed it is relatively easy to pick up how a given tune should be accompanied, particularly when a standard 32-bar form is in play. My broader point is this: although there is considerable regional diversity in North American fiddling, and although there are no North American universals, there do seem to be musical practices—including the harmonic and formal structures just discussed—that extend across regions and unite many musical traditions across the continent. Ethnic and regional differences—but also individual creativity—become apparent when musicians stray from, or elaborate, these commonalities.

THE AFRICAN AMERICAN CONTRIBUTION TO NORTH AMERICAN MUSIC

One of the most characteristic aspects of North American music—and particularly music of the United States—is the important contribution of African American music and musicians. This is not to say that black music has not also made a significant contribution in other parts of the world (as Chapters 9 and 10 illustrate). It is rather to say that African Americans, despite being demographically in the minority in the United States, and subject for centuries to slavery and, later, to legalized forms of discrimination, have played a central role in shaping that country's traditional, popular, and art musics. During the long twentieth century of America's global influence in matters economic, political, and musical, moreover, African American music has exerted an unprecedented influence upon the rest of the world. Many of the genres that emerged in the United States and went on to have a global impact during this period came into existence thanks to originating or otherwise significant contributions by African Americans, including ragtime, blues, jazz, rhythm and blues, rock and roll, soul, funk, disco, hip-hop, and electronic dance music. Other American musical genres would be unimaginable in their present forms without the influence of African American music and musicians: these include country music and bluegrass, the Broadway musical, and American art music, whether in its more tonal manifestations or in its avant-garde expressions.

Culturally speaking, at least two factors seem to be responsible for the prominence of African American contributions to the music of the United States and to musical practices in many parts of the world. First, music has been an important means of creating and expressing collectivity for African Americans themselves. Second, African American music has long been a central element of American musical life more generally, and as such has continually been incorporated into the musical traditions of European-Americans and others. African American music has been an object of fascination for other North American music cultures—and in sustained and at times problematical fashion, as during the era of minstrelsy (further discussion follows). It is probably for both of these reasons that music has been a consistent site of African American cultural innovation and creativity.

Expressing Collective Experience and Resistance

Millions of Africans were forcibly taken across the Atlantic Ocean to the Americas during the centuries in which the slave trade was legal. With them they brought a number of musical practices and technologies that survived despite the crushing circumstances of slavery. Dena Epstein (1975) has suggested that louder African wind and percussion instruments were regarded with suspicion by slave owners, and that for this reason quieter instruments such as the banjo (and the fiddle) became particularly important amongst African Americans. But it is in the realm of musical structures rather than instruments that key African retentions are most evident. Many of the characteristics of sub-Saharan African music (identified in Chapter 7) are present in African American music, including cyclical forms, interlocking parts, dense timbres, and musical divisions into core and elaboration parts. So it is that even as African American musics make use of a wide variety of structures of European origin, they have transformed these to bring them into line with an African American aesthetic. These have, in turn, been incorporated in North American music more generally.

Early accounts suggest that music played an important role in the collective expression of the experiences of slave life. Epstein's research points to an array of musical practices, including work songs, sacred music, and music for socializing and dancing on days of rest. Music expressed sorrow, it protested the conditions of slavery, and it expressed hopes for a better life. Early accounts make it clear, too, that music was useful as a means of resistance, both overt and covert. Drumming, singing, and dancing accompanied an uprising that occurred in Stono, South Carolina, in 1739 (Epstein 2003) in which slaves fought for freedom from their oppressors. And song often enabled the expression of sentiments and the passing of information that would have been dangerous to convey in speech (Maultsby 2011).

African American music was not strictly separate from other forms of American music, however, but stood in complex relationships of exchange. Black fiddlers were particularly common in early American life, for instance, and they appear to have accompanied the dances of both blacks and whites using Anglo-Celtic tunes and genres (see Wells 2003). Whites borrowed practices of music and dance they understood to come from black practice; thus a description of Virginia life published in 1776 remarked, "Towards the close of an evening, when the company are pretty well tired with country-dances, it is usual to dance jigs; a practice originally borrowed . . . from the Negroes" (Epstein 2003: 121). Moreover, the complex syncopation frequently found in American fiddle music seems to have been an African American innovation that was appropriated by whites and then spread across the continent to become the characteristic sound of American fiddle music.

In fact, African American music became an object of considerable fascination for white Americans. Or perhaps it would be more accurate to say that the music became the object of ambivalent fascination, for there existed simultaneously a love for African American music and a refusal to respect the people who made it. This was most evident in the phenomenon of minstrelsy, which emerged around the middle of the nineteenth century. In minstrel shows, white actors and musicians blackened their faces with cork and played parts as stereotypical African Americans. These minstrels played instruments commonly used by blacks and made music that drew upon African American performance practices, but their representations of blackness consisted of grotesque caricatures. Minstrelsy was immensely successful as a popular culture movement, and continued in various forms well into the twentieth century. Its prevalence suggests that, however negative and stereotypical white representations of blacks were—however much whites asserted a distance between themselves and blacks—black music was becoming a central element of white expressive culture.

African American Music: From Emancipation to Today

In the decades following Emancipation (1865), black music continued to offer possibilities for collective expression and action even as it held an enduring fascination for non-blacks. New technologies—beginning with newspapers and other print media, then recording and radio, and finally the Internet—helped spread local musical traditions to new audiences. Many forms of black music became more prominent and more widely dispersed as a result. A few examples will illustrate this point.

Sacred Music   Listen to "Precious Lord, Take My Hand" as performed by the singers of the First Independent Holy Church of God—Unity—Prayer from Marion, Alabama (CD III, 25). Frederic Ramsey, who recorded the song in 1954, described the church as a tiny congregation ("more than eight persons") that met every Wednesday evening in the front room of the cabin of church elder Effie Hall (Ramsey 1962). Both the music and lyrics of the song are striking. The singing is propelled by the insistent rhythmic accompaniment of a bass drum, tambourine, and guitar, the latter played almost like a percussion instrument in its own right (and in a manner that does not always correspond to the harmonies implied by the vocal line). In dramatic contrast, the lyrics project absolute despondency ("I am tired, I am weak, I am worn") and plead for divine help.

As the lyrics of "Precious Lord, Take My Hand" suggest, African American religious observance and sacred song often focused on life's difficulties (see Maultsby 2010). These tended to be considerable in an era when blacks faced not only the same concerns faced by many other Americans—poverty, illness, crime, and the uncertainties of love (though in greater proportion)—but also the crushing effects of legalized racism. In these circumstances, gospel song offered opportunities for collective reflection upon shared circumstances, for mutual affirmation, encouragement, and support, and for expressions of solidarity. This in part helps to explain the quick dissemination of Dorsey's song, which had reached even tiny congregations like the one in Marion, Alabama some two decades after it was first published.

LISTENING GUIDE

PRECIOUS LORD, TAKE MY HAND

GO TO www.mymusiclab.com for the Automated Listening Guide CDIII • Track 25/Download Track 70

Elder Effie Hall and congregation of First Independent Holy Church of God—Unity—Prayer. With Annie L. Fitts, Elma Sawyer, Jennie Jackson, and Brother Williams. Recorded Marion, Alabama, 15 April 1954.

Slaves and free blacks seem to have begun to adopt Christianity widely in the nineteenth century (Epstein 1963) and, as they did so, they adapted it in ways that suited African American sociability and aesthetics. For instance, in the realm of worship, African American congregations tended not to practice the more staid forms of observance characteristic of other Christian traditions, rather incorporating elements such as rhythmic movement and spontaneous spoken and sung expression (Burnim 2001). Worship became a way of expressing and affirming the shared African heritage of participants, shaped by the experience of slavery and the encounter with Christianity. African Americans adopted Christianity, but in doing so they transformed it into something that was their own.

The early decades of the twentieth century saw many African Americans move from rural southern contexts to urban northern ones. Coinciding with this Great Migration to the cities of the north was the emergence, in the 1930s, of a dynamic form of gospel music that fused black gospel hymns, elements of secular popular music, and a spontaneous, unconstrained performance style (Burnim 2001). Thomas A. Dorsey, a former blues and jazz musician who moved from Atlanta to Chicago during World War I (Oliver 2011), was a key figure in this development. It was he who composed the song, following the death of his first wife in 1932.

TIME	SECTION
0:00–0:06	Introduction
0:07–0:28	**Chorus:** Notice the prominent voice of the female leader and also the percussion that is added to the accompaniment as the singing begins.
0:29–0:49	**Verse 1:** See if you can hear the way that the guitar serves more percussive than harmonic functions here. There are a few moments when the chord implied by the melody is not performed on the guitar, for example at [0:37–0:39] and again at [0:46–0:47]. But the strumming pattern remains consistent and insistent throughout, driving the singers through the verse.
0:49–1:09	**Chorus:** Now that you're hearing the chorus again, listen carefully to how the whole performance hangs together, with percussion and guitar driving the singers through each section of the song.
1:10–1:29	**Verse 2:** Now turn your attention to the subtle differences you can hear in each singer's approach to the melody. Some singers are adding harmony, others are embellishing the melody in their own way. You should get the distinct impression of a spontaneous and partially improvised rendition of a song well known by all the participants.
1:30–2:10	**Chorus:** Repeated twice here for emphasis as the song comes to an end.
2:10–2:23	**Conclusion:** Listen for the informal way that the guitarist brings the song to an end here.

The emerging gospel music movement preserved many valued elements of African American musical and religious practice. For instance, Dorsey's gospel songs were notated in a style that left room for improvisation and free elaboration, in keeping with African American performance practice (Maultsby 2010). Perhaps not surprisingly, the melody of the performance you have just heard differs from the published version in a manner that suggests local elaboration. Songs like the foregoing circulated through print and, later, by means of radio and recordings. In this way, they connected local communities and congregations to a broader, continental group of African American musical practitioners. Put another way, the dissemination of musical publications, and their performance from week to week in local congregations, helped to build a black American musical public, distinguished from the Euro-American public not only by the history of slavery and experiences of racism, but also by the collective development and elaboration of shared musical practices. This is not to suggest any sort of strict insularity, however. In fact, Dorsey's "Precious Lord, Take My Hand" became one of the most widely known gospel songs of the twentieth century, thanks in part to recordings by Mahalia Jackson and Elvis Presley, made just a few years after the one you have heard.

Secular Music   Listen to 'Matchbox Blues' by the Texas blues musician Blind Lemon Jefferson (CD III, 26). This is an example of rural blues, a style that appears to have come into being in the southern United States in the early twentieth century. Paul Oliver (2011) suggests that the blues drew upon the solo vocal style of post-Emancipation work songs called field hollers and musical elements of black ballads, and that the earliest blues probably circulated in the repertories of traveling "songsters."

Jefferson's lyrics suggest areas of similarity and contrast with sacred music. On the one hand, the blues, like gospel music, were a genre that allowed singers and listeners to reflect on unhappy circumstances. On the other hand, the blues were more amenable than gospel music to discussions of earthly love, sexuality, money, and the various ways they intersect—in terms both euphemistic ("If she flag my train, papa Lemon's going to let her ride") and direct ("Seems like my heart going break"). It can be added that while this example paints a picture of strained relationships between the sexes from a man's point of view, these relationships were explored from quite distinct perspectives by women blues singers.

Although there are notable differences between the subject matter treated in sacred and secular songs, it is important not to draw too strict an opposition between them. In fact, the same musicians were often active in both areas: as we saw, Thomas Dorsey was a blues singer before he became a composer of gospel music, and Blind Lemon Jefferson sang and recorded sacred songs alongside blues numbers. Moreover, both repertoires played an important part in the work of building a black musical public, circulating through print, broadcasts, and recordings, and connecting local, particularized practices to a broader imagined community.

Importantly, none of these genres has had a solely black listenership, or remained an entirely black practice. Non-black audiences have also been

Blind Lemon Jefferson. *Source:* GAB Archive/Redferns/Getty Images

LISTENING GUIDE

"MATCHBOX BLUES"

GO TO **www.mymusiclab.com** for the Automated
Listening Guide CDIII • Track 26/Download Track 71

Blind Lemon Jefferson
Recorded: Chicago, c. Apr. 1927

Following a brief instrumental introduction, you should be able to hear that the song moves through a repeating lyrical and harmonic pattern seven times. Each of these verses comprises two rhyming lines, the first sung twice and the second only once. The same harmonic progression supports each verse, Jefferson elaborating it in creative ways from iteration to iteration. The tonic chord, I, accompanies the first statement of the first line. In the second statement of that line, the harmony moves to the subdominant, chord IV, for a time, and then back to the tonic. The final line moves to the dominant, chord V, and then back to the tonic. So, the structure of the song's verses can be sketched as follows:

I sat there wondering: will a matchbox hold my clothes?
Tonic (I)
I sat there wondering: will a matchbox hold my clothes?
Subdominant (IV)   Tonic (I)
I ain't got so many matches, but I got so far to go
Dominant (V)   Tonic (I)

This formula is well established and indeed might be thought of as the basic pattern elaborated in many other blues songs. It is important to note, however, that Jefferson frequently breaks away from it in other performances (see Evans 2011), as do many other blues performers.

This recording was made using the acoustic equipment of the day, and existing copies tend to be well-worn; therefore it is difficult to transcribe the lyrics with complete certainty. This transcription attempts to capture what is actually sung, but there is a chance that some words are inaccurate, or that you may hear something differently!

I sat there wondering: will a matchbox hold my clothes?
I sat there wondering: will a matchbox hold my clothes?
I ain't got so many matches, but I got so far to go.
I said, "Fair brown, who may your manager be?
Oh, mama, who may your manager be?
We've asked so many questions; can't you make arrangements for me?"
I got a girl across town: she crochet all the time;
I got a girl across town: she crochets all the time;
Mama if you don't quit crocheting, you going lose your mind.
I can't count the times I stole away and cried;
Can't count the time I stole away and cried;
Sugar the blues ain't on me, but things ain't going on right.
If you want your lover, you better pin him to your side;
I say, if you want your baby, pin her to your side;

If she flag my train, papa Lemon's going to let her ride.
Ain't seen my good gal in three long weeks today;
Ain't seen my good gal in three long weeks today;
Lord it's been so long, seems like my heart going break.
Excuse me mama for knocking on your door;
Well, excuse me mama for knocking on your door;
If my mind don't change, I'll never knock here no more.

captivated by these musical styles, and non-black musicians have performed them and contributed to their histories. These genres appealed to a broad audience for a variety of reasons: the frank discussions of love and money in blues lyrics, for instance, addressed subjects that were of concern to many North American whites as well. In some ways their appeal probably continued the dynamic of ambivalent fascination and imitation evident in minstrelsy (an enthusiasm for musical styles that, while enjoyed, could nevertheless be dismissed as "foreign"). But the immense social transformations that accompanied Emancipation, Reconstruction, and the Civil Rights Movement gradually and insistently pointed white North Americans toward a more productive engagement with African Americans and their musical expressions (a transformation that continues into the present moment).

Changes in the social status of black musicians are especially evident in the history of jazz, and even more particularly those musicians who became active during the 1940s, 1950s, and 1960s—the period immediately leading up to the civil rights reforms in the United States. Perhaps the most iconic musicians in this respect are those associated with the bebop movement. Bebop, emerging in the 1940s, was a demanding style that required great musical facility and flexibility. Musicians improvised at extremely fast tempos, negotiating intricate musical structures at speed. They elaborated preexisting musical and harmonic forms—including the basic blues pattern just introduced—by means of complex harmonic progressions. Consequently, although jazz musicians of previous eras earned renown as artists, it was bebop that definitively won jazz recognition as an art music. Indeed, as George Lewis (1996) has argued, its complexities seem to have spurred developments in other western art music traditions, including a new emphasis on **indeterminacy** and improvisation. As a complex, cutting-edge practice in which black musicians played a particularly prominent role, and which emerged at a moment when blacks were still regularly denied the same rights as white Americans, bebop made a powerful argument for equality.

Although bebop innovators were by and large African American, their audience extended well beyond that community. Moreover, the language of bebop was widely adopted by non-black musicians. The style is now a central component of the training of young jazz musicians around the world (McGee 2011) and an important part of the musical language of many performers. Here again the migration of musical practices between social groups and across social boundaries is evident. Jazz—speaking broadly here, and not simply about

INDETERMINANCY
A term used to describe a compositional technique, increasingly common in Western art music composed after World War Two, in which elements of the composition are left to chance or the preference of the performer.

bebop—incorporates fundamental African retentions, including collective improvisation, and integrates elements of older African American traditions, most notably the blues. At the same time, it has seen important contributions from non-black and non-American musicians, and been a site for collaborations between jazz performers of many backgrounds. Further, its influence is extensive: it is evident in the swung rhythms of classic country music and the improvisatory elements of postwar avant-garde performance. So it is at once a fundamentally African American practice and one that has shaped music making across North America and the globe. In this sense it epitomizes the centrality of African American music to the United States. It also underscores the paradoxical way in which North American music is deeply felt to belong to particular groups even as it regularly makes itself at home elsewhere.

NORTH AMERICAN MUSICAL CONCEPTS

One embarrassing but useful activity I sometimes undertake in the first world music class of a semester asks students to compile a list the songs they can sing. The responses often reveal a division of the class into two groups. The smaller group comprises singers—amateurs, semiprofessionals, and music students—who claim to know some songs, whereas the larger group consists of students who claim to know few or none. "I know a bit, but not all the words," is a common response. It soon becomes apparent that many students believe they are being asked whether they know any "real" songs—pop tunes, jazz standards, art song—and whether they know them in full. Only when asked if they know the national anthem or "Twinkle, Twinkle, Little Star" is it evident that the larger group of students possess a fairly large musical repertory after all: children's clapping games, simple lullabies, sacred music, "Ninety-nine Bottles of Beer on the Wall."

Responses to that exercise suggest a number of things about how music is frequently conceptualized in North America. First, it tends to be understood as something done by professional or specialist artists. Second, it is typically imagined to be something that one encounters in, and performs for, the public sphere. Music learned from intimates—schoolmates, schoolteachers, parents, fellow congregants—is less likely to spring to mind than music that is made available in a somewhat more formalized way, as printed sheet music, an mp3, or a concert performance. Third, music tends to be understood as "music for music's sake" rather than music that is associated with the daily and weekly lives and everyday activities of the people who make it. To some degree, this chapter has sought to balance out these default understandings of music by examining several examples of music performed by non-professionals in everyday settings that is being performed not simply for its own sake, but also to accomplish something, or help accomplish it. To this end, in addition to music played by professional musicians, we have discussed congregational worship, dance music, children's music, and music of welcome and protest.

There are a number of reasons why North Americans tend to conceptualize music in the ways listed above (keep in mind I am suggesting that this is a particularly common way to think of music, not the only one!). Prevailing social and economic conditions have a great deal to do with it. First, North American societies are highly specialized economically, and this professionalization extends to the musical world. Music is thus widely perceived to be the purview of artists who devote the majority of their efforts to it. Second, North American societies are capitalist, and consequently the work of musicians is often understood as a commodity—goods or services available to the public by the unit or the hour. It follows that music is often conceived as something you hear at a concert, or purchase from iTunes, or watch between ads on YouTube. It is perhaps also easy to understand how lullabies and children's games—which circulate in the alternative economies of the home and playground—sometimes come to mind a little later.

So, North Americans often understand music as a commodity produced by specializing artists. Interestingly, the two elements in play—commodification and specialization—do not always mesh smoothly. For they are associated with two different, and sometimes opposing, ways of valuing. From an economic perspective, it is financial success that is esteemed, whereas from a specialist or professional perspective, it is artistic excellence that is measured. Producers of commodities are expected to make music with a wide appeal, whereas artists are expected to make music that evidences talent and craft and pursues excellence. These ends are not always the same.

Indeed, art and commerce often stand in a tense relationship. Fans of popular music will be familiar with certain forms the conflict between them takes: when a metal, country, or indie rock band moves to a major label or starts to court a mainstream audience, concerns are often voiced that the music will lose its authenticity and artistic vitality. Critics worry that, in seeking to fill concert halls, symphonies are relying too much upon familiar works and shirking the artistic imperative to program challenging new ones. Lovers of old-time music express concern that fiddlers are abandoning local styles and taking up more virtuosic national ones in order to win contests and cultivate professional careers (for a discussion of how local styles are defended see Goertzen 1996). Commercially successful music is often alleged to be artistically compromised, and it is sometimes argued that it is pushed on relatively helpless audiences by companies with no interest in art, craft, or tradition. Looking at the conflict from the other side, it is sometimes alleged that art music is too subtle (or even too deliberately abstruse) to be of any value to a wide audience. Its failure as a commodity is deemed to be a symptom of a deeper inability to communicate, and therefore both predictable and deserved. Such quarrels, again, exemplify the tensions that arise in a society where both artistic and commercial success are valued.

However unresolved these arguments, North American behavior suggests that one set of values has precedence over the other. Year upon year, North Americans pour vast amounts of effort into developing and refining musical skills—playing virtuosic guitar solos, improvising in contemporary jazz styles, writing thoughtful lyrics, entering "battle of the bands" contests, and interpreting challenging classical compositions. They do so in full knowledge that their efforts may see little or no financial reward.

Nevertheless, music lovers still get into heated discussions about, for instance, whether avant-garde music should be subsidized, or whether a beloved artist has sold out. But to devote too much space to the tensions between art and commerce—a generative paradox of valuing that isn't going to disappear any time soon—is potentially to ignore two other important issues. The first is that music extends beyond the worlds of art and commerce. It is also a democratic, participatory, and everyday phenomenon. A culinary analogy might be helpful here. The existence of fast-food chains and Zagat-rated restaurants does not change the fact that people still cook at home (and that they garden, fish, and hunt). As this chapter has illustrated, music continues to play a role in the home, the playground, and the community. It acknowledges the passing of the year, assists in rites of passage, coordinates playground games, puts babies to sleep, and teaches the alphabet. And it continues to be implicated in moments of solidarity, helping families, communities, and larger groups to express and experience their bonds to one another. The second concern is North American diversity. Concepts of art and commerce stand in complex and contradictory relationships, not only to one another, but also to ethnic, regional, and community musical priorities. They need to be understood, not as universal North American structures, but rather as two particularly powerful ways of valuing among many. Our task, then, is to consider how the dominant ways of valuing music in North America are challenged and qualified by various ethnic and local ways of assessment.

✓● ⌐**Study** and **Review**
on **mymusiclab.com**

SUMMARY

As we have seen, music helps to give meaning to the passing of time, assisting in the cultural work that vests the daily, weekly, and yearly cycles with significance, and in the rituals that effect transitions between stages of the life cycle. Just as it helps to do the work of shaping temporality, it plays a part in other kinds of organization and differentiation. It coordinates and integrates the efforts of persons and groups (whether under the banner of a nation or some other form of affiliation) and it distinguishes communities, ethnic groups, regions, and nations from one another. Clearly, some kinds of differentiation are unhappier than others, and they are imposed from without by powerful forces, as the legacies of colonialism, slavery, and minstrelsy illustrate. On the other hand, many North American ethnic groups actively pursue cultural and musical paths that distinguish them. Musical differentiation can come from without or within.

In the process of considering differentiation, some interesting complications became evident. First, many North American groups have borrowed musical technologies and stylistic elements from neighbors, as the use of the banjo by Appalachian whites and the presence of German dance rhythms in Mexican-American popular music demonstrate. Nevertheless, these musics are closely associated with their practitioners, by insiders and outsiders alike. Second, despite extensive local and regional variation, widely generalized musical practices can be identified: for instance common-practice harmony, or the **AABB** song form. Third, certain musical particularities seem particularly subject to cross-cultural appropriation, as the extraordinarily broad circulation of African-American musical practices shows.

Finally, many of our examples have suggested a close connection between music, ethnicity, performance, and the everyday. The performance of ethnic music does not simply symbolize difference, but rather actively produces it. Singing improvised gospel music on a Sunday morning, playing the fiddle at a local dance, or turning the radio to the station that plays duranguense at work are generative acts that help bring ethnicity into being. And this North American diversity is not simply produced and reproduced during heightened moments of solemnity and celebration, as in, for instance, the welcoming ceremonies described at the opening of this chapter. It also involves day-to-day activity, and the ongoing practices of musicians both ordinary and extraordinary.

BIBLIOGRAPHY

Works Cited and Consulted   Philip V. Bohlman, "Ethnic North America," Bruno Nettl et al., *Excursions in World Music*, 5th ed. (Upper Saddle River, NJ: Pearson Prentice Hall, 2008); Horace Clarence Boyer, "Black Gospel Music," Harry Eskew et al., "Gospel music," *Grove Music Online, Oxford Music Online* (accessed February 17, 2011); Mellonee V. Burnim, "Religious Music," pp. 624–636, "African American Musics," Ellen Koskoff, *The United States and Canada*, *The Garland Encyclopedia of World Music*, Vol. 3 (New York: Garland Publishing Company, 2001); John Burrison,"'James Harris' Britain Since Child," *The Journal of American Folklore* 80 (1967): 271–284; Martin Clayton, Rebecca Sager, and Udo Will, "In Time with the Music: The Concept of Entrainment and its Significance for Ethnomusicology," *ESEM Counterpoint* 1 (2007): 3–75; Edna Smith Edet, *Songs for Children from New York City*, Folkways 07858, liner notes (1978); Dena J. Epstein, "Slave Music in the United States before 1860: A Survey of Sources (Part 1)," *Notes* 20.2 (1963): 195–212; Dena J. Epstein, "The Folk Banjo: A Documentary History," *Ethnomusicology* 19.3 (1975): 347–371; Dena J. Epstein, *Sinful Tunes and Spirituals: Black Folk Music to the Civil War* (Urbana, IL: University of Illinois Press, 2003); David Evans, "Musical Innovation in the Blues of Blind Lemon Jefferson,"*Black Music Research Journal* 20.1 (2000): 83–116; Alisoun Gardner-Medwin, "The Ancestry of 'The House-Carpenter': A Study of the Family History of the American Forms of Child 243," *The Journal of American Folklore* 84 (1971): 414–427; Kyra Gaunt, *The Games Black Girls Play: Learning the Ropes from Double-Dutch to Hip-Hop* (New York: New York University Press, 2006); John Murray Gibbon, *Canadian Mosaic: The Making of a Northern Nation* (Toronto: McClelland and Stewart, Limited, 1938); Chris Goertzen, "Balancing Local and National Approaches at American Fiddle Contests," *American Music* 14.3 (1996): 352–381; Alan Govenar, "Blind Lemon Jefferson: The Myth and the Man," *Black Music Research Journal* 20.1 (2000): 7–21; Sydney Hutchinson, *From Quebradita to Duranguense: Dance in Mexican American Youth Culture* (Tucson: The University of Arizona Press, 2007); Alan Jabbour, "Fiddle Tunes of the Old Frontier," lecture delivered as the Joseph Schick Lecture at Indiana State University, December 6, 2001, accessed online

<http://www.alanjabbour.com/Fiddle_Tunes_of_the_Old_Frontier_Schick. pdf> (17 February 2011); Will Kymlicka, *Multicultural Citizenship: A Liberal Theory of Minority Rights* (Oxford: Clarendon Press, 1995); Dwight Lamb, liner notes to *Dwight Lamb: Joseph Won a Coated Fiddle and Other Fiddle and Accordion Tunes from the Great Plains*, Rounder CD 0429 (1999); George E. Lewis, "Improvised Music after 1950: Afrological and Eurological Perspectives," *Black Music Research Journal* 16.1 (1996): 91–122; Portia K. Maultsby, "African American," Richard Crawford et al., "United States of America," *Grove Music Online, Oxford Music Online* (accessed February 17, 2011); Kristin McGee, "'New York Comes to Groningen': Jazz Star Circuits in the Netherlands," Jason Toynbee and Byron Dueck, eds., *Migrating Music* (London: Routledge, 2011); Paul Oliver, "Blues," *Grove Music Online, Oxford Music Online* (accessed February 17, 2011); Peña, Manuel. 1985. *The Texas-Mexican Conjunto: History of a Working-Class Music.* Austin: University of Texas Press; Frederic Ramsey, Jr., *Music from the South*, Vol. 9, *Songs and Worship*, Folkways FW02658, liner notes (1962); Helena Simonett, *Banda: Mexican Musical Life Across Borders* (Hanover, CT: Wesleyan University Press, 2001); Harry Smith, *Anthology of American Folk Music*, Smithsonian Folkways Recordings SFW 40090, liner notes (1952); Eileen Southern, *The Music of Black Americans: A History*, 3rd ed. (New York: W. W. Norton, 1983); Thomas Turino, *Music as Social Life: The Politics of Participation* (Chicago: University of Chicago Press, 2008); Paul F. Wells, "Fiddling as an Avenue of Black-White Musical Interchange,"*Black Music Research Journal* 23.1/2 (2003): 135–147; Helmut Wulz, "Musical Life among the Canadian Hutterites," Philip V. Bohlman and Otto Holzapfel, eds., *Land Without Nightingales: Music in the Making of German-America* (Madison, WI: University of Wisconsin, 2002).

General Works on North American Music   Marius Barbeau and Edward Sapir, *Folk Songs of French Canada* (New Haven, CT: Yale University Press, 1925); Richard Crawford, *The American Musical Landscape* (Berkeley: University of California Press, 1993); Beverley Diamond and Robert Witmer, eds., *Canadian Music: Issues of Hegemony and Identity* (Toronto: Canadian Scholars' Press, 1994); Charles Hamm, *Yesterdays: Popular Song in America* (New York: W. W. Norton and Company, 1979); Charles Hamm, *Music in the New World* (New York, W. W. Norton, 1983); Ellen Koskoff, *The United States and Canada, The Garland Encyclopedia of World Music*, Vol. 3 (New York: Garland Publishing Company, 2001); Helmut Kallmann, Gilles Potvin, and Kenneth Winters, eds., *Encyclopedia of Music in Canada*, 2nd ed. (Toronto: University of Toronto Press, 1992); a more recent online edition is available at <http://www. thecanadianencyclopedia.com/index.cfm?PgNm=EMCSubjects&Params= U2>; Conrad Laforte, *Le Catalogue de la chanson folklorique française*, 6 volumes (Quebec City: Les Presses de l'Université Laval, 1977-87); Kip Lornell and Anne K. Rasmussen, eds., *Musics of Multicultural America* (London: Schirmer Books, 1997); Timothy J. McGee, *The Music of Canada*, 2nd ed. (New York, W. W. Norton and Company, 1985).

African American Music   Paul Berliner, *Thinking in Jazz: The Infinite Art of Improvisation* (Chicago: The University of Chicago Press, 1994); Samuel A. Floyd, *The Power of Black Music: Interpreting Its History from Africa to the United States*

(Oxford: Oxford University Press, 1995); Ted Gioia, *The History of Jazz* (Oxford: Oxford University Press, 1997); Glenn Hinson, *Fire in My Bones: Transcendence and the Holy Spirit in African American Gospel* (Philadelphia: University of Pennsylvania Press, 1999); Charles Keil, *Urban Blues*, 2nd ed. (Chicago: The University of Chicago Press, 1991); Ingrid Monson, *Saying Something: Jazz Improvisation and Interaction* (Chicago: University of Chicago Press, 1996).

Asian Music in North America   Deborah Anne Wong, *Speak it Louder: Asian Americans Making Music* (New York: Routledge, 2004); Adelaida Reyes, *Songs of the Caged, Songs of the Free: Music and the Vietnamese Refugee Experience* (Philadelphia: Temple University Press, 1999); Su Zheng, *Claiming Diaspora: Music, Transnationalism, and Cultural Politics in Asian/Chinese America* (Oxford: Oxford University Press, 2001).

Latino and Hispanic Music   Vernon Boggs, *Salsiology: Afro-Cuban Music and the Evolution of Salsa in New York City* (New York: Greenwood Press, 1992); Cathy Ragland: *Música Norteña: Mexican Migrants Creating a Nation between Nations* (Philadelphia, Temple University Press, 2009); John Storm Roberts, *The Latin Tinge: The Impact of Latin American Music on the United States*, 2nd ed. (Oxford: Oxford University Press, 1999); Daniel Sheehy, *Mariachi Music in America: Experiencing Music, Expressing Culture* (Oxford: Oxford University Press, 2005).

Music of European Ethnic Groups in North America   Bertrand Bronson, *The Singing Tradition of Child's Popular Ballads* (Princeton, NJ: Princeton University Press, 1976); Philip V. Bohlman and Doris J. Dyen, "Becoming Ethnic in Southwestern Pennsylvania," paper given at the annual meeting of the American Folklore Society in October 1985, Cincinnati; Philip V. Bohlman and Otto Holzapfel, eds., *Land Without Nightingales: Music in the Making of German-America* (Madison, WI: University of Wisconsin, 2002); Aili Kolehmainen Johnson, "Finnish Labor Songs from Northern Michigan," *Michigan History* 31.3 (1947): 331–343; Doreen Klassen, *Singing Mennonite: Low German Songs Among the Mennonites* (Winnipeg: The University of Manitoba Press, 1989); Robert B. Klymasz, "'Sounds You Never Before Heard': Ukrainian Country Music in Canada," *Ethnomusicology* 16.3 (1972): 372–380; Alan Lomax, *The Folk Songs of North America in the English Language* (Garden City, NY: Doubleday, 1960); Barbara Lorenzkowski, *Sounds of Ethnicity: Listening to German North America 1850–1914* (University of Manitoba Press, 2010); Miller, Rebecca S., "Irish Traditional and Popular Music in New York City: Identity and Social Change, 1930–1975," Ronald H. Bayor and Timothy J. Meagher, eds., *The New York Irish* (Baltimore: The Johns Hopkins University Press); Colin Quigley, "Catching Rhymes: Generative Musical Processes in the Compositions of a French Newfoundland Fiddler," *Ethnomusicology* 37.2 (1993): 155-200; Paula Savaglio, "Polka Bands and Choral Groups: The Musical Self-Representation of Polish Americans in Detroit," *Ethnomusicology* 40.1 (1996): 35–47; Mark Slobin, *Tenement Songs: The Popular Music of the Jewish Immigrants* (Urbana: University of Illinois Press, 1982).

Music and Multiculturalism   Pauline Greenhill, "Backyard World/Canadian Culture: Looking at Festival Agendas," *Canadian University Music Review* 19.2

(1999): 37–46; Marina Peterson, *Sound, Space, and the City: Civic Performance in Downtown Los Angeles* (Philadelphia: University of Pennsylvania Press, 2010); Robert Cantwell, *Ethnomimesis: Folklife and the Representation of Culture* (Chapel Hill: University of North Carolina Press, 1993).

Sacred Music in North America   Philip V. Bohlman, Edith Blumhofer, and Maria Chow, eds., *Music in American Religious Experience* (New York: Oxford University Press, 2006); Kay K. Shelemay, "Music in the American Synagogue: A Case Study from Houston," Jack Wertheimer, ed., *The American Synagogue: A Sanctuary Transformed* (Cambridge: Cambridge University Press, 1986); Jeffrey Summit, *How Shall We Sing? Music and Identity in Contemporary Jewish Worship* (Oxford: Oxford University Press: 2000); Jeff Todd Titon, *Powerhouse for God: Speech, Chant, and Song in an Appalachian Baptist Church* (Austin: University of Texas Press, 1988).

Monographs Focusing on Specific Genres   Robert R. Faulkner and Howard S. Becker, *"Do You Know...?" The Jazz Repertoire in Action* (Chicago: The University of Chicago Press, 2009); Fox, Aaron A., *Real Country: Music and Language in Working-Class Culture* (Durham, N.C.: Duke University Press, 2004); Gage Averill, *Four Parts, No Waiting: A Social History of American Barbershop Harmony* (New York: Oxford University Press, 2003); Gillian Mitchell, *The North American Folk Music Revival: Nation and Identity in the United States and Canada, 1945–1980* (Aldershot, United Kingdom: Ashgate, 2007); Roger Wood, *Texas Zydeco* (Austin, TX: University of Texas Press, 2006).

DISCOGRAPHY

Song   An immense array of North American ethnic music is available on disc and via streaming or purchased download. Given this abundance, some general orientation is followed here by a short list of recordings, in sections corresponding to the genres introduced in the preceding chapter.

The Library of Congress offers a collection of mp3s of traditional music and spoken word on their website <http://memory.loc.gov/diglib/ihas/html/afccards/afccards-home.html>. The library's Archive of Folk Culture has released many compilations of American folk music over the years; see <http://www.loc.gov/folklife/folkcat.html>. Several of these have been rereleased by Rounder Records (as described in the sections that follow) on CD; others remain available from the Archive of Folk Culture on audio cassette.

Smithsonian Folkways offers recordings of folk music from around the world; its North American collections include field recordings of a scholarly nature, popular music, and albums for children. A good place to start for American music is Harry Smith's *Anthology of American Folk Music* (SFW 40090) originally released in 1952 and now available on compact disc with an extensive set of liner notes. For a compilation of Canadian music, see *Classic Canadian Songs from Smithsonian Folkways* (SFW40539). Rounder Records also offers a significant selection of folk music, especially old-time music, although it is more commercially oriented than Folkways. New World Records offers some recordings of folk and ethnic music. So far as early popular music is concerned, JSP Records issues remastered compilations of early blues, country, jazz, and popular song recordings.

Smaller independent labels continue to produce recordings of music oriented primarily to ethnic communities. One such is Sunshine Records, a Canadian company that publishes recordings of fiddle music, gospel song, Ukrainian music, and polka.

Children's Music For a list of recordings of children's folksongs housed in the Archive of Folk Culture at the American Folklife Center, see the following online resource: <http://www.loc.gov/folklife/guides/Children.html>.

Anglo-American Ballads *Anglo-American Ballads*, Vols. 1 and 2, recorded in various parts of U.S. by Alan Lomax and others in 1934–41 (Vol. 1) and 1937–42 (Vol. 2), Rounder CD 1511 and Rounder CD 1516 [originally released by Archive of Folk Song as AFS L 1 and AFS L 7].

Ballads and Songs of the Blue Ridge Mountains: Persistence and Change, Folkways FW 03831.

Fiddle Music *American Fiddle Tunes*, Rounder CD 1518 [a wide ranging collection of American fiddle music, edited and with extensive liner notes by Alan Jabbour, originally released by the Archive of Folk Song as AFS L 62]; *Ashley MacIsaac: fine® thank you very much (a traditional album)*, Ancient Music 79602 2002-2 [Cape Breton fiddle music]; *Old Time Fiddle Tunes Played by Jean Carignan*, Folkways FW03531, 1960 [Quebec fiddle music].

Duranguense and Tecnobanda *Banda Maguey: La Estrella de los Bailes*, Fonovisa [tecnobanda]; *Los Creadorez del Pasito Duranguense: Recio, Recio Mis Creadorez*, Disa Records [duranguense]; *Grupo Montéz de Durango: De Durango a Chicago*, Disa Records [duranguense].

Gospel Music *The Clark Sisters: The Definitive Gospel Collection*, Word Entertainment; *Mahalia Jackson: The Apollo Sessions 1946–1951*, Pair; *Precious Lord: Recordings of the Great Gospel Songs of Thomas A. Dorsey*, Columbia.

Blues *Negro Blues and Hollers*, recorded in Arkansas, Mississippi and Tennessee by Alan Lomax, Lewis Jones, and John W. Work, Rounder 1501 [originally released by the Archive of Folk Song as AFS L 59]; *Rural Blues: A Study of the Vocal and Instrumental Resources*, Folkways FWRF202.

GLOSSARY

Abhinaya: (India). Gestural interpretation of text in dance.

Aerophone: Scientific term for all types of wind instruments, including trumpets, flutes, and the organ.

Ageng: (Indonesia). Large, as in gong ageng (Jv.).

Ageuta: (Japan). A type of song in higher vocal range used in Noh plays.

Agogó: (Africa). Double bell of West African origin, also used in Brazil.

Akadinda: (Africa). Large twenty-two-key xylophone of the Ganda.

Akan: (Africa). A major ethnic group in Ghana.

Akía: (Latin America). An individually owned and sung song of the Suyá Indians of Brazil.

Alap(anam): (India). Raga improvisation in free rhythm.

Angklung: (Indonesia). A kind of pitched bamboo rattle.

Anupallavi: (India). Second section of kriti or other Carnatic song form.

Apache fiddle: (North American Indian). Bowed instrument with one string, probably made in imitation of the Western violin, used in the culture of the Navajo and Apache peoples.

Aragoto: (Japan). Rough-style acting in the kabuki theater.

Aria: (Europe). A self-contained, often highly virtuosic piece for solo voice, most commonly used in opera, that affords the character a moment of reflection on a particular sentiment, issue, or dilemma taking place within the plot.

Arja: (Indonesia). A type of Balinese opera.

Asheq: (Middle East). Middle Eastern singer of romantic narratives.

Asymmetrical phrases: Phrases not equal in length.

Atabaques: (Latin America). Drums of West African origin, used in Brazilian candomblé music.

Atan: A circle dance considered the national dance of Afghanistan.

Atouta: (Japan). The last song in the jiuta cycle.

Atsimevu: (Africa). Large Ewe (Ghana) lead drum.

Atumpan: (Africa). Paired drums central to the Akan people of Ghana.

Avaz: (Middle East). In Persian classical music, the improvised, nonmetric section, rendered vocally or instrumentally, that is central in the performance.

Axatse: (Africa). Ewe shaker with beads on a net on the outside the gourd.

Ayin: (Middle East). A cycle of Mevlevi (Sufi) ceremonial music.

Aymara: (Latin America). Indigenous Andean language, second-largest indigenous ethnic group in the Andean region.

Bajo sexto: (Latin America). A twelve-string guitar used in Mexican norteño music.

Bakhshi: (Middle East). Iranian folk singer of narratives about war and romance.

Balo: (Africa). A Mande xylophone.

Balungan: (Indonesia). Skeletal melody in Javanese music.

Ban: (China). Generic term for Chinese clappers.

Bandura: (Europe). Ukrainian plucked lute of different sizes and ranges, often played in ensembles.

Bandúrria: (Latin America). A mandolin-shaped instrument with four courses of strings.

Bansuri: (India). Hindustani flute.

Bantu: (Africa). A major group of African languages.

Barong: (Indonesia). (1) A mythical lion-like creature in Balinese sacred dramas; (2) a trance dance ritual adopted for performances for tourists.

Barung: (Indonesia). Specifying the middle range of some types of Javanese gamelan instruments.

Baya: (India). Small, bass kettle drum of tabla pair.

Becar: (Europe). Instrumentalist and musical specialist in southeastern Europe, often distinguished by great mobility.

Bedhaya: (Indonesia). Sacred court dance of Java.

Beshrav: (Middle East). Introductory metric ensemble piece in Turkish classical music.

Bhajan: (India). Hindu devotional song.

Bhangra: (India). Pop music of the South Asian diaspora combining aspects of hip-hop, trance, and remix techniques with a traditional folk dance music from the state of Punjab.

Bharata Natyam: (India). Major dance style of South India.

Bin: (India). Hindustani plucked lute associated with dhrupad style.

Bira: (Africa). A Shona religious ceremony involving spirit possession.

Birimintingo: (Africa). An instrumental interlude or "break" during which a Mande jali departs from the basic ostinato.

Biwa: (Japan). A type of lute.

Bol: (India). Rhythmic syllable in Hindustani music.

Bonang: (Indonesia). Multioctave bronze instrument responsible for elaboration in Javanese gamelan.

Bonsan: (Japan). Japanese Buddhist chants in Sanskrit.

Brahmin (Brahman): (India). The highest varna, or caste, in Indian society.

Broadside ballad: (North America). A printed version of a folk song, usually combining a well-known melody with a topical text; printed on large sheets and sold inexpensively.

Bubaran: (Indonesia). A small-scale Javanese gendhing having sixteen beats.

Buddhism: Religion of compassion and salvation based on the teaching of the Indian prince Siddharta ("the Buddha,"

563–483 BCE). Influential in Chinese, Japanese, and Korean societies.

Bugaku: (Japan). Japanese court dance with instrumental accompaniment.

Buka: (Indonesia). Introduction to a Javanese gendhing.

Bunraku: (Japan). The main form of puppet theater in Japan.

Cadence: A pause or ending in music.

Cai Yuanpei (1868–1948): (China). Chancellor of Peking University (Beida) from 1916 to 1926. Important supporter of the May Fourth Movement.

Caja: (Latin America). A large, indigenous snare drum used to accompany pinkillu ensembles.

Cajun: (North America). French-speaking culture of Louisiana, with historical links to French-speaking Canada.

Call-and-response: The alternation or interlocking of leader and chorus musical parts or of a vocal and instrumental part.

Canboulay: (Caribbean). Processions that commemorated the harvesting of burnt cane fields before emancipation.

Candomblé: (Latin America). An Afro-Brazilian religion heavily involving West African religious beliefs and musical practices.

Canto pop: (China). Popular song genre sung in the Cantonese dialect produced in Hong Kong since the 1970s.

Caranam: (India). Last of three sections in Carnatic kriti or other song form.

Carnatic: (India). In music, referring to South Indian music style.

Cariso: (Caribbean). Traditional French creole song. Early form of calypso, often employing insulting or satirical lyrics.

Celempung: (Indonesia). The plucked zither of Javanese gamelans.

Chaharbeiti: A form of slow, soloistic, unmetered, and improvisatory quatrain singing in Afghanistan.

Chahargah: (Middle East). One of the twelve dastgahs, or modes of Persian classical music.

Chahar mezrab: (Middle East). Virtuosic composed metric solo piece in Persian classical music.

Charango: (Latin America). An Andean ten-string guitar variant, the size of a ukulele.

Chen Gexin: (China). Composer of popular songs active in Shanghai between the 1930s and 1940s.

Chilenos: (Latin America). Dance drama group of Paucartambo, Peru representing Chilean soldiers from the War of the Pacific.

Chobo: (Japan). The Gidayu (musico-narrative) duo on the kabuki stage.

Chord: A group of at least three tones sounded simultaneously in combination.

Chordophone: Scientific term for all types of string instruments, including violins, guitars, and pianos.

Chou: (China). Generic name for a clown role in Chinese theater.

Chowtal: (Caribbean). A form of folk music associated with phagwa (holi) in Trinidad and having roots in Indian (Bhojpuri) folk music.

Chunchos: (Latin America). Dance drama group of Paucartambo, Peru, representing jungle Indians.

Church modes: (Europe). Seven-note scales, thought by many to characterize more recent styles of folk music.

Chutney-soca: (Caribbean). Popular music style of Trinidad that combines elements of two earlier styles, soca and chutney.

Cinquillo: (Caribbean). A rhythmic cell common throughout the Caribbean, containing five separate articulations and organized into a long-short-long-short-long pattern.

Colonialism: The administrative, economic, and political control of a territory (colony) by a colonial power (such as the British Empire). This condition is maintained through exploiting unequal power relationships and by force, benefiting the colonial power and its center (the métropole) to a much greater degree than the colony itself in the process.

Colotomic (Japan). Marking or delineating major phrases in a musical composition. Used to describe percussion instruments that have this function.

Colotomic structure: (Indonesia). The marking of fixed beats within the metric structure of a musical piece by particular instruments; in gamelan music these include gong, kenong, kempul, and ketuk.

Colotomy: (Indonesia). The structure of a Javanese gendhing determined by the total number of beats it contains and which of those beats are sounded on particular instruments.

Concertina: (North America). The button-box accordion favored in polka bands of the Midwest.

Confucianism: System of ethics based on the teachings of Kongfuzi (Confucius, 551–479 BCE). Confucianism formed the dominant ethic of Chinese social units from the imperial government to the peasant family. It is also influential in Korean and Japanese societies.

Conjunto norteños: (Latin America). Popular dance bands originally associated with northern Mexico and southern Texas, featuring three-row button accordion, bajo sexto (12-string guitar), bass, and drums.

Contra dance: (Latin America). A type of partnered line dance in which couples arrange themselves in two facing lines.

Copla: (Latin America) (Caribbean). An Iberian-derived verse form with four octosyllabic lines per stanza.

Corrido: (Latin America). Mexican ballads usually on historical or topical themes using the copla text form.

Counter-Reformation: (Europe). A period of Catholic revival (mid-16th to mid-17th centuries), energized in response to the Protestant Reformation.

Criollo: (Latin America). In some regions criollo refers to American-born Spaniards, or largely European-derived ethnicity in Latin America, "white."

Cultural Revolution: (China). Complex social and political upheaval that began as a struggle between Mao Zedong and other top Communist Party leaders for domination of the Party and went on to affect all China with its calls for "continuing revolution" and "class struggle." Dates for the movement are usually given as 1966 to 1976.

Currulao: (Latin America). Afro-Colombian, Afro-Ecuadorian dance context in the Pacific Coast region in which marimba is featured.

Da-daiko: (Japan). The largest of gagaku drums.

Dahina: (India). Treble drum of tabla pair, having a tunable head.

Dalang: Master puppeteer of the Javanese shadow-puppet play.

Daluo: (China). Big Chinese gong.

Dan: (China). Generic name for a female role in Chinese theater.

Dan: (Japan). A musical section in Japanese music of various forms.

Dangdut: (Indonesia). Popular Indonesian musical style that combines Western rock and Indian film music influences.

Danmono: (Japan). Sectional form.

Danpigu: (China). A single-headed drum used in Chinese theater.

Darbucca: (Middle East). (Also Darrabuka). A single-headed drum ordinarily made of fired clay, used mainly in Arabic popular and classical music and in popular music throughout the Middle East.

Darvish: (Middle East). Leader of a community of Sufis and, in rural Iran, street singer of religious narratives.

Dastgah: (Middle East). The mode or scale of a piece in Persian music.

Datangu: (China). A big Chinese barrel drum.

Debayashi: (Japan). The on-stage musicians of the kabuki theater.

Décima: (Caribbean). An Iberian-derived, octosyllabic verse form with ten octosyllabic lines per stanza. The rhyming scheme is **ABBAACCDDC**.

Degatari: (Japan). On-stage musicians in Kabuki theater. This group is divided functionally into two separate ensembles, called the chobo (storytellers) and debayashi (ensemble specializing in performing nagauta, or "long song").

Demung: (Indonesia). The low-range saron.

Devadasi: (India). A Carnatic dancing girl whose art was dedicated to temple deities.

Dhalang: (Indonesia). Puppeteer of wayang kulit.

Dhrupad: (India). A severe classical song and instrumental form of Hindustani music.

Dhun: (India). A regional song of North India sometimes borrowed for Hindustani performance.

Diaspora: (Caribbean). A term describing the movement of a group of people (generally sharing ethnic or national history) into forced exile. This exile in a place other than the group's ancestral homeland generally also precludes the possibility of return. The Jewish and African diasporas are two paradigmatic examples.

Diatonic: Refers to the European, seven-note (do-re-mi) scale.

Didgeridoo: Long trumpet, made of a hollowed eucalyptus branch, used in Australian aboriginal cultures as a drone accompanying singing, and more recently, a general symbol of Australian musical identity.

Disike (Disco): (China). A recent Chinese popular song style.

Dizi: (China). A Chinese transverse bamboo flute with six finger holes.

Doctores: (Latin America). Dance drama group of Paucartambo, Peru, representing lawyers and government officials.

Dombak: (Middle East). Term used for various single-skin drums in the Middle East, but principally for the goblet-shaped drum used in Persian classical music. In Indonesia, a Middle-Eastern hourglass drum, used in gambus.

Dondon: (Africa). Ewe hourglass-shaped "talking drum."

Donkilo: (Africa). The basic sung melody of Mande jali songs.

Dotar: (Middle East). Large lute with long neck, frets, and two or three strings, used in folk music in Iran and in folk and classical music of Afghanistan and Central Asia.

Drut: (India). Fast.

Dùndún: (Africa). Hourglass-shaped "talking drum" of the Yoruba of Nigeria.

Duranguense: (North America). A popular dance music that developed in Chicago. A variant of tecnobanda, the musical style is derived from blending banda with electronic instruments. It is notable for its emphasis on percussion lines and for the generally faster tempos at which the repertory is performed. The accompanying dance is characterized by western attire and a typical dance step, called pasito, derived from the traditional dancing in Durango, Mexico. Duranguense is popular in both Mexico and the United States.

Eduppu: (India). The beginning of a phrase in Carnatic music used as a cadence for improvisations.

Elima: (Africa). A Pygmy puberty ceremony for which women are the primary singers.

Ennanga: (Africa). Ganda bow-harp.

Entenga: (Africa). Royal Ganda tuned drum ensemble.

Erhu: (China). A two-stringed Chinese spike fiddle with hollow wooden cylindrical sound box.

Erhuang: (China). Basic aria-rhythmic patterns used in the Peking Opera.

Eurovision Song Contest: (Europe). The largest popular-song contest in the world, established in 1956 by the European Broadcasting Union and pitting national entries against each other in an annual spectacle judged by telephone voting from the entering nations.

Fangman jiahua: (China). Literally, "making slow and adding flowers." A technique through which the tempo is slowed to achieve temporal space between the notes of the melody. This space is then ornamented with additional notes.

Fei Shi: (China). The pseudonym of an early twentieth-century Chinese reformer.

Filmigit: (India). Popular songs composed for Indian films.

Flat: Pitch lowered by a half tone.

Fret: A device of metal or string that divides the fingerboard of plucked instruments and against which the player presses the playing strings to get different tones.

Fuga: (Latin America). A term used throughout Peru to indicate an animated concluding section to a dance piece.

Fujian nanqu: (China). A genre of song suite with instrumental accompaniment popular in Fujian province in southern China and in Taiwan as well.

Fushi: (Japan). A term for melody in general.

Gagaku: (Japan). Japanese court orchestral music.

Gaku-so: (Japan). The gagaku zither.

Gambang: (Indonesia). A xylophone instrument in the Javanese gamelan; an archaic instrument, g. gangsa, is related to the saron.

Gambuh: (Indonesia). An archaic type of Balinese court opera and its accompanying orchestra.

Gambus: (Indonesia). A type of Islamic song having Arabic influence; the name of the plucked lute used to accompany this song.

Gamelan: (Indonesia). An ensemble of instruments such as those found in the central Javanese courts.

Gamelan Arja: A type of Balinese opera.

Gamelan Gambuh: An archaic type of Balinese court opera and its accompanying orchestra.

Gamelan Gong Gede: Older Balinese court music, used for court and temple rituals, similar in sound and style to the Javanese gamelan.

Gamelan Gong Kebyar: A modern type of Balinese music and the dance it accompanies, which is noted for its virtuosic and unpredictable playing style.

Gamelan Semar Pegulingan: Large, Balinese court orchestra that plays instrumental versions of gamelan gambuh melodies.

Gankogui: (Africa). Ewe double bell.

Gatra: (Indonesia). A four-beat phrase in Javanese music.

Gat-tora: (India). The section of Hindustani instrumental performance, accompanied by tabla, in which a short composed melody, the gat, is alternated with improvisational passages, tora.

Gboba: (Africa). Large Ewe (Ghana) lead drum.

Gede: (Indonesia). Large, as in gamelan gong gede.

Gender: (Indonesia). An instrument having thin bronze slab keys individually suspended over tube resonators.

Gender Wayang: (Indonesia). Four-piece ensemble of genders that typically accompanies the Balinese shadow play.

Gendhing: (Indonesia). A piece of Javanese music for gamelan.

Gerongan: (Indonesia). A male chorus that sings with Javanese gamelan.

Gesangbuch: (North America). Meaning "songbook," a printed collection of Amish religious songs, many entering from outside the community.

Gesellschaft für Musikfreunde: (Europe). "Society for the Friends of Music"; institutional home to concert halls, archives, and artistic monuments that recognize the past history of Austrian music.

Geza: (Japan). The off-stage music of the kabuki theater.

Gharana: (India). A school of professional musicians who originally traced their heritage to a family tradition but which now includes nonbiological descendants as well.

Ghazal: (India). A form of poetry associated with Perso-Arabic Muslim culture enthusiastically taken up by Urdu speakers in North India and Pakistan, where it is often sung.

Ghost Dance: (North American Indian). Native American (principally Plains) religious movement of protest against U.S. government excesses of the 1880s.

Gidayubushi: (Japan). A major Japanese musical narrative style accompanied by the Shamisen created by Takemoto Gidayu.

Gong: (Indonesia). Gong.

Gongan: (Indonesia). A phrase concluded with a stroke on gong ageng or siyem.

Gottuvadyam: (India). A Carnatic plucked string instrument whose strings are stopped with a sliding ball of glass, like the Hawaiian guitar.

Gu: (China). Generic name for Chinese drum.

Guangdong yinyue: (China). A genre of Chinese instrumental ensemble music originating in Guangdong province, which became popular not only in other parts of China but also Chinese ethnic enclaves in the West known as "China Town."

Guiro: (Caribbean). A rattle made out of a vegetable gourd.

Guitarrón: (Latin America). In Mexico, a large acoustic bass guitar with a convex back.

Guru: (India). A Hindu teacher.

Gusheh: (Middle East). Subdivision of a dastgah, and smallest constituent part of the radif, in Persian classical music.

Gusle: (Europe). Bowed lap fiddle, played throughout southeastern Europe, especially to accompany narrative epic repertories.

Haji: (Indonesia). A male Muslim who has made a pilgrimage to Mecca.

Hako: (North American Indian). A complex ceremony of the Pawnee, carried out for the general welfare of the tribe and the world, requiring four days of singing, dancing, and ritual.

Halam: (Africa). A West African banjo-like lute with a neck, gourd sound box, and skin stretched over the face of the sound box.

Hanamichi: (Japan). A ramp used in the Kabuki theater that connects the back of the theater to the stage.

Hardanger fiddle/Hardingfele: (Europe and North America). Elaborate Norwegian folk fiddle, with elaborate woodwork and extra resonating strings.

Harmonium: (India). Portable reed organ, with a single keyboard and a handoperated bellows; of European origin, but used widely in the sacred and semiclassical musics of Pakistan and North India.

Hayashi: (Japan). Generic name for ensembles of flute and drums.

Heterophony: Two or more performers play the same melody, but with small differences in timing or ornamentation.

Heuriger: (Europe). Austrian wine garden, which is often a site for traditional music.

Hexatonic: A scale of six tones.

Hichiriki: (Japan). A double-reed gagaku instrument.

Highlife: (Africa). A form of urban-popular dance-band music of Ghana; also played in Nigeria and elsewhere in West Africa.

Hindustan (India). Region of North India, with a distinct musical tradition—Hindustani.

Hindustani: (India). In music, referring to North Indian musical style.

Hispaniola: The name of the large Caribbean island shared by the modern nation-states of Haiti and the Dominican Republic.

Hocket: (Latin America). Interlocking pitches between two or more sound sources to create a single melody or part.

Hogaku: (Japan). Native Japanese music.

Hogoromo: (Japan). A noh play.

Hosho: (Africa). Large gourd shakers, used in Zimbabwe to accompany mbira music.

Huapanguera: (Latin America). A Mexican guitar variant from the huasteca region, larger and deeper than a normal guitar with eight strings in five courses.

Hua San Liu: (China). A Chinese instrumental piece belonging to the Jiangnan sizhu repertory.

Huasteca: (Latin America). A Mexican region including northern Veracruz State and Tamaulipas, and the musical style from that region.

Huasteca ensemble: (Latin America). Musical ensemble hailing from Northern Veracruz and Tamaulipas state, featuring violin accompanied by two types of guitars.

Hui: (China). Position markers on the qin.

Hummel: (Europe). Dulcimer played widely throughout Sweden and associated historically with Swedish folk styles.

Iberian: Referring to Iberian Peninsula, Spain and Portugal.

Idiophone: Scientific term for all instruments whose bodies vibrate as the principal method of sound-production, including rattles and many other percussion instruments.

Ikagura (Japan). Japanese court religious (Shinto) music.

Improvisation: Performance that is spontaneous rather than predetermined.

Incomplete repetition: (Native America) (North American Indian). A song structure common in intertribal and Plains style and consisting of two sections. The first section includes a short melodic phrase, called a "push up" or "lead," followed by a repetition of that melody by another singer. This repetition is called the "second." The second section, called the "chorus" generally consists of two or more phrases and is, itself, repeated.

Indeterminacy: (North America). A term used to describe a compositional technique, increasingly common in Western art music composed after World War II, in which elements of the composition are left to chance or the preference of the performer.

Interlocking: The practice of fitting one's pitches and beats into the spaces of other parts, or alternating the pitches or phrases of one part with those of others to create the whole; hocket.

Intertribal: (North American Indian). Songs or dances based on the Plains styles with which traditions of various other tribes are combined, developed for performances at modern powwows.

Interval: The distance between two pitches.

Iqa': (Middle East). Generic name of rhythmic modes, or type of musical meter, in Arabic classical music. Called usul in Turkish.

Jaipongan: (Indonesia). Popular Indonesian music that is derived from the native folk entertainment of Sunda (West Java).

Jalatarangam: (India). A set of small bowls partially filled with water to tune their pitches and struck with thin sticks.

Jali. pl. jalolu: (Africa). The term for a hereditary professional musician in Mande society, who serves as an oral historian and singer/performer.

Jarana: (Latin America). In the jarocho region of Mexico, a small guitar type with eight strings in five courses; in the huasteca region, a small five-stringed guitar variant.

Jarocho: (Latin America). A Mexican region on the Gulf Coast in the state of Veracruz, and the musical style of that region.

Jarocho Ensemble: (Latin America). Musical group from the rural, southern coastal region of Veracruz state. It includes a large diatonic harp, a four-string guitar (requinto), and one or more jaranas (a small guitar with eight strings).

Javali: (India). A lyrical song form of Carnatic music.

Jenglong: (Indonesia). An archaic Javanese instrument.

Jhala: (India). The concluding section of instrumental improvisation following jor in Hindustani music during which the performer makes lively and fast rhythmic patterns on the drone strings of an instrument.

Jiangnan sizhu: (China). A type of Chinese chamber instrumental ensemble made up of strings ("silk") and winds ("bamboo") popular in the areas around Shanghai.

Jianzipu (Abbreviated characters tablature): (China). Tablature for the Chinese seven-stringed zither, the qin; it is made up of clusters of abbreviated Chinese characters.

Jing: (China). Generic name for a painted-face role in Chinese theater.

Jingge: (Energy Song): (China). A recent Chinese popular song style.

Jinghu: (China). The leading melodic instrument in the Peking Opera theater. It is a two-stringed bamboo spike fiddle with a very high and piercing range and timbre.

Jingju: (China). Chinese term for Peking Opera. It means "theater of the capital."

Jit, also jiti: (China). Informal Shona village dance, song, and drumming. Also a genre played by electric guitar bands in Zimbabwe.

Jiuta: (Japan). A major koto genre that combines techniques of both kumiuta and danmoto. Sometimes also called tegotomono.

Jo-ha-kyu: (Japan). A basic aesthetic concept in Japanese music. Jo denotes "introduction"; ha denotes "development"; kyu denotes the final section of a composition.

Jor: (India). The section of Hindustani instrumental performance that follows alap and introduces a pulse.

Jùjú: (Africa). A form of Nigerian popular music associated with the Yoruba that combines electric instruments with indigenous drums and percussion.

Junkanoo: (Caribbean). A Bahamian festival, celebrated on Boxing Day (December 26) and New Year's Day and including music, costume arts, and dance.

Kabaka: (Africa). King of Buganda.

Kabuki: (Japan). The main form of Japanese popular musical theater.

Kaganu: (Africa). Small ewe (Ghana) accompanying drum.

Kagura: (Japan). A generic term for Shinto music.

Kagura-bue: (Japan). A flute used in Shinto music and court music.

Kakegoe: (Japan). Vocal drum calls used in noh theater.

Kakko: (Japan). A small horizontal drum used in court music.

Kamancheh: (Middle East). Spiked fiddle, with three or four strings, bowed with horsehair bow, used throughout the Middle East.

Kang Youwei (1858–1927): (China). Confucian scholar, influential in late Qing reform movements.

Kansan: (Japan). Japanese Buddhist chant in Chinese.

Karawitan: (Indonesia). Learned music in the Javanese tradition.

Kathak dance: (India). Major style of Hindustani dance.

Kebyar: (Indonesia). A modern type of Balinese music and the dance it accompanies.

Kecak: (Indonesia). A type of dance drama accompanied by a large male chorus that chants rhythmically, usually performed for tourists.

Kempul: (Indonesia). A type of small suspended gong in the Javanese gamelan having a colotomic function.

Kena (quena): (Latin America). An indigenous Andean end-notched flute of pre-Columbian origin with six top finger holes and one back hole.

Kendang: (Indonesia). Javanese double-headed drum.

Kenong: (Indonesia). A relatively large horizontal gong in the Javanese gamelan having a colotomic function.

Kenongan: (Indonesia). A colotomic phrase in Javanese music marked by a kenong stroke.

Ketawang: (Indonesia). A type of Javanese gendhing having thirty-two beats.

Ketuk: (Indonesia). A small, horizontal gong in Javanese music having a colotomic function.

Ketuk tilu: (Indonesia). A small, Sundanese ensemble consisting of rebab, gong, three ketuk, and drums. This ensemble accompanies a female dancer/singer.

Key: The pitch at which the major or minor scale begins.

Khandan: (Middle East). To sing, recite, or read, literally. In practice, the highest form of Middle Eastern music, used primarily in chanting the text of the Qur'an.

Khorasan: (Middle East). District of Iran located in the northeast corner of the nation.

Khurdak: (India). Small kettle drums used to accompany shehnai.

Khyal: (India). The major vocal style of Hindustani music.

Kidi: (Africa). Middle-sized ewe accompanying drum.

Klezmer music: (Europe). Jewish instrumental music, performed in social events and rites of passage in Eastern Europe prior to the Holocaust and revived in Europe and North America at the end of the twentieth century.

Klezmer musicians: (Europe). Jewish instrumental ensembles that performed, often professionally, for both Jewish and non-Jewish social functions.

Koma-bue: (Japan). A flute used in court music.

Koma-gaku: (Japan). Japanese court music of Korean origin.

Kontingo: (Africa). A five-stringed plucked lute played by Mande jalolu with a skin head stretched over a gourd sound box.

Kora: (Africa). A twenty-one-string bridge harp played by Mande jalolu.

Kotekan: (Indonesia). Often virtuosic and rapid interlocking rhythms important within gamelan kebyar performances and consisting of two parts (a lower part and a higher part) played on two separate instruments. Generally, multiple pairs of instruments are simultaneously involved in performing kotekan.

Koto: (Japan). A thirteen-stringed zither with movable bridges. It is Japan's main zither.

Kotoba: (Japan). A heightened speech style used in the noh theater.

Ko-tsuzumi: (Japan). A small hourglass-shaped drum.

Krakowiak: (Europe and North America). Duple-meter folk dance, associated with the region near Cracow.

Kraton: (Indonesia). Javanese royal court.

Kriti: (India). The major song type of Carnatic music, divided into three parts: pallavi, anupallavi, and caranam.

Kroncong: (Indonesia). A type of popular Indonesian music originating from Portuguese derived sources.

Kumbengo: (Africa). The basic instrumental ostinato, which serves as the foundation for Mande jali performance.

Kumiuta: (Japan). A suite of songs accompanied either by the koto or the shamisen, or by both.

Kunqu: (China). Classical Chinese musical drama.

Kuse: (Japan). The dance section of the first act of a noh play.

Kushaura: (Africa). "To lead the piece"; the first part, or lead part played by one Shona mbira player.

Kutsinhira: (Africa). "To accompany"; the second accompanying part played by a second Shona mbira player.

Kyogen: (Japan). Literally, "mad words"; it is a comic play inserted between noh plays.

Kyogenkata: (Japan). The clapper player in the kabuki theater.

Ladino: (Europe). The pre-Italian Latinate dialects of the southern Alps in Italy and Switzerland. Ladino is also the Romance vernacular language historically spoken by Sephardic Jews.

Lamellaphone: A general class of musical instruments that have tuned metal or reed tongues set on a bridge mounted to a soundboard or box; it is played by striking the keys. The mbira is but one example of this instrument type. Other lamellaphones used in Zimbabwe include the karimba, njari, and matepe.

Laras: (Indonesia). Javanese tuning system; there are two primary types (1) slendro (with a five-note scale) and (2) pelog (with a seven-note scale).

Lay(a): (India). Tempo.

Li Jinhui (1891–1967): (China). Modern Chinese composer and innovator of the first modern Chinese popular song genre, the liuxing gequ of Shanghai.

Li Shutong (1880–1942): (China). Poet, educator, and pioneer of the modern Chinese School Song. He later became a Buddhist monk.

Liang Qizhou (1873–1929): (China). Student of Kang Youwei and also an influential reformer. He used his writings to raise support for the reform movement.

Liu Jinguang: (China). Famous composer of Shanghai liuxing gequ and younger brother of Li Jinhui.

Liuxing gequ: (China). Popular song produced in Shanghai since the late 1920s that is a hybrid of various Western and Chinese musical genres. Its lyrics are sung in the Chinese national tongue, the so-called Mandarin.

Lute: A stringed instrument with a sound box and a distinct fingerboard, the strings stretching over both.

Maeuta: (Japan). The first song in a jiuta cycle.

Mahour: (Middle East). One of the twelve dastgahs, or modes, of Persian music, using a scale like Western major.

Majeños: (Latin America). Dance drama group of Paucartambo, Peru, representing drunken liquor traders.

Majles: (Middle East). In Persian classical music, a small, informal gathering of men assembled to hear a concert.

Major: Referring to the quality of a scale having its pitches arranged as follows: tone, tone, semitone, tone, tone, tone, semitone.

Makam: (Middle East). Turkish spelling of maqam.

Mao Zedong (1893–1976): (China). An early member of the Chinese Communist Party who rose to party leadership in the 1930s. Led the Party on the Long March and then to establish the People's Republic of China in 1949. Until his death in 1976, he was the paramount political leader and theorist of Chinese communism.

Maqam: (Middle East). Generic term for mode, or system of composing melody, in Arabic classical music. The term is used throughout the Middle East, and the concept occasionally appears with different names such as dastgah and gusheh in Persian, or mugam in Azerbaijan.

Mariachi: (Latin America). Ensemble type originally from Jalisco, Mexico, consisting of two or more violins, vihuela, guitarrón, two trumpets, and various guitars.

Marimba: (Latin American). Wooden keyed xylophone, originally from Africa, that is widely popular in Latin America.

Marímbula: (Latin America). A large box lamellaphone used as a bass instrument in a variety of Caribbean ensembles.

Marinera: (Latin America). Mestizo song–dance genre of Peru in sesquialtera rhythm.

May Fourth Movement: (China). Term used to describe student demonstration that took place in Tiananmen Square on May 4, 1919, in protest against unfair terms of the

Treaty of Versailles. Also refers to the period of iconoclastic intellectual ferment that followed the protest.

Mazurka: (Europe). Polish and Polish American folk dance, often stylized in art-music compositions.

Mbaq'anga: (Africa). A South African urban-popular music featuring electric instruments and horns, with the bass often particularly prominent.

Mbira: (Africa). A twenty-two-key Shona lamellaphone, originally associated with the Zezuru Shona of central Zimbabwe.

Mbube: (Africa). "Lion," one name for Zulu migrant choral music.

Melismatic-syllabic: (Europe). Performing a single syllable of text by singing multiple notes or pitches is called a melisma (melismatic). Syllabic singing, by contrast, matches one syllable to a single note or pitch.

Membranophones: Scientific term for all instruments using a stretched membrane for sound production, that is, all true drums.

Mentalité: A collective way of thinking, expressed in the cultural activities of a group or community.

Merengue: (Caribbean). Popular dance music of the Dominican Republic.

Mestizo: (Latin America). A relative term referring to people and a social identity involving the blending of European and Amerindian beliefs and cultural practices. Although in the past used as a racial category, it now more accurately denotes the variable incorporation of Iberian (Spanish and Portuguese) and indigenous cultural heritages.

Metallophone: An instrument classification term for idiophonic instruments made of metal.

Meter: A measure of musical time that organizes beats into larger units also called *measures* or *bars*.

Métropole: From Metropolis, or "mother city." Also used for any colonizing "mother country."

Mevlevi: (Middle East). Order of Sufis (members of the mystical movement of Islam) in Turkey, in which the preservation of classical music plays an important role.

Mikagura: Japanese court religious (Shinto) music.

Minnesinger: (Europe). Medieval singer, who often accompanied himself on the lute and was one of the first musical professionals.

Minor: Referring to the quality of a scale having its pitches arranged as follows: tone, semitone, tone, tone, semitone, (tone, tone) or (tone and a half, semitone).

Mode: Generic term for a concept indicating tendencies or rules for composing melody. Examples of modes include Indian ragas, Persian dastgahs, and Arabic maqams.

Molimo: (Africa). A Pygmy ceremony for the forest; a straight valveless trumpet used in the ceremony.

Monaqeb-khan: (Middle East). Singer of narratives about the virtues of Imam Ali, in small-town Iranian musical culture.

Monophonic: Referring to music comprising a single melody; without chords or other melodic or harmonic parts.

Monophony: One melody line is played by all musicians, with no harmonic accompaniment.

Morshed: (Middle East). Reciter of heroic verse such as *Shahnameh* to accompany exercises in the Zurkhaneh, traditional Persian gymnasium.

Motreb: (Middle East). Generic name for musician in various Middle Eastern cultures; performer of vocal and instrumental music at teahouses in Khorasan.

Mridangam: (India). Double-headed, barrel-shaped drum of Carnatic music.

Mugam: (Middle East). Term for maqam in Azerbaijan (Caucasus).

Mukhra: (India). Initial phrase of a khyal or gat used as a cadence for improvisational passages in Hindustani music.

Mushaira: (India). A traditional poetry-reading session.

Música Duranguense: A popular dance music that developed in Chicago. A variant of tecnobanda, the musical style is derived from blending banda with electronic instruments. It is notable for it's emphasis on percussion lines and for the generally faster tempos at which the repertory is performed. The accompanying dance is characterized by western attire and a typical dance step, called pasito, derived from the traditional dancing in Durango, Mexico. Duranguense is popular in both Mexico and the United States.

Musica humana, musica mundana, and musica instrumentalis: (Europe). Medieval distinction of different domains of music-making: humanly made music, music of the spheres, and music played by instruments.

Musical bow: (Africa). A bent stick with a single string that is struck with another stick or plucked; a gourd resonator is attached to the bow or, on a second type, the mouth cavity serves as resonator.

Music area: (North American Indian). A group of Native American tribes who share similar musical styles, roughly corresponding to the cultural areas (but not by language).

Musiqi: (Middle East). Classical and folk forms of music in the Middle East that have less prestige than the religious khandan.

Muyu (Wooden fish): (China). A carved, hollow, wooden Chinese instrument struck with a pair of wooden sticks.

Nagasvaram: (India). Carnatic double-reed instrument.

Nagauta: (Japan). A lyric genre of shamisen music.

Naoba: (China). A small pair of Chinese cymbals.

Naqqal: (Middle East). Reciter of the *Shahnameh*, Iranian national epic, in teahouses in small-town Iran.

Narodnik Movement: (Europe). A Russian agrarian socialist movement of the late nineteenth century.

Natural: A pitch that is neither raised (sharped) nor lowered (flatted).

Natyasastra: (India). An early Indian treatise on the performing arts attributed to Bharata and concerned with music, dance, and theater and drama.

Nautch: (India). An English colonial name for various kinds of Indian dance, derived from a word in Indian languages for "dance."

Nay: (Middle East). End-blown flute (ordinarily with five finger holes) used throughout the Middle East; sometimes spelled *Nei* or *Nai*.

Netori: (Japan). Introductory section of gagaku music.

Niraval: (India). A type of improvisation in Carnatic music that retains the text and its rhythmic articulation but alters the pitches of the melody.

Ngelik (Indonesia). A section in ketawang pieces that contrasts with the surrounding material (ompak) and is usually longer than one gongan. It is also usually where the gerongan sings the melody of the ketawang composition.

Noh: (Japan). Japanese classical drama that originally developed in the early fourteenth century.

Nohkan: (Japan). The flute used in noh.

Notation: Graphic representation of music.

Nritta: (India). Abstract Kathak dance.

Nyamalo: (Africa). Craft specialists in Mande societies, a category including professional musicians.

Obeah: (Caribbean). Bahamian folk belief and practice derived from African religious models and concerned with controlling and deploying powers in service of both good (i.e., healing) and evil (i.e., vengeance).

Oberek: (North America). Polish and Polish American folk dance in triple meter.

Office (Divine Hours): (North America). Organized to correspond to the canonical hours, the Office (also called the Divine Hours) is a set of daily worship services in which certain prayers, readings, and chants are performed at fixed times. The services include matins, vespers, and compline, among others, and the practice is generally associated with Catholic, Orthodox Christian, and Anglican/Episcopal traditions, though other traditions include these services in their worship as well.

Old Style and New Style: (Europe). The major stylistic categories of Hungarian folk music.

Ompak: (Indonesia) Refers to the opening, usually repeated gongan in ketawang pieces.

Organology: The study of musical instruments.

Orisha: (Caribbean): A spirit understood as one of the manifestations of God within Yoruba and Yoruba-derived religious practice.

Orixa: (Latin America). A spirit or deity in the Yoruba religion of Nigeria.

Orquesta: (Latin America). Orchestra.

Orquesta tipica: (Latin America). A mixed ensemble of European instruments and indigenous Andean flutes.

Ostinato: (Africa) (Caribbean). A repeated or cyclical melody or rhythmic pattern.

O-tsuzumi: (Japan). A large hourglass-shaped drum.

Oud (or ud): (Middle East). Principal lute of the Middle East, and most characteristic instrument of Arabic cultures, with eight strings, no frets, used mainly in classical music. The European lute is derived from it, as is the word *lute* (from al-Ud).

Pachamama: (Latin America). Earthmother, an Andean concept of the living, spiritual earth.

Padam: (India). A lyrical type of Carnatic song that may accompany dance.

Pakhavaj: (India). A double-headed, barrel-shaped drum of Hindustani music associated with dhrupad.

Pallavi: (India). The opening section of a Carnatic song form.

Panerus: (Indonesia). The types of saron or bonang having the highest ranges.

Papai benta: (Latin America). A lamellaphone ("thumb-piano") with reed keys mounted on bridges that are secured to a flat board. Utilized by the Saramaka of Suriname.

Parallel harmony: Refers to two or more melodic lines moving in parallel motion, or consistently remaining the same harmonic interval apart, for example, parallel thirds, a common trait in Latin American music.

Parallel polyphony: (Middle East). The same melodic line is played at different pitch levels by two or more performers.

Parlando rubato: (Europe). Identified by Béla Bartók and characterized by a speechlike style that stresses the words while incorporating a great deal of give-and-take in the rhythmic structure. It is associated most closely with "old style" Hungarian folk song.

Pathet: (Indonesia). A particular way of using a scale or laras in Javanese music.

Peking: (Indonesia). The saron with the highest range.

Peking Opera (Jingju Theater): (China). The main type of Chinese popular musical theater that first emerged in the Chinese capital Beijing (Peking) in the later eighteenth century.

Pelog: (Indonesia). The heptatonic tuning system of Javanese music.

Pentatonic: Having five pitches.

Pentatonicism: Melodic structure based on scales with five pitches, often revealing an historically early stage of folk-music style.

Peshrev: (Middle East). Alternative spelling of beshrav.

Pesindhen: (Indonesia). Javanese female vocal soloist.

Peyote music: (North American Indian). Songs, in a characteristic style, accompanying a ceremony surrounding use of peyote, a drug derived from a cactus. The peyote religion is a major component of twentieth-century Native American culture of the Plains and Southwest.

Pinkillu (Aymara, pinkullu, Quechua): (Latin America). Andean vertical duct flute usually made of cane, but also of wood in some regions.

Pipa: (China). A pear-shaped, four-stringed plucked lute with a short bent neck and many frets.

Pishdaramad: (Middle East). Literally "before the introduction." Introductory piece, composed, metric, and usually played by an ensemble, in a performance of Persian classical music.

Pitu: (Latin America). Andean cane side-blown flute.

Polka: (Europe and North America). Dance in duple meter, originally Czech but disseminated throughout European and North American regions and ethnic groups.

Polyphonic: (Europe) (Native America). Generic term referring to all music in which one hears more than one pitch at a time, for example, songs accompanied by guitar, choral music, orchestral music, or two people singing a round together. Refers more specifically to music which incorporates two or more simultaneous melodic lines or parts.

Pongzhong: (China). A pair of small Chinese handbells.

Portamento: A slide or sweep between two pitches.

Potlatch: (North American Indian). A ceremony once common among the peoples of the North Pacific Coast, held to exhibit personal wealth and family status, and often commemorating important events in the life of the host (i.e., marriage, death, birth of a child, etc.). Potlatch ceremonies usually included a feast and the giving of gifts.

Powwow: (North American Indian). Tribal or intertribal gathering in twentieth-century Native American culture; a principal venue for performance of traditional and modernized music and dance.

Punta rock: (Caribbean). Popular music style developed by the Garifuna, featuring call-and-response vocals and a rich percussion accompaniment derived from traditional punta music.

Pusaka: (Indonesia). Javanese royal heirloom.

Qanun: (Middle East). A type of Middle-Eastern plucked dulcimer.

Qin: (China). A Chinese seven-stringed zither. It is the most revered instrument and was patronized by members of the educated class.

Qinqin: (China). A two- or three-stringed plucked lute with a long, fretted neck.

Qiuge (Jail Songs): (China). Popular Chinese songs of the 1980s and 1990s. Their lyrics deal with convicts' lives in labor reform camps.

Qollas: (Latin America). Dance drama group of Paucartambo, Peru, representing high altiplano traders.

Quadrille: (Caribbean). A dance, originating in Europe and adapted to Caribbean contexts. It was historically performed by couples arranged in a square formation and following a series of set dance figures.

Québecois: (North America). French-speaking residents of the Canadian province of Québec.

Quebradita: (North America). A dance craze, accompanied by tecnobanda ensembles and privileging cumbia dances, which became especially popular in Los Angeles, northern Mexico, and throughout the Southwest. Characterized by western attire, hat tricks, and flips.

Quechua: (Latin America). The most widespread indigenous Andean language; the state language of the Inca, largest indigenous ethnic group in the Andes.

Qur'an: Sacred book of Islam.

Radif: (Middle East). In Persian classical music, the body of music, consisting of 250–300 short pieces, memorized by students and then used as the basis or point of departure for improvised performance.

Rag(a)(m): (India). A scale and its associated musical characteristics such as the number of pitches it contains, its manner of ascending and descending, its predominant pitch, and so forth.

Ragam/Alapanam: An improvisation performed before the kriti, that demonstrates the musician's abilities to interpret the ragam (or mode) in which the kriti is written.

Rai: (Middle East). A modern popular music developed in Algeria and Morocco that combines traditional singing styles and Arabic modes with Western-style synthesized accompaniments.

Rake 'N' Scrape: A traditional Bahamian music, usually played on accordion, saw, and goatskin drum.

Ranchera: (Latin America). A Mexican song genre with rural and working-class associations.

Rasa: (India). The affect or emotional state associated with a raga or other artistic expression.

Rebab: (Indonesia). A type of Javanese bowed lute.

Recitative: (Europe). A style of barely sung recitation in which the action or plot is carried forward. Often used in operas, oratorios, and cantatas, it imitates the rhythm and cadence of speech and is generally sparsely accompanied.

Reng: (Middle East). In Persian classical music, the final piece of a performance, based on the musical traditions of folk dance.

Requinto: (Latin America). A small four-string guitar variant in the jarocho region, more generally simply a slightly smaller six-string Spanish guitar.

Rig-Veda: (India). A collection of poems that tell the stories of the Indian gods. There are three other Vedic texts, called the Yajur-Veda, Sama-Veda, and Atharva-Veda.

Ritsu: (Japan). A basic Japanese scale.

Roma (Europe). Transnational communities of people pejoratively referred to as Gypsies; active participants in Europe throughout history and across the continent.

Rouzeh-khan: (Middle East). Singer of narratives about the martyrdom of the Imam Hossein, in small-town Iranian musical culture.

Rumba: (Caribbean). Cuban dance form that developed at the end of the nineteenth century. The typical Rumba ensemble consists of a lead vocalist, a chorus, clave, palitos, and congas.

Ryo: (Japan). A basic Japanese scale.

Ryuteki: (Japan). A flute used for Togaku music in the gagaku repertory.

Saami: (Europe). Circumpolar peoples, living in northern Norway, Sweden, Finland, and Russia, whose musical practices in Europe mix indigenous and modern sounds.

Sageuta: (Japan). A type of song in lower vocal range used in Noh plays.

Saibari: (Japan). Shinto songs meant to entertain the gods.

Sam(am): (India). The first beat in a tala.

Samagana: (India). Special tunes for singing vedic hymns.

Samba: (Latin America). The most important Brazilian musical genre often associated with Carnival in Rio but performed in other rural and urban contexts.

Samurai: (Japan). Warrior.

Sanghyang: (Indonesia). A heavenly spirit who may possess certain performers in Javanese and Balinese trance dances.

Sangita: (India). Music and associated performing arts.

Sangitaratnakara: (India). This thirteenth century treatise on music, the last to be referenced by both Hindustani and Carnatic musical traditions, marks the beginnings of a distinction in style between the Northern and Southern classical traditions.

Sankyoku: (Japan). Jiuta music played by a trio.

San-no-tsuzumi: (Japan). An hourglass-shaped drum used in court music.

Santour: (Middle East). Trapezoid-shaped hammered dulcimer, played with two balsa wood mallets, used throughout the Middle East but particularly in Iran and Turkey.

Santur: (India). A Kashmiri hammered dulcimer now used in Hindustani music.

Sanxian: (China). A three-stringed plucked lute with a long, fretless neck and an oval-shaped sound box.

Saqras: (Latin America). Dance drama group of Paucartambo, Peru, representing devils.

Sarod: (India). A fretless, plucked string instrument of Hindustani music originally coming from Afghanistan.

Saron: (Indonesia). A type of Indonesian instrument having thick bronze slab keys lying over a trough resonator.

Sataro: (Africa). A speechlike vocal style performed by Mande jalolu.

Satokagura: (Japan). Folk Shinto music.

Sawal-jawab: (India). "Question–answer," rhythmic challenges between soloist and accompanist in Hindustani music.

Saz: Lutelike instrument used widely in Turkish art music and spread throughout the regions of southeastern Europe, into which the Ottoman Empire extended.

Scale: A set of pitches arranged in ascending or descending order.

Schrammelmusik: (Europe). "Schrammel-Music": urban folklike music of Vienna, named after a family of musicians.

Sema: (Middle East). A Mevlevi (Sufi) ceremony of mystical ascent involving a whirling dance accompanied by music.

Sesquialtera: (Latin America). The combination/juxtaposition of duple and triple rhythmic patterns, both simultaneously in different instrumental parts, or sequentially in the same part, hemiola.

Session: A traditional gathering of musicians at an Irish pub to play together in an intimate jam session.

Setar: (Middle East). Small, long-necked, fretted lute with four or (sometimes) three strings, plucked with the nail of the right index finger, used in Persian classical music.

Shagird: (India). Pupil of Muslim master.

Shahnameh: (Middle East). National epic of Iran, dealing with mythology and pre-Islamic history, written by Ferdowsi in the tenth century CE, and ordinarily performed by singing in teahouses.

Shakubyoshi: (Japan). Clappers used in court singing.

Shakuhachi: (Japan). An end-blown flute.

Shamisen: (Japan). A three-stringed plucked chordophone.

Sharp: A pitch raised by a half tone.

Shashmakom: (Middle East). Body of composed music of Uzbekistan (literally, "six makams"), the Central Asian counterpart of the Persian radif and of the Middle Eastern maqam system generally.

Shenai: (India). A Hindustani double-reed instrument.

Sheng: (China). A Chinese free-reed mouth organ; also generic name for a male actor in Chinese theater.

Shen Xingong (1870–1947): (China). Educator and pioneer of modern Chinese School Song.

Shinnai-bushi: (Japan). A musical narrative form accompanied by the shamisen, found in Shinnai Tsuruga.

Shinto: (Japan). Native religion of Japan literally meaning "the way of the gods."

Shishya: (India). Pupil of a Hindu master.

Shite: (Japan). Principal actor in noh.

Sho: (Japan). A mouth organ.

Shoko: (Japan). A suspended bronze drum used in gagaku.

Shomyo: (Japan). Japanese Buddhist chanting.

Shur: (Middle East). The most important of the twelve dastgahs, or modes, of Persian classical music.

Siku: (Latin America). Andean instrument consisting of different lengths of reed or cane tubes, lashed together, each tuned to a specific note. The performer blows across the top of a cane to make it sound. The siku is a double-row panpipe, divided between two players, the pitch row alternating between the two rows.

Sinti (Europe). One of the largest communities of Roma, with a particularly strong presence in Central Europe.

Sitar: (India). Primary plucked string instrument of Hindustani music.

Siyem: (Indonesia). The smaller of the two large gongs in the Javanese gamelan.

Slendro: (Indonesia). The pentatonic tuning system of Javanese music.

Sogo: (Africa). Middle-size ewe (Ghana) accompanying drum.

Sokyoku: (Japan). Popular koto-and-vocal music of the Edo period in Japan.

Son: (Latin America). Mexico's most important songdance genre, a strophic song usually on romantic themes and in many regions characterized by sesquialtera rhythm.

Songs for the Masses: (China). Chinese communist political songs.

Soundscape. A combination of "sound" and "landscape" to indicate how sounds are experienced within a particular area.

Speech Islands *Sprachinseln*, or the German-speaking cultural islands in Eastern Europe, given nationalist significance by Germany prior to World War II.

Sruti: (India). The twenty-two subdivisions of the octave within Indian classical music theory.

Staatsoper: (Europe). National, or "State," Opera of Austria, serving the Habsburg court during the Austro-Hungarian Empire, until World War I.

Steel band: (Caribbean). A band composed of oil drums that have been "tuned" to play a range of pitches.

Strathspey: (North America). A dance tune, associated with Scotland, in 4/4 meter. Characterized rhythmically by dot-cut, or Scotch "snaps" (a short note followed by a dotted note).

String quartet The ensemble of European chamber music that idealizes the social and musical equality of the modern era—two violins, viola, and violoncello.

Strophic form: Song form in which the verses change but the music used to accompany each verse remains the same.

Sufism: (Middle East). The principal mystical movement of Islam, in which the activity of music is regarded as "another way to know God"; found throughout the Middle East and elsewhere in the Islamic world, but as a force in musical life, Sufism is particularly important in Turkey, Iran, and Pakistan.

Sula: (Africa). Social category in Mande societies, referring to "ordinary people" in contrast to craft specialists.

Suling: (Indonesia). Indonesian vertical flute.

Suona: (China). A Chinese conical double-reed oboe.

Suyá: (Latin America). Amazonian Indian group of Brazil.

Suzu: (Japan). A small bell tree used in some Shinto dances.

Svarakalpana: (India). Improvised singing of pitches using their names in Carnatic music.

Syncopation: Accenting rhythms where they would not normally be accented.

Tabla: (India). A pair of drums used in Hindustani music.

Taiko: (Japan). A generic term for drum; also a drum struck by a pair of sticks used in the noh theater.

Takht: (Middle East). Literally "platform." An ensemble of musicians, often including violin, santour, flute, and two drums, used to accompany singing and sometimes dancing in performances of Arabic popular music.

Tal(a)(m): (India). Meter.

Tamboo bamboo band: (Caribbean). Bamboo percussion band that accompanied cariso songs during the late nineteenth and early twentieth centuries.

Tambura: (India). A stringed drone instrument.

Tamburitza (Tamburitza orchestra): (Europe). String ensemble of southeastern Europe and in the diasporas of ethnic and national groups from the Balkans, with distribution of voices from low to high.

Tan: (India). A rapid and florid kind of improvised melodic passage in Hindustani music.

Tanam: (India). The improvised instrumental or vocal performance that follows Carnatic alapanam and that introduces a pulse.

Tanjidor: Musical ensemble from the outskirts of Jakarta that blends European-derived band instruments with local instruments.

Taqsim: (Middle East). Nonmetric improvised instrumental piece consisting of several short sections, in Arabic and Turkish classical music; spelled Taksim in Turkish.

Tar: (Middle East). Lute with long neck, frets, six strings, and heavy, waisted body, plucked with a pick, used in various parts of the Middle East but principally in Iran, in classical but also popular and folk musics.

Tarka: (Latin America). An Andean wooden duct flute.

Tasnif: (Middle East). Type of composed, metric song in Persian music, with words (though sometimes performed instrumentally), and a part of a full classical performance though also found in popular music.

Tavil: (India). A double-headed barrel drum played with a stick and thimble-covered fingers to accompany nagasvaram.

Tecnobanda: (North America). A Popular dance music derived from blending the instruments and repertory of traditional banda ensembles (brass bands) with electronic instruments.

Tegoto: (Japan). Instrumental interludes in koto music.

Tegotomono: (Japan). A generic term for instrumental koto music; it is also used as another term for jiuta.

Tempo giusto: (Europe). Identified by Béla Bartók and characterized by a dancelike style that stresses strict adherence to meter. It is associated most closely with "new style" Hungarian folk song.

Terraced melody: (North American Indian). A melody structured so that it begins in a high register and "steps" or "cascades" down to a low concluding pitch.

Thumri: (India). A lyrical type of Hindustani song and a style of instrumental performance modeled on it.

Tihai: (India). A formulaic cadential pattern, normally repeated three times with calculated rests between each statement so that the performance ends on sam.

Togaku: (Japan). Court music of Chinese and Indian origin in the gagaku repertory.

Tongsu yinyue (Light Popular Music): (China). Chinese popular music of the 1980s and 1990s.

Torimono: (Japan). Shinto songs in praise of the gods.

Trajes de charro: (Latin America). Fancy western Mexican "cowboy" costume worn by mariachis.

Triadic harmony: A European style of harmony with three pitches sounding simultaneously, each a third apart.

Trikala: (India). A type of Carnatic improvisation in which the durational values of the notes in a phrase or piece are systematically augmented or diminished.

Tritone: The interval, or distance between two pitches, whose dissonant character caused it to be associated with the devil.

Tsuri-daiko: (Japan). Suspended drum used in gagaku.

Tsuyogin: (Japan). A strong-style noh music.

Twenty-one Demands: (Japan). Issued by Japan in 1915, in which Japan demanded various economic and political concessions from the Chinese government touching off popular Chinese protests.

Ud: *See* Oud

Ustad: (India). A Muslim teacher.

Usul: (Middle East). Turkish term for the Arabic iq'a.

Varna: (India). Division of society in Indian culture, sometimes translated as "caste."

Varnam: (India). A type of song with which Carnatic recitals generally begin. Sometimes compared to the Western classical "etude" or "study."

Vedic chant: (India). Intoned verses for ancient religious ceremonies performed by Brahman priests.

Venu: (India). Carnatic flute.

Vichitra vina: (India). A Hindustani plucked string instrument whose strings are stopped with a ball of glass; *see* Gottuvadyam.

Vihuela: (Latin America). In Mexico, a small five-string guitar variant with a convex back, used for percussive strumming.

Vilambit: (India). Slow.

Vina: (India). Primary plucked string instrument of Carnatic music.

Vocables: (North America). Nonsemantic syllables that are sung; "nonsense syllables."

Volkslied: (Europe). German term for "folk song," coined by the philosopher Johann Gottfried Herder at the end of the eighteenth century.

Volkstümlich: (Europe). "Folklike" music of Central Europe, in which traditional folk and modern popular musics are often mixed.

Wagon: (Japan). A six-stringed zither.

Waki: (Japan). The supporting actor in noh.

Wankara: (Latin America). Sometimes called bombos, these large, double-headed drums are used to accompany siku ensembles.

Wasan: (Japan). Buddhist hymns in Japanese.

Wayang kulit: (Indonesia). Indonesian shadow play accompanied with gamelan music.

Wayno, or huayno: (Latin America). The most widespread Andean mestizo song-dance genre in Peru, also performed by some indigenous musicians. The song texts are strophic, and the tunes comprise short sections in forms such as **AABB.** Waynos are in duple meter with a rhythmic feel varying between an eighthand-two-sixteenth-note figure and an eighth-note triplet.

Wenchang: (China). The instrumental ensemble in Peking Opera made up of melody instruments.

Wenzipu (Prose Tablature): (China). Archaic Chinese tablature for the qin written in prose.

Wuchang: (China) (Japan). The instrumental ensemble in Peking Opera made up of percussion.

Xiao Youmei (1884–1940): (China). Chinese composer, music educator, and reformer. He established the first modern Chinese music department at Peking University in 1920, and in 1927 he established the first modern Chinese music conservatory in Shanghai, the Shanghai Conservatory of Music, which is still in existence today. Xiao served as its director until his death in 1940.

Xiao: (China). A Chinese end-blown flute with six finger holes.

Xiaoluo: (China). Small Chinese gong.

Xiaotangu: (China). A small Chinese barrel drum.

Xibei feng (Northwestern Wind): (China). Popular Chinese song genre of the 1980s and 1990s. It combines a disco beat with Chinese folk music, and its lyrics are deliberately artless and simple.

Xipi: (China). Basic melody-rhythmic patterns used for arias in the Peking Opera.

Xylophone: An instrument with keys made from wooden slabs.

Yangqin: (China). A Chinese dulcimer struck with a pair of bamboo sticks.

Yaraví: (Latin America). A slow, sad, lyrical mestizo song genre from Peru.

Yayue: (China). Literally meaning "elegant music," it was Chinese court music of imperial China.

Yeibechai: (North American Indian). A major curing ceremony, lasting nine days, of the Navajo; also known as "Night Chant."

Yoiking: Traditional vocal repertory of the Saami people of circumpolar Europe, reflective of the Saami interaction with the nature of the Arctic, for example, reindeer herding.

Yokyoku: (Japan). Choral singing in noh.

Youlan (Orchids in a Secluded Valley): (China). The earliest extant qin piece; it was notated in "prose tablature" in a manuscript dating from sixth century CE.

Yowagin: (Japan). Soft-style noh music.

Yuan Shikai (1859–1916): (China). Leader of the powerful North China army who was instrumental in arranging the abdication of the Qing emperor in 1912. Because of Yuan's strength, Sun Yat-sen, the founder of the Chinese republic in 1912, offered Yuan the presidency of the new republic. Yuan abused the office and proclaimed himself emperor in 1915, but he died six months later.

Yueqin: (China). A four-stringed Chinese plucked lute with a round sound box.

Yunluo: (China). A Chinese suspended gong set.

Zarb: (Middle East). Literally "drum." In Persian music, alternate name for dombak.

Zeng Zhimin (1879–1929): (China). Modern Chinese music educator and a pioneer in writing modern School Song.

Zhao Yuanren (Y. R. Chao) (1892–1982): (China). Influential modern Chinese composer of songs, choral works, and piano compositions, Zhao was also an internationally known linguist. He received his education first from Cornell University and then from Harvard University; he later joined the faculty of the University of California at Berkeley.

Zither: An instrument with strings that stretch along the whole length of the sound board.

Zouk: (Caribbean). Popular music style of the French Antilles, popularized in the 1980s by the band Kassav'.

Zurkhaneh: (Middle East). Literally "house of strength." Traditional gymnasium in Iran, used by men to exercise, accompanied by a morshed reciting heroic verse with percussion.

Zydeco: (North America). African American popular music from Louisiana, also including Caribbean and Cajun elements.

INDEX